By the same author:

Under the pen name Robert Black:

Workers Councils in the Hungarian Revolution, 1966
With L. Trotsky and B. Pearce, *A Moscow Trials Anthology*, 1967
With J. Crawford, *Conflicts in the Bolshevik Party in 1917*, 1967
The Ironies of Isaac Deutscher, 1967
Stalinism in Britain, 1970
The Fight for Bangladesh, 1971
Fascism in Germany 1975

Under his own name:

The Seeds of Evil, 1995
Through Frosted Glass, 2018

Socialism of Fools

The Rise and Fall of Comrade Corbyn

Part II

By Robin Blick

Published by New Generation Publishing in 2022

Revised Third Edition

Paperback ISBN: 978-1-80369-355-2
Hardback ISBN: 978-1-80369-356-9

www.newgeneration-publishing.com

New Generation Publishing

'Yes my dear, all white people are racists.' (Marley K. Age, Age of Awareness, June 6, 2020)

'...all men are created equal...' (United States Declaration of Independence, July 4, 1776)

'I look to the day when a person will be judged not by the colour of their skin but by the content of their character...' (Dr. Martin Luther King Jnr, Washington, August 28, 1963)

'Problem solved'. (Added on August 5, 2014, by Labour MP for Bradford West Naz Shah to posting which said: 'Solution for Israel-Palestine conflict: Re-locate Israel into United States.' As of October 2021, Shah was Labour Shadow Minister for Community Cohesion [sic].)

'If the Jews want a Jewish state, they should establish Tel Aviv in America.' (Benito Mussolini to Amin al-Husseini, Grand Mufti of Jerusalem, Rome, October 27, 1941.)

Contents

Appendices

A Are Zionists Nazis?

'Zionism is Nazism in a new guise.' *La Documentation Catholique,* July 17, 1949.

'Brooklyn-born [Jewish] settlers are Nazis, racists. They should be shot dead.' Tom Paulin, poet, BBC broadcaster and Lecturer in English at Hertford College, Oxford, interview in the Egyptian weekly *Al Ahram*, cited in the *Guardian*, April 12, 2002.

'The Zionists claiming Palestine speak with the accents of Mussolini claiming an Empire, or Hitler, or Japan in China'. *Daily Worker,* Communist Party of Great Britain daily, August 14, 1937

Are Zionists Nazis? And is Israel a Nazi state? In act of despicable bad taste, Labour MP Jeremy Corbyn chose Holocaust Memorial Day of 2010 to host a meeting in Parliament titled, 'From Auschwitz to Gaza', the theme of the event being that the Jews of Israel were no less guilty of a genocide of the Palestinians than the Nazis were of one of the Jews. Pursing the same tack, the next year, Corbyn supported a motion in the House of Commons to change the name of Holocaust Memorial Day to Genocide Memorial Day, effectively decoupling it from Hitler's bid to exterminate the Jews of Europe. It received a derisory 23, votes, 21 of them Labour. Equating Zionism with Nazism has become one of the standard ploys of the far left in its obsessional campaign of vilification of the state of Israel, but the tactic in fact dates back to the time of Stalin, when he slandered his opponents on the left as agents of the Nazis, and 'social fascists', only then to sign a pact of friendship with Hitler in August 1939. Today, there are those on the left who go one better than Stalin in duplicity, denouncing Zionists as Nazis while *simultaneously* collaborating with Muslims who advertise their genocidal intentions towards the Jews and their admiration of Hitler.

Let us begin with Noam Chomsky, a professor of linguistics, a discipline that concerns itself with the meanings of words. However, when it comes to the word 'Nazi' we find Professor Chomsky putting his academic skills to one side in using, or rather abusing this term to describe the policies and actions of the Israeli government, so much so that a survey of his writings conducted by Werner Cohn has revealed that in nearly every case, Chomsky uses the word Nazi almost exclusively in this sense, and not in connection with the policies and deeds of the Third Reich. In fact, Professor Chomsky has never evinced the least interest in the Nazi regime except to equate it with Israel. For example, his anti-Zionist diatribe, *The Fateful Triangle,* highly recommended and advertised by the Neo-Nazi Holocaust-denying *Journal of Historical Review*, contains twelve references to Hitler, each one of them likening his policies to those of Zionism. And while by comparing Zionists to Nazis, Chomsky pioneered what has become the fashion on the left today, nowhere in any of his writings on the Middle East has he made any reference to the one political leader in that troubled region who not only openly

1

admired the Nazis, but as we have seen, in 1941, made his way to Berlin to begin more than three years of intimate collaboration with the chief architect the Jewish Holocaust, Adolf Hitler. We speak of course of the Grand Mufti of Jerusalem, Haj Amin al-Husseini.

If there is one policy that in the informed public mind, the Nazis are identified by, it is their fanatical persecution of the Jews, and their near-successful attempt to wipe them off the face of the planet. But as I have demonstrated in the main body of this work, there are those, non-Muslims as well as Muslims, for whom the two questions I have posed are not absurd in the least. It is to the former group, those belonging to what I have termed the Sharia left, that they are primarily addressed. When the Hamas Charter refers in Article 20 to the 'Nazism of the Jews', (not of Israel); when diaspora Muslims chant 'Nazi' at Jews they encounter and even physically assault on university campuses, on anti-Israel demonstrations, pickets outside Jewish-owned stores and during attacks on synagogues; when Fatah Central Committee member Jamal Muhaisen says there is 'no [sic] difference between [Israeli Prime Minister Binyamin] Netanyahu and Hitler' while in the West Bank, bookshops stock copies of the Arabic edition of *Mein Kampf;* when Hezbollah, a movement whose leader dreams of completing Hitler's Holocaust of the Jews, stages rallies in London (addressed on more than one occasion by Labour's Jeremy Corbyn), displaying banners and posters likening Israel to of all countries, the Third Reich; in each case, such Muslims not only display their visceral anti-Semitism, but an ignorance of the historical and political nature, meaning and significance of Nazism that is so profound, and is motivated by hatreds which run so deep, that attempts to overcome it by rational argument and the presentation of historical facts will, in nearly every case, prove to be a sheer waste of time.

What can one say possibly to convince a gang of Muslim storm troopers who broke up a meeting of the Kings College London Israel Society to chants of 'two, four, six eight, Israel is fascist state' that it is their own conduct, and the doctrine that feeds it, that are fascist, and that Jews have always been fascism's victims? Then there is the glib comment which has become common coin amongst non-Muslim critics of Israel that its Jews are no better than the Nazis. Only those who know nothing of what the Nazis did to the Jews or are no less badly informed as to the history of Israel, could make such remark, unless it is motivated not by ignorance, but as it is for example with the Labour Party's most notorious Jew-baiter, Ken Livingstone, by anti-Semitic malice. The same applies to those on the right who share the mind set of Paddy Sing, the UKIP Parliamentary candidate for North Wiltshire in the general election of June 2017. Three weeks before the election it emerged that in 2014, he had tweeted that Israelis were 'basically Nazis in mentality', 'Nazi Jews like wild dogs on the rampage'. So by a process of elimination, I address myself to a movement that I was once part of and which, for all its blinds spots and illusions, taught me political and historical lessons I could not have learned elsewhere. I speak, of course, of the far, predominately *Trotskyisant* left

True, by surrendering its principles in its pursuit of an alliance with Jihadi Islam, it has completely lost its political and moral bearings. But this movement has its origins in a tradition in which honesty, facts and rational thinking mattered. For those who claim to subscribe to his teachings, Trotsky's legacy is essentially threefold. First, he was with Lenin, the organiser of the Bolshevik seizure of

2

power, and then, as Commissar for War, of its defence and eventual victory; secondly, from 1923, he headed the opposition to the rise to total power of Stalin, a resistance that led in his years of final exile to the foundation of the Fourth International as a rival to the Third controlled by Stalin; and finally, perhaps his greatest intellectual legacy, there is his analysis of the rise to power of the Nazis. Not only did Trotsky more than any other commentator of the time accurately dissect the forces that brought into being the Nazi movement and propelled its path to power. He also foresaw with uncanny prescience the consequences of Hitler's victory not only for the German worker's movement and Germany, but for Europe, the world...and the Jews.

When the Nazi share of the vote surged from 2.6% in 1928 to 16% in the Reichstag election of September 1930, Trotsky warned communist workers that unless their party leaders abandoned Stalin's policy of denouncing the Social Democrats as 'social fascists', by exploiting the disunity in the ranks of the left, the Nazis would 'ride over your skulls and spines like a terrific tank'. As early as 1931, ten years before the actual event, he predicted that 'a victory of fascism in Germany would signify an inevitable war against the USSR'. Not only after, but before the Munich Agreement of September 30, 1938, with the USSR officially opposed to the appeasement of Hitler (but already engaged in secret exchanges with the Nazis), Trotsky foresaw that Stalin would seek a deal with Berlin. George Orwell wrote in 1944 that so far as he was aware, no one on the left foresaw either the Stalin-Hitler Pact or grasped that 'the Nazis were dangerous even when they were on the verges of seizing power.' He obviously had not had full access to Trotsky's writings of the period. In December 1938, while statesmen pursued their fool's gold of 'peace in our time' with a Third Reich preparing itself for the conquest of Europe, and as the world offered platitudes but denied refuge to Jews fleeing mounting Nazi persecution, there came from Trotsky's final Mexican exile another unheeded warning, not only of impending world war, but of what today we know as the Holocaust of the Jews:

> The numbers of countries that expel the Jews grow without cease. The number of countries able [or willing] to accept them decreases...It is possible to imagine without difficulty what awaits the Jews at the mere outbreak of the future world war. But even without war the next development of reaction signifies with certainty *the physical extermination of the Jews.* [the emphasis is Trotsky's]

Those who claim to be the defenders and continuators of Trotsky's theoretical legacy should surely be obliged to answer the following question: how can their current practice of equating Zionism with Nazism, and of accusing the Jews of Israel of complicity in a crime uniquely associated with the Third Reich, namely the attempt to exterminate an entire race, be reconciled with the assessment of Nazism contained in the writings of their mentor? Are they right when they claim Israel is a Nazi state, and that all Jews who support it are Nazis? Let us begin with Trotsky's definition of Nazism, and the regime that it created, and then see if it can in any way be made to apply to Zionism and the state of Israel as it is today.

Trotsky undertook his first detailed analysis of Hitler's version of fascism when as we have said, the Nazis increased their vote from 2.6% in the Reichstag elections of May 1928 to 16% in September 1930. The distinction between German and Italian fascism is important because Muslims and the Sharia left, if they so wanted, could just as easily call Zionists fascists. But they rarely if ever do, because the intention is to depict Zionists as *racists*, not totalitarians. And it is indeed the case that unlike Italian fascism, which described itself as totalitarian and placed not race but nation and state at the centre of its doctrine, Hitler's ruling obsession, and that of his party and Reich, was anti-Semitic racism, as Trotsky readily acknowledged. Hitler was totally in thrall to the same fantasies of the *Protocols* that so captivate Hamas and the preachers of the West Bank and in the UK, frequenters of Corbynista websites. As Trotsky himself said, for Hitler, anti-Semitism was a 'universal key to all the secrets of life', a 'zoological materialism.' As for Nazi 'socialism', this too reduced itself to a struggle against what the theorists of national socialism called 'international Jewish capital'. 'Bowing down before capitalism as a whole, the [Nazified] petty bourgeoisie declares war against the evil spirit of gain in the guise of the Polish Jew in a long-skirted kaftan and usually without a cent in his pocket'…Bebel's 'socialism of fools'… and of hundreds if not thousands of members of the Corbynised Labour Party.

As a Marxist would do, Trotsky sought the explanation for this sudden rise in the fortunes of the hitherto marginalised Nazi Party in social and economic factors. First of course was the economic crisis that overwhelmed Germany in the wake of the Wall Street crash the previous year. Already burdened by reparations payments, and heavily dependent for its economic survival on massive US loans, when after the crash, markets for German exports began to contract, and US loans to be called in to meet rising debts at home, the German economy plunged into recession faster and more deeply than any other. Already by the winter of 1929, unemployment had reached two million. A year on it stood at three million. On the day of Hitler's appointment as Chancellor on January 30, 1933, it had peaked at six million. Germany's worsening economic plight inevitably had far reaching political consequences, as they did in every country affected by the depression. In the USA, there was a sharp swing to the left, with the election of Roosevelt, a surge in trade union membership, strikes and factory occupations, and the adoption of the interventionist New Deal. In the UK, events followed an opposite course, with the collapse in 1931 of a minority Labour administration and the formation of a Tory-dominated 'National' coalition headed by Ramsey MacDonald committed to *laisser faire* austerity. In less industrialised France, where the depression as a result came later and less severely, there was a gradual but powerful swing to the left, culminating in 1936 in the formation of a 'Popular Front' Socialist-Radical coalition under the Jewish socialist Leon Blum, followed as in the USA by radical reforms and an unprecedented wave of strikes and factory occupations. In the same year, Spain plunged into civil war as the propertied classes and the Catholic Church threw their weight behind General Franco's military rebellion in a bid to reverse the newly-elected centre left government's programme of land reform, regional autonomy and improved conditions for urban workers.

In Germany the onset of the world depression ended the series of centre-left coalitions that with only brief interruptions, had dominated political life since the end of the First World War. As was the case in the UK with the bulk of the Labour Party, the Social Democrats (SPD), under pressure from their Trade Union partners, found it impossible to endorse the austerity policies of their liberal and Catholic Centre Party coalition partners. Hermann Mueller, Weimar's last Social

4

Democratic Chancellor, resigned in March 1930, to be replaced by the Centre Party's Heinrich Bruening. Lacking a majority in the Reichstag, Bruening now governed by presidential decree in accordance with the notorious Article 48 of the Weimar Constitution. As the recession deepened, cuts in wages, unemployment benefit and welfare services progressively eroded the living standards of all but the upper and upper middle classes. The communist party (KPD) began to gain votes at the expense of its larger Social Democratic rival, the SPD, which although now officially in opposition, chose after much agonising to sustain Bruening in office as the 'lesser evil' to a cabinet dominated by the extreme right. On the more moderate right, the conservative big business-oriented People's Party (DVP) and the more liberal Democratic Party (DP) lost votes not only to the Nazis, but also, initially, to the anti-Weimar and mainly agrarian Nationalists (DNVP) and a host of smaller parties representing regional and small business and rural interests. As the crisis deepened, the Nazis emerged as the most dynamic force on the far right, mopping up not only the votes of the sectional parties, but biting deeply into the support of the much larger DNVP. This is the backdrop to Trotsky's writings on Germany between 1930 and 1933.

Unlike Stalin and his servile but still frequently purged retinue, Trotsky was a highly sophisticated thinker, one of, if not the most perspicacious political minds of the 20th century. This enabled him to understand that for all its hostility towards the left, the Nazi movement and what passed for its ideology were neither tame creations or creatures of Germany's ruling classes: the Junker landowners and officer caste, the big industrialists and the bankers. Trotsky regarded National Socialism in every sense as an outgrowth of the diverse social strata ranged immediately below these groups and above Germany's most numerous and well organised class, the urban industrial proletariat:

> Under the impact of the crisis, the petty bourgeoisie swung, not in the direction of the proletarian revolution, but in the direction of the most extreme imperialist reaction...The gigantic growth of National Socialism is an expression of two factors, a deep social crisis, throwing the petty bourgeois masses off balance, and the lack of a revolutionary party that would be regarded by the popular masses as the acknowledged revolutionary leader...fascism, as a mass movement, is the party of counter-revolutionary despair.

Recent historical research into voting trends in the late Weimar period has established that the picture presented here by Trotsky is not the whole story. And of course, he understood that no political party, however obviously it gears its appeal to one or more social interests, only attracts support from those groups, any more that it gains the support from all those who comprise them. Political life is much more complex than that. And, by advertising themselves as both 'national' and 'socialist' the Nazis deliberately challenged, with much success, the traditional lines of demarcation that apart from the denominational and aptly named Catholic Centre Party, defined and separated the established political parties of the Weimar Republic. As the deepening crisis of Weimar exposed the bankruptcy of Germany's traditional ruling class parties, significant numbers of Germany's elite switched their political allegiance, giving the Nazis not only their votes but in some cases, their money and influence. Down below, while the Nazis failed to make any inroads into the left vote, which remained split between the SPD and the

KPD, they picked up significant support from what one analyst has called nationalist-minded 'Tory' workers who, repelled by the internationalism of the left parties, had been previously voting for parties of the traditional right, but were now attracted by the Nazi's strident nationalism combined with a promise of a better deal for the neglected 'little man'. However, with these qualifications, Trotsky's depiction of Nazism as essentially a movement of the urban and rural lower middle classes stands. We must bear this in mind when we come to contrast National Socialism with the movement that pioneered, created, built and for most of its seven decades, ruled the state of Israel...*Labour* Zionism.

Issuing out of Germany's intermediate strata, Trotsky foresaw that the Nazi Party, more specifically its paramilitary formations, the SA and the SS, would, if the opportunity and necessity arose, be used to crush the German workers' movement, just as the Mussolini's Black Shirted private army had been in Italy:

> The period of half-way measures has passed. In order to try to find a way out, the bourgeoisie must absolutely rid itself of the pressure exerted by the workers' organisations; these must be eliminated, destroyed, crushed. At this juncture the historic role of fascism begins. It raises to their feet those classes that are immediately above the proletariat and are ever in dread of being forced into its ranks. It organises and militarises them at the expense of finance capital under the cover of the official government and directs them to the extirpation of proletarian organisations from the most revolutionary to the most conservative

Left, or as it was generally known, Labour Zionism, as distinct from, and to a large degree, opposed to General Zionism, neither in its social composition, circumstances of origin nor principles, bore any resemblance to what Trotsky defines here as the salient features of Nazism. It was in no sense a movement of the Jewish petty bourgeoisie, called upon by the Jewish bourgeoisie, such as it was, to crush the Jewish proletariat. It was itself, if not the only, then certainly the chief movement of the Jewish proletariat both in the heartlands of the Jewish diaspora and in its new home in the Mandate, in the creation and building of Israel. Nazi propaganda was for once not so wide of the mark when it depicted the impoverished Jewish masses of the east as the seedbed and carriers of 'Jewish Bolshevism'. According to one Nazi specialist on the 'Jewish question', Professor Walter Recke, 'the Jewish proletarian is the real solicitor of Bolshevism in Poland'. Of the country's 3,5 million Jews, 'ninety per cent [were] proletarians of the worst kind'.

To return to Trotsky. Does the system he describes here bear any resemblance to modern Israel and, if it does, in which respects?

> The system of fascism is based on the destruction of parliamentarism...At the moment the "normal" police and military resources of the bourgeois dictatorship, together with their parliamentary screens, no longer suffice to hold society in a state of equilibrium - the turn of the fascist regime arrives...finance capital gathers into its hands, as in a vice of steel, directly and immediately, all the organs and institutions of sovereignty, the executive, administrative and educational powers of the state: the entire state apparatus together with the army, the municipalities, the universities, the schools, the press, the trade unions, and the co-operatives.

One can argue that Trotsky erred in his expectation that what he described as 'finance capital' would 'gather into its hands', 'directly' all the levers of state power in the Third Reich. The Nazi leadership made it clear from the very beginning of their rule that they were not the agents or servants of 'finance capital' or anyone else for that matter, that they would delegate political power to no-one outside their own ranks. But the point stands that a Nazi regime spelt death not only for the workers' movement, but every last vestige of liberal democracy in every sphere of life, to be replaced by a regime that in its quest for complete domination over society, is usually classified as totalitarian and described by Trotsky as one which necessitates the 'annihilating [of] the worker's organisations' and 'the destruction of parliamentarism'. Do Israel's leftist, in some cases, Trotskyist enemies really believe that Israel is a totalitarian state, governed not by a freely elected parliament based on universal suffrage, with its free press, religious pluralism, leftist and Palestinian parties and free trade unions, but one ruled by a gang of paramilitary thugs on behalf of 'Jewish 'finance capital', where trade unions and strikes are illegal, where the press, academic and cultural life are regulated by the leaders of these same thugs according to the doctrine of the state's one and only party?

If Israel is indeed a Nazi state, and has been, so the story goes, from its very beginning, 'a racist endeavour' then those who created it must have also been Nazis. Who were they, these Jewish Nazis? It is no coincidence that most of the pioneers and early settlers of Israel hailed from eastern Europe. Until the establishment of Israel in 1948, the Jewish diaspora lived in countries whose history and political systems varied enormously, and therefore likewise their attitude towards and treatment of their Jews. While the French Revolution opened up the possibility in the west of emancipation and, especially for more prosperous Jews, assimilation, in the east, well into the twentieth century it was a different story entirely. There a lower level of culture of the host nation prevailed, with its primitive, often murderously violent religiously-inspired anti-Semitism. Tsarist Russia up to 1917 legally confined its five million Jews to the so called 'Pale of Settlement' in the western border regions, where they faced official policies of segregation and discrimination, combined with government-instigated or connived at pogroms by anti-Semitic gangs, the loyalist 'Union of the Russian People', the Black Hundreds. This all-pervading persecution, together with the most terrible economic exploitation and living conditions, convinced large numbers of Jewish workers and the growing Jewish intelligentsia of the necessity to become involved in leftist secular politics. Around the turn of the 19th century, assimilationist intellectuals gravitated towards the Marxist Russian Social Democratic Labour Party, founded in 1898, where after the split of 1903, they comprised the majority of the leadership of the Menshevik faction. Most Jewish workers belonged to the Bund, by far the largest of Russia's labour organisations. Its leaders, while opposed to Zionism, argued in opposition to both Bolsheviks and Mensheviks (who each demanded the Bund dissolve itself and its members individually join the RSDLP) that like the Polish socialists of the Russian Empire, who were allowed to affiliate as a separate party, the Jews were also a nation, and should therefore have the same rights of separate organisation and affiliation.

Both the Bolshevik Russian Lenin and the Menshevik Jew Martov, unlike Trotsky in his last years, vehemently opposed the idea that the Jews constituted a nation, and when the Second Party Congress of 1903 endorsed this position, rather than dissolve itself as required, the Bund withdrew from both the congress and the

7

party, by so doing, providing Lenin's Bolsheviks ('majoritarians') with a narrow lead over Martov's Mensheviks ('minoritarians'). Yet for all its opposition to Zionism, the Bund's insistence on the reality of Jewish nationhood, with its own history, religion, culture, language, literature, aspirations and inner political life, was a harbinger of what was to become Labour Zionism. For what the Jews still lacked was a territory and a state which, like other nations, they could call their own, and where they would be free from persecution and the ever-present threat of pogroms. By 1917, while the membership of Bund stagnated at around 30,000 the movement that would evolve into Labour Zionism counted ten times that number in its ranks.

In the west, where the Jews, at least on paper, had achieved legal equality, the question of a separate organisation for Jewish workers never arose. Just as the more prosperous and better educated Jews assimilated into the liberal bourgeoisie, so Jewish workers and radical intellectuals were absorbed into to the trade unions and parties of the left. True, anti-Semitism was never far away...the Dreyfus Affair, and periodic anti-Jewish riots in London's East End were just the visible tip of the iceberg...but it was anti-Semitism of a different order to that prevalent in the east, rarely violent, never officially instigated or tolerated, and always resisted not only by the Jews, but most of the left and the more enlightened of the middle classes.

As the years passed, apart from the activities of fringe parties and leagues, in the west political anti-Semitism went underground, to ruminate, but not to die. Understandably then, even though the modern Zionist movement was launched in the west by Theodore Herzl in the wake of the conviction in 1894 of the Jewish Captain Dreyfus on a framed-up charge of spying for Germany, it was in east that the appeal of a return to Israel was greatest. And it was this eastern predominance that from the beginning gave Zionism its plebeian, we could even say proletarian character. Not for the comfortable assimilated bourgeois Jew of Paris, Berlin, New York, Vienna, Amsterdam or London the backbreaking slog of turning barren desert into a land of plenty. And so Labour Zionism was born, a Zionism of collective labour and collective ownership in the form of the *kibbutzim,* in which for the first time in over two thousand years, Jews freed from persecution and discrimination, and the ever-present fear of something far worse, could live and work under a government and laws of their own making. The emergence of the principles of Labour Zionism predated by many years its rise to predominance in the Zionist movement of the 1930s. Despite Jews being confined over the centuries by Christian legislation to marginal and despised occupations such as petty trade and money lending, the ideal of collective ownership and labour remained deeply embedded in Jewish culture and re-emerged with the onset of emancipation in the later 19th century.

In 1862, Karl Marx's friend Moses Hess set out his programme for a socialist Jewish state in Israel in his *Rome and Jerusalem: The last National Question.* In this work, he developed for the first time an idea that would recur time and again in writings on the subject of Jewish settlement in Palestine: the Jews must finish with their humiliating semi-parasitic role as marginal petty traders, and return to the soil to engage in honest and honourable productive collective labour. Here already is the germ of the Israeli *kibbutzim.* Other writers on the same theme followed, all stressing that Zionism was pre-eminently a movement of and for the marginalised, oppressed and impoverished Jews of Europe and the Middle East, and that the Israel that Zionism created would be a socialist one and, as has been the case from its birth in 1948, in which any Arab minority would have equal rights of citizenship. Though Herzl saw his role as pre-eminently political, drumming up support where he could amongst Jew and gentile alike for his project, his social and economic programme for a Jewish homeland was well to the left of centre by any standards, with proposals for a comprehensive welfare state, public ownership of all-natural resources and co-operative ownership of industry, agriculture and trade.

After the First World war, Labour Zionism in Palestine was initially represented by Poale Zion, which in time split into two parties, the smaller Marxist Mapam, and the larger reformist Mapai. In a speech to the Poale Zion congress held in Jaffa in February 1919, David Ben Gurion, destined to become Israel's first Prime Minister in 1948, defined the guiding principle of what in 1930 was to become Mapai as an 'organic fusion of two worlds, Jewish national redemption and the social liberation of man'. However construed, in no sense can this be represented as in any sense sharing an affinity with the racial exclusiveness of Nazi 'socialism'. To rebut such accusations, I cite at some length from a speech given by Ben Gurion in 1922 to the third convention of the forerunner to Mapai, the United Labour Party, in Hebrew, *Adhut Ha'avoda*:

> For Zionism, the struggle of the working class is daily labour, the organization of the workers as a unified body in control of its class affairs, their organisation in trade unions for offensive and defensive action in the private sector, their struggle for positions of influence in the economy and the national institutions, the setting up of collective farms, increasing the political power of labour in national and civic governmental institutions, the struggle of the Jewish working class for its national rights, the struggle to increase settlement and to direct immigrants toward productive work, socialistic pioneering activities, cultural creativity, and collaboration with the international labour movement. Adhut Ha'avoda considers it the duty of the Jewish worker to take part in all struggles, to impose labour in the life of the people, the land, and the economy. This must be the role of the Jewish worker in creating a socialist society in Israel.

It is irrelevant to the case under consideration whether this goal has been achieved, which it self-evidently has not. The question is, are these goals in any way Nazi? And has the actual result been the creation of a Nazi state or one similar to those of the liberal democratic west? Even Zeev Sternhell, possibly the most trenchant Jewish critic of Labour Zionism, had to concede in his *The Founding Myths of Israel* that 'of all societies that gained independence after the Second World war, Israel was undoubtedly the one in which political liberty, a multi-party system and the supremacy of civilian government were most completely assured'. And, we could add, has remained so to this day, despite being from its birth constantly threatened and periodically attacked by states and movements that have sought its annihilation.

As we have seen, integral to Labour Zionism was its overriding emphasis on the organisation of the Jewish workers in the newly-established British Mandate into a unified trade union movement, a goal that was achieved in 1920 under the auspices of United Labour. The *Histadrut* or General Federation of Jewish Workers, grew in direction proportion to the rate of Jewish settlement in what was to become Israel. In 1948 its membership had reached 330,000, 48% of the adult

Jewish population, organising and representing by far the highest share of the work force of any trade union in the world, either then, now or at any other time in history. In the early years of the new Jewish state, the trade unions took on a whole range of functions normally provided by either the public or private sectors, such as banking, insurance, health, publishing and education. These the Federation continues to provide today, while other once-wide ranging economic interests have largely been sold off to the private sector. Initially founded to organise settler Jewish labour, the *Histadrut* now organises all Israeli workers irrespective of religion or ethnic origin, and is affiliated, like the UK.'s Trade Union Congress, to the International Confederation of Free Trade Unions, despite the campaign in the 1980s by Corbyn and Livingstone to bring about their disaffiliation. So to those who claim that Zionists are Nazis, I say, the Nazis destroyed trade unions, the Zionists built them.

The ascendancy of Labour Zionism in the 1930s came as a direct response to the rise to power of the Nazis in Germany, and the re-emergence of anti-Semitic movements right across the rest of Europe. The idea of a safe haven for Jewry was no longer just a dream and a hope, but a matter of urgent practical action. For millions of Jews, neither assimilation nor emigration was the answer to the 'Jewish Question'. While some host nations persecuted their Jews, those who did not refused to accept any more. Discrimination, segregation, deportation, extermination: these were the solutions to the 'Jewish Question' that now forced their way onto the agenda. It was in these times of growing alarm amongst European Jewry that Labour Zionism came to the fore as the most outspoken and militant advocates of action, of the organisation of mass migration to the British mandate as both the only viable means of escape from persecution and worse, and the achievement of the goal of a state, no matter how small, in the ancient homeland of the Jews.

Already by 1933, Mapai, the voice of Labour Zionism, had won 44% of the votes in elections to the Executive at the 18th Zionist Congress in Prague. So great was the danger facing European Jewry that a number of prominent assimilated Jews who had previously declined to endorse the Zionist project now publicly declared their support for the Labour Zionists, most famous among them being Albert Einstein. He felt able to do so because as a socialist and secularist he shared both of the aims of Labour Zionism, the creation of not only a socialist Israel but a secular one. Here too Herzl pointed the way. Like nearly all the founders of Israel, Herzl was an atheist, and would have no truck with any Jew who tried to impose a clerical agenda onto the Zionist enterprise. It was an entirely secular venture. 'Matters of faith' were to be 'once and for all excluded from public influence'. Whether anyone 'sought religious devotion in the synagogue, in the Church, in the Mosque, in the art museum, or in the philharmonic concert, did not concern society. That was his own private affair.'

While denial of the existence of a Jewish nation leads on, naturally, to the denial of the right of Jews to their own nation state, a belief in its existence does not necessarily lead to the opposite conclusion, as in the case of the Jewish Bund, which argued instead for Jewish 'cultural autonomy' within the Russia empire. Interestingly from the standpoint of the matter under review, unlike both the Bolshevik and Menshevik factions, who despite their differences at the Second Congress of the RSDLP in 1903, both denied the existence of a Jewish nation, Trotsky, contrary to his epigones today, in his third and final exile came to recognise both Jewish nationhood and the Jews' right to their own state.

> At one time I thought that the Jews would assimilate into the people and cultures they lived among...But now [this was 1937] it was impossible to say this. Recent history has taught us something about this. The fate of the Jews has been posed as a burning question, particularly in Germany, and the Jews who had forgotten their ancestry were clearly reminded of it.... The Jews...can and should lead their own lives as a people, with their own culture. The territorial question is pertinent because it is easier for a people to carry out an economic and cultural plan when it lives in a compact mass. Under socialism, that question will arise, and with the consent of those Jews who desire it, there might be a free mass emigration...why shouldn't they be able to do this?

While warning in July 1940, and with good reason, against the dangers of seeking a homeland for the Jews in Palestine at a time when 'further military developments' could 'transform Palestine into a bloody trap for several hundred thousand Jews', which was indeed precisely the objective of the agreement concluded by the Grand Mufti and Hitler in Berlin in November 1941, Trotsky insisted that the Jews had a right to their 'own autonomous republic as the arena for their own culture'. Trotsky therefore did not in principle, unlike the Sharia left, oppose the creation of a Jewish state in Palestine. However, he believed that the Zionist goal of a Jewish state in what was then still the British Mandate was a 'tragic mirage' not least because the British 'were interested in winning the sympathies of the Arabs who are more numerous than the Jews'. This was indeed the case and continued to be so after the war until the creation of Israel in 1948. However, Trotsky's conclusion that Zionism was 'incapable of resolving the Jewish question' because it sought to do so independently of what he still believed was an impending world socialist revolution and was therefore 'utopian and reactionary in character', was wrong. History has passed its own judgement on which of the two paths to Jewish nationhood has proved a utopian mirage

To return to where we began. It is immaterial whether one agrees or not, or to what extent, with Trotsky's definition and appraisal of the role of National Socialism. The question to be answered by Israel's leftist enemies is, does that definition and appraisal apply in any meaningful sense to the nature and policies of the Israeli state, and the political doctrine of Zionism? For Trotsky, fascism was not a term of abuse, as Nazi is today for the Sharia left, to be hurled at anyone with whom one has serious political differences. It was a very specific form of political rule, none of whose essential features exists in the Israel of today. However, for the sake of the argument, let it be granted that all the accusations made against Israel are true: They are as follows:

1) Israel is Nazi or fascist because it occupies (but, save for East Jerusalem, has not annexed) disputed territories beyond its own internationally recognised (but not by all) borders. But nowhere in Trotsky's definition of fascism is there any reference to colonialism or illegally occupied territories. In fact, the Versailles Treaty stripped Germany not only of all its colonies, but national territories in the north, west and east. When the Nazis came to power, Germany had still three years to wait before it regained full sovereignty over the de-militarised zone of the Rhineland, while at the insistence of France, the Saarland remained an 'occupied territory', not of Germany, but of a League of Nations mandate exercised until 1935. If the possession of colonies is the indicator of fascism, then despite its

having fought a six-year war against a Nazi Germany which possessed none, it would have not been the Third Reich but the United Kingdom which would have been ranked as the world's leading fascist power.

If the illegal or disputed occupation of territories, as distinct from colonial possessions, is a sufficient criterion, then Jordan's illegal annexation of the West Bank in 1948, after the territory had been designated by the United Nations the previous year as part of an independent Palestinian state, would have qualified the kingdom as fascist, as it would for Egypt for its parallel seizure of the Gaza Strip. But since the illegal occupations were the work of Arab Muslims, no-one then or since who claims to support or represent the Palestinian cause has spoken of an illegal occupation of Palestinian territory by Egypt or Jordan, let alone by so doing their becoming fascist states. That only became the order of the day when the occupying (and not annexing) power in 1967 became Jewish. Similar considerations apply to the Soviet invasion and attempted occupation of Afghanistan between 1979 and 1989. Because the occupation was in response to a puppet regime's request, at the instigation of its Soviet masters, for an invasion by the Kremlin to rescue its tottering client, we had a *de facto* rather than technically illegal occupation. But the results were the same. Millions of Afghan Muslims were subjected to a near-genocidal reign of terror that resulted in the deaths of approximately one million civilians. But here too, except on outer fringes of the Maoist far left, no-one described the USSR as a fascist or Nazi state, and those few that did, did so on account of its internal regime, and not its external policies.

2) Israel is a Nazi state because it imposes a racist policy of apartheid on the Palestinians. This is a lie. But even if it were true, following Trotsky, this would not be sufficient grounds to call Israel a Nazi state. Even in the extreme case of South Africa, its apartheid system left intact a whites-only parliament in which, though dominated by the racist Afrikaner National Party, legal opposition of a limited kind was still possible by its three other (white) parties, a luxury not afforded even to pure blooded Aryans by Hitler's one-party Reich. There were also whites-only trade unions, whereas in Nazi Germany there were none. If indeed pre-Mandela South Africa was a Nazi state, it would be unique in history as the first one of its kind to be dismantled peacefully by its own ruling (Nazi) party, release all its political prisoners, conduct free and equal elections and then have its leaders retire either into obscurity or permanent opposition. As the examples of Franco Spain and Mussolini's Italy up to 1938 prove, segregation, whether of race, gender or religion, is not integral to fascism, though it could be pursued by it, as it was in the Jewish ghettos created in Poland by the Third Reich as the prelude to the Holocaust. However, Jews were for centuries also forced by law to live in walled and guarded ghettoes by a 16th century ruling of the Vatican. Did this make the Roman Catholic Church Nazi? Or Tsarist Russia, which enforced a similar servile condition on its Jews? Well into the second half of the twentieth century, blacks in the deep south of the United States were legally as well as socially segregated from whites. Again, one must ask: did this make the USA a Nazi state?

3) Israel is a Nazi state because it is perpetrating the genocide of the Palestinians, just as the Nazis did of the Jews. The first statement is a lie, while many of the Shari left's Muslim friends either deny or celebrate the second. While neither genocide nor anti-Semitism are integral to fascism, in Germany, where its fascism from the outset was obsessively racist, they become its main

distinguishing feature. In the case of Italy up to 1938, and Franco Spain, they were not. However, what have been described as genocides by agencies or states that in no sense can be described as fascist...the catastrophic decline in the native populations that followed the conquest and colonisation of the two Americas and Australasia for example...prove the point.

4) Israel is a Nazi state because Zionism subscribes to the belief that the Jews are racially superior to the Arabs. This too is a lie. Nether in law or in ideology are Israeli Palestinians treated or regarded as racially inferior to Jews, and not even the most vehement anti-Zionist has been able to prove they are. While racist parties in Israel are illegal, Israel has on its borders Arab regimes that promote religiously-inspired race hatred against the Jews as a matter of official state policy. As the *Koran* says, they are 'apes and swine', 'the worst of creatures'. But of course, this in in no sense racism, just theology.

Replicating, albeit in a different context, the lunacy of Stalinist 'social fascism,' these accusations constitute the basis of the claim that Israel is a Nazi state, that Zionism is a racist, Nazi doctrine, and that the vast majority of Jews who live in or support Israel are, *ipso facto,* likewise Nazis. Significantly, all three criteria refer exclusively to Israel's relationship with the Palestinians and not its internal political system, which is a western-type liberal parliamentary democracy, of just the kind which, according to Trotsky, Hitler was bent on destroying in Germany. Since its creation in 1948, Israel has conducted 24 Parliamentary elections on a universal franchise that includes the Arabs it is alleged to be either exterminating, segregating or both. The most recent, in 2021, was contested not by one, as in Nazi Germany, but 13 parties, including two that are explicitly anti-Zionist and attract most Arab voters. The Palestine Authority held its most recent election in 2006, since when Israel has held eight. Therefore, none of the aspects ascribed, rightly or wrongly, to Israel's political system or policies even remotely resembles those that for Trotsky or, for that matter, any serious analyst of the subject, are integral to a fascist or Nazi regime, namely:

a) The emergence of anti-democratic, chauvinist and, in the case of Germany, also anti-Semitic paramilitary movements of the extreme right, drawn mainly from the lower middle classes;

b) The deployment of these movements by the ruling class, or a faction within it, for the destruction of all labour organisations and institutions of parliamentary democracy,

c) Once in power, the creation by the fascist or Nazi movement of a one-party state that obliterates all political freedoms and democratic practises and institutions, and in quick time, stamps out all ideas opposed to its own doctrine by establishing total control over news reporting and all aspects of political, social, cultural and intellectual life. However, there is a regime which today closely approximates these three criteria more than any other in the world today. It is the former employer of Livingstone, Galloway and Corbyn, the Islamic Republic of Iran.

Addenda: The Sinking of the *Struma*

That Trotsky predicted correctly when he said the makers of British imperial policy would always side with the Arabs against the claims of the Zionists was nowhere better proven than by the decisions of British officials that led on

February 19, 1942, to the sinking in the Black Sea of the *Struma*, a ship carrying more than 750 Jewish refugees fleeing from Romania to what was then the British mandate in Palestine. They were enforcing a policy the diametric opposite to that being pursued today towards Muslims seeking entry into Europe, the majority of whom are not refugees but illegal economic and welfare migrants. By contrast, all on board the *Struma* were Jews fleeing a regime that has already massacred tens of thousands of Romanian Jews, and whose armed forces, acting jointly with the Third Reich in the invasion of the USSR on June 22, 1941, had committed identical atrocities on Soviet soil. When the ship put in at Istanbul, the Turkish authorities asked the British ambassador whether they should let the vessel continue on its chosen course. If not, it would be refused passage through the straights and its passengers denied asylum in Turkey. The ball was now in the British court.

While making it clear to the Turks that his government 'did not want those people [sic] in Palestine', Hughe Knatchbull-Hugesson, the British ambassador, suggested the Turks let the ship proceed in the hope that on its arrival, its passengers might receive 'humane treatment.' This was not at all what his political masters in London had in mind. E.H. Boyd, a Foreign Office official, condemned Knatchbull-Hugesson for missing a 'heaven sent [sic] opportunity of getting these people [sic] stopped at Istanbul and sent back to [the Romanian port of] Constanza'...and near certain death. An extraordinary pretext for this decision, which in reality was motivated by what Lord Cranborne, the Colonial Secretary, described euphemistically as 'the extremely delicate position in the Middle East' was concocted by his predecessor Lord Moyne who, in a memo to Foreign Secretary Anthony Eden, claimed that 'we have good reason to believe that this traffic [in refugees] is being favoured by the Gestapo, and the [British] Security Services attach the very greatest importance to preventing the influx of Nazi agents under the cloak of refugees'.

So, hidden among the passengers on the *Struma* were Jews, or 'Aryans' posing as Jews, in the employ of the Gestapo. Not a shred of evidence for this claim had been or was later found among all the many thousands of Jewish refugees who arrived, by one means or another, in the British Mandate during the war. Even so, Moyne proposed that the ship be sent back whence it came. On February 19, the Turks ordered the *Struma* to return into the Black Sea, where it struck a mine and sank with the loss of all but one of its passengers and crew. Undeterred by this tragedy, for which the British authorities were wholly responsible, three weeks later, on March 2, 1942, the War Cabinet resolved that 'all practicable steps be taken to discourage illegal [obviously Jewish] immigration into Palestine.' One of the consequences of this decision was the denial by the Colonial Office of asylum to several thousand Bulgarian Jewish children on 'security grounds', since they 'came from a country which we are at war.' Perhaps among them too were child Gestapo agents. (Today, the UK has adopted a more flexible policy, admitting Muslim men posing as children half their age.) To enforce this strategy of bottling up the Jews in Nazi-controlled Europe, where they faced almost certain death, British warships were diverted from the war against the Third Reich to impose a naval blockade against Jewish refugees fleeing the Holocaust, simply to placate the anti-Semitism of Palestinian Muslims, a policy also being pursued by the Nazis, who, as we have seen (Chapter Six), were playing the same Arab card. Certainly not Churchill's, nor for that matter his deputy Clement Attlee's finest hour.

Refutation

Definitive refutation of the lie that Israel is an apartheid, genocidal, Nazi state (or one or two of the three) came on June 3, 2021, when after four inconclusive general elections in two years (the Palestinian Authority has held none since 2006) an anti-Netanyahu coalition was formed comprising eight parties. Among them were the Labour Party and Ra-am, representing Arab/Palestinian voters. As I am sure those making these allegations would agree, Nazi regimes are not in the habit of holding frequent free elections, or of sharing power with left wing parties, any more than are genocidal ones with their victims, and regimes that practice segregation with those they regard as racially inferior.

B Traison Des Clercs Encores

'Give me the liberty to know, to utter, and to argue freely according to conscience, above all liberties.' John Milton, *Areopagitica*

'Freedom is always for the one who thinks differently.' Rosa Luxemburg.

Article 19 of the United Nations Universal Declaration of Human Rights, adopted in 1948: states that

'Everyone has the right to freedom of opinion and expression; this right includes freedom to hold opinions without interference and to seek, receive and impart information and ideas through any media and regardless of frontiers.'

The First Amendment to the US Constitution, ratified in 1791:

> Congress shall make no law restricting an establishment of religion or prohibiting the free the free exercise thereof, or abridging the freedom of speech, of the press; or the right of the people peacefully to assemble, and to petition the government for a redress of grievances.

By instructing the US delegation to the United Nation Human Rights Council to vote, in November 2009, for a resolution criminalising 'racial and religious stereotyping', President Obama opposed the spirit and letter of both of the above resolutions. So did what follows. On December 17, 2015, the following resolution was brought before the United States House of Representatives by 82 Democrat members of Congress. Published on the Congress website, and titled 'Condemning violence, bigotry, and hateful rhetoric towards Muslims in the United States', it read as follows:

> Whereas the victims of Muslim hate crimes and rhetoric have faced physical, verbal and emotional abuse because they were Muslim or believed to be Muslim;
> Whereas the constitutional right to freedom of religious practice is a cherished United States value and violence or hate speech [N.B. See below] towards any United States community based on faith is in contravention of the Nation's founding principles;
> Whereas there are millions of Muslims in the United States, a community made up of many diverse beliefs and cultures, and both immigrants and native-born citizens;
> Whereas this Muslim community is recognized as having made innumerable contributions to the cultural and economic fabric and well-being of United States society;
> Whereas hateful and intolerant acts against Muslims are contrary to the United States values of acceptance, welcoming and fellowship with those of all faiths, beliefs, and cultures;
> Whereas these acts affect not only the individual victims but also their families, communities, and the entire group whose faith or beliefs were the motivation for the act;

16

Whereas Muslim women who wear hijabs, headscarves, or other religious articles of clothing have been disproportionately targeted because of their religious clothing, articles, or observances; and

Whereas the rise of hateful and anti-Muslim speech, violence and cultural ignorance plays into the false narrative spread by terrorist groups of western hatred of Islam, and can encourage certain individuals to react in extreme and violent ways: Now, therefore, be it

Resolved, That the House of Representatives –

1) expresses its condolences for the victims of anti-Muslim hate crimes ['hate crime' being undefined];

2) steadfastly confirms its dedication to the rights and dignity of all its citizens of all faiths and beliefs and cultures;

3) denounces in the strongest terms the increase of hate speech [again], intimidation, violence, vandalism, arson and other hate crimes targeted against mosques, Muslims, or those perceived to be Muslim;

4) recognizes that the United States Muslim community has made countless positive [but as always, unspecified] contributions to United States society;

5) declares that civil rights and civil liberties of all United States citizens, including Muslims in the United States, should be protected and preserved;

6) urges local and Federal law enforcement authorities to work to prevent hate crimes and prosecute to the fullest extent of the law those perpetrators of hate crime; and

7) reaffirms the inalienable right of every free citizen to live without fear and intimidation and to practice their freedom of faith.

If this bill, which sought to suppress criticism of Islam by creating a law banning so-called, but undefined 'hate speech', had been passed by both Houses of Congress, and then assented to by President Obama, it would have conflicted with the First Amendment, which when approved, set no limits on the right to freedom of speech and of the press. The drafter of the proposed law or laws ingenuously conflated speech that supposedly causes upset to Muslims with acts of physical violence against Muslims and Mosques, both of which are already illegal under existing US laws covering crimes of violence against the person and damage to property, irrespective of religion. That part of the proposed law being therefore redundant, the target was obviously the expression of opinion concerning Islam which, under the First Amendment, is not a criminal act. Passages from the *Koran* which both Christians and Jews could find highly offensive were not however covered by this resolution. Here we had again the usual politically correct one-way street, along which Muslims are at the same time entitled to protection afforded to no one else, while being allowed to say what they like about everybody else.

So, while reference was made in the preamble to United States values and traditions of religious freedom and tolerance (but not free speech be it noted) no attempt was made to require or even claim that Muslims share them, only that they should be their beneficiaries. Was the mover of the bill, Donald Beyer Jr. (Democrat, Virginia) aware that Sharia law and the 1990 Cairo Declaration of Human Rights adopted by the Organisation of the Islamic Conference are both incompatible with the spirit and the letter of the US First Amendment? No doubt to the chagrin of the Democratic Party's speech police and, we can reasonably assume, President Obama, on July 18, 2017, the US Supreme Court unanimously ruled that restricting speech expressing ideas that may offend…strikes at the heart of the First Amendment. Speech that demeans on the basis of race, ethnicity, gender, religion, age, disability or any other similar ground is hateful; but the proudest boast of our free speech jurisprudence is that we protect the freedom to express 'the thought that we hate'. [Bravo!]

Nothing deterred, and following the path taken by Corbynista Labour in the UK, the descent into dhimmitude of the increasingly Sharia-leftist Democratic Party continued apace, with the election to Congress in 2018 of two anti-Semitic Muslim women; BDS supporter Rashida Tliab, who made her debut in the Chamber sporting the colours of the Palestinian flag, and Ilhan Omar, the first woman to wear a hijab in Congress, who shortly after her election, claimed that the American-Israel Public Affairs Committee was paying US politicians to back Israel. Her take on 9/11 was 'some people did something'. A subsequent resolution to Congress condemning anti-Semitism proposed by Democrat leaders to placate the party's large Jewish constituency was vetoed by Omar's supporters, and replaced by one that condemned all forms of bigotry. This was followed by a boycott of the annual conference of AIPAC by nine Democratic Party Presidential candidates, and the Democratic majority in the House of Representatives not only inviting an imam to deliver a prayer at the opening of one its sessions, but one, Omar Suleiman, who has called for a third *Intifada*, or 'uprising', against Israel, likened it to Nazi Germany, backs the boycotting of Israel and called Zionists 'the enemies of God'.

Nowhere in the West are the Enlightenment's values of the primacy of reason and the inalienable right of free expression more under attack than on its university campuses, institutions once esteemed as their custodians, where leftist academics and their student camp followers see it as an obstacle to the advancement of what they term 'social justice' on behalf of the ever-expanding number of self-proclaimed victims of the ruling sexist, racist, LTGBist, genderist, fatist, ableist and Islamophobic white heteropatriarchy. If SJWers were as genuinely concerned with combating patriarchy as they claim, then their prime target would not be its so-called 'white' manifestations, but the one exerted over Muslim women by Muslim men, not just in the Islamic world, but increasingly in the diaspora. It is a patriarchy which, unlike its supposed 'white' counterpart, is re-enforced by barbaric laws and imposed by male violence. Not only this. The laws which under Islam consign woman to second class status are claimed to be of divine origin, the *sharia*, laws compared with which the so-called 'glass ceiling' fades into insignificance If It exists at all, and which impose often unspeakably brutal sanctions when women are found guilty by all-male 'courts' of violating them. But the Islamic subjugation of women is necessarily a SJW taboo subject, because Muslim men no less than women comprise an integral component of the 'intersectional' alliance of the oppressed, despite the reality that if they follow the dictates of their faith, Muslim men are not only the vilest oppressors of women but would, if they could, impose draconian punishments, including death, for the life-style and sexual preferences of many of their SJW cohorts. Because Islam, supposedly quintessentially the religion of the oppressed, trumps all, even in matters of race, sexual orientation and gender, a white male convert to Islam should, at least in in theory, be able to beat and rape his black Muslim wife with impunity, simply because his holy book tells him he can. But beneath Muslim men in the SJW pecking order, all is not sweetness and light. A very unsisterly fight has irrupted between feminists and transgenderists over men who claim to be women competing in women's sports events and who are invading women-only facilities and environments.

Another flagrant contradiction in the SJW movement is the demand by its Black Lives Matter contingent to 'resist white capitalism', one akin to the Nazis' equally selective condemnation of 'Jewish interest slavery'. This slogan cannot sit too well with white feminists who complain of their under-representation at the summits of western ('white') big business. (There is no equivalent outrage concerning their even greater under-representation in admittedly substantially less glamourous and remunerative, but infinitely more essential occupations as garbage collection and sewer maintenance.) In view of the inference to be drawn that only 'white capitalism' is to be condemned, it would be an instructive exercise for those who advance this slogan to conduct a comparative global study of the wages, working conditions and trade union rights of workers employed by capitalism's white patriarchal and non-white versions. As for 'patriarchy', there are entire continents, comprising the majority of the world's population, that are ruled by patriarchies of all skin colours other than white and where, in most cases, the status of women would be anything but the envy of their sisters supposedly languishing under the rule of the eastern patriarchy's western counterpart. Ignorant though they are of world affairs, given the non-subjects they have opted to qualify in, even SJWers must know this, but who would dare say it?

The contortions and feuding of SJWers over who is most victimised has deservedly been the butt of ridicule by non-believers. However, the goals the movement seeks, and is some way to achieving, are no laughing matter. The totalitarian ideology which fuels this lumpen new campus left has as one of its central goals the denial of the right of dissenters to freedom of speech, the foundation stone of not only America's but the entire West's freedoms and prosperity. It is captured to perfection by Barbara White, (sic) an (oppressed) Women's Studies (sic) Professor (sic) at the University of New Hampshire. Free speech is, it seems, and always has been, the means by which the white (heterosexual) patriarchy maintains its rule:

> Academia has traditionally been dominated by white heterosexual [how does she know this?] men, and the First Amendment and Academic Freedom (I'll call them FAF) have traditionally protected the rights of white heterosexual men. Most of us are silenced by existing social conditions before we get the power to speak out in any way where FAF might protect us. So forgive us if we don't get all dewy-eyed about FAF. Perhaps to you it's as sacrosanct as the flag or the national anthem; to us, strict construction of the First Amendment is just another noose around our necks.

So much for free speech, a 'noose around the necks' of the downtrodden and the oppressed. It follows therefore that the first step on the path to their liberation is its abolition. Another conquest of the Enlightenment, the concept of objective truth and the right and duty to pursue it by unfettered inquiry, fares no better at the elite universities of the USA, where 'mission statements' no longer speak of truth and knowledge but of respecting 'inclusiveness' and welcoming 'diversity', though not to be sure one of ideas, where a mind-numbing conformity prevails, but of race, gender and sexual orientation. And as the categories of 'diversity' multiply, so does, at the same rate, the propensity for giving offence. Under the new dispensation of combatting 'triggers' and 'micro-aggressions', we can therefore express this relationship in mathematical terms: As 'diversity' of 'identity' increases, in order to avoid giving offence to their sundry manifestations, the expression of diverse opinions must diminish at the same rate. Exactly the same holds if we substitute 'inclusivity' for 'diversity', and for the same reasons. Just as 'diversity' requires conformity, so does 'inclusion' exclusion, of ideas that might upset those to be 'included'. This is the world of 1984, where peace is war, and freedom slavery. An Open Letter, so obviously the fruit of tutorial spoon-feeding, from black students to David Oxtoby, President of Pomona College, protesting against his policy of upholding free speech, not only denounced it as 'a tool appropriated by hegemonic institutions'(sic) which enabled them to 'perpetuate systems of domination'(sic) by providing 'a platform to project their bigotry'. The letter also declared that 'historically, white supremacy has venerated the idea of objectivity' as 'a means of silencing oppressed peoples' and that the idea that there is 'a single truth' is 'a construct of the Euro-west that is deeply entrenched in the Enlightenment'.(sic) The idea of a 'single truth' was 'a myth, and white supremacy, imperialism, colonisation, capitalism and the United States of América are its progeny. The idea that the truth is an entity for which we must search in matters that endanger our ability to exist in open spaces is an attempt to silence oppressed peoples.' Far better, then, to feed non-white students patronising lies. The result one can see on a YouTube video where a black student at a Cape Town University seminar is denouncing the scientific method as 'white' and 'colonialist', and advocating, unchallenged, its replacement by what she calls 'black magic'. This not funny. It is tragic. This, the Nazi doctrine of 'race truth' at a *university?* And what is worse, in a country where its black majority was not so long ago liberated from the biblically-derived 'race truths' of its white supremacist minority.

In the same spirit, a feminist posing as an academic has given Einstein's epoch-shaping E=MC squared short shrift, denouncing it as a 'sexed equation' that 'privileges' the 'masculine' speed of light over slower feminine speeds no less essential. Newtonian physics fares no better. Since it treats only of the movements of solids, it too is guilty of male privileging. This is attributed to 'men having sex organs that protrude and become rigid', while 'woman have openings that leak menstrual blood and vaginal fluids'. QED. Gravity and the laws of motion, just like everything else we fondly once thought we knew about the universe, are genderist constructs. Such are the fruits of 'different ways of knowing', when two plus 2 can equal anything but 4.

The creators of humanity's most sublime and until 'de-constructed' by post-modernist 'critical theory', universally revered works of philosophy, art, literature and music are likewise found to have white male feet of clay. Introducing criteria of 'identity' of race and gender into the world of the creative arts has led to what one critic of 'third wave' feminism, US scholar Christena Hoff Sommers, described as a situation in academe and beyond where 'the very idea of "genius" is regarded with suspicion as elitist and "masculinist"'. Who needs Bach or Beethoven? Anyone, so long as they have the right genitals and/or skin, can compose a B Minor Mass or Choral Symphony. Plato and Aristotle are now

20

routinely derided as white patriarchs by classicists who are themselves white. The intrusion of the poison of 'identity' politics into the world of classical music has led in the UK to demands by feminazis for concerts to be devoted exclusively to compositions by women composers conducted by women conductors, and for orchestras always to be comprised 50% of women, selected not purely on merit, as is currently the practice, with anonymous auditions from behind screens, but also for their genitals. And at the 2019 Musicians Union conference a motion was carried endorsing this very demand, calling for 'equal representation of female musicians in live music performance and on radio and television'. Indicative of the shape of things to come in the world of music, when interviewed by a white male before the performance of her work on BBC Radio 3, a teenage woman composer was applauded by her audience when she said the purpose of her choral composition was to 'challenge the white male patriarchy'. Racial as well as gender engineering has also been catered for, with the formation of the segregationist Chineke orchestra, which excludes on principle all 'white' musicians, and which, as matter of principle, that of prioritising merit irrespective of race or gender, I will not listen to. Likewise, what goes by the name of 'sexual orientation'. In the USA, which always takes the lead in such innovations, we have had since at least the 1990s the New York Gay Men's Chorus. How one proves one's eligibility for membership is something best left unexplored.

Contrary to the literal meaning of the word, 'diversity' in practice today means the opposite, segregation and exclusion, always at the expense of equal opportunity, merit and quality. The irony is, this racist and genderist onslaught on the humanist tradition, rejected for its assertion of the intrinsic unity of mankind, and on science, high culture and more generally, all evidence-based and creative thinking, comes today in the USA not from the Christian fundamentalist right but increasingly from the so-called 'woke' left, in a country where already, half its population still rejects the evidence-based findings of biology, geology and cosmology, fully a third believes aliens have visited earth, and ten percent that Elvis lives. In the land of Yale and Harvard, an increasing number of its academic staff and students have succumbed to post-modernist mumbo-jumbo, resulting in 'learned' journals publishing in good faith spoof articles arguing that gravity and the penis are 'social constructs', the latter perhaps being a parody of 'deconstructionist' guru Jacques Lacan's claim that the penis can be in expressed in a series of equations, climaxing, appropriately, in the square root of minus one.

Far removed from the realm of pure numbers, an SJW activist at Chicago University appeared on Fox TV claiming the right to use violence to prevent a politician he disagreed with speaking on his campus. He was opposed to 'discussing in sanitised [sic] environments' and 'moderated conversations', meaning those conducted according to the traditional rules of debate and discussion, where there is no ever-present threat of the disruptive and intimidatory violence which has become the norm on so many US campuses. As he put it so well, 'it's not about who's right, it's about who has power.' Not the Enlightenment's power of truth, but the totalitarian principle that power defines what is true. This over-privileged (he was a white, male, probably heterosexual student at one of the USA's most expensive universities) barbarian thug unashamedly proclaimed his contempt for the achievements and indeed glories of more than two thousand years of civilisation when he wrote in his college's newspaper that 'deliberation, analysis and "hearing out both sides" is no longer viable...we must take action and dispense with all this sophistry, all these abstract notions of civility'. How would this ignoramus have known that 80 years previously, with his invasion of Poland only days away, Hitler had similarly instructed his military chiefs to cast all scruples aside: 'What matters is not to have right on our side, but simply to win'.

The contempt for logic, evidence and learning, and the free debate and exchange of ideas, first came to fruition in the fascist era, when reason was supplanted, as it is now, by the claimed higher truths of 'feeling' and of an 'identity' then white and hetero-male, and now their inverses. In its new, pseudo-leftist, guise, the same contempt for reason and knowledge dominates most US campuses today. Of America's 4,298 degree-granting colleges and universities, little more than one per cent, 58 as of March 2019, had endorsed Chicago's statement in defence of absolute academic freedom and the right to free speech and peaceful assembly as defined by the First Amendment. Of the ten elite 'Ivy League' Universities, only two had seen fit to support it; Princeton and Columbia. But not Yale and Harvard, Brown and Cornell, Tuck, Dartmouth, Wharton and Pennsylvania; yet more proof that the USA's institutions of higher learning are now in free fall. And there is every indication that the rest of the Anglo-Saxon world is only too eager to follow suit. For example, after engaging the psychologist Dr Jordan Petersen of the University of Toronto to give a series of lectures on the Old Testament Chapter of Exodus, Cambridge University's Department of Divinity reversed its decision in March 2019 after objections were made by academics and students to his well-advertised rejection, one shared by all biologists worthy of the name, of the claim that gender is purely a 'social construct' and not determined by physiology. What price Genesis 1: 27: 'Male and female He created them'? The university which in better times, when inquiry was unfettered by political correctness, had been the alma mater of some of the world's most illustrious scientists - Darwin, Rutherford, Eddington, Hawking, Crick, Franklin, Maxwell, Chadwick, David Attenborough, Oppenheimer - justified its reversal on the grounds that engaging Dr Petersen would be contrary to its policy of 'inclusiveness', Trigger Police code for *excluding* from campus ideas that students may find upsetting but are incapable of debating and refuting. As on a growing number of US campuses, Cambridge's 'snow flake' divinity students become the arbiters of what can and cannot be said and taught, and by whom. On September 28, 2019, Edinburgh University was the venue for an SJW extravaganza, billed as a Q and A session on the theme 'Resisting Whiteness 2019'. To further this 'resistance to whiteness', white participants were barred from asking questions, and excluded from a 'safe space' reserved for non-whites who felt 'overwhelmed/overstimulated [sic] or uncomfortable', presumably when in too close a proximity to those with a white skin.

In the USA, where SJW lunacy first surfaced, anti-free speech tactics by self-styled 'Social Justice Warriors' are given free rein by college authorities, involving not only the shouting down of speakers whose opinions they disagree with, but mob violence, designed to enforce on all and sundry what Milton described as a 'gross conforming stupidity'. For example, faced with the threat of SJW storm trooper assault, the Jewish libertarian Ben Schapiro had to pay $600,000 out of his own pocket for police protection from SJW mobsters when he spoke at Berkeley University, the home of the 1960s campus Free Speech movement. (With Jewish students subjected to abuse and even violence, their societies in the UK have also been obliged to pay for their own security.) Perhaps the most notorious example of SJW thuggery occurred at Evergreen Washington State College when in May 2017 biology Professor Bret Weinstein refused to comply with demands by SJW activists that white students and staff absent themselves from the campus for one day as an act of atonement for their racist guilt. Acting out, we can be sure unwittingly, since history and its lessons are a closed book to them, the role of Mussolini's 'dynamic minority' and Lenin's 'revolutionary vanguard', student rioters, some armed with baseball bats, stormed the college building, where they sought out and confronted Professor Weinstein as he lectured his class of multi-race students, swearing at and verbally abusing him as a white supremacist. They then besieged and imprisoned in his office, with his consent, the college's Principle, presenting him with a list of demands designed to enforce racial and gender 'equity' (not be it noted, equality), the only one of which he rejected being the summary dismissal of Professor Weinstein. In the following years enrolments plummeted. Betrayed by most of his academic colleagues, some of who agreed with his stand but, like the majority of the college's students, were afraid to say so, Professor Weinstein resigned later that year, after negotiating a pay-out of $500,000.

This strategy of intimidation, one that replicates the methods used by Nazi students in the early 1930s to subdue their embattled Jewish and democratic opponents, is often not only approved of but even incited by 'progressive' academic staff. If SJW mobsters fail to have a meeting banned by college authorities (who more often than not comply) they attend it not to participate in the question and answer sessions that are always a feature of free speech events, but to drown out the speaker by co-ordinated inane chants and to disrupt it by storming the platform, seizing the microphone, shouting abuse though megaphones, and setting off fire alarms... all with impunity, because they are the good guys, fighting for social justice. The appeal of these tactics is that they require next to no brain power. Like all totalitarian movements, the new campus left, unable by reason, logic and the marshalling of evidence to refute ideas it disagrees with, since all that counts are supposedly wounded 'feelings', instead uses a combination of administrative bans and gangster tactics to silence its opponents and intimidate college officials.

Belying their pretentious name, SJW activists are not driven by compassion but an ego-centric craving to be seen as virtuous. It is a second coming of the 'me' generation, whose spoiled brats they mostly are, only this time round, their self-centredness masquerades as altruism. Their claim on a monopoly of virtue, one that out-Robespierres Robespierre's, has been taken to such ludicrous extremes that it is an article of faith amongst SJWers that non-white people cannot be guilty of racism or any other prejudice, itself a racist proposition. Yet numerous scenes on YouTube show black faces distorted by a murderous loathing chanting racial and sexual obscenities at those cursed for being born with the wrong colour skin and genitals, the SJW version of original sin. Orwell's 'hate week' is no longer a dystopian fiction.

What fuels this movement is indeed pure groupthink fanatical hatred, one of race and of gender. It is now preached in what were once places of learning that all self-respecting women, LGTBs and non-whites must hate all heterosexual white men, while to have any prospect of purging their original sin, straight white men must hate and debase themselves, not necessarily for what they do, *but for what they are.* So much for Martin Luther King's dream of a time when people will be judged, 'not by the colour of their skin, but by the content of their character', and Schiller's hope, immortalised by Beethoven's Choral Symphony, that 'all men shall brothers be'. SJWers subscribe to a contrary doctrine of eternal enmity, that a heterosexual white man's character is defined by the colour of his skin and, for good measure, also the function of his genitals. And yes, out-doing the lynch mentality of the KKK, one popular 'feminist' hash tag demands, 'Kill all White Men', while 'Woman's Studies' 'Professor' Suzanna Walters titled her *Washington Post* diatribe against patriarchy 'Why can't we hate men?', after objections, subsequently racially re-calibrated to target only white men.

The SJW crusade against the white patriarchy is not merely a matter of verbal abuse. If a white man so much as displays a passing romantic interest in a member of the opposite sex ('opposite'? Careful...that's binary talk, a microaggression) he faces the very real risk of having his life ruined by accusations of attempted rape. Even 'suggestive staring' can lead to disciplinary proceedings against a man who casts a fleeting appreciative glance at an attractive female student. By running tearfully to Sir every time they are triggered and microaggressed, 'social justice' activists demonstrate that they are more wimps than warriors, throwing tantrums more appropriate for a spoilt child in a nursery than an adult in an institution of higher learning. Reared from the cradle to their late teens and even beyond by ludicrously over-protective 'helicopter parents' who have shielded them from what were in saner times regarded as not only the unavoidable but necessary bumps and bruises of the process of growing up, infantilised millennials arrive at university expecting its student body to function as a substitute family, and its staff as surrogate helicopter parents.

Not the pursuit of knowledge but a womb-like 'safety' is what they crave above all and are given, affording them round-the-clock protection from the slings and arrows of outrageous opinions. Consequently, after being cocooned in their racially and gender-segregated safe spaces, they will leave university more ignorant than when they entered, clutching their worthless degrees in race, gender, queer, disability, women's and fat studies. Yes, Fat Studies is now an accredited academic discipline, totally dominated by women 'professors' waging the good fight against yet another man(sic)ifestation of the white patriarchy, namely, 'thin privilege,' with its false claim that obesity is determinantal to a women's mobility, employment prospects, attractiveness and therefore, dare I say it, marriage prospects, longevity, health and happiness. Not only will graduates in this nonsense have been cheated of a once-in-a-lifetime opportunity to enhance their mental powers. It will leave them emotionally and morally retarded, unable to take responsibility for their lives as adults in a world that neither owes them a living nor excuses, scapegoats and alibis for their own shortcomings and failures.

As an experiment, I typed into Google the name of a number of academic disciplines, followed by either 'racist' or 'white patriarchy'. Up came page after page of expositions on the topic, nearly all either explicitly or implicitly inspired by so-called 'critical race theory', this being a derivative of the post-modernism that held swathes of third-rate leftist intellectuals in its thrall in the 1980s. The difference between the two is that the second denies the possibility of knowing objective reality, whereas the first confines this inability to white heterosexual men, the 'cis-white patriarchy', which, because of its biologically inherited power and privileges, is incapable of or, at the least, inhibited from seeing the world, and its privileged position within it, as it really is. It follows, so the theory goes, that access to the truths of reality is confined to the powerless, to those oppressed in various ways by the white patriarchy because of their race, gender or sexual orientation. These truths are discovered and explored, not by the methods of their oppressors - empiricism, logic, analysis etc - but through 'feeling', 'intuition' and 'lived experience'. Rousseau, an opponent of the rationalist Voltaire and the entire Enlightenment project, thought along similar lines, elevating feeling and sentiment over reason, as did the ideologists of National Socialism and Italian fascism, and the 'integralist' school of philosophy.

We need to be aware that 'critical race theory' is not just a theory, but is geared to an aim, a society where racism as defined by CRT has been totally abolished, a state of affairs where, in the name of 'equity', in every sphere of public life bar none, whether they wish it or, far more likely, do not, the various racial/ethnic groups will be represented in exact proportion to their share of the total population. As has been said by critics of this dystopian project, its achievement would involve, especially in an ethnically diverse society such as that of the USA, racial engineering on a scale requiring a state bureaucracy dwarfing in its size and exceeding in its levels of coercion the machinery and methods of rule employed by Nazi Germany, Stalinist Russia and today's North Korea.

What follow are examples of how 'critical race theory' has invaded and poisoned almost every academic discipline, including not only soft targets such as women's, black, gender and fat 'studies', but the 'hard' sciences and maths, disciplines which one would once have thought would have been impervious to its mumbo-jumbo. I will cite brief excepts from various, mainly American sources which, I believe, capture the essence of this exercise in academic suicide.

'Teaching maths perpetuates white privilege says professor.'

'We [mathematicians] must determine collectively what anti-oppressive, and specifically anti-racist, mathematical research looks like.' (Good luck with that one.)

'Systemic racism is everywhere, even – and oddly – in math.'

'Aristotle, father of scientific racism.' (So racism can be 'scientific', just as the Nazis claimed. So much the worse for science then.)

'How [not 'did'] western philosophy become racist.'

'Race and racism in economics'.

Music theory is 'latent white supremacy'.

'Music theory's white racial frame.'

Terms used in music such as 'harmony, pitch and scale' are the products of 'an intellectual lineage of elitism, Euro-centrism, colonization, patriarchy and ultimately [sic] white supremacy.' So much then for Beethoven and his fifth symphony, one of the most performed of all orchestral compositions, and regarded as a watershed in the history of music for its representation in sound of the triumph of the human spirit over adversity but, since the death of George Floyd, condemned as a 'symbol of exclusion and elitism.'

A similar adjustment to BLM reality was underway across the Atlantic, where a prominent figure in the UK musical establishment announced on the BBC's radio three channel that 'the murder [sic - the trial had not even begun] of George Floyd and Black Lives Matter' should 'affect how we think about classical music.' Precisely how was wisely left unsaid. This left me wondering...how should I now listen to a Beethoven string quartet, or a Bach prelude and fugue? Or, given the new racial and gender dispensations, should I even be listening to them at all?

A posting on the theme of 'the under-representation of black women in astronomy.'

An academic symposium with an all-female platform (none of whom was an astronomer) debated and assented to the proposition that space travel was a colonial enterprise of the white patriarchy.

'There's a lot of bias in astronomy and women of colour are hurt [sic] the most.'

'Professional astronomy has benefited [suffered, surely...otherwise, wherein the problem?] from settler colonial white supremacist patriarchy.' Granted, Keppler, Copernicus and Galileo were male and white. But 'settler colonial'?

'The long history of how gender dynamics have *shaped* astronomy.' (emphasis added)

'Too many scientists and scientific organisations are eerily [is a white patriarchal conspiracy afoot?] silent on the issues of racism and justice – issues that are *embedded* into the history and *practice* of science.' (emphasis added)

These last two quotes are quite extraordinary. How can the results of an observation of an eclipse of the sun, such as that which proved the white patriarch Einstein's theory of relativity, be affected in any way by the race, gender or, since we are going the whole woke hog, sexual orientation of those conducting the observation?

Finally, we have the *piece de la resistance*, the article titled *Making Black Women Scientists Under White Empiricism*. To clarify matters, 'empiricism' in its white-patriarchal manifestations is the search for, and the cognizance, recording, classification, analysis and interpretation of evidence, facts. In its challenging the objective, race-free nature of these procedures, which are not only integral to science but to any discipline worthy of the name, we see critical race theory at its most sinister, namely, its insistence that the validity or otherwise of the means by which knowledge is acquired and interpreted, and therefore of knowledge itself, is conditioned, even determined, by the *racial identity* of those engaged in these operations. The thesis of this article says exactly this, that 'race and ethnicity impact *epistemic outcomes* in physics, despite the universality of the laws that undergird physics, and we introduce the concept of *white empiricism* to explain why.' (emphasis added) On precisely this basis, two Nazi physicists, Nobel Prize winners Philipp Lenard and Johannes Stark, both of whom also accepted the 'universality of the laws that undergird physics', nevertheless, as proponents of an 'Aryan' physics, rejected relativity because it had been discovered by a Jew.

I would like to make two further observations regarding this racist garbage masquerading as scholarship. Firstly, nearly all the quotations are from the publications of top-ranking American universities and prestigious academic journals. Secondly, of the scores that I scrutinised, nearly all dated from some weeks or months after the death of George Floyd. Not only that, of these, a goodly number specifically not only referenced that event, but were explicitly in response to it, and with patent difficulty, attempted to associate it with their own vastly different circumstances. One example of many, titled, 'Confronting Racism in Chemistry, begins thus: 'We confront the terrible reality that systemic discrimination impacts the daily personal and professional lives of many members of the scientific community and broader society. In the U.S., the brutal killing of George Floyd in police custody is one of the most recent examples of the centuries of systemic violence suffered by Black Americans.' And so in a few lines, the reader is segued from what we are expected to believe is the 'terrible reality' of a university chemistry department to the truly appalling eras of slavery and Jim Crow and a 'brutal killing' in Minneapolis, as if the first is connected or comparable in any way with what follows. Let me cite another example from the same discipline: 'On June 29, 2020, graduate students in the department of Chemistry' (of the University of California) gave a virtual presentation titled 'Becoming anti-racist in the physical sciences.' And a third, dating from the same month: 'Black chemists [at Berkeley College] discuss strategies for dismantling systemic racism in science.' Given that it is supposed to be 'systemic', meaning a policy of consistent, all-pervading racial discrimination and bias that cannot possibly spring into existence overnight, how come that prior to the death of George Floyd, nobody seems to have noticed it?

From their content and forced tone, it was palpably obvious that such articles were not the product of some new discovery or insight into their respective fields of inquiry, but were a panic-stricken response of spineless academics and their charges to the very real possibility that failure to add their craven voices to the BLM chorus would leave them exposed to accusations of racism, or in the case of black students and academics, of being an 'Uncle Tom' or, as one Oxford BLM activist had it, a 'coon'. That is why I regard their capitulation to ideological conformism as equivalent to the title of the book by Julien Benda, *The Treason of the Intellectuals*, which indicted those French men of letters who, by joining the Jew-baiting pack that hounded Dreyfus, sacrificed truth to political expediency.

Those academics who have betrayed their calling by promoting ideology instead of pursuing and encouraging in their charges a love of and respect for knowledge are no less despicable than Nazi doctors at Auschwitz, the only difference being they are performing experiments on immature and impressionable minds, not emaciated bodies. They no longer see their role as teaching students how to think critically, but what to think, uncritically, not to

27

revere knowledge for its own sake, but to see it cynically in functional terms, purely as a means to exert or acquire power. Their aim is to replicate themselves not only in the relatively toothless world of academe, but to prepare their charges for entry into those of the media, culture, schools, and above, all politics, where this strategy is already visibly bearing fruit in the increasingly leftist and Woke-friendly orientation of the Democratic Party. Duly lobotomised and then suitably re-programmed, the long-term goal is for SJW graduates to ascend to the upper echelons of the elite they effect to despise, there to steer the bad ship America onto the path of a frictionless dystopia where all speak, if not think the same. It is indeed one of the many contradictions within the SJW movement in the USA that it presents itself as 'anti-elitist', or 'anti-establishment', doing battle against various forms of 'privilege', even though its activists are themselves the beneficiaries of an education far too expensive for most children from a working-class background. What passes for the movement's ideology, mainly a meagre repertoire of chants, is anything but the product of a spontaneous movement of the masses, but a greatly simplified version, doled out to captive student audiences, of the latest fashionable trends in 'humanities' academe. As for its policy of enforced political correctness being 'anti-elitist', in the UK, where successive governments have criminalised 'hate speech' while imposing and promoting a segregationist programme of 'multi-culturalism' and 'diversity' at every level of society, often with disastrous consequences as evidenced by the Muslim gang rape scandal, the movement is pushing on a door long since opened wide by 'the establishment'.

If this war on reason and intellectual inquiry currently being waged by the totalitarian left achieves its goal of stamping out free thought, inquiry and expression in the west, as it has in the past elsewhere, then our liberal democratic civilisation will be heading, not for what the German philosopher Oswald Spengler predicted a century ago would be its unavoidable decline, but its suicide, laid low by cowardice and a self-imposed conformity that is the mortal enemy of the creative spirit. And if we in the west submit willingly, that is what we will deserve.

As a first line of defence against this assault on free speech and the right of peaceful assembly in the USA, the wording of the First Amendment is now patently inadequate to the task, and is therefore itself in urgent need of amendment, since it was based on the mistaken but at the time of its adoption, entirely reasonable presumption that no one would ever seek to prevent their exercise by a fellow citizen. How could those who drafted and approved the First Amendment have imagined that two centuries on, American university students, the most privileged generation in the history of the human race would, while righteously proclaiming and wallowing in their ever-expanding categories of simulated victimhood, not only demand, but successfully enforce by illegal riotous assembly - the so-called 'hecklers' veto' - their imagined right to silence dissent from their opinions on of all places, a university campus? The determination to protect the freedom of expression was not exclusive to the pioneers of the United States. Perhaps its most eloquent and celebrated (at least for those who share it) advocacy is Voltaire's 'I despise what you say, but I will fight to death for your right to say it'. Less dramatic but even more to the point, is that of Kant's 'freedom of the pen is the only safeguard of the rights of the people'. And, unlike the Founding Fathers and the scheme spinners of the French and English utopians, ever the realist, he understood the divided nature of the human species, that while 'as a rational creature', man 'desires a law to impose limits on the freedom of all, he is still inclined by his self-seeking animal inclinations into exempting himself from the law when he can.' *Ecclesiastes* puts it even more bluntly, as would two thousand years later, a deist or pantheist:

> I said in mine heart concerning the estate of the sons of men, that God might manifest them, and they might see that they themselves are beasts. For that which befalleth the sons of man befalleth beasts; even as the one dieth, so dieth the other, yeah they have all one breath; so that a man hath no preminence above a beast, for all is vanity. All go unto one place; all are of the dust and all turn to dust again. (Ecc. 3: 18-20)

Contrary to the Founding Fathers, believers in the perfectibility of humankind, Kant recognised that the 'beast' endured in a species that had evolved socially from one that in Rousseau's state of nature cared only for itself and at best its immediate kin to one that by virtue of its unique powers of reason, was capable of creating ever more complex civilisations, but yet was one that still remained an animal. Unless compelled to do otherwise, mankind, as in Hobbes' war of 'each against all', mankind would therefore continue as it did in its primitive state to seek its freedom at the expense of everybody else's. This conclusion led Kant to propose a 'constitution allowing the greatest possible human freedom in accordance with laws which ensure that the freedom of each can co-exist with the freedom of all the others.' And contrary to the racist cultural and moral relativism that increasingly holds sway today on university campuses across the western world, Kant believed that with one exception, that of the franchise, which, like all liberals of his day, he limited to the propertied classes, all humanity was entitled to the same rights and freedoms, irrespective of physical features, place of birth, social station or location. Unlike those legislators who drafted and adopted the First Amendment, Kant anticipated and in his political proposals provided for the possibility, and as recent events have proved, certainty, that private citizens no less than the state could suppress the freedoms of others. As a counter to this threat, and to uphold what Kant called the 'Universal Principle of Right' (a concept adopted by the United Nations in its founding charter of human rights) he argued that 'if a certain use to which freedom is put is itself a hindrance to freedom in accordance with universal laws', such as the organised shouting down of public speakers exercising their right to freedom of speech, 'any coercion which is used against it [such as the removal, by force if necessary, of those disrupting the proceedings] will be a hindrance to a hindrance of freedom'.

I agree. So, in accordance with Kant, as the purpose of speech is for it to be heard by those to whom the speech is directed, it logically follows that preventing such speech or rendering it inaudible constitutes a violation of free speech, as it does no less the right of others who have peacefully assembled to hear what is being said. Such an amendment as I propose would therefore stipulate that it is unlawful, either by word of mouth or any other action, to impede the exercise of free speech by another citizen or group of citizens.

Addenda:

'Give me the child, and I will give you the man.' (Ignatius Loyola, founder of the Jesuits)

There is nothing new under the sun, so the saying goes. Back in the late 1860s, a century and half before, under the banner of anti-racism, the leftist intelligentsia (sic) unleashed its onslaught against 'white' learning, a certain Russian self-styled anarchist, Michael Bakunin, from the safety of his Swiss exile, called on his student compatriots to 'leave [Russia's] universities, its academies, its schools.' They were instructed 'not to bother with [official] learning, in the name of which they [the Tsarist patriarchy...the Tsars were called 'little fathers'] would bind you, castrate you.' Marx publicly denounced Bakunin for 'preaching to Russian youth the cult of ignorance, under the pretext that modern science is merely official science'. He asked, rhetorically, believing the notion to be absurd, 'can one imagine an official maths, physics or chemistry?', perhaps forgetting that dissenting from the Catholic Church's official astronomy got Bruno burned at the stake and Galileo condemned to house arrest for the remainder of his life. What Marx could not imagine has become all too real and, irony of ironies, in its most recent version, in the guise of a so-called 'cultural Marxism'. Its predecessors were first, Nazi 'Aryan science', then followed by Stalinist 'Soviet science', the former exemplified by racist mumbo-jumbo, and the latter by the anti-Darwinian quackery of Lysenko. As Stalin in his last years became more overtly chauvinist and anti-Semitic, 'Soviet' morphed into 'Russian science' which, in the name of combatting 'rootless cosmopolitanism' (code for the Jews – see Appendix W) broke all its connections with world science. One of its results was that in a classic left-right convergence, pure-blooded 'Russian science', like its Nazi analogue, rejected Einstein's theory of relativity.

Now we have their American equivalent, a no less racist, totalitarian hocus pocus, one which has invaded and, as its practitioners fondly believe, exposed all branches of traditional learning, from philosophy, mathematics, physics and chemistry to history, economics, music and astronomy, as perverted creations of the white patriarchy. Since I cite examples of this onslaught elsewhere, let just three more suffice here, from the world of physics which, we now learn, is saturated with white racism. First, one from the American Institute of Physics *Bulletin* for July 22, 2020, that is, two months after the killing of George Floyd: 'Amid a national reckoning over systemic racism and police violence, the physical sciences community is searching for ways to deepen [sic] its efforts to make physics more inclusive and equitable. [that is, anti-racist]'. Now, another post-Floyd *mea culpa* in *Physics Today* for July 20, 2020, titled *Disentangling anti-Blackness from Physics* and subtitled 'It's not enough to try to be non-racist. The physics community needs to act. It can start by hiring, including and listening [sic] to Black scientists.'

'Disentangling'...'listening to'...as if black scientists possess, by virtue of their skin colour, scientific insights denied to those who skins are white. First we had 'Aryan science', now in the name of anti-racism, its inverted analogue, 'Black science'. Finally, my third example of the new 'Official Science' is an article published on July 14, 2020 by the journal of the Experimental Physics Department of New York University. Titled *Addressing Systemic Racism in Physics*, it describes a global campaign on behalf of 'black scientists' against a

'Universe of Racism', launched by a group calling itself 'Particles for Justice'. It seems that like thousands of academics in other disciplines across the USA, until the killing of Floyd, even scientists able to detect the smallest of sub-atomic particles had not noticed that their work-places and profession were riddled with 'systemic racism'.

Not just in physics, but in all branches of learning, the task in hand was to supplant white knowledge by, to use Marx's term, a new, all-embracing, anti-racist 'official science' derived from 'critical race theory', an ideology which, to the shame of American academe, has enthroned itself as the new and viciously intolerant orthodoxy in what were once the world's finest institutions of learning. Now it seeks new fields to conquer...the schools. Because as with all totalitarian movements, be they religious or secular, it is the minds of the young that the high priests of critical race theory see as their prime target for indoctrination.

That is why in the USA, failure to comply with this 'official science' in the teaching profession can have serious career repercussions, as is evident from an academic paper published in the American journal *New Directions* [sic] *for Teaching and Learning* for December 2014, titled, *Addressing Racial Awareness and Colour-Blindness in Education.* Not beating about the bush, its synopsis announces that 'Racial awareness is a critical foundation to racial sensitivity, and it is necessary [sic] for future professionals who want to be prepared to succeed in an increasingly diverse society.' This 'necessary preparation' requires trainee teachers to undergo 'programmes with a focus on racism *using a Critical Race Theory paradigm.*' (emphasis added) The message could not be clearer. Embrace the new 'official science', or look for another job.

(In the UK, Leicester was the first university off the mark in the scramble to get up to speed with the new learning when in January 2021, it unveiled a 'decolonised' syllabus for its English literature students. Among the classics to be flushed down the memory hole were Geoffrey Chaucer's *Canterbury Tales*, Sir Thomas Malory's *Mort D'Arthur*, John Milton's *Paradise Lost* (sic), poems by John Donne and the early Anglo-Saxon epic poem *Beowulf*. They were to be replaced by modules focusing on 'race, ethnicity, sexuality and diversity', promoted as 'excitingly innovative' and providing 'what students expect of an English degree'...one divested of some of the classics not only of English but world literature and replaced by ideological indoctrination. Old-style historians accustomed to thinking logically and requiring evidence will no doubt be puzzled - since one of the stated aims of the course is to eliminate literature dating from before 1500, how can their purging be described as 'de-colonising' when the founding of the first English colonies dates from the 16th century? Leicester was joined in its Wokist exercise in racial engineering by the University of Hull, which in April 2021 announced that it would be removing what it called 'barriers to learning', one of which was marking students down for bad spelling, grammar and punctuation. 'Technical proficiency' in the various disciplines was described as 'homogenous, northern European [sic...that's a new one!] white, male and elite'. Instead, students from minority backgrounds would be encouraged to develop their 'own authentic academic voice'... as in black maths and chemistry, to cite but two of many examples where knowledge has acquired a racial dimension. Such are the fruits of a patronising white racism, of 'low expectations'...fobbing off 'minority' students with dumbed down, third rate degrees because, it is assumed, they can't do any better. As for 'northern European'...a nebulous entity to be sure…let us assume that it lies north of a latitude midway between the southern and northern extremities of the continent, Gibraltar and Norway's North Cape. Well below it lie the cradles of European civilization, Greece and Rome, who more than two thousand year ago, bequeathed to us all the academic disciplines that until the advent of the current prevailing imbecilities of culture-destroying wokery, were justly regarded as the bed-rock of modern learning. Far to the north of that meridian are the Mongol by origin Sami people of Lapland, who, through no fault of their own, are the least numerate and literate people of the entire continent. Such are fruits of Hull's non-elitist history and geography. The drive to racialise knowledge gathered momentum when In April 2022, Durham University announced it would be 'de-colonising' its math syllabus. This would involve making the subject 'more inclusive', with teaching staff being required to question why they were relying on the work of white and male mathematicians, and to consider the 'cultural origins' of the concepts they teach. The seeds of this sinister development, which calls to mind the 'Aryanisation' of academic disciplines in Nazi Germany, were sown in 2020 with the publication by the university's 'Decolonise Durham Network' of its *Manifesto for Decolonising*. It demanded a 'decolonised curriculum' informed by critical race theory, one that 'challenges white euro-centric knowledge and canons.' Yes, 'knowledge', knowledge as abstract as the discipline of number, has a colour, the colour of the skin of those who practice it. White knowledge bad, non-white knowledge, good; for example, as we shall see, as in Orwell's *1984*, with two plus two not necessarily equalling four.)

Critical race theory is running riot, virtually unchallenged, at every level and in every branch of US academe. Another American publication, the *Journal of Diversity* [sic] *in Education,* in September 2014 featured a paper titled, *Are Perfectionism, Individualism And Racial Colour-Blindness Associated With Less Cultural Sensitivity? Exploring* [sic] *Diversity Awareness In Prospective Teachers.* This is just one of many 'academic' broadsides against the attitude to race advocated by the Rev Martin Luther King, namely, 'colour blindness'. One appropriately struck a religious note, with the title, *My Eyes Have Been Opened: White Teachers And Racial Awareness,* while another described in glowing terms a 'struggle for a just society' led by 'students of colour working *in opposition to a colour blind society'.* (emphasis added) If only they could be teleported back to the days of racially sensitive Jim Crow or apartheid South Africa, they could experience at first hand what living in a full-on non-colour blind society would be like. ('Colour blindness' is listed among examples of 'covert white supremacy' in 'racial equity training' materials for Google employees. Others include 'there's only one human race' [Nazis and Klansmen also strongly disagree with that], 'bootstrap theory' [that is, saying blacks are able to help themselves], 'paternalism' [that is, saying blacks can't help themselves…either way, whites are racist] and 'calling the police on black people.' [The rate for murders by blacks in the USA is eight times that for whites.])

Libraries have also been targeted for de-colonisation. There already exists in the USA a segregationist 'Council of Librarians of Colour', with one of its leading lights, a devotee of critical race theory (there's a surprise) complaining that 'our library collections' are 'mostly written by straight white men', a 'physical manifestation of white men ideas [so ideas have both colour and gender] taking up all our space in our library stacks.' There is a simple answer to this problem, and the Nazis demonstrated how it can be solved in Berlin's Odeon Platz on the night of May 10, 1933. All you need is a box of matches and a highly flammable liquid. But then the question arises - with what to fill the empty shelves?' We continue: 'Libraries and librarians have a long history of keeping people of colour out. They still do so.' That is a lie. Next, we are assured that the prevalence of 'white' books in libraries has nothing to do with their merit. 'Most of the collections are written by white dudes writing about white ideas [again]'. Except for 'things they stole from people of colour', 'white' books only contained 'so-called knowledge' (like 2+2=4). Books were forms of property akin to slaves, a means of racial domination, proof that 'white people want to stay being white [so do they have a choice?] because of the privilege and protection whiteness offers them under the law they created.' What law? 'The laws they created' were the Civil Rights acts of 1964 and 1965 abolishing all forms of racial discrimination, and eight 'Affirmative Action' measures and acts implemented by US governments since 1961 that favoured blacks over whites in employment and education.

Across the pond, this obsession with racial difference was naturally all the rage at Goldsmiths University, London, a lunatic asylum run by its inmates masquerading as an institution of higher learning. It offered a course titled 'A practical approach to developing [not combatting] racial awareness in schools'. Perhaps with the same goal in mind, the presenter of a children's Promenade concert provided the BBC with the opportunity to introduce its young audience to a racialised, and fictitious version of the genesis of Dvorak's ninth symphony, the 'New World'. Its themes, the presenter said, had been inspired by songs the composer had heard sung by black slaves during his stay in the USA when he was Director of the National Conservatoire. What she did not tell her audience, and those like me listening at home to the broadcast, was that Dvorak was in the USA between 1892 and 1895, and that slavery was abolished in the USA in 1864. The result of this outrageous falsehood will have been that 5,000 or so school children were leaving the Albert Hall believing that the USA was still practicing slavery 30 years after its abolition by Lincoln's Emancipation Proclamation of January 1, 1864

To return to the proselytes of the 'new learning'. Like the first paper cited, the explicit message of the September 2014 paper is that sharing King's stance on the race question can and should raise questions as to one's fitness to be an educator, as it indeed once did with mine:

Cultural ideologies of meritocracy and individualism [sic] act as strong barriers for college students in understanding the most complex systems of inequity across racial, cultural and gendered lines. The dichotomous thinking patterns of maladaptive perfectionists [!!!] may also relate to resistance of [sic...'to', surely] multi-cultural awareness. This study examined whether perfectionism, individualism and *racial colour blindness* predicted [negative] cultural diversity awareness of prospective teachers. (emphasis added)

And of course, they did because, given the terms in which the question was posed, there was only going to be one answer. Those of the 239 white students in the study (only whites are racists, remember) who exhibited symptoms of 'dichotomous thinking' by judging students on merit alone, treating them as unique individuals and not according to their 'identity' as members of a racial group, and of 'maladaptive perfectionism' by encouraging non-white students to do their best and not use race as an excuse for failure, were judged to be lacking in the required 'awarenesses' that made them suitable for the teaching profession. As the cure for these deficiencies, the paper proposed that (white, obviously} prospective teachers should be subjected to 'strategies involving assessment and self-reflection [admission and confession of one's thought crimes], cognitive dissonance instruction ['How many fingers am I holding up, Winston?'] and perspective enhancement and immersion ['brain-washing'].' Maoists called this 'thought reform', induced by protracted 'struggle sessions' and 'self- criticism'. Then we have the religious equivalents, the Holy Inquisition's 'pear of anguish', an expanding metal device inserted into the vaginas of women suspected of 'dichotomous [heterodox] thinking' – witchcraft - and the Puritan Pilgrim Fathers' burning out the tongues of blaspheming Quakers with red hot pokers for uttering thoughts deemed 'cognitively dissonant'. The methods vary, but the end in each case is the same...a mind-numbing, sheep-like conformism to a doctrine that stultifies the questioning intellect.

What we have here, in the guise of anti-racism, is a patronising 'racism of low expectations', the belief that only by racial engineering will black students achieve 'equality of outcome' with white students. This claim is empirically (yes, a white concept) refuted by the staggering academic success of Jews (25% of all Nobel science prizes won by 0.2% of the world's population), a people who, after emerging not from 400 but 2,000 years of dispersal, persecution, exclusion, segregation, discrimination, enslavement (by the Nazis), pogroms and, finally, genocide, neither asked for nor were afforded such favours and allowances as those being demanded by and provided for America's (non-Asian) ethnic minorities.

The tsunami of wokery, much of it simulated, that followed the murder of George Floyd, even lapped the shores of Norway in 2021, with demands that race and gender should be taken into consideration when awarding Nobel Prizes. Just for once, they were met with a firm rebuff. Merit, and not skin colour or reproductive functions, would remain the sole criteria for awards. Goran Hanssen, Head of the Nobel Prize Science Awards Academy, said science prizes should be awarded to those who 'made the most important discovery'. Arbitrarily increasing the number of prizes given to women would result in it being thought that 'those laureates got the prize because they are women, not the best.' Exactly. After all, it is not the Nobel committee's fault that many women students prefer to graduate in women's or gender studies, and blacks, in black or ethnic studies, rather than maths or physics. So despite the woke clamor, there would be no awards made on the basis of skin colour or reproductive functions: 'We have decided we will not have quotas for gender or ethnicity. We want every laureate to be accepted because they made the most important discovery, and not because of ethnicity or gender.'

There was once a time when such a statement would have been unnecessary, and if made, superfluous. No longer. In the toxic political climate of the post Floyd era, it was heroic. I suspect this refusal to give an inch to the battalions of intersectionality was born of an awareness that had the Nobel Prize committee done so, they could have been bombarded with further demands that to ensure each race, gender and sexual orientation received its due, all of these 'identities', together with their ever-expanding sub-categories, should be awarded their own prizes. Given the number of variables involved in this operation, guaranteeing equitable treatment for all aspirant laureates will require not a little fine tuning and tweaking …as with the Black Gay Transvestite Prize for Chemistry.

The UK Musicians Union had for some years also been demanding a similar policy of 'diversity' and 'inclusivity' in the music industry, as we have seen, approving at its 2019 conference a resolution calling for concerts devoted entirely to compositions by women composers, and mandatory 50% female orchestras. However, as is often the way with the pursuit of 'equity' as distinct from 'equality', the union's stance on 'diversity' has not been consistent, for it has never condemned the total *exclusion* of white musicians from the racially segregationist Chineke Orchestra. In September 2021, a matter days before the announcement of the 2021 Nobel Prizes that occasioned the above comments, 14 white musicians, some with more than 20 years' service, were summarily dismissed by English Touring Opera, half of its orchestra, to make way for those with skins of darker hues. Defending its decision, a spokesperson for the company said it was acting on a requirement by its main source of funding, the Arts Council, to 'improve diversity'. Some of the 14 sacrificed on the altar of racial correctness would in all likelihood have approved, and possibly even voted for the 2019 'diversity' resolution, never suspecting this policy would come back two years later to bite them in the bum. As the saying goes, 'take care what you wish for.' The union said it was 'appalled' and that there had been an 'understandable outcry' from members. (See below for other instances of this discriminatory policy of racial quotas, first enforced against the Jews, one that historically goes by the name of *numerus clausus*, 'closed number'.) Imagine the uproar had the reverse action been taken - not to speak of the legal consequences. But in the event, apart from the protest by the MU, scarcely a ripple. The union said it would be taking legal advice, though on what grounds was not stated.

Like the BBC, also committed to a similar operation of genetic engineering (see Footnote to Appendix B) the Arts Council objective would seem to be one of making the demographic of recipients of their funding reflective of the racial profile of the general public. Even if we assume that all of the ETO orchestra had been white, sacking half of its members and replacing them with musicians of other races will in no way create an ensemble racially representative of the UK population any more than it will, I suspect, of opera audiences, since only 13 % of that population was classified by the 2011 census as belonging to ethnic minorities. If any evidence existed that audiences attend concerts not only to listen to music, but to see themselves reflected (proportionally of course) in the racial and sexual identities of the musicians performing it (presumably by counting who is what), we would have heard about it long ago. There is no such demand. Audiences pay good money to hear great music played by musicians chosen on merit alone, not to be witnesses to an exercise in, I repeat, genetic engineering.

What failed with Nobel, but succeeded with English Touring Opera, has also been attempted with some success at other institutions such as the BBC (whose white staff have been accused of 'unconscious racism'), the British Museum committed to 'recruiting and developing a diverse staff' and the British Library 'committed to promoting equality and diversity in the workplace', all being institutions which were originally dedicated solely to the provision to the public of culture and enlightenment of the highest possible quality. In each case the goal is now one of harnessing these public institutions to social and political agendas totally at odds with that original objective. Why else the assertion by the library's Chief Librarian Liz Jolly that 'racism is the creation of white people' and that as pursuant to the 'decolonisation' of the library, it was considering removing the statues of the humanist Beethoven and the Jew Mendelssohn (both of whose statues in Germany had been subjected to the same treatment by the Nazis) as symbols of 'white supremacy'? Why else the preposterous claim of library chief executive Roly Keating that 'the killing of George Floyd and the Black Lives Matter movement are the biggest challenges to the complacency of organisations, institutions and ways of doing things that we are likely to see in our lifetimes'? This nonsensical hyperbole was followed by the British Museum's announcement that the hitherto exalted status of Charles Darwin was under review in the light of his alleged role in promoting British colonialism. Darwin was in fact an outspoken opponent of American slavery.

In the light of such pronouncements, the question needs to be asked; if the British Museum truly believes, as it should, in staffing based purely on merit, why did it feel necessary to adopt an 'Equality *and* Diversity' policy statement? (Perhaps a clue is the date it was adopted…post Floyd, on November 5, 2020.) 'Equality' in this context can only have one meaning, that staff will be employed purely on merit. So why add 'diversity', and then list no fewer than 17 'identities' (surely a record) that will not be discriminated against? Why should they be, since the Museum says it is already committed to 'equality'? Instead of putting job applicants in umpteen boxes, balkanising what is one race, the human race, why not just treat them as unique individuals, and judge them on that basis alone? I suspect that like the BBC, which has announced its actual target race, gender and disabled quotas, and the Arts Council, the British Museum management could well be engaged in a similar operation but has chosen not to advertise it. One thing is certain. Along this road lies not racial harmony, but only cultural decline.

Some would say, with the example of the Jews in mind, that overcoming adversity by one's own efforts can prove to be an advantage over those for whom life has been made all too easy. As Nietzsche put it, 'what does not kill me makes me stronger.' I am not arguing that life should be made more difficult than it is for America's blacks, only that making it easier than it is for everybody else, for society and the state to treat them as over-protective 'helicopter parents' do their children, is demeaning, even infantilizing, as indeed Obama has argued with respect to absent black fathers delegating their paternal responsibilities to the state. And what is equally to the point, it does them no favours. Several studies have suggested that 'affirmative action' has not enhanced black academic performance, but rather, by lowering entrance qualifications below those of all other ethnic groups, dispensed with the requirement and therefore incentive to do one's best. If this is true…and having seen the evidence, for example, the above-average drop-out rate for black students, I happen to think that it is…surely the Jewish experience provides a lesson for those genuinely concerned to improve the academic performance and life opportunities of the USA's blacks?

Room 101

'When I use a word', Dumpty said in a rather scornful tone, 'it means just what I choose it to mean, neither more nor less.' (Lewis Carroll, *Alice Through the Looking Glass*)

'What seems to me white, I will believe black if the hierarchical church so defines.' (Rule 13 of the Jesuit's 'Rules for Thinking'.

'The idea of 2 + 2 equaling 4 is cultural, and because of western imperialism/colonialism, we think of it as the only way of knowing.' (Brittany Marshall, maths PhD student [sic] at Rutgers University and Math Ed Collective activist)

'Freedom is the freedom to say two plus two equals four. If that is granted, all else follows.' (George Orwell, *1984*)

When referring to 'critical race theory', I prefer to put it in quotes, because its fixation on race to the exclusion of all other determinants of human behavior and social evolution renders it neither critical nor a theory, and therefore, not a science, but an ideology masquerading as one. (As it occurs so frequently in the text, I shall abbreviate it as 'CRT' but without the quotes.) Science is *self*-critical and skeptical, divided up into a range of disciplines, each with its own methods of analysis particular to the aspect of reality scrutinised, with its practitioners submitting their work to peer review by specialists in the relevant fields. None of this applies to the *modus operandi* of the apostles of CRT and its dystopian policy panaceas. It is more of a movement than a discipline, akin to a Manichean religious cult whose devotees, when invited or challenged to do so, refuse to engage with anyone outside their closed ranks, while inside, all speak with the same voice. Instead of participating in a debate with disbelievers they are decried as apologists for racism, and their books denied reviews in leftist publications and academic journals.

The definition of 'Critical Race Scholarship' provided by the University of Denver's 'Critical Race and Ethnic Studies Guide' (see below) provides the explanation as to why this is so. Like a religion, which it closely resembles, CRT rests on a number of assertions, or rather, articles of faith, for which it offers no evidence, hence the refusal to engage with its critics. The two most important, from which the rest flow, are that firstly, the USA is a racist society in which the white (male) majority oppresses a non-white and female majority, and secondly that it has created and used the US constitution to do so. And it must be stressed that CRT is not just an explanation of how things are, but a *movement*, a call to bring about racial change by political activism. As regards the first assertion it is refuted by the statistical analysis in Charles Murray's *Coming Apart: The State of White America 1960-2010,* which charts the relative and, in some respects, absolute economic and social decline of a large proportion of the USA's white working and lower middle classes, a process that other statistics prove is accompanied by a comparable rise in a number of ethnic minorities. The end result of these two recent developments is that today, US white household income has declined to the national average, while two thirds of US national and ethnic minority households now rank above it, some by 20% or more.

In terms of personal income, whites, at $37,000 per annum, are ranked below all Asians, on $41,000, with Indians on $55,000, and Chinese on $53,000.

Apologists for the excesses of 'critical race theory' may well object, 'but whites predominate among the super-rich', which indeed they do, partly because whites, even if we exclude Latinos, comprise two thirds of the US population. But CRT does not say that the USA is ruled by a super-rich white elite both male and female, but by a 'privileged' white patriarchy consisting of all the USA's 118 million white males, irrespective of their wealth, income or any other criteria than those of gender and race.

The reality is that race and gender divisions in the USA tell us very little about the distribution of wealth and the power that goes with it. 76% of US millionaires are white, 8% black, 8% Asian and 7% Hispanic. These percentages do not deviate radically from their respective shares of the total population, and the gap, which once seemed unbridgeable, is now rapidly narrowing. Only at the very top is it substantial, but even here, there is movement in the same direction, creating absurdities like the following. Oprah Winfrey's wealth in 2021 was rated at $2.7 billion. Yet according to 'intersectionality', as a black woman, she is doubly oppressed on account of her race and gender, while millions of white men existing on a pittance and with nothing in the bank except debts are ranked among her oppressors on account of their race and gender. Thus CRT - very conveniently for some - conjures out of existence material wealth as the prime determinant of power and privilege in the USA, and replaces it with genes. And this is supposed to be 'Marxism'? In its denial of class, CRT resembles *fascism*, and in its obsession with 'race', *national socialism*. Yet there are millions on both sides of the political divide in the USA who are convinced that CRT has something to do with socialism, even with Marxism. As to the latter, those that think thus should count the number of times the word 'race' and its cognates appears in the *Communist Manifesto*, the definitive statement of Marx's materialist conception of history and politics, and compare that number with that of 'class'. They will find that 'race' occurs but once, though not in its 'critical theory', biological, usage, but as an alternative to 'class' in a reference to a 'race' of 'proletarians'. 'Class' however occurs 107 times, and terms that imply it, such as 'bourgeoisie' and 'proletariat', occur even more frequently. If CRT does have a political kinship, it is to be found at the other end of the political spectrum.

Angelo Olivetti, like nearly all the founders of fascism, began his political career as a theorist of Italian syndicalism, a movement that advocated and attempted to practice militant trade unionism as a revolutionary alterative to reformist socialism. With its failure, Olivetti, together with others of his persuasion, most of them, like today's critical race theorists, academics, performed a spectacular ideological *volte face* (as also like the critical theorists), rallying to the national cause in the First World War, and then after it, to fascism. Olivetti was also one of the first to define the new doctrine: 'The nation is above classes, and all considerations of class should give way to considerations of a national character.' Replace 'nation' and 'national' with 'race' and 'racial' and you have a no less succinct definition of CRT ...and National Socialism.

CRT says that in the USA, all women and all racial minorities are oppressed in various ways by a privileged white, male (in some versions, only heterosexual) 'patriarchy', one defined not in terms of class, but those of biology, of race and sexuality. Therefore the 'theory' necessarily takes no account of the following: as of 2021, 13.5% of American billionaires were women, 1.2% were black, and 2% either Indian or Chinese. All, just like Winfrey, and for the same reason, are ranked by CRT as belonging to America's under-privileged and oppressed, while the 9% of US white males who are below the official US poverty line are included among their oppressors, even though for all the contact they have with each other, they could just as easily be inhabiting separate continents as different zip codes. If you were to ask any of America's so-called trailer park trash if they are enjoying their white privilege, do not expect a polite answer.

It remains something of a mystery that highly educated people could invent or believe such absurdities when not only economic but other indicators such as education and occupation all pointed to the same conclusion, one that before their abandonment of the traditional leftist, class-based analysis of society, the creators of CRT would have endorsed; that as in any capitalist society, what we see predominating in the USA today, *and more so than at any other time in its history, and of any other western country*, is the 'privilege' of *class*, a stain on the USA that will not be erased one iota by the politics and policies of race, whether they come from the left or the right. One of the services that CRT renders to the US upper class is its concealment of the great divide in the USA today; which is not the one of skin colour (or for that matter of gender), but of *wealth*. And as the former narrow, the latter widens. In 1978, 0.1% owned 7% of the nation's wealth. (yes, 0.1, not 1.0%) Forty years on, and the 7% had become 20% and the 0.1% that owned it, *less white and less male*. It is not difficult then to see why so many of America's great, good and well-healed, and even some of its super-rich, have embraced, and on Wall Street by huge subventions to Black Lives Matter, helped to promote the ideology and policies of CRT. It also helps to explain why CRT and the movements it has spawned largely leave cold the USA's great unwashed, be they white or black.

Here we have an entirely orthodox exposition of that 'theory' by the University of Denver:

Critical race scholarship [sic] is unified by two tenets; the first is to understand that a regime of white supremacy and its subordination of people of colour have been created and maintained in America [i.e., by 'systemic' and 'institutional' racism] and in particular, to examine the relationship between that social structure and the professed ideals such as 'the rule of law' and 'equal protection'. The second is a desire not merely to understand the vexed bond between law and racial [n.b.] power but to *change* it. (emphasis in original)

This last is an obvious crib from Karl Marx's 'the philosophers have only interpreted the world, in various ways. The point, however, is to change it.' Also to the point is that Marx believed it would be changed not, as with CRT by the politics of race, that as it did in Nazi Germany, will leave the existing economic order undisturbed, but by the struggle of *classes*.

As befits a celebrated high priest of the CRT cult, like the University of Denver, Ibram X. Kendi has excluded entirely the notion of class from his analysis of society. He makes the following claim in his best-selling *How to be an Anti-Racist*: 'Every [sic] policy in every [sic] institution in every [sic] community in every [sic] nation is producing or sustaining either racial inequity or equity between racial groups.' Note that as all devotees of the cult do, he speaks only of 'equity' not 'equality'. The difference is a crucial one. In 'critical race theory' lingo, 'equity' means 'equality of outcome', not equality under the law and of opportunity which, as we have seen in the above citation, are depicted as legal and constitutional devices to conceal and maintain white rule. Since for Kendi everything revolves around racism, we would expect that he can offer a clear, succinct definition of what he means by that word. When asked to so in the course of a lecture on CRT, this is how he responded: 'I would define racism as a collection of racist policies that lead to racial inequity that are substantiated by racist ideas.' This is a classic example of a circular argument: racism = racism = racism = racism. Correct.... but useless. How is it possible to take seriously anything Kendi says when he cannot offer a coherent, let alone plausible definition of his central concept? Yet hundreds, probably thousands of academics do.

Then there is the 'theory' itself. Kendi says there is no such thing as a race neutral policy. Really? Then which race would be favored (or penalised) by a US state raising its highway speed limit by five miles per hour? Or making safety belts mandatory for all car users? Then he says 'in every nation'...but what of nations that comprise only one racial group, as is the case with a number of Arab and African states, Mongolia, and the Pacific Island peoples of Polynesia, Micronesia and Melanesia? As for 'communities', this term usually describes a people who *are* ethnically homogenous. So, right from the outset, his 'theory' collapses under the weight of its unsustainable universalist claims.

But it gets worse, if that is indeed possible. He gives an example of racial 'inequity', housing: '71% of white families [in the USA] live in owner occupied-homes compared to 45% of Latinx [sic] families and 41% of black families.' (In wokespeak, gender neutral 'Latinx' replaces the 'binary' and masculine case 'Latino'. So should 'Gerx' replace 'Germans'?) Racial equity would therefore be achieved, says Kendi, when as a result of government policy, these percentages become equal. This would require the state acquiring the power to, if necessary, compel families and individuals to relocate from their current accommodation, either to force home-owning whites to move to rented accommodation, or in some cases, compelling reluctant blacks to buy property they possibly could not afford or when they would prefer to carry on renting. And so on across the entire board of policy, until in every aspect of society, irrespective of cultural traditions that have little or nothing to with race, from jazz, where blacks, at 24%, are over-represented, to airline pilots, at 2%, where the opposite is the case, the point is reached where all races will be represented, *whether they like or not*, in the exact same ratio as their share of the total population. I can conceive of no policy more likely to generate racial friction in a country that more than any other, values its individual freedoms. Just imagine having to justify to the USA's black jazz musicians, among them the best in the world, that in order to achieve 'equity' in their calling, one half of them will have to make way for the less talented of other skin colours, or in the UK, the reaction of players, managers and, bar a few racists, fans, to an identical command to reduce to 3% the current 25% of professional footballers who are black.... 0.75% of one black player per regulation premiership squad of 25.

These and countless other - let us call them 'anomalies'- are still only the beginning of Kendi's problems. In his example of how to achieve 'equity', he presents the reader with what on the surface seems a simple problem with a simple solution, the latter involving a property adjustment between three racial groups. Would it were that straightforward. Under the heading, 'Rate of home ownership in the USA by race, 2018', the website *Statistica* lists not three but five racial groups, whites, blacks, Asian, Hispanic and American Indian or Alaskan native, each with a different and, over time, varying rate of home ownership that will periodically require either levelling up or down. And this is still letting Kendi off lightly. Official US household income statistics list not five, but 94, repeat, 94 distinct racial/ethnic groups. No wonder Kendi prefers to talk only about whites, 'Latinx', and blacks. And even if we confine ourselves to these three racial groups, the mind bogles at the level of state intervention and, inevitably, coercion that would be required to implement just this one policy, bearing in mind we are considering here not a conventional voluntary property swap between two families, but a compulsory one imposed on a nation of 123 million households. And that is but one of a vast range of similar 'adjustments' that need to be implemented in order to reach Kendi's goal of across the board racial 'equity'.

Even a Stalin, who deported entire nations, a Hitler, who went two thirds of the way to deporting and then exterminating all Europe's Jews, and a Pol Pot, who in a matter of days, evicted the entire population of Cambodia's capital (with the approval of Noam Chomsky) would be hard pressed to carry through this unprecedented exercise in racial engineering. But not so, it seems, for the reviewer of Kendi's book in the *Guardian* (yes...I cannot resist saying it, because it is true... where else?) a journal which in its first Manchester incarnation, was the UK's staunchest defender of *laissez faire* and individual freedom. Kendi had put forward a 'brilliantly simple [sic] argument. We are either racist or anti-racist, there is nothing in between, argues this powerful memoir and political guide.' The reviewer happened to be black, and therefore had no apparent reason to fear the consequences of Kendi's policies. But had it occurred to those predominately white academics, journalists and commentators who enthused over Kendi's 'brilliantly simple argument' that they could be among its first victims, that maybe one day, or, more likely, in the middle of the night, as was the routine with Stalin's NKVD, there would be a hammering at the door, followed by a command to load all the family's possessions into an unmarked removals van?

Kendi's assumption that in each case, whites are the current beneficiaries of racial iniquities, and all other racial groups, their victims, is precisely where his argument breaks down at the most fundamental level, income 'inequity', from which stem nearly all others. Median white household annual income in the USA in the year 2018 was ranked *two thirds of the way down*, 60th out of 94 ethnic/racial groups, at $65,902, almost exactly the national average. For Asian households, it was $87,204. Those households with an Indian background ranked the highest - $135,705 – *more than double that of the white*. So, according to Kendi's definition, US whites are victims, along with blacks and 'Latinx', of serious racial, in this instance, economic 'inequity'. Native black Americans ranked 86, at $43,862. They would rank substantially higher, but for the fact that around 70% of black American households have no bread-winning father and as result, a mother probably on welfare. Nigerian American households, which mostly do have a father *in situ*, rank above not only native black Americans *but also native US whites*, at 55, on $68,658. The redressing of this particular 'inequity', in which several categories of non-whites would be losers, and whites, winners, would require either racially targeted income taxes, or a totally state-controlled economy paying equal wages/salaries to the entire working age population, whatever their personal circumstances, thereby relacing one kind of inequity by another.

Other US statistics abound with similar anomalies that render Kendi's all-encompassing 'theory' worthless...university admissions for example, where Chinese out-perform all other ethnic groups to such an extent that Ivy League universities have devised ways of restricting their admission, while favoring 'affirmative action' applications from less qualified black students. Perhaps the biggest elephant in Kendi's racial room is the statistic about which, at least in the short run, government policy can do little, if anything to impact...life expectation. As of 2018, for all US citizens, it was 78.7 years, for all whites, 78.5, again, like household income, virtually bang on the national average. For all blacks, it was 75, for Hispanics, 82, and Asians, *86* (an obvious case of Indian and Chinese privilege). And as with income, whites rank below halfway.

One of the factors contributing to the low life expectancy for blacks is the life, or rather death style, of far too many in the age group between 15 and 34, for whom the most common cause of death is murder, statistically most likely to be at the hands of someone in the same demographic. For white males in the same age group, it is by car accident. For blacks of all ages, homicide is the fourth ranked cause of death, 5% of the total, while for whites, homicide does not appear on a list of ten causes of death, the last being chronic liver disease, at 1.7%. In 2018, of the 3,175 black victims of homicide, 2,430 were male. Thus, the percentage of black males dying of homicide is not 5%, which is the percentage of all blacks, but 8%, meaning that something like 1 in 12 black males, most of them below 40, will die, not of 'natural' causes or accident, but murder, with more than 90% killed by other blacks. These appalling statistics are totally ignored by (Some) Black Lives Matter, because they tell a 'wrong narrative', just as for the same reason they are passed over in silence by the bulk of the media, who only show an interest when blacks are killed by police, preferably by a white officer. The number killed by police in 2018, legally or otherwise, armed or otherwise, was 228, 8% of those killed by other blacks, whose lives did not matter.

The US life expectancy figures for individual states also throw up data that do not confirm to Kendi's race narrative. In Idaho, for example, life expectancy for blacks was 81.3, and whites, 79.1, Maine, 80.9, and whites, 78.6, Montana, 81.9, whites 79.3, New Hampshire, 80.8, whites 79.3, South Dakota, 81.2, whites 80.0, North Dakota, 82.1, whites, 80.1, Wyoming, 80.2, whites 79.0, Utah, 80.2, whites 79.6. I would suggest that the key factor producing these apparent anomalies is Kendi's great unmentionable, class. What these states have in common is low-density, predominantly middle-class populations, prosperous, low-crime small towns, and an absence of run-down, 'rust-belt', socially deprived, crime-ridden urban jungles. There are also large state-wide variations in white populations that can only be explained by class, to which we should add culture. In Washington DC, the gravitational centre of the US's political and media elites, life expectancy for whites was 87.5, nine years above the national average for whites of 78.5, and *thirteen* above that for West Virginia whites, the lowest, at 74.8. As of 2019, whites comprised 93.5% of West Virginia's population, the third highest in the USA, blacks, 3.6%. Like life expectancy at 74.4 years, the state's average annual household income was also the lowest in the USA, $46,700, $20,000 below the national average. 'White privilege'? Washington DC, with a white population of 37.5%, the lowest in the USA, not only has the highest life expectancy, but the highest average household income in the USA, at $85,000. Even Kendi would be hard put to explain these correlations and variations by any other than the income/class factor.

Then we have Illinois, with its South Side Chicago as a centre of black crime and social and economic deprivation. In that state, the life expectancy for blacks is 73.9, and in Michigan, with a similar demographic in Detroit, 73.5, compared to the blacks of North Dakota at 82.1, 8.5 years higher. Again, we must ask...how can such a vast discrepancy be due to an all-pervading, nation-wide, 'institutional' and 'systemic' racism'? In Chicago, a city of 2.7 million, in the year 2018, there were 653 murders, the vast majority being blacks, mostly killed by other blacks, at a rate of one murder per 4,134 of the city's population. In just one weekend, July 16-17, 2021, 56 people, including several children, were shot, eleven fatally. In Fargo, the largest town in North Dakota, with a population of 121,000, it was five in the whole year of 2018, one per 24,000 of the population, six times less than Chicago's.

Think on this: If the annual rate of black-on-black murders in cities like Chicago was the same as that in Fargo for all murders, the life expectancy of US blacks would begin to approach the national average for whites. The wide variations in black life expectancy, *in eight states exceeding that of whites*, prove that whatever Kendi might say, it is not US government policy for blacks to die younger than anyone else, nor is it an unintended consequence of any other policy. The simple, undeniable, even by Kendi, fact is, blacks do not have to kill each other, any more than they have to be absent fathers, the prime cause of juvenile black crime and death. The racial engineering proposed by Kendi will have zero impact on both, because each are expressions and products of a number of deep-going economic factors and cultural problems, not racial ones. Black men in states where they have a higher life expectancy than whites do not kill each other or routinely abandon their children to a life of crime, gang warfare, jail and possible death. Instead, they share the same peaceful culture and obey the same laws as their white neighbors.

The solution of America's 'black question', of which low life-expectancy and a high crime rate are two of its most troubling manifestations, is not dependent upon token acts of contrition by the 'white patriarchy'. It requires on the part of blacks a total rejection of the fatalistic black 'victimology' and 'white-blaming' promoted by CRT and applied by Black Lives Matter, and instead, as a growing number of prominent black academics have argued, a radical movement for black self-reform comparable in several important respects to the *Haskalah*, a 'self-help' Jewish Enlightenment movement of the 18th and 19th centuries that prepared the way for the Jewish renaissance of the 20th and 21st. Those who say otherwise, that deliverance must come from above, from a guilt-ridden white patriarchy, are themselves guilty of a 'racism of low expectations', one that treats black adults as if they were children, incapable of taking responsibly for their own lives...just as white slave-owners once did.

The statistics that I have cited (and others I have not) point to only one conclusion, one totally at odds with CRT: the largest single (I do not say only, because unlike Kendi and his co-thinkers, I do not subscribe to monocausal explanations of complex social phenomenon) determinant of life expectancy is income, and therefore, class, which in its turn, either influences or determines so much else - health, education, housing, diet, exercise etc etc. Class not only explains divergencies between racial groups, but also within them, as in the examples cited above, and as illustrated by the response of two wealthy black women to the surge in urban violence following the murder of George Floyd in May 2020. Both Patrisse Cullors, co-founder of Black Lives Matter (resigned in May 2021) and Democratic Congresswoman for Missouri Cori Bush support the defunding (abolition by another name) of the police, a policy actually implemented by some Democrat Party authorities, with the results that many predicted. In the year 2021, as of June 24, there had been 296 mass shootings, with nearly 10,000 homicides, 24% up on same period of the previous year and 49% on 2019, putting the USA on track for the highest annual murder rate in two decades. In Chicago in the first three weeks of July 2021, 395 were shot, of whom 81 were killed. Anyone who says de-funding the police will protect black lives is either an imbecile, a liar or a gangster. As across the USA, the murder rate for working class blacks soared, nearly all killed not by police, but by other blacks, millionaires Cullors and Bush were able to insulate themselves from this carnage by paying for their own private security, Bush at $30,000 per month, while continuing to call for a defunding of the police that will lead to yet more deaths of working-class blacks and their children. In 2021, violent crime in St Louis, Bush's home town, was four times the national rate. Not only did an undisclosed proportion of the $30,000 she spent on protecting herself from it come from Democratic Party sources. Two police officers were sacked when caught working extra shifts as her private bodyguards. Some police are less defundable than others. Challenged as to her hypocrisy, Bush replied, 'you would rather me die?... So suck it up. [sic!] Defunding the police has to happen…I have private security because my body is worth being on this planet right now'. Some black bodies matter more than others.

Following the pattern described above, Asians, who are not classed as 'white', (though often treated as such because their spectacular success does not 'fit the narrative'…Kendi excludes them from his housing example) have by far both the highest income and life expectancy, followed by Latinos for both, then whites, with US average income and life expectancy, and blacks, less than average of both, with deviations from the mean by whites and blacks that again, can only be explained by variations of income, as between North Dakota and Michigan, and Washington DC and West Virginia. Can these correlations of income with life-expectancy be sheer co-incidence? Kendi would like us to think so. Yet a scholarly survey, based on 1.4 billion tax records between 1999 and 2014, established, quote, that 'higher income was associated with greater longevity throughout the income distribution' and, quote that 'the gap in life expectancy between the richest 1% and the poorest 1% of individuals was 14.6 years.' Not only this. 'Inequality in life expectancy increased over time', bearing out my claim that the USA is becoming a more class, not race, divided society. (A matter of hours after I wrote this, I experienced a rare moment of serendipity when in the course of an interview by Coleman Hughes, the renowned journalist, constitutional lawyer, free speech advocate and author Glenn Greenwald said that 'for me, the primary division in America is not race or gender or sexual orientation but class. That for me shapes our experience far more than any other of those categories.' Hughes concurred.) The statistics I cite that prove it are not good news for the race industry, so perhaps that is why they get little if any publicity. Neither do we learn of such facts from Kendi, because he only cites those few statistics which he - mistakenly as we can see - believes bolster his case, while ignoring the mass of evidence that refutes it. So much for 'everything is (white) racist'.

What Kendi and those who share his particular brand of anti-racism are proposing is in fact itself racist, being an all-embracing *numerus clausus*, or 'closed number', a device used to restrict, or exclude entirely from certain occupations and institutions of learning a particular category of a country's population, usually on racial or religious grounds. Historically, going back to medieval times, it was deployed only against the Jews, who were confined to occupations either deemed forbidden to Christians, such usury, or regarded as degrading, like the so-called 'rag trade'. This practice continued well into modern times, for example in tsarist Russia, and even the USA, where Ivy League universities restricted Jewish entry in favour of applicants from elite WASP families. (Today, those excluded are another too clever by half, work-ethic driven ethnic group, the Chinese.)

Ironically, if Kendi's anti-racism were to become official government policy as he and his co-thinkers intend, then its main victims would be the same as they were under the Nazis...the Jews. Thomas Mann records in his diary entry for March 28, 1933, the introduction by the Nazis of 'quotas for the number of Jews in the academic and legal professions *based upon their percentage in the total population*.' (emphasis added) This is exactly the 'equity' policy proposed by Kendi, the only difference being, it is now coming from the far left, not the extreme right. As I have said in this work in another context, having endured for the best part of two millennia unceasing and at times, horrendous, even genocidal persecution, over the last century, despite the ravages of the Holocaust and comprising only 0.2% of the world's population, the Jews have outperformed gentiles in almost every field of intellectual endeavor, as reflected in their share of 'hard' Nobel Prizes...currently, around 25%. That is why the Jews will be the prime target for Kendi's all-embracing 'equity', penalized for being too industrious and successful. As in Nazi Germany, and in other countries that even before the war came under its sway, such as Austria and Rumania, Kendi's 'anti-racist' *numerus clausus* will require a massive purging of Jews in the elite professions...law, academe, medicine, the various branches of science as well as in the arts...cinema, music, literature, the stage...so as to make room for those racial groups correspondingly under-represented. As a result, Kendi's world will be one where merit, and the motivation to succeed, count for nothing, and race, again as in Nazi Germany, everything. This will create a society in which, possibly, all will be equal (though, as in *Animal Farm*, with some, the policy enforcers, necessarily more equal than others), but certainly one where nearly all will be poorer, conforming exactly to what Karl Marx described as a 'barracks communism', one ruled by 'assessors and officers regulating education, [n.b.] production, consumption, in a word, all social activity'. It is a sad comment on our times that such a society as Marx described and as Kendi proposes can be acclaimed by so many of the US leftist intelligentsia as the answer to their country's race problems.

But we have been here before, when in the 1930s, at the height of the Stalin terror, the slave barracks that was the USSR was hailed, in the title of the Webbs' book on the Soviet Union, as a 'new civilisation', and at the time of the famine caused by Stalin's collectivisation of farming, in which at least ten million died of hunger and cannibalism was rife, the leftist American journalist Walter Duranty could dismiss in the *New York Times* reports in the *Manchester Guardian* of a Soviet famine as a 'big scare story'…rather like the more recent dismissal, in the *Times'* sister journal, the *Guardian*, as 'horror stories' reports about the way Muslim men treat their wives (See Chapter 3) and, even after the revelations in the Khrushchev and Gorbachev eras of the enormity of Stalin's crimes, Corbyn press officer Seumas Milne's insisting that they had been 'wildly exaggerated' and that their perpetrators were motivated by 'genuine idealism.' (Although full appraised of the scale of his rural genocide, Stalin likewise dismissed a report of its consequences in the Ukraine - four million deaths by starvation – as 'fabricating a fairytale about famine'.)

Those academics and their allies in the media who promote CRT mean business. According to the *National Review* of February 5, 2021, like Black Lives Matter, with which it is ideologically aligned, it has 'proliferated into K-12 classrooms, federal, state and local government, businesses and even pre-schools.' 'CRT training' was established practice at 'more than 200 colleges and universities across the country.' In 2021, Brandeis University authorised the introduction of a 1984 wokespeak, with its newly-appointed Assistant Dean, Kate Slater, fresh from her award of a PhD in CRT, drawing up a list of forbidden words, terms and phrases, and replacing them with an officially approved vocabulary. Her starting point, to quote her, is that 'all white people are racist' (including, she readily admits, herself…a case of the blind leading the blind). All men - at least white ones - are also sexist. So, words and phrases deemed 'masculine dominant' such as 'you guys', 'policeman', 'congressman' and 'freshman' are out, as is the gender-binary 'ladies and gentleman'. (For the same reason, the Head Girl of the London elite St Paul's girls school is now called 'Head of School'.) Racial terms hitherto universally regarded as politically correct were deemed no longer so. 'Afro-American' and 'People of Colour' are out, and 'black' is back in, and who knows, soon to be replaced in its turn by 'negro'. More obscure is the banning of 'picnic', the reason given being that whites used to eat snacks while watching a lynching. The recommended replacement was 'outdoor eating'. Even 'trigger', introduced by wokista academics as an advanced warning to snow flake students that they might be traumatised by a class topic, is itself rejected for its fear-inducing 'connections to guns', and should be replaced by 'content note.'

Granted, this word-play has its comic aspects. But the joke ends when it is decanted down from campuses of adult students, many of whom, while perhaps deciding it might be unwise to say so, will dismiss it for the garbage that it is, to impressionable and in many cases, vulnerable school children. White pupils are being taught they have been born in sin as inheritors of white privilege, no matter what their personal circumstances, and black ones, that they are condemned to a life-time of victimhood (albeit noble) and failure – neither being propositions likely to encourage the will to succeed.

CRT has even extended its reach from academe down through teaching-training academies and schools to new-born babies, with the publication in 2021 of another of the anti-racist fraudster Kendi's best-sellers, *Antiracist Baby Picture Book*. (Yes, this is the title) The Amazon promo informed its white, upper middle class, guilt-tripping potential buyers that the '[32-page] full-sized picture book empowers parents and children [specifically, those of the age "baby-3 years"] 'to uproot racism in society and in ourselves', in racist babies as well as their racist parents. This baby will do by looking at the illustrations on Kendi's book and then 'taking nine easy steps to build a more equitable world.' Some babies! Kendi's crash course on infant anti-racism calls to mind a saying attributed to Ignatius Loyola, the founder of the Jesuits; 'give me the child for the first seven years, and I will give you the man.' In Kendi's case, more like a guilt-ridden, nervous wreck.

Kendi's new money-spinning literary, or rather pictorial scam furnishes yet more proof that like others of his persuasion, he regards racism as an inborn, genetically inherited characteristic of exclusively white *homo sapiens*. As such, it is ineradicable, and will therefore prove impervious to Kendi's remedies. But then logic, like much else issuing from the white mind, counts for little when weighed against the noble goal of racial equity. Those like myself whose thinking is trapped in the confines of white empiricism will perhaps ask themselves, as the babies will be in every case the offspring of white parents, and will have siblings, if any, also white, against whom will their racism be directed? As a child is able to articulate its thoughts coherently only after it no longer belongs to the target age of the book ('Baby – 3 years'), how will it express its inborn racism? Unless it learns it by rote from its parents, with what vocabulary?

Kendi is not alone in his absurdities and self-contradictions. The entire movement driven by CRT is shot through with ideological and logical inconsistencies. Here is one. For racism to exist (and for sure it does, not least amongst the professional anti-racists) there must be different races, each with physical characteristics that distinguish them from all others. Apart from a few outliers who argue that race is a 'social' not biological/physiological 'construct', critical race theorists necessarily accept this to be the case, since their entire 'theory' hinges on the significance of this difference. In fact, as we have seen, at every possible opportunity these differences are emphasised and dwelt upon to exclusion of all other factors that shape human behavior. But when it comes to matters concerning gender, the same term that defines race - biology - is deemed inadmissible, even though the differences it refers to are not superficial, as with race, but absolutely fundamental. And yet, as in other policy areas, so here, despite vociferous protests by high profile feminists, public institutions have endorsed the woke agenda, with biological men, some convicted of rape but 'identifying' as women, being incarcerated in women's prisons. The result? In 2018, self-confessed rapist and biological male 'Karen' White was convicted of sexually assaulting two women prisoners while on remand for rape in the woman's section of Wakefield prison, Yorkshire. Occurrences like this - for there have been others like it – give a whole new meaning to an old song, whose chorus goes:

Put me among the girls!
Do me a favour do,
You know I'd do as much for you.
Put me among the girls!
Those with the pretty girls:
They'll enjoy themselves and so will I
If you put me among the girls.

For all its success with the wokistas, amongst ordinary folk, racist anti-racism in the USA had few takers as parents of all social and racial backgrounds and political persuasions staged often angry organised protests against its divisive, odious, evil brainwashing of their children. This was no racist movement, but an anti-racist one. Parent after parent could be seen on YouTube citing Martin Luther King's axiom that a person should be judged not by the colour of their skin but the quality of their character. CRT does the exact opposite, pitting white children in their ascribed role of oppressors against black children as their victims. What particularly enraged parents was that on entry into a new class, pupils were required to define themselves according to the 'identities' of race, gender *and* sexual orientation (yes), and were then divided into those with privilege and those without. One school in California teaching CRT conducted Jim Crow parents' meetings in separate rooms according to race. Teachers in the same state - also home, not co-incidentally, to the Flat Earth Society- were instructed to, quote, 'identify and challenge the way maths is used to uphold capitalist, imperialist and racist views'...like, for example, as we shall see, by insisting that everywhere and always, $2 + 2 = 4$.

As in California so across the USA, parents objected to the dilution of subject content with racially divisive ideology. This had become standard practice at teacher training colleges, illustrated by an article in an academic journal advocating training maths teachers in what it called 'racial noticing' of pupils, as if the brains of different races in the same class required different approaches to questions of number: 'Race-focused teacher education centered on noticing the impact of race and racism in learning settings can make the practice of anti-racist teaching more tractable for pre-service teachers.' As in all other subjects, here, 'race-focusing' and a spurious 'anti-racism' had displaced subject focusing as the prime objective.

Maths has been singled out for special treatment precisely because its abstract and value-free nature and content poses a special challenge to wokistas in their campaign to colonise the entire US educational system, from nurseries and infants to post graduate studies. That is why Seattle public schools do not teach a conventional maths course to its K-12 (5-6 years to 12) pupils, but one titled 'Math Ethnic Studies Framework'. It is divided into four headings, each of which focuses on a different aspect of race and/or ethnicity. The second, 'Power and Oppression' (bear in mind, this a maths, not history, politics or sociology syllabus) begins by asserting that 'power and oppression, as defined by ethnic studies, are the ways in which groups and individuals define mathematical knowledge so as to see "Western" mathematics as the only legitimate expression of mathematical identity and intelligence. This definition of *legitimacy is then used to disenfranchise people* and communities of colour. This erases *the historical contributions* of people of colour and communities of colour.'(emphasis in original) Thus 'Western' or white maths, according to which 2 plus 2 always equals 4, is a tool of white oppression. It necessarily followed therefore that one of the 'learning targets' of this module was to enable pupils (beginning with those aged 5/6 remember) to 'identify how math has been and *continues to be* used to oppress and marginalise people and communities of colour.' (emphasis added) What more could be done to ensure that ethnic minority children should for the rest of their lives remain at best semi-numerate and that as a consequence, be un-employable in any occupation that required basic skills in 'western' maths?

The purposes and methods of CRT are so patently racially divisive and educationally counter-productive that even ultra-liberal white parents rebelled against them at an elite New York private school where, said one parent, 'every class this year has had an obsessive focus on race and identity', with '"racist cop" reenactments in science [!!!], "decentering whiteness" in art class [!!!], and learning about white supremacy in health class. [!!!]' No wonder the performance of black pupils in US public schools is in free fall. A California guide for teaching maths titled *Deconstructing* (a hang-over from post-modernist lingo) *Racism in Mathematics* begins with the bald assertion that 'white supremacy infiltrates [sic] classrooms in every day teacher actions', followed by an example which 'deconstructs' the very foundation of maths: 'There is a greater focus on getting the "right" [note quotes] answer.' It does not say, however, what the 'greater focus' should be. Another reads: 'Contrived [sic] word problems [i.e., that involve mathematical calculations] are valued over the math in students' lived experience [e.g., 'how old will you be at your next birthday?'].' We shall encounter the term 'lived experience' again, because, as here, it plays a key role in the epistemology of CRT. It is also worthy of note that while CRT introduces into the classroom the notion that precision is so much 'white' pedantry, lacking the validity of the 'lived experience' of non-white pupils, its own methods of teaching have to be rigidly enforced, whatever the negative 'lived experiences' of those subjected to them.

The claim made by CRT that the USA is a nation afflicted by an all-pervading racial 'inequity' is riddled with internal inconsistencies. One, perhaps the most controversial, is its treatment of racial minorities whose academic performance and professional success does not 'fit the narrative' of a dominant white elite. We have already seen that 'over-performing' Chinese students have been subject to a secret, but when challenged, ruled to be legal *'numerus clausus'* at Ivy League universities. In July 2021, the *Wall Street Journal* published two letters exposing an identical policy towards students of Asian heritage at two of the USA's elite high schools, Thomas Jefferson in Virginia and Stuyvesant in New York. Both schools had conducted what one letter described as a 'purge' of Asian students, denying them admission in order to admit less qualified applicants from other minority races, thereby applying to the letter Kendi's policy of 'equity'. I quote from one of them, whose author turned critical theory's own lingo against itself:

After Idi Amin's 1972 ultimatum, my family left Uganda in the Indian exodus with $500, two suitcases and a plane ticket. Purged in an overt act of discrimination, we ran from the country we had helped to build for generations. Now discrimination against Asians will again affect my family...Equity [sic] cannot be achieved with discrimination, justice [sic] is empty without basic fairness. America and the American dream are unsustainable platitudes without meritocracy. The irony is, my children, who have worked hard and attended elite universities, have four generations of African ancestors - but they are not black. For this reason, they and their children will have to endure new purges. For them and America, I am heartbroken.

Does this require comment?

Here are some examples of the issues and incidents that aroused ire and even outrage at parents meetings in response to the new 'anti-racist' curriculum imposed on their children. Third grade pupils (7 or 8-year-olds) at a California elementary school were compelled, in what was timetabled as a maths class, to 'deconstruct' (again) their racial 'identities' and then rank themselves according to their 'power [of a seven-year-old] and privilege'. White middle school students in North Carolina were instructed to stand up in class and apologise for their 'privilege'. Buffalo schools taught that the USA is 'built on racism' and that all white people perpetuate racism and are guilty of 'implicit racial bias.' An elite New York school practiced apartheid by requiring its third to fifth grade pupils to separate themselves into groups according to race - what is called in wokespeak (and by Hitler in *Mein Kampf*) as encouraging 'racial awareness'. A New York head teacher was caught on tape saying that his white students were 'inherently evil', 'demonised for being born.' At one parents meeting, a father was ruled out of order by the chair for using the term 'critical race theory' since it did not appear on the school syllabus he was referring to. Another parent was instructed to cease speaking altogether when he pointed out that Nigerians were the most successful recent immigrant group in the USA. As I have said elsewhere, CRT does not like facts, (a manifestation of 'white empiricism'), least of all those based on 'white' statistics.

One tactic used by school boards to smuggle CRT into the classroom was reminiscent of failed attempts by advocates of biblically-based 'creationism' to rebrand it as 'intelligent design'. The brainwashing exercise was redefined as one of promoting 'equity', 'inclusivity' and 'diversity', a ruse that cut no more ice with parents than did creationism's with courts which ruled its new guise to be no less a violation of the First Amendment's separation of state and religion than the original version. Perhaps the most sensational development was the exposure in August 2021 of a fully-fledged, illegal, Jim Crow regime at Atlanta's Mary Lin Elementary School operated by its black (yes, black) Principle. Contrary to Title Six of the Equal Rights Act of 1964, pupils were segregated by race, with six classes composed entirely of white children, and two of black. When a black parent insisted that her child be enrolled in an all-white class, because she liked the teacher, the principle refused, saying her child would be 'isolated' and that pupils learn better when racially segregated. On September 25, 1957, at Little Rock, Arkansas nine black girls arrived for their first day at a newly-integrated school, protected by two lines of fully-armed national guards from a mob of white trash holding aloft placards which proclaimed 'Race Mixing is Communism'.

The classroom battle over CRT really began in earnest when President Biden, on his first day in office, rescinded the Executive Order issued by President Trump on September 22, 2020 banning its use in, amongst other public places and institutions, schools. If we put aside the usual *ad hominem* objections, and focus only on what it says, I cannot see how any parent concerned with the educational progress and moral and mental well-being of their child could have found fault with the Order's stated objective, which was to 'combat offensive and anti-American race and sex stereotyping', both being goals that were once upon a time integral to the left and liberal agenda. Specifically, the Order was aimed at the 'pernicious and false belief that America is an irredeemably racist and sexist country; that some people simply on account of their race or sex, are oppressors, and that racial and sexual identities are more important than our common status as human beings and Americans.' That is an accurate representation of what CRT says, because the Order cited examples that proved it.

Biden's Order, possibly motivated more by the need to appease his party's left and ethnic minority constituencies than genuine conviction and for that reason, although couched in the terminology of CRT, did not specifically mention it, served as a green light for 'progressive' school boards to resume their interrupted exercise in racial engineering. This in turn unleashed the backlash from parents referred to above.

No such resistance to the 'critical theory' onslaught was in evidence at the world-famous Juilliard School of Music and Drama, where its governing body capitulated totally to the demands of an activist black-separatist clique after objections were made to a showing of the 1970's TV anti-slavery series *Roots*. Black students claimed they had been 'broken' by the experience, reviving traumatic race memories of a slavery they had never experienced, while white students had found it profoundly moving. The (black) tutor who had shown the film had his course cancelled. A petition followed, demanding the 'de-colonisation' of the Drama Division and the hiring of an outside consultant to investigate the 'inequitable, anti-black and racist structures and system that are built into the architecture of the Juilliard culture.' (So racist and exclusionist is it that 50% of Julliard drama students are black.) There were also demands to shift the curriculum away from a 'Euro-centric' culture to a black one, and to cease penalizing black students who arrived late for classes, punctuality, like so much else in the USA, being a distinguishing trait of 'white privilege'. The result of focusing only on 'black' drama would be equivalent to excluding, on the same racial grounds, Louis Armstrong, Duke Ellington, Charlie Parker, Dizzy Gillespie and Miles Davis from a course on jazz. What these privileged, over-indulged cry-baby brats need to be told, preferably by a black Julliard alumnus like trumpeter Wynton Marsalis, famed for excelling in both jazz and white colonialist genres, is to stop the infantile, victim play-acting and start acting like adults, literally.

In June 2021, Ivy League Cornell hit the headlines with a story on a subject that normally would not have been the concern of tabloids, because it was about astronomy. But since it was about woke lunacy, it was, and rightly so. To refer to 'black holes' as 'black holes', it would seem, is racist, like calling black boards black boards was for UK leftist educational authorities back in the 1980s. (Now schools use white boards and call them such, which, it is assumed, does not traumatise pupils with white skins.) Under the same 'loony left' dispensation, 'baa baa black sheep' became 'baa baa bleat sheep', as if there was something inherently wrong about an animal (or anything else save a human being for that matter) being (correctly) described as black. And this was anti-racism? As for black holes, they are so described, not because astronomers are racists, but because that is what they are, 'holes' from which light cannot escape, due to the extreme gravitational attraction of collapsed, concentrated 'dark matter' acting upon it. (light is composed of particles, and therefore subject to gravity) This cut no ice with astronomy Professor Nicholas Battaglia and literature Professor Parisa Vaziri. They devised a course titled 'Black Holes: Race and the Cosmos', which challenged the (correct) assumption that there is no connection between race and astronomy, and 'subverted racist assumptions about blackness'. Just as Kendi says, everything is racist, even gravity, empty space and the big bang.

Perhaps white men like myself should be grateful that Kendi's final solution of the equity question does not involve, as did Hitler's of the Jewish one, our physical elimination. But an article in the on-line magazine *The Root* by its editor Damon Young can be construed as pointing in that direction. Back in the Middle

Ages, the Jews were accused of spreading the Black Death. (In 2020, it was Covid19) In an updated version of the same fable, a Nazi propaganda film depicted Jews as plague-spreading rats. Young goes one step further in race hate. Whites are not spreading a plague; *they are the plague itself*. In his article, *Whiteness is a Pandemic*, Young, after attributing all the ills that beset blacks in the modern world to crimes and deeds collectively committed by whites going back four centuries and more (and as always, with no reference to the Arab/Muslim slave trade of far older and longer lasting vintage), he draws the following conclusion: 'White supremacy is a virus that, like other viruses, will not die until there are no more bodies left for it to infect. Which means that the only way to stop it is to locate it, isolate it, and kill it.'

Without it being acknowledged as such, because it originates from within the same 'intersectional' camp, perhaps the most serious challenge to 'critical race theory' is mounted by another spurious mono-causal hypothesis, one claiming, in the words of one of its most vociferous exponents, the lavishly-funded, man-hating Anita Sarkeesian, that 'everything is sexist'. (Unlike many of her kind, she is quite attractive.) This proposition has spawned an entire school of feminist 'ways of knowing' analogous to and necessarily competing with those founded on race, and which, again, like 'critical race theory', has set out to colonise the world of academe in a campus turf war over whose 'ways of knowing' are truest, those of genes that determine skin colour or those that determine gender. (I provide examples of the latter below.) Both, however, have the same origin, emerging in the mid-1990s out of the dying embers of post-modernism. The seminal moment was perhaps the publication in 1996 of a special issue of the prestigious academic journal *Social Text*, titled *Science Wars*. It set itself the goal of 'uncovering the gender-laden and racist assumptions built into the Euro-American scientific method [destined to make way for feminist algebra, queer maths etc]'. The aim was to 'talk about different ways of doing science [from which came "different ways of knowing"], ways that downgrade methodology and evidence [sic!!!!... and replace them with the "feelings" and "lived experiences" of various oppressed "identities"]'. Unbeknownst to its editors, evidently on a high from their ground-breaking venture, one of the articles was a spoof, a grotesque parody of post-modernism by a traditional physicist, the white patriarch Alan Sokol, one so extreme that anyone whose thinking was grounded even only marginally in reality would have spotted it at once. The very title should have alerted the editors that something was afoot: *'Transgressing Boundaries: Toward a Transformative Hermeneutics of Quantum Gravity* - sheer gibberish, a cocktail of post-modernist buzz words and a dash of *bona fide* physics. Such was their gullibility that they either failed to notice, or even (and if true, this is truly mind-boggling) agreed with Sokol's insistence that reality itself, and therefore the article itself and anyone reading it, including the editors who approved and published it, did not exist.

This would have been a new departure for post-Modernism, the existing 'orthodox' position being that reality existed, but all 'discourse' about it was shaped and therefore limited by language and, as such, could not be said to be objective truth about that reality, but a 'social construct' of 'competing narratives', one as valid as any other. (On no account should this be confused with Kant's eminently arguable proposition that our knowledge of objective reality, the 'thing in itself', 'noumena', is refracted, or filtered, not through language, but by and through our senses' perception of that objective reality, hence, 'phenomena'.) One consequence of post-modernism's epistemological agnosticism was that its historians found themselves in deep moral water when it was pointed out that the equal validity (or non-validity) of competing 'narratives' about the history of the Third Reich legitimised Holocaust denial. The weaker spirits among them gave ground, eventually conceding that the greatest crime in human history did actually happen, while others stood firm, insisting that 'debates over evidence are largely diversionary', calling them the 'fetishising of documents'. This, from *professional historians*?

Ironically, the failure of either the editors or academic readership of *Social Text* to detect Sokol's spoof or to find fault with its thesis anticipated the transition from post-modernism to 'critical theory'. When Sokol poured scorn on the idea 'that there exists an external world whose properties are independent of any individual human being and indeed of humanity as a whole; that these properties are encoded in "eternal laws" and that human beings can obtain, reliable, albeit imperfect, knowledge of these laws by hewing to the "objective" [note the tongue in cheek quotes] procedures and epistemological structures prescribed by the (so called) scientific method', he was identifying precisely those principles that came to be rejected in favour of a 'science' whose validity or otherwise was determined by the 'identities' (of race, gender and sexuality) of those who performed it.

In the fiercely competitive, backbiting, hothouse world of academe, what counts more than anything today is sensing the right moment to jump from a sinking ship to one newly-launched and hopefully, seaworthy. This is what Professor Jodi Dean accomplished in 1998 with her *Aliens in America: Conspiracy Cultures from Outerspace to Cyberspace*. Conventional wisdom says that aliens may exist, but there is not a scrap of verifiable evidence they do. Dean had no time for that kind of thinking, a burdensome inheritance from the Enlightenment: 'Alien narratives [sic] challenge us to face head on ([not dismiss as absurd] *the dissolution* of *notions of truth, rationality and credibility.*' (emphasis added) In other words, anything goes, even green aliens landing on your front lawn...anything, that is, except evidence and rationality: 'Argument, thought by some [sic] to be an important part of the process of democracy, is futile [sic!!!!], perhaps because democracy can bring about Holocaust.' (That is, assuming it did actually happen.) So, we have an equation of sorts: Reason + Evidence = Holocaust. So, best not to argue - which is exactly what Dean is doing...against arguing - or thinking rationally.

Here were, albeit in embryonic form, some of the essentials of 'critical theory', a 'theory' that asserts much...too much in fact for its own good...but proves nothing, because it explicitly rejects all the rules and procedures that proof demands...objective evidence and reason...as themselves tainted by their intrinsic 'whiteness', 'maleness' or 'straightness'. Perhaps that is why Dean, a Professor of Political Science (sic), seems to be unaware, firstly, that it was only Hitler's *destruction* of German democracy that made possible the Holocaust, and that it was precisely the *rejection* of rational argument and thinking, and its replacement by the mystique of race, that provided its justification. How did Ivy League Cornell come to publish this nonsense? Was it peer reviewed? If so, who approved it? Whatever the answers to these questions, the book was clear evidence, if its author will permit the use of that word, that the floodgates of unreason were opening. Sustaining the aquatic imagery, perhaps it was not entirely accidental that the publication of Dean's book coincided with a surge in the USA of quackery of another kind, with the use of homeopathic 'remedies' more than doubling between 1990 and 1997. By the end of the decade, 87 million Americans were spending $27 billion a year on the medical equivalent of Dean's scholarship, with both being diluted to zero percent content.

While inheriting post-modernism's subjectivist methodology, one key new departure of 'critical theory' was the replacement of language and 'discourse' as the determinants of what deluded rationalists call knowledge by 'identity', racial and sexual. Another was that instead of all 'discourses' being equal, since none reflects reality, certain 'ways of knowing' now endowed those who possessed them, by virtue of certain inborn characteristics, with genuine 'insights' that are denied to those who did not, a claim akin to that made for 'lived experience'. Sokol had anticipated this development when in his spoof, he argued for a feminist 'liberatory mathematics'. (It came to pass with 'feminist algebra' - see below.) But herein lies the problem and the sleight of hand. There is no way that I as a white heterosexual male can know what it is like to be on the receiving end of white racism, misogyny, or homo and trans phobia. Those who have can describe it to me, but that is a world away from it being for me a 'lived experience', just as, by the same token, it is impossible for blacks, women, gays and trans people to comprehend what it is like for someone sharing my characteristics to be falsely accused, as so many have been in these woke and politically correct times, of racism, misogyny or homo and trans-phobia. Again, for essentially the same reason, it is impossible to reproduce in words the 'lived experience' of hearing a musical composition, because it too is pre-eminently an *emotional reaction,* whereas the process of solving algebraic equations is a purely *intellectual activity* that can be explained and taught to others. When someone says, 'I know how you feel', they mean well, but they cannot, because everyone's 'feelings' are unique and confined to the person who experiences them. No two griefs are the same, or joys. But a person can share with someone else information that is external to them both, like the time of day, or the speed of a car both are travelling in.

But CRT erodes this crucial distinction between emotion and reason, between the subjective and the objective. Instead it elides them; hence its claim that simply being black, female, gay or trans not only generates unique 'lived experiences', which I agree it does, but also provides 'ways of knowing', insights into *academic disciplines* that were hitherto considered unaffected by the 'identities' and 'lived experiences' of those practicing them; that, for example, to put it at its most basic, the correct (itself now a questionable concept) answer to 2 + 2 will not always be 4, that it can vary, as it can to questions in a wide range of academic disciplines, according to the culture, genes, sexual orientation and even belief system of the person making the calculation. Surely not, you may well say. If you do, you are mistaken. By way of an introduction to this subject, I provide one example of many, some of which I have already cited. Just listen to Maria Akindele, PhD, expounding on the subject of black 'ways of knowing': 'I think black people are relationable [sic] people, people of context. It's very western and European to dissect and analyse and take apart things [what is known as the scientific method] whereas referral-centric schooling or Afro-centric spirituality, African epistemology or *ways of knowing* [is one in which] everything is connected…this is why education is not working for so many students of colour because we are

54

context-driven people...we can't tell a story without telling the ten things that happened that led up to that moment. There's no such thing as thinking in isolation, isolating yourself from nature, from your family. It's just not part of our ways of knowing [again] and being in the world. So when we tap into the ways that we [that is, 'people of colour'] understand the world, students are able to make wonderful connections and unleash their brilliance and their wisdom.' (emphasis added)

A number of important questions arise from this exposition of black 'ways of knowing'. If we take the study of STEM subjects (science, technology, engineering and maths), what are its specific achievements? Why has the claimed 'brilliance' and 'wisdom' of these 'ways of knowing' not been acknowledged with the awarding of Nobel prizes? Is this perhaps due to racial bias on the part of the judges? Looking at specifics, in what ways do 'Afrocentric spirituality' and African 'ways of knowing' equip maths students to solve quadratic equations? Or provide chemistry students with an understanding of the periodic table of elements? How does the 'context' of a student's family help to explain Newton's three laws of motion, or Darwin's theory of evolution? 'Western' scientists worth their salt would argue that to claim African 'ways of knowing' are not only distinct from, but superior to science as it has been understood and practiced since the ancient Greeks, is to put in question the laws that science has proved govern not only our planet, but the entire universe. Finally, to extol the superior qualities of an 'African epistemology' is to subscribe to a black equivalent of the Nazi doctrine of 'race truth' or 'thinking with the blood'; one with its roots in Germany's romantic, *Volkische,* reaction to the Enlightenment and the French Revolution, with their commitment to the universal rule of reason and the equality of the human race.

For the Nazis and its *Volkische* precursors there was a single patriarchal, misogynist, heterosexual, white and Germanic, Nordic truth, rooted in race. Now, according to CRT, we have a multiplicity of truths, or 'ways of knowing'; matriarchal, misandrist, gay and transgenderist as well one of race, with its origins not in the north, but the African tropics. Despite their remoteness in place and time and for all their antinomies, what *Volkische* and African truths share in addition to being rooted in race and place is a belief in the mystical, knowledge-giving qualities of 'nature', a perverted, racialised pantheism that has nothing in common with the rationalist, cosmic universalism of Spinoza's. Black Africans supposedly 'tap' into nature as *Volkische* Germans, especially anti-Semitic middle-class male youth of the *Wandervögel*, forerunner of the *Hitlerjugend*, once 'tapped' into the countryside as a life-affirming alternative to the soullessness of the city, with Berlin as 'the playground of the Jews'. Like the *Volkische* movement's view of the Jews, Akindele believes that 'western', 'analytical' thinking is deficient because it lacks 'spirituality' and a rootedness in 'nature' and 'family'...the repositories of a racial or tribal wisdom. This is a notion not so different from the *Volkische* idealisation of the peasant, with his sense of place, 'folk memory' and respect for tradition, each of which under the Nazis were subsumed into the overtly racist doctrine of 'blood and soil', in which the honest, loyal, life-sustaining and eternal peasantry, custodian of the race, was contrasted with the Jews, who were parasitical, (thus 'moon creatures', with Germans as 'sun people'), dishonest, scheming, alienated from nature, rootless, the architype of the 'wandering Jew'; given to 'dissecting' and 'analysing' but incapable of feeling;

and being nationless, at home only in the anonymous metropolis. In an attempt to validate this racial stereotype, Nazi neurologists took measurements of the skulls of murdered Jews that, so they claimed, proved a Jew's 'way of knowing' was that of a materialist, grasping sub-human, lacking the honesty, uprightness and 'spirituality' of an 'Aryan'.

Akindele's negative view of (obviously white) 'western' or 'European' academics as lacking, for want of a better word, in soul, was advanced by a black academic as far as back as the 1990s, leading to a legal case that attracted considerable attention not only in the world of US scholarship but, because of its political implications, far beyond it. Leonard Jeffries was a professor of Black Studies at the prestigious New York City College. Well before the idea became mainstream, he proposed that public school syllabi should become less 'Euro-centric' by incorporating some of the achievements of Black Africans and Americans which thus far, had not been acknowdged by the white academic establishment. Here he was pushing on an open door. But not so with his allegation, one that has gone the rounds on the Corbynista left, that Jews financed the trans-Atlantic slave trade, and another, that Jews use their control of the movie industry to harm black people. The final straw which led eventually to his dismissal was Jeffries' advocacy of black mental superiority, which was later to resurface in the guise of black 'ways of knowing'. According to Jeffries, whites were 'ice people', violent, cruel, lacking in feeling and spiritual qualities, unlike blacks, who were 'sun people' (again), attuned to nature, compassionate, peaceful. Jeffries subscribed to the so-called Melanin Theory, that by absorbing the sun's rays, the melanin in black skin transmits to black brains mental powers superior to those of whites. (A female, Muslim, Black Lives Matter activist has declared her support for this nonsense, adding to it that whites are 'subhumans' deserving only of elimination.) The 'Melanin Theory' gained considerable traction over the years among some black academics, and judging by her comments on the superiority of African 'ways of knowing', I would not be at all surprised if Professor Akindele was one of them.

If, as is clearly the intention, African, or more generally, black 'ways of knowing' are to be introduced (as in some states they already have been) into all subjects taught at US public schools, a number of practical issues will necessarily arise. Will 'African' and 'Western' methods be taught alongside each other in the same class, as was unsuccessfully proposed by creationist opponents of evolution for biology lessons? Or will 'decolonisation' prevail, with an all-'African' syllabus? A third solution would be a reversion to Jim Crow, with each race being taught separately, according to its ways of knowing (as in Atlanta's Mary Lin school). To further complicate matters for 'progressive' educationalists, there are other ways of knowing than those of race. Gender and sexual orientation are no less vigorously bidding for a place in the academic sun to promote their own unique truths, and it is difficult to see how they can all be accommodated in the same curriculum.

I have deliberately chosen as examples of female 'ways of knowing', as I have done for their 'black' equivalents, mainly those pertaining to what I call the 'hard' disciplines - the sciences, maths etc - because their subject matter, until the advent of post-modernism and now its CRT derivatives, has been universally regarded as having an objective character unaffected by the 'identity' of its practitioner. In those with a 'softer', subjective content, such as literature and the arts generally, 'lived experience' can legitimately be said to contribute to their appreciation and understanding.

Thus we have books, papers and articles with titles such as: *On the Possibility of* [a] *Feminist Philosophy of Physics; Moving Towards a Feminist Epistemology of Mathematics; Gender in the Substance of Chemistry; Stars, Planets and Gender: A Framework for a Feminist Astronomy; A Feminist's Guide to Botany; Glaciers, Gender and Science: A Feminist Glaciology Framework for Global Environmental Change Research; Talking Feminist Astro-Physics with Chandra Prescod; Feminist Geography in Practice; An Introduction to Feminist Theology; How Feminist Biology is Challenging Science's Gender Biases; Feminist Empiricism; Egyptology, Feminist Theory and Alterative Worlds; Limits of Experimental Knowledge: A Feminist Perspective; Neuro-Feminism and Feminist Neuro-Scientists: a critical review of contemporary brain research; Feminist Geography in the UK: the dialectics of women-gender-feminism-intersectionality and praxis; Feminist Approaches to Musicology; Feminist Practices: Interdisciplinary Approaches to Women in Architecture; Zoology from a Liberal Feminist Perspective; The Limits of Experimental Knowledge: A Feminist Perspective; Towards a Feminist Algebra* [my favorite – R.B.]*; Feminist Economics: Theoretical and Political Dimensions; Theories put forth by Evolutionary Theory are Testament to what happens when the Field of Science is restricted to Upper Class White Men* [Mendel and Darwin were white and male, but not 'upper class']; *The Talking Feminist Astro-Physics; Neurofeminism and Feminist Neurosciences - A Critical Review; A Brief Introduction to Feminist Engineering; Implementing Feminist Theory in Engineering* and *A Feminist Approach to Teaching Quantum Physics.*

This upsurge in books and articles devoted to female 'ways of knowing' marks a regression in four ways, each well illustrated by a Wikipedia entry on 'Feminist Philosophy'. The most obvious of the four is the repudiation, in most cases explicit, of the objective, rational methods of scientific inquiry. We read that 'feminist epistemology' (that is, precisely, 'female ways of knowing') 'challenges traditional philosophical ideas of knowledge and rationality as objective, universal or value neutral.' These concepts also happen to constitute the Enlightenment principles on which has been built, at enormous human cost, today's western liberal, democratic civilisation, one that, ironically, has for the first time in human history, enshrined in law the equality of women with men. Secondly, this attack on reason, objective truth and universal values (such as those enunciated in the United Nations Universal Declaration of Human Rights, which also includes the equality of women with men) is not only intellectually reactionary in its advocacy of feeling, intuition and subjectivity as against reason and evidence. It is equally so ethically, with its denial of universal morals, which has led some feminist advocates of moral and cultural relativism to oppose the criticism of the subjugation of women by Islam. (See chapter three) Thirdly, with its rejection of rationality and emphasis on feeling, instinct and intuition as uniquely female 'ways of knowing', it also projects an image of women conforming to the traditional, 'Victorian era' stereotype that pioneer feminists, beginning with Mary Wollstonecraft, always rejected and rebelled against. Finally, and perhaps most concerning, these 'ways of knowing' also reprise, in a feminist guise, the quasi-mystical, anti-positivist, 'integralist' school of philosophy that in Italy and France in the first two decades of the 20th century (as exemplified by Henri Bergson and

Georges Sorel), sowed the ideological seeds of fascism.

That is why serious political thinkers in the USA, both black and white and from the moderate right to the moderate left, have taken issue with the official endorsement by public institutions of CRT, with its elevation of feeling and identity over reason and evidence, seeing it as an attack on the Enlightenment foundations of the United Sates, and more broadly, western civilisation. As I say elsewhere, this highly authoritarian (per)version of 'leftism' contains the potential, in ways that should be apparent to the discerning reader, for evolving into a *sui-generis* totalitarian, collectivist movement, one neither exclusively of the left or right, but containing, in a distorted form, elements of both (as did national socialism and fascism), with its goal of a state-imposed 'equity', racial obsessions and contempt for individual liberties. (In a survey conducted in 2017, 62% of pro-Democrat students believed they had the right to shout down speakers they disagreed with, even though the so called 'hecklers' veto' had previously been ruled by the Supreme Court to be a violation of the free speech clause of the first Amendment. 20% advocated *using violence* to the same end, and as I record elsewhere here in this work, some have done so. More recent surveys, and the continued rise of campus thuggery, suggest these percentages are increasing.)

Conservative academics and politicians use the term 'cultural Marxism' to describe (and discredit) CRT for two reasons; that like Marx, it projects a conflict model of society; and that those academics who first devised and now propound the theory are without exception in origin leftists of one kind or another. As to the first, the same can said of any system of ideas or movement that sees the world in binary terms, though it should be born in mind that Marx only did so in relation to capitalism. All three monotheisms project a picture and tell a story of a humanity griped in a battle between God and Satan, spawning throughout their histories a multiplicity of Manichean and Millennial movements that have often taken it to violent extremes. So while there is a certain substance to the claim that CRT has substituted Marx's struggle of classes with one between a privileged white, heterosexual ('cis') patriarchy and a multiplicity of oppressed 'identities' of race, gender and sexual orientation, it is by doing so that it ceases to be in any meaningful sense 'Marxist'. Race and gender differences cut across those of class…today, in a variety of countries, not least in the USA, we see the rise of both a none-white and a female 'bourgeoisie', and it is because all the relevant statistics bear this out that they are never cited by 'critical' theorists. Neither is it the case that like CRT, which sees people purely through the prisms of their immutable racial and gender 'identities', Marx negated the individual. On the contrary, his aim was the *abolition* of classes, creating a society 'in which the free development of each is the condition for the free development of all'…as concise a definition of classic liberalism as any coming from the pen of a Mill or Macauley. And while Marx said, 'unto each according to their needs', Kendi's message is, unto (and from) each according to their race.

All that being said, we are still confronted with the reality that an entire generation of former leftist, in some cases '*Marxisant*' US academics have been involved in an ideological undertaking that in certain respects re-enacts the beginnings of the transition a century previously of a number of prominent French and especially Italian political thinkers from socialism to fascism. Five of the seven who founded the Italian fascist movement in March 1919, were from the far left; three being former leaders of the Socialist Party, including Mussolini, who until October 1914, had been the editor of the party official daily, *Avanti*, and two revolutionary syndicalists.

In his *The Birth of Fascist Ideology*, Zeev Sternhell describes some basic features of fascism, and the circumstances in which they arose, that have an uncanny resemblance to the emergence of the US woke left, and its underpinnings in 'critical race theory': 1: 'It [fascism] expressed a revolutionary aspiration based on a rejection of individualism' (today replaced by CRT with group 'identities' based on race and gender). 2: 'It created the elements of a new and original political culture.' (The current predominant political conflicts in the USA have been defined as 'culture wars.) 3: 'This political culture, communal, anti-individualistic and anti-rationalistic represented a rejection of the heritage of the Enlightenment and the French Revolution.' (Thus today, we have 'ways of knowing' and 'group think'.) To which I add a fourth: None of pioneers of fascism was a conservative. Those of the traditional right had no taste or aptitude for mass politics, their natural habitat being the debating chamber, not the street. That is why it is wrong to describe former Republican President Donald Trump as a conservative, with his promise that he would 'shake things up'. His record both in and out office revealed him as a not very bright *populist demagogue*, one devoid of any ideology, but with more than a sneaking regard for dictators and 'strong men' past and present - he is alleged to have said that Hitler 'did a lot of good things'. Nevertheless, he has proved himself capable of mobilising millions behind a conspiratorial agenda no less threatening to US liberties and race relations than the divisive 'anti-racism' of the far left. But contrary to what some on the left claim, neither Trump nor the vast majority of his deluded followers are even proto-fascists, let alone the fully-developed article. Their main arena remains that of electoral politics - hence the cry of 'stop the steal' and the abortive bid to prevent the confirmation of Biden's election victory. Despite his endorsement of the 'Proud Boys', Trump has no standing militia to call on remotely comparable to that of Mussolini or Hitler, or even the far left's Black Lives Matter and Antifa

Then there is the matter of ideology. While it is true that a number of academics and political commentators, (black as well as white, female as well as male, Jewish as well as gentile, gay as well as straight), have identified themselves to one degree or another with Trump, or at least supported him, however critically, as what they see as the only viable alternative to the left, they all define themselves as, and indeed are, conservatives and, as such, criticise the left for its 'cancel culture' attacks on free speech...hardly an indicator of fascist leanings.

Where is the USA headed? Its democratic institutions and liberal culture are without doubt menaced by the growth of extremes within the party system, leaving millions of Americans who value both without an electoral voice, voting against a party they want to lose, rather than for one they want to win...hardly a sign of a healthy democracy. In so far as the genuinely liberal middle ground finds an coherent expression, it is in the immense popularity of political thinkers and commentators like the black academics Coleman Hughes, Glen Lowry and John McWorter, the neurologist Sam Harris and evolutionary biologist Bret Weinstein, each of whom, like their followers on YouTube, are repelled no less by Trumpist conspiracy theories and populist demagogy as they are by Biden's indulgence of 'critical race theory' and its street counterpart, Black Lives Matter.

Without in any way belittling the threat from the right, as an ante-diluvian (that is to say, pre-Corbyn) leftist, my prime interest, as the reader will by now have gathered, is compable in some ways to Orwell's, whose overriding concern as a libertarian democratic socialist was also a threat to individual freedom issuing from a part of the Left. Today, we face another, originating not in Russia, but in of all places, the USA, under the banners of CRT and a racial 'social justice'. It has been joined in Europe, especially in the UK (viz. Labour Corbynistas and academe) by a left that lends its support to states and movements ranged against what it calls 'western imperialism' (for example backing the Ayatollahs in Iran, the Taliban in Afghanistan and Hamas in Palestine) and as integral to that, an obsessive, unrelenting hostility towards the state of Israel. In both (related) movements there is a defining racial dimension, explicit in the USA, with its ferocious attack on 'white privilege', and in the UK and on the continent, one coded as anti-Zionism, but correctly understood as anti-Semitism by those Muslims attracted to it both as voters and political activists.

While history never repeats itself exactly, it does furnish patterns and precedents that can give insights to the present and hints of a possible future. Today's attack on liberal democracy most certainly has its precedents. A century ago, they took the form of fascism and then, Bolshevism, each, like the USA today with Trumpery and wokery, feeding off the other. It is beyond dispute that CRT, and the deeply reactionary, viciously racist movement it has spawned, are both creations of leftist academics and intellectuals, just as in both Italy and France, fascism began as movement of dissident radical intellectuals and academics. They too were looking for new paths, disillusioned by what they saw as the inertia of mainstream leftist movements, brought about, so they argued, by their adaptation to the institutions of 'bourgeois' liberal democracy and 'bread and butter' trade unionism. Georges Sorel, like his Italian co-thinkers, initially an advocate of militant, even violent trade unionism (known as 'syndicalism'), looked for a substitute for a passive proletariat, and located it in the nation. CRT has found it in race, and the European far left, also in Islam.

What is common to such movements, whatever their political coloration, is a predilection for organised violence. Instead of the game of parliamentary politics that had become the main pre-occupation of the socialist party following the extension of the franchise to male workers, the pioneers of Italian fascism advocated 'direct action' - a euphemism for organised violence - by what Mussolini called 'dynamic minorities'. After his swing to the far right, and now financed by business and agrarian interests, beginning in the Autumn of 1920, his black-shirted *squadristas,* many of them ultra-nationalist ex-army officers, unleashed an orgy of organised violence against the Left, assaulting and even killing trade unionists and socialists, and wrecking and burning down the offices and looting the co-cooperatives stores of the Italian workers' movement. Exactly a century on, the world watched with a wide variety of reactions as on its screens it saw the *squadristas* of Black Lives Matter (also funded by business interests), some wearing masks and parading, like the Italian fascists, in all-black uniforms and with semi-automatic rifles, unleashing a similar orgy of violence on the streets of the USA, with assaults, some lethal, on police, bystanders and shop keepers; looting, vandalism, arson and attacks on synagogues, Jewish-owned stores, police stations, court houses and other public buildings, causing damage and losses through theft (in mainly black neighbourhoods) estimated at more than five billion dollars

The violence on the streets has its intellectual counterpart - and also been provided with its ideological justification - in the explicit disillusionment among the US intelligentsia with what has been called 'the American way' - individual freedom and equality of all under the law. This has been found wanting by leftists, because it does not facilitate 'social justice', or, as Kendi and his ilk would have it, 'equity', an 'equality of outcomes', a utopia in which everyone is a winner, instead of 'equality of opportunity' in which the dice, despite 'affirmative action', are allegedly deliberately loaded in favour of the 'white patriarchy'. Add to this, further disillusionment caused by 1: the world-wide monopoly of capitalism following the collapse of the Soviet bloc and the restoration of a (partial) market economy in China and, domestically, 2: the domination of the Democratic Party by mainstream liberalism; 3: a mainly white the working class totally disinterested in when not hostile to any kind of socialism, resulting in 4: this increasingly conservative and mainly white working class being replaced in the scheme of things, not by 'nation' (the US far left despises everything the USA stands for) as with fascism, but an anti-national 'intersectional' alliance of the supposedly oppressed and disaffected - all women, and a range of racial and sexual minorities. Taken together, here we have many, if not yet all, of the ingredients necessary for an explosion of frustration on the US left similar to those of the early 20th century that gave rise to fascism....revolt on the street against the institutions of democracy, and against reason and evidence on the campus. From these events and developments spring the *enragé* mood of leftist students, the 'extra-parliamentary' and often illegal tactics of the various branches of the woke movement - Black Lives Matter, Antifa (sic) etc - with their undisguised contempt for the 'system' and its constitution, and a readiness to silence or 'cancel' all opposition, as did Mussolini's *Squadristas*, 'by any means necessary'.

The similarities, indeed, in some instances, identities, between the revolt against 'orthodox' Marxism by a part of the left in the early 20th century and, a century later, the rise of its 'social justice' or 'woke' counterpart, are uncanny. Sternhell is describing the first, but in so many ways it could easily be, *mutatis mutandis*, the latter. (my parallels in square brackets):

A total moral revolt [c.f., against 'equality', for racial/gender, not class, 'equity'] would replace the struggle for better conditions, psychological methods [c.f., 'lived experience'] would replace the traditional mechanist [c.f., 'white' empirical/rational] approach, and irrationalism [c.f., 'ways of knowing'] would replace the classical Marxism concept of socialism. ['race' replacing 'class'] Since it appeared that the masses could not be activated by reason [c.f., again, 'white' empiricism etc]...and since capitalism did not collapse [instead, in 1991, it was the 'socialist' USSR that 'collapsed'] and social polarisation [of class] did not happen, one had artificially to create a process of rebellion of a new type [c.f., of 'intersectional' racial and gender 'identities' and by 'culture wars'] suitably adapted to new social conditions [c.f., social media, street violence, monument vandalism, campus politics etc].This was the function of the theory of myths that lay at the heart of the anti-materialist revision of Marxism.

Sorel advocated the propagation of 'myths' that need not be true, but could serve to generate a mass movement, for example as the Nazis did with the lie of a 'world Jewish conspiracy', the fascists, with their claim that Italy was a cheated, exploited, 'proletarian' nation, and today, the equally unfounded 'woke' claim of a 'systemic' or 'institutional' racism in the USA. The proponents of 'critical theory' in its various manifestations are untroubled by accusations, such as those made against Kendi, that it does not rest upon proven facts, since it is the denial of the very notion of objective truth, condemned and rejected for its intrinsic 'whiteness', and its replacement by 'lived experience' and 'ways of knowing', that are, as we have seen, its governing principles. The only criterion is, does a 'myth' work, does it legitimise and galvanise a movement for goals that are held to worthy, as with critical theory's 'social justice' and 'equity'?

Sam Harris has called the new anti-racism a secular religion. If it is - and there are good grounds for saying so – it is not the first. Following the First World War, the pioneers of totalitarian movements both left and right did what all organised religions have done since time immemorial, re-enforcing their respective 'myths' with carefully-staged mass rallies, rituals, rhythmically chanted slogans and displays of flags and symbols, each designed to appeal, not to reason, but the movement's unique 'way of knowing'. BLM's 'knee-taking' resembles genuflection in the Catholic Eucharist, as does the martyrology surrounding the death of George Floyd that of the crucifixion of Christ. Street 'happenings' play the same role...the ceremonial pulling down of statues of historic figures that not only personify slavery, but also of those who led the war that abolished it, the laying siege to buildings that symbolise the authority of the enemy. SJW slogan-chanting at rallies and on marches has both positive and negative functions; the first, group-bonding around a small number of primitive ideas (akin to prayers) and second, to silence those who do not share them. Then of course there are the uniforms, matching the uniformity of thought, or rather, feeling, that defines such movements, be they of the left or right. Finally, there is the matter of social composition. No political movement has ever been 'chemically pure' in respect of its following. It is where the balance lies that lends a movement its character and political style. Both Italian fascism and German Nazism drew most of their support from the middle strata, as do the various branches of the woke movement in the USA and the UK, with young white women, many if not most students, being the most prominent in both. Conspicuous by its absence, and even more so than was the case with fascism and national socialism, is the traditional, unionised working class, for whom the divisive politics of race have no appeal whatsoever, since they undermine, as they always have done, its unity in action.

Those academics who created 'critical theory' were not fools or ignoramuses, or university common room windbags. They knew exactly what they were doing, and no less that it violated all the procedures and traditions of genuine intellectual inquiry. That is why they invented the myth of their 'whiteness' to justify their abandonment in favour of an anti-Enlightenment, subjectivist epistemology in which almost anything goes. Objective truth - even if it is attainable - counts for nothing. In fact, it is the enemy. Winning is everything. Here we have three examples of that 'pragmatic' attitude to truth and morality: 1) 'We have created our myth. The myth is a faith, a passion. *It is not necessary that it shall be a reality*. It is a reality by the fact that it is a goal, a hope, a faith...' (emphasis added) 2) 'What matters is not to have right on our side, but simply to win.' 3) 'It's not about who is right. It's about who has power.' The first is Mussolini, the second, Hitler, the third, a student 'Social Justice Warrior' at the University of Chicago.

Another similarity between fascism and movements influenced by CRT is their shared predilection for redemptive violence. In his *Reflections on Violence*, the work that marked his break with the mainstream left, Sorel sees violence as a moral act, 'very beautiful and very heroic', 'serv[ing] the primary interests of civilisation' by 'sav[ing] it from barbarism', by which he meant the debilitating conventions and institutions of 'bourgeois' liberal democracy. In the same spirit, if not in the same elevated terms, Black Lives Matter organiser Ariel Atkins justified the orgy of massive and pre-planned looting that engulfed downtown Chicago on August 10, 2020. It too was a moral act, one of restitution and retribution for four centuries of black slavery, and not, at least in her eyes, to be seen as theft: 'The whole idea of criminality is based on racism, because criminality is punishing people for things that they have needed to survive.... I will support the looter till the end of the day, if that's what they need to do to eat.' Is that why looters loaded up vans with items from fashion and tech shops, while ignoring food stores?

As I have said, BLM violence is, not, generally speaking, spontaneous, as most riots are, but organised, however chaotic it may seem, especially when it is joined by elements of the local black criminal under-class, who though maybe not up to speed on BLM ideology, must surely endorse its policy of abolishing the police and justice system. In a short film on BLM consisting partly of interviews with activists, at a 'riot' in Minneapolis, one justified vandalism, arson and looting as 'necessary to get rid of the whole shit', and another, that it was OK to 'burn the whole fucking lot down...if there's no change, there might be whole lot more destroying until there is.' And others: 'riot is a voice to [i.e., 'of'] the unheard...destruction and looting kinda sends a message to the people. So when we take it back [i.e., loot] or burn it down we're getting back what's ours...this country was built on violence [a central axiom of CRT - but what country wasn't?] so we're giving it back to you...Do you need violence? yes...as a school...you've got to have violence...looting and rioting is part of the protest...' A slogan inscribed on a wall read: 'Vandalism: As beautiful as a rock in a cop's face.' Others read 'Kill the pigs', 'Today's Cops, tomorrow's pork rinds' and 'All Cops must die'. All this is pure hate, pure nihilism, pure criminality, none of disowned, and much of incited and explicitly justified by the BLM leadership, and even by a CNN newsreader, despite it being a calculated violation of that clause in the First Amendment which specifies that the right of assembly is to be exercised peacefully.

As was fascist violence a century previously, BLM's is designed to weaken the institutions and discredit the norms of liberal democracy, all of which are, according to the University of Denver's definition of CRT', simply means to uphold the rule of the white patriarchy and therefore destined to be 'abolished', along with much else, by any means that come to hand. A century previously, with Mussolini on his corpse-strewn road to power, Sorel acknowledged that his pupil's black-shirted desperados had 'very clearly demonstrated the value of triumphant violence.'

And, of course, as well as BLM and fascist violence, there is a shared anti-Semitism, true, not a feature of Italian fascism until near its end, but very much that of the French version. Sorel, in his more orthodox socialist years, was a Dreyfusard, but then, after his open break with Marxism and his alliance with the ultra-right, monarchist *Action Française*, he became a vocal anti-Semite, demanding that 'the French must defend their state, their customs and their ideas against the Jewish invaders who want to dominate everything.' As there was no Israel to disguise it as anti-Zionism, as many on the far left do today, anti-Semitism could only express itself in those times as an open hostility towards to the Jews, as Sorel does here. BLM co-founder and 'trained Marxist' Patrice Cullors, now departed for lucrative and luxurious pastures new, would, of course, deny she is an anti-Semite. (Unlike Black Muslim *Fuehrer* and BLM enthusiast Louis Farrakhan, who makes no secret of it, any more than he does his admiration for Hitler.) Why then, her opposition to the existence of the only Jewish state on this planet, and to no other, not even those guilty, she would claim, of 'institutional' and 'systemic' racism, and a history of black slavery? Here she is, addressing a BLM meeting: 'If we don't step up boldly and courageously to end the imperialist project called Israel [aka 'Zionist entity'] we are doomed', a similar message to that delivered by a BLM activist at an anti-Israel rally in London in May 2021. One could legitimately construe this as, it's either us...we blacks... or them...the Jews, a warning certain, if not calculated, to incite hostility towards them. And sure enough, after a BLM demo in LA, two graffiti on a synagogue wall read: 'Fuck Israel' and 'Free Palestine'.

To return to Atkins, one of BLM's more articulate spokespersons. The reason why she scorned peaceful action and working through existing democratic institutions was because 'winning has [only] come through riots'. If by 'riots' she means violence, then that is true of fascism in Italy, a movement that in a free election, never came remotely near winning a majority in the Italian parliament, any more than did the Nazis in Germany's *Reichstag*. But in the USA of today, this is a lie, one no less false than the belief of the Black Panthers that 'with the gun' the 'black masses' would 'capture their dreams and bring them to reality'. Their urban terrorism did nothing for the USA's blacks, any more than has BLM looting, vandalism and arson, which serve only to leave a trail of devastation in black neighbourhoods that drives out businesses and discourages investment, thereby generating yet more social deprivation. Martin Luther King understood this. He rejected rioting and other forms of violent protest (he was however always prepared to defy racist laws peacefully) not only for moral reasons, but because, in his own words, 'rioting is not revolutionary but reactionary'. Waging what will always in the end be a losing battle against the superior forces of the state, it 'invites defeat'. But King's strict, disciplined, unvarying adherence to non-violent, but always militant methods of protest, more than any other factor, helped to deliver the Civil Rights Acts of 1964 and 1965 that put a legal end to Jim Crow. Atkins' lame attempt at a sophisticated justification of looting as 'reparations' for slavery demonstrates the pernicious, self-defeating impact of CRT as it decants from leafy campuses down onto the streets of Chicago's crime-blighted South Side, where at weekends, without any condemnation by Atkins or her Black Lives Matter comrades, black children are caught in the crossfire of shoot-outs between rival gangs.

If we shift our focus from the street to the world of academe, we see both the ideological justification and reflection of this transition from rational, pluralist democratic politics to sheer gangsterism in the multiplication and spread of logic-defying variants on the regressive, deeply reactionary ideology that drives and fuels the action on the streets. Here, for example, we have it taking a step further down the same subjectivist, even solipsist path, claiming that not only genes, but also the sexual orientation and belief system of those practicing a range of

64

academic disciplines *determine the validity or otherwise of their findings.* Let me quote from an article which explores the part played by not only the ideological but the sexual orientation of mathematicians in their researches. Its title is: *A Queer Turn in Mathematics Education Research: Centering the Experience of Marginalized Queer Students.* But before I do, let me make the following point. I readily grant that creative activity such as the writing of poetry or a novel will reflect in some way the beliefs, ideals and, quite possibly, sexuality, of the author. However, while the creative artist, if they are true to themselves, cannot but help reveal something of who they are through and in their work, I cannot see how this can be the case with mathematics or physics, the most abstract of all the disciplines. *1984* tells us a great deal about Orwell's politics, but E = MC squared tells us absolutely nothing about Einstein's, any more than it does about his sexuality.

But it seems I am wrong. The argument is as follows: 'The knower and the known are intertwined [a sensuous image to be sure] ...a science without humanity - without values, purposes, beliefs - is a *false science, the false science of the spectator* who always stays outside the arena of action, removed from the existential happenings of life - the "pure scientist" as the phrase goes. This spectator view of science, of knowledge and of teaching is a *thing of the past.*' (emphasis added) Here the author echoes, we can be sure without realizing it- the words of another Professor, Ernst Krieck. The '*old idea* of science' as 'pure rationality', with its validity 'unlimited by time', 'detached', was dead. Science 'depended on the scientist', all knowledge was therefore subjective, 'a decision, a *valuation*'. (emphasis added) Who is, or rather was, Professor Krieck? Although seemingly up to speed on the new woke science of 'identity', he was in fact a prominent and much-published German academic of the Third Reich, an exponent of Nazi 'race truth'.

For all its failings...objectivity, lack of *engagement* and of values other than the quest for knowledge... this 'dead', 'false' 'thing of the past' gave us the discoveries of Galileo, Newton, Darwin, Mendel, Einstein, Plank, Bohr, Heisenberg, so it is legitimate to ask: what does the author of the article in question, a professor at the University of Michigan, offer us? 'I choose to dwell in the borderlands between queer theory and mathematics, not only to challenge the border between them [n.b.] but to push on the borders of mathematical educational research.' So I ask again...what achievements does this 'challenging' and 'pushing' have to its credit? Has it cracked Fermat's last theorem? Well...not just yet. There is much preparatory work to done before that stage is reached: 'I offer ways in which mathematics education researchers can take a queer turn in mathematics education research by generating queer curriculum, engaging in queer pedagogy, and queering mathematical content.' So it would seem, as with other comparable revelations in 'ways of knowing,' we must be patient. Nevertheless, I think is it is reasonable to insist that only when queer maths begins to deliver solutions to unresolved problems such as Hilbert's Sixteenth and answers to Kaplansky's Conjecture can 'straight' mathematicians be expected to take its claims seriously.

And yet, in anti-imperialist as opposed to queer maths, when it comes to 'ways of knowing', or rather, in this case, of counting, things are already on the move, heralding the era of Big Brother. The correct answer to 2 plus 2 may not yet have been 'queered', but it has certainly been de-colonised. Brittany Marshall is a US school teacher (a truly terrifying state of affairs), PhD student at Rutgers University (likewise) and 'critical [sic] mathematics researcher', who defines herself as a 'social justice change agent', BLM supporter and 'wannabe math person'. In the latter capacity, she tweeted on July 5, 2020 (yet again, post Floyd) that 'the idea of 2 + 2 equaling 4 is cultural, and because of western imperialism/colonialism, we think of it as the *only way* of *knowing*.' (my emphasis) 'How many fingers do you see, students?' George Orwell predicted this, now it is upon us, heralded by a PhD student at a university promoting itself as an 'academic, health and research powerhouse'. And there is more. She is not alone. Far from it. Responding to a number of derisory comments on line and in the media, the 'Math Ed Collective' rallied to her defence, calling on sympathisers and academic institutions to support the 'scholarship of students of colour'. Endorsement of the new anti-imperialist/colonialist maths of colour was also forthcoming from Amanda Jansen, Professor of Mathematics no less at the University of Delaware, author of *Attitudes, Beliefs, Motivation and Identity* [sic] *in Mathematics Education* and, predictably, also, like a growing number young, mainly female academics at otherwise reputable US universities, a member of the 'Math Ed Collective': 'I support Brittany Marshall. Critical [n.b.] mathematics education research has an important role in dismantling injustices.'

According to its website, the 'Math Ed Collective' is a 'collective of mathematics educators fighting for freedom'…from the rules of maths I suspect. Be that as it may, the 'collective' has in all probability contributed to the decline in maths performance by US students. In 2018, they were ranked *30th* repeat, *30th* out of 79 countries by the Organisation for Economic Co-operation and Development, with a score of 478, *below the OECD average of 489*. Among the many countries outperforming the US, while still teaching racist, sexist, imperialist and homo/trans phobic maths, were Singapore, 569, Taiwan, 531 and Japan, 527. In science, the US ranked 11th with a score of 502, again far behind Singapore with 551, followed by Macao, 544 and Estonia, 530. Evidently, performance in maths and science is not simply a matter of resources, but also how they are taught.

I am not a mathematician, but even so, I have four issues with anti-imperialist/colonialist maths of colour. First, if 2 plus 2 no longer necessarily equals 4, and perhaps never did, what does it equal? Or is the act of addition itself tainted by its association with imperialist/colonialist rationalism/empiricism? Second, there is no such discipline as (white) 'colonialist' maths, even on CRT terms. The numerical symbols universally used today are not a creation of white imperialism/colonialism. They are Arab/Islamic imperialist in origin, supplanting those evolved by Roman imperialism/colonialism, while the number zero was invented, independently, by the Sumerians, the South American Mayans, and the Indians. Third: maths as a means of measurement and calculation was created by the Egyptians and the Babylonians around 2,000 BC. Granted they too were imperialists…but also ones 'of colour'…surely a redeeming feature. Fourth: How, precisely, does questioning two plus two equals four 'dismantle injustices?

No doubt those academics and school teachers who disseminate this poisonous, mind-crippling nonsense to their charges believe they are striking out on a new, radical path, one informed by the conviction that maths is subject to racial influences. We shall see they are mistaken. It has been done before…long before. California now teaches an anti-racist maths, like Professor Akindele's, according to the state's *Mathematics Project*, 'rooted in culture and values', and consequently, one whose problems can have more than once answer. Of all academic disciplines maths, being totally abstract, is the one that, at least until the advent CRT, could be said with total certainty to have 'roots' neither in 'values' nor 'nature' and least of all, race. With pre-CRT maths, 2 plus 2 = 4 was not a value-laden moral judgment but a calculation, and the correct answer was the same whether the calculation was made in a jungle or a desert. No longer. The Oregon 'Math Equity Tool Kit' (sic) explicitly rejects the notion that maths is 'a culturally or politically neutral subject,' while California's teacher instructional manual, *Dismantling Racism in Maths* asserts that 'the concept of maths being purely objective is *false*. Right and wrong answers *perpetuate objectivity*.' (emphasis added...and I am not making this up) And as every educationalist should by now know, 'objectivity', once the bedrock of all genuine academic disciplines, is a manifestation of whiteness, and therefore, racist. And again, we have been here before, to the same place and time, and issuing from the same racist doctrine: 'Two times two equals four is somehow [sic] differently tinged in the minds of a German, a Frenchman and a negro.' Yet but for the use of 'negro' rather than 'person of color' or 'Afro-American', who would doubt that this nostrum issued from the 'Math Ed Collective' or a California school board rather than from its actual author, the pro-Nazi catholic theologian Jacob Hommes, expounding in 1934 the Nazi doctrine of 'race truth', in his book, *Lebens und Bildungsphilosophie als volkische und catholische Aufgabe*? (Philosophy of Life as a Racial and Catholic [sic!] Task)

Oregon's math teachers have been equipped with their 'Toolkit' not to enhance their teaching of maths as it used to be, purely about number, but to 'dismantle racism in mathematics instruction' by 'transforming traditional approaches to anti-racist practices'. But even this is not the whole story. The ultimate goal is not educational, but political: 'We can no longer believe that a focus on curriculum, instruction and assessment alone will be enough to prepare our children for survival [sic!] in the world. We need anti-racist conversations for ourselves and our children.'

The project is itself racially selective, and therefore discriminatory, being 'targeted for [sic] Black, Latinx [sic] and Multilingual students'. Thus, for everybody but students with 'white privilege'. Lucky white students. The entire prospectus is based upon the same subjective, even solipsist principles enunciated by California's (miss)educators: 'The concept of mathematics being purely objective is *unequivocally false*, and teaching it is even much less ['more', surely] so. Upholding the idea that there are always right and wrong answers *perpetuates objectivity* as well as *fear of open conflict*.' (emphasis added) Conflict between whom and about what, one may well ask. About whether 2 plus 2 still equals 4? Quite possibly, because maths is no longer 'objective', there are not always right or wrong answers, perhaps not even to something as elementary as the sum of 2 plus 2. Granted, there can be no 'right' answer to the question, what is value of P if P = X + 10, because X has no numerical value. But that has always been the case. The 'Tool Kit' is talking about something entirely different, maths problems that *do* have numerical answers. If there may not necessarily be a single 'right answer' to a normal maths question that does have numbers, e.g., X = 7 + 15, that can only be the case if the value of one (or more) of its numbers is not constant, is not always equal to itself, changing and thereby creating more than one answer.

This overturns the foundational principle of Aristotelian logic, that a given finite entity, in this case a number, *is* always equal to itself, the so called 'principle of non-contradiction': 'The same thing cannot at the same time belong and also not belong to the same thing and in the same respect.' But if the answer to 2 plus 2 is not necessarily 'always' 4, then 2 is not 'always' 2. So much then for the white, 'western', 'European' Aristotle.

With numbers not necessarily constant in their value, or who knows, even perhaps having more than one value at the same time, this must render invalid addition, subtraction, multiplication, division...even counting...together with measurements of length, volume, weight, speed, temperature, time...spelling death to any academic subject or human activity such as medicine, engineering, manufacturing or architecture dependent on their constancy, uniformity, objectivity and precision. Instead, we have an 'anti-racist' racial negation of 'white' maths, one in all likelihood inspired by the lunacies of the Math Ed Collective's anti-'imperialist/colonialist' maths 'of colour', which as we have seen, also puts in question the 'colonialist/imperialist' answer to 2 + 2, and one also calling to mind the 'African epistemology' advocated by Professor Akindele, and Professor Jeffries' 'Melanin Theory'.

I suspect that what we have in Oregon and elsewhere is not only a racialisation of maths. In accordance with CRT 'intersectionality', there could also be afoot a feminisation, or even perhaps a maternalisation of the subject, if there is such a word. As far as I have been able to ascertain, all those involved in devising and promoting the Oregon maths project were women, with not even a 'man of colour' in sight, as is also the case with the Math Ed Collective. Those who specialize in such matters might see in this predominance of mainly young women operating at the schools rather than ideological level of the movement evidence of a primal 'nurturing' instinct at work, triggered by an unspoken (albeit 'soft') racist assumption that 'students of colour' lack the capacity to cope with a 'white' centered curriculum, and therefore need to be provided with one attuned to their own less academic, 'nature rooted' 'ways of knowing'.

True or not, there is one very obvious and unmistakable clue as to the ideological inspiration of this drive to racialise school syllabi and teaching methods...the repeated use of the word 'equity' instead of 'equality'. 'Equality' is now in bad odor among 'progressives' because it (correctly) implies 'equality of opportunity', with everyone, irrespective or race or gender, being treated the same. That notion, the bedrock of the 'American Way', is anathema to those who devised the Oregon 'Math Equity Toolkit'. At the outset, we are told that '*all* levels of teaching mathematics are *imbued* with the same racism *and violence* that *permeates all schooling*.' (emphasis added) If this allegation bears any resemblance to the real state of affairs in Oregon schools, then the first priority is not a new teaching syllabus, but an investigation by the police and child protection agencies. (Oregon banned corporal punishment in its public schools in 1989.) As we progress through the presentation, we learn what this 'racism' and 'violence' consists of. Pupils are not being abused with racial insults and epithets, illegally beaten by (white) teaching staff, or attacked by pupils of other races. What this 'racism' and 'violence' amounts to is teachers failing to adjust to the new, anti-racist ethos by treating all students the same, irrespective of skin colour, thereby displaying a lack what is called in the trade (and by Adolf Hitler on at least two occasions) 'racial awareness'.

Central to the imposition of the new 'anti-racist maths' agenda is the need to bring about a transformation in pedagogic principles, eradicating all traces of their humanist ethos and replacing them with an all-embracing focus on racial difference. Thus we have teachers undergoing Maoist 'thought reform' or Stalinist 'self-criticism', requiring that they 'examine their actions, beliefs [sic] and values [sic] around [sic] teaching mathematics.' They need to be made to understand that teaching anti-racist maths is not primarily, if indeed at all, about imparting knowledge to and developing skills in students, but a 'holistic' undertaking and process, in which everything in the teaching environment, including not only the race of the student, the ambience of the classroom and society at large, but most important, the private, personal 'beliefs' and 'values' of the teacher, which hitherto were rightly thought to have no bearing whatsoever on the subject matter being taught. No longer. The assumption is that all (white) teachers are racists. 'White supremacy culture infiltrates [sic] math classrooms in *everyday teacher actions.*' (emphasis added) For example, like 'focusing on the right answer' (especially as there may not be one). That is racist, as is 'addressing mistakes', requiring students to 'show their work' (!!!) and using 'state standards' to guide 'learning in the classroom' (these standards obviously being 'white'). Also racist is the presumption on the part of teachers that 'teachers are teachers and learners are learners', and teaching maths 'in a linear fashion', with skills taught 'sequentially', that is, beginning with fundamentals and first principles, and then progressing by steps to more complex levels, a method once universally regarded as the acme of good teaching, whatever the subject. Perhaps the greatest racist sin of all is a teacher's reluctance to abandon methods now judged to be racist, exemplified by a teacher's belief that not anti-racist hectoring, but '"good" [note quotes] math teaching' is 'an antidote to mathematical inequity.'

I could go on, but the reader surely by now has a pretty clear idea of what 'anti-racist maths' is and is not about. It is not focused exclusively on improving the mathematical skills of all pupils, irrespective of their genes (that is now deemed racist). Instead, it promotes among teachers the racism of low expectations, treating ethnic minority students as helpless victims of a racist educational system and nation who, to make any progress, need a syllabus tailored to accommodate their racial characteristics and background. The message is that black students fail to make the required progress at maths, not because of any shortcomings on their part, but because the subject has been 'colonised' by 'white' culture. It does no service to ethnic minority students to reassure them that all their academic difficulties are due to the 'institutional' racism of the educational system, and not to any failings on their part, and that therefore it is the 'system' that has to change, not the student his or her attitude. Thus, instead of racist 'white maths', students of colour are introduced to a decolonised 'ethnomathematics', in which they 'reclaim their mathematical ancestry'. Whatever that might be, it is self-evidently not the maths of Euclid, Pythagoras, Newton, Gaus, Leibnitz, Russell and Wittgenstein. How well this maths of 'ancestors' will serve them in the USA of the 21st century is another matter.

As a collectivist development of the ubiquitous 'ways of knowing', instead of being treated as unique individuals and encouraged to be self-reliant in their academic endeavors, acquiring and developing the work ethic essential for success, non-white maths students are to work in teams, to 'embrace multiple and variable *ways of sharing, showing and communicating* knowledge'…such as it is.

(emphasis added) I predict with total confidence that the imposition of anti-racist maths on teachers, and from them to their charges, will lead to a catastrophic decline in mathematical ability among Oregon's public school pupils, not least those of an ethnic minority background, for whom, so we are told, it was specially designed. Proof of this came in July 2021, when Oregon Governor Kate Brown signed a bill, passed by the Democrats, ending the requirement for high school graduation that students should able to read, write and do math. A spokesperson for the Governor explained that ending these requirements would benefit 'Black, Latino, Latinx [how do they differ?], Indigenous, Asian, Pacific Islander, Tribal and students of colour'...by rendering them illiterate and innumerate. Meanwhile, the woke machine churns out convoluted gibberish, like the following, from an on-line seminar by Danny Bernard Martin of the University of Illinois:

> Equity and inclusion for Black learners in mathematics are delusions in the fictions of white imagination contingent on appeasing white logics [sic] and sensitivities and characterised at best by incremental changes that do little to threaten the maintenance of racial hierarchies inside or outside of mathematics education. Mathematics identity [sic] encompasses a person's self-understanding as well as how they are constructed by others in the context of doing mathematics. Mathematicise identities can be expressed in narrative form as a negotiated self, a negotiation between our own assertions and the external ascriptions of others. Maths identities are always under construction...Over the last 20 years, conceptual and methodological space has opened up for non-deficit, phenomenological perspectives of Black learners focusing on socialisation, identity, resilience, agency, and success.

I challenge anyone to explain, in plain, white English, what any of this means, if anything. However, what we can learn from its author is that black students in Illinois, as in Oregon, are having a rough time in math classes: 'Many black children continue to experience dehumanising and violent forms of mathematics education. These dehumanising and violent experiences are rooted in white supremacy, anti-blackness and racial [sic] capitalism.' Illinois banned corporal punishment in its public schools in 1993.

To conclude this journey through the land of wokethought, let us move up a level, from the school back to where all this brain-pickling nonsense began, the university, where an identical development has long been in train, embracing not just those of race, but all the 'identities' that comprise the grand 'intersectional' alliance. Here are seven more examples of these new pathways to unlocking the secrets of the universe that have eluded the 'false science' of the past, pathways which multiply in direct proportion to the number of 'identities' that have been exploring them on US and now UK campuses. We have: *Space is Gay: How We Can Use the Cosmos as a Model of Inclusivity; Fat Studies: The Oxford Handbook of the Social Science of Obesity; Non-Binary Geometry and Feminist Expanded Painting; X-Static Process: Intersectionality within the field of Fat Studies; Transgender researchers want to make an impact: Trans and non-binary people are becoming more visible in science and engineering; How Do We Make Math Class More Inclusive Of Trans And Non-Binary Identities* (good question) and *Gender Parity and Queerness Needed in Mathematics.*

The fissiparous nature of intersectionality, a feature common to all would-be radical movements, has generated a most unsisterly civil war between traditional feminists and the trans-movement, with the later claiming that men can become women (and vice versa) by simply 'identifying' themselves subjectively as such, and the former saying that men and women are defined exclusively by objective, scientific, specifically biological criteria. (If Labour Shadow Foreign Secretary Lisa Nandy had her way, saying this this would be sufficient grounds for expulsion from the party.) Conducted over the heads of 'ordinary folk', as are all the arcane quarrels within the woke camp, this dispute is of course nowhere more bitterly fought out than on university campuses, as in the case of mature student Lisa Keogh. In 2021, she underwent an investigation on a charge of 'misconduct' by the University of Abertay, Dundee, after a student (or students) complained that they had been offended by her saying that 'women have vaginas', and men were on average physically stronger than women. Instead of the complaint being dismissed out of hand, as in saner times it would have been (given the remote possibility that one would have been made in the first place) it took *two months* of deliberations for the university disciplinary board to decide that she had no case to answer. Let us note that the student(s) had complained that her remarks were 'offensive'...*but not untrue,* further evidence that universities are now becoming 'safe spaces' where young people go, not to seek truth, but to avoid being offended. Hence the need for bans on 'trigger' words and phrases...flat earthers may well find the statement that the earth is a sphere offensive, as might Holocaust and Covid 19-deniers that both are facts, and creationists that the universe is not 6,000 but 14 billion years old.

Friction within what might defined broadly as the distaff branch of the grand and ever-expanding intersectional alliance is not confined to trans issues. Far from it. In recent years, a truly venomous attack has been launched on white feminists by ones of other hues. Because of the nature of intersectional theory, sooner or later it had to happen. One can liken the power struggles that erupt within the woke movement to a game of cards, each category of membership having a different value card according to the ranking they have either been awarded, or more likely, as in this instance have awarded themselves. Moving from the bottom, we have the lowest value card in the woke pack, held by people like me - male, white, straight, the oppressor of everybody else, and therefore ranked zero. Next come white gay men, followed by white women and men who claim to be women, and then white lesbians. Now it gets more complicated, because once we move up to another level of virtue and victimhood, from sexual orientation and gender to 'people of colour', the plus points begin to multiply and accumulate. (One must never say 'coloured people' because even though it is grammatically if not politically correct, as in National Association for the Advancement of Coloured People, and means exactly the same thing, for some obscure reason it is deemed racist, as Football Association Chairman Greg Clarke discovered when he had to resign after using it.) Women who are black will score more than women who are white, and women who are both black and lesbian will score more than white lesbians, as will black gay men (if they admit to it) more than straight black men and white gay men. Then to add to the mix, we have physical features such as obesity, which scores another plus point, while 'thin privilege' and 'fatophobia' lose one. (Ironically, one of biggest boosts for woke ranking came when a white, male, heterosexual, President Joe Biden, possibly as an act of contrition - he is a devout Roman Catholic - announced in January 2022 that he would be appointing a black woman to the Supreme Court as the replacement for the retiring left-leaning Stephen Breyer. Implementing this choice, one based not on merit but race and gender, would necessarily require excluding as candidates not only all men, black as well as white, but all but 6% of women...94% of the US population. Inevitably, as would have been the case had the demand for the racialisation and gendering of Nobel Prizes been acceded to, many will question whether Biden's appointee was chosen because of her genes and skin colour, and not because she was the best qualified person for the post.)

Thus far, the system as outlined above works according to the set values of the various forms of victimhood. However, there then comes into play at least one joker in the pack, and in certain circumstances, two. The first joker is Islam. Almost universally on the left, and without exception among wokistas, Islam is seen not only as a religion of peace, but as one of the oppressed, like King Salman of Saudi Arabia or the Supreme Leader of Iran, Ali Khamenei. This should then add plus points for all Muslims, be they male, female. or whatever. But this not how it works in practice. Muslim men will indeed score above non-Muslims of the same gender, all other factors being equal. But Muslim women, because of their *Koran*-sanctioned abuse by Muslim men (wife beating and marital rape for example), cannot enjoy a superior status to non-Muslim women or Muslim men in the woke movement. Allowing them to denounce their treatment at the hands of their own Muslim patriarchy as white women do theirs would put in question the status of Islam as a victim religion, and by so doing, play into the hands of white, male, racist, Islamophobic imperialists. (cf. Chapter Three) Insofar as Muslim women are regarded as victims, it is only in countries ruled by the white patriarchy, and even then, only when they are said to be subject to discriminatory laws or treatment, such as the French ban on the public wearing of burqas. Not a word will be uttered either by themselves or by their infidel sisters about and against their domestic oppression at the hands...or rather fists...of Muslim men, whether it takes place in the 'warm', 'vibrant', 'closely knit' Islamic 'community' of western Muslim ghettoes, or countries officially ruled by Sharia law. Once again then we have the usual wokist double standards on display where and when Islam is involved. Western feminists celebrate annual World Hijab Day to affirm the right of Muslim women to wear what they like in western countries, but never display the same sisterly solidarity with courageous women who risk floggings and jail sentences for refusing to wear what they don't like, the hijab and the burqa, in Islamic countries, a textbook example of the religious card trumping that of gender. The gender card can also be trumped by race. The fact that feminists of all races denounce only the many misogynistic sins of the white patriarchy could lead one to suppose that 'men of colour' are by contrast, paragons of virtue when it comes to their relations with women. No rapes, no wife beating etc etc. The reality is, shall we say, somewhat at variance with that assumption, at least when comes to rape, for which, unlike wife-beating and the rest, we have data. In the USA, according to the FBI, black men annually commit around 28 % of all rapes, while constituting only 12% of the USA's male population. Comparing 'black' and 'white' countries, the rape rate in Botswana is 90 per 100,000 of the population, the highest in the world, compared with Canada's 1.7 per 100,000, one of the lowest. To merely allude to these contrasts would be deemed the wrong narrative. So nobody does. There is rape...and rape.

Once the principle of intersectionality has been grasped, it become obvious that friction and open rivalry will inevitably occur between immediate neighbours in the victim pecking order as they jostle each other in their bid for a place in the woke sun. Such is the only plausible explanation for the truly vicious onslaught that has been unleashed on white feminists by their (mainly black) sisters 'of colour'. They have accused white feminists of seeking to cancel out or override their 'white privilege' by simulating the symptoms of a suffering and oppression that is only genuinely experienced by 'women of colour' (though obviously not at the hands of 'men of colour') - hence the accusation that 'white women's tears are racist.' I will repeat that, that 'white women's tears are racist', for example, after being raped or beaten, or on the death of a loved one. The titles of the articles in question convey the level and nature of their invective, which never varies: 'The Destructive Power of White Women's Tears'; 'How White Women's Tears Oppress Women of Colour'; 'I Refuse to Listen to White Women Cry' (*Washington Post*); 'Why white women crying is still racist'; 'How white women use strategic [sic] tears to silence women of colour' (yes, it's the *Guardian*); 'The destructive power of white women's tears'; 'White Women Crying Is Racist'; 'White feminism and how it betrays women of colour' (needless to say, by crying); 'Deconstructing White Privilege: When white women cry'; 'What's up with the white women doing this fake crying?' (*Tick Tok*); 'White Tears/Brown Scars: How White Feminism Betrays Women Of Colour'; 'Crying Shame: the power of white women's tears'. And so it goes. But enough. What with all this unsisterly bitching which, I have heard traditional feminists admit, can be the norm when women contest the same political territory, 'Intersectionality' resembles more of a battlefield than an alliance.

(Let me provide two examples, both featured on YouTube, of just how far this wokery has gone down the path of racism. One is titled 'Everything Gonna Be All White'. Its opening shot is of a black woman pretending to cry and saying, 'I think what annoys most about white people [note, not just men] is when they pretend to be the victim', an obvious allusion to 'white women's tears' being racist. But the real venom is reserved for white men: 'What's also annoying is when they kill us'. (According FBI data, in 2019, of a total of 3,299 white victims of homicide, 566 were killed by blacks, 17%, compared to 246 out of a total 2,96 black victims of homicide killed by whites, 8.5%. But then this is only according to 'white' maths.) Then we have a white man, in full self-flagellation mode, asking, 'what is fragile about whiteness when everything has been constructed around it?' - an obvious allusion to the seminal CRT screed, '*White Fragility*' by Robin DiAngelo. Next comes a hijabed Muslim women, declaiming that 'every part of who I am has been distorted [not by FGM one hopes] or criminalised', followed by a black 'street' youth on a skateboard: 'it's just a bunch of white lies'. Then we see a shot of white men storming of the Capitol on January 6, 2021, and a Oriental lady saying 'you're not patriots, you're ridiculous.' (In that case, so were the women, blacks, Asians Latinos and Arabs who also took part in Trump's assault on US democracy.) A black woman tells us that 'whiteness is ignorance' and a black man tells white people 'we are not your problem, you are.' Another black man says 'Jesus was not white' because 'there ain't no way Jesus walked around with blonde hair and blue eyes'....or also not, if he was a Jew as the Bible says, a man with a black skin. 'White culture', we are told, 'fears the end of the world', whatever that might mean. No rational person would disagree with the black woman who says that 'the truth has to be told about history', but I for one would disagree that as a black man then puts it, 'we have to make sure that these stories are told from our perspective.' No. We have to 'make sure' that history, like all other academic disciplines, is based on objective facts, not racial 'perspectives'. And so it goes. All race and gender bases are covered and neatly stereotyped, good and bad alike. I was immensely heartened by the reception this screening received from black commentators, all of whom, some with evident disgust, rejected it as racist...against whites. Several gleefully revealed that when the dislikes broke all records by reaching over 100,000 compared to only a few hundred 'likes', the tally was deleted, a sure sign that the mass of the US public, black and white alike, does not buy into CRT and BLM race-baiting. Another racist woke production evoked an identical reception, not for an assault on 'whiteness' but for its racial stereotyping of black men. Produced by the social activist and businesswoman Tina Knowles, aka Celestine Beyoncé, and titled 'Profile : The Black Man', it listed all the qualities that set black men (we are led to assume all black men), not only apart from but above their white counterparts. Black men were: 'beautiful, magnificent, innovators, brainy, compassionate, intelligent, complex, critical necessary, everything.' As one amused black commentator put it 'they're saying we are some kind of superman.')

Readers unacquainted with the often-arcane ways of wokery may well be asking themselves...why this masochistic obsession with victimhood, which has privileged, prosperous, highly educated middle class women verbally scratching each others' eyes out over who is the most oppressed? The answer is quite simple. Today, victimhood, or rather what passes for it, *empowers, enriches* and *entitles*. It facilitates, legally and otherwise, preferential treatment in all walks of life that count, from the media, culture and business to employment, politics and education, as evidenced by the adoption of racial, gender and disability quotas independent of merit in the private sector, public institutions and political parties. By the same token, it of necessity, and by intention, discriminates against those who lack victimhood status... people like me. But now, it would seem, not only me. If successful, the ferocious and it would seem, synchronised, campaign unleashed by 'women of colour' to deprive their white sisters of victimhood status will mean that that its benefits...and they are substantial...will be distributed among a much smaller number of claimants. Substantial, but not limitless. So, rather like a game of musical chairs, the purging process could continue until there remain to enjoy the rewards of their oppression only those possessing the combination of victim categories producing the highest possible score. I have often entertained the idea of marketing a board game called 'Victim' that reproduces this process. Like Monopoly, it is based on the same Darwinian principles that we see operating in the woke movement, the aim being to accumulate the most victim points and thus buy out or bankrupt all the other players. At the throw of the dice, instead of Mayfair for example, one can land on and buy Obese Black Lesbian, or Tearful White Feminist instead of Old Kent Road, and instead of 'Go to jail', land on 'Your skin has turned white and you have sprouted a penis...miss three turns'....and so on. All good, clean non P.C. fun.

Assuming the role of informer was of course expected of students in Nazi Germany and Stalinist Russia, as it was of everybody else. Now, with the connivance and, one suspects, encouragement, of university authorities, it has become an accepted practice in the UK and the USA. In 2020, Sheffield University appointed 20 students as official informers, designated 'race equality champions'. Paid at the rate of £9.34 per hour, they were to report anyone

74

committing 'micro aggressions' and to 'lead healthy [sic!] conversations'...in wokespeak. The aim of this campus Stasi/Gestapo/KGB/NKVD Thought Police was, explained Vice Chancellor Koen Lamberts, to 'change the way people think [sic] about racism'. Change it to what? Examples of Thought Crime included 'stop making everything a race issue' and 'why are you searching for things to be offended about?' To the second, I could suggest an answer. 'I get paid to do it.' To pre-empt his being reported by his students for the speech crime of genderism, a professor at the University of California stopped short in the middle of a lecture to apologise for using the term 'pregnant women'. 'If you can summon some generosity to forgive me, I would really appreciate it...it was not my intention to offend anymore. The worst thing I can do as a human being is being offensive.' So, saying something that is true, that women can become pregnant (not even the transphobic that 'only women can become pregnant') is worse than committing murder, rape or any other crime that carries a lengthy prison sentence and, in some US states, in the case of murder, the death penalty. Did he really mean what he was saying? Surely not. But, to protect his job, he felt he had to pretend he did. These are but three of many examples of how universities today are succumbing without a struggle to the tide of wokery which is engulfing academe in the Anglo-Saxon world, and to the prejudices and intellectual inhibitions of a generation of 'snow flake', 'virtue signaling', mainly female students who do not see their time at university as an opportunity to encounter and explore new ideas and re-examine their own, to pursue knowledge and enhance their powers of reasoning, but as one to 'have fun' and as a means to re-enforce, massage and legitimise their 'ways of knowing'. And, as is now the case in the USA, there is a more than sufficient supply of university teaching staff who are only too happy to oblige, as their published offerings demonstrate.

Though a sceptical reader will find it hard to credit, of all the examples of this 'new learning' cited above, only one is a spoof. But a goodly number, indistinguishable in their absurdities from the remainder that are not, have been generated by old-fashioned academics such as Sokal, who are vainly resisting the trendy new-wave nonsense engulfing the campuses of the Anglo-Saxon world. They first made their mark with a number of post-modernist hoaxes, one of which we have visited, and two others, gravity and the penis as 'social constructs', both of which were published in academic journals, presumably after being peer and who knows, queer-reviewed. More recently, they have trained their sights on post-modernism's bastard offspring, 'critical theory' in its various guises. I have included in the list above one of their hoaxes that was also published in good faith by a prestigious academic journal. I challenge the reader to identify it. (The reader perhaps may have noticed that three of the titles I have listed, like others of this genre, have a cautionary prefix, one a 'possibility' and two a 'towards', suggesting a work still in progress, one that to deliver its stated goals, will need more time, and perhaps more funding and an 'affirmative action' staffing programme.)

One consequence of this mumbo-jumbo masquerading as genuine scholarship is that competition for victimhood status amongst all categories of homo sapiens other than white, straight males (not surprisingly, a threatened - in more ways than one - species on university campuses) has led to a surge of hoax hate crimes, as each 'intersectional' racial and sexual 'identity' has contrived, illegally, to lend substance to its bogus claims of persecution and discrimination and in doing so, to the authenticity of its own special, unique 'way of knowing'. In his study of the subject, *Hate Crime Hoax: How the Left is Selling a Fake Race War,* based on reported hate crime statistics, the black academic William Reilly reveals that one third of all reported hate crimes are faked, and of this one third, fully one third occur on US university campuses...rape claims boosting feminist allegations of endemic, toxic, male sexual violence, trans and homophobic incidents, postings etc, sightings by black students of a hooded Klansman wielding a noose, anti-trans graffiti, swastikas, abusive emails...all of it either a hoax, self-generated or faked.

It seems that certain 'ways of knowing' can morph into ways of thinking bordering on the lethal, what one might call 'ways of killing', judging from comments made by the appropriately named Dr Aruna Khilanani in the course of her guest lecture to Yale (yes, *Yale*) students in April 2021 on the subject, 'The Psychopathic Problem of the White Mind'. It only requires a few citations from her lecture to capture its flavour, and to leave one wondering, who is the psychopath and who is the racist? She admitted (if that is the right word) to having had 'fantasies of unloading a revolver on any white person who got in my way, burying their body and wiping my bloody hands as I walked away relatively guiltless with a bounce in my step.' Discussing race with white people was 'a waste of our breath. We are asking a demented, violent predator [sic] who thinks they are a saint or super-hero to accept responsibility. [For what, she does not say. Maybe just for having been born with the wrong colour skin.] They have five holes in their brain. [?] It's like banging your head against a brick wall...Addressing racism assumes that white people can see and process what we are talking about. They can't. That's why they sound demented...There are no good apples out there. White people make my blood boil.' Just imagine, if you can, the reaction if a white speaker had substituted black for white. Or to this, a tweet by sociology professor Dr Rita Repulsa (sic) of the University of Iowa: 'Lately, I try to limit my reactions with white people as much as possible'?

One naturally wonders...what would justly famed pioneer women (not feminist) scientists have made of all this flavour of the month flim flam...the Hellenist pagan philosopher and mathematician Hypatia, murdered by a Christian mob in 415, Voltaire's mathematician and physicist mistress, Madame du Châtelet, Madame Curie, with her Nobel Prizes for chemistry and physics, biologist Rosalind Franklin, denied one after her work on DNA, and the astronomer Jocelyn Bell, likewise, after discovering pulsars?

But back to my main point: In this undeclared 'intersectional' contest between race and gender, which is it to be? Since the epistemological claims for both are all-embracing, they can't both be right. In fact, both are wrong, partly for that reason. Any hypothesis that seeks or claims to explain everything by the action of one single cause, either of race, as does CRT and as did Hitler and his ideologists, of sex, as did Freud and his disciples (Marx made no such claims for class, as we have seen with his exploratory observations on oriental despotism) or, as monotheisms do by attributing the creation of the entire universe and its workings to the will of an all-powerful creator is, *ipso facto*, worthless. One size does not and cannot fit all. A 'theory of everything' is an explanation of nothing. But the heart of the matter is this; for a proposition to pass the test of being a theory it must, contrary to the popular saying, 'it's all right in theory, but it won't work in practice', say something about reality that precisely *does* 'work', that has been proven to be true by having *predictive capacity*, by resting on a body of verifiable and verified empirical and, in certain cases, depending on the subject matter, statistical data. It must be testable, and, though this sounds paradoxical, be refutable by hypothetical alternative data. Darwin's theory of evolution, Einstein's of relativity and Newton's of gravity and motion each share all these essential qualities, while 'critical' race, feminist, fat, trans and queer 'theory', with their ludicrous advocacy of an anti-racist, feminist, trans, gay, fat maths, chemistry, astronomy and the rest, have none.

Specifically, the claim that CRT is a scientific theory has been demolished by a multitude of statistical studies of aspects of the race question in the USA; for example, income, crime and policing. Its advocates claim that their 'theory' explains everything of importance about the workings of society, but it cannot account for something as basic and straightforward as the two Presidential election victories of Barak Obama in a society that was, according to their 'theory', 'systemically' and 'institutionally' racist. Neither can it explain the following; that as long ago as 1954, the US Supreme Court, by a vote of 9 to zero, ruled racial segregation in public schools as un-constitutional, being contrary to the 14th Amendment of 1868; that with the Civil Rights Acts of 1964 and 1965, Congress abolished the last legal vestiges of Jim Crow; that beginning in 1961, a series of Congressional acts and Supreme Court rulings established preferential educational and employment rights for blacks - so called 'affirmative action' programmes; that the only name day in the US calendar is for Dr Martin Luther King Junior; that in four successive Presidential elections, from 2008 to 2020, the explicitly anti-racist Democratic candidate had a clear majority over their Republican rival, in the 2020 contest, Biden's vote being 7.25 million more than Trump's; that as of 2021, more than one third of the mayors of the USA's 100 largest cities were black, compared to the black share of the US population of 12.5%, and that 13% of members of Congress were black, the highest proportion in US history. 'White privilege'?

Neither can CRT explain why the average annual household income of a white patriarchy family approximates both in the UK and the USA to the national average, while the income for Indian and Chinese households respectively is 20% higher, any more than it can account for why Nigerians and West Indians…and they don't come any blacker…are the two most successful recent immigrant groups to the USA. CRT also cannot explain how it is that in a UK ruled by a privileged 'white patriarchy', white male students are significantly under-represented at the top levels of the UK's educational system and under-perform at all the others, while females and all other ethnic groups, including blacks, are over-represented, or why Indians along with Jews are the most over-represented ethnic group in the higher professions. It cannot do so because its fixation on gender and race excludes consideration of the impact of culture and class on educational performance, in which white working-class males come last. Likewise, 'everything is sexism' cannot account for the 'gender gap' at UK and US universities…57% of students in both are female and the percentage in both is still rising.

UK converts to CRT must surely have been thrown into confusion, if not perhaps plunged into despair, by the publication in July 2021 of a report by the Office of National Statistics (yes, again, those damned white statistics) which showed that far from suffering all manner of 'institutional' and 'systemic' social deprivations injurious to their physical well-being, life expectancy for the UK's black Africans was substantially longer than for UK whites. For black women of African origin, it was 88.9 years and for white women, 83.1. For African men, it was 83.3, compared to white men at 79.7 So once again, the white patriarchy comes at the bottom of the heap.

Yet even though on nearly every count, in every field, the claims of 'critical theory' in its various manifestations have been refuted by the empirical evidence, its triumphant march through academe continues almost unresisted, as it cynically deploys the charge of racism, transphobia and the rest to bludgeon into silence or grudging acquiesce those few daring to resist this tide of intellectual charlatanry. Slander, a block on promotion and tenure, and loss of access to publishers, (this is already happening) fear of dismissal after denunciation by students and ostracism by fellow staff as a racist, sexist or transphobe…each have played their part in generating an atmosphere of intellectual and ideological conformism redolent of the McCarthy era, only this time it comes from the left. But the goal is the same, control over what can be said, and, over time, what will be thought. I know of no better, and at the same time, for this reason, chilling description of awaits the west if it succumbs to the power-hungry high priests of 'critical theory' than the reaction by Thomas Mann to the first weeks of Nazi rule in Munich. In his diary entry of March 17, 1933, he writes:

> Discussed the brazenly sadistic plans announced by the German government, the heralded crushing of public opinion [today, so-called 'hate speech'] and imposition of total conformity [yes], eliminating all adverse criticism and crippling any opposition [yes]. The disgusting modernist twist [yes…out with the 'false science' of the past], the psychological opportunism [everything is 'racist', 'sexist' etc] in view of what is actually cultural, intellectual and moral regression ['ways of knowing']. The boldly modern, fast moving futuristic approach put to the service of an anti-future, a philosophy devoid of all ideas, a mammoth campaign for nothingness. [The elevation of 'experience' and 'identity' over reason and evidence] Horrible and base.

But just as Galileo, after renouncing to the Inquisition his conviction that the earth revolved around the sun, muttered under his breath, 'but still it moves', so, despite the successes of the campus inquisition in stigmatising the heretical 'false science' that since the time of Galileo, has served humanity so well, the truth still remains the truth, facts remain facts, 2 plus 2 still equals 4, only women have vaginas, and there will never be a trans/queer/anti-imperialist/anti-racist /anti-sexist refutation of the white patriarch Pythagoras's theorem that the square of the longest side of a right-angled triangle is equal to the sum of the squares of the other two sides. And for all their deficient genes, Newton and Einstein still managed, somehow, to devise the equations that took man (and yes, they were men, white, and for all I know, 'straight') to the moon and back.

Footnote

Determined to prove it was up to speed with the latest woke buzz words, in 2021, the BBC published its 'Diversity and Inclusion Plan'. Whether or not it was inspired by Kendi's declared goal of 'equity', the plan certainly set out to achieve it. The goal was a BBC work (or rather 'woke') force comprising 50% women (that is, one assumes, those with vaginas...but who knows?), 20% ethnic minorities, and 10% disabled. Perhaps because they are relatively new to the game, those who arrived at these percentages seriously miscalculated two of them, and marginally so the third. Because they tend to live longer than males, in 2019, females comprised slightly more than half of the UK population, 50.6%. (But for Muslim female, mainly pre-natal infanticide, it would be slightly higher. 51% of those of Pakistani heritage are male, of Bangladeshi, 52% and Arab, 58% [!], compared with male Chinese, Africans and West Indians, 48%.) In the UK census of 2011, 12.9%, not 20%, defined themselves as non-white, while 18%, not 10% of the adult UK population are officially disabled.

Leaving aside the issue of these two substantial disparities, which could either reflect racial bias against whites and prejudice against the disabled, or just woeful levels of incompetence at the highest levels, we have the prime cause for concern, which is that as a publicly-funded public service, one charged with providing the highest possible quality of programmes to its viewers and listeners, it has no business promoting politically-motivated gender, disability and racial agendas that potentially undermine the performance of that duty. Defending the corporation's triply selective staffing policy, a BBC spokesperson explained in wokebabble that 'the BBC is a welcoming, inclusive organisation committed to representing and reflecting our audiences' - not, as was once the case, in the words of its founder, Lord Reith, to one providing 'all that is best in every department of human knowledge, endeavor and achievement'. (If the BBC is really serious about enforcing a *numerus clausus* accurately 'reflecting' its 'viewers and listeners', where are the quotas for the LGBTs among us?)

If a survey was conducted on this issue, I am certain that save for a handful of trans activists and feminanzis on the far left, and race zealots on both the far left and right, the public would agree that the skin colour, genitals, sexual orientation, mobility, sartorial preferences etc of BBC employees are irrelevant, that BBC should cease its doubly racist policy of advertising posts from which white applicants are excluded and as if non-white applicants are incapable of competing on equal terms with whites, and that instead, staff should be selected on merit alone, and if that means having more or less women staff than men, so be it, or more or less ethnic minority and disabled staff than their shares of the total population, then also so be it. People watch and listen to the BBC, not to be 'represented' or 'reflected' - that is what political parties and pressure groups are for - or to keep a count of the number of wheel-chairs and female and black faces they see on their TV screens each evening. They simply want to be informed and entertained by the best talent available.

Let us next see how Kendi's *numerus clausus* works out when applied to another great UK public service...the NHS. Currently, of its 1.3 million staff, 21% are from ethnic minorities, over-represented by a little under a factor of two. So as to 'represent' and 'reflect' both the overall ethnic balance of UK society, and of the public it serves, thereby achieving the over-riding goal of 'equity', (to which that of the health of its patients necessarily takes second place) the NHS will have to dismiss nearly half of its ethnic minority staff, and hire, and if necessary, conscript white staff in their place. People may die as a consequence - coerced and unwilling labour is always the least efficient - but then progress never comes without sacrifices.

Finally, a third British public institution...its state educational system. To the trained eye, the 2022 election addresses of candidates for posts in the University and College Union displayed clear evidence of the battle being waged between advocates of united action in defence of members rights, pay and working conditions and those whose agenda has nothing to do with traditional trade unionism. The latter are organised under the banner of 'UCU Left', an amalgam of far leftist grouplets dominated by the Sharia left Socialist Workers party and Labour Party Corbynistas. (Corbyn's former Shadow Chancellor and fellow anti-Zionist zealot John McDonnell was the featured speaker at the UCU Left's election campaign rally.)

Seven candidates stood for the two posts of Trustees., whose sole task is the management of the union's finances, as one candidate, obviously opposed to UCU Left, made clear: 'The Trustees attend and may contribute to Congress, NEC and Strategy and Finance Committee but they have no role in making policy.' But the UCU Left candidate evidently did not agree, because he ended his address with a rousing call for 'freedom of speech' for 'supporters of Palestinian Civil Rights' - as if any campus had been denying it to them. On the contrary, as I show elsewhere in this work, it has been open season for Zionist-baiting and worse on UK campuses and in student unions for more than three decades. And as we have also seen; the reverse has been the case for supporters of Israel's right to simply exist.

(The union's stance on Israel was nowhere better exemplified than in the case of Shahd Abusalama, a PhD student at Sheffield Hallam University who had applied for a teaching post at the same university. Attention had been drawn to her on-line comments on the Jews, many of which, as they promoted Jewish conspiracy theories and opposed the right of Israel to exist, flagrantly conflicted with the university's endorsement of the definition of anti-Semitism adopted by the EU, the US Department of State and Senate, the UK Parliament, the Labour Party and the 31 countries comprising the International Holocaust Remembrance Alliance. Abusalama's comments included 'Somehow Zionist lobbies control all this for their interest. They buy Presidents/slaves', praise for terrorists who killed Jewish civilians and endorsement of a video that she said 'tells the truth about #Zionist #Jews' who 'take their legitimacy from the Talmud.' The video in question claimed 'the Talmud permits stealing from non-Jews' and that Jews had 'robbed the banks of America' just as they 'steal the Palestinian land'. When her comments were investigated by the university, her UCU branch quite rightly took up her case. But in doing so, it went beyond the call of duty, just as Chomsky did in his defence of Faurisson, another ant-Semite, by not only defending her right to express her opinions, but endorsing them, saying they fell 'entirely [sic] within the boundaries of acceptable [to whom?'] political commentary'. Would the UCU had said this in defence of a member who had made identical comments about blacks or Muslims? [In fact, Abusalama had a pretty low opinion of Barack Obama, in one of her postings describing him as 'bastard' and a 'Zionist puppet'.] After the university cleared her of any wrong-doing, they appointed her as an associate lecturer, while issuing a statement upholding the 'principles of free speech and academic freedom'. All well and good. But as an employer, there is also the question of competence and professional standards of objectivity, and it is hard, if not impossible to see how someone so wedded to the dissemination of racially-motivated lies and conspiracy theories, and no less approving of anti-Jewish terrorism, can be expected to conduct themselves with objectivity in their teaching duties (what they say and do outside them is their own affair), especially in view of the fact that her special area of interest was 'Palestinian Cinema'.)

Even if candidates running on the UCU Left slate for Vice-President, Trustees (two posts), Women's Representatives (three posts) and for Migrant members (one post) had not announced their support for it, they would have been easily identified as such, with their use of critical race theory terms such 'decolonising the curriculum' 'intersections of race, colonialism, age and gender' (but not, one notes again, 'class'), the 'intersecting matrices of oppression',' 'interacting inequalities', 'intersectional gendered problems'…and so on and on…

One UCU Left candidate proudly related how she had had 'practised intersectional [sic] anti-sexist, anti-racist pedagogy for over twenty-five years' (I weep for her students), while another announced, somewhat opaquely, that she supported 'gender equality' in 'areas like design of personal protective equipment'. The UCU Left candidate for Migrant Members (sic) complained that 'migrant staff are least represented in high ranking positions in British universities and colleges', seemingly oblivious to the reality that quite apart from migrants being relatively very few in number compared to the UK's total higher education staff of 450,000, not to speak of the UK's population as a whole, as recent arrivals in the UK, most will be without the necessary language skills and far fewer again with the necessary professional qualifications and experience to take up high ranking positions at UK universities..

Another distinguishing feature of UCU Left candidates (seven in all) was an obsession with 'identity', mainly their own, which goes a long way to explaining why there was only one representative of the white patriarchy, sis or otherwise, on the UCU Left slate. Even a candidate who wasn't on the slate felt it necessary to announce that she was a 'working class, disabled queer women' with 'an in depth, practically focused understanding of gender-based oppression [there is no 'oppression' in UK universities of anyone] and how it intersects [sic] with industrial discrimination, through issues such as domestic violence [which by definition, does and cannot take place on university campuses] and harassment, precarity and disability.' Another non-UCU Left candidate for one of the three women's slots let it be known that she was a both a professor of 'Gender Studies' and 'an intersectional inclusive feminist'. With a keen eye for the 'intersecting [sic] matrices of oppression that affect our most vulnerable colleagues and students', she was working 'for and with trans and queer colleagues in the face of bigotry, racism, transphobia and misogyny', standing in 'unequivocal [who would expect anything less?] solidarity with trans and non-binary comrades, women of colour [we are all 'of colour'] and migrant members [the latest addition to the victim list].' It is as if she is saying to her UCA Left rivals, 'Beat that if you can'. And yet for all the rampant campus oppression wrought by the white cis patriarchy on all these categories of intersectional victimhood, contrary to what one might expect, the percentage of white male students in higher education has fallen by 10% between 2014 and 2021.

Two black women contested the single post of UCU Vice President. The UCU Left candidate for Vice President had the advantage that unlike her rival, Maxine Looby, her surname, Ojinnaka, clearly suggested an African heritage. She was currently a member of the 'Black Members Standing Committee', and was deeply into a range of 'black' issues – 'Black women and the gender pay gap', 'Black worker's and mental health', 'de-colonising the curriculum' and 'black women's and girls' education'. Her black rival had also served on the Black Members Standing Committee, as co-chair, and as 'NW [North West] black representative and regional chair'. Also like her rival, she used the word 'black' four times in her address. She too favoured what she called an 'intersectional approach' to 'our bargaining agenda' - one hardly like to appeal to straight white male union members. Thus far, very 'orthodox' wokery. But there was a distinctly heretical sting in the tail, which explained why she was running against her black sister. She ended her address with what was, given the 'context', a brave advocacy of pre-woke trade-unionism: 'We are nothing without our collective voice. A united fighting voice [which] supports our members, students and communities. We may work in different areas, and may hold different views [sic], but we have more in common than divides us.' If only...

Several rungs down the academic ladder, in the schools, an identical operation is under way. Plans are afoot in its largest teachers' union, the far left-dominated National Education Union, to introduce into the classroom the same curriculum innovations that provoked a furious parental backlash in the USA. In July 2021, the union announced guidelines for teachers urging them to combat 'white privilege' in its various manifestations: 'From curriculum to routines to classroom layout [?] our educational system has been shaped by colonisation and neo-liberalism.' The teaching in UK schools lacked 'honesty and transparency' due to the 'silence around [sic] British imperialism and racism in the British education system, as well as a lack of histories around the world.' (The grammar is shocking, and gets worse) 'British culture is saturated with a longing for [no indefinite article] return to empire without any understanding into [should be 'of] what empire is/was.'

The (semi-literate) statement proposed 'strategies for decolonizing education in our nurseries [yes, that is what it says], schools and colleges.' So, a nursery child, aged no more than four, yet already 'saturated with a longing for return to empire', will be told, perhaps as she plays in the Wendy house, that the British empire, the only empire in modern history, beginning with India in 1947, to voluntarily relinquish its colonies, while Germany, France, Japan, Russia, Holland, Portugal, Belgium and Spain fought doomed military campaigns to retain them, was an unmitigated evil, while all non-white empires - the Egyptian, Hittite, Babylonian, Sumerian, Pre-Columbian, Persian, Assyrian, Chinese, Japanese, black African, Islamic, Ottoman and Mongol - were philanthropic undertakings.

To prepare staff for the transition to the new anti-colonial curriculum, 'specialists' should be hired to 'train teachers and schools on [sic - wrong preposition] whiteness, anti-racism, creating tools for critical [sic] self-reflection [presumably only for white staff – non-whites can't be racist] and understanding the system.' Schools should 'make white privilege and colonialism visible' - quite how was not said, but I assume that this would involve wall displays - pictures of black slaves and their white masters, (none, we can be sure, of black slaves with their black African masters, and black and white slaves with their Arab/Muslim masters), maps of the British empire (but not of anyone else's) etc. Then comes an allusion to CRT: Schools should 'move beyond diversification of literature to look at critiquing [sic] the ideas and knowledge [sic!!!] we perpetuate and transforming pedagogical methods.' [not a proper sentence] So even 'knowledge', i.e., *that which is known to be true,* (i.e., that the UK once had an empire) is suspect. Mark this well.

Teaching having rid itself of the constraints of 'knowledge', i.e., evidence and fact, the decks will be clear (and the desks re-arranged) for the indoctrination of pupils in anti-racist, anti-(British) imperialist history, chemistry, maths...the full CRT package...creating, if everything goes to plan, a generation of unemployable and resentful ignoramuses, innumerates and illiterates. A matter of days after the release of the NEU's de-colonisation proposals, an elite Edinburgh high school, James Gillespie's, announced that it would be removing 'outdated' texts from its literature syllabus, including two hitherto regarded as anti-racist classics, *To Kill a Mocking Bird*, and *Of Mice and Men*. The reason given was that they both contained a 'white saviour' motif, that is, white men opposing white racism. Both would be replaced by racially correct novels featuring 'people of colour'. A school withdrawing works hitherto recorded as classics is bad enough, but in re-enacting what the Inquisition and the Nazis did to texts likewise deemed incorrect by burning 4,700 books on identical grounds, which is exactly what 30 Canadian schools did in 2019, is to commit the ultimate crime against human culture. Compounding this atrocious act of vandalism, it passed almost without comment in the world's media or condemnation by Canada's super-woke Prime Minister Justin Trudeau.

The Anglo-Saxon world seems incapable of resisting the lunacy that is wokery, but on the continent, it has fewer takers, especially in France, the land of Voltaire and a constitutionally entrenched secularism. President Macron made it very clear, much to the chagrin of some of the left, where he stood on this defining principle of French political culture in his speech at the funeral of Samuel Paty, and he did it again in an interview with *Elle* that appeared at the beginning of July 2021. This time, his target was not the threat to social peace posed by Islamic intolerance, but one issuing from the left, aimed at *egalité* and *fraternité.* Concerned that France was becoming 'progressively more racial', he said 'I am on the side of universalism.' Hitherto, racism had come from the right. But, having 'freed ourselves from this approach, now we are once more categorising people according to their race'...an unmistakable reference to CRT. Unlike Biden, Macron was having none of it. Instead, the President, ironically a (in view of his office, very private) Roman Catholic, gave a humiliating lesson in authentic Marxism to critical theory's leftist converts: 'Social difficulties are not only explained by gender and the colour of your skin, but also by social inequalities'...i.e., *class.* Bravo, Comrade Macron!

A New Physiology – 'Privileged Pain'

Always at the cutting edge of progressive groupthink, the *Guardian* coined for its well-heeled readers a new SJWspeak term when, in its online edition of September 15, 2019, it published an editorial which took to task former Tory Leader David Cameron for advertising in his memoirs his 'privileged pain' at the death of his six year old son, afflicted from birth with cerebral palsy. The offending passage read:

> When you watch your tiny baby undergoing multiple blood tests, your heart aches. When they bend him back into the foetal position to remove fluid from the base of his spine with a long, threatening-looking needle, it almost breaks...He could have

20 or 30 seizures a day, lasting for minutes, or sometimes hours, his small frame racked with spams and what look like searing pain. By the end his clothes would be drenched in sweat and his poor body exhausted.

This elicited from the *Guardian* the following obscene response: 'Mr Cameron has known pain and failure in his life but it has always been limited failure and privileged pain'. Former *Daily Mirror* editor Piers Morgan put it well when he asked, 'What kind of mind would write that?' What indeed? Perhaps one that can also believe that like grief, race and gender are also 'social constructs', and who knows, even gravity and the penis. At the very least, we now know that genuine grief of a parent for the death of their child can only be experienced by those without privilege...like, for example, the editor of the *Guardian*. On June 9, 2020, in its birthday greetings column, the *Guardian* said 'happy birthday' to the Jazz musician Gilad Atzmon who, amongst others comments hostile to the Jews, has claimed that the Grenfell Tower fire tragedy was the work of 'Jerusalemites' (sic) and that 'the Jews were expelled from Germany for misbehaving'. He also believes, as does another Hitler apologist and BLM promoter ('these are our leaders of the future'), the Black Muslim *Fuehrer* Louis Farrakhan, 'the Left should decide whether it is pro-Jewish or pro-Black cos the two contradict each other.' What kind of journal would send birthday greetings to someone who could say that?

C Swedish Syndrome

Named after the reactions of hostages held captive for six days in a raid on a Stockholm bank in 1973, Wikipedia defines the so-called 'Stockholm Syndrome' as one where 'hostages express sympathy and have positive feelings for their captors.' Today, the hostages are again Swedes, chiefly women, and the reactions are frequently the same. However, their captors are not fellow Swedes, but male Muslim migrants. In 1975, when its Parliament voted to embrace multi-culturalism, Sweden had the lowest incidence of rape in the entire world. Today, it is the second highest, having increased since then by fourteen times. What follows is first, a chronology of incidents in just one month November 2015.

I

November 6: The Gronkulla School in Alvesta closed after reports of a rape at the facility spread on social media. A Somali boy had apparently been sexually harassing a 12-year-old girl for some time. On October 17, he allegedly took his attentions a step further, pulled the girl behind a bush and raped her. The girl's father had been unsuccessful in trying to get the school to address the problem earlier, but even after the reported rape, the school's management did not act. The boy was allowed to continue going to school - just on a schedule different from the girl's. Her distraught parents told the news website *Fria Tide,* 'We are being spat on because we are Swedish'. In protest against the school's management, many parents, viewing the school as having sided with the perpetrators, moved their children to other schools.

November 9: Social commentator and whistle-blower Merit Wager revealed on her blog that administrators of the Immigration Service had all been ordered to 'accept the claim that an applicant is a child, if he does not look as if he is over 40 [sic].' (In the UK, two approximately thirty-year-old migrant 'children' were removed from their schools, but only after protests by parents.) 32,180 'unaccompanied refugee children' arrived during 2015 by December 1. After another 1,130 arrived, the government finally decided to act. Everyone who looks adult is forced to go through a medical age-determination examination. The UK government has refused to adopt this procedure.

November 10: A 28-year-old Iraqi man was prosecuted for raping a woman on a night train between Finland and Sweden. The man had originally planned to seek asylum (illegally) in Finland but had found the living conditions too harsh. He had therefore taken a train back to Sweden. In a couchette (sleeping car where men and women are together) the rapist and two other asylum seekers met one of the many Swedish women whose hearts go out to 'new arrivals'. The woman bought sandwiches for the men; they drank vodka. When two of the men started groping the woman, she told them to stop, yet chose to lie down and go to sleep. Sometime during the night, she was awakened by the Iraqi as he raped her. The woman managed to break free and locate a train assistant. To the attendant's surprise, the woman did not immediately want to press charges. The court documents state: 'The train attendant asked if he should call the police. At first, the woman did not want him to do so, because she did not want to put N.N. [the rapist's initials] an asylum seeker, in a tough spot. She felt sorry for him and was afraid he would be deported back to Iraq.' The man was given a sentence of one year in prison, payment of 85,000 kroner (about $10,000) in damages and deportation - but would be allowed to come back to Sweden after five years.

An Algerian and a Syrian asylum seeker were indicted for raping a Swedish woman in Strangnas. The men, a 39-year-old Algerian and a 31-year-old from Syria, met the woman in a bar one night in August. When the woman left, one of the men followed her, pulled her to the ground, and assaulted her. Afterwards, the woman kept walking, and ran into two other men – the Syrian and another unidentified man - and was raped again. The Syrian reportedly also spat her in the face and said, 'I'm going to fuck you, little Swedish girl.' The men, who live at the same asylum house, denied knowing each other when questioned by police. The verdict was announced on December 1. Rapist number one was sentenced to two and half years in prison, 167,000 kroner in damages, and deportation to Algeria. Rapist number two was convicted of aggravated rape and sentenced to four years in prison. He cannot be deported, however, because 'there are currently hindrances towards enforcing deportations to Syria.' He was also ordered to pay the woman 117,000 kroner in damages.

November 13: A trial began against eight Eritrean men, between the ages of 19 and 26, who according to the District Court, 'crudely [sic] gang-raped' a 45-year-old woman. She had been waiting in a stair well for a friend when the men invited her into an apartment. Inside, she was thrown on the floor, held down, beaten and brutally raped. When questioned by police, she said, 'It felt as if there were hands and fingers everyplace. Fingers penetrated me, vaginally, anally. It hurt very much. I could feel the finger nails.' She said she could also hear the Eritreans laughing and speaking in their own language while they raped her. 'They seemed to be enjoying themselves', she said. When two of the men started fighting over who should rape her next, she tried to flee, but one of the men hit her over the head; she fell unconscious. After coming to, she escaped out of a window and was able to reach a neighbour. The District Court of Falun established that several men had taken part in the attack, but the District Attorney was unable to prove who had done what. Therefore, only one man was convicted of aggravated rape, and sentenced to five years in prison. The others were sentenced to only 10 months in prison for helping to conceal a serious criminal offence. After serving their time, the men will be allowed to stay in Sweden.

November 23: Hassan Mostafa Al-Mandlawi, 32, and Al Amin Sultan, 30, were indicted in the Gothenburg Municipal Court suspected of having travelled to Syria in 2013 and murdering at least two people there...The accused men came to Sweden, one from Iraq, and one from Syria, as children. Both grew up in Sweden and are Swedish citizens. They travelled to Syria in 2013 and joined one of the many Islamist terror groups there. According to the prosecution, they murdered two captured workers in an industrial area of Aleppo by slitting their throats (as per the *Koran*, Chapter 8, Verse 13). The prosecutor wrote that 'Al-Mandlawi and Sultan have both expressed delight at the deeds.' During the trial, films of the executions were shown, but both men still denied having committed the crimes. First the films show a man having his throat slit, the blood gushing before he dies. Then, the other victim's head is severed from the body, and the killer holds up the severed head to loud cheers from the other. The verdict was announced on December 14. Both men were convicted of terrorist crimes and sentenced to life in prison. The verdict will be appealed, defence lawyers said.

November 28: A large mob at an asylum house on Nora tried to break into a room where a woman had barricaded herself along with her son. Some 30 Muslim men apparently thought the woman was in violation of Islamic Sharia law, by being in Sweden unaccompanied by a man. They thought that she should therefore be raped and her teenage son killed. Asylum house staff called the police, who averted the plan

II

Juden Raus

In 1936, the German firm of Günther and Co. marketed a new children's board game. Advertised as 'entertaining, instructive and solidly constructed', it was called 'Juden Raus'. Played with dice, the objective, as the name suggests, was to be the first to round up six Jews and deport them from the Third Reich. I see no reason why, if adapted for use by Sweden's Muslim migrants and those Swedes who see it as their life's duty to indulge their Islamic guests' every appetite, whim and prejudice, it should not enjoy a renewed popularity. Readers will recall that the Sharia leftist Mayor of Malmo justified Muslim migrant assaults on the Jews of his city as warranted by their presumed support for Israel. What follows is a brief survey of similar attempts by Swedes to appease Muslim anti-Semitism.

November 9, 2015: An anti-racist demonstration is held in Umea to commemorate the *Kristallnacht,* the night of crystals or broken glass, when on the night of November 9-10, 1938, urged on by Propaganda Minister Goebbels, Nazi thugs unleashed a pogrom on Germany's Jews, vandalising their property, burning down at least 200 synagogues, murdering more than a hundred Jews and dispatching another 30,000 to concentration camps, to be followed by death in the gas chambers of Hitler's Final Solution. In commemorating what proved to be the prelude to the Holocaust, here was Sweden at its very liberal, tolerant best, one might assume. And indeed, the demonstration had the support of four of Sweden's political parties. But participation in this event was not open to everyone. Incredible as it may seem, Jews, whose persecution was supposedly being commemorated, were barred from attending because, as Jan Hagglund, an organizer, explained, they would perceive the demonstration 'as an unwelcoming or unsafe [sic!] situation for them'...just like Nazi Germany on the night of November 9-10, 1938, or pro-Hamas demonstrations in the summer of 2014. 'Unwelcome and unsafe'? What, one wonders, could possibly give Sweden's Jews that impression? Could it have been because the purpose of the event was not to combat anti-Semitism, but to welcome the arrival of illegal and in many cases, anti-Semitic Muslim migrants in their new home?

January 2009: A pro-Israel demonstration in Malmo was attacked by Arabs chanting 'fucking Jews' and assailing marchers with exploding fireworks, bottles and eggs. Instead of arresting their attackers, police pushed the marchers into a back alley.

2010: Malmo: A series of attacks on the city's synagogue, resulted in a warning by the Simon Wiesenthal Centre in Los Angeles to Jews not to visit

87

Malmo, 'due to harassment of Jewish citizens'. At the most recent count, 30% of Malmo's population was reported to be Muslim, though the actual percentage is probably higher, and certainly rising.

2015: Malmo: In the first six months of 2015, police recorded 30 grenade explosions in the city, parts of which had become Muslim no-go areas for public officials.

October 2015: Malmo: Two members of the Swedish Parliament took part in an anti-Israel demonstration that featured anti-Semitic chants and support for the stabbing attacks on Jews then gathering pace in Jerusalem.

October 2012 The reader will recall that a Bavarian State Minister criticised visits by children of Muslim parents to Holocaust museums. Teaching the history of the Holocaust to Muslim students has also has its opponents in Sweden, just as it does in the West Bank and the Gaza Strip in schools administered by the anti-Semites of UNRWA, the Palestinian Authority and Hamas. Helena Mechlaoui, a High School history teacher, put the case for blotting out the greatest crime in the history of mankind like this: 'If we talk about students from the Middle East, it may be because many of them bear the traumatic experiences that are related to either Israeli or American policies. And the two states are often seen as one'. So? '...the two states are often seen as one'? Then surely it is a history teacher's job to rectify such misapprehensions, not defer to them. But perhaps Mechlaoui shares them. She continues: 'They may [sic] have lost one or more siblings, cousins or peers in an Israeli or American bombing.' Even if true, why does that require excluding the Holocaust, and only the Holocaust, from a history syllabus? The US Eighth Air Force dropped bombs a plenty on Germany in the Second World War, but German schools nevertheless teach the history of the United States.

All states have taken lives, and lost them, in warfare of one kind or another. If applied consistently, this principle would result in the total abolition of all history teaching. But that is not the intention here, which is to abolish only the teaching of the Holocaust to Muslims. Although Mechlaoui's version of the history of the Middle East is, to say the very least, debatable, the main point at issue is that she is prepared to use it to erase or, if you will, trump, the teaching of the true history of the Holocaust. After listing the deprivations that she believes her Muslim pupils may have suffered at the hands of Israel and not, as is so often the case, by fellow Muslims, she concludes: 'In this context [there we have it again: 'context', this time invoked to justify telling lies about history] it is perhaps not desirable to start talking about the Holocaust'. Palestinian Authority President Mahmoud Abbas, David Irving and the Holocaust-denying associates of Jeremy Corbyn would surely agree.

February 2015: Teaching politically correct but factually incorrect history is not only for school children. At an adult education class in Helsingborg, a student questioned whether the Holocaust actually happened. (I leave to the reader to hazard a guess as to the religious affiliation of the student in question.) In reply, the teacher, who being a substitute was evidently not up to speed on the new Sharia history curriculum, outlined the evidence which proved that the Holocaust was a historical fact. The teacher quickly learned that in the new Islam-friendly Sweden, this was not the correct response. Following a complaint by a student (again, guesses as to their religious identity are in order) the teacher was reprimanded by the school administration for defending historical truth: 'What is history for us is not the history of others. When we have students who have studied other history books, there is no point in discussing facts against facts'.

'*Facts against facts*'? *No point*'? The mind boggles. Here we have the leftist, post-modernist and Sharia-correct variant of Trump's 'alterative facts'. Purely in order to appease the ingrained anti-Semitism of Sweden's Muslim migrants, Sweden's educational system is trampling underfoot the conquests of centuries of rational, logical, scientific, empirically-grounded thought and inquiry, reaching back through the Enlightenment to classical Greece. Here we have the fruits of the much celebrated 'cultural sensitivity', 'diversity' and 'inclusivity', and its analogue, cultural relativism; the emergence, in of all places, Sweden, of the Nazi doctrine that there is no objective truth, that each people 'thinks with its blood' and has its own 'race truth', in this instance, Swedes theirs, and Arab Muslims theirs. 'Fact against fact'…as if facts were mere opinions, resting on nothing, one as good or bad as another, with no objective criteria and method by which to judge what is truly fact and what is merely fiction and fancy. Some say the Holocaust happened, while others, Muslim migrants, 'who have studied other books', produced we can guess by whom, say it did not. Who are we to judge between them? There is 'no point' in challenging those who deny the Holocaust. Worse, it causes offence. It's simply a case of 'facts against facts'. It's a 'fact' that it happened, and another that it did not. Who knows? Corbyn's 'friends' could well be right.

But why just the Holocaust? If the principle of epistemological solipsism is valid for history, it surely needs to be extended and applied to every other branch of what we once fondly took to be human knowledge. Some say the earth is a sphere, and goes around the sun, others that it is flat, and some, Saudi Muslim clerics for example, add to this that the sun goes around the earth. Fact against fact. Some say the universe is 13.7 billion years old, while others, Christian 'young earth creationists' as they call themselves in a rare moment of lucidity, say that it is six thousand. Fact against fact. Some say the various species have evolved over a period of four billion years by a process of natural selection, others, Muslims as well as Christians, that they have all been created simultaneously in a matter of hours by an entity called god.

Tens, possibly hundreds of millions of Muslims, and also millions of non-Muslims, believe that the Jews, and/or President George Bush were responsible for 9/11, while others, including many millions of Muslims approvingly and correctly, believe it was the work of 19 Al-Qaeda Muslim martyrs acting on behalf of Allah. Fact against fact. There are Christians today who still say the Jews once used to drain the blood of Christian children to mix with Passover unleven bread, and Muslim preachers, including one praised by Corbyn, who agree with them, while the rest of mankind says it is all lies. Fact against fact. Take your pick. But what about evidence, you may ask. Doesn't it count for *anything*? No longer, especially in Sweden when the subject is the Holocaust and the students are Muslims. In the war against 'Islamophobia', if the first casualty proves to be the truth, as in this instance it surely did, then so be it. As in the Doublethink of Orwell's Oceania, two plus two can equal both four and five.

2015: Complaints are made to Sweden's top television channel, TV4, for featuring in a 'reality' show the rapper Dani M, who specialises in promoting Jewish conspiracy theories in the tradition of *The Protocols of the Learned Elders of Zion*. Putting to one side the related issue of whether anti-Semites should be banned from appearing on television (though for the record, as a believer in free speech, I say no - there is always the off-button or other channels), it is the reply of the show's Executive Producer, Christer Anderson, that interests us here: 'TV4's core values are zero racism and always have been, so long as I can remember, but we cannot cut people off who do not feel the same way. TV4 is a portal through which people with different opinions pass and we must have a broad level of acceptance'. Anti-Semitism and the advocacy of the existence of a world Jewish conspiracy 'a different opinion'? Here we go again. Surely it was possible to defend the channel's right to allow such views to be aired, and at the same express its disagreement with them? When a TV4's employee used the word 'nigger' in a YouTube clip, she was promptly sacked. What happened to the channel's 'broad level of acceptance'? Evidently some racist opinions are more acceptable than others. There are good grounds for suspecting that with the current wave of Islamophilia that is enveloping Sweden, in the unlikely event of even the mildest of critics of Islam appearing on the same show, the complaints would have been far more numerous, and the channel's response cringingly apologetic.

In 2010, the Swedish TV celebrity, Gina Dirawi, who is of Palestinian origin, wrote in her blog that Israel's policies were similar to those of the Nazis, and in 2012, that her fans should read a book which (as neo-Nazis do) denied the Holocaust...both being what one might expect from some Palestinians. These are just two samples of her many anti-Jewish postings. But her well and proudly advertised anti-Semitism has proved no impediment whatsoever to her continued rise to mega-stardom. Today, she hosts a number of shows on SVT, the Swedish public broadcasting network, and although a Muslim, was chosen to host SVT's Christmas show. She was also selected to host the prestigious 2016 Meodfestivalen, one of Sweden's most popular music events of the year.

May 2015: The Swedish think tank Perspektiv Pa Israel released evidence that the director in Sweden of the Swedish government-funded Islamic Relief was disseminating anti-Semitic postings on Facebook. All Sweden's major media companies refused to take the story. One, Nyheter24, explained why: 'Readers are, to say the least, [!!] not interested in this particular issue', the 'particular issue' being Muslim anti-Semitism and its funding by the Swedish taxpayer. But how could Nyheter24 be so sure, since a news blackout of the issue had ensured that the public knew nothing about it? All this and more happened, and is happening now, in of all countries, Sweden. Sweden, the beacon and exemplar of democratic socialism: liberal, cultured, tolerant, relaxed, secular. If it can happen to Sweden, it can happen to any western country that in order to placate Islam, first dilutes, then surrenders and in the end, comes to despise the very values which are the foundation of western civilisation. Be warned.

Malmo, April-May 2016: Under the auspices of the city's ruling Social Democratic and Green Party administration, a number of events were held featuring speakers from the Middle East. One of the participants, specifically invited to attend by the Green Party, was the Saudi imam Salman Al Ouda, referred to in the Swedish media as a 'Salafist megastar'. He was a notorious anti-Semite. He can be seen on YouTube explaining why the Holocaust was a 'myth of tremendous proportions', a 'sacred myth'. The Jews themselves were 'carrying out a Holocaust in Gaza and the occupied land', 'under the pretext of the Holocaust they are trying to substantiate'. 'The role of the Jews is to wreak destruction, to wage war, to practice deception and extortion'. He claimed to have found proof that even today, Jews were 'making matzos with human blood. They eat it, claiming that it brings them closer to their false god Yahweh'. Malmo's Municipal Council has a policy which states that 'racism, discrimination and hate crimes do not belong in open Malmo.' But anti-Semitism does.

Evidently those who determine who can and cannot air their views in Malmo believe like fellow Sharia leftist Ken Livingstone that anti-Semitism is 'not the same thing' as racism. Neither did the policy apply when another invitation was extended to another anti-Semite, the former Grand Mufti of Jerusalem, Sheikh Ekrima Said Sabri, to address the fourteenth 'Palestinians in Europe' event at the prestigious Malmomassan conference centre. Following the precedent set by his most illustrious predecessor, the Nazi collaborator Haj Amin al-Husseini, Sabri had advertised, only now not on a Nazi radio station but democratic Swedish TV, his belief in the authenticity of the *Protocols:* 'Anyone who studies the *Protocols of the Elders of Zion* will discover that one of the goals of these *Protocols* is to cause confusion in the world and to undermine security throughout the world.' When it was pointed out to the event's hosts that Said's anti-Semitism violated Malmo's anti-racist policy, the reply was that 'we do not take positions on the substance of the matter'...that is, unless it is deemed 'Islamophobic'.

Following President Trump's announcement that the USA recognised Jerusalem as the capital of Israel, in Gothenburg, three Muslim asylum seekers were arrested after attempting to stage an Islamic re-enactment of the Nazi Crystal Night by fire-bombing a synagogue, while in Malmo, Muslim storm troopers took the street chanting 'We're going to shoot the Jews'. More than 2,000 Muslim anti-Semites also ran amok in Berlin, burning Israeli flags at the Brandenburg gate. One speaker declared that Israel 'should disappear once and for all.' Berlin police union chief Rainer Wendt blamed such outrages on politicians for 'illegally allowing in more and more foreigners from the most anti-Semitic region in the world and then not even deporting the offenders among them', while at the same time 'proclaim[ing] they are doing everything against anti-Semitism.' Interior Minister Thomas de Maiziere called for the appointment of a Commissioner to combat the recent surge of hatred against Jews and Israel.

III

Bath Time for Muslim Men

Different cultures habituate the people reared by them to do the same things in different ways. We have seen how this plays out when Muslim migrant men encounter the life styles, laws, customs and moral standards of Europeans, and nowhere more so than when it involves relationships between the sexes. Take swimming. Mixed bathing was pioneered by the Swedes (who else?) as long ago as the late nineteenth century, and over time, it has become a norm throughout the western world, the assumption being that increasingly scantily clad women would not have to contend with the unwanted sexual attentions of men. All that changed with the arrival in Sweden of young male Muslim migrants from countries whose Islamic culture had over centuries inculcated the belief that outside her home, a female must be accompanied by a male relative; and no less important, when in public, that her entire body has to be covered up. Swedish women do neither, and therefore, like thousands of other women in other European countries that have played host to Muslim migrants, have found themselves the target of sexual attacks by Muslim men who saw them as fair game for rape. For reasons that should not need stating, the most frequent venue for these attacks has been public swimming baths.

Let us begin in Malmo, now a city with a Muslim population fast approaching a majority. As long ago as 2003, gangs of Muslim youths became so disruptive at the city's indoor water park, Aq-va-kul, that the facility had to be converted into a fortress. It was temporarily closed to install extra security devices and equipment, including taller entrance gates to keep out intruders, a glass security panel around the reception desk to protect staff from attack, surveillance cameras and an Arabic-speaking 'pool host' to deal with the facility's unruly Muslim patrons. Far from solving the problem, the situation rapidly became much worse. These measures were - correctly - seen by young Muslim men as intended to curb their fun, and they reacted as some Muslim men can do when their honour is at stake, with violence. Gangs ambushed staff on their way home, so the pool had to hire security staff to provide escorts. More confrontations ensued when Muslim youth who did use the facility disobeyed hygiene rules, refusing to shower before entering the pool, and swimming in their underclothes. And so the running battle continued until 2013, when a gang of Muslim youths broke into the pool, smashed the protective glass around the reception desk, threw the shards into the water and assaulted swimmers. The pool was again closed, the pool drained and cleaned, and the damage made good. When finally, re-opened, it was closed to the public, and can now only be used by swimming clubs and for competitions.

Muslim trouble in Stockholm's Hushbybadet swimming pool began in 2005, when a 17-year-old girl was raped by a 16-year-old boy. The rapist received a three-month sentence in a juvenile facility. The girl was so traumatised she attempted suicide on several occasions. As more Muslims used the pool, in 2007, city authorities had to build a separate sewage facility to cope with the high levels of nitrogen caused by Muslims swimming in their sweaty dirty underwear and urinating in the pool. With the arrival in Sweden of 163,000 migrants in 2015, the majority being young men, the number of sexual assaults on women swimmers surged dramatically. This was mainly because despite past problems with Muslim males abusing swimming pool facilities, refusing to observe hygiene rules and pestering women swimmers, in their multicultural wisdom, local authorities allowed migrants to use pools free of any charge. Consequently, in the first week of January 2016, Stockholm's national swimming facility, Eriksdalsbadet, introduced gender segregation in its hot tubs after a series of sexual assaults by migrant men on women. This decision proved controversial, as it failed to tackle the cause of the problem, which was sexual aggression by Muslim men. It can also be seen as an accommodation to Sharia law, which enforces segregation of unrelated men and women.

January 15: a local paper reported that two girls had been sexually assaulted in the lift at the Oasen baths in Kungalv. The two perpetrators were described as 'unaccompanied refugee children'. The response of the town's Social Affairs department was to stress the need to 'step up the work concerning issues of equality and interaction [sic] among our new arrivals'. Three days later, the management of the Fyrishov pool in Uppsala belatedly revealed that in the previous year, there had been seven reported cases of child molestation. The suspected offenders were all newly-arrived teenaged migrants.

January 22: local news media carried reports of a sudden increase in sexual assaults at the Aquanova adventure pool in Borlange. While in 2014, there was only one such incident, in 2015, the number jumped to 20. Women had their bikinis ripped off, were groped on the water slide and attacked in the changing rooms.

January 25: press reports of a girl being raped at the Stockholm Eriksdalsbadet pool. Police began regular patrols of the facility.

January 26: reports of sexual assaults at the Storsjobadet pool in Ostersund on two girls and a woman by a group of migrant boys. However, pool staff allowed the boys to remain in the facility.

January 27: Vaxjo municipality announced that it will hire a security guard to patrol its pool after two 11-year-old girls were sexually assaulted by a group of migrant boys.

February 1: local media, again belatedly, reported that over the previous few weeks, five girls and a woman had been sexually assaulted at a pool in Vanersborg.

February 25: another sexual assault is reported at the Eriksdalsbadet pool. A group of girls had been surrounded, Cologne fashion, by ten or so young men, who then started to grope them. A staff member called the police, but there were no arrests.

Given this surge of sexual assaults by migrants at Sweden's pools, it remained for some a mystery why none had been reported at Malmo's recently opened Hylliebadet pool. In the first few days after its opening in August 2015, 27 'incidents' had been reported, but officially at least, none was of a sexual nature. Off the record however, one pool employee confided to a reporter that staff had been instructed not to report certain incidents and never to identify by ethnicity or religion those who had caused trouble at the pool. Another employee, again off the record, was more specific:

> Of course, we have incidents here, particularly involving Afghan men groping girls. Not long ago, a man of Arab descent was caught masturbating in the [mixed] hot tub. But we are not allowed to report things like that. These men understand that it is forbidden when we tell them, but they keep doing it anyway. They just smile and keep doing it.

While Sweden's public officials continue to display their customary indulgence towards Muslim sexual misconduct, when asked to give his opinion of the behaviour of his fellow Afghans, the manager of a large hotel in Kabul adopted a much more enlightened, though politically incorrect, stance:

> What the Afghans [in Swedish pools] are doing is not wrong in Afghanistan, so your rules are completely alien to them. Women stay at home in Afghanistan, and if they need to go out, they are always accompanied by a man. If you want to stop Afghans from molesting Swedish women and girls, you need to be tough with them. Making them take classes on equality and how to treat women is pointless. The first time they behave badly, they should be given a warning, and the second time, you should deport them from Sweden.

Islamophobe...Racist...*Nazi*.

And what of |Muslim women who might want to swim? Those few who do, conform to the Sharia dress code, by covering their entire bodies in an aquatic version of the burka, known as the burkini. For Allah is not only merciful, but resourceful. Responding to news that Marks and Spencer and House of Frazer had launched new lines in Sharia fashions, the staunchly Tory and female reader-oriented *Daily Mail* hailed their burkinis as 'ultimate proof that Britain is truly multicultural.' French feminists, who tend to be made of sterner stuff than the Anglo-Saxon variety, and politicians, defending both their secular constitution and a law which bans the public wearing of the burka, denounced the product. Minister of Families, Children and Women's Rights Lawrence Rossignol went to the heart of the matter:

> What is at stake is social control over the bodies of women. When European brands invest in the lucrative Islamic fashion market, they are shirking their responsibilities and are promoting a situation where women are forced to wear garments that imprison the woman from head to toe...Our role should be to help Muslim women, to support them by putting them in a position to confront radical Islam.

Whereas Sharia feminists hailed the arrival of the burkini as yet another opportunity for Muslim women to celebrate their 'personhood', when interviewed by *Le Monde,* the traditional feminist Elisabeth Badinter argued that 'tolerance has been turned against those it was intended to help', with the result that 'the veil has spread among the daughters of our neighbourhoods' due to 'mounting Islamic pressure'. Fashion mogul Pierre Berge was if anything even more blunt:

> Fashion designers have no business being in Islamic fashion. I am outraged. I have always believed that the job of designers is to make women more beautiful, to give them their freedom, not to be an accomplice of this dictatorship which imposes this abomination that hides women and makes them live a hidden life...I do not understand why we are embracing this religion and those manners that are incompatible with the freedoms that are ours in the west. Creators who are taking part in the enslavement of women should ask themselves some questions. All this to make money? Excuse me, but I think that belief should come before money. Give up the money and have some principles.

Vive la France!

As for Muslim men who cannot keep their groping hands off women in *kuffar* bikinis, as our Afghan Islamophobe proposes, it is high time they took an early bath and were returned pronto to their misogynist homelands.

D Germany Says Enough

'And whosoever migrates from his country in the way of Allah will find in the earth an abundant place of refuge and plentifulness.' *Koran,* Chapter 4, Verse 101

'We can do it.' German Chancellor Angela Merkel, September 15, 2015

Everything has its limits, even prosperous and liberal Sweden's ability and readiness to accept an ever-growing flow of Muslim migrants. The number of migrants who had arrived since 2012 reached 342,625 at the end of 2015, easily the highest proportion in relation to population of any EU country. And still they kept coming, many attracted by the prospect of an easy but largely unproductive life in Sweden's justly famed welfare state. With entry applications running at 10,000 per week and predictions that another 1.5 million migrants would arrive in Europe in 2016, on January 4, Sweden's coalition of Social Democrats and Greens followed the example of Norway by abandoning their increasingly unpopular policy of an open door for all comers. For the first time in over half a century, all those seeking admission to Sweden by train, boat or bus from Denmark were now required to produce a valid photo ID, such as a passport. Those who failed to do so were turned back. Justifying the *volte face,* the Deputy Prime Minister explained that 'the current situation, with a large number of people entering the country in a short space of time, poses a serious threat to public order and national security.'

Naturally, Denmark, like its northern neighbours also feeling the cultural, social, political and economic stresses of mass Muslim migration, did not want to become a haven for Sweden's rejected migrants, so it too introduced similar controls on its border with Germany. And so the ripple effect worked its way back to where the wave began, with even Merkel, for similar reasons to the Scandinavians, reluctantly considering similar measures to check the flow before Germany, and indeed the European Union as presently constituted, gave way under the strain of importing three million Muslims in two years. The Cologne-based Institute for Economic Research calculated that the cost to Germany of providing care for migrants in 2016 would be 22 billion euros, rising to 27.6 billion in 2017. This bill would not have been footed by those whose decisions have created it, or those who from far, decry those who say enough is enough. The cost measured in increased taxes, strains on services of all kinds, crime, and social tensions would inevitably fall largely on the shoulders of those least able to bear them. As of February 2016, 81% of Germans polled believed Merkel's migrant policy to have been a disaster. By May, only 22% of those polled believed Islam had a place in Germany, a result which gave the lie to the claim that opposition to the religion was confined to the far right. In fact, Muslim migration had become an issue no European leader could afford to ignore. Convened primarily to discuss economic matters, the World Economic Forum at Davos instead found itself exploring emergency measures to prevent the never-ending flow of Muslim migrants from not only undermining the Schengen Treaty on free movement within the EU's borders, but the very existence of the European Union itself.

The Schengen Agreement, first adopted in 1985, then supplemented by Schengen Convention, and incorporated into EU law in 1990, while allowing for freedom of movement between its signatories, does not in any way modify their pre-existing right to control the movement of people across their external borders. The arrival in 2015 of more than a million migrants in Italy and Greece had put that agreement under severe strain, with the result that in 2016 six countries, Sweden Denmark, Austria Poland, Germany Norway and France, temporarily re-imposed internal border controls. That did not, however, resolve the problem of what to do with those who had already arrived, 70% of whom, according to the United Nations High Commissioner for Refugees, were not refugees, but migrants. Some put the percentage even higher. One Muslim migrant/refugee explained in very candid terms what he saw as the future of his new German home:

> We are multiplying faster and faster. At most you get two children. We are making seven or eight children. And then we take four wives each. Then we have 22 children. So make it Allah, blessed be his name, make it that we conquer you, not with war, here in Germany, but with birth rates, firstly, and secondly, we will marry your daughters, and your daughter will wear a Muslim headscarf. And your daughter will marry a bearded man.

True, it is possible to argue this is the opinion of just one migrant, and therefore not representative of the majority. Those so inclined should listen to what Muslims higher up the Islamic ladder had to say on the same subject. First, and most recently, the Islamising President of Turkey, whose mainly Muslim population of 75 million the Chancellor of Germany would dearly love to enrol as citizens of the European Union, had to say on May 30, 2016: 'I say it clearly; we need to increase the number of our descendants…People talk about birth control, about family planning. No Muslim family can understand and accept that'. Then in a speech mocking rather than marking International Woman's Day earlier the same year, he asserted that 'a woman is above else a mother'. It was a claim which outraged Turkish feminists, but not the western Sharia variety, since they had more pressing tasks on hand, such as campaigning for a university campus ban on the *Sun* and no 'platforming' ex-Muslim campaigners for women's and gays rights in Islamic countries. Birth control, Erdogan declared in 2014, was 'treason'. This was par for the course for a Muslim politician. Although his geography was a little hazy, the warning former Algerian President Hourari Boumedienne issued in the course of a speech to the United Nations General Assembly in 1974 was deadly serious: 'One day millions of men will go from the southern hemisphere to the northern hemisphere. And they will not go there as friends. Because they will go there to conquer it. And they will conquer it with their sons. The wombs of our women will give us victory.' The late but not lamented, except by the Sharia left and the beneficiaries his largesse, Libyan dictator Colonel Gaddafi predicted the same future for Europe: 'There are signs that Allah will grant victory to Islam in Europe without swords, without guns, without conquest. We don't need terrorist; we don't need suicide bombers. The 50 million plus Muslims [already] in Europe will turn it into a Muslim continent within a few decades.'

The Hamas Charter, Article 17, defines the role of women as 'the factory of men', pumping out an endless supply of warriors, suicide bombers and, Corbyn's 'friends' hope, one day soon the conquerors of and settlers in a Jew-free greater Palestine. Finally, we have Yasser Arafat, whose specific target for uterine conquest was Israel. He told a closed meeting of Arab diplomats in Stockholm on January 30, 1996, that is, three years after singing the Oslo Accords that committed Israel and the PLO to a 'two state' solution to the Palestine issue, 'we will make life unbearable for the Jews by psychological warfare and *population explosion*. We Palestinians will take over everything, including Jerusalem'. (emphasis added) Barbra Lerner Spectre [sic], a US Jewish high priestess of multiculturalism, embraces this future of a mass Muslim migration (that is for Europe) with open arms and joy in her heart. Unlike Merkel, what she proposes is not an open door just to those claiming to be refugees, but to all migrants, no matter who, why, how many or from where: 'Europe has not yet learned how to be multi-cultural. And I think that we [that, is the Jews] are going to be part of the throes [sic] of that transformation, which must take place. Europe is not going to be the monolithic societies they once were in the last century. Jews are going to be at the centre of that.'

Spectre's claim that that Europe is not multicultural is sheer nonsense. In the true sense of the word, it is now, and has been for thousands of years. Quite apart from the recent arrivals of diasporas from other continents and climes, Europe has for centuries, and in many cases for far longer, been the home to a vast kaleidoscopic array of peoples of widely differing cultures, faiths and languages. Just within the European Union, there are 23 officially recognised languages and more than 60 indigenous regional dialects, together with a wide variety of tongues brought to and used in Europe by migrants from other continents. The ethnic variety is also broad. From beyond the Urals came the Finno-Ugric peoples, distant cousins of the native Americans, today comprising the Hungarians, Finns, and Estonians, and in the Arctic the Sami and the Laps. Then there are the Teutonic peoples, in the north, the Scandinavians, and at Europe's core, the Germans, Dutch and Flemish. To the far west, there are the Celts, and to the east, the Slavs, and to south, the Mediterranean Latins and Greeks.

However, for all their diversity…and it is immense…they all share, to varying degrees, a commitment to values, principles and institutions that have come to make Europe what it is today… a beacon and fortress of western civilisation, where 'diversity' has made for mutual enrichment, and not exclusivity and endless friction. This is because the vast majority of Europeans believe in and practice democracy and individual freedom, a secular system of justice and the rule one law for all, the equality of men and women and the rights of children, the toleration of differing opinions, beliefs, life-styles and sexual preferences, the separation of state and faith, freedom of speech, press and artistic expression, the right of labour to organise and the access by all to free public education and welfare. If there was no broad consensus in these matters, the creation and progressive enlargement of the European Union would have been impossible. However, the experience of Muslim migration has proved that these values are not shared by those whose ethos and conduct is determined by slavish adherence to Islam. Far from the passing of time aiding integration, not only the recent emergence of the 'home grown' Jihadi, but numerous surveys have shown that the younger the Muslim, the less favourably disposed he or she is likely to be to the values that underpin the host nation's way of life. No less crucially, unlimited Muslim migration into Europe, quite aside from its inevitable political repercussions, will impose on the continent burdens that simply cannot be sustained without causing possibly irreparable damage to its economic and social infrastructure.

Those celebrities who from within their privileged bubble demand a world with open borders simply have not thought through how it will affect those hundreds of millions of less fortunate Europeans who live outside it. They should ask themselves what the consequences will be of a one-way flow of tens of millions of people from those many countries where the quality of life is substantially lower than the world average, to a much smaller number where it is far higher. As we saw in 2015, this immense migration of peoples will naturally target those relatively few nations which offer the highest standards of living and are most indulgent towards the life styles of new settlers, for example the Scandinavian states and Germany. But as we have also seen, the ability to absorb far less than the numbers of migrants that a permanent open border policy would entail reached its limits in less than a year, along with the tolerance of migrant life styles. Say, for example, that ten million migrants from Africa, the Middle East and South Asia wish to settle in Switzerland, current population, eight million, or Denmark, 5.6 million. Given this opportunity and considering the huge disparities in the quality of life, pitching their number at ten million is conservative in the extreme. And we must bear in mind that the advocates of open borders not only say they must be admitted as of right, regardless of number, but that they must not be treated as second class citizens and should have the right to expect that their everyday needs will be met by the host nation. For otherwise, why migrate in the first place?

Like the planet, the territory and natural resources of a state are finite, and likewise, over the short run, its social and economic infrastructure. To describe, as some do, those who oppose the open border policy on these entirely practical grounds as racist bigots is a slander, though it may salve the consciences of those who claim that all the problems of the poor nations are 'our fault'. It is incredibly naïve, at best, given what we have already witnessed in Europe with 'only' one million plus Muslim migrants arriving in one year, to assume that immigration on such an unprecedentedly colossal scale will have no negative economic and social repercussions upon the host nation's less prosperous classes and its political equilibrium. Then of course there will also be enormous and unprecedented cultural consequences. We are assured by open border advocates that just as in the past, when migrations have resulted over time in the migrants being integrated and, to a lesser or greater extent, assimilated into the host nation (though this is palpably not true of Muslims), this will happen again as a result of the adoption of an open border policy. The 'home grown' gang rapists and pimps of Rotherham, Rochdale, Oxford, Keighley, Sheffield, Aylesbury and elsewhere all had decades to settle down and assume the ways of their host nation, but they chose instead to behave like barbarians.

References to previous mass migrations also fail to take into account what made them fundamentally different from those that are taking place today, and far more so, from what the advocates of open borders are now demanding. In complete contrast to what is happening with Asian and African Muslim migration, with the exception of a far more protracted flow within Europe from a backward and repressive east to an advanced and liberal west, the great migrations of earlier eras have always been in the opposite direction to today, away from Europe to other continents. Between 1821 and 1932, 32 million Europeans migrated just to the United States. In the same period, nearly seven million migrated to Brazil, over five million to Canada, 3.5 million to Australasia, and from 1856 to 1932, 6.4 million to Argentina. In each case, the movement of peoples was from a continent and countries that were densely populated and becoming more so, to vast territories that in most cases were by comparison sparely settled. In little more than a century, a global European diaspora was generated by 60 million migrants. Such an unprecedented movement of peoples was only possible because in the first place there existed the means to transport them, and once they had arrived, the space to accommodate them, land to feed them and work to employ them. This was the time of the spread of the industrial revolution from Europe to the world, a process that drew in its wake vast armies of migrant labour to build cities and railways, dig canals and coal, and toil on farms and in mills and factories.

Apart from the massive relocation within Europe of so-called 'displaced persons', the last great migration after the Second World War found millions of Asians and Africans, mostly from former or existing colonies, settling in western Europe, initially finding mainly semi or unskilled employment in a continent struggling to rebuild itself with a severely depleted indigenous male labour force. With the exception of Muslims, today, the children and grandchildren of this post war migrant wave have, to a greater or lesser degree, integrated themselves into their host societies. Some have intermarried with the native population, and their children and grandchildren, if not themselves, have become fully assimilated. This development is quite normal and is surely to be welcomed by all concerned. Not of course by racists, but sadly also not by many Muslims. Islam's rules on sexual conduct constitute one of the most effective barriers to Muslim integration. Gang raping a *kuffar* girl is one thing, but marrying one unless she converts, another entirely, and for most Muslim families, strictly *haram,* as is a Muslim woman marrying or taking up with a *kuffar* man, the punishment for which can be so-called 'honour killing'. By in-group marriage, either arranged or forced, to close relatives, sometimes much older than the bride, diaspora Muslims have succeeded in isolating themselves biologically as well as socially and culturally from their host societies, the price for which is the well-documented but rarely acknowledged prevalence of genetically transmitted physical and mental disabilities markedly more widespread and severe than in the non-Muslim host population. The success of self-ghettoisation has led even mainstream European politicians who cannot resist singing the praises of Islam to frankly admit that the integration of Muslims, insofar as it has been seriously attempted, has totally failed. All that unlimited Muslim immigration will do is make a hard task impossible. But then, that is what Spectre appears to be advocating.

Assuming that an open border means exactly what it says, that there are no legal limits to the number of migrants who will be as of right granted legal entry and permanent settlement in the country of their choice, it is surely reasonable to ask that quite apart from the practicalities of providing for the necessities of their life, what could be the cultural consequences of Denmark admitting, as it would be obliged to do, possibly a total of non-European migrant's greater than that of its own native population? One result is certain. Denmark as Danes know it today would cease to exist. Barbra Lerner Spectre would doubtless believe this to be a splendid vindication of multiculturalism. And if there is one country more than any other that would be the target of mass migration should the unrestricted opening of borders become a legal obligation on the part of all member states of the United Nations, that country would be Israel. What an Allah-sent opportunity to at last and forever 'wipe off the map' the accursed 'Zionist entity' by flooding it with a sufficient number of Arabs to convert its current 80% Jewish population into a minority that can then be either driven out, exterminated, as proposed by Corbyn's 'friends' Hamas and Hezbollah, or at best, reduced to the status of second-class *dhimmis* under Sharia law.

Once cold numbers and economic realities are brought to bear on the wishful thinking of champagne internationalists, the whole idea collapses upon itself. Not only that. Quite aside from the impact on the economy, politics and culture of the host nations targeted by unlimited migration, by encouraging and facilitating the draining of failing nations of their most active elements of the population, leaving behind the old, the very young, the mainly female and the infirm, opening borders would condemn these nations to an ever-sinking spiral of demographic distortions, decay, poverty, corruption and lawlessness. Is that what the open doorers want? Let them also consider the following: In 2010, that is, five years before the arrival in 2015 of over a million Muslim migrants and refugees, the continent's Muslims numbered 44 million, six per cent of the total population. Discounting new migrations, this Muslim share of Europe's population, because of various demographic factors, is projected to reach eight per cent by the year 2030, 58 million Muslims. As previously, we can expect that this increase will not be evenly distributed across Europe, or within its individual states, but concentrated in a growing number of large cities in the west, where for some years now, Muslim enclaves have taken root, some of them to the extent that while living off the host society, they are off-limits to its security forces, legal systems and other public agencies.

In every European state where such statistics are available, Muslim unemployment is chronic, in some cases 50% and more, and always greatly in excess of other migrants from a non-European background. In Denmark, Muslims comprise 5% of the population, but draw 40% of its welfare payments, eight times more than the average. According to Germany's former Interior Minister Otto Schily, '70% of newcomer's land on welfare on the day of their arrival'. This applied to migrants arriving *prior* to the current surge of Muslims, all of whom 'land on welfare' and in all probability will, in their vast majority, stay there for the foreseeable future. Given what the statistics tell us about the situation of most Muslims in the Europe of today, we have no reason to suppose that newly-arriving Muslims will be any more successful at integrating themselves into their host nations than those who are already here. And what incentive is there for them to do so, given that current state of affairs works so well in their favour? In 2015, unemployment just in the European Union stood 24 million, 10% of its working population. Since the onset of the recession in 2008, the European economy has struggled to reach let alone sustain a growth rate that matches its annual 2% increase in productivity. Until it exceeds that rate of increase, the jobs market will remain static at best. And the bulk of the new vacancies that are created will be filled by those with high levels of technical, literacy, numeracy and language skills. Are Muslim migrants, at least 60% of whom are functionally illiterate even in their own language, likely to be, assuming that they want to be, first in the queue for jobs in what is an ever-higher tech economy? Leaving to one side welfare payments to jobless migrants, as a direct result of the arrival of well over a million non-contributing potential claimants to its state-of-the-art health service, Germany faced a shortfall in 2017 of one billion euros in its health budget, the balance of which had be made good by raiding the social insurance funds paid in by German workers.

Despite the lenient approach to migrant crime adopted by politically corrected police forces, Muslims, unlike other 'Asians', are still vastly overrepresented in crime statistics and prison populations. 70% of French prisoners are Muslims, while they make up ten per cent of the country's population. 70% of Spain's prisoners are also Muslim, even though they comprise only 2.3% of Spain's total population. And throughout Europe's jails, the trend is for that share to increase. In England and Wales in 2002, 5,502 prisoners said they were Muslims. Twelve years on, and the number had jumped to 12,225. Saxony, which in 2015 received 'only' 45,000 migrants, in the same year experienced a 47% increase in migrant crime, with one migrant in ten being an offender. Included in these offences were 17 murders and five rapes.

Quite apart from the irreconcilable cultural tensions that mass Muslim migration has generated, even Germany, the economic powerhouse of Europe, and the highly organised and prosperous Nordic states have rapidly found themselves unable to withstand the demands placed on their welfare and security infrastructures. So what hope is there for the main recipients of migrants, bankrupt Greece and Italy, and Spain, with 20% unemployment, and the less developed states of the European East? In the radiant, brave new Musli-cultural Europe that so excites the Spectres, will there be any losers? Since according to her, it is the Jews' mission to persuade Europe that it needs to absorb an unlimited number of migrants whose religion demands that they despise Jews, it was not hard to predict who they going to be, and Spectre made no attempt to hide it. In fact, she embraces the prospect, at a distance of 3,000 miles: 'It's a huge transformation for Europe to make. They are now going into a multicultural mode and Jews will be resented [sic!] because of our [i.e., Jewish] leading role. But without that transformation and without that transformation, Europe will not survive.' But will the Jews? The surge in Jewish migration to Israel suggests that with their not so disant history in mind, many are not prepared to risk waiting to see.

As if they did not have enough trouble on their hands with Sharia left anti-Zionism, Neo-Nazi and Muslim anti-Semitism and Jihadi terrorism, the Jews of Europe, for some unexplained reason, and at the cost of incurring hostility from fellow Europeans, have to be at the forefront of encouraging the immigration of yet more millions of potential Muslim anti-Semites, a role that in the unlikely event of their being so foolish as to take it on, would indeed ensure the enmity of those many Europeans who see this policy as tantamount to inviting cultural and economic suicide. Thus the Jews would be trapped on both sides in an anti-Semitic vice of their own making. But their sacrifice will not be in vain. The only hope for Europe is more and yet more Muslims, and if this leads to yet more Jews packing their bags and heading for Israel, then so be it. Muslims in, Jews out. And not only Jews. As more Muslims continue arrive, despite nation-wide protests, through Merkel's illegal open door, so more Germans leave. 2 million Muslims arrived in Germany in little more than a year, while 1.5 million Germans have left over the last ten years, 138,000 in 2015 and many more again in 2016. And they were Germans the country could ill-afford to lose. According to *Die Welte,* 'German talent is leaving the country in droves'. However, the official attitude is, good riddance. Those Germans who disagreed with Merkel's immigration policy were advised by Walter Lubcke, President of Kassel, that they were 'free to leave Germany at any time', a sentiment shared by a young Syrian migrant writing in the on-line *Der Freitag*: 'We refugees do not want to live in the same country with you. You can, and I think you should, leave Germany. Germany does not fit you. Why do you live here? Why do you not go to another country? We are sick of you.' Muslims in, Germans out.

French Prime Minister Manuel Valls, whose country had become the prime target for Muslim terrorism, and whose government, unlike Spectre, had understandably shown no great desire to add to its country's six million largely unintegrated Muslims, feared that unless the flow was halted, 'our societies will be totally destabilised. If Europe is not capable of protecting its own borders, it's the very idea of Europe that will be questioned.' In an obvious allusion to Merkel's migrant policy, Valls warned that the message 'come you will be welcome' was producing a major shift in the balance of Europe's population. More than that, Merkel's open-door policy must share part of the blame, together with the people traffickers and the Muslim states that have refused to accept refugees, for the deaths by drowning of those attempting the crossing in overloaded and unseaworthy dinghies from Turkey to Greece, and north Africa to Italy and Spain. Why has Turkey not been instructed to round up its people traffickers and instead allow refugees a safe land route into Europe? Instead, the resulting migrant drownings have been cynically exploited by much of the media and publicity seeking celebrities to urge an ever widening of the EU's door, a policy which will only result in yet more of the drownings they claim to abhor. Madness.

Like all the other European leaders present at Davos, Valls was careful not to directly criticise Merkel's open-door policy, but he did not have to, since its consequences, dramatized by the mass migrant sexual assaults of December 31, 2015, and the participation of Muslim migrants in terrorist attacks in Paris, were all too clear. If the Schengen Treaty does have to be revised, or possibly even torn up, then it will be the German Chancellor who will have to take most of the blame. The Dutch Prime Minister Mark Rutte was no less emphatic. Europe was 'at breaking point, and its leaders need[ed] to get a grip in the issue in the next six to eight weeks'. 'We can't cope with the numbers any longer. We need to get a grip on this.' Yes...but how...and who was going to do it? Germany's Finance Minister Wolfgang Schauble admitted that 'the abilities of the EU countries are not inexhaustible'. My very point. So why then did Merkel conduct her migrant policy as if they were? Schauble claimed that the EU was 'united on the need to reduce the migrant pressure [no longer were they refugees]', ignoring the fact that many EU member states were seeking not a reduction, but an end to this pressure, and even its reversal. Schauble's solution to the migrant crisis could not have appealed to his EU partners, not only because it was totally unrealistic, but would if attempted be both immensely costly and. almost certainly counterproductive: 'We Europeans need to invest billions [sic] in Turkey, Libya [sic!] Jordan and other countries in the region as quickly as possible.' This proposal to bribe corrupt Muslim regimes to stop driving and passing on millions of migrants into Europe...we can call it Allah geld...not surprisingly met with no takers. There is a far cheaper and infinitely more humane and effective alternative, the return of all those except proven genuine asylum seekers who are already in the EU to their countries of origin, and strict enforcement of the EU's asylum rules for all those seeking entry. Faced by the prospect of another 2.6 million migrants arriving in Europe over the next two years, EU leaders at an emergency meeting in Amsterdam on January 25 finally decided, a year late, to stem the tide by agreeing to seal off Greece by closing its border with Macedonia, together with the temporary re-introduction of internal border controls within the EU.

With 110,00,000 migrants arriving just in January 2016, ten times the number in the same month of the previous year, the Dutch government proposed that all new arrivals should be immediately ferried back to Turkey. NATO announced that it would send three warships to patrol the Turkish coast to deter new migrant arrivals. Meanwhile, Sweden and Finland had already announced they would between them be expelling as many as 100,000 bogus asylum claimants, that is, approaching half of the total number of migrants that arrived in the two countries in 2015. Totally isolated in Europe, and increasingly so in her country, where around half of all Germans were supporting calls for her resignation over her handling of the migrant crisis, to save her own political skin, Merkel announced at the end of January that once it was safe to do so, all refugees would be returned to their countries of origin. Even if the Religion of Peace were to weary of its fratricidal slaughters, the success of Merkel's plan of course depended on whether her guests could be tracked down. By January 2016, as many 600,000 had already disappeared under the radar, many of them men of military age fit enough in some cases to have walked hundreds of miles on their journey from the south of Greece and Italy to Germany, after allowing vastly inferior numbers of fellow Muslims to take over huge areas of their countries almost unopposed, leaving behind their children, womenfolk and the aged to face the consequences. .

Figures released by the BBC on February 18, 2016, revealed the scale of the number of migrants falsely claiming asylum status. We must exclude from any calculations those who are or claim to be Syrians who arrived in Europe in the twelve months between October 2014 and October 2015, 250,000 in all, even though many would, on closer scrutiny than they underwent on arrival, prove to be migrants. Then we have 110,000 Afghans, some of who will have fled locations where the Taliban is engaged in killing fellow Muslims, though how many are from these areas it is impossible to know. Iraqis number 70,000, again, some from areas either occupied or under attack by the Islamic State, or in the throes of inter-Muslim strife between Shi'a and Sunni. Between them, these three countries generated 430,000 asylum claimants, most, let us grant, genuinely so. But the next country on the list is Kosovo, with 80,000, followed by Albania with 60,000 and then Pakistan, with 40,000! Far away Nigeria has contributed 25,000. In the case of Kosovo, this number compromises over 4% of the country's total population! Given that the majority of migrants are young men, the most active and productive sector of the population, this is certain to have negative demographic, social and economic consequences in their homelands on a scale that that will simply encourage yet more migration. Even Ukraine and Serbia have each supplied 20,000 migrants to add to the unchecked flow of bogus refugees wending its illegal way to the rich feeding grounds of western and northern Europe. The extent to which migrants had been posing as asylum seekers was revealed when after the EU concluded an agreement with Turkey to return all those unable to establish their *bona fides,* the number making the crossing to Greece fell by *90%*. As for the impact on Europe, even in politically correct Scandinavia, its Social Democrats, hitherto the most enthusiastic of all parties in the encouragement of a Muslim immigration that had provided them with an ever-growing supply of voting fodder, began to sing a new tune when at last, they woke up to the threat that mass Muslim migration posed to their justly famed welfare states and to their traditional support in the working class. Henrik Sass Larsen, the leader of the Danish Social Democratic Party Parliamentary group, spelled out the new line:

> We will do all we can to limit the number of non-European refugees and immigrants to this country. That is why we have gone far, much farther than we ever dreamed of. We do this because we do not want to sacrifice the welfare state in the name of humanism. Because the welfare state is the political project of the Social Democrats. It is a society built on the principle of freedom equality and solidarity. Mass immigration - look at Sweden for example - will undermine the social and economic foundation of the welfare state.

When the full history of this unprecedented episode comes to be written, its prime cause will inevitably be located in a crisis of Islam that set Muslim against Muslim throughout the Middle East, South Asia and North Africa. But such an account, if it is to be true to the facts, will also have apportion considerable blame to European politicians, in the first place Chancellor Merkel, for not only allowing but actually encouraging a mass Muslim migration to Europe that was not only illegal, but, more to the point inhumane in the extreme. The illusion was fostered that Europe, in the first place those countries with the most developed welfare provisions, could absorb unlimited numbers of culturally backward Muslims from the Middle East, Africa and even further afield, on a permanent basis, irrespective of whether they were genuine asylum seekers or simply economic and welfare migrants, and without any serious adverse impact on the economy, security, social stability and politics of the countries foolish enough to accept them on such a basis and scale. It took only a matter of a few months after Merkel announced that Germany's door was open to all comers to demonstrate how wrong this assumption was. Disgusting and for the victims, traumatic though the sexual assaults of New Year's Eve were, they shrink almost to insignificance compared with the drowning of thousands lured on by the promise of a new life in Europe. Their deaths are on Merkel's hands no less than the traffickers who packed them into unseaworthy vessels, and the Turkish authorities who turned a blind eye to this sordid trade in false hope, misery and despair.

Inevitably, the Islamophile lobby, located mainly in countries that have accepted few if any migrants, sanctimoniously depicted any measure taken to stem their flow in the most lurid colours imaginable. When Denmark introduced the long overdue requirement that migrants seeking entry who had the means to do so should contribute towards their upkeep by surrendering valuables (excluding jewellery and items of a sentimental value) or cash in excess of a total value of £1,000, the measure was compared to the Third Reich's pre-war practice of confiscating the property and savings of Jews fleeing Nazi persecution. Firstly, the migrants/refugees in question were not fleeing from Denmark, but to Denmark. Secondly, many had been able to pay extortionate sums to people traffickers to ferry them either from north Africa across the Mediterranean or from the Middle East and even much further afield via Turkey to Italy or Greece, and then the fare to be transported northwards the best part of two thousand miles through either Austria or the Balkans and Germany to Denmark And if they refused to comply, there was always the option of staying in Germany as a guest of Angela Merkel. Ignoring the sanctimonious clamour, several other European countries adopted the same measure.

Here we had yet another case of branding as a Nazi anyone who does not dance to the Sharia leftist tune Only those who are totally ignorant of the history of Nazi Germany, and/or have an agenda that has nothing to do with the welfare of migrants, can possibly make such a comparison between the two situations. Firstly, the Danes had not driven any Muslims out of their homeland, which is what the Nazis did to the Jews. Although it is not politically correct to say so, this has been solely the doing of their Jihadi co-religionists. Secondly, it is the infidel Danes who welcomed some 200,000 Muslim migrants into a country with a total population of only 5.6 million, one migrant for every 28 Danes, with the result that the strain on their tiny nation's resources had reached a level that had become unsustainable without some help from the migrants themselves. The revenues thus raised would be used to help provide for their upkeep, whereas the assets stolen from fleeing German Jews were used to help fund the Nazi war machine and the extermination of the Jews themselves. How can these two situations be compared?

If those, not least publicity seeking celebrities, who parade their concern about the welfare of migrants, regard these regulations as unfair, why have they not demanded of the oil rich despotisms of the Middle East that as they have refused to offer sanctuary to fleeing fellow Muslins, the least they could do would be to contribute towards their upkeep in infidel countries that have, instead of devoting their spare billions to the financing of Jihadi armies, yet more European Mosque building and the distribution of anti-Semitic propaganda? And, crowning irony, it is a reasonable assumption that among those Muslim migrants already safely accommodated in Denmark at the expense of its tolerant and industrious people, there will those who took part in the riots which followed the publication of the so-called Danish cartoons back in 2006. These included attacks on Danish embassies, along with a world-wide Muslim campaign to boycott Danish goods. If the Danes were the vindictive people they are portrayed to be by the critics of their migrant policy, they could have quite easily sought redress by denying any entry to the followers of a faith that sought their destruction for the sake a few cartoons. But they did not. Surely there is a lesson here somewhere.

Rather late in the day...some would say too late...even politicians who not only welcomed the Islamic invasion of Europe, but encouraged it, have now had second thoughts about its consequences, which have been, as those familiar with the ways of Islam have predicted, sexual assaults on women, including gang rape, and attacks on Jews, including their murder. The main accessory to this Muslim crime wave, German Chancellor Merkel, admitted on April 23, 2018, that 'we have a new phenomenon, as we have many refugees among whom for example there are people of Arab origin who bring another form anti-Semitism in the country.' She neglected to point out that this 'form of anti-Semitism', far from being 'new' is in fact as old as Islam. Moreover, it is not confined to migrants from Arab countries but can be found everywhere that Islam has spread its poisonous, genocidal message that Jews are not human, but apes and swine.

Seven decades after the Holocaust, Merkel found herself in the humiliating situation of having to announce that she had appointed a government commissioner charged with combatting an anti-Semitism she was responsible for importing illegally and *en masse* into Germany, in an interview on CNN in May 2019, referring to the 'dark forces' not only in Germany but across Europe that were now menacing the continent's Jews, though neglecting to identify who or what they were. In the main body of this work, I predicted that one of the consequences of her decision in the summer of 2015 to illegally open her country's border to uncontrolled Muslim immigration would be a 'bumpy ride' for Germany's Jews, and that is exactly what has happened. Merkel admitted that 'there is not a single synagogue, not single day care centre for Jewish children, not a single school for Jewish children that does not need to guarded by a German policeman'. But again...from whom or what?

The answer came from her own security agency, the Federal Office for the Protection of the Constitution, which Merkel's migrant policy had violated. (See Addendum) Among the more than a million Muslim migrants that had arrived in Germany since 2015 were activists of anti-Semitic Islamic movements such as the Muslim Brotherhood, Hamas and Hezbollah. According to Germany's Ministry of the Interior, anti-Semitic incidents, had increased in 2019 by 20%, with violent attacks up by 86%. In response to this surge in anti-Jewish crime, Felix Klein, Germany's Anti-Semitism Commissioner' (sic) admitted that he could 'no longer recommend Jews wear a kippa at every place and time in Germany'. This was not Hitler's Germany, *circa* 1938, but Merkel's, 2019.

Germany's President, Frank-Walter Steinmeier, had been far less inhibited than his Chancellor in identifying Germany's new Jew-baiters when, in December 2017, he defied the fashionable conventions of multicultural moral relativism by declaring he was 'horrified and ashamed' that Muslims were burning Israeli flags in Berlin in protest against US President Trump's decision to recognise Jerusalem as the capital of Israel. Anti-Semitism was 'showing its face in many evil shapes, including public acts with hate-filled slogans...they do not understand, or do not respect, what it is to be German.' In the light of the Holocaust, Germans more than any other people, he continued, had a special responsibility to oppose anti-Semitism, 'and this responsibility does not recognise caveats for migrant backgrounds and exceptions for newcomers. It is non-negotiable for everyone who lives here and wants to live here.' In secular France, unlike the UK, a tradition endures that one can speak one's mind publicly about matters religious without the same fear of prosecution. In the wake of the murder of a Holocaust survivor by her Muslim neighbour in April 2018, 300 prominent public figures, mainly from the arts, academe and politics, signed a declaration condemning Muslim (not Arab) attacks on and murder of Jews. There had been public outrage that her killer, who as he stabbed her, cried 'God is Great', was declared unfit to stand trial because, at the time of the crime, he had been allegedly under the influence of marijuana. Acknowledging the fact that Jews are 25 times more likely than Muslims to be the victims of racist violence, even though Muslims outnumber Jews by a ratio of 10 to one, and with nearly all of it inflicted by Muslims, the declaration made the unprecedented demand, almost unthinkable let alone sayable in the UK, that 'the verses in the *Koran* that call for the death of Jews, Christians and unbelievers must be excised by [Islamic] theological authorities'. Just as in the UK, and in fact any country with a large and growing

Muslim population, the unassailable assertion was made that in France too, the lack of concern for the well-being of the Jews arose from the fact that 'the Muslim vote is ten times larger than that of the Jews'. And, we can add, precisely because of this at best indifference, Jews will continue to leave, while the number of Muslims increases, further accentuating their leverage within the political life of not only France, but across the whole of Western Europe. And of course, acting on this cynical calculation, just as in the UK and Sweden, to cite but two examples, is a part of the French left, disguising its war on the Jews as anti-Zionism, and depicting Muslim anti-Semitism as a protest against oppression:

> The anti-Semitism of radical Islam is seen by a part of the French elite [given the context, obviously its left wing is meant here] as purely an expression of social revolt...[Thus] the old anti-Semitism of the extreme right has combined with that of a part of the radical left, which uses anti-Zionism as an alibi to transform the tormentors of the Jews into victims of society.

Addendum

Article 16a of the Constitution of the Federal Republic of Germany, titled 'Right of Asylum' specifies, in Paragraph 2, that Article 16a 'may not be invoked by a person who enters the federal territory [of Germany] from a member state of the European Communities or from another state in which the application of the Convention relating to the status of refugees and of the Convection for the Protection of Human Rights and Fundamental Freedoms is assured.' It goes on to say that 'measures to terminate an applicant's stay may be implemented without regard to any legal challenge that may have instituted against them'.

Dublin Convention III, like its two previous versions, binding on all member states of the European Union, stipulates that all applications for asylum must be processed by the first country of the applicant's entry into the EU. This law was also flouted by Merkel. In July 2017, the European Court of Justice ruled that despite the unprecedented influx surge of Muslims migrants into Europe, EU member states retained the right to lawfully deport migrants back to their first country of entry into the EU.

E Spoils of War

'The spoils of war are for Allah and the Messenger.' *Koran,* Chapter 88, Verse 2.
111

I

By the Book

Everywhere in Europe where they are available, official government statistics show that inward Muslim migration has been accompanied by a rise, sometimes spectacular, of sex crimes, as in Sweden (by 14 times) and in the case of the UK, by the organised grooming, trafficking and gang rape of several hundred thousand vulnerable non-Muslim girls, some barely in their teens, with the full knowledge and in some cases connivance of the police, public authorities, Islamic clerics, and government and local politicians. In Pakistan, Christian girls are similarly regarded and treated, often with the same impunity, as rape fodder by Muslim men. On January 13, 2016, in Lahore, three Christian girls who resisted the sexual advances of a gang of wealthy Muslim men were pursued in a car and assaulted, one of them later dying of her injuries. During the assault, one of the attackers shouted: 'Christian girls are meant for only one thing, the pleasure of Muslim men.' Local police seemed to agree, because just as in the UK, they showed little interest in pursuing the case. Should we be surprised? As we shall see, however ignorant they may be in matters pertaining to proper conduct in a modern civilisation, Muslim men know their rights under Islamic law when it comes to raping non-Muslim women.

Rape as we understand it today must have been practised before recorded history, despite taboos that sought to regulate relations between the sexes. But it is the sanctioning of rape by religion that concerns us here. And the simple truth is that religion and rape have gone hand in hand over the millennia. We are not talking here about priests raping altar boys in the crypt, but rape explicitly sanctioned by the texts of a faith. But first there is the question of religion and slavery, the latter being in some ways not only morally but physically akin to rape. It is generally known, or at least it should be, that devout Muslims and Christians upheld and practised slavery up until very recent times, Christians well into the 19th century, and Muslims as far into the twentieth…Saudi Arabia and Yemen only abolished slavery, on paper, in 1962. But how many know that the world's two most widely disseminated and influential holy books, the Bible and the *Koran,* both explicitly sanction not only slavery, but the enslavement of women for the purposes of sexual intercourse?

It can be objected that so far as observant Jews and practising Christians are concerned, excluding from consideration religious cults whose gurus practise polygamy, neither today use holy texts to justify rape, and at this distance in time, it is impossible to know to what extent this occurred when both faiths were young and still all-powerful. Even then, there were laws relating to rape, but only because women were seen as the property of men (in Islam they still are) and since rape could involve the infringement of male property rights, it was punished as such, for example in the code of King Hammurabi of Babylon, dating from BC 1685. The right of a woman not to be raped is a relatively recent legal concept, and a wife by her husband, more recent again. Both these women's rights owe nothing to the so-called Judeo-Christian values that we are told are the foundation of western civilisation.

The original Anglican marriage vow of the bride, dating from 1549, obliged her to 'love, cherish and obey' her husband. More than four centuries later, in 1980 to be precise, in addition to the original vow of 1549, the choice of two more vows was made available in the Alternative Service Book. Option A was the same for bride and groom and therefore omitted 'obey', while option B, though amended as compared with the vow of 1549, still retained the bride's pledge to obey her husband. Then in 2000, yet another version, replacing both that of 1549 and those of 1980, was introduced. It too, like that of 1980, offered two versions, one with obey, and one without. It is difficult to see how the Anglican Church can totally rid itself of the vow to obey without doing violence to the book on which in theory its teachings rest, namely the Bible. Paul, in Ephesians, Chapter 5, Verses 22 and 23, reads: 'Wives, submit yourselves unto your husbands, as unto the Lord. For the husband is the head of the wife, even as Christ is the head of the church'. And in Peter 1, 3,1: '...ye wives, be in subjection to your own husbands...'

Since the Marriage Act of 1949, applicable only in England and Wales, the wording of the civil marriage vows makes no reference to a god, is the same for bride and groom, and does not include a bride's vow to obey. A rare victory for secularism as well as one for gender equality. The ritual of the father 'giving away' what has been, since her birth, 'his' daughter to another man also originates from a time when a woman was either by custom or law, the property of a man as indeed they still are where Sharia law holds sway. Then of course there is the dowry, the payment in money or kind made by the owner or owners of the bride, who is therefore judged to worth less than nothing, a burden, who needs a bribe to persuade another man to assume ownership and upkeep of her. Again, 'giving away' conveys with it the notion that what is being given has no value, hence the need for a bribe.

As one would expect, in the *Koran*, we find the same idea as in Paul, though in this case, it defines the relationship not between husband and wife (or wives) but men and women in general: 'Men are guardians over women because Allah has made some of them excel over others'. (Chapter 4, Verse 34) A Muslim woman's marriage vow reflects this relationship, with its pledge to 'be for you an obedient and faithful wife'. Under Sharia law, there are no restrictions on the age of the wife taking this vow. The founder of Islam is said by all Islamic sources to have married his last wife, Aisha, when she was six, and consummated the marriage when she was nine. True or not, this has become the template for paedophilic Islamic marriage laws and practices, with the predictable result that child and even new-born baby brides, often bought by much older relatives, are a commonplace in a number of Muslim countries, including Yemen and Pakistan. In Pakistan, in January 2016, the ruling Muslim League Party's bid to enforce a law, dating back to British rule in 1929, limiting the minimum age for marriage for women to 16, was decreed to be 'blasphemous' by Pakistan's Council of Islamic Ideology. The Council's Chairman, Mohammad Khan Sheerani, ruled that 'Parliament cannot create legislation that is against the teachings of the Holy *Koran* or Sunnah'. The bill was promptly withdrawn, thereby confirming child rape as lawful in Pakistan. And, as before, our Sharia feminists will continue to rail against 'horror stories' of Muslim misogyny, while they prattle on about the glass ceiling in the boardroom and the 'sexism' of page three of the *Sun.*

In the west, until the advent of laws protecting wives from rape by their husbands, a husband's sexual rights within marriage were usually referred to as conjugal rights, and the wife's as duties. Islam, being perfect and therefore unchangeable, to this day does not recognise rape within marriage (*Koran,* Chapter 2, Verse 223, and Bukhari v.4, b.54 No.460) while English law only ceased doing so in 1991 when not an Act of Parliament, but a ruling by the Appellate Court in the House of Lords made non-consensual sexual intercourse by the husband a crime under Common Law. A survey conducted by the UN in 2006 found that rape within marriage was outlawed in 106 countries, leaving nearly as large a number where it was not. A classic statement on the Islamic denial of the very concept of rape within marriage was made as recently as 2014 by the Lebanese cleric Sheik Ahmad al Kurdi. He complained that criminalising rape within marriage 'could lead to the imprisoning of the man where in reality he is exercising the least [sic] of his marital rights'.

Again, unlike the Muslim world, civilised countries also outlawed, long ago, another ancient right of husbands, namely that of wife-beating. In England, it was called 'the rule of thumb', this being the legal limit under Common Law of the width of the implement used to administer the beating. Wife-beating was outlawed, though of course not eliminated, in the UK by the Aggravated Assaults Act of 1853. The MP Thomas Phinn moved an amendment to stipulate flogging as the punishment for wife beating, but it was defeated by 108 votes to 50. Another attempt to introduce flogging was made in 1856 but was defeated by 135 votes to 97. But such was feeling on this issue, that a third attempt to render the act's enforcement more effective was made in 1860 by Lord Raynham, but it was again defeated, by 221 votes to 81, though not out of any sympathy for the wife-beater who, and I agree with them, was judged to have deserved it, but chiefly on the reasonable grounds that wives would be less likely to report the crime if it led to their husbands being flogged as many believed they deserved. True, no civilised country would or should today contemplate the use of such methods to combat this or any other crime, no matter how barbaric, but one can understand the anger and frustration felt by those who with the best of motives, were ready to resort to flogging as the only means to deter husbands from assaulting their defenceless and more often than not, economically dependent wives. The popular journal *John Bull* captured the mood of the time: 'The brutal bully that maltreats a defenceless woman is, as a rule, a baseless coward, and the dread of retaliation provided for him by the law is the best guard that can be placed on his unruly fists.'

We are now a century and a half on from the time when in England, a women's right not to be beaten by her husband was recognised, if not effectively enforced by law. In the savage, bestial, viciously misogynist world of Islam, wife beating is not only permitted under Sharia law, but in the *Koran,* specifically *recommended,* in Chapter 4, Verse 34. We have encountered it before, but it is worth repeating for the benefit of *dhimmi* feminists:

> 'And for those [wives] on whose part you fear [only fear, not have committed] disobedience, admonish them and keep away from them in their beds and chastise them. Then if they obey you, seek not a way against them. Surely, Allah is High and Great'. (Some translations use 'beat' instead of 'chastise', which is the correct translation of the Arabic *idrib*'.

There is also a passage in the *Koran* where Allah relates how he commanded Job (in Arabic *Ayyub*) to 'take in your hand a green branch and beat her [his wife] with it'. (38: 41-43) Unlike in the civilised world, where wife beating not punished by the law is a shame and outrage of the distant past, Muslim clerics uphold it today just as it was written in the book of the prophet:

> The *Koran* says 'and beat them'. This verse is of a wondrous [sic...this is not a misprint] nature. There are three types of woman with whom a man cannot live unless he carries a rod on his shoulder. The first type is a girl who was brought up this way...So she becomes accustomed to beatings. We pray Allah will help her husband later. He will only get along with her if he practises wife beating. The second type of woman is the one who is condescending towards her husband and ignores him. With her, too, only a rod will help. The third type is a twisted woman who will not obey her husband unless her oppresses her, beats her, uses force against her, and overpowers her with his voice. (Qatar TV, August 27, 2002. After bribing a sufficient number of FIFA officials, Qatar was selected as the venue for the 2022 World Cup.)

And more recently:

> Islam instructs a man to beat his wife as a last resort before divorce so that she will mend her ways, treat him with kindness [sic] and respect and know that her husband has a higher station than her...A good woman, even if beaten by her husband, puts her hand in his and says: 'I will not rest until you are pleased with me'. This is how the Prophet Mohammed taught his women to be. (Al-Nas TV, Egypt, August 17, 2012)

When we compare the unspeakably vile subjugation of wives under Islam today with their status in marital law in the west, we should take note of the fact that whereas in England, male politicians of the mid-nineteenth century wanted to flog men to enforce a law enacted by men to protect women from male violence, today, in at least two Muslim states, Iran and Saudi Arabia, women are flogged by men for alleged infractions of sex and dress codes devised by men. With the right of a Muslim husband to beat and rape his wife or wives set in stone for eternity by no less an authority than Allah and his prophet, it was inevitable that when the United Nations adopted its Declaration on the Elimination of Violence Against Women in 1993, it would meet with organised and determined opposition by a phalanx of Muslim regimes, some today in the forefront of the heroic struggle to eliminate the state of Israel, where wife beating and marital rape are of course illegal. Typical of this resistance was the objection by Iran's theocratic rulers to a resolution of the UN Commission on the Status of Women calling upon all governments to 'condemn violence against women and refrain from invoking any custom, tradition or religious consideration to avoid their obligation with respect to its elimination'.

If the Ayatollahs were to comply with UN policy in this matter, they would have to forgo, amongst other sub-human abuses of women, the popular (amongst men) spectator participatory sport of stoning to death women accused of violations of Sharia law sex codes. The *Koran* also sanctions, in fact, encourages, the stealing (that is, abduction) of a non-Muslim woman from her previous owner, be he husband, father or brother, and her sexual subjugation by her new one, so becoming what it calls the 'spoils of war'. This is an Islamic euphemism for what is the most vicious, intrusive and hence degrading form of slavery, sexual slavery.

First, as regards slavery *per se,* (though the Bible, in all its versions, prefers the milder and more politically correct, but inaccurate 'servant'), Timothy 1, Chapter 6, Verse 1 says: 'Let as many servants as are under the yoke [sic] count their master's worthy of all honour, that the name of God and his doctrine be not blasphemed'. Honour those who place you 'under the yoke'…such is God's 'doctrine'. And to rebel against the yoke is to blaspheme. And we know what happened to blasphemers. Then we have Paul again, this time to Titus: 'Exhort servants to be obedient unto their own masters, and to please them well in all things; not answering again'. (Chapter 2, Verse 9) In other words, grin and bear it, and suffer in silence. Peter 1, in Chapter 2, Verse 18, if anything goes further, demanding submission to masters cruel no less than kind: 'Servants, be subject to your masters with all fear; not only to the good and gentle, but also to the froward'. Currently available English translations of the *Koran,* unlike those of the Bible, have no problem with retaining the original word slave. Its usage also occurs in those verses that deal with the rules for the sexual enjoyment of captured women, though in this particular verse, selected because here the issue is simply one of slavery *per se,* male slaves are also referred to: 'And marry those among you who are single and those who are fit among your male slaves and your female slaves.' (Chapter 24, Verse 32) A *Hadith* of Bukhari provides an insight not only into the kind of treatment a slave might expect at the hands of his (or her) owner, but also the nature of the sexual relations between a Muslim man and his wife (or wives). Mohammed is reported as saying: 'It is not wise [sic] of you to lash [sic] his wife like [sic] a slave, for he might sleep with her the same evening'. (6: 60: 466) When it comes to the abduction of women for the purposes of sex, both the Bible and the *Koran* are quite explicit. First Deuteronomy:

> And when the Lord thy God hath delivered it [a captured city] unto thy hands, thou shall smite every male therefore with the edge of the sword: But the women and the little ones and the cattle, and all that is in the city, even all the spoil therefore, shalt thou take under thyself, and thou shalt eat the spoil [sic. like the *Koran*] of thine enemies, which the Lord thy God hath given thee. (Chapter 20, Verses 13 and 14)

The fate of the abducted women is described in Chapter 21, Verses 10-13:

> When thou goest forth to war against thine enemies, and the Lord thy God hath delivered them unto thine hands, and thou hath taken them captive, and several among the captives a beautiful woman, and hast a desire unto her, that thou wouldst have her to be thy wife; then thou shall bring her home to thine house; and she shall shave her head, and pare her nails; and she shall put the raiment of her captivity from off her, and shall remain in thine house, and bewail her father and mother a full month; and after that thou shall go in unto her, and be her husband, and she

114

shall be thy wife.

First comes abduction as spoils of war, then 'going in unto her', that is to say, rape, accompanied by forced marriage. It sounds like the Islamic State, or the Afghan and Pakistan outback but, as every observant Jew and practising Christian should know, it is the Old Testament. Ownership also looms large in Deuteronomy's rulings on rape within the community, that is, according to whether the victim belongs to her husband or her father. But location also plays its part, as does the behaviour of the victim. In the first case, 'if a man be found lying with a woman married to an husband, then both of them shall die'. (22: 22) Next, 'if a damsel that is a virgin be betrothed unto an husband, and a man find her in the city, and lie with her; then ye shall bring them both out unto the gate of that city and ye shall stone them with stones that they die, the damsel, because she cried not, being in the city'. (22: 23,24) But 'if a man find a betrothed damsel in the field, and the man force her, and lie with her; then the man only that lay with her shall die', obviously because no-one can hear her protests. (22: 25) Finally, there is the case where a man rapes an unbetrothed virgin: 'Then the man that lay with shall give unto the damsel's father fifty shekels of silver, and she shall be his wife; because he hath humbled her, he may not put her away [i.e., divorce her] all his days.' (22: 28,29)

Now the *Koran*: 'Oh prophet! We have made it lawful to thee thy wives to whom thou hast paid their dowers and those whom thy right hand possesses [i.e., slaves] out of the prisoners of war whom Allah has assigned to thee'. (Chapter 30, Verse 50) And: 'O Prophet! We have made it lawful to thee thy wives who thou hast paid their dowries, and those whom thy right hand possesses [i.e., concubines] from among those whom Allah has given thee as gains of war...' (33: 51) The reading here implies a private arrangement between Allah and Mohammed to satisfy the prophet's legendary sexual appetites. The following verse suggests a more general application, one which sanctions the rape of enslaved married women, since they previously belonged to infidel men: '...all married women are forbidden unto you, save those whom you right hand possesses.' (4:24) Then there is Chapter 8, Verse 69: 'But now enjoy what ye took in war, lawful and good.' All told there are four verses which sanction the sexual enslavement of infidel women. That is why Muslim theologians and clerics down the ages have upheld this Allah-sanctioned right to the human spoils of war, not least, captured and enslaved women. They continue to do so to this day. On June 8, 2011 the Egyptian cleric Abu Ishak Al-Heweny expounded to a live and internet audience the finer points of Sharia law as they pertain to this question:

When I talk about religion, what I say is fixed...according to the rulings of Jihad, if we fight polytheists, the Prophet Mohammed told the military commander he should do three things. This *hadith* appears in the Muslim collection. If you fight polytheist enemies, offer them three options: first call them to join Islam. If they join Islam, let them be...If they refuse to join Islam, they should pay the *jizya* poll tax [that is, become *dhimmis*]. If they refuse to pay the *jizya*, seek the help of Allah and fight them...The basic pre-requisite of Jihad is that your enemy be non-Muslim. If we are the winners, it is only natural [sic] to impose the rules of Islam on the country we invaded. According to the rules of Islam, all the people in that country become booty and prisoners of war: the women [just for once, women come first], the men, the children, the money, the homes, the fields. All these become the property of the

Islamic State. [sic] What is the fate of the prisoners of war according to the Sharia? Since they constitute booty, they should be divided between the *mujahidin*. According to the *hadith*, the law states that anyone who did not participate in the raid does not get a share of the booty...Let's say we invaded a country with a population of half a million...Let's say there were some 100,000 *mujahidin*. That's it then. Each *mujahidin* gets five of them...You can take two men, two women, and a child, or the other way round. You divide them up. Great. {sic} As soon as this system is in place, there has to be a slave market where you can sell slaves, slave girls and children...We are talking about the rulings that are fixed in the *Koran*.

This is not the Saudi desert of the 7th century, the birth place of Islam, or the Islamic State, the Taliban or Boko Haram, but 'moderate' Egypt, in the year 2011. One of the world's leading modern authorities on Islamic law, Majid Khadduri, had this to say on the same subject in his *War and Peace in the law of Islam:*

The term spoil (*ghanima*) is applied specifically to property acquired by force from non-Muslims. It includes, however, not only property (moveable and non-movable) but also persons, whether in the capacity of *asra* (prisoners of war) or *sabi* (Women and children) ...If the slave were a woman, the master was permitted to have sexual connection [sic] with her as a concubine.

In other words, rape her. Open season? Not quite. It seems that the warriors of the Islamic State, schooled though many are in their holy texts, mistakenly assumed that they had given them what amounted to a blank cheque from Allah to seize and rape any non-Muslim women they fancied. *Fatwa* Number 64, issued on January 29, 2015 by the ISIL Committee of Research and *Fatwas*, disabused them of this understandable error. Its preamble reads as follows:

One of the graces which Allah has bestowed upon the State of the caliphate is the conquest of large surface areas of the country, and one of the inevitable consequences of the jihad of establishment is that women and children of infidels will become captives of Muslims. Consequently, it is necessary to clarify some rules pertaining to captured prisoners to avoid any violations in dealing with them.

As we have seen, Allah has rules for nearly everything, and rape is no exception. Of the 15 rulings on Muslim rape etiquette (and we are not dealing here with Muslim marital rape) perhaps the most revealing is number five:

If the owner [sic] of a female captive, who has a daughter suitable for sexual intercourse [i.e., rape] has sexual relations with the latter, he is not permitted to have sexual intercourse with [i.e., rape] her mother and she is [therefore] permanently off limits to him. Should he have intercourse with [i.e., rape] her mother, then he is not permitted to have intercourse with [i.e., rape] her daughter and she is to be off limits to him.

The interested reader can access the entire *fatwa* online, so let us close with the fifteenth and final ruling. When trading in or selling on a sex slave, the following rule applies: 'The owner of a female captive should not sell her to an individual whom he knows will treat her badly or do unto her what Allah has forbidden'. Who says Islam treats its women badly?

II

From Rotherham to Cologne

Europe: December 31, 2015. In Germany, in the cities of Cologne, Leipzig, Berlin, Bremen, Bielefeld, Stuttgart, Frankfurt, Dusseldorf and Hamburg, and in 12 of Germany's 16 states, and elsewhere in Europe in Helsinki, Zurich, Malmo, Kalmar, Vienna, Innsbruck and Salzburg, as in other cities and towns across Germany and Europe, the traditional New Year's Eve celebrations get under way. This year, the festivities in these locations are joined by some of the continents recently arrived guests from Muslim lands at the (illegal) invitation of German Chancellor Angela Merkel, all seeking refuge, so we are assured, from the terrors inflicted on them by their co-religionists. According to reports that in a sinister throwback to earlier times, were initially subject to a total news black-out and only made public by the media after a delay of five days, in Hamburg, women reported more than 400 assaults, and in Cologne, 2,000, including not only robbery and sexual assault, but rape, by men whom victims and police described as 'of Arab or North African appearance', in other words, Muslims. In cities across Germany, in all, more than 3,000 women were the victims of premeditated attacks, many sexual and including rape, by Muslim migrants. By July 2016, there had been only four convictions. Two of the four, both Muslims, after being described by the presiding judge as 'animals', walked from the court laughing after receiving *suspended* sentences.

As in other cities subjected to organised Muslim sex attacks, the initial Cologne police report nevertheless said the evening in the city centre had been 'relaxed' with a 'jolly atmosphere'! No less relaxed was the initial reaction the next day of the Minister President of Baden-Wurttemberg, Winfried Kretschmann. In an interview with *Die Welt,* he dismissed as absurd fears of an Islamisation of Germany. 'If you look at the facts, this fear is unfounded. We have a stable democracy and a free society. State and religion are separated [not strictly true]. How should Muslims, who represent a minority, Islamise our society?' The 'fact' was that the previous evening the centre of one Germany's largest cities had been well and truly 'Islamised', and those responsible for defending Germanys 'stable democracy' and 'free society' had not only done nothing to prevent it but even tried to suppress reports of what had occurred.

However, one local politician, perhaps better appraised of the real state of affairs in Cologne, begged to differ with Kretschmann's assessment of the threat, insisting quite truthfully that the city centre had been turned into a 'no go' zone for German women. Yet as of January 6, police had made no arrests, and admitted that none were likely in the future. This was because on the night of the attacks, they followed the usual practice when dealing with troublesome Muslim migrants of avoiding confrontations, allowing them, many of whom were reportedly drunk, to gather in large numbers at the station prior to launching their assaults. Then, just as they did in Rotherham, the police allowed the sex attacks to proceed without any restraining action on their part, a decision in all probability fuelled by the same fear as in the UK that protecting women from Muslim sex criminals could lead to career-threatening accusations of Islamophobia and racism. Even after the attacks, Cologne police lyingly told inquiring journalists that the night had passed off peacefully. Rather hypocritically, in view of the fact that the Cologne police were simply following guide lines issuing from his own department, Interior Minister Thomas de Maziere complained that 'the police cannot operate like this'.

For at least a decade previous to these attacks, not only the police, but Germany's courts had been following a policy of either ignoring or adjusting to Muslim ways. In 2006, after years of violent abuse, a Moroccan-born woman separated from her Muslim husband and sued for divorce. Forced to leave their marital home, the husband then issued death threats against his estranged wife. Her response was to apply through her lawyer for a speedy divorce, hoping that this would put an end to the threats. In January 2007, the judge handling the case rejected the application on the grounds that the *Koran* permits a husband to discipline his errant spouse, and therefore this was not sufficient cause for a speedy divorce: 'The exercise of the right to castigate [sic] does not fulfil the hardship criteria as defined by paragraph 1565 of German Federal law.'

If Judges were prepared to defer to Muslim cultural practices and indeed Sharia law where women were concerned, why not the police? Just how the police did operate in Cologne, and what they confronted, only became public knowledge when on January 7, the mass circulation tabloid *Bild* published a leaked report by a senior police officer who witnessed the sex assaults in Cologne on the night of December 31. He described in his report how young men involved in the attacks mocked and humiliated police by tearing up their resident permits, one of their number saying as he did so, 'I am Syrian, you have to treat me kindly. Mrs Merkel invited me.' Which of course she did. Another rioter tearing up his permit taunted, 'You can't do anything to me, I can get a new one tomorrow'. Which of course he could. The officer making the report had been in command of a unit of 100 extra police drafted into Cologne's city centre to help cope with what was regarded as an emergency situation, one 'far more serious than previously thought', in which 'there could have been fatalities'. 'Relaxed'? 'Jolly'? The report continues:

> When we arrived, our vehicles were pelted with firecrackers. About a thousand people, mostly males of an immigrant background, were indiscriminately throwing fireworks and bottles into the crowd. Around 10.45 PM, the station forecourt filled with people of an immigrant background. Women literally had to run the gauntlet through a mass of drunken men, in a way you can't imagine. We concluded that the situation threatened chaos or serious injury, if it didn't lead to fatalities...Many women came to officers shocked and crying and reported sexual assaults. Police officers were unable to respond to all the events, assaults and offences. There were just too many at the same time...

It also emerged that the police had prior knowledge of the impending assaults. On December 29, Peter Roemer, the officer in charge of Cologne security, wrote in a report that migrants were planning 'tumultuous [sic] offences and massive thefts' in the city centre, and that 'larger crowds and a larger consumption of alcohol is to be expected with the typical dangers associated with them.' The 'offender clientele [sic]' who were expected to be the cause of the 'tumultuous offences' were described as 'substantially North African repeat offenders'. So not only were the attacks known to be impending, but also the identity of those who were about to carry them out. Yet after they happened, both were initially denied. And to cap it all, no special measures were taken to deal with the attacks until it was too late. In total, 2000 assaults…but on the night, no arrests and, as of March 5, only one conviction…for robbery. So initial police reports were able to claim that as in previous years, everything had passed off peacefully. The police swung into action however when days later, German men vented their anger against the assaults on their wives, sisters, girl-friends and daughters, only to be drenched with water cannons, while *dhimmi* feminists, unmolested by police, protested against… 'racism'.

Some, as we shall see, simply refused to believe migrants/refugees had been responsible the assaults, even though in their aftermath, one police officer revealed that his colleagues had been given 'strict instructions not to report offences by refugees' (shades of Labour Home Secretary Jacqui Smith), and two local Cologne newspapers, the *Express* and the *Kolner Stadtanzeiger*, both carried the story that an internal police report had identified large numbers of the attackers as recent migrants from Syria, Iraq and Afghanistan. The same 'hands off' policy for migrants was also being applied in Frankfurt, where a senior police officer told *Bild* that 'for offences of criminal suspects who have a foreign nationality, and are reported [to be] in a [refugee] reception centre, we put the case on the desk immediately to the side'- just like in Rotherham and several dozen other towns and cities across England. Based on eyewitness and victim accounts, internal police reports and other leaks, it is beyond any doubt the case that that nearly all, if not all sex and other assaults were carried out by Muslims. That is why the question of their race, or rather, races, is irrelevant. What took place was not the product of so-called ethnicity or skin colour but of a particular religion. Misogyny is not inherited via male genes, as some feminists claim, but from and via a culture, in this case, an Islamic one.

Perhaps because of these and other similar revelations from *bona fide* police sources, the Interior Ministry came clean and revealed that of 31 men suspected of committing assaults of one kind or another in Cologne on New Year's Eve, all but two were foreigners, including 18 asylum seekers. Of the 29, four were Syrians, and one an Iraqi. The other 24 were from countries where there were no war zones: five Iranians, eight Moroccans, nine Algerians, one Serb (!) and one from the USA (!!). Again, the common denominator is not 'ethnic origin', a term much favoured by those who want to avoid using religious descriptions, but Islam. So, in this admittedly small sample, only five were from countries where there were conditions that generate genuine refugees, and no fewer than 24 from countries where no such conditions existed. Why then was this second and much larger group awarded refugee status? If it had not, there would have been at least 24 fewer sexual predators on the loose in Cologne on the night of December 31. After such a spectacular and, for Germany of all countries, humiliating failure to enforce the law on its own streets and protect its women from an army of sexual assailants, a scapegoat had to found. With the storm of criticism of the 'softly softly' method of dealing, or rather not dealing with migrant sex crimes growing louder by the hour, the buck was passed down to Cologne's police chief, Wolfgang Albers who, it was subsequently claimed, had covered up the whole affair because it was 'politically awkward'…just as his counterparts did in Rotherham and a score or more police authorities across England. He was summarily sacked on January 8, as a punishment for implementing what he believed was the official, if never stated policy for handling migrant anti-social behaviour and, possibly on his own initiative, for falsifying reports on the events of December 31. One can indeed sympathise with the predicament that faced Cologne's police chief and his understaffed and politically hamstrung force on the night of December 31, faced as they were with a thousand-strong army of young Muslim men intent on seizing and enjoying their 'spoils of war'. The assaults, aimed exclusively at young women and teenage girls, were conducted with military precision, with groups of thirty or so attackers targeting and overpowering their prey, and then subjecting them to sexual assaults, including rape, and robbing them of their possessions. A man described how his partner and 15-year daughter were sexually assaulted outside the station: 'The attackers grabbed her [his daughter's} and my partner's breasts and groped between their legs'.

There is a video on YouTube of a far worse attack, in which a gang of twenty or more migrants surround a young woman and drag her screaming down some steps into what looks like an underpass. Police are nowhere to be seen. What happened next, we can easily imagine. Some women were not only groped, raped and robbed, but had lighted fireworks thrown at them, one being stuffed inside a young English woman's clothes, leaving her, she said, 'scarred for life'. There were no reports of any attacks on German men. True to past form, the Jihadis preferred to attack 'soft' targets.

As outrage at the news spread across Germany, Justice Minister Heiko Mass described the attacks, according to Cologne police pre-arranged and co-ordinated by mobile phones, as 'a completely new dimension of organised crime'. Departing from her mantra that Germany has nothing to fear from the influx of more than one million Muslim migrants, even Merkel found herself obliged to promise that the perpetrators of the 'disgusting assaults' would be brought to book 'without regard to their background or origin'. But then she added the caveat that it was 'completely improper to link a group that appeared [sic] to come from North Africa with [sic] the refugees'. Then why the reference to 'background and origin? The reason why they 'appeared' to come from North Africa, was because they *did* come from North Africa, unless, that is, they were Germans disguised as such with the intention of inciting yet more Islamophobia. And why was it wrong to 'link' them with the refugees'? Surely, they *were* refugees, or at least claimed to be such, and it was Merkel who had invited them in.

Once the German media broke its deplorable self-imposed silence on the events of December 31, the taboo on discussing and challenging Merkel's Muslim migrant policy was dead and buried. It now became possible for mainstream politicians to talk of 'background and origin' without being automatically accused of Islamophobia or, however illogically, of racism. The already-mentioned Justice Minister Heiko Mass, whose Social Democratic Party had hitherto been the most supportive of Merkel's 'open door' policy, had evidently had enough. 'Nobody can tell me this [the Cologne assaults] was not co-ordinated or prepared, when such a horde meets to commit such criminal acts, it looked like it was planned in some form.' The Bavarian Christian Social Union Interior Affairs spokesman Stephan Mayer, whose party is also a member of Merkel's coalition, warned it would be 'fatal' to remain silent when such crimes were being committed by those 'to whom we have granted a generous welcome in our country'. Indeed, especially since it was at Munich's main railway station that his fellow Bavarians, rather naively in retrospect, had greeted with applause, embraces, banners and balloons the first wave of migrant arrivals. Ordinary Germans, who for the best part of a year had borne the brunt of the consequences, all negative, of their establishment's policy of encouraging illegal and uncontrolled Muslim migration, were enraged. Non-*dhimmi* women took to the streets holding placards that asked, 'Mrs Merkel, where are you?' Where indeed.

As if co-ordinated migrant sex assaults in seven German cities were not enough embarrassment for Merkel, on January 10 she learned that the Muslim terrorist who attacked a Paris police station on the first anniversary of the *Charlie Hebdo* massacre had, like two of the assassins involved in the Paris massacres of November 2015, passed through Germany posing as an asylum seeker *en route* to his suicide mission, having previously stayed in a refugee centre in western Germany. The worst blow all to Merkel's illegal migrant policy however fell the next day, when after a week of dissemblement, prevarication, leaks to the press and frantic back-peddling, the Interior Ministry finally came clean on those responsible for the attacks of December 31: 'Based on testimony from witnesses, the report [presumably a revised and more truthful one] from the Cologne police and descriptions by the Federal police, it looks [sic] as if people with a migration background were almost exclusively [sic] responsible for the criminal acts.'

However, 'improper' Merkel believed it was to say the sex assaults were the work of migrants, finally the truth was out…they were, 'almost exclusively'. Even so, the devoutly Lutheran and politically conservative Merkel found what was on the face of it, highly improbable support for her resistance to acknowledging migrant, and therefore her own responsibility for the events of December 31. It came, again almost exclusively, from women, mainly *dhimmi* feminists, who were far more concerned with protesting against what they claimed was the greater threat of racism than denouncing gang rape, demanding justice for its victims and better police protection for women. Whereas a number of male politicians and government officials had been prepared to unequivocally condemn the attackers and, equally to the point, to say who they were, with one exception, this was not the case with women politicians and social activists. Cologne's ultra Islamophile Mayor, the aptly named Henrietta Wreker, like Merkel, warned against 'jumping to conclusions' about the identity of their attackers, even though both their victims and the police were certain as to what that identity was. Echoing Merkel's disclaimer almost word for word she said 'It's completely improper [sic] to link a group that appeared [sic] to come from north Africa with the refugees'. 'Improper'…. but not untrue, as her police, belatedly, confirmed. One of the sex attackers, when later questioned by police, said 'I am a Syrian. You have to treat me kindly. [sic] Mrs Merkel invited me'…which she did. And yes, a leaked police report did indeed say said that 'some of the Cologne sex attackers claimed to be Syrian refugees.' One police officer told a Cologne newspaper, 'we arrested 15 people. These people have been in Germany for only a few days or weeks'. As tourists? No. 14 were from Syria and one from Afghanistan. The officer continued: 'This is the truth, even if it hurts. I had young women standing next to me crying because they no longer had any underwear after the mob had spat them out.' Police found sheets of paper with Germany translations of Arabic phrases to facilitate their amorous approaches to German women, such as 'Busty I want to kiss you', 'I will kill you' and 'I want to fuck'. Shades of the Arabian Nights.

122

If Wreker was justified in expressing her doubts about the identity of the attackers, she needed to explain how it was that before the arrival in 2015 of one million mainly young male Muslims, no such events even remotely resembling these had ever occurred before in post-war Germany. Instead of denouncing as barbarians the (Muslim) men who organised and carried out the assaults, she placed the responsibility for preventing them in future on their potential victims. Her solution, justly treated with derision (by men but not feminists) was to propose that women should 'stick together in groups' and 'keep at a certain distance of more than an arm's length' from men 'with whom they do not have a trusting relationship'. (A group of young women did in fact adopt this very tactic but succumbed to vastly superior numbers of migrant attackers.) What could be easily inferred from Wreker's anti-rape precautions is that if women failed to follow this advice by continuing to behave normally, potential sexual predators could assume they were 'asking for it', a presumption shared by many Muslim men. So although the problem was presented as of one male behaviour in general (and not men of a certain religious persuasion, culture and age) it was women, the potential victims, and not men, their potential assailants, who had to change their behaviour. And this from a woman who doubtless regards herself as a full-on feminist.

As, thanks to Merkel, the Muslim rape rate soared in Germany during 2016, public officials offered women advice on how best to protect themselves. One suggested that they should stay indoors, another that they should stop wearing high heels so that they could make good their escape from a potential attacker. Anything rather than confront the issue...Muslim misogyny. The idea that women had to change their public behaviour now that Merkel's Muslim guests were on the prowl had already been proposed in a much more extreme form by the Norwegian anthropologist and Sharia apologist Unna Wikan back in 2014. Norwegian woman had been 'inviting rapes' (sic) by 'acting [sic] like Norwegian women' instead of 'internalising that we live in a multicultural society and accommodating that fact. In most Muslim countries, it is assumed that the woman is at fault for being raped, and it is only fair [sic] that Muslims bring these kinds of opinions with them when they move to Norway.' Will the reader please read this again, several times, before continuing, and, as they do so, keep reminding themselves that this was written by a highly-educated European woman.

Following this prescription, what Wikan called 'multiculturalism' becomes in reality the imposition of a misogynistic Islamic monoculturalism, one which requires the adoption by the host nation of the culture and mores of the Muslim male migrant. Hence her demand that Norwegian women should cease thinking and acting like (emancipated) Norwegian woman and start thinking and acting like (subjugated) Muslim women. If they don't, they will only have themselves to blame if they are raped ('fairly') by Muslim men. Another Norwegian academic, the historian of religion Hanne Herland, also placed the blame for Norway's spectacular increase in rape squarely on the culture of the victims. 'Africans rape when they come to Norway', she explained, because they 'discover what a low value Western culture places on a woman's sexuality', presumably, because unlike where they come from, it outlaws rape and wife-beating. Once again, it is 'our fault'.

Canadian Sharia feminists have already begun to move in the direction proposed by Wikan. At their instigation, on February 25, 2016, Ottawa officially celebrated 'Hijab Solidarity Day' with the city's *kuffar* women being urged to sport the Muslim symbol of female oppression by 'walking with our Muslim sisters'. There was a time long ago when feminists would have not have demonstrated their approval of this cowl of servitude, but their solidarity with the brave and genuine feminists in Iran who refuse to conform to dress codes imposed by misogynist Muslim men. Now the solidarity is with the dress code and, necessarily, with the men and the draconian laws which enforce it. Perhaps on future such occasions, Ottawa's *dhimmi* feminists can shift up a gear by holding a Burka Solidarity Day, shuffling around town, heads down and peering through the eye slits of their brand-new burkas. The day's festivities could then be rounded off in Ottawa's central square with an exemplary simulated stoning of an Islamophobic sister who refused to celebrate her subjugation in the approved manner. Lowered down to her waist in a personhole cover, she could be bombarded with papier maché replica Iranian regulation size stones by enthusiastic male Muslim volunteers from the local diaspora.

Token hijab days are all very well, but Canada's feminists still have a long way to go before than can truly claim to have fully embraced the enriching life of a Muslim woman. The ultimate test of their sisterly solidarity would be to take regular thrashings from their male partners…and enjoy it. In Toronto, one the of texts distributed free of charge by the York University Muslim Students Association at its 2015 Annual Islamic Awareness Week (sic) in a section titled 'Wife Disciplining' says the following: 'Submissive or subdued women may even enjoy being beaten at times as a sign of love or concern', while a Montreal imam, Hussein Amer, has defined wife beating as 'a type of education'. If any of Canada's playacting *dhimmi* feminists intend to go the whole hog and convert, as indeed some inadequate, desperate, naïve or just plain stupid women do, then before embarking on this one-way path to marital slavery, listen first to Calgary imam Abdi Hersy advising Muslim husbands of their rights:

> The husband has many rights on his wife. First and foremost, she has to obey you. He comes with the orders. You come with the orders and she has to obey you. She cannot leave the house without your permission.' [He then addresses himself to their wives] You have to choose either Allah or your country. Canada is a feminine [he means feminist] country. So, ladies, the other thing I want to quit from your life is feminism.

Not to be outdone by their transatlantic *dhimmi* sisters, British Sharia feminists acted out a no less ludicrous scene than in Ottawa when, on August 25, 2016, to the certain delight of any Muslim misogynist who may have passed by, they proudly sported their shrouds of submission outside the French embassy in London to protest against the French ban on Islamic swimwear. Their slogan 'wear what you want' presupposed that Muslim woman who cover up their entire bodies in public have in every case freely chosen to do so, something they surely must have known was not the case. If the demonstrators really believed what their slogan said, why then had they not mounted similar protests outside the embassies of the many Islamic countries, in the first place Saudi Arabia and Iran, that not only deny precisely this choice to their Muslim sisters, but inflict on those brave few who do exercise it the cruellest punishments? I think I know the answer. Any such action would be deemed 'Islamophobic'. A matter of days later, a poll found that the UK favoured the banning of the burka by a majority of two to one, while in the Syrian city of Manbij, Muslim women celebrated their liberation by a Kurdish army from Islamic State Sharia tyranny by burning their sartorial symbols of female enslavement.

Another variation on the theme of embracing the Islamic life-style was offered by the former UK race relations industry supremo Trevor Phillips, in comments made after the Cologne events, to the Policy Change 'think tank'. It showed the 'deepest lack of respect' towards Muslims to ask or expect them to change their ways, because 'they see the world differently from us'. But what if these 'ways' include those that were demonstrated in Rotherham for more than thirty years, and Cologne on New Year's Eve, when in both cities they displayed their 'deepest lack of respect' towards *kuffar* girls and women? Coming from another angle, but homing in on the same target, Labour MP Jess Phillips claimed on BBC TV's Question Time that in Birmingham's Broad Street, there was 'every week' a 'very similar situation' to what took place in Cologne, only the culprits were not Muslims. So the problem was men in general, not young male Muslims. Like Rotherham perhaps? If her claim is true, there must be hordes of up to a thousand or so drunken non-Muslim young men gang-raping and robbing young women and girls 'every week' in her Birmingham constituency. Well, not exactly. What she described as 'violence against girls' turned out to be women being 'baited and heckled'. Unpleasant, to say the least, and in certain given cases, quite possibly illegal. But not organised mass physical sexual assault and rape. And local women were quick to deny that Broad Street in any way resembled Cologne on New Year's Eve. Some of her constituents, disgusted by what amounted to a belittling of the Cologne assaults, demanded her resignation.

Finally, there are those who not because of political correctness, but just plain stupidity or even worse, exhibit the symptoms of the Sharia Stockholm Syndrome without themselves having been victims of Muslim sex crime. The classic case is that of Deborah Green, aged 47, a juror in the 2014 trial of the Sheffield Muslim child rapists. After their conviction and sentencing, it transpired that during the trial, she had been writing to one of the rapists, Shakeal Rehman, encouraging him to 'keep you chin up, sexy' and letting him know that in the jury room she was arguing for his acquittal. In the event, her efforts proved in vain. Her 'sexy' child rapist was given a jail term of twelve years. Signing herself 'Dee', other letters offered money to the accused men. When subsequently appearing herself in court on a charge of contempt of court, she explained that she felt sorry for the rapists, and just wanted to make sure they were alright. Could it be that she was hankering after the treatment Rehman had been dealing out to his 13-year-old 'spoil of war'? Because here for sure we have the kind of sad loser who writes to the Yorkshire Ripper with proposals of marriage, or converts to Islam as a last desperate attempt to get a bloke.

To return to Cologne and its Stockholm Syndrome Mayor. With the money-spinning Cologne carnival due in a month, and fears that thousands would keep away for their own safety, Mayor Wreker made the following suggestion, which I assume she expected to be taken seriously: 'We will explain our Carnival much better to people who come from other cultures [sic] so there won't be any confusion [sic] about what constitutes celebratory [sic] behaviour in Cologne, which has nothing to do with sexual frankness [sic!]'. What? Rape is '*sexual frankness*'? And those engaged in it were simply 'celebrating' in their own multicultural fashion a festival that their own religion's calendar does not recognise? The Mayor of Cologne evidently believed in all seriousness that all that was required to avoid any repetition of the New Year's Eve events was to explain to 'confused' Muslim migrants that whatever it might mean in Islamic countries, in Germany, 'celebration' is not another word for rape, or rather, 'sexual frankness'. In line with this policy, in the run-up to the carnival, leaflets (presumably not in German) were distributed explaining to migrants the does and don'ts of celebratory behaviour, among which were not urinating in public and requesting permission for kissing German women. Not everyone appeared to have got the message, because just on the first day of the carnival, despite a massive security presence double that of previous years, police reported 190 arrests, with 22 sexual attacks, including rape, 143 bodily assaults and 30 thefts. Eleven police were injured defending themselves from assaults, and a women TV reporting covering the event was groped while on camera. A case of Muslim 'sexual frankness', or just another migrant 'misunderstanding'? As in the wake of the New Year's Eve assaults, police declined to provide details as to the background of the culprits. And as in other German cities, women continued to be targeted by Muslim men, especially at swimming baths. On March 6, six migrants were arrested by Cologne police after a sexual assault on a 12-year-old girl in a swimming pool.

Handing out leaflets cannot eradicate literally overnight beliefs and patterns of behaviour that have been ingrained in a culture and sanctioned by a religion over centuries. The delusion that it is simply a matter of rectifying a 'misunderstanding', akin perhaps to Brits being reminded to drive on the right-hand side of the road when arriving on the continent, is the result when Sharia feminism meets political correctness. Perhaps the Wrekers of this world feel guilty about what must surely be their initial instinctive revulsion at gang rape, and so feel compelled to demonstrate to all and sundry that they are neither racist nor Islamophobic by devising the most preposterous and self-demeaning arguments to prove it. Though Muslim men were the culprits, it was their intended victims who had to learn to modify their public behaviour or face the consequences. No wonder sales to women of self-defence devices boomed in Germany.

There was however one woman who had the civic courage and honesty to draw the correct conclusions from outrages that are unprecedented in the history of post-Nazi Germany and, save for the Balkans in the 1990s, of the entire western world. Mina Ahdi, who headed the German Council of ex-Muslims, is an Iranian apostate from Islam who has been under a death sentence imposed by the Religion of Peace, Love and Tolerance since 1981. Like many others in her predicament, she is under constant police protection from the attentions of this same Religion of Peace, Love and Tolerance. So understandably, she did not mince her words: 'For them [the Muslim gropers and rapists] women are dirty. They are sex objects to be enjoyed in the home and allowed outside only in a burka in the company of a man.' There spoke the voice of bitter experience, and not *dhimmi* delusion and wishful thinking.

Sharia feminists can always be relied upon on when Muslim men behave badly to deny, divert attention from or excuse Islamic misogyny, and so it proved again in the aftermath of the Cologne sexual assaults. For Wreker, the problem was not Islam, but 'misunderstandings' and men. For others, there was the ever-present danger of racism, German racism. One woman demonstrator held aloft a banner with the slogan 'Against Sexism [is rape just 'sexism'?], against Racism', while young leftist women displayed a large banner demanding a 'Nazi Free Zone' in Cologne *but saying nothing about a rape-free zone.* Had Nazis, German ones that is, been doing the raping, perhaps disguised as migrants to stir up racial tensions? Apparently not. Neither were the young ladies, posing as 'Young Socialist German Workers', alluding to anti-Semitic Muslims who carried out the sex attacks on December 31, because this slogan, was in fact aimed at those 'Nazis', among whom we must we must include Mina Ahdi, who had the temerity to protest against them. As for 'sexism', this term is traditionally reserved by feminists to denote gender-based discrimination against women. However, the issue on this occasion was not one of gender bias, but something much worse, namely one of massive sexual violence against women, *including rape.* So why not a banner that simply said: *Gegen Vergewaltigung* - Against Rape? And why racism? The only racism on display in Cologne, Dusseldorf, Stuttgart, Frankfurt, Berlin, Bremen, Bielefeld and Hamburg on New Year's Eve had been that of Muslims treating white *kuffar* German women as mere objects for sexual gratification. But I have a sneaking suspicion that Muslim racism was not the one that the woman holding the banner had in mind.

Another line of approach was to canvas the idea there were as bad or even worse things that could happen to a German woman than being gang raped (that is, when the rapists are Muslim migrants). In the considered opinion of the (male) Interior Minister of North Rhine-Westphalia, 'what happens on right wing platforms and in chat rooms is at least as awful as the acts of those assaulting the women'. *At least!* Whatever might take place on 'right wing platforms' and in 'chat rooms', it is not gang rape by rampaging mobs of drunken Muslim migrants and, given the choice, with the possible exception of lobotomized Sharia feminists, no woman would think twice before deciding which experience to undergo. There was a time, and it seems so long ago now, when if an official charged with upholding the law were to publicly trivialise the crime of rape, in this case *gang rape*, it would have been regarded as grounds for automatic dismissal, No longer. Today such views, endorsed of course by feminists, are judged to be the acme of enlightened, progressive thinking, and those that dissent from them run the risk of being accused of racism.

While some public figures frantically rummaged around for the most improbable explanations and excuses for Muslim sexual predators, another male commentator distinguished himself by dispensing with excuses altogether. Mass sexual assault by Muslims, including we must always remember, gang rape, must not be seen as a crime, *but as a form of social rebellion.* But let us begin at the beginning. The initial response of the inventor of this theory was to deny that there had been any sexual assaults, and only subsequently, when it was impossible to sustain this lie, did he then find it necessary to celebrate them. Ridiculing reports that Muslim migrants could have been responsible for sex attacks in Cologne on New Year's Eve, *Der Speigel* columnist Jakob Augstein wrote on his Facebook page: 'We are so racist. Everyone immediately wanted to believe that 1,000 North Africans were committing mischief.' Rape was in his book, not 'frankness' but simply 'mischief'. In fact, we have seen that there were others in positions of authority and influence who like Augstein, also refused to believe it. He continues: 'One thousand. This is a fairy tale figure. Just like the three golden hairs of the devil. Or the seven dwarfs. Or the thirteenth fairy.'

Once the scale and nature of the attack, and the number and identity of their perpetrators became impossible to deny, Augstein decided that only option left was to transform his fairy tale mischief-makers into real-life warriors for social justice. Armed with this new truth, he returned to his Facebook page on February 23:

> The victims of Cologne were inferior to their perpetrators only in the immediate moment of the attacks. These women were powerless and helpless at the moment they were assaulted and robbed [by 'seven dwarfs' perhaps?]. But before the attacks and after, they were their [presumably social] superiors.

Now Augstein drew the threads together, leading to the conclusion that the rape of German women by Muslim men is, in its way a kind of (admittedly rough) social justice:

> The lawbreaking [sic] in Cologne brought a brief rupture in the social hierarchy, a reversal of the true balance of power. The reason is that in this moment the relationship between victim and perpetrator [that is to say, the raped and the rapist] was reduced to physical strength [i.e., a gang of thirty men overpower and rape one woman]. In all other respects, the victims of Cologne are superior to their perpetrators [to save his Sharia left blushes, Augstein never once uses the words 'rapists' and 'rape']; in language, nationality, education, social status, wealth, legal certainty, self-confidence.

Now we had three more definitions of rape to add that of Mayor Wrecker's 'sexual frankness'; namely, 'mischief', a 'brief rupture in the social hierarchy' and 'a reversal in the true balance of power'. Perhaps that is also what it was in Rotherham, Sheffield, Oxford, Rochdale, Aylesbury, Keighley, etc etc... We await comment by our Sharia feminists.

In the wake of the attacks, *dhimmi* feminists queued up to denounce the public outcry, such as it was, against the Cologne assaults, one claiming that 'the debate [sic] about Muslim immigrants [surely she means 'refugees'] has reached its recent hysterical [sic] climax'. What she found 'disgusting' was not the rapes, but 'the debate' about the identity of the rapists. She complained of 'lurid descriptions of tattered underwear and fingers to body orifices', oblivious perhaps to the fact that these were accounts of the victims themselves. As to the identity of the perpetrators, which was her sole interest, their 'origin was not clear'. So there is rape and rape, depending on the 'origin' of the rapist. Another from the same stable confessed that 'on New Year's Eve, something happened that I don't really want to talk about'. A feminist who 'doesn't want to talk about' the premeditated and organised sexual assault of women? This is because in the arcane pecking order of 'intersectional', 'identity'- driven 'Third Wave' feminism, Muslim men, rapists or no, rank above white non-Muslim women, even when the former are raping the later. Yet another feminist piled in, arguing that the Cologne attacks had been 'set upon enthusiastically by those who wish to turn emotions against the new arrivals [sic]' and who had in fact 'little respect for women'...who knows, perhaps even less than those who had been sexually assaulting them. Concerned to conform to the already referred to pecking order, she continues: Feminists 'are finding it difficult to speak up about the event [sic]' because 'it might be used to encourage aggression against refugees. I can't say I blame them.' So, better keep *shtum* about organised sexual aggression against her sisters. Now that really is showing respect for women.

Finally, inevitably, we had the Pope, as always in times of stress and tragedy ready to offer kind words of solace, understanding and hope. He urged angry Germans, presumably also those hundreds of fathers, husbands, brothers and boyfriends of as well as the actual victims of sexual assault and rape, 'not to lose the values of humanity however much they prove in some moments of history, a difficult burden to bear'. Such words come all too easily from someone who so far as I am aware, has neither suffered the trauma of being raped (unlike so many sexual victims of his clergy) nor offered sanctuary to a single refugee, and is the head of a State which has as a matter of policy, consistently concealed and protected those of its clergy guilty of sexual abuse of their charges, and at the time of the Holocaust, not only turned a blind eye to the extermination of six million Jews, but did all it could to help those responsible for their murder evade justice by aiding their escape via the Vatican's infamous 'rate line', to sanctuary in Catholic South America and a Muslim Middle East.

But the Pope's exercise in clerical hogwash was not done. Instead of condemning those who, lacking any 'values of humanity', were responsible for the outrages, and advising Germany's Muslim guests to be in future on their very best behaviour, he drew a picture of Germany's migrants that with the best will in the world, few, especially women, who had unwillingly encountered them sexually at first hand, would not easily recognise: 'Many migrants from Africa and Asia see Europe as a beacon for principles such as equality before the law and values inherent in human nature'. But as the 1990 Cairo declaration of the Organisation of the Islamic Conference made very clear, Islam utterly repudiates the idea of human values. All values, all rights, such as they are, come only from Allah (just as for the Pope they come from god) as does the Islamic system of justice, the Sharia, which in its treatment women and infidels likewise rejects the idea of 'equality before the law'.

As for Europe as a 'beacon', judging by their choice of country, the only beacon most migrants are drawn towards is that of a free ride on the welfare states of Germany, the UK and Scandinavia. And data released in January 2016 showed that despite talk of tighter controls, an ever-increasing proportion of migrants arriving in Germany were from countries that in no way can be described as war zones. In just one month, December 2015, 2,300 Algerians and 3,000 Moroccans applied for asylum, compared with 4,000 from the two countries in the whole of 2014. The two questions that have to be asked and answered are, firstly, given that their nationality was known, why were they not refused asylum and returned to their country of origin on arrival in the EU; and, secondly, why were they allowed to travel north from Italy, their country of entry in the EU, through Austria to be illegally admitted by Germany? As of January 2016, only 53 had been returned to their country of origin. This massive official encouragement of the abuse of asylum will for certain lead to its discrediting in the eyes of the public not only in Germany but right across Europe for the foreseeable future, which will be a tragedy for those whose need for it is genuine…exactly what the xenophobic right wants. Well done Merkel, well done Sharia left, well done *dhimmi* Stockholm Syndrome feminists.

Addenda

i

1) In a belated attempt to curb the surge in sex assaults committed by Muslim migrants, on July 7, 2016, the German Bundestag unanimously approved an amendment to the existing law relating to sexual assault, including rape. Hitherto, the relevant law followed the Old Testament principle that a woman had to provide proof that she had physically resisted her assailment. This is now no longer necessary. Sharia law requires the unanimous testimony of four reliable male witnesses that the woman (or girl) had resisted her rapist, while Deuteronomy Chapter 22 requires that in a city, a married woman must cry out and presumably be heard, otherwise she will be stoned to death together with her rapist. If the victim is an unmarried virgin, the rapist is obliged to marry her, and pay 50 silver shekels to her father. However, Jews and Christians today neither approve of nor apply their rape laws, but many Muslims do theirs.

2) According to statistics released by Germany's Federal Criminal Police Office, migrants committed 142,500 crimes in the first six months of 2016, an increase of 40% over the whole of 2015, and at a rate of 380 crimes per day.

3) According to former MI6 head of counter-terrorism Richard Barrrett, as of December 2016, there were in Germany 'hundreds of really extreme terrorists on the books. In addition to that, if you include all the Lander [states] in Germany, they have about 7,000 cases.'

ii

Unlike Germany, France is habituated to Muslim gang rapes, known in the trade as *tournantes*, or 'pass-arounds', which average between 5,000 and 7,000 per year. Even so, one case attracted much outrage, not only for the crime itself, but the leniency shown by the court to its perpetrators. In October 2012, two girls reported to police being repeatedly gang-raped between 1999 and 2005 by on one occasion as many as 50 young males in a Muslim suburb on the outskirts of Paris. When the case came to court, ten men were acquitted, and four found guilty, three receiving suspended sentences, and the fourth, one year in prison that he had already served on remand. All 14 walked from the court free men. In 2002, French and Arab feminists founded the movement *Ni Putes Ni Soumises* – neither whores not doormats - to campaign against Muslim gang rape, only to be promptly denounced, as in the UK after protests against Muslim rape gangs in Rotherham and elsewhere, as Islamophobic by *dhimmi* feminists, male Muslims and leftists

iii

The 'night of the Muslim rapes' broke the spell of collective denial imposed on Germany by its political establishment in the wake of Merkel's illegal decision to invite into her country an unlimited number of Muslim migrants, irrespective of their countries of origin, status and motives. After nearly a week of self-imposed censorship, the press began to report the events and politicians confront the issues that millions of ordinary Germans had been only too well aware of since Merkel opened her door back in the summer of 2015, but about which they had often been afraid to publicly voice their concerns lest they be accused of racism or worse. For obvious reasons, when it came to silencing critics of Merkel's migrant policy, nothing worked better in Germany than the charge that it is Nazi to doubt the wisdom of unlimited Muslim immigration. Starting on January 1, 2016, that tactic no longer worked. A series of opinion polls charted an ever-growing majority of Germans who judged Merkel's open-door policy to have been mistake, and even amongst her own party's voters, a sizable minority who believed she should resign. What follows is a summary of some of the incidents in the month after the Cologne events that continued to force the question of unlimited Muslim migration out into the open, and public comments and official statements that reflected this radical change of mood.

January 1: The International Monetary Fund estimates that 2.6 million more migrants will enter the European Union in the next two years.

January 2: Fighting that breaks out among children as young as 11 at a refugee shelter in Stockach in south Germany is joined by parents. Seven people are injured before police restore order

January 3: The Chairman of the Bremen, north Germany, Police Union, Jochen Kopelke, says that migrants are attacking police with increasing frequency: 'The tone has become extremely aggressive; sometimes the police must apply massive force to get a situation under control.' Bremen Senator Ulrich Maurer says 'the excesses of violence against police officers show that these people have no respect for our constitutional order and its representatives.'

January 3: In one of many similar incidents, more than 50 migrants are involved in a mass brawl at a refugee shelter in Ellwangen, near Stuttgart. Migrants attack each other with fire extinguishers, metal pipes, rocks and stones.

January 3: A leading German economist cites estimates that German taxpayers could pay up to 450 billion euros for the upkeep of the million migrants who arrived in 2015. If as expected a similar number arrive in 2016, in total, the bill would be in the region of one trillion euros.

January 4: *Der Spiegel* and *Bild* both publish a leaked report by a senior police officer that in the centre of Cologne on New Year's Eve, women were forced to 'run a gauntlet' of drunken men 'of a migrant background' to enter or leave the main train station. 'Even the appearance of the police officers and their initial measures did not stop the masses from their actions.'

January 5: Cologne Mayor Henriette Wrecker says: 'There is no [sic] reason to believe that those involved in the sexual assaults in Cologne were refugees'. Cologne Police Chief Wolfgang Albers says: 'At this time we have no information about the offenders.'

January 6: Former Interior Minister Hans-Peter Friedrich says: 'It is scandalous that it took the mainstream media several days to report on the sexual assaults in Cologne.' He adds that the public media were a 'cartel of silence' that exercised censorship to protect migrants from accusations of wrongdoing.

January 7: The charity Refugees Welcome Bonn which organised a Rhine cruise to welcome migrants to Bonn apologises to German female guests who were sexually assaulted by migrants on the boat.

January 10: Three teenage migrants from north Africa try to stone to death two transsexuals in Dortmund. After being rescued by police, one of the victims says: 'I never could have imagined that something like this could happen in Germany.'

January 11: A 35-year-old migrant from Pakistan (sic) sexually assaults a three-year-old girl at a refugee shelter in the Ruhr town of Kamen.

January 12: Following an interview with *Bild*, Christian Democratic Party politician Frank Oesterhelweg is met with outrage from political correctors when he demands that police should be prepared to use force to protect women from sexual assaults by migrants: 'These criminals deserve no tolerance, they have to be stopped by the police. By force if necessary and, yes, you read correctly, even with firearms. An armed police officer has a duty to help a desperate woman. One must, if necessary, protect the victims by means of force: with truncheons, water cannon or firearms.'

January 12: A YouGov poll finds that 62% of Germans believe the number of refugees is too high, up from 53% in November. Most of those opposed are women.

January 13: A 20-year-old Somali migrant is sentenced to four (sic) years in prison for raping an 88-year-old woman in the Rhineland town of Herford. In Gelsenkirchen, also in the Rhineland, four migrants attack a 45-year-old man when he tries to prevent them from raping a 13-year-old girl.

January 14: A Bavarian politician sends a bus load of 31 migrants on a seven-hour journey to Chancellor Markel's office in Berlin as a protest against her open-door policy. Merkel sends them back to Bavaria.

January 14: Unable to guarantee the safety of women revellers, city officials in Rheinberg cancel the annual carnival.

January 15: A 36-year-old migrant sexually assaults an 8-year-old girl in a park in the Rhineland town of Hilden. A 31-year-old Moroccan migrant is arrested after attempting to rape a woman in Dresden. Two women are sexually assaulted by migrants in separate attacks in Mainz. An African migrant sexually assaults a 55-year-old woman in Mannheim.

January 16: A 19-year-old migrant from Afghanistan sexually assaults four (sic) girls between the ages of 11 and 13 at an indoor swimming pool in Dresden. The migrant is arrested and then released. A migrant from Syria sexually assaults a 12-year-old girl in the Rhineland town of Mudersbach. A 36-year-old migrant sexually assaults an 8-year-old-girl in Mettmann, near Dusseldorf.

January 16: A group of between 6 and 8 African migrants are ejected from a discotheque in Offenburg after sexually molesting women clients. They then ambush three people leaving the discotheque with metal rods, street signs and garbage cans.

January 17: Holger Munch, President of the federal Criminal Police, tells *Bild am Sonntag* that the number of crimes in migrant shelters has increased 'significantly' since 2015. Those most responsible are from the Balkans (sic!!) and north Africa, especially Algerians (!), Tunisians (!) and Moroccans (!). Most offences involve physical assaults, with a growing number of homicides and sexual crimes.

January 17: Berlin clergyman Gottfried Martens accuses politicians and church leaders (but of course) of ignoring the persecution of Christians by Muslims in refugee shelters. Christian refugees are facing 'verbal threats, threats with knives, blows to the face, ripped crucifixes, torn bibles, insults of being an infidel, and denial of access to kitchens because of their alleged uncleanness'.

January 18: A migrant from the Sudan who receives 300 euros a month in welfare payments drops his trousers in a Hanover Street and exposes himself, shouting, 'Who are you? You cannot do anything to me. What I cannot get from the state I will steal.' Held for questioning by the police, he is then released.

January 19: A 28-year-old migrant from Iran (sic) pushes a 20-year-old under an oncoming train in Berlin. The woman dies.

January 20: Male migrants invade female changing rooms and showers at two swimming baths in Leipzig. They then jump into the pools in their street clothes. City officials try to supress reports of the incidents, but the story is leaked to the media.

January 22: A report is leaked to *Bild* that migrants are defecating in public swimming pools in the Saxon city of Zwickau. Security cameras film migrants harassing women in a public sauna and storming the female dressing room.

January 22: In Stuttgart, a migrant attempts to rape a 16-year-old girl, and four migrants sexually assault a 23-year-old woman.

January 23: Two migrants sexually assault an 18-year-old woman in Weisbaden, and a 35-year-old migrant sexually assaults a woman in a toilet on a train in Dusseldorf.

January 26: In an interview with the public radio station Deutschlandfunk, retired public media personality Wolfgang Herles reveals that public broadcasters receive 'instructions from above' concerning the reporting of certain topics:

> We have the problem that we are too close to the government. The topics that we cover are determined by the government. But many of the topics the government wants to prevent us from reporting about are more important than the topics they want us to cover. We must report in such a way that serves the European Union and the common good, as it pleases Mrs. Merkel. There are written instructions. Today we are not allowed to say anything negative about the refugees. This is government journalism, and this leads to a situation in which the public loses their trust in us. This is scandalous.

January 26: The Mayor of Freiberg, Dieter Salomon, orders police to crack down on migrants snatching purses and assaulting women in the city's clubs. Migrants are robbing women on the dance floor and raping them in cloakrooms. Club owners say the migrants 'know that nothing will happen to them'.

January 28: *Bild* reports that politicians in Kiel have ordered police to ignore crimes committed by migrants. Similar instructions have been given to police in North Rhine-Westphalia, where Cologne is situated, and Lower Saxony.

January 29: A vocational school in Hamburg cancelled classes for migrants after they sexually harassed dozens of female students.

January 30: A gang of Afghan migrants on a Munich subway train are filmed attacking two elderly men who try to stop them groping a woman.

January 31: Migrants deface more than 40 gravestones at a cemetery in Konstanz with slogans, among them 'Germans out of Syria [sic]', 'Christ is dead' and 'Islamic State'.

On January 1, the Minister President of North Rhine-Westphalia asked what he clearly intended to be understood as a rhetorical question, 'how could Muslims, who represent a minority, Islamise our society?' The events and facts listed above suggest an answer.

On New Year's Eve, 2021, Muslim rape gangs struck again in force, only this time in Italy, at Milan and Turin. As in Cologne and across Germany in 2015, the massed attacks on young women included sexual assaults and robbery. Also as in Germany, police did little or nothing to protect women who were being targeted by what were described as men of 'north African origin'. In Milan, two young women were pushed up against barriers and sexually assaulted by dozens of young men. One said 'I realised they were touching me and we wanted to escape but there were too many of them.' Her friend fell, and at once, she was groped all over her body. As of January 12, although police had CCTV images of some the attackers, there had been no arrests, once again, like Cologne.

F 9 or 19?

References to Mohammed's sexual prowess are legion in the *hadith*, as are those describing his sexual relations with his last wife, Aisha, whom he married when he was 51 and she was six. As to the first, Bukhari 5: 268 records the following superhuman display of sexual stamina: 'The prophet used to visit all his wives in round, during the day and the night and there were eleven in number. I asked Anas, "has the prophet strength for it?" Anas replied, "we used to say the Prophet had the strength of thirty men".' We must assume that the need for relief from the burdens of leadership entitled the Prophet to exceed by seven the number of wives he permitted to his followers. Bukhari, regarded by all schools of Islam as the most reliable of all the *hadith* collections, says this of his sexual relations with Aisha: 'Narrated Aisha, that the Prophet married her when she was six years old and he consummated his marriage when she was nine years old, and then she remained with him for nine years [until his death]'. (Bukhari: *Book of Wedlock, hadith* Number 64)

With numerous other *hadith* collections telling the same story of a middle-aged man having his holy way with a nine old child, this was a challenge the Sharia left could not afford to ignore. So on September 17, 2012, the Islamophile *Guardian* carried a feature by the *dhimmi* feminist Miriam Franceois-Cerrah, the purpose of which was to combat 'Islamophobic' criticisms of Mohammed's sexual conduct by situating it in what she regarded as its proper historical and cultural context. Consequently, calling the Prophet a paedophile was a 'slander'. 'Aisha may [sic] have been young, but she was not young for the time.' Well, that's all right then. Slavery, torture, capital punishment, child labour and a lot else we, or at least most of us, now abhor was also the norm 'for the time'. See how post-modernist cultural relativism sits so easily with, and re-enforces, moral relativism or, as in this case, moral nihilism. This extraordinary article can be accessed on line, so I will cite only its conclusion. Having argued, without citing any alternative sources, that all *hadith* accounts of Aisha's age are unreliable, and that the consummation of her marriage could have occurred when she was as old as 19 (sic!!!), Francois-Cerrah nevertheless was prepared to claim that these very same unreliable sources mysteriously became totally reliable when they described their 'loving and egalitarian relationship, which set the standard for reciprocity, tenderness [sic] and respect enjoined by the *Koran*.' How naïve can one get? 'Egalitarian'? Could she be alluding to the verse (Chapter 4: 34) which says 'men are guardians over women because Allah has made some of them excel others'? 'Tenderness' and 'reciprocity', when the same verse advocates wife beating and Chapter 2, Verse 223, marital rape? Yes...they were normal 'for the time' too. And for many Muslim men, they still are.

G Under the Ayatollahs

'Those who know nothing of Islam pretend that Islam counsels against war. Those who say this are witless…I spit on the foolish souls that make such a claim.' Ayatollah Khomeini, *Islam is not a Religion of Pacifists.*

I

The Iranian theocracy is not only admired by the Sharia left for its resolute stand against the American 'Great Satan', and of course the 'Zionist entity' that it says it will one day 'wipe off the map'. Some of the Sharia left's most prominent representatives have gone beyond praise by actually serving as its paid broadcasters on Iran's English language channel 'Press TV'. Amongst those so honoured are, as of writing, the current Labour Party Leader Jeremy Corby who, in the year 2012, as an MP, registered four payments totalling £20,000, as remunerations for appearances on the State-funded channel. When these payments from the murderous theocracy came to light, Corbyn's cynical response was to quip that '£20,000 is not a lot of money'. Well, that all depends on one's personal circumstances. Corbyn is a multi-millionaire currently drawing an annual salary of £79,458 as an MP, £49,191 as Leader of Her Majesty's Opposition, sundry sums for extra-parliamentary engagements and activities, and an undisclosed income from two pensions. Being paid £5,000 a time for a four hour appearance on an Islamic TV chat show in a comfortable studio in west London, which works out at £1,250.00 per hour is, all but devotees of the Corbyn cult would surely agree, a different proposition to the pittance - at a rate of no more than 50p an hour, 2,500 times less than Corbyn's - paid to those workers who in the non-union sweat shops of Haiti, Bangladesh and Nicaragua, manufactured the Corbyn T shirts that selling at £10.00 a time, raised £100,000 to fund Corbyn's election campaign for the Labour leadership.

Interviewed on BBC TV by Andrew Marr on January 28, 2018, and asked about his employment by Press TV, inveterate liar that he is, Corbyn claimed that he had worked for the station 'a very long time ago', whereas his last appearance had been on August 12, 2012, even though he falsely claimed that he stopped working for Press TV when his employers violently supressed Iran's green movement (10,000 arrests and over a hundred killed) which arose in response to the rigging of the Presidential elections of 2009, the year Corbyn made his *first*, not last appearance on Press TV. (This is confirmed by his declaration in the House of Common Register of MPs financial interests) What was worse, Corbyn continued to work for the station even though in December 2011 it had been fined £100,000 and banned from broadcasting in the UK by Ofcom for screening a forced confession, extracted under torture, of an Iranian political prisoner. (Press TV is not the only Islamic broadcaster to get into Ofcom's bad books. In August 2021, it took to task Sheffield-based but Pakistan-owned Link FM for transmitting a call to Jihad in Arabic.)

Useful idiot Corbyn's last appearance on the channel came *nine months later*, on August 12, 2012, and can be seen on YouTube. And what an appearance it was, shared with Muslim convert Lauren Booth, Islamophile Cherie Blair's sister. One of the topics discussed was a Jihadi attack in Egypt's Sinai that left sixteen police officers dead. Corbyn, in denial mode about Muslim involvement in an act of terrorism, predictably pinned the blame on Israel: '...you have to look at the big picture [Always the 'big picture']. In whose interests is it to destabilise the new government in Egypt? In whose interest is it to kill Egyptians, other than Israel, concerned at the growing closeness between Palestine and the new Egyptian government?'

As we have seen, this kind of pseudo-reasoning proliferates on a number of Corbynista websites, where the hand of Mossad is detected behind every act of terrorism, beginning with 9/11, carried out in the name of Islam. Booth naturally endorsed the Jewish conspiracy theory advocated by Corbyn. The evidence which she presented for it was laughable: 'Would a Muslim go against his Egyptian brother?' To which Corbyn, warming to the idea, replied 'It seems a bit unlikely that would happen during Ramadan, to put it mildly, and I suspect *the hand of Israel* in this whole process of destabilisation.' (emphasis added)

Also to put it mildly, both Booth and Corbyn were talking bollocks, specifically, anti-Semitic, *Protocols* conspiracy theory bollocks. First, Booth's ludicrous claim that Muslims do not kill their Muslim brothers. In Egypt alone, in the upheavals which followed the so-called 'Arab Spring' that began in 2012, nearly 5,500 Egyptians were killed by their Muslims brothers. Taking a wider view, in the war between two Islamic states, Iraq and Iran, which began in 1980 and ended in 1988, the number of deaths...all, *pace* Booth, the result of Muslims killing their Muslim brothers...was in excess of half a million. Thousands have died in Afghanistan as a result of terrorist operations by the Taliban and clashes between the Taliban and government forces. In Yemen, a proxy war rages between Houthi rebels, sponsored by Iran, and government forces backed by Saudi Arabia. In Syria and Iraq, the death toll generated by the emergence of the Islamic State and clashes between a range of Islamic factions that have been at each other's throats for centuries runs into the tens, possibly even hundreds of thousands. Algeria's ten-year civil war, from 1992 to 2002, cost at least 50,000 Muslim lives, and Saddam's genocide of Kurds, an estimated another 100,000. The Religion of Peace. The University of Maryland's Global Terrorism data base has recorded 167,221 terrorist fatalities between 2001 and 2015, 75% of which occurred in 25 Muslim majority countries. And so on. Yet Booth tells us that Muslims do not kill each other. As for Corbyn's claim that Muslims do not wage war in Ramadan, an Islamic website, *Muslimink*, proudly lists six battles that Muslims have fought in Ramadan, the first being the battle of Badr, fought by Mohammed on the 17th of Ramadan, (March 24) in the year AD 624, with the permission of a verse, so says his biographer, conveniently sent down by Allah on the eve of battle. Thus a precedent had been set and, being sanctioned by Allah, it is one which operates until the end of time. The practise has therefore continued into the modern era without any censure on the part of Muslims versed, unlike Corbyn, in Islamic law. For example, there were no Ramadan cease-fires in the eight-year war between Iran and Iran. But, Booth and Corbyn still insisted, without a shred of evidence to support their accusation, it had to be the Jews wot did it.

Was it for services such as this, telling lies about Islam and disseminating conspiracy theories about the Jews, that Corbyn, instead of being paid the normal rate of £500.00 per appearance, received *ten times* that amount? In the four years of his employment, 2009 to 2012, there were 2,204 executions in Iran, which works out at just over £9.00 per execution, probably more than paid to those doing the actual hanging. Nice work if you can get it, and the Parliamentary register of MP's financial interests, which I have checked personally, proves that Corbyn, avowed opponent of capital punishment, certainly did. (Corbyn asserted on Press TV in 2011 that he 'profoundly disagreed with the death penalty in any circumstances for anybody', but this was said in response, not to any one of the thousands carried out by his employers, but the US 'execution' of Osama Bin Laden, architect of 9/11.) Others hiring themselves out for their theocratic pimps include, as one would expect, the seasoned Sharia leftists Ken Livingstone and George Galloway, but also from the Liberal Democrats Lembit Opik MP and Baroness Tonge, the Tory Party Dereck Conway MP, and from the far right, former KKK Grand Wizard, Corbyn enthusiast and professional Jew-baiter David Duke, Holocaust denier Kevin Barret, Jewish conspiracy theorist James Thring, the German neo-Nazi Manuel Ochsenrieter and Corbyn associate, Palestine Solidarity Campaign activist and Jewish conspiracy theorist the Rev. Stephen Sizer.

Corbyn's final appearance on Press TV in August 2012, did not bring to end his association with the Holy Hangmen of Tehran. From January 6 to 10, 2014, he and his wife, together with a 'research worker', enjoyed the hospitality of the 'Iran-UK Parliamentary Friendship Group of the Iranian Parliament', jointly funded by the Iranian Parliament and the UK-based Iranian billionaire Ardeshir Nagashineh. A month later, on February 9, Corbyn addressed what was billed as a 'seminar marking the 35th anniversary of the Islamic revolution in Iran' at the Maida Vale Islamic Centre of England. Corbyn chose as the title of his address, 'The Case for Iran'. (see below for excerpts) As of 2009, the year Corbyn began his employment by Press TV, the official number of children awaiting execution in Iran was 137. A kinder politics.

The governing principles of the regime Corbyn was being paid to promote were clearly set out by its founder and, after the crushing of the Iranian left, undisputed ruler, Ayatollah Khomeini, in his *Green Book,* relevant excerpts of which are reproduced here:

The leaders of our country [this text dates from the time of the Shah] have been so deeply influenced by the West that they have regulated the standard time of their country upon that of Europe…Greenwich Mean Time. What a nightmare! In the past century, during which European medicine and surgery have been introduced into Iran, our leaders have forgotten our traditional medicine and encouraged a handful of inexperienced young men to study this cursed European medicine. Today we realise that illnesses such as typhus, typhoid fever and the like are curable only by traditional remedies. [Like the quack homeopathic potions recommended by Corbyn...and the no less gullible Prince Charles.]

The clergy must undertake no functions other than religious ones which serve monotheism, virtue, the teaching of divine laws, and the upholding of public morals. The army must also be under the control of the clergy in order to be efficacious and useful. We clergy forcefully affirm that refusal to wear the veil is against the law of Allah and the Prophet, and a material and moral affront to the entire country. We affirm that the ludicrous use of the Western hat [sic] stands in the way of our independence and is contrary to the will of Allah. We affirm that co-educational schools are an obstacle to a wholesome life; they are a material and moral affront to the country and contrary to the divine will. We affirm that Music engenders immorality, lust and licentiousness, and stifles courage, valour and the chivalrous spirit; it is forbidden by Koranic law and must not be taught in the schools. Radio Tehran, by broadcasting Western music, Oriental and Iranian music, plays a nefarious role by introducing immorality and licentiousness into respectable families...

We see today that Jews - may Allah bring them down! - have manipulated the editions of the *Koran* published in their occupied zones. We have to protest, to make everyone understand that these Jews are bent upon the destruction of Islam and the establishment of a universal Jewish government. [like the Hamas Charter, lifted straight from the *Protocols*] And since they are a cunning and active people, I fear - may Allah protect us from it - that sooner or later they may succeed in attaining this goal, that through the weakness of some among us we may one day find ourselves under Jewish rule - Allah preserve us from it!

An Islamic government cannot be totalitarian or despotic but is conditional and democratic. In this democracy, however, the laws are not made by the will of the people, but only by the *Koran* and the *Sunnah* [the traditions, e.g., the *hadith*] of the Prophet. The constitution, the civil code and the criminal code should be inspired only by Islamic laws contained in the *Koran* and transcribed by the Prophet. Islamic government is the government of divine right, and its laws cannot be changed, modified or contested. The Islamic government is subject to the law of Islam, which comes neither from the people nor from its representatives, but directly from Allah and his divine will [And this is 'democracy'?]...The Prophet, the Caliphs and the people owe absolute obedience to these eternal laws of the Almighty, transmitted to mortals through the *Koran* and the Prophet, which remain immutable until the end of time...the imam and the clergy have the duty to use the political apparatus to apply the laws of Allah to bring about a system of equality for the benefit of the people. Governing for them means nothing but pain and duty, but what else can they do? The rule of the clergy is an obligation they must fulfil.'

II

Iranian Nights

'Oh, Allah's Apostle! We get female captives as our share of booty, and we are interested in their prices, what is your opinion about *coitus interruptus*?" The Prophet said, "Do you really do that? It is better for you not to do it. No soul that which Allah has destined to exists but will surely come into existence".' Bukhari *Hadith*, Volume 3, Book 34, Number 432

'I drove them [captured female slaves] along until I brought them to Abu Bakr, who bestowed that girl upon me as a prize, So we arrived in Medina. I had not yet disrobed her when the Messenger of Allah met me in the street and said, "Give me that girl".' Salih Muslim *Hadith*, Book 19, Number 4345.

Both major branches of Islam, the Shi'a and the Sunni, seek, through the enforcement of Sharia law, total control over the lives of Muslims. This is nowhere more obvious and explicit than in the sexual act, the human activity that is in its very nature the most personal and private, or at least should be. That is of course why Islam goes to the most inordinate and extraordinary lengths to regulate it, and it must be conceded that Ayatollah Khomeini's *Green Book* admirably and appropriately rises to the challenge. What follows is a representative sample of the rules that the leading modern authority of Shi'a Islam believed were necessary to regulate human sexual activity in accordance with the will of Allah. Some the reader may find hard to credit. If so, then the full text is readily accessible on line in several English language translations. On a technical point: Sharia law divides human behaviour, all human behaviour, into five categories: that which is: Forbidden, Disapproved, Permitted, Approved and Obligatory:

If a man has had sexual relations with his wife during periods of prescribed abstinence, such as the fast of Ramadan, he must avoid saying his prayers so long as he still has upon him the traces of post-coital sweat...Sperm is always impure, whether it results from actual coitus or from an emission while one is either conscious or asleep, whether it is abundant or not, whether or not it results from sexual pleasure, whether emission is intentional or not....During sexual intercourse if the penis enters the woman's vagina or a man's anus [sic] fully, or only as far as the circumcision ring, both partners become impure, even if they have not reached puberty [nb re Islamic paedophilia]; they must consequently perform their ablutions. If the man thinks he has not entered the woman's vagina beyond the circumcision ring, ablution is not required. If a man - Allah protect him from it – fornicates with an animal [sic], ablution is necessary. If a sperm moves inside the penis, but does not come out, or if there was doubt about whether it was actually emitted, ablution is not required... [While defecating or urinating] it is not sufficient to turn one's sex organs away while facing or turning one's back on Mecca; and one's privates must never be exposed either facing Mecca or facing directly way from Mecca...It is recommended to urinate before prayers, before going to bed, before having sexual intercourse, and after ejaculating.

[Eating] the meat of horses, mules and donkeys is not recommended. It is strictly forbidden if the animal was sodomised while alive by a man. [sic] If one commits an act of sodomy with a cow, a ewe or a camel [as one does] their urine and their excrements become impure and even their milk may not be consumed. The animal must then be killed as quickly as possible, and the price of it paid to its owner by him who sodomised it... If one performs his ablutions after having ejaculated and one has a verse of the *Koran* or the name of Allah written or tattooed on his body, one's hand must not touch that part of the body during the ablution, but that part must be washed without being touched...If a man [it is always a man] becomes aroused by a woman other than his wife but then has intercourse with his own wife, it is preferable for him to pray if he has sweated; but if he first has intercourse with his spouse and then with another woman, he may say his prayers even though he be in a sweat. A man who has ejaculated as a result of intercourse with a woman other than his wife and who ejaculates again while having coitus with his legal wife, does not have the right to say his prayers while still sweating, but if he had intercourse with his wife first and then with a woman not his wife, he may say his prayers even though still sweating... [Obviously...anyone could have worked that out. But now it gets highly technical]

Sexual intercourse is a breaking of the fast, even if the penis enters only as far as the circumcision ring, and even if no ejaculation results. If the penis enters less

140

deeply into the vagina, the fast has not been broken. If the man cannot determine with certainty what length of his penis entered the vagina, and if he has gone on beyond the circumcision ring [and only Allah would know this] his fast has not been broken. If a man has intercourse because he has forgotten he is in a fasting period, or someone forces him to have intercourse [sic!] his fast has not been broken. But if he remembers the fast while the sex act is taking place [hold it...I've just remembered...it's Ramadan!] or if he is no longer forcibly constrained [?] to complete the coitus, he must interrupt it immediately. [Sharia *coitus interruptus*] If a man during a fasting period masturbates and brings himself to ejaculation, his fast has been broken. During the time a woman is menstruating, it is preferable for a man to avoid coitus, even if it does not involve full penetration...it is also highly inadvisable to sodomising her during this time...If a man sodomises the son, brother or father of his wife after their marriage [again, as one does] the marriage remains valid...A woman who has contracted a continuing marriage [Shi'a Islam in Iran permits 'marriages' as brief as a few minutes for the purposes of prostitution] does not have the right to go out of the house without her husband's permission; she must remain at his disposal for the fulfilment of any one of his desires, and may not refuse herself to him except for a religiously valid reason.

III

Filling the Vacuum

In the February 2009 number of the Socialist Workers Party journal *Socialist Review,* in line with the party's orientation towards Jihadi movements and the most resolutely anti-western Islamic regimes, it was argued that in the Middle East generally, and specifically Iran, 'Islam has filled the vacuum left by the bankruptcy of Stalinism and [secular] nationalism'. It therefore followed, the article continued, that 'any Left in Iran or the region must now relate to this reality if it is not to make the same mistakes'. I reproduce below the nature of this 'reality' the Sharia left now relates to, as described by one of its countless victims. Let the three doyens of Sharia leftism, Corbyn, Galloway and Livingstone, who have over the years served as propagandists and apologists for Islamic terrorism and theocracy, answer this question: *What has been the fate of the Left under Islam?*

> I have lived thousands of days in Iran when Islam has shed its blood. In the name of Allah, a hundred thousand have been executed in Iran since 1979. I have lived days when I, along with thousands of men and women throughout the country, looked for the names of our lovers, husbands, wives, friends, daughters, sons, colleagues, and students in the papers that announced the names of the executed on a daily basis. Days when the soldiers of Allah attacked bookstores and publishing house and burned books. Days of armed attacks on universities and the killing of innocent students all over the country. Weeks and months of bloody attacks on workers' strikes and demonstrations [nb]. Years of brutal murder and suppression of atheists, freethinkers, socialists [nb], Marxists [nb], Baha'is, women who resisted the misery of *hijab* and the rule of sexual apartheid, and many others who were none of these, those who were arrested in the streets and then executed simply because of their innocent non-Islamic appearance. Years of mass killing of youth that kept the keys to heaven in their fists during the Iran-Iraq war. Years of brutal assassination of opponents inside and outside of Iran.

I, along with thousands of political prisoners, was tortured by order of the representative of Allah and *Shar'ia*. Tortured, while the verses of the *Koran* were played in the torture chambers. The mechanical voice reading the *Koran* was mixed with our cries of pain from the lashes and other forms of brutal torture. Thousands were shot by execution squads who recited koranic verses while conducting the killings, regarding as blasphemous those who were simply political opponents of the regime, the death of blasphemers is required by the *Koran*. They prayed before raping female political prisoners for the sake of Allah and in order to enter heaven. Those who were in prisons and not yet executed were awakened every day at dawn only to hear more gunshots aimed at their friends and cellmates. From the numbers of gunshots, you could find out how many were murdered on that day. The killing machine did not stop for a minute. Then, fathers and mothers, husbands and wives who received the bloody clothes of their loved ones had to pay for the bullets. [The Nazis also billed relatives for the cost of executions] Islamic Auschwitz was created. Many of best, the most passionate and progressive people were massacred. The dimension was and is beyond imagination.

Excerpted from: Azam Kamguian: *Leaving Islam and Living Islam*

III

Jeremy in Ayatollahland

'The Zionists are crooks. A small handful of Zionists, with a very intricate organisation, have taken over the power centres of the world'. (President Mahmoud Ahmadinejad of Iran, September 18, 2008)

Hundreds of celebrity pilgrims to Stalinist Russia, after being taken on the same conducted tour of Potemkin showpiece prisons, collective farms, industrial projects and other wonders of the Five-Year Plan, returned to their homes in the capitalist west convinced, in the words of one dupe, the American journalist Lincoln Steffens, that 'they had seen the future, and it worked.' For some two decades now, Islam in its most militant manifestations has replaced Soviet-style communism as the longed-for alternative sought by western radicals to what they perceive as the failings of western liberal democracy. And perhaps the prime example of our later-day political pilgrims is Labour Party Leader Jeremey Corbyn, whose admiration for the theocracy that rules Iran is such that he has over the years taken up paid employment, together with fellow Sharia leftists Livingstone and Galloway, along with a team of far right anti-Semites, as a propagandist for the Ayatollahs on the London-based Iranian Press TV channel. As revealed in the *Daily Telegraph* of July 18, 2015, Corbyn's travelling and other expenses incurred in his trips to Iran have met in part at least by an extremely wealthy British-Iranian businessman (see below). This is in addition to payments Corbyn has received from organisations linked to the Iran-sponsored anti-Semitic terrorist movement Hamas which, as everybody by now should know, the Labour leader chose to call his 'friends'. He is also on record as claiming, ludicrously, that this same Jew-killing, homophobic, misogynist, genocidal, *Protocols*-citing collection of theocratic thugs 'is an organisation that is dedicated towards bringing about long-term peace and social justice in the whole region.' If the infinitely gullible Corbyn had taken the trouble to read the Hamas Charter, perhaps even he might have noticed that is dedicated not to peace, but to the destruction of the state of Israel and the extermination of the world's Jews.

In addition to numerous public speeches, articles in the Communist Party's *Morning Star* and statements in the House of Commons in support of the Iranian theocracy, the nature of the services Corbyn has performed over the years for the Ayatollahs is captured in one appearance on Press TV, screened in 2010. Corbyn could be seen responding to phone-ins by viewers. One complains that the BBC are 'Zionist liars' to which Corbyn replies that the caller had a 'good point' and suggests that the caller complain directly to the BBC. Another describes Israel as 'a disease' that the Arabs must 'get rid of'. Assuming, perhaps too charitably, that he may have wanted to dissent from such an opinion but feared that doing so could well have endangered his continued employment, because the destruction of Israel is the declared aim of Iran's Supreme Leader, Corbyn instead replies, 'OK. Thank you for your call'.

As it was for those millions whose misery, and even slavery Stalin's so easily bamboozled guests were never allowed to see, actually living, and dying, in Iran can be a very different experience compared to that of the likes of Corbyn, who on their fleeting visits to confer with and promote to the world the regime of their clerical pimps, only see what they are allowed, or want to see. They are unconcerned, because it is hard to credit that they do not know, that for every day they spend as propagandists for or guests of the Ayatollahs, it can happen that a dozen or more Iranians will die at the hands of the executioner, among whom there will be, as the account above and the reports below tell us, those whose only crime is their beliefs, their writings, their sexual orientation, their desire for the rights of labour, individual liberty and justice. It is not as if Corbyn is unaware of these abuses. However, his response has always been, as he explained to MPs in the House of Commons on January 11, 2012, that 'any change within Iran is more likely to come from internal opposition and internal organisation than from anything done from the outside or any outside pressure.' But that precisely is the point! As Corbyn knew only too well, the Iranian theocracy does not allow 'internal opposition' and anyone who attempts to create one is likely to be arrested, and possibly tortured and then executed. (For details, see the UN Secretary-General's report below.)

Yet on another occasion, he tried to convince sceptical MPs that 'a lively, if [sic] robust and sometimes very dangerous [!!!] debate is going on in Iran'. How can a debate be at the same time 'lively', 'robust' and yet 'very dangerous'? Let us recall that Iran ranks 150 in the world democratic index, and has by far the world's highest per capita execution rate. When it comes to Israel, which ranks 120 places higher, and executes no one, not even terrorists who kill its civilians, Corbyn tactics are reversed. Even though Israel's pluralist multi-party-political system does allow 'lively debates' that are not 'very dangerous', a free press and a legal 'internal opposition', including that of parties representing Palestinian voters, Corbyn has for decades been actively involved in numerous campaigns and with movements that apply 'outside pressure' on Israel's government including not only boycotts (never demanded by Corbyn for any Islamic state, or any other for that matter, no matter how repressive) but the indiscriminate murder of its civilians, including children, whose aim is not to bring about reforms within Israel, but its total destruction and the extermination of its entire Jewish population. Yet it is Corbyn who accuses the west of having 'double standards' on human rights issues.

Do not, then, expect those like Corbyn who make their subsidised pilgrimages to Iran to apply any 'outside pressure' on their hosts, as we were once invited to, and rightly, to Apartheid South Africa and the Chilean Junta. They see only the official Iran, and only meet with its official representatives. But the other Iran, the real Iran of Kurds denied their national freedom, of the torture chamber and the gallows, of the public hanging from cranes, of the compulsory hijab and the stoning to death of women who stray from the path of Sharia, of mobs chanting death to the Jews, of Iran's Supreme leader boasting of his intention to wipe Israel off the map within twenty five years, and who in 2016 on International Holocaust Day released a video in which he questioned whether the Holocaust was 'reality or not', of anti-Semitic cartoon competitions…righting these wrongs (if indeed wrongs they be), even though a 'very dangerous' task, is best left to Iran's 'internal opposition'. Neither should we expect Corbyn, when he mounts the rostrum to address Jew-baiting al-Quds Day rallies in honour of Ayatollah Khomeini, to speak of the Iran of the *pays real,* but only of the fake *pays legal* Iran of the political tourist and the hired propagandist, the Iran insulated from any criticism of its abysmal human rights record by the mutual protection mafia of its Muslim and other Third World partners in crime, who sit by rotation on the United Nations Human Rights Council, directing all their diversionary venom at only one state...Israel.

In February 2014, Corbyn was a guest of honour at a function at the London Islamic Centre of England celebrating the 35th anniversary of the murderous theocracy that today goes by the name of the Islamic Republic of Iran, and whose guiding principles, and some of their consequences, are contained in the previous three items and the two following. These are excerpts, with interpolations, from his sycophantic speech, titled, *The Case for Iran'*:

When the Director spoke in opening this conference, I thought it was a very interesting address, and it is one that I wish a much larger number of people in this country could have heard, because he was describing the history and traditions of Islam, but he was also describing the inclusivity, the tolerance and the acceptance of other faiths and other traditions and other ethnic groupings within Iran. I think that is something that most people in the West simply do not understand [If so, it is because they do not exist] … Iran is a member of the United Nations Human Rights Council, which I also attend. Iran, like every other country, must undergo its universal periodic review, and I raised these [human rights?] questions with the [Iranian] Foreign Minister during our visit and the assurance was given that the full response will be given at the UN Human Rights Council in June [2014] as is required.

[This is a pack of lies. The clerics who rule Iran have never in the past co-operated with UN in any investigation into their abuses of human rights, and the Human Rights Council session of December 22, 2014, and UN Secretary-General's report of March 3, 2016, excerpts of which are reproduced below, make it clear even to regime stooges like Corbyn that they have no intention of doing so now or in the future. Corbyn surely also must have known when he made this speech that his Iranian friends would be given a clean bill of health by its partners in human rights violations sitting on the Council. (Examples of this practice are also reproduced below) The UN General Assembly and its General Secretary are however not quite such a soft touch. See below for details]

144

The message I got from my visit was that Iran is a country that is strong, a country with the most amazing history and a country that has suffered very grievously during the Iran-Iraq war. [Initiated, as I recall, by fellow Press TV broadcaster Galloway's 'indefatigable' anti-imperialist hero and paymaster, Saddam Hussein] ...Are we to go down [the road of] yet more wars? [Jihad excluded of course] Or are we to bring up our children to understand our history, to understand the principles of Islam as one would the principles of every other faith? There is a commonality [between them] of humanity, of understanding, of acceptance.

[Here I must interrupt Corbyn's homage to the Religion of Peace to remind readers not only of Islam's doctrine of Jihad and aim of world conquest, but of the well-advertised pledge made by Iran's current Supreme Leader' Ayatollah Ali Khamenei, that within twenty-five years, 'there will be no more Israel'. And it is indeed ironic that the anti-American Corbyn shares US President Obama's delusion that Islam embraces with the infidel or, to use the Arabic vernacular, the *kuffar* a 'commonalty of humanity' when the *Koran* not only says exactly the opposite, (16: 93, 49: 10, 32: 3, 3: 38) but on no fewer than six occasions, instructs Muslims 'not to take Jews and Christians as your friends'. There must have been many in his Muslim audience who knew that Corbyn was either lying about or totally ignorant of the faith he was extolling.]

I respect Iran's history. I respect what brought about the revolution in 1979. ['understand' surely?] And I hope I understand the need and wish of the people of Iran to have a peaceful relationship with the rest of the world.

[But that is not the wish of its rulers, who in addition to their long-standing support for the anti-Semitic terrorist movements Hamas and Hezbollah and intervention in the wars in Syria and Yemen, to complement their nuclear programme, are with Putin's help busily constructing long range ballistic missiles than will be able to reach the 'Zionist entity' and even the 'Great Satan', the United States.]

It was my pleasure [sic] to go to Iran and I am very much looking forward to returning, and I have been invited to go again to talk about British politics and all that sort of thing [sic]...Thank you very much for the honour of inviting me today.' [Applause]

Corbyn speaks of Iran's 'amazing history', though what he has to say about it is confined to those times and events in which the west, principally the UK and USA, were to their shame, ranged on the side of the Shah and the western oil companies against its people. Since Corbyn is a veteran leftist who writes for the Stalinist *Morning Star,* some, though not myself, might find it strange that in his entire speech of some fifteen minutes' duration, he had nothing at all to say about the 'amazing history' of what was once Iran's major left-wing party, the Tudeh, which in all but its name, was also communist. He could, for example, have made the telling point that it was his leftist comrades, not the Islamic clergy, that bore the brunt of the repression under the Shah's police regime, and that the clergy had collaborated with the CIA-sponsored overthrow of the leftist and secular Mosaddegh government in 1953, which it rightly saw as a threat to its power and immense wealth.

After the Shah's coup, again with the technical assistance of the CIA and the support of the clergy, the Shah's secret police, SAVAK, rounded up no fewer than 4,121 Tudeh Party militants. Massive protests in the west succeeded in saving the most prominent Tudeh leaders from execution, though the party was viciously persecuted and driven underground until the overthrow of the Shah in 1979. Naively applying the classic Stalinist strategy of the 'popular front', the Tudeh

Party then sought an accommodation with the Islamic forces mobilised under the leadership of the returned Ayatollah Khomeini. The party was following the Kremlin line, now taken up by all the Sharia left, that by overthrowing the pro-western Shah, the 'Islamic Revolution' had ranged Iran in the camp of the progressive anti-imperialist forces. Be that as it may, along with the national minorities and other secular and western-oriented groupings, the Tudeh Party very quickly found itself under attack by the Khomeinists, whose objective was not the replacement of the Sha's police regime by a genuine democracy, but the establishment of a fully-blown totalitarian theocracy, one that by its ruthless suppression of all political opposition, rapidly proved itself to be far more repressive than the worst the Shah's regime had to offer.

Yet it is at this point, the post-1979 crushing of Corbyn's leftist comrades, that his 'amazing history' with the omissions I have outlined, stops, and it cannot be because he does not know it, but rather because of the audience he was addressing. If he was not such a wretched, craven opportunist, always telling audiences what they wanted to hear rather than what they needed to be told, Corbyn could have and should have related to his all-Muslim audience how their hero, the Supreme Leader Ayatollah Khomeini, presided over the arrest of at least 10,000 members of the Tudeh Party, followed in many cases by Stalinist-style show trials, tortures, forced false confessions of collusion with Zionism and the CIA, forced conversions to Islam and of course executions. The number of all leftist victims is known to run into the tens of thousands. None of this mattered to Corbyn, who was instead 'looking forward' to meeting again representatives of the regime that murdered them, and is still murdering them today.

But events have a way of exposing such dupes, if that, to be charitable, is what they are. First came one of Corbyn's other loves, the authoritarian regime of Venezuelan President Maduro, whose repression of demonstrators in the summer of 2017 protesting against the corruption, economic bankruptcy and electoral frauds he has inflicted on his people resulted in over a hundred dead and many more wounded and imprisoned. Then at the end of the year came the turn of Iran, with mass protests against the identical abuses of power by the clerical regime, with the same result, dead bodies on the streets, and mass arrests, followed in the Spring of 2018 by the killing of more than 200 demonstrators protesting against the bankrupt authoritarian regime of Nicaraguan President Daniel Ortega and his wife, Vice President Rosario Zambrano. And also, just with Venezuela and Iran, no protest from Corbyn. In the case of Iran, fronting for her boss, his Shadow Foreign Secretary, Emily Thornberry declared that the Labour Party could not condemn the killings or support the demonstrators because it was not clear who was wearing the 'white hats' (sic). And anyway, her master's voice argued in the classic cultural relativist manner, 'we can't simply impose our views on other countries'.

Yet the left once supported boycotts of South Africa to impose an end to apartheid did it not? No one would expect the Labour Party to 'impose' anything on Iran's theocratic rulers - how could it? - but simply to condemn their killing of unarmed demonstrators. But she knew she couldn't, because Jeremy was a friend and former employee of the regime doing the killing. Then on June 25, 2018, thousands took to the streets of Tehran to protest against the cripplingly costly foreign involvements of the Ayatollahs, chanting, not the state-sponsored 'death to Israel', but death to *Palestine*, and 'no to Gaza, no to Lebanon, leave Syria'.

Corbyn must have been mortified, because here for once was a genuine 'stop the war', or rather wars, protest, directed against his former theocratic employers and terrorist 'friends'. Five weeks later, they were back on the streets again in cities and towns across Iran, again chanting 'death', not to America or Israel, but to 'the Dictator', Corbyn's former employer 'Supreme Leader' Ayatollah Ali Khamenei, with one of the targets of their anger not the US embassy, but a religious school near Tehran. Millions of young Iranians have had more than their fill of a clergy and religion that has nothing to offer them except repression and economic decline at home, and abroad, proxy wars with Saudi Arabia, hatred for the West in general and for the Jews in particular.

IV

I want a kinder politics

So said Jeremy Corbyn to the 2015 Labour Party Conference. However, his friends Hamas and Hezbollah would make an exception when it comes to the Jews, whom they are both sworn to exterminate. But what of his former theocratic employers? The answer is to be found in what follows, beginning with an article from the *Daily Telegraph* of January 4, 2001, titled, 'Khomeini fatwa "led to killing of 30,0000 in Iran"':

Children as young as 13 were hanged from cranes, six at a time, in a barbaric two-month purge of Iran's prisons on the direct orders of Ayatollah Khomeini, according to a new book by his former deputy. More than 30,000 political prisoners were executed in the 1988 massacre - a far larger number than previously suspected. Secret documents smuggled out of Iran reveal that, because of the large numbers of necks to be broken, prisoners were loaded onto forklift trucks in groups of six and hanged from cranes in half-hourly intervals. Gruesome details are contained in the memoirs of Grand Ayatollah Hossein-Ali-Montazeri, one of the founders of the Islamic regime. He was once considered Khomeini's anointed successor, but was disposed of for his outspokenness, and is now under house arrest in the holy city of Qom. Published privately last month after regime attempts to suppress it, the revelations have prompted demands from Iranian exiles for those involved to be tried from crimes against humanity.

The most damning of the letters and documents published in the book is Khomeini's fatwa decree calling for all Mojahedin (as opponents of the Iranian regime are called) to be killed. Issued shortly after the end of the Iran-Iraq war in July 1988 and an incursion into western Iran by the Iranian resistance, the fatwah reads: "It is decreed that those who are in prisons throughout the country and remain steadfast in their support for the Mojahedin are waging war on God and are condemned to execution." It goes on to entrust the decision to "death committees" - three-member panels consisting of an Islamic judge, a representative of the Ministry of Intelligence [sic] and a state prosecutor. Prisoners were to be asked if they had changed their loyalties, and if not, were to be executed. Montazeri, who states that 3,800 people had been killed by the end of the first fortnight of executions, includes his own correspondence with Khomeini, saying that the killings would be seen as a "a vendetta" and would spark opposition to the regime. He wrote: "The execution of several thousand prisoners in a few days will not have positive repercussions and will not be mistake-free." The massacre, which came just before the Lockerbie bombing, were seen as a sop to the hardliners at a time when Khomeini was already in failing health and the battle for the succession had begun between fundamentalists and moderates. He died the following year.

According to testimony from prison officials - including Kamal Afkami Ardekani, who formerly worked at Evin prison - recently given to United Nations human rights rapporteurs: "They would line up prisoners in a 14-by-five-metre hall in the central office building and ask them one simple question, 'what is your political affiliation?' Those who said the Mojahedin would be hanged from cranes in position in the car park behind the building. He went on to describe how, every half hour from 7.30am to 5pm, 33 people were lifted onto three fork lift trucks to six cranes, each of which had five or six ropes. He said: "The process went on and on

148

without interruption". In two weeks, 8,000 people were hanged. Similar carnage took place across the country. Many of those in the ruling council at the time of the 1988 massacre are still in power, including President Mohammed Khatami, who was the Director of Ideological and Cultural [sic] Affairs.

"The massacre may have happened 12 years ago, but the relevance is that these atrocities are still happening" said Mohammed Mohaddesin, the Chairman of the Foreign Affairs Committee of the Iranian Council of National Resistance, (NCR) the main opposition group, who was in London last week to present evidence to MPs. The NCR has prepared files on 21 senior members of the regime whom it alleges were "principal protagonists of the massacre" including Mr Khatami and Ayatollah Ali Khamenei, Iran's 'Supreme Leader'. Mr Mohaddesin will travel to New York to present the files to the UN and call for a tribunal to try them for crimes against humanity. Mr Mohaddesin said human rights abuses were continuing in Iran despite the election of Mr Khatami, who "presents himself as a reformist".

V

Allah Rules OK

As we have seen, Islamic states such Iran, together with many other member states of the United Nations no less guilty of human rights violations, have managed to frustrate any effective indictment of or action against their crimes by participation in a mutual protection cartel operating within the UN Human Rights Council. However, this strategy does not work quite so well at the level of the General Assembly, where representation is more diverse and, with a large number of western states committed to liberal democracy, not so easily either intimidated or manipulated. Even so, just in 2015, Israel was condemned 20 times, all but five in matters relating to the Palestinian issue, and nearly always by huge majorities averaging around 150. In the same year, the General Assembly recorded only *three* other votes critical of member states: Iran, where the voting was 81 for, 37 against and 67 abstentions, Syria, 104, for, 13 against and 47 abstentions, and North Korea, 119 for, against 19 (sic!!!) and 48 abstentions. If all we had to go on were these results, we would have to conclude that the Jews of Israel are by far the biggest criminals on this planet, being responsible for nearly 90% of all its human rights abuses, twenty time worse even than North Korea where human rights are non-existent, and the regime of Syria's Bashar al-Assad, which in 2015 killed 200,000 of its own people and drove out millions of others as refugees. And even here, 61 members found themselves unable to condemn these unprecedented crimes. As for other states where rights are abused as a matter of course on a daily basis, such as Saudi Arabia, China, Russia and its client states, and by a host of other similarly repressive regimes...nothing. In fact, they are the ones setting the pace for the onslaught on Israel.

However, because the UN General Assembly ranks above the Human Rights Council, and its Secretary-General therefore not only acts and speaks on behalf of the higher body, but is also empowered to ensure that the subordinate Human Rights Council carries out its duties objectively, and has the right to take to task any member state of the UN that fails to respond positively to demands for information or action in connection with human rights issues, this has resulted in Iran finding itself in the unaccustomed situation for an Islamic regime of being held to account for its notorious human rights abuses, even if only by a minority vote. Contrary to the lie told by Corbyn that Iran honours its duty to comply with UN Human Rights investigations and recommendations, this is of course what its clerical rulers, safe in the knowledge that no punitive measures will ensue, has consistently failed to do, as the report cited below proves beyond all doubt. On December 7, 1984 Iran's representative to the UN General Assembly, Rajaie-Khorassani, explained why:

> Iran recognises no authority or power but that of Almighty God and no legal tradition apart from Islamic law...declarations and resolutions or decisions of international organisations which are contrary to Islam have no validity in the Islamic Republic of Iran...The Universal Declaration of Human Rights, which represents a secular understanding of the Judeo-Christian tradition, cannot be implemented by Muslims and does not accord with the system of values recognised by the Islamic Republic of Iran. Iran will therefore not hesitate [nb] to violate [nb] its provisions, since it has to choose between violating the divine law and violating secular conventions.

One of the tragic consequences of this quite open flouting of human rights as defined by the United Nations is Iran's legalisation of paedophilia. Even though having signed in 1994 the UN Convention on Rights of the Child, in which a child is defined as 'a human being below the age of eighteen years', Iran's clerical rulers have since the Islamic Revolution of 1979 enforced a law legalising marriage for females at the age of nine, this being the same age that all Islamic sources state Mohammed consummated his marriage to his last wife Aisha, whom he married when she was six years of age. Child marriages in Iran are on the rise, in 2016 accounting for 24% of all marriages, more than double the rate of a few years previously.

The following excerpts are taken from a lengthy report by the UN Secretary General on the human rights situation in Iran, submitted to the Human Rights Council after Iran's failure, *pace* Corbyn, to comply with repeated requests by the General Assembly to cease a large number of human rights abuses. Dated March 3, 2016, the Report followed on from *non-binding* resolutions adopted by the UN's so-called Third Committee, 'on the human rights situation in Iran', which were adopted as far back as October 27, 2011. They called on Iran 'to positively avail itself of the opportunity to co-operate fully with the Special Rapporteur and other human rights mechanisms, including by allowing the Special Rapporteur unfettered access to the country to carry out his mandate' so that 'credible and independent investigations of all human rights violations can be conducted'. This access was of course denied. What a farce! Sharia leftist pilgrims and propagandists are made welcome and financially rewarded by those who perpetrate and then lie about these crimes, while the denial of UN access to their victims goes unpunished. It is indicative of the reluctance of many UN member states to investigate Iran's notorious human rights abuses that when put to the vote at the General Assembly in 2011, the resolution, which bear in mind was anyway 'non-binding', secured the support of considerably less than half of the UN's total membership, 86 votes, with 32 (the Islamic bloc) voting against and 75 either abstaining or not voting at all. Six year on, and with still no reply from the Ayatollahs, the UN Secretary General felt it was time to give Corbyn's torturer friends a gentle tap on the wrist.

Report of the Secretary-General on the situation of human rights in Iran. (Excerpts)

I. Introduction

3. Since the submission of the report of the Secretary-General to the 70th session of the General Assembly [September 2015] the application of the death penalty persisted at an alarmingly high rate, including in relation to drug-related crimes, and with regard to juveniles. Corporal punishment, including amputation, flogging and forced blinding [sic!!!], was applied against individuals in detention.

4. The crackdown on journalists, human rights defenders, in particular women human rights offenders, intensified, with a large number of individuals arrested, detained and persecuted for the mere and peaceful exercise of their profession or their legitimate rights to freedom of expression and association. No improvement was observed regarding the situation of religious and ethnic minorities, who remain subjected to restrictions. [Contrary to the claim Corbyn made in his Address] Women and girls continue to face discrimination in the areas of marriage, employment and political participation.

II. Overview of the human rights situation in the Islamic Republic of Iran

A. The death penalty. [Corbyn is on record as saying 'I profoundly disagree with the death penalty in any circumstances for anybody' but, so far as I am aware, has never publicly protested its use in Iran.]
   6. The Secretary-General remains alarmed at the staggering rate of executions carried out in Iran. At least 900 executions including women [only when they are flogged, stoned or on the gallows are they equal to men] and children [but surely only Jews kill children?] were reportedly recorded in 2015, with some sources suggesting the figure to be as high as over 1,000, confirming a consistent pattern since 2005…On 26 June 2015 alone, 25 individuals were executed in Rajai Shahr prison.
   8. Executions for drug-related offences, which amount to a violation of international law [but remember that in Iran as in other Islamic states, Allah's law trumps all others] account for over 60% of all executions in Iran. These executions are often carried after trials that do not meet international fair trial standards.
   10. In 2015, at least eight political prisoners were executed for charges such as taking up arms for terrorism and disruption of public safety [sic] and several others were handed down the death penalty for politically motivated charges. On 4 March 2015, six individuals including Hamed Ahmadi, Kamal Malaee, Jahngir Dehghani and Jamshed Dehghani, all members of the Kurdish community, were executed on charges of *Moharebeh* and *Mofsid fil Arz,* corruption on earth. [That is, on theological grounds]
   11. Furthermore, on 5 August, the High Commissioner and a group of Special Procedures mandate holders separately expressed serious concern at the imposition of the death penalty on Mohammed Ali Taheri, the founder of a

spiritual movement, writer and practitioner of alternative medicine theories used in Iran and abroad...Shahram Ahmadi, a religious activist promoting Sunni belief [there's the rub] by distributing books and leaflets, was arrested on 26 April 2009 and sentenced to death in early 2015...He was held in solitary confinement for 33 months and subjected to beatings, psychological attacks, and exposure to extreme cold. Mr Ahmadi was forced to sign a blank paper on which revolutionary guards later reportedly composed a confession. [Is this what Corbyn had in mind when in his address he praised Islam's 'inclusivity, tolerance and the acceptance of other faiths'?]

12. The Secretary-General notes with concern that the practice of public executions continued despite their dehumanising, cruel, inhuman and degrading nature on the victims and on observers. At least 47 individuals were publicly executed in 2015. Despite statements to the contrary by the Government, photos taken at the scene demonstrate that children are often present at these events.

13. On 16 December 2015, several Special Procedures mandate holders expressed outrage at the executions, on 6 and 13 October, of two juvenile offenders. The Special Rapporteur on summary executions described these executions as unlawful killings by the State, comparing them with murders performed by individuals. Underlining that executing a juvenile offender, especially after a questionable trial, directly contravenes international human rights law, the Special Rapporteur urged the Government of Iran to immediately stop killing children...On 25 November, according to a semi-official Iranian news outlet, Mr Alireza, a juvenile offender was sentenced to death for the murder of his friend on 30 October 2008, these cases bring to four the number of confirmed juvenile executions in Iran in 2015.

B: Torture, inhuman or degrading treatment and punishment

16 The Secretary-General remains concerned about the persistent practice of corporal punishment, such as amputation of limbs, blinding and flogging. The Islamic Penal Code, which came into force in June 2013, recognises corporal punishment, including limb amputations, flogging and stoning.

17. At least 21 cases of corporal punishment were reported in 2015, including three cases of forceful blinding, five cases of amputation of limbs, one stoning to death and 12 cases of flogging in public. On 13 December 2015, Iranian media reported that a woman convicted of adultery was sentenced to death by stoning in Gilan province.

18. The Secretary General regrets [sic] the Government' refusal to accept all the recommendations concerning torture and other cruel, inhuman or degrading punishment. [It has rejected] recommendations to outlaw inhuman corporal punishments, revoke all laws that allow corporal punishment of children, and investigate and prosecute all those responsible for ill-treatments or abuse of detainees. The Government also rejected recommendations to ratify the Convention against Torture and Other Cruel, Inhuman or Degrading Punishment and its Optional Protocol.

19. The persistence of torture and other cruel, inhuman or degrading punishment in various places of detention and prisons also remains of serious concern. Beatings, stress positions, denial of medical attention and prolonged solitary confinement are among commonly applied methods of ill-treatment. Such

treatment appears to mainly affect human rights defenders, journalists, social activists, political activists, members of some religious groups and individuals associated with some minority groups.

20. Between January and November 2015, several procedures transmitted 14 communications to the Government of Iran concerning prolonged solitary confinements, forced confessions, flogging, amputations, blindings, virginity tests (also referred to as virginity examinations), pregnancy tests and lack of medical attention to prisoners. For instance, on 13 September 2015, Shahrokh Zamani, a labour rights activist, reportedly died of a stroke in Rajai Shahr prison...The denial of health care, along with severely overcrowded and unsanitary conditions and deficient food, are believed to have caused his death. [How fitting that in the same week that Corbyn the internationalist is elected Leader of the UK's Labour Party, his pimps in Tehran preside over the death of an Iranian labour activist. Three years later, on the eve of another Labour Party Conference, an Iranian court sentenced to 74 lashes and ten years in prison the trade union activist Mohammed Habibi for taking part in a peaceful anti-government protest.]

21. On 10 January 2015, Atena Farghdani, a peaceful activist and artist, was arrested and beaten in front of her parents and later in front of a court judge. In June 2015, she received a sentence of 12 years and 6 months' imprisonment. While in prison, she was reportedly subject to torture, sexual harassment and degrading detention conditions...On 14 October 2015, Fatemeh Ekhtesari, a prominent poet, was sentenced to nine years and 6 months of imprisonment on charges of 'insulting the sacred', 'publishing unauthorized content in cyberspace' and 'propaganda against the state' for the publication of a collection of poetry online titled 'A Feminist Discussion before Boiling the Potatoes'.

C. Restrictions to freedom of opinion and expression.

[Readers will recall that in 2006, Corbyn was a *kuffar* useful idiot speaker at a Muslim rally held in Trafalgar Square to protest against the publication of the Danish cartoons. In the course of his speech he called in effect for the censoring of adverse comments on religion, with his declaration, 'we demand that respect be shown for all faiths'. Such calls are redundant in Iran, where the theocracy ruthlessly controls not only comment on religion, but on just about everything else.]

24. The Secretary-General is particularly concerned about the crackdown on journalists and social media activists ahead of the parliamentary elections scheduled for 26 February 2016. [In which to be allowed to run for office, as in all other elections, all candidates require the approval of the Guardian Council, whose members are in turn selected by the Supreme Spiritual Leader, Ayatollah Ali Khamenei.] On 2 November 2014, five journalists were reportedly arrested by Revolutionary Guards in Tehran on suspicion of taking part in an 'infiltration network' 'seeking to influence public opinion' [something Corbyn is paid to do with impunity in the imperialist west] and undermine the Islamic Republic on behalf of western governments.

25. Iran has one the highest number of journalists and social media activists in detention, with at least 45 being held for their peaceful activities.

26. On 14 October 2015, the Revolutionary Court in Tehran sentenced Mehdi

Mousasi, a poet, to 11 years of imprisonment and 99 lashes on charges of 'insulting the sacred' due to the social criticism expressed in his poetry. The convictions were reportedly based on forced confessions...He refuted the charges against him during his trial.

27. The authorities continued to filter and block social media websites, such as Facebook [used by Corbyn], YouTube, [ditto] Twitter, [ditto] Viber, Tango, WhatsApp [ditto] and Instagram [ditto]...On 20 October, 2015, the Chief Executive Officer of the instant messaging service Telegram, Mr. Pavel Durov, affirmed publicly that the Government [of Iran] has asked the company to spy on its users in Iran. On 15 November 2015, the administrators of more than 20 groups on Telegram were arrested for spreading 'immoral content'...In September 2015, 11 individuals were also arrested in relation to jokes circulated on social media that were deemed offensive to the former Supreme Leader, Ayatollah Khomeini. [A sure indicator of totalitarianism, as it was under Hitler and Stalin.]

D. Rights to freedoms of association and peaceful assembly

28. The Secretary-General deplores the Government's refusal to accept the recommendations that it received during the second cycle of Iran's UPR to 'repeal all legal provisions that infringe the freedoms of peaceful assembly and association.

['UPR' refers to a series of recommendations made to the Iranian government in relation to its failure to respect the above and other human rights. Given that the state under review was Iran, as one would expect, the recommendations only had the endorsement of western, liberal democratic states, including Belgium, Canada, the Czech Republic, Finland, Germany, Netherlands, the UK, Norway and the Great Satan, the USA. The minutes of the session of the UN Human Rights Council which convened on December 22, 2014, to debate the recommendations, illustrates how the Muslim Mafia goes about protecting its own. Rather like judges at the Eurovision Song Contest, where voting is mainly by religious and ethnic blocs, the Muslim Mafia, supported as is the norm by infidel regimes no less unsavoury, speaks with one voice, usually by pre-arrangement, with each delegation focusing on issues designed to distract attention away from the subject under review, which in this case, was Iran's stubborn and long-standing refusal to comply with repeated requests to end, or at the very least, reduce those practices that are in conflict with the UN Universal Declaration of Hunan Rights of 1948.

Reading the report, it is as if the rival camps of democracy and Islam are speaking about two totally different countries. While the Spanish delegate voiced concerns about the 'continued use of cruel punishment' (as specified above), Switzerland's about the 'increasing number of death penalty cases' and that of the USA about the 'harassment of religious minorities and the detention of journalists', the Syrian delegation (closely allied with fellow Shi'ite Iran) 'cautioned against basing human rights reviews on 'confrontation, politicisation and double standards', while Yemen's 'commended the enactment [by Iran] of a number of laws aimed at supporting human rights'. Kuwait 'welcomed the measures taken on behalf of persons with disabilities' but had nothing to say about those caused by physical and mental torture in Iran's prisons. In all apparent seriousness, Qatar, whose own human rights record is not without the occasional blemish, 'commended the inclusion of human rights in school curricula and the organisation of human rights training for Government officials', without making it clear that like all other signatories to the 1990 OIC Cairo declaration, Iran's concept of human rights is defined by Sharia law.

Sharia law was also in perfect working when in March 2002, a fire broke out at a girls' school in Mecca. The Saudi Religious Police (yes, you read aright) prevented pupils leaving the burning building because they were not wearing appropriate Islamic dress. 15 girls were either burned or crushed to death. Men who tried to save them were stopped by Allah's enforcers, who told them, 'it is sinful to approach them'. The father of one of the dead girls said the school watchman refused to open the school gates to allow girls to escape. Saudi Arabia is one the biggest customers of the UK's arms industry. Overall, UK exports to Saudi Arabia amount to £4.2 billion per annum. Joint UK-Saudi business ventures are currently worth around £15 billion. Then there is the funding of university Islamic Studies departments…and the oil. Too bad about the schoolgirls and the floggings, but business is business…

It would be tedious to cite all the many statements made by the Muslim Mafia in support of Iran, since they all followed the same tactic of either diverting attention away from the subject under review, or re-cycling Iranian regime claims that there was no case to answer. Far more interesting is the support Iran received from the lands of the normally despised *kuffar*. Let us begin, appropriately in the circumstances, with Corbyn's Chavista comrades from Venezuela, who declared that 'unilateral sanctions violated the fundamental rights of the Iranian people', even though the proceedings had no bearing whatsoever upon the sanctions then being imposed on the Iranian government in connection with its nuclear programme. (BDS sanctions against Israel are another matter entirely.) Comrade Mugabe's delegation, like Qatar's, commended Iran for its 'organisation of human rights training courses for Government officials, the judiciary and law enforcement officers'. Putin's delegation 'noted the new laws to protect children', such as those that still permit their execution, while his neo-Stalinist colony, Belarus, faithfully echoing its master, 'noted the development of national institutions to protect the most vulnerable.' Yet another prolific human rights abuser, China, called for the UN to 'examine human rights in the country objectively,' that is, to believe what the Iranian government says, while one-party Cuba, another Corbyn favourite, 'noted the progress made by the country in areas such as health and education' but, like the rest of the Ayatollahs' infidel allies of convenience, had nothing whatsoever critical to say about the subject that had necessitated the review in the first place, namely, Iran's proven abuse of human rights.

Finally, we have two contributions to the debate issuing from countries that in almost every way imaginable, are diametrically opposed to each other. First, North Korea, which is officially an atheist state, the only one in the world, and where practising any form of worship other than of its Supreme Leader can have unpleasant consequences. Since North Korea shared with Iran the same principal enemy, the USA, or 'Great Satan', it was only to be expected that following the strategy 'the enemy of my enemy is my friend', the atheists of Pyongyang would follow the example set by other infidel human rights abusers by closing ranks with the theocrats of Tehran, commending Iran's 'achievements regarding economic, social and cultural rights'. But pride of place must go to *Dhimmi*

156

Sweden. In 2014, on the eve of a mass Muslim migration that would find its Islamophiliac establishment in denial at its consequences, and the country's population finally roused from its politically correct stupor, few media outlets or anyone on the public stage would have dared to breath so much as a critical word against the Religion of Peace, Torture, Child Murder, Censorship, Public Executions, Floggings, Stonings, Blindings, Amputations and the rest. And so Sweden's delegation cast its lot with the defenders of the faith along with Mugabe, Putin, the Chavistas and Emperor Kim Jong-un in 'welcoming the President's commitment to reduce [sic] media censorship and promote a less [sic] security-oriented atmosphere'. This, from *Sweden*? Picking up where we left off, the Secretary-General's report continues]:

Between January and November 2015, the Special Procedures transmitted five communications to the Government concerning freedom of assembly and association, drawing attention to its international obligation to respect and full protect the rights of all individuals to associate freely, including individuals adhering to minority views of beliefs, and human rights defenders

29. Article 498 of the Penal Code imposes a punishment of two to 10 years of imprisonment for any individual who 'establishes or directs a group, society or branch, with aims to perturb the security of the country'. [A catch-all clause if ever there was one. So much for Corbyn's 'lively' and 'robust' debate.]
30. The Secretary-General remains concerned about the large number of political prisoners, including members of political parties [mostly of the left be it noted] who continue to serve sentences for charges that are believed to be linked to the exercise of their freedom of association and peaceful assembly...In particular, the house arrest, since February 2011, of the two former presidential candidates and leaders of the 'Green Movement', Mir Hossein Mousavi and Mehdi Karoubi, remains of concern.

[In view of Corbyn's pronouncement, after two decades and more of opposition to UK membership the EU, that leaving the European Union would result in a 'bonfire of workers' rights', and his close relations of late with a number of left trade union officials who sit on the Labour Party's National Executive Committee, the following item is of special interest.]

31. The Secretary-General remains concerned about the ongoing ban on the activities of the Workers' Union and Teachers Association, whose members continue to face judicial harassment, arrest and prosecution for legitimately and peacefully exercising their right to freely associate and assemble. Teachers' unions were targeted in recent months for protesting against inequality, poor living standards and overdue wages. Some of their leaders have been arrested and prosecuted. [A list of such cases then follows]

F. The situation of women

[Islam is notorious amongst civilised people for its subjugation of women, and Iran lacks no zeal in that respect, as the following cases illustrate.]

35. [Iran] is not party to the Convention on the Elimination of All Forms of discrimination against Women.

36. The Secretary-General remains concerned about violations of the human rights of women including in relation to the freedom of movement, the right to health and in work. Following the adoption of the April 2015 Plan to Promote Virtue and Prevent Vice, [here as always since the time of Eve, blamed on women] strict and discriminatory rules on women's and girls' dress are being enforced across the country. On 15 November 2015, police announced that cars driven by women not observing the Hijab will be impounded for a week and fines will be imposed…On December 15 2015, the head of Tehran's traffic police was quoted by media stating that during the previous eight months, Traffic police had dealt with 40,000 cases of 'bad Hijabs, with vehicles seized and their owners brought before courts…The authorities stressed that wearing the Hijab was a moral matter and its imposition in public places is to maintain security. [sic…under the Ayatollahs, every day is a hijab day.]

37. There has been no progress in efforts to end child marriages. According to the Global Gender Gap Report 2015, 21 percent of Iranian women aged between 15 and 19 married as children…the legal age of marriage for girls is still 13 years old, as established by the Civil Code. The same Civil Code allows girls below the legal age to be married with the consent of their father or the permission of a court. In their comments on this report, the authorities acknowledged occurrences of underage marriage in rural areas and noted that it is legitimate in some regions due to geography [sic] and sexual maturity. [sic]

38. Article 1117 of the Civil Code allows men to prevent their wives from being employed in the public and private sector if they consider it to be 'incompatible with the interests of the family or with his or his wife's dignity'. The Code also requires women to be submissive to men *and specifies that they may lose their rights, including to maintenance, if they fail to respond to the sexual needs of their husband.* [Emphasis added. Forget the pathetic Sharia stooge Corbyn for a moment, and ask yet again: Where are the feminist protests in the west on behalf of their Iranian sisters against a law that effectively upholds the Koranically-sanctioned right of a husband *to rape his wife?*]

39. The report ranks Iran 106 out of 145 countries in terms of educational achievement…In this context, the gender gap among out of school children of primary age is particularly alarming, with 63.3 percent of girls not enrolled in primary education compared to 35 percent boys.

40. Iran was ranked 141 out of 143 countries in terms of women's economic participation and opportunity, with unemployment for women reaching 19.8 percent compared with 8.6 percent for men. [As with item 39, these are of course official Government statistics]

VI

Equal…Under the Lash

In the religion so admired by western *dhimmi* feminists, when it comes to the law, in all respects save one, women are deemed to be only half as worthy as men. In the penal code of Jeremy Corbyn's former Iranian pimps, women achieve full equality with men only when they come under the lash, hanged or stoned to death. For example, while Article 75 specifies that 'if adultery is punishable by flogging it may be provable by the testimony of two just men or four just women', when it comes to the infliction of punishment for this crime, Article 88 states that 'the punishment for an unmarried adulterer or adulteress shall be 100 lashes'…exactly the same. The only gender variation allowed for in the execution of this punishment is in posture and state of attire:

> The flogging of an adulterer shall be carried out while the adulterer is standing upright and his body is bare except for his genitals. The lashes shall strike all parts of his body except his face, head and genitals and with full force. The adulteress shall be flogged while she is seated and her clothing tightly bound to her body. (Article 100)

When it comes to stoning, the same commendable concern for the modesty of the female victim is observed:

> The stoning of an adulterer or an adulteress shall be carried out when each is placed in a hole and covered up with soil, he up his waist, and she up to a line above her breasts.' (Article 102) Another variation arises due to biology: 'If an ailing woman or a woman in menstruation has been condemned to death or stoning, the punishment shall be carried out. If, however, she has been condemned to flogging, the punishment shall be delayed until she has recovered or her menstruation period is over.' (Article 93)

The same equation of one man = two women applies even in the case of murder, which is not regarded as nearly so serious a crime as adultery or homosexuality, which carries an automatic death penalty: 'The blood money for second or first-degree murder of a Muslim woman is half that of a Muslim man.' (Article 300)

Likewise, for abortion:

> Blood money for the aborted foetus which has taken in the human spirit shall be paid in full if it is male, one half if it is female and three quarters if its gender is in doubt.' (Article 487) According to Article 297, the blood money, or fine, for killing a man is set at the value of 100 camels, this being the same penalty incurred for irreparably damaging a man's testicles. Since according to the Sharia, a man's left testicle carries the seed for males, and the right for females [another testimony to the superiority of Islamic science over the inferior *kuffar* version] the separate fine for damage to just the left testicle is 66.6 camels, and the right, 33.3. [Sharia maths…66.6 + 33.3 = 100. And what use is 0.6 or 0.3 of a camel? Perhaps Jeremy can tell us.]

As we have already noted, under Sharia law, to prove rape four male witnesses are required. So in a case of gang rape, where all the 'witnesses' are also likely to be participants, it is the victim who can find herself convicted of adultery. This indeed happened in one of Prince Charles' favourite monarchies, where in November 2007, a Saudi woman who had been gang raped by seven men had her sentence increased from 100 to 200 lashes and a prison term of six months, because the court ruled she had invited rape by sitting in a parked car with a man who was not a relative. So, only a mere 100 lashes for being gang raped when accompanied by a male relative. Although this case attracted considerable media coverage, I cannot recall any feminist protests outside western Saudi embassies, or for that matter from Clarence House, official residence of the Prince of Wales.

H Return of the Caliphate?

The fostering by successive UK Governments of a proliferation of faith schools has probably contributed more than any other single external factor to the increased segregation of Muslims from the rest of British society, ensuring as it must do that the children of Muslim parents will have ever fewer opportunities to encounter children from other cultural backgrounds. Ironically, this policy is one of the fruits of what goes by the name of multi-culturalism and promoting diversity. Let us be for once charitable and allow that that those who engage in this act of cultural suicide simply do not know or lack the capacity to imagine what it means to be ruled by Islam. Spain, which only finally liberated itself from nearly eight centuries of Muslim rule in 1492, has no such excuse. And just in case anyone had forgotten what Islamic Jihad is about, they were given a reminder when in March 2004, with a series of bomb explosions, Muslim terrorists killed 192 and wounded another 2,000 at Madrid's main railway station. In 2010, Spain's Muslims numbered just over one million, 2.3% of the country's total population. Even after discounting the impact of the surge of Muslim migrants into Europe since 2014, by the year 2030, the number of Spain's Muslims is projected to reach nearly two million, 3.7% of the total population.

As elsewhere in Europe, the vast majority of Spain's Muslims have shown no desire to integrate themselves into the host society, highlighted by their vast over-representation in crime statistics. Though comprising only a little over 2% of the country's population, Muslims make up 70% of Spain's prison inmates, the highest percentage in Europe. Put another way, a Muslim is at least *thirty times* more likely to end up in jail than any other Spaniard. As of 2010, 42% of Moroccans, the largest Muslim group resident in Spain, were unemployed, double the national jobless rate. And of course, self-ghettoisation has proceeded apace, just as it has in all other European states with a substantial and growing Muslim population. In Salt, a township north of Barcelona, the Muslim population has reached 40% and is heading for a majority any time soon. Until it was exposed, a secret deal, agreed by a Socialist council blatantly bidding for the Muslim vote, would have allowed the construction of Europe's largest Salafist Mosque, funded like so many others across Europe by Saudi oil money. Here in Spain as elsewhere, leftist politicians, unabashed to be riding on the backs of a brutal feudal monarchy, are likewise unperturbed by Salafist preachers publicly advocating the adoption, or rather in this case, the restoration of Sharia law.

Pending Sharia law's formal introduction, Muslims are enforcing it piecemeal. After failing to persuade Lleida city authorities to ban dogs from all public places as Islam requires, local Muslims took the (Sharia) law into their hands. In just one day, 14 dogs were found dead, believed to have been poisoned. In Tarragona, the local Salafi imam was arrested after forcing a 31-year-old woman to wear a hijab. He had threatened to burn the woman's house down for being an infidel. In order to avoid what the court called 'social conflict' (to be precise, Muslim rioting) the imam was cleared of any wrongdoing. In Barcelona, following the ban on bull fighting in Catalonia, Muslim leaders demanded the right to build a mega-mosque on the now disused Coliseum Bull Ring even though Spain already has well over 100 Wahhabi mosques with more, we can be sure, on the way. Wahhabi Islam is the warrior version dominant in Saudi Arabia and promoted worldwide by its mosque and *madrassah* building programmes. It should therefore come as no surprise to learn that when polled on the subject, 7 out of ten Muslims ranked their allegiance to Islam higher than their loyalty, if any, to their host country.

In the light of the above, one would expect public policy, in so far as it relates to the Muslim population, to be one of encouraging, especially amongst the young, a more positive attitude towards the society and culture of their host nation. One might reasonably think so, but one would be wrong. The entire thrust of Spain's conservative government educational strategy was in the opposite direction, one of using the school system to re-enforce what they already have drilled into them at home and in their 'communities', a policy that can only result in accentuating the already deep divisions that exist in Spain between Muslims and non-Muslims. As in the UK with its Muslim faith schools, but more systematically, the solution to the problem of Jihadi terrorism was to ensure that the young are force-fed with Islam 24/7.

In April 2016, Spain's Ministry of Education announced plans to spend vast amounts of mainly non-Muslim tax payer's money on a programme of Islamic instruction aimed at the children of Muslim parents. According to the Education Ministry, this programme would seek to stimulate 'interest in religious and cultural texts' and what it called 'curiosity' for the *Koran* in oral and written language. Pupils would be encouraged to memorise 'Islamic recitations, narration and descriptions', just as they do in Saudi-funded and pupil-beating *madrassahs* across the Muslim diaspora. So instead of special courses designed to acquaint Muslim pupils with the classic texts of western liberal and democratic thought, in the first place those of Salvador Maradiaga, an eloquent and tireless opponent of Franco's fascism, they will chant in Arabic hour after hour verses from a book that preaches contempt for women, hatred of the Jews, and the duty to wage Jihad against their infidel hosts. And it is this policy, claims Spain's Ministry of Education, that will ensure the defeat of Islamic 'extremism'! Perhaps in their eagerness to appease Islam, those who devised this policy forgot the stark warning of George Santayana that 'he who does not learn from history is condemned to repeat it'.

While in the UK, the Department of Education goes through the motions of checking up on what is taught in schools run by Islamic organisations, in Spain, even this pretence of supervision is to be dispensed with. Those who teach the curriculum of Islamic indoctrination, *in state schools, at state expense*, are nevertheless to be chosen by local 'Muslim communities', which in practice will mean their mainly Salafist clerics. The content of the courses, and the textbooks to be used, will also selected in the same way, and will need final approval, not by the Ministry of Education, *but by a Muslim body*, the Islamic Commission of Spain. Let me repeat, for this could well be the music of the near future elsewhere, here we have the scandal of public money, collected almost entirely from non-Muslims, being spent exclusively on Muslims, with private, Muslim, control over how it will be spent. And this is how: Pupils between the ages of 3 (sic) and 18 who undergo this course will be expected to 'emulate the values of Mohammed', many of which have been the subject of a critical evaluation in this work and should require no repetition here. Suffice it to say that should the project achieve this particular goal, it will have trained yet more generations of wife-beaters, thieves, liars, parasites, rapists, paedophiles, anti-Semites and Jihadis. Instead of being encouraged to learn about and appreciate the achievements of the country and continent in which they will grow up, without which there can be no prospect of integration, pupils will be studying the 'achievements of Islamic civilisation', specifically including the 1990 Cairo declaration of the Organisation of the Islamic Conference, which counterposed to the United Nations' secular definition of natural Universal Human Rights the theocratic notion that all human freedoms are defined by and subjected to Sharia law; exactly what Spain's Salafist clerics are demanding. As the old proverb has it, 'those whom the gods would destroy, they first make mad'.

I A Voice in the Desert

On two occasions, in 1991 and 2003, with scarcely a dissenting voice, throughout the West, the far Left mobilised to defend the fascist, genocidal regime of Saddam Hussein against invasions led by the United States. In a political re-alignment redolent of the Stalin-Hitler pact of August 23, 1939, leftists who up until the very eve of Saddam's invasion and annexation of Kuwait in August 1991 had denounced and demonstrated against the Ba'athist dictatorship's relentless persecution of leftists, Kurds and Shi'as, literally overnight began to hail this same regime as a resolute foe of western imperialism. Saddam's useful idiot George Galloway captured perfectly this slavish submission to the butcher of Baghdad when in the presence of his puppet and pay master, he was caught on camera saluting his 'courage, strength and indefatigability'.

As I have tried to demonstrate with many examples, the Sharia left's version of international solidarity almost invariably results in supporting any regime, no matter how reactionary or despotic, that finds itself at odds with the west. And this, as we have seen, is the official policy of the Stop the War Coalition, founded, and from 2011 to 2015, chaired by former Leader of the Labour Party and Her Majesty's Opposition, Comrade Corbyn. As we have also seen, the same principle extends to Jihadist movements, especially those dedicated to the destruction of Israel and the extermination of the Jews. A necessary corollary of this orientation is that there can be no international solidarity of the traditional kind in support of internal oppositions to such 'anti-imperialist' regimes, for example, the Kurds, ('western pawns') secularists, cultural figures, leftists, labour and human rights activists and feminists. In the judgment of Sharia leftists, no less than that of rulers of these states, they are all, consciously or otherwise, by opposing the enemy at home and failing to see the 'bigger picture', simply serving the goals of western imperialism.

What follows is a broadcast on Lebanese TV that puts to shame those on the left who now and in the past have betrayed the cause of democracy and freedom for the Arab peoples by siding with their domestic oppressors. The date is July 31, 2005, at the height of the combined Ba'athist and al-Qaeda terrorist campaign to overthrow the democratically-elected government of post-Saddam Iraq, a war that despite its catalogue of appalling atrocities inflicted on the Iraqi people, the Sharia left falsely depicted and supported as a legitimate 'resistance' to western imperialism. The speaker is Sayyed Ayad Jamal Aldin, an Iraqi Shi'a cleric, secularist intellectual, member of the Iraqi parliament and anti-corruption campaigner.

First of all, no-one can accuse me of sectarianism, because I support a secular regime which will fully separate religion and state. I believe that my freedom as a Shiite and a religious person will never be complete unless I preserve the freedom of the Sunni, the Christian, the Jew, the Sabai [related to Hinduism] and the Yazidi. We will not be able to preserve the freedom of the mosque unless we preserve the freedom of the entertainment clubs. The curricula, both the modern ones in some Arab and Islamic countries, and the books of jurisprudence and heritage, have many flaws that must be fixed once and for all. There are the rulings about *Ahl Al-Dhimma*, [rules governing the treatment of non-Muslims in an Islamic state] even if Allah be praised, no modern regime can enforce these rulings. However, just for the sake of amusement and diversion, I recommend that the viewer read the books of jurisprudence and see how *Ahl Al-Dhimma* are treated. I especially recommend this to a people with a lust for Arab and Islamic history who claim that our history is a source of pride and that others were treated with kindness and love, especially Christians and Jews. [this is a very different appraisal, made from the inside so to speak, from Obama's "proud tradition of tolerance".] Among these rulings, a *Dhimmi* must wear a belt so he would be identifiable [like the yellow star worn by Jews under the Nazis]. Moreover, it is recommended that he be forced to the narrowest paths, and there are even jurisprudents who say that it is recommended to slap a Christian on the back of his neck so he would feel humiliated and degraded. This is how we harass him and then invite him to join Islam.

I can swear that the Prophet Mohammed is innocent of such inhuman jurisprudence. I challenge anyone among our people with a lust for history, to talk candidly to the west, to the advocates of human rights, and tell them that our heritage has such evils and flaws. We are a nation of blackout and darkness. [Not according to the anti-Orientalist Professor Edward Said] We cannot live in the light of day. We do not hold ourselves accountable. This is why America came to demand that the Arabs be accountable. We must have more self-confidence and be accountable before others hold us accountable. We must discipline ourselves before the Americans and the English discipline us. We must maintain human rights that we have neglected for 1,300 or 1,400 years, to this day [that is, throughout the entire history of Islam] until the arrival of the Americans, the Christians, the English, the Zionists, the Crusaders - call them what you will. They came to teach you, the followers of Mohammed how to respect human rights.

The Arab governments should support the Iraqi government, which was legally elected. I think this is the only government in our Arab region that was formed following free and fair elections. The Arabs must stop meddling in Iraq's affairs and stop inciting hatred, violence and terrorism. *They should not call these terrorist attacks resistance.* [emphasis added] There isn't any kind of resistance in Iraq, these are terrorist attacks under the guise of patriotism and of claims about defeating the occupation. They have nothing to do with the Americans or others. *They are scum, remnants of the previous corrupt regime.* [emphasis added] They attracted all the Arab terrorists, this riffraff, which entered Iraq in order to kill according to ethnicity. [Not according to Corbyn, who from the safety of London proclaimed his support for what he described as 'the resistance', 'engaged in a titanic struggle to rid their country of occupying forces'.

They kill the Shiites in public. We have not heard a single Arab jurisprudent condemn the terrorist attacks that target Shiites [nor a Sharia leftist]. We are killed because of our identity. They kill Shiites became of their identity and the killers are the dirtiest riffraff among the Arabs. Nevertheless, we have heard no condemnation of Al Zaqawi [Al-Qaeda terrorist leader in Iraq] and his followers. If we were English or Americans, you would see the court jurisprudents of the Arab regimes and all the Arab governments that stand behind them convene thousands of summits to condemn terrorism, but they remain silent about what happens in Iraq. [again, like the Sharia left] Moreover, we saw the President of a large Arab state say: "We call for national reconciliation", as though there is a real problem among the Iraqi people. There is no problem. There is the tyrannical Saddam Hussein regime, which is the only legitimate heir to the Arab and Islamic civilisation. [sic…what would the late Professor say to *that*?] This corrupt regime, which has been toppled, and on whose ruins a modern and democratic state will be established, this is not what the Arabs like. The Arabs want tyrannical regimes, in line with their backward culture.

165

If we were English or Americans, you would see how the Arabs would raise an outcry over every [civilian] casualty. Today, dozens of people and children queuing in front of bakeries are killed and we hear no condemnation from any jurisprudent, quasi jurisprudent or any government.

What is happening in Iraq is a real massacre and a real war between truth and falsehood, between a democratic government that relies on the public, and the remnants of the Umayyad, Abbasid [early Sunni caliphates] and Ottoman tyranny. Iraq will be a cemetery for them and those behind them. The terrified and self-defeated Arab states who fear the establishment of a democratic regime in Iraq would prefer a stupid and reckless dictator like Saddam to a democratic regime in Iraq because the epidemic of democracy and the winds of freedom will reach them whether they like it or not.

J Back Channel to Allah?

In 2016, while several western powers, including the USA, France and the UK, conducted military operations against the Islamic State, two contestants for the leadership of the Labour Party advocated an entirely different approach. As someone who, when it is a matter of combatting Islamic terrorism, is invariably devoted to the cause of peace, the incumbent, Jeremy Corbyn, felt obliged to seek what he called a 'political solution' to the rise of ISIS, one that, in an BBC TV interview on January 17, he described as a 'back channel' approach to the Islamic State, leading to what he termed on another occasion as a 'peace process', analogous presumably to that negotiated between the IRA and the British government in the 1990s. His opponent, Owen Smith, favoured exactly the same policy, announcing in a televised husting on August 16 that the aim should be to get 'all of the actors' (sic) 'around the table'. In both cases, the assumption was that the Islamic State could be negotiated with, and would sooner or later be prepared, perhaps even obliged, to sit at the same table with those who are currently at war with it. This assumption in turn rested upon another, that the Islamic State was, for all its religious nomenclature, rhetoric and claims, essentially a secular political entity, and that its leaders were therefore driven primarily by worldly concerns.

As a corrective to this widely shared and dangerous delusion, and as proof that the Islamic State Caliphate was exactly what its leaders said it was, the instrument of Allah's will on earth, I have reproduced below an item from number 15 of the Islamic State's official journal, *Dabiq,* titled, appropriately, *Why We Hate You, and Why We Fight You.* What they hated about 'us', that is, the infidel west, was not our foreign policy. As the article makes clear, this was the very least of our sins. The Islamic State hated and fought us because we infidels had refused to worship Allah and because we denied the teachings of his prophet. What our clerics, Corbyns, Smiths, Camerons, Clintons, Obamas, Merkels and Hollandes simply could not accept was that *this war was about theology, that and nothing else.* Of this issue's 80 odd pages, well over half are devoted purely to theology, the bulk of the remainder comprising accounts of various terrorist operations (a term they gladly embrace since it is in the *Koran*) against the enemies of Allah. There is also the by now familiar graphic depiction of a beheading, captioned, 'The Sword is Part of Allah's Law'.

No amount of searching for 'back channels' or tables to sit around was going to convince the rulers of the Islamic state, and those who had left Europe to kill and be killed for its cause, that they were in error in matters theological, and that Islam is a faith of peace, love and tolerance. And the same applies to all other Jihadi movements that fight for the same cause, Corbyn's Hamas and Hezbollah friends included. What they do is in accordance with commands inscribed in a thirteen-hundred-year-old book they believe was transmitted from an all-powerful god to his last prophet, Mohammed, a god to whom his Muslim slaves are alone answerable. The mandate of the Caliphate that ruled the Islamic State did not come from those it governed, but from heaven. The terms that we in the west employ to conduct our political discourse, like freedom, democracy, accountability, either have a totally different meaning, or mean nothing at all. Instead, the reader will see that at every step, what the Islamic State did, and why, is purely religious in content and purpose, and justified and buttressed with citations from Islam's highest authority, the *Koran*. It therefore follows, as indeed the article states, that any negotiations with the Islamic State would have had to have been conducted on these terms, and these alone. What in the end defeated it was not Corbyn's 'back channel', but Kurdish bullets and Western bombs.

Why We Hate You and Why We Fight You

Shortly following the blessed attack on a sodomite Crusader night club by the mujahid Omar Mateen, American politicians were quick to jump into the spotlight and denounce the shooting, declaring it a hate crime, an act of terrorism, of senseless violence. A hate crime? Yes. Muslims undoubtedly hate liberalist sodomites, as does anyone else with any shred of their fitrah, (their inborn human nature) still intact. An act of terror? Most definitely. Muslims have been commanded to terrorise the disbelieving enemies of Allah. [The author of this text missed a trick here. He (it is safe to assume it must be a 'he') should have quoted at this point the *Koran,* Chapter 8, Verse 12: 'I will strike terror into the hearts of those that disbelieve'.] But an act of senseless violence? One would think that the average Westerner by now would have abandoned the tired claim that the actions of the mujahidin - who have repeatedly stated their goals, intentions and motivations - don't make sense. Unless you truly - and naively - believe that the crimes of the West against Islam and the Muslims, whether insulting the prophet or burning the *Koran* or waging war against the Caliphate, won't prompt brutal retaliation from the mujahidin, you know full well that the likes of the attacks carried out by Omar Mateen, Larossi Aballa and many others before and after them in revenge for Islam and the Muslims make complete sense. The only senseless thing would be for there to be no fierce, violent retaliation in the first place.

Many Westerners however are already aware that claiming the attacks of the mujahidin to be senseless and questioning incessantly as to why we hate the West and why we fight them is nothing more than a political act and a propaganda tool. The politicians will say it regardless of how much it stands in opposition to facts and common sense just to garner votes for the next election cycle. The analysts and journalists will say it order to keep themselves from becoming a target for saying something that the masses deem to be politically incorrect. [This is wrong. In fact, the reverse is the case. Living as they do in daily contact with, and now fear of Islam, the 'masses', who care nothing for political correctness, have a pretty clear idea of what the Jihadis are about. It is the politically correct establishment that has tried to persuade them, with diminishing success, that the real Islam has nothing to do with terrorism.]

The apostate 'imams' in the West will adhere to the same tired cliché in order to avoid a backlash from the disbelieving societies in which they've chosen to reside. The point is, people know that it's foolish, but they keep repeating it regardless because they're afraid of the consequences of deviating from the script. There are exceptions among the disbelievers, no doubt, people who will unabashedly declare that jihad and the laws of the Sharia - as well as everything else deemed taboo by the Islam-is-a-peaceful-religion crowd - are in fact completely Islamic [those we in the west condemn as Islamophobes] but they tend to be people with far less credibility who are painted as a social fringe, so their voices are dismissed and a large segment of the ignorant masses continues believing the false narrative. As such, it becomes important for us to clarify to the West in unequivocal terms - yet again - why we hate you and why you fight you.

1. We hate you, first and foremost, because you are disbelievers [so, not because we are imperialists]; you reject the oneness of Allah - whether you realise it or not - by making partners for Him in worship, you blaspheme against Him, claiming He has a son, you fabricate lies against His prophets and messengers, and you indulge in all manner of devilish practices. It is for this reason that we were commanded to openly declare our hatred for you and our enmity towards you. There has already been for you an excellent example in Abraham and those with him, when they said to their people, "indeed, we are disassociated from you and from whatever you worship other than Allah. We have rejected you, and there has arisen, between us and you, enmity and hatred forever until you believe in Allah alone." (*Koran,* Chapter 60, Verse 4)

Furthermore, just as your disbelief is the primary [sic] reason we hate you, as we have been commanded to fight the disbelievers until they submit to the authority of Islam, either by becoming Muslims, or by paying jizyah [the tax on non-believing monotheists] - for those afford this option - and living in humiliation under the rule of the Muslims. Thus, even if you were to stop fighting us, your best-case scenario in a state of war would be that we would suspend our attacks against you - if we deemed it necessary - in order to focus on the closer and more immediate threats before eventually resuming our campaigns against you. Apart from the option of a temporary truce, this is the only likely scenario that would bring you fleeting respite from our attacks. So in the end, you cannot bring an indefinite halt to our war against you. At most, you could only delay it temporarily. 'And fight the until there is no fitnah [paganism] and [until] the religion, all of it, is for Allah.' (*Koran,* Chapter 2, Verse 193)

2. We hate you because your secular, liberal societies permit the very things that Allah has prohibited while banning many of things He has permitted [such as slavery, wife beating marital rape, female genital mutilation and paedophilia], a matter that doesn't concern you because you separate between religion and state, thereby granting supreme authority to your whims and desires via the legislators you vote into power. In doing so, you desire to rob Allah of His right to be obeyed and you wish to usurp that right for yourselves. 'Legislation is not but for Allah'. (*Koran,* Chapter, 12, Verse 40) Your secular liberalism has led to tolerate and even support 'gay rights', to allow alcohol, drugs, fornication, gambling and usury to become widespread and to encourage the people to mock those who denounce these filthy sins and vices. As such, we wage war against you to stop you from spreading your disbelief and debauchery – your secularism and nationalism, your perverted liberal values, your Christianity and atheism - and all the depravity and corruption they entail. You've made it your mission to 'liberate' Muslim societies; we've made it our mission to fight off your influence and protect mankind from your misguided concepts and your deviant way of life.

3. In the case of the atheist fringe. We hate you and wage war against you because you disbelieve in the existence of your Lord and Creator. You witness the

extraordinarily complex makeup of created beings, and the astonishing and inexplicably precise physical laws that govern the entire universe [not 'precise', but unvarying], but insist that they all came about through randomness [not so] and that one should be faulted, mocked and ostracised for recognising that the astonishing signs we witness day after day are the creation of the Wise, All-Known Creator and not the result of accidental occurrence [not 'accidental', but natural]. 'Or were they created by nothing, or were they the creators of themselves?' (*Koran,* Chapter 14, Verse 35) Your disbelief in your Creator further leads you to deny the day of judgement, claiming that 'you only live once': 'Those who disbelieve have claimed that they will never be resurrected. Say, "yes, by my Lord, you will surely be resurrected; then you will surely be informed of what you did." And that, for Allah, is easy.' (*Koran,* Chapter 14, Verse 7)

4. We hate you for your crimes against Islam and wage war against you to punish you for your transgressions against our religion. As long as your subjects [sic] continue to mock our faith, insult the prophets of Allah - including Noah, Abraham, Moses and Muhammad - burn the Quran, and openly vilify the laws of the Shari'ah, we will continue to retaliate, not with slogans and placards, but with bullets and knives.

5. We hate you for your crimes against the Muslims; your drones and fighter jets bomb, kill, and maim our people around the world, and your puppets in the usurped lands and oppress, torture, and wage war against anyone who calls to the truth. As such, we fight to stop you from killing, our men, women, and children, to liberate them those of them whom you imprison and torture, and to take revenge for the countless Muslims who've suffered as result of your deeds.

6. We hate you for invading our lands and fight you to repel you and drive you out. As long as there is an inch of territory left for us to reclaim, jihad will continue to be a personal obligation on every single Muslim. [Here too, a Koranic citation would have been appropriate: 'Fighting is prescribed for you, and ye dislike it. But it is possible that ye dislike a thing which is good for you, and that ye love a thing that is bad for you. But Allah knoweth, and ye know not.' (Chapter 2, Verse 216)]

What's so important to understand here is that although some might argue that your foreign policies are the extent of what drives out hatred, this particular reason for hating you is secondary, hence the reasons we addressed it at the end of the above list. The fact is, even if you were to stop bombing us, imprisoning us, vilifying us, and usurping our lands, *we would continue to hate you because our primary reason for hating will not cease until you embrace Islam.* [emphasis added] Even if you were to pay jizyah and live under the authority of Islam in humiliation, we would continue to hate you.

No doubt, we would stop fighting you then as we would stop fighting any disbelievers who enter into a covenant with us, but we would not stop hating you. What's equally if not more important to understand is that we fight you, not simply to punish and deter you, but to bring you true freedom in this life and salvation in the Hereafter, freedom from being enslaved to your whims and desires as well as those of your clergy and legislatures, and salvation by worshipping your Creator alone and following His messenger. We fight you in order to bring you out from the darkness of disbelief and into the light of Islam, and to liberate you from the constraints of living for the sake of the worldly life alone so that you may enjoy both the blessings of the worldly life and the bliss of

170

the Hereafter. [Again, one notes the total absence of any concern for what the Sharia left would describe as the 'struggle against Western imperialism'. The war is against our godlessness, which the Sharia left, for all its simulated enthusiasm for Islam, is guiltier of than most.]

The gist of the matter is that there is indeed a rhyme to our terrorism, [sic] warfare, ruthlessness, and brutality [sic]. As much as some liberal journalist would like you to believe that we do what we do because we're simply monsters with no logic to our action [and which therefore has no connection with the 'real' Islam], the fact is that we continue to wage - and escalate - a calculated war that the West thought it had ended several years ago. We continue dragging you further and further into a swamp you thought you'd already escaped only to realise that you're stuck even deeper within its murky waters…And we do so while offering you a way out on our terms. So you can continue to believe that those 'despicable terrorists hate you because of your lattes and Timberlands, and continue spending ridiculous amounts of money to try to prevail in an unwinnable war, or you can accept reality and recognise that we will never stop hating you *until you embrace Islam*, and will never stop fighting you until you're ready to leave the swamp of warfare and terrorism through the exits we provide, the very exits put forth by our Lord for the People of the Scripture: Islam, jizyah, or – as a last means of fleeting respite - a temporary truce. (emphasis added)

[Corbyn seeks a 'back channel' to the Islamic State, Owen Smith a place with it at the same table. My advice to them both is, mind you head.]

K Volunteers for Genocide?

For obvious reasons, estimates of the number of Arabs who have illegally migrated into Israel, excluding the 'occupied territories', since 1967, vary. All however agree that the number is at least in the tens of thousands, and probably higher. In addition, there are the approximately 70,000 Arabs who have returned legally since 1948 in accordance with Israel's policy of re-uniting families lies torn apart by the Arab invasion and ensuing war of that year, and those many thousands more who have in recent years taken up legal employment in Israel. There has also been a much larger movement of Palestinian Arabs from Jordan into the West Bank since it came under Israeli administration following the June of war of 1967. Again, accurate figures are hard to come by, since this migration is also mainly illegal, but the number is in the region of half a million.

All this must seem inexplicable to anyone who is gullible or prejudiced enough to take seriously the often-repeated allegation emanating from all quarters of the political spectrum that the Jews of Israel are set on a course of exterminating the Palestinians. Why risk the hazards and endure the upheaval involved in illegal migration only then to knowingly put you head in the Zionist noose? I say knowingly, because as we have seen, around the clock, 24/7, the Palestinian Authority and Hamas media, clergy and public institutions, in the first place, naturally, their partly UN-funded schools, from infancy drum into the brains of every Palestinian that the Zionists seek their deaths.

And yet they still come, while virtually no Arabs move in the opposite direction, fleeing to escape what their political and clerical leaders assure them is, according to the two versions, either an impending or actual genocide. (Arabs comprise barely 5% of those annually migrating from Israel.) It is as if millions of Jews, in the full knowledge that they faced near certain death in the gas chambers of Hitler's Final Solution, chose nevertheless to migrate into Germany at the height of the Holocaust. So why do so many Palestinians apparently prefer to risk an early death in an Israeli Auschwitz rather than continue to savour the many joys and blessings of life in the West Bank and the Gaza Strip? Let us attempt to answer that question with a number of facts.

Just in one year, 2015, 180,000 Palestinians crossed the border into Israel, not as illegal immigrants (or suicide bombers) but for treatment in an Israeli medical facility. In addition, there are many who also prefer to work for their Zionist enemies rather than their fellow Palestinians. Speaking on Palestinian Authority TV on March 16, 2016, the Palestinian labour lawyer Khaled Fukhi said the following:

> The Palestinians female workers in the Israeli agricultural sector enjoy many rights, like any Israeli worker in the agricultural sector. The salary is higher than the minimum wage, fourteen vacation days a year in the first four years, 2,000 shekels convalescence pay yearly, payment for holidays, whether Islamic or Jewish. But in reality, Palestinian workers - and especially the female workers - do not receive these things....The Palestinian middleman takes 50%, 60% and even 70% of her salary. If her daily salary is 180 shekels, in the end she receives 60 shekels....

Excuse the word steals, but that is the exact word.

On February 4, 2016, speaking on the same TV channel, Qassem Abu Hadwah, a labourer from Hebron said the following:

The lack of monitoring of Palestinian owners or companies and factories and their exploitation of workers is what has forced people to Israel...If only the salary in the Palestinian Authority was at least half of the salary in Israel, no one would work in Israel. However, workers have to go to Israel, because no one in the PA gives them what they deserve for their work.

According to the official PA daily, *Al-Hayat Al-Jadida*, of February 26, 2016, 'the average daily wage for employees in the West Bank was 94.1 shekels, and 61.9 shekels in the Gaza Strip, while the average wage for employees in Israel and the [Jewish] settlements is 198.9 shekels' and 'the number of [Palestinian] workers from the West Bank who work in Israel and the [Jewish] settlements reached 112,300.' As of 2018, the unemployment rate in the West Bank was 18%, Gaza 52%, and Israel, 3.6%.

L The Religion of Jihad

'Islam is a religion that preaches peace.' (Barak Obama, September 28,2014)

'I will cast terror into the hearts of those who disbelieve. Therefore strike off their heads and every fingertip of them.' (*Koran*, Chapter 8, *The spoils of War*, Verse 12)

There is an historic precedent for the failure of western politicians, academics, journalists and other opinion formers to fully comprehend, and therefore to effectively resist the gathering threat to modern civilisation posed by Islam. Whether it was the extermination of the Jews, crushing the left, war in the East for *Lebensraum*, or reversing the Treaty of Versailles, Hitler never made any secret of his strategic aims, which were first set out systematically and at some length in 1925 in his *Mein Kampf* and subsequently in innumerable public speeches. On the sixth anniversary of Hitler's appointment as Chancellor on January 30, 1933, he announced to the world what his plan was for the Jews:

> If the Jewish financiers in and outside Europe should succeed once in plunging the nations once more into a world war, the result will not be the Bolshevisation of the earth, and thus the victory of Jewry, but the annihilation of the Jewish race in Europe.

On January 30, 1941, Hitler repeated this threat, but minus the reference to the 'Bolshevisation of the earth,' out of deference to his Bolshevik colleagues in the Kremlin, together with whom he, and not 'Jewish financiers' had launched the Second World by conquering and partitioning Poland. In these speeches, Hitler could not have made his intention to go to war and exterminate European Jewry any clearer. Yet hardly anyone took him seriously, least of all those whom he threatened, in the first place, the Jews, or those who had to the power to prevent him carrying out his programme. In the latter case, this was due not so much to stupidity or gullibility, though there was that in plenty, but a lack of imagination or, if you will, to wishful thinking, the false assumption that modern politics would always be played according to the same set of rules by all its participants - for example those of the Geneva Convention and the League of Nations.

Today, exactly the same mind set is preventing the West, with its declarations, conventions and courts of Human Rights, each of which are rejected by all 57 Islamic states, from properly comprehending, and therefore combatting, the Jihad being waged against the liberal democracies by Islam, even though, just like Hitler's speeches, its founding text, readily available in all the world's major languages, makes no attempt conceal its objective of world conquest. For example, the genocidal intentions of Hamas and Hezbollah towards the Jews are no less specific than were those of Hitler, but this has not prevented Corbyn from emulating Chamberlain's peace in our time by praising them as movements dedicated to the cause of 'peace', 'understanding' and' dialogue'. Likewise, the faith that inspires these two terrorist organisations is not only assumed to be a religion just like any other, but even depicted, in defiance of its declared aims and methods to achieve them, as 'a (sometimes even 'the') religion of peace'. But then did not Neville Chamberlain, after handing over to him a chunk of Czechoslovakia, come to the same conclusion about the pacific intentions of Hitler?

After each terrorist atrocity committed by Muslims in the name of Islam and, more often than not, accompanied by exultant cries of '*Allahu Akbar*', 'God is Great', comes the refrain from all and sundry, be they politician, cleric, academic or journalist, 'Nothing to do with Islam', though what it is to do with is a matter of some confusion and no little disagreement. Anyone who dares say it is to do with Islam (and, as we have seen, there are Muslims who do) will invariably be branded by all right-thinking people as racist, Islamophobic and far rightist, by so doing even running the risk in some countries of prosecution for 'hate speech'. What we have here is, to use an expression now much in vogue, a state of denial, one no less monumental or fraught with tragic consequences than that concerning Hitler's declared intentions and his ability to come perilously close to achieving them.

This paralysis of minds steeped to varying degrees in the traditions of the Enlightenment and principles of secular liberal democracy, minds that cannot conceive of a degree and nature of evil so utterly alien to their own culture, is well-described in Walter Laqueur's *The Terrible Secret*, which meticulously documents the failure to either believe or comprehend, and in some cases, even more reprehensibly, when accepted as true, to make public the scale of the Nazi Holocaust of European Jewry. In the passage I cite below, nearly every word applies with equal force to the same lack of imagination that is preventing the West, with the exception of the Jews, from understanding the nature and objectives of Islam's global Jihad against the infidel:

> Democratic societies demonstrated on this occasion as on many others, before and after, that they are incapable of understanding regimes of a different character. Not every modern dictatorship is Hitlerian in character and engages in genocide but every one has the potential to do so. Democratic societies are accustomed to think in liberal, pragmatic categories; conflicts are believed to be based on misunderstandings and can be solved with a modicum of goodwill [viz Corbyn's 'peace process' with the Islamic State]; extremism is a temporary aberration, so is irrational behaviour in general, such as intolerance, cruelty etc. The effort to overcome such basic psychological handicaps is immense. It will be undertaken only in the light of immediate (and painful) experience. Each new generation faces this challenge again for experience cannot be inherited.

David Hume, the 18th century Scottish sceptic, came to exactly the same sobering conclusion: 'There is a universal tendency among mankind to conceive all beings like themselves and to transfer to every object those qualities with which they are familiarly acquainted, and of which they are intimately conscious.' Exactly. This insight explains why, for example, Prime Minister David Cameron sincerely believed that young Muslim men could be weaned from terrorism by enabling them to climb the property ladder. And so it is that like the opponents of and refugees from the tyranny of Hitler and Stalin, only the apostates from Islam, because they have endured and rejected it, can truly comprehend its totalitarian nature and barbaric methods. The unwelcome message the apostates from Islam bring of a religion dedicated to the overthrow of western civilisation is dismissed as 'horror stories', 'Islamophobia' and even criminalised as 'hate speech', even though it is there for all to read in the faith's holiest texts as it was in the writings and speeches of Hitler, Lenin and Stalin

Readers by now should be familiar with some of the many pronouncements by liars or ignoramuses (and in some cases by those who are both) that Islam is a religion of peace. Earlier in this work, I made what I assumed was the correct observation that one of the few places in the UK where it is possible to speak the truth about Islam without reprimand or fear of prosecution is a court of law, together with Parliament a place where free speech is privileged. Now I am not so sure. Justice Haddon-Cave, the judge presiding over the case of the Parsons Green bomber Ahmed Hassan, when sentencing Hassan to life imprisonment, in the opinion of the National Secular Society, went beyond his brief by extoling what he saw as the peaceful nature of Islam. The Judicial Conduct Investigation Office to which the NSS made its case did not agree, ruling that that the judge's reference to the *Koran* as 'a book of peace' was 'founded on case law' (not what its text actually says about Jihad), and that there was a 'legitimate public interest' in making such statements to 'address Islamophobia', presumably even if such statements might not necessarily be true. This is what Judge Haddon-Cave actually said to Hassan: 'You will have plenty of time to study the *Koran* in prison. The *Koran* is a book of peace...Islam is a religion of peace...the *Koran* and Islam forbid terror'. Only the first of these statements is true. The rest are outright falsehoods, all the more despicable because they have been made by a judge in his capacity as a custodian of English justice. The *Koran* does not 'forbid terror', it explicitly prescribes it, as in Chapter 8, Verses 13: 'I will cast terror into the hearts of the disbelievers. Smite them above their necks [i.e., decapitate them] and cut off their fingertips.'

This ruling may well have profound implications. Are we to understand that, based upon case law, it is now part of Common Law that that *Koran* and Islam are a book and religion of peace, and that to say otherwise in a court is inadmissible evidence and/or to be in contempt of court, and outside of court, can constitute an indictable offence? We shall see.

While not always agreeing on the exact total, scholars of Islam, whether they be themselves Muslims or infidels, agree that the number of Koranic verses advocating Jihad exceeds one hundred. Jihad, strictly speaking, does not mean 'holy war', as some infidels believe, just as Islam does not mean peace, as some Muslims duplicitously claim and infidel dupes, including, so it would seem, Justice Haddon-Cave, believe. The Arabic for peace is *salaam*. Islam means 'submission' and Jihad means 'struggle', of which it is claimed by some, falsely, there are two kinds; what is sometimes referred as the 'greater' Jihad, the 'internal' struggle of a Muslim within him or herself to become a good Muslim, and the 'lesser' Jihad, an 'external' struggle against the enemies of Islam. This 'inner Jihad' against oneself has no Koranic foundation whatsoever, first appearing in what most Muslim scholars have always regarded as a spurious *hadith* dating from the 12th century, that is, at the end of a 'chain' five centuries long. Even if authentic, the so-called 'greater' Jihad does not concern us here, except inasmuch as it should lead to the better pursuing of the 'lesser', the 'struggle' or 'striving' against the enemies of Islam that is incumbent on all those Muslims who are in a position to wage it. Generally speaking, Jihad is translated into English as 'strive' or 'struggle' and their various derivatives. It has not escaped the notice of some critics of Islam that the German equivalent of Jihad is *Kampf*, as in in Hitler's work of that name.

The following selection of 61 citations from the *Koran* include some that are not complete verses, but only those passages which invoke Jihad. Since many of such verses are similar, near-duplicates have in some cases been omitted. The reader will easily detect a common theme to many of them, one that in addition to the 'spoils of war' - human and otherwise - also promises rewards in the afterlife in return for the sacrifice of oneself in the cause of Islam in this. The numbering of the verses might not always exactly tally with some English translations of the *Koran.*

Chapter 2

And say not of those who are slain in the way of Allah that they are dead; nay, they are living, only you perceive it not. (155

And fight in the way of Allah against those who fight against you, but do not transgress. Surely, Allah loves not the transgressors. (191)

And slay these transgressors wherever you meet them and drive them out from where they have driven you out, for persecution is worse than slaying. (192)

And fight them until there is no persecution, and religion is professed only for Allah. (194)

Fighting is ordained for you though it is repugnant to you. (217)

Persecution is worse than killing. (218)

Those who believe and those who emigrate and strive Hard in the cause of Allah, it is these who hope for Allah's mercy, and Allah is Most Forgiving, Merciful. (219)

Hast thou not heard of those who went forward from their homes, and they were thousands, fearing death? And Allah said to them, 'Die, and then He brought them back to life.' (244)

And fight in the cause of Allah and know that Allah is all-hearing and all-knowing. (245)

Chapter 3

And remember when thou didst go forth early in the morning from thy household, assigning to the believers their positions for battle. (122)

Yes, and if you be steadfast and righteous, and they come upon you immediately in hot haste, your Lord will help you with five thousand angels, attacking vehemently. (126)

Do you suppose that you will enter Heaven while Allah has not yet caused to be distinguished those of you that strive in the cause of Allah and has yet caused to be distinguished this steadfast? (143)

And you used to wish for such a death before you met it, now you have seen it face to face, then why do some of you seek to avoid it? (144)

And if you are slain in the cause of Allah or you die, surely forgiveness from Allah and mercy are better than what they hoard. (158)

And if you die or be slain, surely unto Allah shall you all be gathered together.

(159)

Think not of those who have been slain in the cause of Allah, as dead. Nay, they are living, and are granted gifts from him. (170)

Those who answered the call of Allah and the Messenger after they have received an injury – such of them as do good and act righteously shall have a great reward. (173)

So they returned with a mighty bounty from Allah and a great bounty, while no evil had touched them; and they followed the pleasure of Allah; and Allah is the Lord of great bounty. (175)

Those, therefore, who have emigrated and have been driven out from their homes, and have been persecuted for My cause, and have fought and been slain, I will surely remit from them their evil deeds and will cause them to enter gardens through which streams flow- a reward from Allah, and with Allah is the best of rewards. (196)

Chapter 4

O ye who believe! Take your precautions for security, then go forth in separate parties, or go forth all together. (72)

Let those who fight in the cause of Allah who would sell the present life for the Hereafter. And those whoso fights in the cause of Allah, be he slain or be he victorious, We shall soon give him a great reward. (75)

Those who believe fight in the cause of Allah, and those who disbelieve fight in the cause of the Evil One. Fight ye, therefore, against the friends of Satan; surely, Satan's strategy is weak. (77)

And when fighting, behold! A section of them fear men as they should fear Allah, or with great fear; and they say, "Our Lord, why hast Thou prescribed fighting for us? Wouldst thou not grant us respite yet a while?" Say, "The benefit of this world is little and the Hereafter will be better for him who fears Allah; and you shall not be wronged a whit." (78)

Fight therefore in the way of Allah - thou art not made responsible except for thyself – and urge on the believers to fight. (85)

Those of the believers who sit at home, excepting the disabled ones, and those who strive in the cause of Allah with their wealth and their persons, are not equal. Allah has exalted in rank those who strive with their wealth and their persons above those who it at home (96)

And whoso goes forth from his home, emigrating in the cause of Allah and His Messenger, and death overtakes him, his regard lies on Allah. (101)

Chapter 5

The only reward of those who wage war against Allah and His Messenger and strive to create disorder in the land, is that they be slain or crucified or their hands and feet be cut off on account of their enmity, or they be expelled from the land. (34)

Chapter 8

They ask thee concerning the spoils. Say, the 'the spoils of war are for Allah and the Messenger'. (2)

I will cast terror into the hearts of the disbelievers. Smite them above the necks and smite off all finger-tips. (13)

O ye who believe! When you meet those who disbelieve, advancing in force, turn not your back to them. And those who turn his back to them on such a day, unless manoeuvring for battle or turning to join another company, he indeed draws upon himself the wrath of Allah and Hell shall be his abode. (16-17)

And fight until there is no more persecution and religion is wholly for Allah. (40)

And know that whatever you take as spoils of war, a fifth is for Allah and for the Messenger and the kindred and the orphans and the needy and the wayfarer. (42)

So, if thou overcomest them in war, then thereby strike fear in those that are behind them, that they be mindful. (58)

And make ready for them who fight you whatever you can of armed force and of mounted pickets whereby you may frighten the enemy of Allah and your enemy and others beside them who you know not, but Allah knows them. (61)

O Prophet, urge the believers to fight. If there be of you twenty who are steadfast, they shall overcome two hundred; and if there be a hundred of you, they shall overcome a thousand of those who disbelieve because they are people who do not understand. (66)

So, eat of that which you have won in war as lawful and good and fear Allah. Surely, Allah is Most Forgiving, Merciful. (70)

Chapter 9

And when the forbidden months [the four months of pilgrimage] have passed, slay idolaters wherever you find them and take them captive and beleaguer them and lie in wait for them at every place of ambush. (5)

And if they break their oaths after their covenant and attack your religion, then fight these leaders of disbelief. (12)

Fight them, that Allah may punish them at your hands, and humiliate them, and help you to victory over them, and relieve the minds of a people who believe. (14)

Those who believed and left their homes for the sake of Allah and strove in the cause of Allah with their wealth and their lives have the highest rank in the sight of Allah. (20)

Surely, Allah has helped you on many a battlefield. (25)

Fight those from among the People of the Book, who believe not in Allah...until they pay the tax considering it a favour and acknowledge their subjection. (29)

And fight the idolaters all together as they fight you altogether; and know that Allah is with those who fear Him. (36)

If you will not go forth to fight, in the cause of Allah, He will punish you with a painful punishment and will choose in your stead a people other than you. (39)

Go forth, light or heavy, and strive with your wealth and your lives in the cause of Allah. That is best for you, if only you knew. (41)

O Prophet! Strive hard against the disbelievers and the Hypocrites. And be firm against them. Their abode is Hell, and an evil destination it is. (73)

But the Messenger and those who believe with him strive in the cause of Allah with their wealth and their persons, and it is they who shall have good things, and it is they who shall prosper. (88)

Surely, Allah has purchased of the believers their persons and their property in return for the heavenly Garden they shall have; they fight in the cause of Allah, and they slay and are slain. (111)

O ye who believe! Fight such of the disbelievers as are near to you and let them find hardness in you; and know that Allah is with the righteous. (123)

Chapter 17

And when We intend to destroy a township, we command its people who live in comfort to adopt the way of righteousness but they transgress therein, so the sentence of punishment becomes due against it, so We destroy it with utter destruction. (17)

Chapter 22

Permission to take up arms is given to those against whom war is made, because they have been wronged, and Allah, indeed has power to help them. (40)

Those who leave their homes for the cause of Allah, and are then slain or die, Allah will, surely, provide for them a goodly provision. And, surely, Allah is the best of providers. (59)

And strive in the cause of Allah as it behoves you to strive for it. (79)

Chapter 33

Say, 'Flight shall not avail you if you flee from death or slaughter; and even then you will not be allowed to enjoy yourselves but little.' (17)

Verily, Allah knows well those among you who hinder others from fighting and those who say to their brethren, 'come and be with us', and they themselves come not to the fight but little. (19)

And He brought those of the People of the Book who aided them ['the disbelievers'] down from their fortress and cast terror into their hearts. Some you slew, and some you took captive. And He made you inherit their land and their houses and their wealth, and also a land on which you have not yet set foot. And Allah has power over all things. (27-28)

Chapter 47

And when you meet in regular battle those who disbelieve, smite their necks; and when you have overcome them, by causing a great slaughter among them, bind fast the fetters – then afterwards release them as a favour or by taking ransom - until the war lays down its burdens. (5)

And those who believe say 'Why is not a Surah [a chapter in the *Koran*] revealed?' But when a decisive Surah is revealed and fighting is mentioned therein, thou seest those in whose hearts is a disease, looking towards thee like the look of one who is fainting on account of approaching death. So woe to them! (21)

So be not slack and sue not for peace, for you will certainly have the upper hand. And Allah is with you, and He will not deprive you of the rewards of your actions. (36)

Chapter 48

Those, who contrived to be left behind, will say, when you go forth to the spoils to take them, 'Let us follow you.' They seek to change the decree of Allah. Say, 'You shall not follow us'. (16)

Allah has promised you great spoils that you will take and He has given you this in advance. (21)

And if those who disbelieve should fight you, they would, certainly turn their backs; then they would find neither protector nor helper. (23)

Chapter 49

The believers are only those who truly believe in Allah and His Messenger, and doubt not, but strive with their possessions and their persons in the cause of Allah. (16)

Chapter 50

The believers are only those who truly believe in Allah and his Messenger, and then doubt not, but strive with their possessions and their persons in the cause of Allah. It is they who are truthful. (16)

Chapter 59

But Allah came upon them whence they did not expect, and cast terror into their hearts, so that they demolished their houses with their own hands and with the hands of the believers. So take a lesson, O ye who have eyes. (3)

And whatever Allah has given to the Messenger as spoils from them is of Allah's grace. (7)

Chapter 100

In the name of Allah, the Gracious and the Merciful, by the snorting chargers which strike sparks of fire with their hoofs, making raids at dawn and rising clouds of dust thereby and thus penetrate into the centre of the enemy ranks. (1-7)

The book of *peace*, Judge Haddon-Cave?

Addendum

'Verily, you have in the Prophet an excellent model'. *Koran*, Chapter 33, Verse 21

So far as its believers are concerned, and in the first place, its theologians and clerics, the sources of Islamic doctrine are, in order of precedence of authority, the *Koran*, conveyed by Allah via the angel Gabril to his prophet, and the *Sunnah*, the sayings and deeds of Mohammed as recorded in the *Hadith*, and as related by his biographer Ibn Ishaq, born in Medina in 702 AD, 70 years after the death of the prophet in 632, and died in Baghdad in 768. This last is regarded by Muslim scholars as the most trustworthy account because, as with the equally respected Buhkari *Hadith*, it has the shortest 'chain' connecting it with Mohammed and his immediate contemporaries. A reading of this work undoubtedly helps to further round out the picture that we already have of the founder of the religion of peace as a war-lord, mass murderer, plunderer, slave-holder, Jew-killer, liar and rapist. Here I focus only on his role as military leader. An overview of this aspect of his activities in the service of Allah can be partly at least gleaned from some of the book's chapter headings:

Jewish opponents
Jews joined by hypocrites among the Helpers
The chapter [of the *Koran*] of The Cow and Jewish opposition
The first raid on Waddin
Raid on Buwat
Raid on al-'Ushayra
Raid on al-Kharrar
Raid on Safawan
Fighting in the sacred month [re Corbyn's assertion on Press TV to contrary]
The chapter [of the *Koran*] of The Spoils [of war]
Names of the Emigrants who fought at Badr
Names of the Helpers who fought at Badr
Names of the [Jewish tribe of] Quraysh prisoners
Verses on the battle [20 pages]
Raid on B. Salaym
Raid on Dhu Amarr
Raid on al-Furu
Killing of Ka'b b. al-Ashraf
Battle of Uhud
Names of Muslims slain at Uhud
Names of polytheists slain at Uhud
Verses on Uhud [23 pages]
Raid of Dharu'l-Riua
Last expedition to Badr
Raid on Dumatu'l-Jandal
Battle of the Ditch
Attack on B. Qurayza
Poetry thereon [six pages]
Killing of Sallam
Attack on B. Libyan
Attack on Dhu Qarad
Attack on B. al-Mustaliq
Expedition to Khaybar
Division of the spoils of Khaybar
Raid on Mu'ta
The occupation of Mecca
Battle of Hunayn
Verses thereon [15 pages]

Capture of al-T'a'if
Division of the spoils of Hawazin
Raid on Tabuk
Those who hung back from the raid on Tabuk
Destruction of al-Lat
Hassan's odes on the campaigns [3 pages]
A summary of Muhammed's raids and expeditions.

Of these last, Ibn Ishaq says: 'The apostle took party personally in twenty-seven' and that 'he actually fought in nine engagements' ...peacefully, naturally.

Mohammed only gets into his stride in the ways that by now should be familiar when he and his small band of proselytising followers are unceremoniously bum-rushed out of Mecca by the pagan Quaraysh tribe and head north to Medina. Here too his message falls on largely stony ground, rejected by the Jews, who 'became insolent towards God and rejected His gracious purpose,' that is, to convert to Islam. This time, however Mohammed does not intend to undergo a second humiliation. Allah 'gave permission to His apostle to fight and to protect himself against those who wronged them and treated them badly'. Conveniently, as on so many other occasions when Mohammed was in a tight spot, Allah sent down a new verse, instructing him to 'fight them so that there be no more seduction...and the religion is God's, until God alone is worshipped.' And so was born Islam Mark Two, which would now involve the cancelling out, or 'abrogation' of all earlier verses that spoke of peaceful and tolerant relations between Mohammed's followers and those who rejected his message.

One of the prophet's early encounters with the Jews of Medina involved a battle of wits with a delegation of rabbis, who put four questions to him. If he answered them correctly, they would convert to Islam. One is worth repeating as perhaps the first example of 'Islamic science': To the question, 'Why does a boy resemble its mother when the semen comes from the man?' Mohammed replied: 'Do you not know that a man's semen is white and thick while a woman's is yellow and thin and the likeness goes with that which is on top?' On another occasion, a married man had committed adultery with a married woman, and Mohammed was asked to provide the appropriate punishment. 'The apostle ordered them to be stoned, and they were stoned at the door of his mosque. And when the Jew felt the first stone, he crouched over the woman to protect her from the stones until both of them were killed. This is what God did for the apostle in exacting the penalty for adultery for the pair.' Mohammed had passed the test with flying colours, and in doing so, had proved himself truer to the *Torah* than the Jewish elders, who had advocated a less harsh punishment. 'Woe to you Jews! What has induced you to abandon the judgment of God which you hold in your hands?' Evidently tiring of these fruitless contests, Mohammed moved up several gears, because we soon find him plotting the first of what would be a string of caravan raids: '...when the apostle heard about Abu Sufyan coming from Syria, he summoned the Muslims and said: "This is the Quaraysh caravan containing their property. Go out and attack it, perhaps God will give us a prey."'.

Sure enough, Allah came through for his apostle, just as he always would in future. *En route* to Mecca, the caravan was ambushed by Mohammed's followers at Badr, the first battle of the religion of peace. It was also the prophet's first opportunity to savour the 'spoils of war'. As we shall see, here too Allah was more than a little helpful, 'abrogating' one of his hitherto immutable laws concerning the distribution of the spoils. The battle of Badr looms large in the life story of Mohammed, because here for the first time, he was operating as military leader and not, as previously, a peaceful advocate of a new religion. (Hence the need for Koranic textual 'abrogation'.) The prominence awarded the engagement and its aftermath by Ibn Ishaq is quite extraordinary. Of the 463 pages describing Mohammed's life following his *Hijra*, that is from the time he left Mecca for Medina in 622, no fewer than 71 are devoted to this one single battle. In view of its historical significance, some of its features are worth relating. one of them being that his biographer tells us it began 'on Friday morning on the 17th of Ramadan', even though on an Islamic website, *My mercy embraces all things*, Farhana Qazi expressed his astonishment that 'religious extremists choose to kill during one of Islam's holiest months'.(Recalling his claim on Press TV, so would have Corbyn.) The founder of Islam an *extremist*? Another feature of the battle worthy of note was its being a purely offensive undertaking which, according to legend, was contrary to the rules for Jihad. A third gives us a revealing glimpse of the prophet's sexual proclivities. While at Badr, he saw a certain Ummu'l-Fadl 'when she was a baby and crawling before him. Said Allah's apostle, if she grows up and I am still alive I will marry her.' Fortunately for Ummu'l-Fadl, in view of his consummation of his last marriage to Aisha when she was 'grown up' at nine, he died before he could have his holy way with her.

Badr was a desert watering hole, and it was there Mohammed's forces ambushed the Quaraysh as they watered themselves and their camels: 'And when Quaraysh encamped, some of them went to the cistern of the apostle to drink. "Let them be", he [Mohammed] said; and every man that drank of it on that that day was killed'. We are not spared the gory details of the slaughter. One Quaraysh had his 'foot and half his shank sent flying' and lay by the cistern, 'blood streaming from his foot', while another had his leg cut off, with 'marrow oozing from it'. It was at Badr that the prophet first sanctioned an Islamic practice we have become all too familiar with…decapitation. One of his warriors, Ibn Mas'ud, related that he brought him the head of a Quaraysh: "This the head of the enemy of God, Abu Jahl." He [Mohammed] said, "By God than Whom there is no other, is it?" "Yes" I said and threw his head before the apostle and he [the prophet] gave thanks to God.'

Here too for the first time we encounter the prophet enunciating the doctrine of Muslim martyrdom: '70,000 of my people shall enter Paradise like the full moon'. Rather like the three robbers in Chaucer's *Pardoner's Tale*, no sooner was the battle won than Allah's warriors fell out over the proceeds of their victory. So, 'when Badr was over, God sent down the whole *Sura* [chapter] *Anfal* about it. ['The Spoils of War'] With regard to their quarrelling about the spoils there came down [via Gabril to Mohammed, who unlike his trusting followers, claimed to have a direct line to heaven]: "They will ask you about the spoils, say, the spoils belong to God and [of course] the apostle, so fear God and be at peace with one another, and obey God and His apostle if you are believers".' This evidently did not go down too well with those who done the fighting and the plundering, so down came another verse: 'He [Allah] taught them how to divide the spoil', only now, they were to have four fifths, while of 'what you take, a fifth belongs to God and his apostle and the next of kin and orphans the poor and the and wayfarer.'

184

Nice one, Allah. Or should I say, Mohammed?

Supported by a growing band of followers eager for booty, human and otherwise, all that was now needed was a verse from above conferring upon Mohammed the right and in fact duty to wage war against the unbelievers. And down it came, as always, bang on time: 'And then He [Allah] said, "Fight them so that there is no more persecution [sic] and religion, all of it, shall belong to God".' And so, in the midst of plunder, rape, beheadings, blood, gore and marrow, was born the religion of peace. Having, at least temporarily, squared accounts with the Quaraysh, it was the turn of the Jews of Medina, the tribe of B. Qaynuqa, to feel the wrath of Allah. Right on cue, down came a verse authorising another punitive military action against the infidel: 'Say to those who disbelieve, you will be vanquished and gathered to Hell, and evil resting place.' Said one participant in the ensuing battle, 'our attack upon God's enemy cast terror among the Jews, and there was no Jew in Medina who did not fear for his life.' 'And the apostle said, *"Kill any Jew that falls into your power".*' This is the language of Nazi-style genocide and it is back today in the manifestos of Corbyn's 'friends' Hamas and Hezbollah. But those who attribute Muslim anti-Semitism to the sins of Zionism need to take note: the Jews were despised as the prime enemy of Islam and the Arabs more than thirteen centuries before the birth of Israel.

Terror and conversion went hand in hand. One Jewish captive asked of his captor,' By God, if Mohammed had ordered you to kill me would you have killed me?' His captor answered, 'Yes, by God, had he ordered me to cut off your head I would have done so.' The captive Jew then replied, '"By God, a religion which can bring you to this is marvellous!", and he became a Muslim.' Could this be the first recorded instance of the Stockholm Syndrome? Having twice tasted victory and the fruits thereof, the prophet now began a series of military campaigns that he waged to the end of his life, and which his successors have continued until the present day. Returning home after one such engagement, the battle of Uhud, a return match against the Quaraysh, 'he handed his sword to his daughter Fatima, saying, "Wash the blood from this, daughter, for by God it has served me well today".'

It served him even better after his victory over the Jews of B. Qurayza. Their men having surrendered, 'the apostle confined them in Medina the quarter of al-Harith, a woman of B. al-Najjar. Then the apostle went out to the market of Medina and dug trenches in it. Then he sent for them [the Jewish prisoners] and struck off their heads in those trenches as they were brought to him in batches...There were 600 or 700 in all, though some put the figure as high as 800 or 900'. Those familiar with the Holocaust of the Jews will, save for the use of a sword rather than firearms, recognise at once the identical method employed by the Nazi murder squads, the *Einsatzgruppen*, on the Eastern front during the Second World War, filling up trenches with massacred Jews. 'Then the apostle divided the property, wives and children of B. Qurayza among the Muslims.' For his own sexual needs, 'the apostle had chosen one of their women', a wife of a Jew he had just beheaded. In his infinite wisdom, god chose this very moment to send down another verse, one that to this day provides a *carte blanche* for every Muslim man to rape, plunder and murder in the name of Allah: 'In God's apostle you have a fine example'. Now see what follows.

185

M Anything You Can Do...

For decades now, western liberals and leftists have allowed their thinking on serious matters to be warped by what is commonly known as post-colonial guilt. Starting with the Crusades, then Christian slavery, and ending with the era of empire (while by-passing Islamic slavery and the vast empires of Allah), the western radical intelligentsia has taken upon itself the guilt of their forebears to such a degree of self-abasement that it has blinded its members to the failings and misdeeds of any culture other than their own. The high priest of this latter-day flagellant cult is of course Noam Chomsky. Islamic imperialism, with its avowed goal of world conquest in the name of and for Allah, is not now, and never has been troubled by such qualms of conscience. Its cause is noble, therefore its means are justified, even if they exceed in brutality and savagery those of the despised infidel West. Reproduced below is a text from the same issue number 15 of the Islamic State journal, being part of an article titled *By the Sword*. To drive home its message, as if that were necessary, the article is accompanied by a photograph of an Islamic State executioner caught in the act of slicing off the head of a sinner against the laws of Allah, a spectacle watched by an audience of men, male youths and young male children.

By the Sword

The clear difference between Muslims and the corrupt and deviant Jews and Christians is that Muslims are not ashamed of abiding by the rules sent down from their Lord regarding war and the enforcement of divine law. So if it were the Muslims, instead of the Crusaders [by which is meant the infidel West] who had fought the Japanese and Vietnamese or invaded the lands of the native Americans, there would have been no regrets in killing and enslaving [sic!] those therein. And since those mujahidin would have done so bound by the Law, they would have been thorough and without some 'politically correct' need to apologise years later. The Japanese, for example, would have forcefully converted to Islam from their pagan ways - and if they stubbornly declined, perhaps another nuke [sic!!!] would have changed their mind. The Vietnamese would likewise be offered Islam or beds of napalm [sic!!!]. As for the Native Americans - after the slaughter of their men, those who would favour small-pox to surrendering to the Lord – then the Muslims would have taken their surviving women and children as slaves [sic!], raising the children as model Muslims and impregnating [by rape] their women to produce a new generation of mujahidin. As for the treacherous Jews of Europe and elsewhere - those who would betray their covenant – then their post-pubescent males would face a slaughter that would make the Holocaust sound like a bedtime story, as their women would be made to serve their husbands' and fathers' killers. Furthermore, the lucrative African slave trade would have continued [sic!], supporting a strong economy. The Islamic leadership would not have bye-passed Allah's permission to sell captured pagan humans, to teach them, and to convert them, as they worked hard for their masters in building a beautiful country.

N Goodbye to All That

I first conceived of this work seven years ago, at the time when anti-Zionists ranging from the infidel far left to the Islamic and Neo-Nazi far right were storming through the streets of western Europe in support of the anti-Semitic Hamas regime in Gaza. Little did I or anyone else for that matter then suspect that a year later an identical combination of forces would succeed in securing the election of one of their own to the leadership of the UK's major leftist party. The letter below is my response to this succession of events:

September 24, 2016

To whom it may concern:

The purpose of this communication is to formally inform you of my resignation from the Labour Party, effective as from the date of this email. I owe it both to you and myself to provide the reasons for this decision, which I can assure I have not taken lightly. I joined the Labour Party forty-two years ago, believing that it was the only political organisation that could represent and advance the interests of working people. The re-election of Jeremy Corbyn as party leader has convinced me, and I have good reasons to believe many others, that this is no longer the case. The party has allowed itself to be hi-jacked by infiltrators, many of whom have been proved to have either belonged to or voted for parties other than Labour, or to be members of organisations whose ethos and methods are totally opposed to those of the Labour Party and incompatible with its rules of membership.

Since the election of Corbyn and the emergence of Momentum as the dominant force in the party, electoral support has been in catastrophic decline in those very areas of the country that are its traditional strongholds, not least because the party has become the vehicle for the ambitions of self-indulgent political play-boys who care nothing for those the party was founded to represent. However, important though they are, these are not my main reasons for leaving the Labour Party.

As a life-long opponent of anti-Semitism, I cannot remain in a party led by someone who throughout his career as an MP, has collaborated with individuals and movements who make no secret their enmity towards the Jews, and in the cases of his 'friends' Hamas and Hezbollah, have as their avowed goal not only the destruction of Israel but the murder of its entire Jewish population. Corbyn has also taken paid employment with the state-run Iranian Press TV channel, that is, with a regime whose Supreme Leader proclaims that it is his aim to 'wipe Israel off the map' and which amongst its many victims that include poets, secularists and Kurds, publicly hangs homosexuals from cranes.

I do not believe that it was by coincidence that Corbyn's election as leader was accompanied by an upsurge of quite open hostility towards the Jews, to such a degree that he was with some reluctance compelled to commission what predictably proved to be a toothless inquiry into Labour Party anti-Semitism. What sort of a party has Labour become that a Jewish MP critical of Corbyn's leadership, after receiving 25,000 abusive messages, some of them death threats and many of them anti-Semitic, has found it necessary to attend the party conference accompanied by a body guard?

Robin Blick, membership number A314906

Swansea East CLP.

O When Did You Last Beat Your Wife?

We have seen how some Muslim clerics based in the west have tied themselves in semantic knots in their attempts to present Islam as a humane faith, especially so with regard to its treatment of women. We have also seen that in this endeavour, they have been able to enlist the invaluable support of quisling western feminists engaged in the same enterprise. In the Middle East, where the whole filthy business began, no such subterfuges are called for. There, Islam is served up to the faithful hot and strong, and in no subject more so than the noble task sanctified by Allah of keeping Muslim wives in line. What follows is a verbatim transcript of a Friday sermon preached on Qatar TV on August 27, 2004. It is readily accessible on YouTube. But first, the Koranic verse which the preacher invokes as the authority for this barbaric practice. It occurs in Sura (Chapter) 4, *An Nisa*, meaning 'The Women'. The number of the verse varies, being either usually 34 or, less often, 35. The translations from the Arabic that I have consulted translate the Arabic word '*daraba*' as either 'beat', 'chastise' or 'scourge'. So far as the wife on the receiving end of the operation is concerned, it makes no difference. The source I have used for Verse 34 is from the Islamic website Ayyid Ahul Ala Maududi - Tafhim al - Qur'an: The Meaning of the Koran. It reads:

Men are the managers of the affairs of women because Allah has made one superior to the others and because men spend of their wealth on women. Virtuous women are, therefore, obedient. They guard their rights carefully in their absences under the care and watch of Allah. As for those women, whose defiance you have cause to fear, admonish them and keep them apart from your beds and beat them.

Now the Sermon:

We must know that wife beating is a punishment in Islamic religious law. No one should deny this because this was permitted by the Creator of Man, and because when you purchase an electrical appliance or a car, you get a manual, a catalogue, explaining how to use it. The creator of man has sent down this book, the *Koran*, in order to show man which ways he must choose. We shouldn't be ashamed before the nations of the world who are still in their days of ignorance to admit that these beatings are part of our religious law. We must remind the ignorant from among the Islamic nation who followed the West that those Westerners acknowledge the wondrous nature of this verse. There are three types of women with whom life is impossible without beatings. The *Koran* says 'and beat them'. This verse is of a wondrous nature. There are three types of women with whom a man cannot live unless he carries a rod on his shoulder. The first type is a woman who was brought up this way. Her parents ask her to go school and she doesn't – [so] they beat her. 'Eat' – 'I don't want to' – so they beat her. So she becomes accustomed to beatings, she was brought up that way. We pray Allah will help her husband later. He will only get along with her if he practices wife beating. The second type is a woman who is condescending towards her husband and ignores him. With her, too, only a rod will help. The third type is a twisted woman who will not obey her husband unless her oppresses her, beats her, uses force against her, and overpowers her with his voice.

Here we have another Muslim cleric, Sa'id Arafat, expounding on what he calls 'the etiquette' of wife-beating:

Allah honoured [sic] wives by installing the punishment of beatings…The Prophet Mohammad said, 'don't beat her in the face and do not make her ugly.' See how she is honoured…Even when he beats her, he must not curse her…He beats her in order to discipline her. In addition, there must not be more than ten beatings and he must not break her bones, injure her, break her teeth, or poke her in the eye. There is a beating etiquette. If he beats to discipline her, he must not raise his hand high. He must beat her from chest level. All these things honour a woman. [sic] She is in need of discipline…He can beat her with a short rod…The honouring of the wife is also evident in the fact that the punishment of beating is permissible in one case only: when she refuses to sleep with him.

P Dutch Cowardice

Of all Europe's peoples, it is the Dutch who over the centuries have arguably given more proof than any other of their commitment to liberty, both of their nation, and of the individuals who have lived within its borders. Beginning with their revolt against the tyranny of Spanish rule in the sixteenth century, which after their victory, made Holland a haven for those persecuted for their beliefs, through to their resistance to Nazi occupation, when the workers of Amsterdam staged a general strike against the deportation of the Jews to the gas chambers of the Third Reich, the Dutch have deservedly won for their country a global reputation for their respect for personal freedom and acceptance of the widest variety of life styles and beliefs. But tragically, that reputation is now in tatters. Holland is no longer a land of the free, but one ruled by politicians who rather than resist the assault of Islam on their hard-won freedoms, have chosen to capitulate to it, and persecute with all legal means at their disposal those who fight back.

The alarm was first raised by Pim Fortuyn. Being by profession a sociologist, and by sexual orientation a homosexual, Fortuyn was more attuned than most to the impact of large-scale immigration Islam on a society that shared little, if any of the life-style and beliefs of the large numbers of Muslim migrants their hosts had naively assumed would in time exchange for Dutch ones. Based on his observations of the failure, in fact refusal, of Muslim immigrants to integrate into liberal Dutch society, in 1997, Fortuyn published his book, *The Islamisation of Our Culture*. His next step was to enter politics as the leader of his Livable Netherlands party to defend the traditional Dutch commitment to individual freedom, in particular freedoms fanatically opposed by Muslims; those of sexual equality and orientation, and of expression. While he made it clear in an interview that he believed Islam to be 'an extraordinary threat, a hostile religion' to Dutch values, he also insisted, contrary to the lies of his opponents, 'I want to live together with the Muslim people', adding, correctly, 'but it takes two to tango'. In an allusion to his own sexuality, and to the vicious persecution and even murder of gays in Islamic countries, Fortuyn made a point that once upon a time any leftist would be only too willing to endorse had it been made by one of their own: 'Look at the Netherlands. In what country, an electoral leader of such a large movement as mine be openly homosexual? How wonderful that that is possible. That's something that one can be proud of. And I would like to keep it that way, thank you very much.'

But for some, especially those on the left, such libertarian statements today constituted proof, along with his unconditional support for free speech above all other rights, that he was a fascist. (And as anyone conversant with its history knows, fascism has always been foremost in upholding the rights of gays and the protection of free speech.) It rapidly become obvious however that despite all the slanders, Fortuyn had struck a chord with millions of Dutch citizens who shared his concern about the failure of Holland's political elite to defend their country's liberal values and way of life, either out of fear of a Muslim backlash or because their brains had been addled by the new fads of political correctness and multi-culturalism. Sensing that Fortuyn now had a powerful wind in his sails, the establishment almost to a man launched a campaign of vilification, denouncing him as a fascist, a slander echoed by the *New York Times* with its headline that Fortuyn was 'marching the Dutch to the Right', seemingly oblivious to the fact that it was Islam that was marching Holland to the right, and Fortuyn, by defending his country's secular democratic values and institutions, who was resisting it.

On May 6, 2002, only a matter of days before a general election that would have resulted (and fact did result) in his party making sweeping gains, Fortuyn was assassinated by a far leftist, Vokert Van der Graaf, because, so he said at his trial, of his views on the impact of Muslim migration on Dutch society. Even after his murder, the slanders continued: 'Dutch Len Pen Assassinated' proclaimed the UK's pro-Labour *Daily Mirror*. The mould had been set: he or she who criticises Islam, no matter from what standpoint, is, necessarily, by that fact alone, a far rightist, possibly even a fascist. Fortuyn had been slain, but the cause he represented was taken up by three courageous critics of Islam, each of whom we have already encountered: the film-maker Theo van Gogh, murdered by a Muslim in revenge for his film *Submission* (in Arabic, *Islam*) depicting the plight of Muslim women; his Somali-born collaborator on the film, the atheist ex-Muslim writer Ayaan Hirsi Ali, no-platformed by Brandies University for her outspoken attacks on the Islamic oppression of women, and the MP Gert Wilders, denied entry to the UK to show his anti-Islam film *Fitna* to MPs at Westminster.

Van Gogh's assassination on November 2, 2004 triggered identical reactions to those that would eleven years later be displayed in response to the *Charlie Hebdo* massacre. He had been 'insensitive' to 'Muslim feelings', and if not in so many words, 'had it coming'. Naturally the *Guardian* hastened to advertise its 'understanding' for the motives of Van Gogh's killer. Belying without any sense of shame its own title, *Index on Censorship* denigrated Van Gogh as a 'free speech fundamentalist' (sic) who had been 'on a martyrdom operation, roaring his Muslim critics into silence' with his 'abuse of the right to free speech'. Indeed, so lacking was there any solidarity with the victim or the cause for which he had been slain that Peter Whitehead of the New Culture Forum felt obliged to complain that the film-maker's murder had elicited 'no significant expressions of outrage from Britain's creative figures and institutions', a sure indicator that amongst the literati, Sharia leftism was already well and truly on the march. So was Sharia self-censorship.

A showing of *Submission* at a Dutch festival of censored films was cancelled because of a fear of Muslim reprisals. The film's producer, Gijs van de Westelaken, frankly admitted that he was 'yielding to terror'. What Fortuyn had feared had now come to pass. The pattern had been set. It now became *de rigueur* to counterpose to free expression the sensitivities of Muslims, invariably to the advantage of the latter. Where they did not already exist, laws would be enacted to ensure that those who chose to act otherwise would be punished. Such would be the fate of Geert Wilders. In November 2007, Associated Press reported that the Dutch MP was planning to make a film highly critical of Islam; a brave, some would say foolhardy venture in view of the fate that befell van Gogh. The same report revealed that Dutch 'Interior and Justice Ministers said they were concerned but believed they had no authority to prevent Wilders from screening

194

his film'. Bear in mind that even though the two ministers could have had only the haziest idea of what the film might contain, they were already seeking ways to prevent its being shown. And this was not China, Iran, Saudi Arabia or North Korea, but once liberal Holland, the land of the free. And all to protect Muslim 'sensitivities'.

No wiser than the two ministers to the film's actual contents, but now alerted as to its imminent showing and galvanised by the prospect of yet more Muslim violence, the forces of political correctness mobilised. Doekle Terpstra, chairman of the Netherlands Association of Universities of Applied Science, charged Wilders with 'abusing his position and freedom of speech' to divide Dutch society, as if the Dutch, always a quarrelsome people, should all be of the one mind sought by totalitarian dictators. With this end in view, Terpstra assembled an anti-Wilders popular front comprised of Christian and Muslim clerics, politicians from various parties, business leaders and assorted establishment personalities, and led them into battle to the cry 'Wilders is the evil'…all because the MP had announced his intention to make film about Islam, a film, I repeat, that none of Terpstra's army of the great and the good had seen. The Islamic component of the alliance immediately began to flex its muscles, with the Dutch Muslim Council warning that if Wilder's film was screened, 'the youths on the street will have the last word. We can't stop them'. As if they wanted to.

Though no part of his brief, Foreign Minister Maxime Verhagen intoned what has now become a familiar *non-sequitur*, that 'freedom of expression does not mean the right to offend'. Whoever said it does? It simply recognises the possibility, in fact probability, that expressing an opinion freely on a matter of substance can give offence, even if not intentionally so, to someone, somewhere who thinks differently, and that such a possibility should be no grounds for curtailing the right to free expression. If it was allowed to do so, no-one would be allowed to say anything for fear of giving offence to someone, somehow, somewhere. Of course, in this instance, the whole object of the exercise was the suppression of the right to criticise Islam, and the specific target, the film *Fitna,* still as yet to be viewed by its legions of outraged critics

The day of reckoning arrived on March 27, 2008, when the film was released on-line (naturally no cinema would dare screen it). Would it live up to its advanced billing of seeking to 'polarise Dutch society' and the 'stigmatising of entire population groups' (code for Muslims)? Would it be 'hate-inciting or blasphemous' or, as the London *Observer* confidently predicted, define Wilders as a 'new brand of right-wing populist'? For the record, I do not like some of the political company Wilders chooses to keep, but that should not invalidate his right to free speech, and to make and show a film. In the event *Fitna* did none of the things its opponents warned of. Just over sixteen minutes long, to a soundtrack of classical music, the film consisted largely of quotations from the *Koran* on Jihad (also cited in my text) and sermons by Muslim preachers, together with footage of the deaths and destruction caused by Muslims who acted upon them. Excepting the cries of terror victims, all the words spoken were by Muslims.

Wrong footed by the absence of a content they had so confidently predicted, the film's release was accompanied not only in Holland but globally by a surge of simulated *kuffar* outrage. Leading the pack was UN Secretary-General Ban Ki-moon, with his charge that *Fitna* constituted 'hate speech', even though the film's only 'hate speech' were Muslim sermons and citations from the *Koran*. CNN reported that the Bush administration feared 'the film could spark protests and riots'. Jorge Sampaio, the UN Representative for the Alliance of Civilisation (sic), found *Fitna* 'an insulting film on the Holy *Koran*', again begging the same question...how can quoting from a book insult it? In accordance with what had by now become the required norm, Sampaio spelled out the UN's new stance on free expression, one that implicitly repudiated Article 19 of its own founding Universal Declaration of Human Rights, falsely claiming that 'it does not preclude the protection of people from discriminatory and xenophobic language'. To repeat yet again: the only 'language' in *Fitna* was that either inspired by or to be found in the *Koran*. Are we to assume then, as some *dhimmi* law makers have indeed successfully insisted, that only Muslims should be allowed to quote from it?

Dutch courage is no more. Not only in Holland, but across the western world, publishers will not publish books and TV and internet channels will not screen programmes critical of Islam and of Muslims who commit crimes inspired by its teachings, even when their authors and makers are highly respected academic authorities on the subject. Bookshops will not sell such books. Journals and newspapers will not review them, but they will invariably slander their authors as 'far right' for opposing in the name of individual freedom a doctrine that is itself analgous to fascism. But, unfortunately for Allah's *Kuffar* Thought Police and his army of terrorist enforcers, in the era of the internet, the self-publishing of such books is booming.

Q Sweated Labour

In the darkest days of the Second World war, George Orwell took comfort from his conviction that the British, for all their faults, and he was never slow to criticise them, were by tradition resistant to the appeals of the totalitarianism and leader cultism that had extinguished democracy on the European continent. 'No party rallies, no Youth Movements, no coloured shirts, no Jew-baiting, or spontaneous demonstrations.' That was then. Following his election as Labour Party Leader in September 2015, in addition to Nuremberg-style chanting of his name at pop festivals, we had a Jeremy pop song, oil painting, T-shirts and umpteen memorabilia, including life-size cardboard cut-outs of the Dear Leader, Jeremy underpants, Lego, garden gnomes, shopping bags, pillow cases, colouring-in books, teddy bears and fake tattoos.

Helping to fund Corbyn's campaign for the Labour leadership, the T-shirts were priced in the UK at £10.00, while being produced at minimal cost by third world sweated labour. In Nicaragua, where workers were paid under £6.00 for a 12-hour day to make T-shirts for Corbyn, they toiled under a regime headed by the husband and wife team of President Daniel Ortega and his wife, Vice President Rosario, one that in the spring of 2018, emulating the example of Corbyn's Chavista comrades in Venezuela, unleashed a repression of street protests against poverty and cuts in welfare that led to the killing at least 170 demonstrators by security forces. A kinder politics. Among items advertised on the Nicaraguan Solidarity (with the regime, naturally) website are Jeremy mugs (sic) and Jeremy magnets.

In Bangladesh, the going rate for Jeremy shirt-makers was even lower, at £3.00 for a ten-hour day. One worker commented, 'I feel angry that a politician is using T-shirts created with our back-breaking work to make a statement about workers' rights when he clearly doesn't care about our rights at all.' Corbyn T-shirts were also made in Haiti, where the rate was £20.00 for a six-day week. In all, proceeds from the sale of Corbyn T-shirts netted £100,000. Corbyn had pledged to raise the minimum wage for British workers to £10.00 an hour, more than twenty times the rate paid to those workers who helped to finance his leadership campaign. When working for Iran's Press TV channel, Corbyn was paid £1,250.00 an hour. He also received a payment of £5,000 for a single appearance on Al-jazeera TV. His combined annual income as MP and Leader of the Opposition is £128,559. According to the magazine *Spears,* multi-millionaire Corbyn's private fortune stood at £3,000,000. On his retirement as MP, he will receive a pension of another £1,600,000.

As I scrolled through Corbyn's numerous entries on the register of MP's financial interests, I came across one item that in view of his pecuniary and political relationship with the hangmen of the Iranian theocracy, merited closer scrutiny. It concerned Corbyn's visit to Tehran (accompanied by his wife and a 'research worker') from January 6 to 10, 2014, on behalf of the 'All-Party [UK] Parliamentary Group on Iran at the invitation of the Iran-UK Parliamentary Friendship Group of the Iranian Parliament'. The junket was funded by two donors, again quoting Corbyn's register entry, 'the Parliament of the Islamic Republic of Iran' and 'Ardeshir Nagashineh, Chairman of Targetfellow Group Ltd', based in Norwich. Just as has been the case with Jew-killing Jihadis, there is nothing out of the ordinary in Corbyn's 'friendship'(or as he likes to say, 'solidarity') with regimes which, as matter of course, jail, torture and murder their opponents and rig elections to rubber-stamp 'parliaments'. What is of special interest is the profile of Mr Nagashineh. A little digging uncovered the following: Listed as a billionaire, Corbyn's benefactor is an Iranian-born property tycoon, as of September 2019 holding directorships in *sixty-five* companies, out of total of 227 in his entire business career. Undeniably an exemplary case of 'For the very Few' and, as such, unless considerations of a political nature come into play, surely a prime candidate for expropriation under a Corbyn regime.

.

R Dialogue?

After meeting Hitler in Berlin in April 1937, George Lansbury, the pacifist Leader of the Labour Party from 1932 to 1935, returned to England convinced that 'history will regard Hitler as one of the great men of our time...with no love for pomp and show, Christianity in its purest form might stand a chance with him.' One can still see on-line a YouTube video where Corbyn is uttering no less delusional platitudes about his anti-Semitic terrorist 'friends' Hamas and Hezbollah:

> It will be my pleasure and my honour to host an event in Parliament where our friends from Hezbollah will be speaking. I have also invited friends from Hamas to come and speak as well...so we can promote that peace, that understanding and that dialogue. The idea that an organisation that is dedicated towards the good of the Palestinian people and bringing back long-term peace in the whole region should be labelled as terrorist organisations by the British government is really a big, big, historical mistake. [Corbyn's customary hapless syntax has the 'idea' making the mistake, not the government.]

Like his predecessor in his estimation of Hitler as a man of peace, it was Corbyn who was making a 'really big, big, historical mistake'. The only difference was the religion. The way Corbyn described Hamas and Hezbollah, they could easily be taken for the Middle Eastern equivalents of a European social democratic party rather than terrorist movements dedicated to the elimination of a member state of the United Nations. In fact, both Hamas and Hezbollah are religiously-driven anti-Semitic war machines pure and simple, awash with the most advanced conventional weaponry that money can buy, and they make no secret of it. The Shia militia, Hezbollah, does not attempt to disguise that it is little more than an Irian proxy, and its sponsors have seen to it that it is better equipped for war than the armed forces of its Lebanese hosts. Both movements' genocidal intentions towards the Jews and Israel, defined with total clarity in their respective charters and numerous public statements by their leaders, those whom Corbyn described as his 'friends', are no different in intention and no less transparent than were those of Hitler towards the Jews. Given his close relationship with his Hamas and Hezbollah 'friends' and the Iranian theocracy, Corbyn must be fully aware of this.

Just one example of many of Hezbollah's dedication to peace is the tenfold increase in its stock of missiles, a purely offensive weapon, in the period between 2006 and 2015, giving it the capacity to launch 1,000 missiles *per day* into Israeli territory for a period of two months. Yet although equipped for and pledged to a war of aggression and elimination against the 'Zionist entity', in true Orwellian fashion, Hezbollah invariably refers to itself in its *Manifesto* as a 'resistance' movement...just like Hitler's Waffen SS. And how does Corbyn reconcile his description of Hamas as a movement dedicated to 'bringing back long-term peace' with its suicide attacks on Israeli restaurants, cafes, markets and school buses, its tunnelling into Israel's territory, the kidnapping and murder of its civilians and the bombarding of civilian targets with thousands of rockets, and the round-the-clock pumping out of genocidal hatred towards the Jews on its TV channels? Just between January 2000 and August 2005, during the so-called 'Second Intifada', Hamas was responsible for more than 40% of all suicide attacks carried out in that period, nearly all of them on civilian targets, such as the Tel Aviv Dolphinarium discothèque of June 1, 2001, with 21 victims, the Haifa bus bombing of December 2 of the same year, with 15 victims, and on March 31, 2002, the Mazta Restaurant bombing, also in Haifa, with another 15 killed. The list goes on. According to Wikipedia, in the twelve years between 1993, the year of the adoption of the Oslo Accords, and 2005, the end of the second 'Intifada', there were 171 suicide attacks, nearly all aimed at civilian targets. Of these attacks, 87 were carried out by Hamas, including one against a school and another against a school bus. Hamas subsequently claimed responsibility for nearly all of these attacks. In the same period, as a result of these 'martyrdom operations', 805 Israelis were killed, 503 by those of Hamas. Of the 964 wounded, 388 were caused by Hamas suicide bombers. And this is not terrorism? Corbyn speaks of 'dialogue', knowing full well that both Hezbollah and Hamas have always on principle rejected any negotiations with Israel on the grounds that the Jewish state has no right to exist. Article 13 of the Hamas Charter says 'there is no solution to the Palestinian problem except by Jihad'. Section Three of Chapter Three of *The New Hezbollah Manifesto* (2009) reads as follows:

> Our stance on the negotiations and compromises made by the Madrid conference, the 'Araba Valley retrospect', the 'Oslo Accords', is a total refusal to any kind of compromise with the Zionist entity, which is based on admitting its legitimate presence and giving in [sic] what it occupied from the Palestinian and Islamic land. This stance is predetermined and permanent [n.b.] and isn't set for any compromise, even if the whole world admits to 'Israel'.

Hezbollah leader Sheikh Hassan Nasrallah goes much further; it is not just Israel, but the Jews, *all the Jews*, who must disappear: 'If Jews all gather in Israel it will save us the trouble of going after them worldwide.' Is this what Corbyn means by 'dialogue'?

S For the Attention of Mr K. Livingstone

Minute of the meeting between Reich Chancellor Adolf Hitler and Grand Mufti Haj Amin al-Husseini; Berlin, November 28, 1941, in the presence of Reich Foreign Minister Joachim von Ribbentrop and Minister Fritz Grobba, Head of the Reich Foreign Ministry Middle East Desk.

The Grand Mufti began by thanking the Fuhrer for the great honour he had bestowed by receiving him. He wished to seize the opportunity to convey to the Fuehrer of the Greater German Reich, admired by the entire Arab world, his thanks of [sic] the sympathy which he had always shown for the Arab and especially the Palestinian cause, and to which he had given clear expression in his public speeches. The Arab countries were firmly convinced that Germany would win the war and that the Arab cause would then prosper. The Arabs were Germany's natural friends because they had the same enemies as had Germany, namely the English, the Jews, and the Communists. Therefore, they were prepared to cooperate with Germany with all their hearts and stood ready to participate in the war, not only negatively but positively by the formation of an Arab Legion. The Arabs could be more useful to Germany as allies than might be apparent at first glance, both for geographical reasons and because of the suffering inflicted upon them by the English and the Jews. Furthermore, they had close relations with all Muslim nations, of which they could make use in behalf of the common cause. The Arab Legion would be quite easy to raise. An appeal by the Mufti to the Arab countries and the prisoners of Arab, Algerian, Tunisian and Moroccan nationality in Germany would produce a great number of volunteers eager to fight. Of Germany's victory, the Arab world was firmly convinced, not only because the Reich possessed a large army, brave soldiers, and military leaders of genius, but also because the Almighty could never award the victory to an unjust cause. In this struggle, the Arabs were striving for the independence and unity of Palestine, Syria and Iraq. They had the fullest confidence in the Fuehrer and looked to his hand for the balm on their wounds, which had been inflicted upon them by the enemies of Germany.

The Mufti then mentioned the letter he had received from Germany, which stated that Germany was holding no Arab territories and understood and recognized the aspirations to impendence and freedom of the Arabs, just as she supported the elimination of the Jewish national home. A public declaration in this sense would be very useful for its propagandistic effects on the Arab peoples at this moment. It would rouse the Arabs from their momentary lethargy and give them new courage. It would also ease the Mufti's work of secretly organising the Arabs against [sic] the moment when they could strike. At the same time, he could give the assurance that the Arabs would in strict discipline patiently wait for the right moment and only strike upon an order from Berlin.

With regard to the events in Iraq [the failed pro-Nazi coup of April 1941], the Mufti observed that the Arabs in that country certainly had by no means been incited by Germany to attack England, but solely had reacted in reaction to a direct English assault upon their honour. The Turks, he believed, would welcome the establishment of an Arab government in the neighbouring territories because they would prefer weaker Arab to strong European governments in the neighbouring countries, and being themselves a nation of 7 million, they had moreover nothing to fear from the 1,700,000 Arabs inhabiting Syria, Transjordan, Iraq and Palestine.

France likewise would have no objections to the unification plan [sic: Palestine was thus not considered by Husseini to be a nation distinct from its Arab neighbours] because she had conceded independence to Syria as early as 1936 and had given her approval to the unification of Iraq and Syria under King Faisal as early as 1933. In these circumstances, he was renewing his request that the Fuehrer make a public declaration so that the Arabs would not lose hope, which is so powerful a force in the life of nations., With such hope in their hearts the Arabs, as he had said, we are willing to wait. They were not pressing for immediate realization for [sic] their aspirations; they could easily wait half a year or a whole year. But if they were not inspired with such a hope by a declaration of this sort, it could be expected that the English would be the gainers from it.

The Fuehrer replied that Germany's fundamental attitude on these questions, as the Mufti himself had already stated, was clear. Germany stood for uncompromising war against the Jews. That naturally included active opposition to the Jewish national home in Palestine, which was nothing other than a centre, in the form of a state, for the exercise of destructive influence by Jewish interests. Germany was also aware that the assertion that the Jews were carrying out the functions of economic pioneers in Palestine was a lie. The work there that was done only by the Arabs, not by the Jews. Germany was resolved, step by step, to ask one European nation after the other to solve its Jewish problem, and at the proper time to direct a similar appeal to non-European nations as well.

Germany was at the present time engaged in a life and death struggle with two citadels of Jewish power: Great Britain and Soviet Russia. Theoretically there was a difference between English capitalism and Soviet Russia's communism; actually, however, the Jews in both countries were pursuing a common goal. This was the decisive struggle; on the political plane, it presented itself in the main as a conflict between Germany and England, but ideologically it was between National Socialism and the Jews. It went without saying that Germany would furnish positive and practical aid to the Arabs involved in the same struggle, because platonic promises were useless in a war for survival or destruction in which the Jews were able to mobilize all of England's power for their ends.,

The aid to the Arabs would have to be material aid. Of how little sympathies alone were in such a battle had been demonstrated plainly by the operation in Iraq [the failed coup of April 1941], where circumstances had not permitted the rendering of really effective, practical aid. In spite of all the sympathies, German aid had not been sufficient and Iraq was overcome by the power of Britain, that is, the guardian of the Jews.

The Mufti could not but be aware however, that the outcome of the struggle going on at present would also decide the fate of the Arab world. The Fuehrer therefore had to think and speak coolly and deliberately, as a rational man and primarily as a soldier, as the leader of the German and allied armies. Everything of a nature to help this titanic battle for the common cause, and thus also for the Arabs, would have to be done. Anything however, that might contribute to

202

weakening the military situation must be put aside, no matter how unpopular this move might be.

Germany was now engaged in very severe battles to force the gateway to the northern Caucasus region. The difficulties were mainly with regard to maintaining the supply, which was most difficult as a result of the destruction of railroads and highways as well as the oncoming winter. If at such a moment, the Fuehrer were to raise the problem of Syria in a declaration, those elements in France which were under de Gaulle's influence would receive new strength. They would interpret the Fuehrer's declaration as an intention to break up France's colonial empire and appeal to their fellow countrymen that they should rather make common cause with the English to try to save what could be saved. A German declaration regarding Syria would in France be understood to refer to the French colonies in general, and that would at the present time create new troubles in western Europe, which means that a portion of the German armed forces would be immobilised in the west, and no longer available for the campaign in the east.

The Fuehrer then made the following statement to the Mufti, enjoining him to lock in the utmost depths of his heart:

1. He, (the Fuehrer) would carry on the battle to the total destruction of the Judeo-Communist empire in Europe.

2. At some moment which was impossible to set exactly today but which in any event was not distant, the German armies would in the course of this struggle reach the southern exit from Caucasia.

3. As soon as this had happened, the Fuehrer would on his own give the Arab world the assurance that its hour of liberation had arrived. Germany's objective would then be solely the destruction of the Jewish element residing in the Arab sphere under the protection of British power. In that hour, the Mufti would be the most authoritative spokesman for the Arab world. It would then be his task to set off the Arab operations, which he had secretly prepared. When that time had come, Germany could also be indifferent to French reaction to such a declaration

Once Germany had forced open the road to Iran and Iraq through Rostov, it would also be the beginning of the end of the British World Empire. He (the Fuehrer) hoped that the coming year would make it possible for Germany to thrust open the Caucasian gates to the Middle East. For the good of the common cause, it would be better if the Arab proclamation were put off for a few more months than if Germany were to create difficulties for herself without thereby being able to help the Arabs.

He (the Fuehrer) fully appreciated the eagerness of the Arabs for a public declaration of the sort requested by the Grand Mufti. But he would beg him to consider that he (the Fuehrer) himself was the Chief of State of the German Reich for five long years during which he was unable to make to his own homeland the announcement of its liberation. He had to wait with that [sic] until the announcement could be made on the basis of a situation brought about by the force of arms that the Anschluss had been carried out [sic]. The moment that Germany's tank divisions and air squadrons had made their appearance south of the Caucasus, the public appeal requested by the Grand Mufti could go out to the Arab world.

The Grand Mufti replied that it was his view that everything would come to pass just as the Fuhrer had indicated. He was fully reassured and satisfied by the words which he had heard from the Chief of the German State. He asked, however, whether it would not be possible, secretly at least, to enter into an agreement with Germany of the kind he had just outlined for the Fuehrer. The Fuehrer replied that he had just now given the grand Mufti precisely that confidential deceleration. The Grand Mufti thanked him for it and stated in conclusion that he was taking his leave from the Fuehrer in full confidence and with reiterated thanks for the interest shown in the Arab cause.'

From the Memoirs of Haj Amin al-Husseini:

> I did not expect that my reception at the famous chancellery would be an official one, but a private meeting with the Fuhrer. I had just arrived at the wide square in front of the chancellery and stepped out of the car in front of the entrance of the great building, when I was startled by the sound of a military band and guards of honour composed of around two hundred German soldiers who gathered in the square. My escorts from the Foreign Office invited me to inspect the guards, which I did. Then we entered the chancellery and passed through its long colonnades and impressive portals until we reached the large reception hall. There, the head of state protocols greeted me, and after a short while led me to the Fuhrer's special room. Hitler greeted me warmly with a cheerful face, expressive eyes, and clear joy...
>
> Our fundamental condition for cooperating with Germany was a free hand to eradicate every last Jew from Palestine and the Arab world. I asked Hitler for an explicit undertaking to allow us to solve the Jewish problem in a manner befitting our national and racial aspirations and according to the scientific methods innovated by Germany [i.e., gassing] in the handling of the Jews. The answer I got was: 'The Jews are all yours.'

Not according to Ken Livingstone and the Secretary-General of the Organisation of the Islamic Conference.

Addendum

Some months before the Mufti's arrival in Berlin, the path of his collaboration with the Third Reich in the extermination of the Jews had been smoothed by Nazi academics specialising in matters racial. At a conference convened at Alfred Rosenberg's Frankfurt 'Institute for Research into the Jewish Question' (sic) in March 1941, speakers were at pains to make a clear-cut racial distinction between their sought-for allies, the Arabs, and their mutual enemies, the Jews. As one explained, 'it would be well for the sake of clarity if the European world in its struggle against the Jews always remained aware of this context and did not call the struggle, as hitherto, anti-Semitism, because it is directed not against peoples of Semitic tongue, but against the unharmonious Near Eastern-Oriental-Mediterranean Jew-people which is being so passionately rejected also by the purely Oriental, Semitic tribes and peoples.' (i.e., the Arabs) When in October 1942 Rashid Ali, the former pro-Nazi Prime Ministry of Iraq, now like the Mufti an exile in Berlin after being ousted by the British, inquired as to the attitude of Germany's racial experts towards the Arabs, one replied that

> the Semitic-Arab peoples, languages and cultures always were the object of affectionate interest on the part of German scholarship. No responsible person or institution in Germany ever said that the Arabs were racially inferior or stood on an unfavourable place in the rank order of human races. On the contrary, National Socialist racial theory considers the Arabs [to be] members of a high-value race that

looks back upon a glorious and heroic history. That is why, too, the struggle of the Arabs for political liberation against the Jewish usurpation of Palestine has always been observed and supported by Germany with particular sympathy.

T Labour's Black-Shirts: Jeremy and the Jew-Baiters

'He who toucheth pitch shall be defiled therewith'. Ecclesiasticus 13:1

'[Jeremy]'s been steeped in anti-Semitism.' Shadow Leader of the House Valerie Vaz, Radio Four, March 25, 2018

Jeremy Corbyn and his apologists have always insisted that his long-standing political collaboration, declared friendship and even brotherhood with Jew-killers, anti-Semites and Holocaust and 9/11 deniers does not constitute proof of his alleged prejudices against the Jews. There are facts that suggest otherwise, and his repeated claim that they do not carries no more weight than a not-guilty plea in a criminal trial. For more three decades, at least since his launching, with the anti-Semite Ken Livingstone, of the forerunner of the Palestinian Solidarity Campaign in 1982, Corbyn's political career has been dominated and his thinking shaped by his obsession with Israel. Of the 834 Early Day Motions sponsored by Corbyn in the 20 years since 1989, 63 criticised Israel. The next highest number concerning a country is 26, on Morocco. As his Press Officer, Seumas Milne puts it, anti-Zionism is 'the great international issue of our time'. And so far as Muslim Jihadis, and much of the Neo-Nazi right and the neo-Leninist left are concerned, this is indubitably true. Like Corbyn's, their anti-Zionism is a Manichean struggle of absolute good, embodied in the Palestinians (or rather those genocidal terrorists who claim to represent them) against absolute evil, personified by the Jewish state of Israel, a mental and moral world not far removed from that inhabited by the Russian clerics who at beginning of the 20th century, conjured up the fabrications of that notorious text commended not only by Hitler and Hamas but as we shall see, websites associated with and visited by none other than Corbyn himself...*The Protocols of the Learned Elders of Zion*. This utterly depraved world has become by his choice Corbyn's natural habitat, one where a virulent hatred of Israel has repeatedly slipped its mask to reveal what it truly is... a loathing of Jews...all Jews.

Corbyn has frequently been accused, and with good reason, of sharing platforms or associating with individuals who before Zionist-baiting became the fashion, would have never been given house-room by the vast majority of the left. Let two instances suffice here, since I have cited many others in the main body of this work. Speaking on the same platform with Corbyn at an event he hosted in Parliament in 2009, was Dyab Abou Jahjah, a Hezbollah supporter. The day before, addressing a meeting of the Stop the War Coalition, Corbyn, in the course of advertising his meeting the next day, famously or infamously, described Hezbollah and Hamas, two terrorist movements dedicated to the destruction of Israel and the extermination of the Jews, as his 'friends'. One of them, his guest speaker at Westminster, in the wake of 9 /11 had hailed the atrocity as 'sweet revenge', and in 2004, told a Flemish magazine, 'I consider every dead American, British and Dutch soldier a victory'. 'Stop the War?' Nor was this all. Prior to the meeting, Jahjah had posted Holocaust-denial cartoons on his website, for which he was convicted by a Dutch court. Appraised of his posting, and the subsequent conviction, the Board of Deputies of British Jews wrote to the Home Security objecting to his presence in the UK to attend the Westminster meeting.

Some six years later, when Corbyn emerged as the leading contender for the Labour Leadership, he was criticised for sharing a platform with a convicted Holocaust denier and apologist for terrorism. Corbyn initially claimed in a BBC Radio 4 interview that he had never heard of or met Jahjah, let alone shared a platform with him: 'I saw the name this morning and asked somebody, "Who is he?" ...I'm sorry, I don't know who this person is.' In a matter of hours, Corbyn's lie was exposed when a photo was produced showing Corbyn and Jahjah siting side by side at their Westminster meeting. Jahjah then confirmed that not only did he know Corbyn, but that 'we worked together closely...we had two lunches or breakfast together...He is a political friend. I am very sympathetic to his political ideas...I am hopeful he will win the leadership of Labour and help build a better future for the British people.' Yet a few hours earlier, Corbyn had said, 'I don't know who this person is'. At the meeting in question, responding to criticism his of sharing a platform with a Holocaust denier and advocate of terrorist attacks on civilians, Corbyn was unrepentant. 'I refuse to be dragged into this stuff [sic] that somehow or other because we're pro-Palestinian we're anti-Semitic. It's a nonsense.' Holocaust denial not anti-Semitic?

Two years after sharing a platform with Jahjah, Corbyn became the subject of another controversy involving a relationship with an anti-Semite who advocated terrorism against Israeli politicians. In 2002, the Polish journalist Ewa Jasciewicz, who writes regularly for the fanatically anti-Israel on-line *Electronic Intifada,* (sic) called, on a pro-Palestinian website, for the assassination of members of the Israeli parliament, the Knesset, saying they should be 'bumped off', preferably while it was in session. Active on behalf of *Kampania Palystina*, the Polish equivalent of BDS and Corbyn's PSC, she has brushed aside accusations of its collaboration with movements that were only too willing, as is the way in Poland, to further their own anti-Semitic agendas. It should have come as no surprise then that in 2010, together with another anti-Zionist activist, she scribbled anti-Israeli graffiti on a wall of the Warsaw Ghetto, where in April 1943, Jews destined for the gas chambers of Hitler's Final Solution staged an uprising against the Nazis. Some of the survivors of the uprising made their way at the end of the war to what in 1948 became the new state of Israel, where they founded a kibbutz that is today run by their descendants. They rose against the Nazis at a time when the Palestinian leader, the Grand Mufti of Jerusalem, together with other prominent Muslim politicians, was collaborating with Hitler in the extermination of the Jews. What Ms Jasciewicz claimed was a protest against what she saw as Israel's exploitation of the Holocaust to justify the 'colonisation and repression' of the Palestinians was in fact a desecration of the memory of the Jews' struggle for their liberation from centuries of persecution, pogroms and finally, genocide. Israel's Yad Vashem Holocaust Museum condemned her action as 'tainted with anti-Semitism', while the Community Security Trust described it as an 'act of arrogance and callousness'.

Not everyone shared that view of Ms Jasciewicz. Speaking at a pro-Gaza, or more accurately, pro-Hamas rally in 2009, Corbyn referred to her as a 'good friend', and her notorious exploit in Warsaw the next year did nothing to harm that friendship. In 2011, the Palestine Solidarity Campaign, of which Corbyn is both a founder and a patron, staged what it called a 'Literary Festival' (sic) in Tottenham, North London. Children from eight local primary schools, that is, those under the age of 12, had been invited to attend the event, where they would be addressed by amongst other speakers, none other than Corbyn's 'good friend', Ms Jasciewicz. As in the case of the Hezbollah Holocaust denier Dyab Abou Jahjah, the Board of Deputies of British Jews understanbly found itself at odds with the organisers of the event. Dismissing their objection to what was obviously his choice of speaker, Corbyn announced he would be attending the event, adding, 'it's great opportunity for children to understand the wealth and joy of Palestinian literature and a little [sic] of the history of the region.' He insisted that the festival would 'not in any way be biased.' 'In any way'? In which case, why invite a notorious anti-Israeli activist? With her track record, which Corbyn must surely have been aware of, what kind of 'unbiased' history of the Middle East would she be instilling into her charges? This one can guess from her comments on the Gaza conflict of 2014 on behalf of 'London Palestine Action', when she defined Israel's polices towards the Palestinians as those of 'massacre', 'apartheid' and 'genocide'. She surfaced again when she was due to share a Momentum platform with Corbyn and his Shadow Chancellor John McDonnell at the September 2018 Labour Party conference. She and Jeremy were obviously still 'good friends'. As Aesop puts it, 'a man is known by the company he keeps'. But such was the outcry, that that she withdrew at the last moment.

From the PSC's inception in 1982, Corbyn has been has been amongst, if not the most frequent and prominent of the campaign's public speakers. Also numbered among its patrons are film director and one-time WRP sympathiser Ken Loach, who is in favour of a re-examination of whether the Holocaust happened, and former Liberal (sic) Democratic Peer Baroness Tonge, who in 2010 retailed the accusation Israel relief workers had harvested body organs from victims of the Haiti earthquake, and who in 2016, resigned from the Liberal Democratic Party after being suspended for hosting a meeting at Westminster where claims were made that Zionists encouraged the Nazis to carry out the Holocaust to gain sympathy for a Jewish state in Palestine, as if they needed any such inducement. She resigned from her sponsorship of the PSC following an uproar when she implied that that the massacre of 11 Jews at prayer in a Pittsburgh synagogue by a Neo-Nazi was caused by Israel's ill-treatment of the Palestinians. With patrons such as these, little wonder that irrefutable evidence has been found of the dissemination within the campaign of the most extreme manifestations of anti-Semitism, giving the lie to the PSC's statement that it is 'opposed to all form of racism, including anti-Jewish prejudice'.

The attacks on the Jews go far beyond the routine denunciations of Zionism that are the stock in trade of the Sharia left and the Neo-Nazi fringe. The target of the invective, with items on Jewish conspiracies and Holocaust denial being the most frequently posted and re-cycled, is not just Israel, but the Jews, *all Jews*. Yet Patron Corbyn has not only failed to denounce and demand the expulsion of these Jew-baiters from the PSC. He is on the most cordial of terms with some of them and can be seen in photos taken with three of these purveyors of the myths of the *Protocols*. And even more to the point, he shares the views of the most extreme of them, to the extent of signing the Declaration 'Against US Hegemony and War on Iraq and in Solidarity with Palestine' adopted at the Cairo conference of

December 18-19 2002, which twice in its text accused Israel of perpetrating, quote, 'genocidal crimes against the Palestinian people' and, for good measure, simultaneously imposing, quote, 'a system of Apartheid on the Palestinian people'. The fascist regime of Saddam Hussein, which was guilty of both crimes against the Kurds, and which the purpose of the conference was to rally world-wide opposition to its removal by an immanent US-led invasion, was praised in the same Declaration for, quote, its 'positive profile according to certain human development indicators'. As someone so passionately committed to the defence of human rights, as in Iran for example, he must have been better informed than most about Sandam's gassing of the Kurds in 1988. But yet he still signed. One must see the bigger picture...an Arab regime that commits genocide must at all costs be defended, while a Jewish state that is the intended victim of Palestinian genocidists must be treated as an enemy, and those who would if they could murder its entire Jewish population, as his friends. One of the proposals endorsed by Corbyn was 'to prepare for sending human shields to Iraq', and another 'the boycott of US and Israeli commodities'. Corbyn's name heads the list of signatories to this lying Declaration, followed by a cavalcade of veteran Zionists-baiters...Andrew Murray, George Galloway, Ken Loach, Tariq Ali, Paul Foot, Alex Callinicos and Lindsey (Shibboleth) German.

Before exploring the nether regions of this fetid world inhabited by Corbyn, let us first look at two examples of the beliefs that led him there, which have him subscribing to two classic Jewish stereotypes, as conspirators and exploiters. They are related by Tom Bowyer in his biography of the Labour Leader, *Dangerous Hero*. In 2003, with Jewish bankers in New York in mind, Corbyn told a meeting of Hamas supporters that in the USA, 'the power of the Israel lobby is truly phenomenal'. 62 years previously, another anti-Semitic politician, announcing to the German Reichstag his declaration of war on the USA, described the USA as a country ruled by a 'Jewish clique which surrounds Roosevelt and exploits the American people'. Racialist minds think...and speak... alike, as also in this next case. In 2015, recalling his time as an assistant researcher for the National Union of Taylor and Garment Workers in the early 1970s, Corbyn called the mainly Jewish employers of the union's members 'scumbags' and 'crooks' for using devious methods to defraud their workers of their wages. This story, like others of Corbyn's about the Jews, proved to be a lie. The union's archives have no record of such exploitative malpractices, and a colleague of Corbyn's assured Bowyer that Corbyn 'never had any contact with our members. He just sat in meetings and passed me information.'

What follows are samples of mainly on-line Jew-baiting by those on the left whose guiding principle, judging by their content, could, with the change of just one letter, easily be a paraphrase of the Corbynite mantra, 'For the Many, not the Few'. They have been selected from a wide range of sources, the most comprehensive being by David Collier, of postings by the Palestine Solidarity Campaign, the Boycott, Disinvestment and Sanctions campaign backed by Corbyn, the Facebook site *Palestine Live*, one of whose secret members was Jeremy Corbyn, and by individual, mainly pro-Corbyn Labour Party members.

Over a period of two years, Collier investigated the on-line activity of members of 31 branches of the Palestine Solidarity Campaign in England and Wales, samples of 17 of which are featured in his 80-page report. (The photos of the saintly Jeremy with his Jew-baiting comrades can be seen on pages 12 and 51)

Collier had very strict criteria for what could be included as examples of PSC anti-Semitism: 'If the worst I found was an activist saying that Israel should be destroyed, is committing genocide, and Zionists are all Nazis, that activist would not have made the grade for this research. Let that fact sink in.'

Now for samples.

Bristol:

'The USA is controlled by Zionists. Israel controls US government and media... Record number of Jews in US government.'
'Did you know that the only people to be arrested on September 11 in connection to [sic] the attacks were 5 Israeli Mossad agents?'
'Report in *Veteran Today* that ISIS is Israeli.'
'Suspicions are growing that Paris shootings are a false flag operation.'
'The genocide of 15 million+ Germans by the Jews.'
'The France attacks. What better excuse to get the France [sic] Jews to move to Israel.'
[This is patently a variant on the oft-repeated claim that the Zionists collaborated with the Nazis in the Holocaust in order to generate sympathy and support for a Jewish state in the British Mandate.]
'ISIS leader Al-Baghdadi is a Jewish Mossad agent.'
'Settler Rabbi publishes *The Complete Guide to Killing Non-Jews.*'
On page 12, Saint Jeremy is posing with each arm around a Bristol Jewish conspiracy theorist, Edward Clarke on his right, and Rita Tiziana to his left. Clarke is the expert on the motive for the *Charlie Hebdo* massacre, Tiziana on Mossad and settler Rabbis.

Cardiff

'Mossad is busy in Paris again.'
'Israel executing Palestinians, harvesting their organs.'
'Bibi [Netanyahu] a suspect in *Charlie Hebdo* massacre.'
'The greatest lie ever told - The Holocaust - 2015 documentary HD.'
'Critical discussion of the Holocaust is dangerous.'
'Auschwitz Museum is a fraudulent enterprise.'
'ISIS is working on a Mossad/CIA plan to make a Greater Israel.'

Durham

'25000 Ukrainian children organs harvested in Israel.'

Jersey

'Israelis - not Muslims - cheered in Jersey City on 9/11.'

Merton, London

'Israelis stealing organs from living people - including testicles and ovaries.'
[This myth has bled into the political mainstream, with PSC Patron Baroness Tonge's insinuation that Israeli relief workers harvested the organs of victims of the Haiti earthquake of 2010, and Rutgers University Professor and former Syrian

diplomat Mazen Adi's allegation at the United Nations in April 2012 that 'international gangs led by some Israeli religious figures are now trafficking children's organs.']

'French journalist arrested after exposing Israel link to Paris attacks.'

'CIA and Mossad are behind Boko Haram and ISIS, says Sudan President.'

'9/11 Tel Aviv-based outside job.'

'The "Zionist Power Configuration" (ZPC) operates at both a global and local level as was indicated on 9/11.'

'Ukrainian General: "Ukraine is under Zionist occupation".'

Richmond, London

'Zionist Broadcasting Corporation forthcoming events: BBC to broadcast Holocaust Memorial Day.'

'There was no Holocaust. It's a pack of lies...Fuck Zionism and fuck its Holy Holocash.'

'The Zionist tentacles on our Parliament almost complete.'

'Jewish donors to the Labour Party run it.'

'The attack by the pro-Israel lobby on the Labour Party 7 days before the election is not just an attack on Jeremy Corbyn...what we are witnessing is an attack on British democracy by a foreign power.'

'The only individuals arrested on 9/11 in connection with the attacks were Israeli nationals.'

Luton

'The belief that the Jews were responsible for the Holocaust is common to orthodox Jews.'

'What is it with Zionists and children, killing children and stealing children to sell them on the black market. And yet we are always told Israel has a right to exist.'

Medway

Advertising a video: 'New world Order as planned in the elders of Zion.'

In a posting advertising a 'Stand up to Racism' public meeting featuring Momentum Vice Chairperson Jackie Walker, twice suspended and eventually expelled from the Labour Party (but not Momentum) for anti-Semitism, we read the following]

"No to Islamophobia, no to anti-Semitism."

[while in another posting *on the same page*]

'Literally a bus load of Zionist Jews arrested for organ smuggling.'

Norwich

'We no longer have a democracy when the Jewish lobby can tell what we can and cannot discuss.'

'Of course, we are used to being [a Freudian slip, or does she mean accused of being?] anti-Semitic all of the time. I can live with it now, knowing that it isn't

true.'
    [but in another of hers]
    'Bodies of murdered Palestinians are being returned with organs missing.'
    [and yet another]:
    'Have questions on the Holocaust? Tony Blair wants you arrested.'

Peterborough

    (Where in June 2019, Labour's conspiracy theorist candidate Liz Forbes [see below] was possibly elected with fraudulent votes.)
    A posting promoting the video titled: 'The Covenant of the Jew Illuminati.'
    'Israeli Jews admit they run America.'

Reading

It is here on page 51 we see Reading PSC's Tony Gratrex, sporting a PSC T-shirt, posing in a photo with a grinning Jeremy Corbyn, who has his right arm around Gratrex's shoulder. They are clearly on more than nodding terms with each other, because Gratrex was also snapped in an identical pose with Corbyn at another PSC function. How does a quite open anti-Semite, Holocaust denier, and Nazi apologist come to enjoy the patronage of the Labour Party's Leader? Another link with Corbyn is Gratrex's membership of the congregation of the anti-Semitic Rev. Stephen Sizer's Anglican Church in nearby Virginia Water. Sizer is a high-profile PSC member, sharing its platforms with Corbyn, while Corbyn, it will be remembered, came to the Reverend's defence when he was reprimanded by his Bishop for claiming that the Jews were responsible for 9/11. Like Sizer and so many other members of the PSC, Corbyn, as we have seen, also does not accept the 'official version' of what happened on that day.
    These are some of Comrade Gratrex's postings:
    'There is still not a shred of evidence in the public domain that a single "terrorist" was involved in any part of 9/11' [Corbyn also believes that 9/11 was 'manipulated']
    'Paris attacks. Another false flag?'
    'Jewish power for you…The Daily Telegraph and other press outlets list the sex abuse allegations against Lord Janner, a 27-year Labour MP. But there is one thing The Telegraph and other British press outlets fail to mention. They omit the fact that at the time Lord Janner was allegedly sexually abusing young British [sic] orphans…he was head of the British Jewish community.'
    'A century of deceit: Iraq, the World Wars, Holocaust, Zionist militarism…In an effort to whitewash their own egregious war crimes, the Allied powers went along with the Zionists' pre-mediated fictional account of six million dead Jews. At the post-war Nuremberg Trials, an Allied-run kangaroo court staffed to the brim by Zionist Jews and their Allied lackeys, the truth was buried ['drowned' surely] under a tidal wave of falsehoods. The Zionist motives for the war itself were purposefully obscured and a cartoonish propaganda narrative of "Nazi evil" was foisted upon the world to advance the victors' post-war aims for Europe and accelerate the Zionists' ambitions for a Jewish ethno-state in Palestine.'
    A posting advertising *The Protocols of the Learned Elders of Labour*:
    'Jewish power is no longer a vague and mysterious concept. We should listen

to the words of a few of the prime Elder Jewish oligarchs and learn from them about the future of the Labour Party and its political role.'

Inevitably, Gratrex detected the hand of the Jews in the anti-Semitic crisis that beset Labour after Corbyn's election as party leader: 'If Jewish power is the power to silence opposition to Jewish power, then the scandal over the alleged anti-Semitism within the Labour Party is a perfect example of that power.'

West Midlands

'The Babylonian Jewish Talmud advocates sex with a child of three years, saying with every tear, the virginity is renewed.'

'Essential reading: Many claims around the Holocaust were debunked long ago, yet they are still regurgitated to this day…Evidence collected by scientists, engineers, historians, scholars and others, some of which [sic] are Jewish, strongly support the conclusion that the facilities alleged to have been homicidal gas chambers could not possibly have been used to exterminate human beings for a number of fundamental reasons.'

'Did you know that just months before 9/11, the World Trade Centre's lease was privatised and sold to Larry Silverstein. Silverstein took out an insurance plan that "fortuitously" covered terrorism.'

Next, PSC Scotland

Posted by some guests at the SPSC Christmas Dinner, 2015, with Scotland's First Minister Nicola Sturgeon in attendance:

'The real Holocaust of World War Two - the genocide of 15 + million Germans.'

'Why does extreme Muslim state ISIS attack Muslim state after Muslim state but never fire a shot at Israel?'

'It is the ghastly truth of the Jewish-orchestrated plundering, mass rape, mass murder, and subjugation of the German people in the latter days of the and aftermath of World War Two, which continues to this day.'

'These were the real death camps of World War Two, not the slave labour and internment camps run by the Germans in the alleged Jewish "Holocaust", which is a Jewish fraud and lie.'

'The biggest single source of Holohoax in modern times is Jewish Hollywood. Most people's views of the Second World War are formed by watching movies and the Jewish propaganda documentaries on Jewish owned or run channels such as the history Channel National Geographic of the BBC.'

West Dunbartonshire

'ISIS leader "Al-Baghdadi" is Jewish Mossad agent Simon Elliot.'

'Mossad agent accidentally admits they did 7/7 London bombings.'

'…Princess Diana was assassinated by Mossad…'

'25,000 Ukrainian children organs harvested in [sic] Israel.'

'Fake Muslim preacher Omar Bakri busted as Mossad Mole - tied to Woolwich'. [i.e., murder of Lee Rigby]

'The fall of the Holocaust lie and the rise of truth and reason.'

Posting promoting 'The Protocols of the Learned Elders of Zion. Zionist plan for world conquest through Jewish world government.'

'Israel murdered 3,000 Americans on 9/11 2001.'

Glasgow

'Nazis and Zionist Jews made a deal behind the real Jewish people's backs and that is how the state of Israel was created with the help of Adolf Hitler.'

'ISIS is a Zionist creation being used to achieve a "greater Israel".'

Posting of speech by Hitler: 'Adolf Hitler talks about the Jews and the Allies.' 'Never mind the alleged Holocaust, just listen to his opening lines and tell me its not happening now.'

'American gas chamber export [sic] Dr. Leuchter visited all sites and testified that supposed gas chambers "incapable" of supporting gas executions.'

'Press TV [Corbyn's former employer]: "9/11 was Zionist coup d'état."'

'How is France under attack? Jewish owners recently sold Paris's Bataclan theatre where ISIS killed dozens.'

'Did Mossad do Charlie Hebdo?'

'David Icke [sic]: The Rothschild Zionist Agenda. New World Order and the Third World War.'

Dundee

'So we have France voting to give Palestine statehood and then all of a sudden they get attacked by ISIS.'

'Paris admits Nice attack was false flag operation.'

'Israel linked to Istanbul Airport terror attack.'

'96% of world's media is controlled by Jews.'

'Israel did 9/11 to destroy "7 countries in 5 years". Trump's Muslim ban targets almost [sic] exactly [sic] the same seven countries.'

Fife

'International Red Cross report confirms the Holocaust of six million Jews is a hoax.'

Aberdeen

'Israel kills its own teenagers. Zionist money owns the mainstream media. Kennedy was assassinated because he wanted to take on the Rothschilds.'

'ISIS belongs to Jew Zionism.'

'Israel injects Palestinian prisoners with dangerous viruses.'

Here are some postings by BDS activists:

'Some Israelis/Jews worked at WTC were tipped off to absent on that day, and those who did die in the attacks ignored or missed the tip.'

'All Zionists must die.'

'ISIS is Israel.'

215

'Because Israel OWNS the USA, all American taxpayers are slaves to the Zionists. Without the US support Israel will collapse.'

'Edward Snowden: Top ISIS leader Abu Bakr Al Baghdadi was trained by Israeli Mossad.'

'ISIS is working on Mossad/CIA plan to create Greater Israel.'

'Complete list of banks owned by Illuminati Rothschild family.'

'Former Italian President says 9/11 solved. It's common knowledge, Mossad, CIA behind 9/11 terror attacks.'

'The "Six Million" Holocaust lie.'

'International Red Cross report confirms the Holocaust of six million Jews is a hoax.'

'They [the Jews] are ALL terribly ugly because of the evil inside them. And they all look alike.'

'A Century of Deceit: Iraq, the World Wars, Holocaust Mythology and Zionist Militarism.'

Video: 'Israeli terrorism against America. By Dr. David Duke.' [Duke is the former KKK Grand Wizard and white supremacist who admires Corbyn and is admired by Green Party members.]

Now the Campaign Against Anti-Semitism's report, based on a month-long monitoring of the PSC's Facebook page during November 2016:

'Sure the Jews own America what do you expect?'

'The Rothschilds run every country in the world except 5. That's why Israel can do this.'

'...the Zionist mafia run the planet.'

'I hate my government. Weak puppets for the Zionists NWO [New World Order] their bankers and their puppet governments and regimes.'

'Pretty much most right-wing organisations around the world including those that claim to be Islamic are actually Zionist funded.'

'They are bloody thirsty. They want to kill entire humanity except America. God will punish them soon.'

'Filthy jew dirtbags.'

'What Jewish Zionist mother*****zzzzz. Inshallah [Allah willing] they will rot in hell for their messed-up actions.'

'Israel is a syndicate crime country. It should be destroyed in the world for ever.'

'Allah will destroy Israel soon.'

Another website devoted to the same subject, Stand for Peace, reports a posting by former PSC West Midlands branch chairperson Sammi Ibrahim. Like Gratrex, he deplores the Nuremberg Trials; 'I bow my head to those who were judicially murdered at Nuremberg. They were the world's martyrs, not villains. Not one of them would have been condemned to death in a fair trial - not one! They sacrificed an entire nation, and in the end, themselves, to save western civilisation. They were defeated by thugs in robes and gangsters in uniform - and conspiracies hatched by shysters from the ghettoes of Eastern Europe.'

To see if PSC Facebook pages were being monitored for racists comments, the

216

Campaign Against Anti-Semitism posted three about a fictitious 'Bangalla people' identical in sentiment to those that had been made about the Jews. *All were removed within six hours.* Those about the Jews remained. As a personal spot check, I scrolled down the PSC national website, and in no time, came across this posting by a Marty Chamberlain, dated December 2, 2017: 'Israel is like a disease on this planet...can we get a vaccine for that?' I toyed with and then rejected the idea of answering: 'Yes, Zyklon B.' (the gas used to exterminate the Jews in the Nazi gas chambers.) Immediately below this posting, blatantly anti-Semitic by any standards other than those of Corbyn's PSC, there was another, which stated, in all seriousness:

'Please help raise money for a legal challenge to the Independent Press Standards Organisation to prevent Palestinian events being smeared [sic] as anti-Semitic.'

From his two-year study of the postings and public activities of the Palestinian Solidarity Campaign, Collier concluded that around 40% of its activists qualified as anti-Semites, attracted to the Campaign like iron filings to a magnet, just as is Corbyn to movements and regimes that propagate the lies they subscribe to. The evidence presented by Collier reveals an on-line culture of festering Jew-hatred, one awash with fake news, 'alternative facts' and demented conspiracy theories that within the PSC are its *lingua franca*. It is a culture which those who inhabit it not only make no attempt to hide but advertise to all and sundry. It is obvious from numerous postings reproduced by Collier that for many PSC activists, the Palestinian issue serves merely as a pretext to spew their venom on the Jews. It was just their kind who back in the 1930s, motivated by the same vile prejudice, would have been activists in LINK, like the PSC infested with anti-Semites and pro-Nazis, which campaigned for what it euphemistically called 'Anglo-German understanding'. Anyone reading their postings and not *au fait* with the PSC's un-hidden agenda would surely ask themselves, what have harvesting body organs, the Nuremberg Trials, and the causes of world wars one and two got do with the Palestine question? The simple answer is, nothing.

In addition to Gratrex, Corbyn appears in numerous other photos in Collier's report, pictured with PSC anti-Semites during the course of his political engagements with the PSC and the Labour Party. They include one with to Corbyn's right, Edward Clarke, one of whose postings refers to an 'ugly Israel species', and another which reads, 'can I tell you how much I hate Israel and its rich western backers'; and another with on his left, Rita Roberta Tiziana, who believes, like many other PSC members, that the Islamic State is a creation of Mossad. She also posted on-line her claim that the Islamic State terror attacks in France were part of a Zionist plot to provide an 'excuse to get the France [sic] Jews [to] move to Israel. They want the Jews out of Europe to populate the stolen land'. Another snap shows Corbyn posing with Dr. Swee Ang, who shared on line a video made by David Duke alleging the existence of a world Jewish conspiracy.

As well as being a patron of the PSC, Corbyn has been a highly visible supporter of Unite Against Fascism from its founding in 2003. The human rights campaigner Peter Tatchell has criticised UAF for being 'silent about Islamic fascists who promote anti-Semitism', and with good reason. We have seen that the 'anti-fascist' Corbyn has no problem in sharing platforms with notorious Muslim anti-Semites, and to be photographed with a neo-Nazi (twice), two Jewish conspiracy theorists and two Holocaust deniers. Just how he conceives of the struggle against fascism is graphically depicted in another photo, this time on a UAF website, where he can be seen holding a UAF poster, inscribed in large letters, NEVER AGAIN. This is an exclusively Jewish slogan, especially popular with Zionists, and it conveys the resolve of the Jews never again to be subject to another Holocaust, such as Corbyn's friends Hamas and Hezbollah have in mind. It is also the title of a book by the founder of the Jewish Defence League, Meir Kahane. But the UAF purloined these two words to give them an entirely different meaning because below them, on the poster held up by Corbyn, there is no reference to anti-Semitism, but instead, 'No to racist Pediga, no to Islamophobia'.

Corbyn also plays a prominent role in Labour Friends of Palestine which, despite its membership being restricted to MPs, is not immune from the kind of Nazi-style thinking that infests the PSC. On September 25, 2017, there appeared on the LFP website a tweet that blatantly alluded to the Holocaust and implied that the final objective was the total elimination of Israel, with the comment that a 'two-state solution will end the occupation - our solution will be the final solution.'(sic) Only two weeks previously, anti-Zionists had demanded at the Labour Party conference that the affiliated Jewish Labour Movement should be expelled from the Labour Party, a demand first raised by Corbyn and Livingstone back in 1984. Then on December 11, in Committee Room 1 of the House of Commons, Corbyn, his Shadow Chancellor John McDonnell, who is on record as being opposed to very existence of Israel, and Bradford West MP Naz(i) Shah, suspended for anti-Semitic remarks about Israel, launched the Labour Muslim Network. This is an organisation based purely on a religion, and not, like the Jewish Labour Movement, on ethnicity, and a religion, moreover, that preaches hatred against the Jews. The Network is headed by Ali Milani, who doubles up as Vice-President of the *dhimmi* National Union of Students, and who in that capacity has made a series of anti-Semitic comments that he was subsequently required to apologise for. He has also declared like McDonnell that 'Israel has no right to exist.' Posing with Milani, Corbyn once again used the occasion to have himself photographed with an anti-Semite. Among other MPs present was Afzal Khan, who during the 2014 Gaza conflict, accused Israel of 'acting like Nazis'. This, from someone whose own religion is saturated with anti-Semitism. Representing the clerical interest was Mohammed Kozbar, who just happens to be Chairman of Corbyn's local Finsbury Park Mosque, where on the first anniversary of 9/11, a packed to overflowing congregation celebrated the attack on the World Trade Centre.

Next, Corbyn as art critic. The following item, titled *There is only one word for Jeremy Corbyn*, appeared in the *Jewish Chronicle* on March 24, 2018:

The word is overused in politics. Politicians rarely lie, if for no other reason than the risk of being caught out. But sometimes it is the only appropriate word when a politician is guilty of a deliberate attempt at distorting the truth wilfully and shamelessly. That time is now, and the politician is Jeremy Corbyn. In November 21015, the *JC* reported that back in 2012, Jeremy Corbyn had defended the existence of a mural which had been widely condemned as being anti-Semitic. The work, *Freedom for Humanity*, was painted near Brick Lane in London's East End by 'graffiti artist' Kalen Ockerman, he goes by the name of Mear One. Its intent was obvious. It showed businessmen and bankers sitting counting their money. Not only did they look like obvious caricatures of Jews - in a style reminiscent of Nazi propaganda in the 1930s - the artist himself confirmed they were intended as such, writing: 'Some of the older white Jewish folk in the local community had an issue with me portraying their beloved Rothschild or Warburg etc as the demons they are.'

Anyone with even a basic knowledge of politics, history and the world would see that the [20 foot-high] work was caricaturing Jews. And, to be blunt, anyone denying that is indulging in the sophistry of the most pathetically unconvincing kind. Indeed, the then Mayor of Tower Hamlets, Lutfar Rahman [certainly no friend of the Jews] himself ordered council officials to 'do everything possible' to remove the mural, agreeing that 'the images of the bankers perpetuate anti-Semitic propaganda about conspiratorial Jewish domination of financial institutions'. But when Mr Ockerman wrote on Facebook that his mural was to be removed, a then insignificant Labour MP expressed his support for the piece, writing in response: 'Why? You are in good company. [Yes, that of the Nazi's *Die Sturmer*] Rockefeller destroyed Diego Viera's [sic] mural because it included a picture of Lenin.' Mr Corbyn was referring to the removal in 1934 of a work by the Mexican artist Diego Rivera from the Rockefeller Centre in New York. When we unearthed Mr Corbyn's 2012 comment in 2015, we contacted his office for a response, asking about his support for a clearly [and expressly] anti-Semitic mural remaining on display.

No response was forthcoming then or, indeed, for over two years - until yesterday, when the Labour MP Luciana Berger came across the story and asked Mr Corbyn's office for a response. That response was perhaps the most appalling single comment by any mainstream party leader of my lifetime. A spokesman for the Labour leader said [why can't leaders speak for themselves?]: 'In 2012, Jeremy was responding to concerns about the removal of public art on grounds of freedom of speech [which Corbyn does not believe in]. However, the mural was offensive [when did he say this?], used anti-Semitic imagery, which has no place in our society [but it does on websites frequented by Corbyn], and it is right that it was removed.' [which Corbyn at the time said it should not be] The more one thinks about this, the more shocking it is. The statement acknowledges what it could hardly deny, that the mural was anti-Semitic. But it also says that Mr Corbyn was defending it on 'grounds of free speech'. [something Corbyn has made it clear that when it comes to criticising Islam, he does not believe in].

In other words, we are expected to accept that it was perfectly fine for the leader of the Labour Party to support the existence of a large public anti-Semitic mural. The free speech argument is of course risible. Few politicians have been less committed to upholding free speech principles than Mr Corbyn. In February 2006, for example, he did not merely attend but spoke at a rally in London against the Danish cartoons of Mohammed published in the *Jyllands-Posten.* The obvious truth of the matter is that he liked the mural and saw it as wrong that it should be destroyed. There is almost no room for ambiguity over this, despite his spokesman's attempt yesterday to create some. But deplorable as this was, it was not even the worst aspect of this affair. The spokesman's comment prompted outrage on social media and from some Labour MPs. Ian Austin, who has consistently stood up to Mr Corbyn and taken him to task over anti-Semitism, tweeted: 'Luciana won't be alone. I think lots of Labour members will want an explanation for this.' [I am not so sure. As we have seen, anti-Semitism runs deep nowadays on the left.] Gavin Shuker, MP for Luton South, said that the statement from Mr Corbyn's spokesman 'isn't even an apology. I know this is like screaming into the wind, it'll make zero difference, but I want to say that this is just so wrong. It's impossible to confront anti-Semitism in our party if this is the response from the very top.' And Mrs Berger said the response was 'wholly inadequate'. Even Mr Corbyn's office could see that its explanation made things worse. So a few hours later, a statement from Mr Corbyn himself was issued:

'In 2012 I made a general [sic] comment about the removal of public art on the grounds of freedom of speech. My comment referred to the destruction of the mural *Man at the Crossroads* by Diego Rivera on the Rockefeller Centre. That is no way comparable with the mural in the original post. I sincerely regret that I did not look more closely at the image I was commenting on, the contents of which are deeply disturbing [so deeply, he did not notice them] and anti-Semitic. I wholeheartedly support its removal. [But at the time, you *opposed* it.] I am opposed to the production of anti-Semitic material of any kind, and the defence of free speech cannot be used as a justification for promotion of anti-Semitism in any form. That is a view I have always held.' [Then, just to give one example of many, why has Corbyn not condemned the genocidal anti-Semitism of the 1988 Hamas Charter?]

As I wrote at the start, the word 'lie' is overused in politics. But it is impossible not to regard this statement as a lie. Mr Corbyn saw the image. He went out of his way to comment on it in Facebook. He knew what the mural depicted; it is not possible not to see that after a moments glance. The Jewish caricatures were the entire point of the mural. This incident must be judged on its own terms and those terms show that Jeremy Corbyn a) defended an anti-Semitic mural b) refused to answer questions on that defence for over two years c) when pushed for an explanation by a Labour MP argued that it was a free speech issue and then d) said that he hadn't really looked at it. But there is a pattern here. Only last week Mr Corbyn was revealed as having been an active member of a private [in fact 'secret'] Facebook group that was suffused with anti-Semitism. His excuse then was the same as his latest excuse yesterday: that he hadn't noticed it. This newspaper has spent the two years and six months since Mr Corbyn's election as Labour leader exposing anti-Semitism within the Labour Party. Barely a day has gone by in that time when another incident has not emerged. During his first leadership campaign in 2015 we posed seven questions to Mr Corbyn on the front page of the *JC* over what we knew already knew back then about his unsavoury associations with anti-Semites. To date, no serious response has been given even to those original questions. Now this, and last week's Facebook story. Mr Corbyn protests that he cares about anti-Semitism 'and all forms of racism', in the formulation he insists on using. Mr Corbyn is a liar.

Corbyn was also caught down-playing the closeness of his relationship with Palestine Live Administrator Elleanne Green, who in one of her many anti-Semitic postings, quoted approvingly from Hitler's *Mein Kampf* a passage attacking Zionism. The Campaign Against Anti-Semitism published on March 27, 2018, the following refutation of Corbyn's claim, reported in the *Guardian*, that she was merely an 'acquittance'.

Last week, Jeremy Corbyn was exposed as being a member of a deeply anti-Semitic Facebook group in which he participated for two years. Now, damning new evidence made available to Campaign Against Anti-Semitism proves that Mr Corbyn or his team were demonstrably lying when, as was reported in *The Guardian* they had said that his relationship with the founder and key administrator of the Facebook group 'Palestine Live' was that of a mere 'acquaintance'. Research and documents in our possession indicate that he had an intimate relationship with Elleanne Green, a woman who has expressed anti-Semitic beliefs and who has prolifically disseminated extreme anti-Semitic material, including neo-Nazi articles. They shared a love of the same poetry and of various common causes even before he joined the Facebook group, almost certainly at her invitation, despite Mr Corbyn implying that he was added against his wishes. [in which case, why did he remain a member for more than two years?] They organised events together, and she proudly noted the two years he spent in the group with her.

Those familiar with Mr Corbyn know well that he was not - before becoming Party Leader - someone who posted frequently on social media, so when he bothers to pay attention to someone publicly, it is noticeable. Mr Corbyn has paid Ms Green a lot of attention, and that attention has been returned. In fact, Mr Corbyn and Ms Green could be described as sharing a personal bond. As early as January 2014, he approved when she spoke of Caroline Kennedy's poetry; when she publicly posted a favourite poem by Rose Milligan, he confessed to her that it contains a sentiment meaningful to him; when she professed her fears for the future of the rhinoceros, he agreed; similarly when she backed an African water charity they shared a little joke together online; and when she was off on her travels to Cuba [together with another anti-Semite, Ken Livingstone, Corbyn is a leading member of the Castroite Cuban Solidarity Campaign] he wished her a 'wonderful time'.

In short, there is not much about Ms Green's tastes and opinions that Mr Corbyn does not seem to know or approve of, and he singles her out to use when he wishes to thank others. She is clearly not just an acquaintance or friend, she is 'special'. However, this is all without their mutually shared passion, even above poetry and rhinos; namely; the Palestinians. So it is no surprise that Ms Green signed Mr Corbyn up to her 'Palestine Live' group, of which, at that time, it appears that she was the only administrator, and Mr Corbyn can be seen, for example, approving of her Palestine-themed posts in August 2014, and again in October 2014. There is evidence that Mr Corbyn joined in late 2013, participated in online conversations, and remained a member for two years.

With regard to 'Palestine Live' and other so-called 'pro-Palestinian forums', Ms Green and Mr Corbyn don't just interact online, but in person (she is also on chatting terms with MPs such as Chris Williamson [praised by Corbyn as a 'very good MP', only to be then suspended, despite Corbyn's attempt to prevent it, for one of a number anti-Semitic outbursts] and John McDonnell [opposed to the existence of the state of Israel] when she sees them.) Finally, her involvement with him is deep enough that at one point they jointly organised a talk to be given by the controversial Max Blumenthal at Mr Corbyn's own office, using Mr Corbyn's staff, as chronicled in detail by David Collier in his report into the 'Palestine Live' Facebook group. Again, the talk having taken place at this venue, Mr Corbyn thanked those who attended on the 'Palestine Live' Facebook group in a thread with Ms Green. But what of Ms Green's views? Ms Green is a prolific and obsessive poster of conspiracy theories. A list of those to which she subscribes constitutes an A to Z of the genre: on more than one occasion she promoted the theory that Israeli intelligence services were secretly behind the 9/11 terrorist atrocities, as well as the terrorist massacres in Paris, able to boast when the celebrated conspiracy theorist who has written the article became a member of the group. She shared a post that suggested that a wife of a witness to 9/11 was deliberately killed six days after meeting President Obama; shared a post suggesting that the BBC is deliberately employing 'obnoxious Jews' in order to encourage anti-Semitism and suggests it 'could even be true'; claimed that Israel bombed its own embassy in a 'false flag' operation; shared a link to an article claiming that ISIS leaders were trained by Israel; supported the idea that London Bridge terrorist attacks may have been a stunt to throw the general election off track; and posted a claim that the BBC is 'completely controlled' by Rothschild influence.

Similarly, the people she supports, and has invited to be members in the group, are a Who's Who of Britain's most infamous anti-Semites. She participates in conversations with Holocaust denier Paul Eisen (a friend of Mr Corbyn's whose work he used to help fund, but with whom he claims no longer to associate) in one of which, Mr Eisen says to Baroness Tonge [together with Corbyn a Patron of the

Palestine Solidarity Campaign] and Ms Green: 'You'll continue feeling depressed, dismal and let down until you start standing up to Jews - not the Israelis, not the Zionists, the Jews', to which Ms Green responds, asking: 'What do you suggest?' Mr Eisen asked of another member, 'but what do you find so unsavoury about Dr Duke?' (Dr Duke is the former Grand Wizard of the Ku Klux Klan). She defended disgraced Baroness Tonge, who resigned from her [Liberal Democratic] party over anti-Semitism allegations, claiming that the notion of her remarks might be anti-semitic is 'appalling'. She shared posts by David Icke. [!!!] She is personally friendly with and supports Gilad Atzmon, who has allegedly said that 'the burning down of a synagogue is a rational act', whose ideas are better described as far-right than far-left [when it comes to anti-Semitism, this distinction no longer applies anyway], and whose book *The Wandering Jew* has been described as 'probably the most anti-Semitic book published in this country in recent years'. She posts his work on the group, and praises his 'truth' when, ironically, Gilad Atzmon is considered so anti-Semitic that 'anti-Zionist' Palestinian groups and activists have taken care to distance themselves from him. Ms Green also appears to be friendly with and supportive of Jackie Walker [of Momentum] who is touring the country describing how she was 'lunched' for claiming that Jews were the 'chief financiers of the slave trade'.

It is difficult to give an account of every example of anti-Semitic discourse in which Ms Green has participated. She has shared a post claiming 'Zionists' are 'killing children to sell them on the black market'. She promotes the London Forum, described as 'a secret Neo-Nazi society'. She has posted an article by an author convicted in a Canadian court for promoting hatred against Jews, a piece that appeared on the Radical Press website that promotes the Protocols of the Elders of Zion and Adolf Hitler's book, *Mein Kampf*. Bearing in mind that the overwhelming majority of British Jews are Zionists, her assertion that 'the time must surely come' when no "friend of Israel" can stand as an MP is chilling. She adored Gerald Kaufman, who claimed that 'Jewish money...biase[s] the Tory Party'. She likes social media posts that suggest Jewish influence in Britain is 'dangerously close to being treasonable'. She shared a post and endorses the author of a raw anti-Semitic diatribe describing Jewish values as 'massacre, rape...torture, sex trafficking and child abuse', describing the author as a "great man". [Possibly a mistake here...could the author in question be referring to the 'values' of certain Muslims?] She refers to 'zios', which even Labour's Baroness Chakrabarti accepts is an unacceptable term of abuse. She was proud to be among those who yelled and intimidated when Haringey Council adopted the International Definition of Anti-Semitism.

So much of what she posts is simply raw Jew-hatred that she seems to have forgotten that she is supposed to be maintaining the fiction of being a mere critic of Israeli policy. However, at one point in the Palestine Live Facebook group she admits that the ideas behind Holocaust denial are 'true and clearly the questions are legitimate...but not HERE' - a cynical admission that while she has sympathies with Holocaust deniers she is, on the group at least, trying to draw a virtuous skein over the views aired. In the end, by commenting positively on a link to the neo-Nazi *Daily Stormer*, all pretence disappears. Elleanne Green is a member of the Labour Party [yes...the *Labour* Party] in the Cities of London and Westminster, who enthusiastically backs the Reverend Steven Saxby - also a member of Palestine Live - as a future Parliamentary candidate; is a representative of Momentum, and a member of the so-called Jewish Voice for Labour. Evidence held by Campaign Against Anti-Semitism shows that she was reported to the Labour Party on 4th September 2017 yet clearly no action has been taken. Instead she is on friendly personal terms with Mr Corbyn, Chris Williamson MP, John McDonnell MP, Clive Lewis MP (who even blows her virtual kisses) journalist Paul Mason and others.

Elleanne Green is not the only individual propagating extreme anti-Semitism on Palestine Live.

As David Collier's research demonstrates, using a sample period to analyse posters and their postings from 1st to 15th February 2018, anti-Semitic postings on the site were ubiquitous and unmissable. Furthermore, witness reports bear testimony to the level of anti-Semitism a member would have to be subjected to during the summer of 2014, when Mr Corbyn was an actively posting member of the group. Members of Palestine Live comprise a roll call of the UK's leading so-called "anti-Zionists" either posting or tolerating nakedly anti-Semitic material that hardly requires the International Definition of Anti-Semitism to assist in its identification. The naked truth laid bare by Mr Collier's report is that in the current culture of the UK's far-left, anti-Zionism and anti-Semitism are indistinguishable...

For Mr Corbyn to suggest that Ms Green is a mere 'acquaintance' [and even if this were true, what an acquaintance!], as he or Labour's press officers have communicated, is demonstrably a lie. Given both their intimacy and the fact that she prolifically posts hardcore anti-Semitic material, to say that he had no knowledge of her anti-Semitism stretches credulity. [as it does with many other of his anti-Semitic 'acquaintances'] Further, to claim that in two years as a member and close friend of Ms Green's he saw no- anti-Semitism posted by her or others on the site itself would be like standing in an open field in a rainstorm and claiming that the raindrops missed you. Perhaps another explanation lies in two posts in which Ms Green says: 'Am disgusted [to be under investigation] but suppose it is inevitable if one speaks up for justice for the Palestinians' and 'I am NOT anti-Semitic'. [that is what they all say - even David Irving.] Ultimately, people like Ms Green are perhaps blinded to their own racism, however extreme., by cloaking it with the virtue of a 'pro-Palestinian' position, both externally for others, but also for themselves. If Mr Corbyn is similarly blind, it is perhaps because he is so similar to his friend, Ms Green.

Joseph D. Glassman, Head of Political and Government Investigations at Campaign Against Anti-Semitism, said 'Jeremy Corbyn said he did not see anti-Semitism in the Palestine Live Facebook group but he wrote comments on anti-Semitic posts during his two-year membership of the group. He said he was added to the group by an 'acquaintance' but in fact it was his intimate friend Elleanne Green, a prolific disseminator of extreme anti-Semitic material. By lying about their relationship and pretending that he saw no anti-Semitism on Palestine Live, he takes the British public for fools, drags the Labour Party into further disrepute and causes yet more fear and anguish for British Jews. But what is most frightening is the lack of public outrage. [Dead right!!!] Where are the cries of 'Not in my name'? Through their silence these past weeks, British politicians are allowing our society to descend deeper into a dark place where anti-Semitism is tolerated, and history shows as where that path leads.' Ms Green did not respond to a request for comment.

Hard on the heels of the mural scandal came the revelation by the *Guido Fawkes* website that Corbyn was a member of two other anti-Semitic Facebook groups, *Labour Party Supporter* (sic) and *History of Palestine*. They feature the same genre of postings as the others he frequents...body organs...Rothschilds...the Illuminati...Again, he saw nothing untoward, and only when outed did Corbyn announce he had left them.

Now, David Collier's report on the cesspit that calls itself *Palestine Live*, where there are featured some of the notorious anti-Semites we have already observed fraternising with Corbyn in other settings. Founded on August 2, 2013, as of February 20, 2018, Palestine Live had 3,279 members. Previously listed as 'closed', Palestine Live had been listed as 'secret' since November 2014, meaning it cannot be accessed by using Facebook search functions. New users have to be invited to join by someone already a member of the group who has been granted permission to add new members. Corbyn interacted with this website at least 30 times.

Introducing his report, Collier says

> It would be easy to start this blog with Jeremy Corbyn. After all, it seems as if he was part of a rabidly anti-Semitic Facebook Group, along with Paul Eisen, Gilad Atzmon, numerous other Holocaust Deniers, hard-core anti-Semites, white supremacists, and all the other wretched political ideologues that gather together to pretend it is about Palestine and not the Jews...I have been engaged in an exercise to analyse a secret [nb] Facebook Group called 'Palestine Live'. Immersed deeply in an anti-Semitic soup was disturbing enough but seeing names there that simply should not ever have stepped foot inside, gave an entirely new, and far darker feel to the entire exercise. Corbyn was there in late 2014, he may have joined a year earlier, and every indication is, that he stayed in the group until shortly after he became leader of the Labour Party. Jenny [body organs] Tonge is still a member. David Ward too. Clive Lewis? Go figure. It just shows how blind everyone is to anti-Jewish racism. I quantified the level of anti-Semitism within the group by analysing all those who shared posts over a two-week period during February 2018. The level was 64% When I extracted the Jewish anti-Zionists, the level rose to 73%. Nobody should be able to spend any time at all in that group, without understanding the twisted anti-Semitism that drives so much of the activity.

The founder of the group, the Jew-baiting, *Mein Kamp*-quoting anti-Israeli activist Elleanne Green, is one of its three administrators, the other two being the ubiquitous photo-op companion of Jeremy Corbyn, the Neo-Nazi Tony Gratrex, and Carol Foster of the obsessively anti-Zionist Socialist Fight. Recruitment is tightly controlled, as is evident from this exchange between Green and Jacquie Walker of Momentum, twice suspended and then eventually expelled from the Labour party for anti-Semitism:

> 'Walker: 'How safe is this group?' [Safe from *what*?]
> 'Green: 'Very. No one allowed in who is not trusted. I am very careful...and it is a Secret Group...so it really is as safe as you will be able to find anywhere...anyone here will be your friend and admirer.' [So, Jeremy was 'trusted'.]

Group Founder and Administrator Green's stance on the 'Jewish question' is reflected in her posting of a lengthy quote from *Mein Kampf* where Hitler engages in an exposure of the aims of Zionism, which are to create in Palestine 'a haven for convicted scoundrels and a university for budding crooks'. Now a sample of the postings by some of Corbyn's fellow members of this 'secret group':

First, Administrator Foster:

> 'The Jewish lobby it's plain to see
> Is full of people unlike me
> They're bigoted and full of bile
> Their talk is cheap and rather vile

From what they say it's really clear
They are everything that they most fear
So it's really clear now is the hour
To rob these demons of their power.'

Here is Corbyn's twice photo partner Administrator Gratrex, riding his favourite hobby-horse:

'Revisionist scholarship has determined that somewhere between 100-150 thousand people perished in Auschwitz mainly as a result of disease and starvation, which was not a deliberate act on the part of the Germans, but rather outcome of Allied carpet bombing of Germany's infrastructure. In an effort to whitewash their own egregious war-crimes, the Allies went along with the Zionists' premeditated fictional account of six million dead Jews.'

Pam Arnold: '...we just do not recognise this barbarian part of that tribe that is lording it over every single government in the world and using their untold wealth to control the agenda for all of us in order to further their nefarious aims for the Jewish state and to wipe out the Palestinians in the process.'

'Am reading Mein Kampf...everybody should be forced [sic!!!] to read it, especially jews who have their own agenda as to why they are not liked.'

Andy Hopkins: 'Perhaps if one asked some very basic questions, they might learn the truth about the HOLOCAUST. Most people have accepted the story given out by a group of people who in reality have EVERYTHING TO HIDE. They were talking about 6,000,000 (6 million) dead for at least 50yrs before Hitler came to power in 1933.'

Hopkins then recommends 'a video about one person awakening to the truth', *A Holocaust Inquiry,* by Corbyn enthusiast David Duke.

Elleanne Green: 'Ex-MI5 Agent knows that Israeli Mossad was behind 9/11.'

'Mossad's fingerprints on Paris attacks.'

'Former CIA Agent: The ISIS leader Abu Bakr Al Baghdadi was trained by the Israeli Mossad.'

Two boosts for Jeremy:

June Tobin: 'We must remember too who owns most of the media [i.e. the Jews] and why Jeremy Corbyn would not be a good appointment for them.'

George Garside: 'The Jewish minority have far too much to say in this country, they are pandered to and over represented in the corridors of power and their influence is dangerously close to treasonable...The people of this country know right from wrong, they are choosing truth, justice and transparency. Jeremy Corbyn will see they get it.'

Tony Gratrex, again: '...a cursory glance using the internet will show that a majority of the media is Jewish owned or controlled'.

'JFK was the last American President who wasn't chosen by the [Jewish] Cabal... [His assassination] was a really a Cabal job...All American elections have been arranged by the Cabal ever since, based on the two principles of Cabal politics, bribery and blackmail. Trump won because he wouldn't succumb to either. These principles are used in the UK as well. We've seen how Jeremy Corbyn has been treated by the Cabal.'

Baroness Tonge (she of the body parts slander) is featured praising fellow Palestine Solidarity Campaign Patron Ken Loach for a 'useful article' rebutting accusations that the Labour Party has an anti-Semitism problem.

Neville Thomas: 'Jews thrown out of 100 countries. Why?'

Michael Summer posts a reproduction of an anti-Semitic cartoon from the Nazi journal *Der Sturmer* of October 1938, the editor of which, Julius Streicher, was hanged at Nuremberg. He archly asks the question: 'Agree he should have been hanged or disagree?'

Benefactor of Corbyn's generosity, Paul Eisen: 'And you'll continue feeling depressed, dismal and let down until you start standing up to the Jews - not the Israelis, not the Zionists, the Jews.'

Eisen again: 'I see anti-Semitism as a legitimate opposition to appalling Jewish behaviour so I accept the label with pride.' (along with Corbyn's donation)

Next, a posting of a page from a Neo-Nazi website, *The Daily Archive*, promoting Nazi memorabilia:

Tony Murphy: 'The Jews are like a cancer, when they enter the host nation, e.g., US and EU, they spread their rotten virus until they take control of all the host nations arteries, media, government, banking etc.'

'I just heard on the radio that Jews do not donate their organs after death. This, in my opinion, lends credence to the theories that is why they murder Palestinians and not inclined to return their bodies to their families so they can harvest their organs.'

A sizable section of Collier's report is devoted to the role played in Palestine Live by Corbyn, both as participant and as source of inspiration for many of its members. As Collier comments, 'Wherever you look in Palestine Live, you find people that shouldn't be there, and endless images of Jeremy Corbyn.' PL Founder and *Mein Kampf* quoter Elleanne Green posted:

'Jenny [body organs] Tonge and Jeremy Corbyn are inspirational here in the UK. I commend them to anyone anywhere who wants to know who the brave and articulate [sic!!!] politicians in my country are.'

And again;

'I do know how much Jeremy Corbyn opposes all these evils though – he is quite astonishing in his energy and efforts.'

And again:

'Jeremy is so active - he cares about Palestine.'

And yet again:

'Gratitude to Jeremy Corbyn.'

Corbyn's services and staff proved invaluable in setting up a meeting at Westminster on October 2, 2014, where the keynote speaker would be the US anti-Zionist campaigner Max Blumenthal:

Elleanne Green: 'Would Jenny Tonge or Jeremy Corbyn know if is possible to organise something in a room at Portcullis House?'

Never one to miss out on a good Zionist bashing, Jeremy is indeed up for it:

Green: 'Have a reply from Jeremy's office. V[ery] helpful indeed.'

Sadly, Jeremy couldn't make the meeting, as 'is away next week…conference on'…guess what? 'Palestine.'

But still, 'kudos and thanks to the office of Jeremy Corbyn MP'.

According to Corbyn, he could not attend because 'Sadly, I was at the funeral of a very old friend, Ron Blanchard, so missed event.'

This posting is proof of his membership of the secret Palestine Live group, and that he has read other posts on its website. Green cannot resist advertising to PL's (secret) members the name of their far and away biggest catch:

'Jeremy Corbyn is even a member of this group' and

'Jeremy was a member of this group for several years ['several years'...and he saw nothing untoward?] until a few weeks after his election as Labour leader...such a friend to Palestine.'

And enemy of Israel. Here is Green again: 'Jeremy Corbyn sparks row by turning down dinner with Israeli MP.'

Rivalling Corbyn in cult status is veteran conspiracy nutter David Icke:

Sandra Wafta: 'British author and lecturer [!!!] David Icke has written 20 books and travelled to over 55 countries since 1990.

Derek Hands, promoting the video *Israel's Fake History: The Cruellest Hoax* by David Icke: 'The David Icke video can be delivered to your email every Sunday.'

Lynn Faulkner, promoting Icke's video, *Rothschild Zionism*: 'His books reveal how a hidden hand is behind world-changing events like the attacks of 9/11 and the manufactured wars in the Middle East'. In the book refereed to, Icke says 'Israel is not the home of the Jewish people, it is the fiefdom of the Rothschild dynast that also controls the American administration, the British administration.'

George Garside posts a photo of Jeremy with the caption, 'Join the Labour Party', followed by a promo for Icke's *The Rothschild Zionist Agenda* and the comment:

'He's on the money on this one and there's no lizards in it.'

And this: 'Why are murdering Jews exempt from criticism and immune from prosecution? By their actions are they not inviting a new Holocaust on themselves?'

Two PL members who joined Labour to vote for Jeremy:

Pam Arnold: 'Once I see what these right-wing fascists [left-wing ones OK?] do to Jeremy I will rescind my labour party membership which I only took up to vote for Jeremy.'

Felix Allen: 'As I haven't received my membership card yet (I allowed my membership lapse) does this mean I cannot vote for Corbyn?'

And we see a posting by Corbynista Allen promoting the video, *Holocaust: The Greatest Lie Ever Told.*

Now yet another Corbynista, Rosemary Henke. First a photo of Jeremy on ITV news, followed by a photo of 9/11, with the caption, 'on 9/11/2001, the laws of physics took the day off, along with NORAD, security cameras, and 4000 Israelis'.

And another: 'The Realist Report: How the "Holocaust" was faked.' According to this Corbynista's posting the Jewish inmates of Nazis camps were 'well-fed, well-provided for, and given medical treatment and entertainment. They were allowed to attend concerts, organise plays, make music and play sports. If the Germans were hell bent on murdering these people, why would they provide medical care for them and allow them to entertain themselves?'

Sarah Scott is an anti-Semite, posting a cartoon of a Jew with a huge hooked nose, with the caption, 'I don't deny the Holocaust...do you?'

Sarah Scott is a big fan of David Icke, posting a clip from his *Rothschild Zionism* video. She is also a big fan of Corbyn: In huge letters: 'I just voted for Jeremy Corbyn', and 'The quicker he is elected as PM the sooner we can rid the Party of Blair for ever.'

Camilla George posted a fake map of the Middle East entirely under Israeli rule, with the caption, 'Greater Israel'.

She also posted 'We support Jeremy Corbyn'.

So does David Birkett.: '…join the Labour Party and stand by the man who looks out for the interests that serve us all.' Birkett is also an anti-Semite: 'Holocaust: Not even one body, of thousands autopsied by US medical examiners across ALL camps after World War II exhibited any signs of dying from ANY type of "Gas poisoning". Nor evidence of any viable gas chambers for the purpose of killing humans.'

David Carter posted a photo of the entrance to Auschwitz, with its legend, *Arbeit Macht Frei* and the caption, 'Why the Holocaust Story was invented'. He also made another posting:

'Thank God for a politician who sticks to his principles and beliefs and won't be swayed to abandon them, just to curry with the political elite and their financial backers.' (who might these be I wonder?)

To cut a long anti-Semitic posting short, Aleksandra Davies believes the Jews 'are beyond evil.' But with Saint Jeremy, the opposite is true: 'That's precisely why we urgently need Jeremy Corbyn to take the lead of this country.'

Simon Massey is yet another Ikista/Corbynista, who believes that 'the Israelis had something to do with the 7/7 attacks in London'.

So is Simon Fox, who posts more Ikisms on the Rothschilds, and then this:

'Last chance for a labour leader that supports Palestine. £3 to join as a supporter and get to vote – come on!'

Palestine Live has proved an irresistible attraction for anti-Semitic and Neo-Nazi crackpots, for whom the group is more about applauding Jeremy and baiting Jews than it is supporting the Palestinians. Yet although the website is awash with their ravings, and despite the fact that Corbyn was a member of the group for more than two years, and as the record shows, worked closely with its leading officials to help further its objectives, he claims he knew nothing about what went on in Palestine Live. Like, for example:

Chaz Labrock: 'International Red Cross report confirms the Holocaust of six million Jews is a Hoax.'

Corbyn's anti-Semitic Vicar friend from the PSC, the 9/11 conspiracy theorist Stephen Sizer:

'Why would the Jews make up the 'holocaust'? Jews want you to feel sorry for them…why? Because any group of people viewed as "victims" tend to be allowed much more leeway within society.'

One of the consequences of Corbyn's election as Leader has been the enrolment of anti-Semites and even Nazis into the Labour Party. Here is a posting by Jake Moose, which carries two images, one of a Labour Poster: 'We're now over 380,000 members strong. Are you one of them yet? Join.labour.org.uk' and another, of white supremacist provenance, from *Renegade Tribune*, which has three guards standing outside a prison cage which has a prisoner inside. The guards are sporting the star of David, and the cage has a sign above it which reads: 'Asked for Proof of 6 Million Gassed During Holocaust'.

Here is Patricia Sheerin-Richman: 'Mossad officer leading ISIS as mosque Imam arrested in Libya', and

'Ukrainian General: "Ukraine is under Zionist occupation"', followed by: 'I'm still confident in Jeremy Corbyn. Do you still have confidence in Jeremy Corbyn? Over the last two days, we have seen a huge swell of support for Jeremy Corbyn from amongst Labour members and Labour voters. We've had hundreds of thousands of people contacting us with messages of support, signing petitions…' [Clearly someone of standing in the Labour Party…and a Corbynista anti-Semite.]

Finally, Dave Christopher: 'Israeli forces bury Palestinian kids alive —The 41 News', and 'The Jews and the Concentration Camps: No evidence of genocide.'

Dave is yet another anti-Semitic Corbynista. He posts a photo of the Dear Leader, and the comment, on the 2017 general election, which Corbyn claimed he had won,

'Jeremy was 2,227 votes away from becoming Prime Minister. So, to all of the fekin dipshits who didn't bother to vote, see what you could have done if you did?'

Collier's breakdown by content of all the postings scrutinised, 794 in total, was 53% anti-Semitic, and at that with the bar raised very high for what constituted anti-Semitism. One of the recurring themes of the postings reproduced above is their concern to solve the mystery posed by the political establishment's parroting of 'nothing to do with Islam' after every Jihadi atrocity. If not Muslims, then whom? The Corbynista websites provide the answer: 9/11, 7/7, Paris, Islamic State, Boko Harem, Al Shabaab…all are manifestations and proof of the world Jewish conspiracy, hell-bent on depicting the religion of peace as one of terror. To paraphrase Voltaire, if the Jews, the all-purpose scapegoat, did not exist, they would have to be invented.

The following item appeared in the *Jewish Chronicle* of October 8, 2017. It throws light on Corbyn's dealings with yet another notorious anti-Semite, this time one who is a member of both the Palestine Solidarity Campaign, Patron, Jeremy Corbyn, and the Labour Party, Leader, Jeremy Corbyn:

A Labour Party member who is reported to have shared anti-Semitic conspiracy theories was manning the Palestine Solidarity Campaign stall at this year's Labour Party conference - and previously enjoyed a guided tour of the Houses of Parliament with Jeremy Corbyn. [Corbyn really has a thing about inviting anti-Semites to be his guests at Parliament] Tapash Abu Shaim, who is now understood to be under investigation by Labour, shared articles on social media claiming that Israel was behind the *Charlie Hebdo* killings and the ISIS terror group, as well as promoting the anti-Semitic conspiracy theory that Israel was behind the 9/11 terror attacks. According to the *Guido Fawkes* political blog, the Labour Party was notified about Mr Shaim's social media activity back in August [2017], with articles earlier in the year noting Mr Shaim's presence at the 2016 Labour Party conference despite his social media posts. However, no action appeared to be taken at the time. In 2012, Mr Shaim shared an article on social media from the far-right anti-Semitic *Veterans Today* website, the title of which was '9/11 Truth Could be the Answer to the Palestine/Israel Conflict'.

Three months later, Mr Shaim was a member of a PSC delegation which enjoyed a guided tour around Parliament, courtesy of Jeremy Corbyn. Mr Shaim later praised Mr Corbyn on Twitter as being 'the best tour guide…your knowledge of history is so deep and clear'. [Maybe even as deep and clear as that of his anti-Semitic comrade, Ken Livingstone.] Mr Corbyn responded by saying, 'it was a pleasure showing PSC supporters around the vagaries [?] of Parliament and British history'.

In a statement given to Guido, Jennifer Gerba, Director of Labour Friends of Israel, said it was 'disgusting that a Labour Party and Palestine Solidarity Campaign activist promotes conspiracy theories about the Jewish state being behind Islamist terror attacks. Given that the Labour Party and the PSC were made aware of Mr Shaim's posts earlier this year, questions must be asked about how this individual was allowed into conference. The Labour Party should expel Mr Shaim immediately and the Palestine Solidarity Campaign, should cease all relations with him.

In view of his prominent role in the PSC, I find it impossible to accept that this orgy of quite open and widely distributed Jew-baiting by PSC members and supporters went unnoticed by the patron saint of British anti-Zionism and Leader of Her Majesty's Opposition. And it certainly cannot have been by those who were responsible for monitoring the PSC's postings, as the test cited above proved. Given that he has never expressed any public disquiet with this scandalous state of affairs but has even chosen to be photographed with a number of the campaign's most notorious Jew-baiters, this is compelling evidence that at best, Corbyn is prepared to turn a blind eye to PSC anti-Semitism, and at worst, does not even see it for what it is, since he shares their prejudices. The un-deleted racist spoof postings cited above make a mockery of the PSC's claim that 'anti-Semitism has no place anywhere [n.b.] in our campaign for Palestinian human rights'.

What follows next is a report by the *Daily Mail* of September 26, 2017, on manifestations of anti-Semitism at the 2017 Labour Party conference, with interpolations by myself:

Labour was branded as the 'new nasty party' last night after an outbreak of intimidation and anti-Semitism as its annual conference. Jeremy Corbyn was urged to act after activists applauded panellists at a fringe meeting who likened supporters of Israel to Nazis. One speaker even suggested Labour should be free to debate whether the Holocaust had happened. [Of course, anyone should be free to say what they like about the Holocaust. But why should whether it happened be a subject for debate in the Labour Party?] Mr Corbyn was also facing a row about intimidation of Laura Kuenssberg. The BBC political editor had been given a bodyguard following threats from left-wingers [sic] at the conference. [Almost certainly because of her name it was wrongly assumed she was Jewish] A Labour shadow minister yesterday claimed using an ex-soldier for protection was a 'ploy' to demonise hardliners. [This was not the first time the BBC had been accused of conspiring, on behalf of whom we are left to guess, against the Dear Leader.] Chris Williamson, who is a close ally of Mr Corbyn, refused to say whether party members who abused Miss Kuenssberg should be expelled. And he questioned whether anyone in Labour was involved, saying, 'People join the Labour Party because they are caring individuals. [Like the Luton Labour Councillor who admired 'my man Hitler'] They are not the sort of people that indulge in intimidation and violence.' But Andrew Percy, a former Tory minister who has also been the target of anti-Semitic abuse, last night described Labour as the 'new nasty party'. He said Labour appeared to be in the grip of a 'frightening cult'. 'What we are seeing is really dangerous', he added. 'The idea that the political editor of the BBC would need a bodyguard to attend the conference of the official opposition should appal all decent people in politics. The kind of anti-Semitic abuse we are seeing is also something that has not been part of our political system until the past couple of years.' [That is, if one discounts the Neo-Nazi fringe]
     There is a cult of personality around Jeremy Corbyn that will not allow questioning him or his views. It is deeply sinister, nasty and quite frightening. These

people are genuinely extreme. Sheryll Murray, a Tory MP who has had swastikas daubed on her general election posters, said: 'From what we've seen today at the Labour conference, it feels like things are getting worse [in relation to anti-Semitism she must mean] rather than better. I worry it's putting good people off from working in politics. It's hardly the kinder, gentler politics that Jeremy Corbyn promised.' Yesterday's events horrified moderate Labour MPs. Former deputy leader Harriet Harman urged Mr Corbyn to condemn the abuse of Miss Kuenssberg. In a message on Twitter, she said: 'Is this from the left? If it is, it's even worse as the Left is supposed to be for equality and women's rights and online trolls is about silencing women.' Fellow Labour MP Jess Phillips said: 'Let's clean up our act please. Women's safety is the reason we champion the Uber action for example Let's walk the walk.' Senior Labour MPs last night urged Mr Corbyn to act against anti-Semitism in the party. John Cryer, who is chairman of the Parliamentary Labour Party, said some social media postings were 'redolent of the 1930s' and 'made you hair stand on end'.

Labour denies building a personality cult around Mr Corbyn. [Stalinists also denied there was one of Stalin] But criticism of the party leader is so frowned upon that senior figure yesterday refused to accept he had even lost the election. Len McCluskey, general secretary of the Unite trade union, yesterday rounded on 'traitors' in the party, telling cheering activists at the Brighton conference: 'Let me say this to those merchants of doom, the whingers and the whiners who say we should have done better, we didn't win. I say we did win.' In which case, why is Theresa May in Number 10, and not Corbyn? Cat Smith, a member of the Shadow Cabinet and close ally of Mr Corbyn, said: 'We didn't win the general election, but we didn't lose the general election either.' A Labour spokesman last night said Mr Corbyn was now tightening up [sic] on the rules on those who make anti-Semitic comments. He said the party 'condemns anti-Semitism in the strongest possible terms' and 'will not tolerate Holocaust denial'. [And yet] Corbyn activists applauded speakers who delivered vile anti-Semitic rants at the Labour conference yesterday. Delegates at a fringe event demanded the expulsion of the Jewish Labour Movement from the party for supporting the state of Israel. One compared 'Zionists' to the Nazis and [yet] claimed it was part of free speech to ask the question, 'Holocaust yes or no.' The event, which took place outside the main conference venue but was listed in its official handbook, was titled, 'Free speech on Israel [where alone in the Middle East, there is free speech]: why we oppose the witch hunt.' Several attendees said claims of anti-Semitism in the Labour Party were part of a plot [why not say conspiracy and have done with it] by the pro-Israeli lobby and the Labour right to stop Jeremy Corbyn from becoming Prime Minister. [Actually, it was voters who did that] And some spoke up in favour of former London mayor Ken Livingstone who remains suspended from the party for claiming that Hitler supported Zionism. The statements exposed that anti-Semitism is still a big problem in Mr Corbyn's party more than a year after he pledged to get to grips with the issue. It came as: A leaflet was circulated at the conference from 'Labour Party Marxists' discussing the 'commonality between Zionists and Nazis' and quoting Reinhard Heydrich, the architect of the Final Solution [who in that capacity chaired the Wannsee conference of January 1942, which planned and authorised the extermination of European Jewry] saying, 'National Socialists had no intention of attacking Jewish people'. [If so, how come the Holocaust? Or perhaps it never happened after all.]

The chairman of the Parliamentary Labour Party, John Cryer, said he has seen tweets from party members which 'made his hair stand on end' and were 'redolent of the 1930s'. Another Labour MP, Wes Streeting, criticised Mr Corbyn, saying there was 'too many people in our party, including at the top of the party, who have adopted an ostrich strategy' on anti-Semitism. ['Too many'? One is one too many]

Fellow MP John Mann said 200 Labour members had forwarded him links to a US white supremacist site to back up Mr Livingstone's claims about Zionism. The Holocaust Educational Trust suggested that in the two years since Mr Corbyn was elected there was a 'fertile ground' for people to express such views. Analysis released last night by the Campaign Against Anti-Semitism found the problem is worse in Labour than any other party. The group looked at 4 million social media posts of 2000 parliamentary candidates and found that 61 per cent of anti-Semitic posts were written by Labour candidates – eight times higher than any other party.

The controversial meeting on Free Speech on Israel was chaired by Naomi Wimborne-Idrisi, who said that there was a 'vicious campaign that's been directed at the Palestinian cause, misusing anti-Semitic allegations.' Although described as a free speech event, audience members were told not to record it. Miko Peled, an Israeli-American who sat on the panel, said 'they'- an apparent reference to Israel or the pro-Israeli lobby - did not want Mr Corbyn to enter Number 10. 'This is about free speech, the freedom to criticise and to discuss every issue, whether it's the Holocaust yes or no, Palestine, the liberation the whole spectrum. [It is a rather narrow spectrum that only encompasses things Jewish.] There should be no limits on the discussion.' [But who was saying there should be?] He adds: 'It's about the limits of tolerance: we don't invite the Nazis and give them an hour to explain why they are right; we do not invite apartheid South Africa racists to explain why apartheid was good for the blacks, and in the same way we do not invite Zionists - it's the same kind of thing.' [One moment there are 'no limits', not even for Holocaust deniers, and the next, there are, and they exclude amongst others, 'Zionists'.] Michael Kalmanovitz, from the International Jewish Anti-Zionist Network, was applauded for calling from the audience for the expulsion from Labour of the Jewish Labour Movement and the Labour Friends of Israel. A Labour spokesman said: 'Labour condemns anti-Semitism in the strongest terms. We will not tolerate anti-Semitism or Holocaust denial.'

And now an excerpt from an article from the *Jewish Chronicle* of August 26, 2015, by Louise Mensch, titled *Corbyn supporters post vile racism and he says nothing*. All that needs to said by way of an introduction is that in the same year that this article was written, a survey revealed that around 40% of the UK electorate was anti-Semitic, and in another, that the Muslim vote could determine which party wins in as many as a quarter of all Parliamentary seats. The votes of Jews, only one tenth that of Muslims, do not determine any. But then, Corbynistas of the kind described below would say that they don't need to, as they already control Britain anyway:

Twitter has given voice and focus to a loud, dedicated minority among Mr Corbyn's wider support; those who dislike, hate or even loath Jews. It is through social media that Mr Corbyn's links to the anti-Semite Paul Eisen were exposed. It was through Twitter that I discovered Jeremy Corbyn's 'friend', the racist and homophobe Abou Jahjah, whom he invited to Parliament. Abou Jahjah has said 'every dead British soldier I consider a victory'. Twitter pointed me to CEC [Citizens Electoral Council], a tiny Australian party, followers of the La Rouche anti-Semitic cultists whom Corbyn brought to Parliament to interview him just this spring. So it was, in that sense, useful. But the more Mr Corbyn's embrace of Eisen, Raed Salah, Hamas and Hezbollah are exposed, the better he did in the swollen electorate that has swamped real Labour members two to one (600,000 now vs 200,000 at the start of the race). And instead of decrying his links to anti-Semites, the left broadly shrugged their shoulders - or rejoiced that Mr Corbyn had given them comfort. The majority of Jeremy Corbyn's supporters are not anti-Semites but hundreds, maybe even thousands of them are. Anti-Semites form a significant minority of Corbynites and they are among the loudest online. [With Salah, the 'embrace', as a subsequently discovered video was to reveal, was literal. It showed Corbyn embracing Salah after the Court of Appeal had found the Hamas preacher guilty of promoting the ancient myth that Jews use the blood of Christian children for mixing with the bread for the Feast of the Passover. Deploring the ruling in one of his many articles for the Stalinist *Morning Star*, Corbyn implied that through their influence in the media, Zionist Jews had been responsible for the hearing's outcome. It was, he said, 'time Western governments stood up to the Zionist lobby [a much-favoured euphemism and/or code for Jewish conspiracy] which seems to conflate criticism of Israel with anti-Semitism'. The blood libel and 9/11 Jewish conspiracy theories 'criticism of Israel'?]

Abuse and Jew-hatred is rife. First you have the open loathers of Jews like Alison Chabloz, a performer at the Edinburgh Fringe who tweeted a quenelle [the much-emulated disguised Nazi salute pioneered by the Holocaust-denying French Muslim comedian Dieudonne M'bala M'bala] then said that Jewish people brought pogroms on themselves. You have those who said Liz Kendall was a 'servile Jewish cow'. You have Fred Litten, who tweeted 'Hitler was right and we were wrong'. You have the commenter on my blog reporting on Mr Corbyn's meetings with anti-Semites who said that the Holocaust was fake but added wistfully: 'I wish there were six million less of them'. Next you have people who are anti-Semitic but do not know they are. Perhaps these are more worrying. 'What, are you saying that all Jews, not just the business owning rich ones, hate Corbyn?' one man asked me. 'Nothing wrong with denying the Holocaust, history is written by the victors', said another. 'Zyklon B was used for delousing'. Another, a Scottish nationalist who likes Mr Corbyn, replied to a tweet saying that he had called for an inquiry into 'Jewish donors to the Conservative party' with 'About time!'. (In fact, Mr Corbyn has supported an inquiry into 'Zionist' donors to the Conservatives, but every name mentioned at the event where he endorsed this was Jewish.)

The anti-Semites are drawn to Mr Corbyn like a moth to a flame. 'The Nuremberg Trials were for show', says Mathew Lees. Susan John Richards, a deselected Tory councillor in 2010, now supports him because of her anti-Semitism. 'All Jews are intermarried anyway' she says'. 'Jews and Zionists own the whole world.' She also believes in the blood libel [Jews murdering Christian children for their blood] and that '9/11 was an inside job'. Respect Party supporters of George Galloway have flocked to back Corbyn. Adnan Sadiq, for example, [previously] condemned by the Corbyn [Labour Leadership] campaign in the Sunday Times for his tweeting, worked for Mr Galloway in Bradford. Joanne Stowell, formerly a staunch Respect supporter, is now a huge Corbyn fan. 'We've had the Holocaust rammed down our throat by the Zionists forever ensuring only Jewish suffering counts', she said. 'Holocaust "denying" is research and fact-finding', she insists. Is Mr Corbyn complicit? He must answer for the known anti-Semites he invited to Parliament and donated to. But he is not responsible for the tweets of his supporters. [I disagree, to the extent that he has not accounted for why these and many other anti-Semites are so taken with him] Yet he is responsible for the shabby silence which greeted this tsunami. All he says is 'no rudeness'. Holocaust denial is not 'rudeness'. '#F**kjews' as Peter Farquhar, a Corbyn supporter, tweeted, isn't rudeness: 'f**kisrael and f**kjews they are the c**ts ruining the planet #F**kJews', he said helpfully. This is hatred, not rudeness.

If Mr Corbyn hates racism and has fought it all his life as he tells us, then he is failing to keep that up at the moment. The Corbyn campaign [for the Labour leadership] has called unearthing these facts a smear. Yet Mr Corbyn is a hypocrite, for he himself said of Nick Griffin of the BNP: 'No one should share a platform with an avowed racist'. That is his standard response. We are simply holding him to it. Mr Corbyn has shared platform with racists countless times. In 2005 he attended a Deir Yassin Remembered celebration with the anti-Semites Eisen and Gilad Atzmon. Now Atzmon is tweeting that Jeremy Corbyn should be voted in because Jews fear him. He wrote a blog post to that effect; anti-Semites who support Mr Corbyn are now re-tweeting it again and again. What can we say of Mr Corbyn's silence? It is not good enough. Were his parents silent at Cable Street?

Mr Corbyn can at best say in the face of the evidence that he never knew his collaborators were racists. But what does that tell us? It says he does not think that the Jewish people are worth even a basic check - that his tax-funded staff should have Googled his guests. In spring of this year [2015] he gave an interview in Parliament to the anti-semitic La Rouche cultist group CEC. Now his campaign says it is 'concerned' to hear of the La Rouche links. But the name La Rouche in bold letters on the group's front page. If Mr Corbyn says he didn't know, then that in itself shows no regard for British Jews, because he is an MP with an office, with a staff, with plenty of resources to check. He has not defended his fellow MP Liz Kendall in the face of tweets like 'Kendal would serve Israel before you or your family'. He has done nothing, said nothing - other than a vague platitude or two. Where is his thundering speech in defence of the Jewish community? Nowhere. Nothing. It is pathetic. This is no smear. This is Mr Corbyn's record in meeting anti-Semites; and it is the record of anti-Semitism of a large, vocal minority of his supporters.

The next survey by David Collier cited here is of 56 Labour Party members who have posted on line their endorsement of Jewish conspiracy theories, many of whom make it clear they have joined the party after and because of Corbyn's election as party Leader in September 2015. Collier categorises their postings under a number of headings: Mossad, Jews, Zionists, Israel and the Rothschilds variously control or are responsible for: 9/11, London 7/7, *Charlie Hebdo*. Nice and Munich, July 2016, Manchester May 2017, London Bridge June 2017, Paris November 2015, Brussels, March 2016, the assassination of President Kennedy, the death of Princess Diana, both World Wars, the Iraq war, the slave trade, child trafficking, paedophile rings, the attacks on oil tankers in the Gulf, ISIS, the Arab Spring, Grenfell Tower, six mass shootings in the USA, blackmailing MPs, MI5, Wahhabism (sic) the media, the myth of the Holocaust, the world's banks, the internet, the Labour Party, the USA, the UK, the royal family, the trade in children's body organs, the poisoning of Sergei and Yulia Skripal, the shooting down over the Ukraine of Malaysia Flight MH1 and sinking the Titanic (sic). These are the delusional ravings of the deranged and the psychopathic. Their natural home would either be an institution that cares for the mentally ill or a viable leftist-tinged Nazi movement, but since none exists, they have gravitated to Corbynised Labour. The websites featuring these blatant and unashamed anti-Semitic postings, all by self-declared Labour Party members, include:

We Support Jeremy Corbyn
Register to vote for Jeremy Corbyn
@Jeremy Corbyn
Join Labour Org UK
On the Left with Jeremy Corbyn
#JC4PM
#keepCorbyn
Supporters Labour Org UK

YourLabourNec.Co.UK
Debating Zionism

And now some of their comments:

Feeling great. Just voted for Jeremy Corbyn.
Jeremy Corbyn for Labour Leader.
These [NEC candidates] are the six to put your cross against for Jeremy Corbyn. Spread the word.
I wouldn't have done this [joined Labour] for anyone else...only Jeremy Corbyn. [This we can believe. She is Elleanne Green, the *Mein Kampf*-quoting Administrator of the secret Palestine Live group.]
I joined the Labour Party to support the wonderful gentleman Jeremy Corbyn.
If they oust Jeremy as Leader, then I will be cancelling my direct debit and terminating my membership tonight.
For the first time in my life (58) I have just registered to vote. Will be voting for Corbyn [not Labour].
I've just joined the Labour Party so I can vote for Jeremy Corbyn.
Corbynites are go! What a privilege to know him. [Which indeed he does. This is the neo-Nazi Palestine Live Administrator Tony Gratrex, pictured, twice, with fellow group member Corbyn.]

Perhaps the most telling evidence of the role played by Corbyn in the rise of Labour anti-Semitism are Collier's surveys of two groups of Corbynistas, one comprised of those who joined the Labour Party expressly to vote for and support Corbyn and who were already posting anti-Semitic materials, and another, whose on-line activity initially displayed no interest in let alone animosity towards either Israel or the Jews but who, after joining Labour, were rapidly sucked into the same Corbynista bubble and became venomous opponents of both. Each group vented their Jew-hatred in a spate of on-line postings, in some cases numbering hundreds, that relied mainly on the recycling of material from white supremacist and neo-Nazi websites, (the mainstream media being rejected as controlled by the Jews) consisting of the usual Jewish conspiracy theories (the Rothschilds, ISIS, the media) and allegations (Israeli genocide of the Palestinians, collusion with or being Nazis) and, as a bonus, the French Yellow Vest accusation that President Macron is a 'Zionist gangster'.
One of the many bizarre features of the postings on websites with a Corbyn connection is the harmony that prevails between those whose anti-Semitism is clearly and, in some cases, explicitly inspired by Nazi propaganda, and those which liken Jews to Nazis and Israel to the Third Reich. There is also a similar perverse division of labour between Holocaust deniers and approvers, just as among Muslims there are those who attribute to Mossad both 9/11 and ISIS, and those who in their thousands celebrated the attack on the World Trade Centre and have volunteered to fight as Jihadis for what other Muslims claim is the Mossad-controlled Islamic State.
Following their mentor's election as Party Leader, rank and file Corbynista Jew-baiters judged the times propitious to advance their careers by selection as local councillors. When Alison Grove Humphries was selected as Labour council candidate in Birmingham's Hall Green Constituency, postings by her came to

light that included a claim that 'the Israel lobby manufactured UK Labour's anti-Semitic crisis', and the recycling of another that Israel was the 'key link in the exporting of ISIS oil'. Although deselected by her local party as an anti-Semite, she was nevertheless allowed to attend the 2017 Brighton Labour Party conference, where she could be seen on her website enjoying herself in Corbynista company at a Momentum event in a photo taken by its founder (and owner) Jon Lansman. Mike Sivier, former editor the *Brecon and Radnor Express*, adopted as a Labour candidate to stand for a seat in the 2017 Powys County Council elections, had among his postings endorsements of Livingstone's claim that Hitler 'supported Zionism' and of former Labour MP Tam Dalyell's that Tony Blair had been 'unduly influenced by cabal of Jewish advisers'. Sivier also endorsed the anti-Semitic postings of the Corbynista MP Naz(i) Shah and defended the exclusion of the Jews from the notorious SWP leaflet listing the victims of the Nazis as 'politically [if not historically] correct'. The media were 'Zionist led', further proof that, at least to comrade Sivier's satisfaction, there was 'no doubt' there was a Jewish conspiracy. When these and other similar postings came to light, Sivier, who claimed he was being accused of 'guilt by association' was not deselected by his local party, though he did fail to get elected.

What follows are some, by no means all, such cases of alleged anti-Semitism by Labour Party members. They are at every level of the party, from constituency activists and local councillors up to MPs and even members of Corbyn's Shadow Cabinet. As of July 2019, of all the several thousand cases of alleged anti-Semitism by Labour Party members, only fifteen had resulted in expulsions.

Let us begin with what surely qualifies as the *piece de la resistance.* 'Anti-racist trainer' Mizanur Rahman, who ran 'inclusivity' workshops for civil servants, at the Cabinet Office no less, was suspended from the Labour Party and sacked from his job in December 2021 after the *Jewish Chronicle* revealed evidence of his blatant anti-Semitism. Among his on-line comments about the Jews were one that likened them to Nazis, and another which responded to a tweet about an Israeli soldier who lost both his hands in an attack by Hamas with the comment: 'Hopefully he, and all IDF soldiers and Zionists [n.b.] will lose more than just their limbs…their lives.' When they and others like them came to light, Rahman claimed they were not 'offensive or controversial in any way'. Maybe not in the Muslim company Rahman keeps where, according to Mehdi Hassan, anti-Semitism is the norm, what he called 'our dirty little secret', 'routine and commonplace' …even for an 'anti-racist trainer' specializing in 'diversity'.

Next, Labour MP Angela Rayner, who served as Shadow Minister for Education following mass resignations from Corbyn's shadow cabinet in 2016, and after backing Corbynista Rebecca Long-Bailey against Keir Starmer for leader, served under him first as Deputy Leader, then Shadow Chancellor of the Duchy of Lancaster and Shadow Secretary for the Future of Work. While serving under Corbyn, she described accusations of Labour anti-Semitism as a 'smear', and praised as 'seminal' Norman Finkelstein's anti-Zionist screed, *The Holocaust Industry',* which claims Jews have milked the Holocaust both politically and economically. No action was subsequently taken against her for these two comments.

Corbynista Unite (sic) official Nick West was suspended after a series of anti-Semitic postings came to light. One was directed at a Jewish Labour MP: 'Margaret Hodge makes millions of us sick to our stomachs. A woman who weaponises both her faith [Hodge is an atheist] and the holocaust to forward her own petty Zionist aims...those like her who wield the bloodshed as a political weapon are beyond redemption. Humanity would not miss her.'

Former Witham Labour Councillor John Clarke, suspended after posting a comment on a Neo-Nazi website which claimed the Rothschilds used Israel to 'take over the world', saying it 'contained a great deal of truth'.

Zafar Iqbal, a Labour Councillor in Birmingham, shared a video by the Neo-Nazi, Corbyn admirer and former KKK Grand Wizard David Duke. No action was taken after he claimed he had no recollection of the video.

Two Jewish Labour Councillors in Haringey, London (a Corbynista stronghold), resigned after experiencing anti-Semitic abuse by fellow party members - 'Jews have big noses' and 'control the world'.

Chesterfield Labour Councillor Andrew Slack, suspended after sharing an anti-Semitic meme of a blood-stained, hooked-nosed Israeli soldier with the comment that 'Israel was created by the Rothschilds, not God. And what they are doing to the Palestinian people now is EXACTLY what they intend for the whole world.'

Teesside Labour Party member and Momentum activist Bob Campbell shared an image of a rat marked with the Star of David which claimed Israel controlled ISIS. No action taken.

Labour Councillor and former Mayor of Blackburn Salim Mulla called Jews a 'disgrace to humanity', endorsed a video which blamed Jews for the school shootings in the USA (at least this was original) and claimed Israel was behind ISIS (which most definitely was not). After being suspended, reinstated.

Tayyib Nawaz, Chairperson of Manchester Labour Students, resigned after tweeting that 'Hitler was Jewish'. (full marks for out-Livingstoning Livingstone)

Former Chairperson of Spitalfields and Banglatown (sic) Labour Party Musabbir Ali, suspended after tweeting a Neo-Nazi 'Timeline of the Jewish Genocide of the British People'

Sean McCallum, suspended after being chosen as Labour candidate for mayor of Mansfield. when a posting came to light claiming Nazism and Zionism were 'equally foul'.

Renfrewshire Labour Councillor Terry Kelly claimed that the 'American Jewish lobby is extremely powerful and it has its boot on Obama's neck', and that the film *The Kings Speech* might not win an Oscar because 'there is a powerful Jewish lobby campaigning against the film because of its historical inaccuracy about Hitler and the anti-Semitism.' Reinstated after a month's suspension.

Josh Simons, former policy advisor to Corbyn, said that one member of the Labour Leader's team referred to a 'Jewish conspiracy' in an office discussion and that Corbyn's chief spokesperson, Seumas Milne, subjected him to an 'inquisition' concerning his Jewishness, his family and his attitude to Israel.

Billy Wells, dropped as a council candidate in Great Yarmouth after writing on Facebook 'It's the super-rich families of the Zionist lobby that control the world. Our world leaders sell their souls for greed and do the bidding of Israel.'

Deputy Leader of Kirklees Council David Sheed tweeted that 'Jewish organisations run a concerted campaign against JC [Jeremy Corbyn]'.

Eleanor Tristam was adopted as a Council candidate for Labour after sharing on Facebook one posting that Jewish MP Ruth Smeeth was funded by the 'Israel lobby' and another claiming that 'the current anti-Semitism witch-hunt' was 'a fraud' and 'a cover for sabotage'.

Mick Bone, adopted as Labour candidate for Middlesbrough Council after sharing an image implying that the BBC is control by the Israeli embassy and a posting demanding that Israeli diplomats should be expelled from the UK. (Corbyn has made the same claim regarding the BBC.)

Anti-Zionist zealot Labour MP for Easington Grahame Morris in 2014 posted a picture of the Israeli flag, with the comment, 'Nazis in my village, do you see the flag they fly'. Later the same year, he compared Israeli soldiers to ISIS. Like other Corbynistas, Morris is always on the look-out for any stick with which to beat the Zionists, no matter how dubious its provenance (he has visited a website that features myths about the Rothschilds conspiracy). More recently, he shared a video which purported to show to show Israeli soldiers beating a child when in fact the soldiers were Guatemalan. No action taken.

Labour MP for Blyth Valley Ronald Campbell told the BBC that 'the Jewish issue' is being used 'as a big stick to beat Corbyn and get rid of him'. No action taken.

Corbynista NEC member Peter Willsman was suspended for alleging that accusations of Labour anti-Semitism were 'all lies' and had been instigated by the Israeli embassy.

Labour activist Frances Naggs authored an open letter endorsed by thousands of party members claiming that Jewish protests against the party's anti-Semitism were the work of 'a very special interest group' that could 'employ the full might of the BBC'. Subsequently adopted as a Staffordshire Council candidate.

Former Labour NEC member Martin Mayer was adopted as a candidate for the EU election of May 2019 after sending an email titled 'How Israel manufactured UK Labour anti-Semitism crisis', in which he claimed that the 'smear of anti-Semitism' was being used 'to undermine Jeremy Corbyn's leadership'.

Momentum activist Marlene Ellis was suspended after saying in an open letter in defence of the suspended Ken Livingstone that Zionists were 'involved with the Nazis and that the Labour Party sought to 'curry favour with the pro-Zionist lobby in and beyond the media'. (This last was indeed actionable. Surely not under Corbyn.)

In December 21016, Corbyn attended the book launch of, and posed for photos with, Hatem Bazian, organised by the Iranian Human Rights Commission. (This is not a spoof. There is such an organisation, and like Corbyn's former employer Press TV, it is sponsored by the human rights-respecting Ayatollahs). Bazian later apologised for anti-Semitic tweets where he shared a picture of an ultra-orthodox Jew with the message: 'Mom, look! I is chosen! I can now kill, rape, smuggle organs [yes...again] and steal the land of the Palestinians. Yay #Ashke-Nazi.' What charming friends Jeremy has.

Former Labour Parliamentary candidate for Woking Vicki Kirby was suspended and then reinstated after tweeting that Hitler might be a 'Zionist God' and Jews have 'big noses'.

Luke Creswell, suspended, reinstated, and then adopted to stand as a Labour Councillor in Suffolk after tweeting an image of a blood-stained Israeli flag with the caption 'Moses must be proud of you'.

North Wales Labour Councillor Max Tasker posted YouTube videos to his Facebook page titled: 'Is ISIS good for the Jews?', 'The whole story of Zionist conspiracy', 'The filthy history of paedophilia, murder and bigotry. Not for the immature!', 'Zionist Antichrist will rule the New World order' and 'Ukraine's anti-Russian stance is a Zionist master plan.' (Here too, a welcome spark of originality)

Nottingham Labour Councillor Ilyas Aziz, was suspended and then reinstated after sharing anti-Semitic posts from the conspiracy theorist crackpot David Icke and one called 'Israel - Rothschilds' Frankenstein Monster.'

Brighton Council candidate Alexandria Braithwaite was suspended for tweeting that the Rothschilds were 'Satanists', 'responsible for every war on earth' and linked to the Illuminati. Brighton has an active branch of the Palestine Solidarity Campaign.

Brighton Labour activist Amanda Bishop, suspended when as a protest against Braithwaite's suspension, she posted that party members 'need to march about this to the Synagogue in Brighton' adding, 'why are we continuing to accept this bullshit? Why aren't we defending ourselves?' There are three synagogues in Brighton. One of them was defaced with pro-Hamas graffiti during the Gaza conflict of 2014. What Bishop did have in mind this time? A Labour version of the Crystal Night?

Manchester Council candidate Jade Doswell posted that seeing the Israeli flag 'made her feel sick'.

Sara Conway stood down as Labour's Parliamentary candidate for Finchley and Golders Green after protests concerning her claim that Labour's anti-Semitism scandal had been 'drummed up' and 'weaponised by certain media commentators'.

Bradford Labour Councillor Mohammed Shabbir tweeted that Israel was behind ISIS and that the BBC was run by a 'hasbar media cartel'.

Mary Bain, a Labour Councillor for Lochgelly, Cardenden and Benarty, Scotland, speculated that Jewish accusations of anti-Semitism in the Corbyn wing of the Labour Party could be a 'Mossad assisted campaign to get rid of Jeremy Corbyn as Labour Leader' and 'prevent the election of a Labour government pledged to recognise Palestine as a State.'

Bognor Regis Labour Councillor Damien Enticott, suspended after sharing a video titled *Jewish Ritual* with a subtitle claiming Jews 'drink blood and suck baby's dick.'

Corbynista Len McCluskey was accused of blatant anti-Semitism when, on October 19, 2020, in a BBC TV Newsnight TV feature on Keir Starmer, the Unite union chief launched into a vicious attack on Peter Mandelson for praising the Labour Leader in the same feature: 'I stopped listening to anything Peter Mandelson says years ago. I would suggest Peter goes into a room and counts his gold and not worry about the Labour Party.' Three years earlier, in a BBC interview on September 26 2017, asked if he recognized Labour had an anti-Semitism problem, he replied: 'I've never recognized that. I believe it was mood music created by people who were trying to undermine Jeremy Corbyn.'

On November 25, 2020, Corbyn supporter Nicholas Nelson was sentenced to 30 weeks jail, suspended for 18 months, for racially abusing two Jewish Labour MPs, Margaret Hodge and Louise Ellman. In December 2018, he had been sentenced to 20 weeks jail, suspended for a year, after racially abusing two other Jewish Labour MPs, again, both women, Ruth Smeeth and Luciana Berger. The judge described his invective as 'the most vulgar, obscene, threatening vocabulary I can think of.' In a phone call to her office, Nelson said to Hodge, 'fuck off, you fucking racist [sic] Zionist cunt. You need to get out of the party and I hope you die, you Tory cunt.' In another call later the same day, he called her 'an apartheid supporting disgusting scumbag bitch.' In an email to Ellman, he called her 'a hypocritical Tory cunt'. Hodge was also the recipient of identical abuse for her insistence that Corbyn should not have the whip restored after his suspension was lifted by the NEC's appeals committee by a vote of 3 to 2: 'Hope she dies soon. Dumb bitch. Member of a rich and powerful Jewish dynasty. Mossad agent. Liar. Rat. Old cunt. Snake. Nazi. [sic] Traitor. Zionist stooge. Evil personified. Cancer. Zionist traitor Pig. Infiltrator. Racist [sic] witch. Controlled and funded by Israel. Palestine child murderer.' A kinder politics.

Labour activist and Corbynista Ash Small, re-instated after being suspended, not expelled, for a series of anti-Semitic postings. One proposed that pro-Israel party Jews should be 'taken out one at a time' and another asked, 'can someone please explain where the figure of 6 million Holocaust victims came from?' He shared an article which objected to what it claimed was 'Jewish and Zionist influence at the BBC', a complaint also voiced by Corbyn on Iran's Press TV, and another which claimed that the USA and the UK were 'slaves of Israel'. One of the Jews scheduled to be 'taken out', Luke Akehurst, Director of We Believe in Israel, said he was 'left wondering what anyone has to say to have disciplinary action taken against them in the Labour Party.'

Angela Ormerod, one of the Corbyn intake joining the Labour Party after his election as Leader, suspended for claiming that 'Jews control the media'.

Pastor (sic) Liam Moore, Labour candidate for Liverpool's Norris Green Ward, tweeted: 'People, understand that Rothschilds Zionists run Israel and world government, don't give a toss about ordinary Jews, Jesus is coming back to his people'; and 'Zionism is not healthy for children and other living things.' Another referred to a 'Zionist coup' by pro-Israel MPs 'infiltrating' the Labour Party and, like Judas, 'selling out for thirty pieces of silver'.

Nottingham Councillor Ilyas Aziz, suspended then re-instated after urging Jews to 'stop drinking Gaza's blood' and comparing Israel to Nazi Germany.

Mohammed Yasin, Labour Party West Midlands Organiser, suspended, not expelled, for a series of anti-Semitic postings on social media, including: 'Jews are responsible for the all the wars in world' and another of a picture of a Rabbi with the caption 'Goyim were born only to serve us'.

Miqdad al-Nuaimi, Labour Councillor for Newport, suspended then re-instated after tweeting that Israel was 'increasingly assuming the arrogance and genocide character of the Nazis.'

Kasey Carver, adopted as Labour Candidate for High Peak Council after posting on the website 'Semitic Controversies', 'just looked at the potential Zionist influences of the BBC'.

Kate Linnegar, adopted as both a Parliamentary candidate for North Swindon and for Swindon Council after sharing an article that alleged anti-Semitism was being 'weaponised' to discredit Corbyn.

Sian Bloor, Secretary of the Trafford branch of the National Education Union, suspended, then re-instated after claiming that Corbyn has 'the 'full force of the Rothschild Zionist agenda drawing down on him', and that 'Jewish Israelis' were behind 9/11.

Council candidate for Kingston-upon-Thames Simon Attwood tweeted that a world Jewish conspiracy controls UK politics and the media, and that anti-Corbyn

Labour MP John Mann, who chairs the all-party Parliamentary Group against anti-Semitism, is a paid agent of Israel.

Ex Labour MP for Paisley and Renfrewshire North Jim Sheridan had his membership restored after being suspended for writing that he had 'lost respect and empathy for the Jewish community and their historic suffering due to what they and their Blairite plotters have done to my party.'

Tina McKay, prospective Parliamentary Candidate for Colchester, posted on Facebook that 'there have been individuals who have said that it [anti-Semitism] has been used as a plot, there is evidence of what they said being true.'

Mike Amesbury, Shadow Minister for Employment, after initially denying it, admitted tweeting an-anti-Semitic cartoon from the website 'IlluminatiAgenda.com'. (sic). It displayed an archetypically hooked-nosed 'Father Christmas' Jew with the caption, 'remember to support the banks and corporations this Christmas in their continued efforts to enslave mankind, by spending money you haven't got on things you don't need'.

Shadow Immigration Minister Afzal Khan, selected Labour candidate for the 2017 by-election in Gorton after being investigated and then and cleared for endorsing a tweet that compared Israel to Nazi Germany.

Naz(i) Shah, MP for West Bradford and Private Secretary to Shadow Chancellor John McDonnell, suspended in April 2016 for tweeting a map which showed Israeli Jews re-located to the United States. In an allusion to US aid to Israel, she added the comment that the move 'saved them some pocket money'. She also tweeted that 'everything that Hitler did in Germany was legal'. Really? So what were the Nuremberg Trials about? After being restored to membership, no action was taken in August 2017 when she endorsed in good faith a spoof tweet which said that 'for the good of diversity', 'those abused girls in Rotherham and elsewhere just need to shut their mouths', and when, following the death of Winnie Mandela in April 2018, she tweeted her image with the quote, 'together, hand in hand, with our matches and our necklaces [sic] we shall liberate this country', a reference to the ANC leader's notorious practice of burning alive her political opponents by setting light to a large tyre round their necks. A kinder politics.

In March 2019, disgraced former Rotherham Deputy Council Leader Jahangir Akhtar, suspected of but never charged with having sexual relations with an under-age gang-rape victim, posted two viciously anti-Semitic cartoons, one with a hooked-nosed Jew. He has reportedly combined with Momentum in a bid to de-select Rotherham Labour MP Sarah Champion, who resigned from the shadow cabinet after coming under fire from Corbyn loyalists for writing in the *Sun* about the Muslim gang rape industry in her constituency.

Lancashire Labour Councillor Pam Bromley posted links to an article titled, 'World War 3: Trump Begins Paying His Homage to Rothschilds. As in all other similar samples, 'Rothschilds' serves as code for 'the Jews'. Here for example

Bromley added the comment that the Rothschilds 'represent capitalism and big businesses'. She also claimed the Manchester Arena terror attack was not the work of a Muslim terrorist but a 'false flag' operation carried out on Prime Minister Theresa May's orders as 'a handy excuse to squash Jeremy Corbyn's growing support'. How this would work was not explained, but Corbyn, obviously out of the loop on this one, unwittingly helped things along by insisting that the massacre was a protest against British foreign policy. But that is so like Saint Jeremy, always trying to see the good in people, so long as they are not Zionists, even when they massacre children at a pop concert.

Hampstead and Kilburn CLP member Terrance Flanagan compared a Jewish Councillor to Josef Goebbels. Suspended, and then re-admitted after a warning.

Former Labour prospective Parliamentary candidate John Clarke shared a neo-Nazi meme saying that the Rothschilds used money lending and Israel to 'take over the world'. The meme, he said, 'contained a great deal of truth'. Suspended, not expelled.

Maureen Madden, Labour Councillor in North Tyneside, shared an image of banker Jacob Rothschild captioned: 'The people who invisibly control the world.' No action taken, re-elected in 2018.

Alex Scott-Samuel, Chair of Liverpool Wavertree CLP, in one of his regular appearances on the David Icke-sponsored Richie Allen Show, claimed that 'the Rothschild family are behind a lot of the neo-liberal influence in the UK and the US. You only have to Google them to look at this.' It was Scott-Samuel who moved the vote of no confidence in Jewish MP Luciana Berger, that led to her resignation from the Labour Party.

Luton Councillor Aysegal Gurbuz tweeted that Hitler was 'the greatest man in history and that if it was not for Hitler, 'these Jews would've wiped Palestine years ago.' After first denying then admitting she was the author (she initially blamed her sister) Gurbuz resigned from the Labour Party.

George McManus of Labour's National Policy Forum, suspended after posting on Facebook; 'Apparently [Deputy Labour Leader Tom] Watson received £50,000 from Jewish donors. At least Judas only got 30 pieces of silver.' His suspension was lifted after the usual ritual apology and appointed Labour Spokesman for the East Riding of Yorkshire.

Chesterfield Labour Councillor Andrew Slack, suspended after sharing a meme of a blood-smeared hook-nosed Israeli soldier. The caption said 'Israel was created by the Rothschilds'. Slack was re-instated and remains a Councillor. Slack indeed.

Former chair of Spitalfields and Banglatown [sic] CLP Musabbir Ali tweeted a neo-Nazi 'Timeline of the Jewish genocide of the British People' claiming that 'Jews control Britain and are committing genocide on us.' Suspended, not expelled. Makes a change from the Palestinians.

Paul Ashworth of Tameside tweeted to his 30,000 on-line followers that 'most of top movers at BBC are Jewish. Their head of news is married to a Jew from a well-known banking dynasty.' (Could it just be the Rothschilds?)

Kensington Labour Councillor Beinazir Lasharie, suspended and then reinstated after sharing a video on Facebook claiming that ISIS is run by Mossad. She commented, 'Many people know about who was behind 9/11 and also who is behind ISIS. I've nothing against Jews…just sharing it.' (sic)

Enfield Labour Councillor Ayfer Orhan had the whip withdrawn after retweeting the same claim.

Lambeth Labour Councillor Irfan Mohammed shared a post that said 'Jews working in the World Trade centre received a text message before the incident "Do not come to work in [sic] September 11."'

Dorian Bartley, a 'Diversity' officer of Lambeth CLP, posted images comparing Israel to the Nazis. He also shared a post defending the anti-Semitic mural approved by Corbyn and an image of Hitler giving the Nazi salute with the caption, 'we are the master race', next to an image of Israel Premier Netanyahu.

Luke Cresswell tweeted an image of a blood-soaked Israeli flag and captioned the image, 'Moses must be proud of you.' Suspended, then re-instated and elected as Suffolk Labour Councillor.

Wiltshire Labour Council candidate Terry Couchman, suspended, then expelled for using social media to attack 'ZioNazi storm troopers of Israel Hell'.

In an interview in the *Radio Times*, Corbynista actress Miriam Margoleyes claimed there was not 'the extent of anti-Semitism in the Labour Party that people seem to imply. It is to do with trying to stop Corbyn from becoming Prime Minister.' On previous occasions, she claimed 'Jews and blacks are stingy', that 'nobody likes Jews', and 'people understandably and correctly associate Israel with Jews and Jews are killing innocent people.'

Rachel Abbotts, elected Labour Councillor in High Peak after posting on Facebook the claim that 'the Jews declared war on Germany' and another which asked, 'is Israel's hand behind the attacks on Jeremy Corbyn?'

Fylde council candidate Harry Verco, suspended after tweeting 'Israel is turning itself into a Neo-Nazi state' and sharing an article with the comment:' Disgusting pair Murdoch/Rothschilds Israel exposed secretly paying Syria rebels to protect Rothschild Murdoch oil'.

Rebecca Massey of Hove tweeted that 'Israel has Tory and Labour Parties under control, and that Labour's anti-Semitism crisis had been 'manufactured'. No action. Instead, she was appointed Treasurer of Hove and Portslade CLP.

Redditch Labour Party Branch Secretary Alan Mason resigned from the party when there came to light a posting which claimed that Jewish Labour MP Ruth Smeeth was funded by an 'Israeli Lobby', that the Rothschilds funded Hitler, that Hilary Clinton's 'Zio strillionaire [sic] friends in London are sucking America and 99% of Americans dry', and that Jewish real estate developer Larry Silverstein profited from 9/11.

Paul Merron, Ealing Labour Party member, and video-maker for PSC and Stop the War Coalition, shared one post saying that 'a 15-year-old girl learns the truth about the Holohoax', and another which claimed that '6 Jewish companies control 96% of the world's media.' Merron says that he 'joined the Labour Party to support Jeremy Corbyn'.

Tony Greenstein, the archetypical 'self-hating Jew', suspended after comments such as 'Zio idiots', 'Zionist scum', that Jewish MP Loise Ellman 'supported Israeli child abuse' and 'gay Zionists make me want to puke'.

Essex Councillor John Clarke and Labour Parliamentary candidate in 2015 tweeted that the Rothschilds have 'used usury as an imperial instrument to take over the world and all its resources, include you and I.'

Former Labour MP Michelle Harris shared a Facebook post from David Icke (sic) titled 'Rothschild Zionist Israel an International Pariah' and others comparing Israel to Nazi Germany. No action taken.

Corbynista MPs Chris Williamson and Dan Carden were present at a Momentum rally where a member of Liverpool Sefton CLP, to a standing ovation, declared, 'What could be greater threat to our democracy than a foreign government who [sic]is trying to veto the person we want for Prime Minister? Of course, I'm talking about the Israelis with their foot soldiers in Labour, the Labour Friends of Israel, the Jewish Labour Movement. They are trying to take out democracy away from us.' Neither Williamson nor Carden challenged this exposition of the World Jewish Conspiracy.

In the same vein, Fife Labour Councillor Mary Lockhart suggested on Facebook that there could be a 'Mossad-assisted campaign to prevent the election of a Labour Government.' Suspended, then reinstated.

Dipu Ahad, a Labour Councillor for Newcastle, posted that he didn't vote for a new mega Marks and Spencer store in Gosforth 'as a matter of principle' because the company was 'directly killing innocent Palestinian people by directly funding the Zionist regime'. In another posting, he claimed western countries went to war in Iraq, Afghanistan and Libya to 'achieve the Zionist goal...to have each country in the debt of the Rothschilds.' Again, a ritual apology for saying something he obviously believed to be true (otherwise, why advertise it?) and no further action. Adopted to stand again as candidate for the Elswick ward.

When Steve Cooke, Secretary of Stockton CLP moved a resolution condemning the Pittsburgh synagogue massacre in which 11 Jews died, objections were made it did not condemn all forms of racism, only anti-Semitism. A previous resolution, condemning 'Islamophobia' was not subjected to the same criticism.

Invited to address a Momentum fringe meeting at a Labour Party conference, Ewa Jasiewicz withdrew when it was revealed that she had daubed 'Free Gaza and Palestine' on the Warsaw Ghetto wall in 2010, and had called for Palestinian 'activists' (sic) to 'do' the Israeli Parliament or 'bump off' a 'sophisticated politician' rather than target Israeli civilians.

Addressing a party meeting in 2014, Labour MP for Leeds East and Corbyn's Shadow Justice Secretary Richard Burgon said that that 'Zionism is the enemy of peace' and that all Labour MP's who are members of Labour Friends of Israel should resign their seats. In a subsequent TV interview with Andrew Neil, he denied using these words: 'I didn't say that. It's not my view'. When a video of the meeting proved that he did, he issued the usual pro-forma apology, claiming that he was only criticising the Israeli government. No action was taken.

Rupa Huq, MP for Ealing Central and Acton, accused of a number of anti-Semitic comments and actions by two of her employees. One was repeatedly asked, 'why do you have the flag of Israel on your bag?' even after being told it was nothing of the sort. A briefing he wrote on the Middle East conflict was criticised for being too pro-Israel. He was subsequently banned from writing any more. For one potential Jewish employee, Huq 'devised a whole separate list of questioning based on Judaism and loyalty to Israel'. The other employee claims Huq regaled an employee with stories about Jewish conspiracies and in her office tore down a 'No tolerance for anti-Semitism' poster, saying that it was not needed any more. No action taken.

Labour's council candidate for Tonbridge Wells Roy Smart, suspended after sharing a series of links on a Holocaust denial website and posting that 'people being allowed to question if the Holocaust happened is not the same as being a Holocaust denier, any more than protesting about the Israeli government's treatment of the Palestinians is anti-Semitic'.

Margaret Tyson of Liverpool Wavertree CLP accused local Jewish Labour MP Luciana Berger of supporting the 'Zionist Israeli government' whose 'Nazi masters [sic] taught them well'. In another posting, she wrote, 'Is it any wonder the Zionest [sic] are hated and despised throughout the world?' No action taken. Berger has been the target for abuse on Corbynista websites that even by their standards are especially vicious: 'She is a vile Zionist'; 'Get rid of this cancer'; 'Deselect the cunt'. A kinder politics.

Former Shadow Fire and Emergency Services Minister Chris Williamson, Labour MP for North Derby, described by his leader Jeremy Corbyn as 'a very great friend', dismissed accusations of Labour Party anti-Semitism, as 'proxy wars' [waged on behalf of whom?], 'bullshit' and 'smears', for which, after an outcry by anti-Corbynistas, despite his very great friend's attempt to save him, he was suspended from party membership. Williamson was speaking at a meeting called to protest at the expulsion and suspension of party members on charges of anti-Semitism, referring to 'dark forces' at work in the media and elsewhere to undermine Corbyn. Nothing deterred, the suspended and unrepentant Williamson provoked more outrage when he 'liked' a Jewish conspiracy posting by expelled Momentum activist Nadeem Ahmed claiming that 'Israel have [sic] offered a £1m bounty for Labour insiders to undermine Jeremy Corbyn.' One of these 'insiders' was said to be Labour Friends of Israel Chair Joan Ryan who, according to Ahmed, had been 'filmed asking Shai Masot [an official at the Israeli embassy] about a list of names that were sent to the Israeli embassy.' Williamson's suspension was lifted in June 2019 by a panel of three NEC members/ by a vote of two to one. Those voting to lift the suspension were Keith Vaz, a close friend of Corbyn's of more than thirty years standing and like his Leader, an Islamophile, leading a demonstration of Muslims in his Leicester constituency in 1989 demanding the banning of Salman Rushdie's *Satanic Verses*, and Huda Elmi of the Palestine Solidarity Campaign and Momentum. Like her Leader, she is a supporter of Venezuelan dictator Nicolas Maduro and an enemy of Israel, posting on *The Electronic Intifada* the warning that 'Israel's [sic] definition of anti-Semitism will unleash havoc in Labour', and at a public meeting, describing Israel as a 'settler-colonial state' and Corbyn as a 'pro-Palestinian leader'. She has called the Human Equality and Human Rights Commission, currently investigating her party's anti-Semitism, a 'failed experiment' (in what she did not say), and demanded that it should be wound up. 120 Labour MPs and peers and 70 staffers protested Williamson's re-instatement, resulting in the withholding of the Labour whip.

In March 2018, actor and Labour Council candidate for Stratford-on Avon Chris Jury posted on-line the allegation that the Israeli embassy had 'aided and abetted' the 'right wing of the of the Labour Party' in its 'cynical abuse' of the Holocaust to undermine the Corbyn leadership. In April, likening Israel to Nazi Germany, Jury said its 'racist, colonial, Eurocentric [sic] moral; degeneracy' was 'still playing out in the Middle East'. Again, in August, Jury claimed that British politics were being 'subverted' and anti-Semitism 'weaponised' by Labour's right wing. In a statement to the online *Daily Mail,* Jury stood by all these and other similar comments. No action taken.

In Peterborough, one of a growing number of Labour's rotten Muslim boroughs, a by-election was triggered by the resignation of Fiona (Jesus Christ) Onasanya following her conviction and jailing for perverting the course of justice. Labour replaced a crook by an exponent of Jewish conspiracy theory, namely Corbyn loyalist Liz Forbes. She had endorsed a posting accusing Theresa May of following a 'Zionist slave masters agenda' and another, one that she 'enjoyed reading so much', claiming that that ISIS was created by Mossad and the CIA. As a PSC activist and supporter of BDS, Forbes also rejected one of the 11 articles in the International Holocaust Remembrance Association's definition of anti-Semitism, adopted with a caveat, and after prolonged resistance, by the party's NEC and opposed personally by Corbyn. She insisted that Labour Party members should be free to criticise Israel's 'system [sic] of apartheid and ongoing ethnic cleansing'. Like other Corbynistas exposed as Jew-baiters, Forbes agreed to undergo 'anti-Semitism awareness training', presumably because like many of her ilk, her racism is so deeply ingrained that it can only be eradicated by a course of intensive re-programming in elementary human decency. Forbes was elected on the lowest-ever percentage vote for a winning candidate…30.9%, compared with

Jesus Christ's 48.1% at the 2017 General Election, and the highest percentage of postal votes. Despite what impartial observers described as flagrant fraud, Labour's vote fell from 22,950 to10,844. Rejecting demands that she be denied the Labour whip, Corbyn insisted Forbes was a 'good woman, not a racist in any way whatsoever'. Jewish conspiracy theories not racist? Not for Corbyn, because he shares them. Corbyn and Forbes were frequently photographed posing and canvassing with convicted and jailed vote-rigger and former Peterborough party secretary Tariq Mahmood, who also featured in a Labour election video. Corbyn was also seen visiting local mosques, again accompanied by election fraudster Mahmood. And why not? Corbyn is, after all, a supporter and in the case of Iran, even the former employee, of regimes that when they deign to hold elections, rig them as a matter of course. Mahmood, expelled from the party after his conviction, describes his services to it as those of a 'freelance Labour campaigner'.

Jo Bird, a Wirral Councillor, in a meeting called to defend party members accused of anti-Semitism complained, to laughter and applause, of what she called 'Jew process'. This, and other similar remarks, led to her suspension, which days later, was lifted.

Conspiracy (again, explicitly Jewish) was the central theme of a meeting convened on March 11 2019, by the far left to rally support for a Comrade Corbyn besieged by false accusations of anti-Semitism. The audience included 60s student protestor and Brexit campaigner Tariq Ali, Glyn Secker, columnist for the Stalinist *Morning Star* and suspended from Labour Party membership for 'comments on social media that may be anti-Semitic', and Gerry Downing, expelled from the Labour Party for *supporting* 9/11, and who publishes *Protocols*-style diatribes against the sinister role of a 'world Jewish bourgeoisie'. Addressing the meeting, Corbyn's old comrade from the Stop the War Coalition Lindsey German, after reading out a letter of greetings to the event by Comrade Corbyn, denounced accusations of anti-Semitism against the Labour Party and its Leader as a 'huge lie'. 'There is one dominant racism that is going on [sic] and that is Islamophobia.' (Yet again, Islam becomes a race when circumstances require it.) Corbyn's leadership was being undermined by a 'wrecking operation' organised by the Jewish MP Margaret Hodge: 'We are here tonight to say we are not going to allow that wrecking operation to continue'. Two weeks later, hard-core Corbynistas gathered again, this time under the auspices of 'Labour Against the Witch-hunt', to listen to Livingstone intone the same tune, that Labour's anti-Semitic crisis was the product of 'lies and smears' peddled by 'ghastly old Blairites'. He said that his own fall from grace as Corbyn's adviser on matters military (sic), which after more than two years of suspension, was climaxed by his resignation, had been engineered by a 'Labour machine staffed by 'Blairites'. Corbyn's own office, he revealed 'did not want it to happen'. That at least we can believe. Unrepentant as ever, he insisted 'it's not anti-Semitic to hate the Jews of Israel'.

The reader will no doubt have noticed several recurring themes in the above citings, two of the most frequent being that ISIS is a Mossad creation and that Labour's anti-Semitic crisis has been artificially fomented and then exploited by Jews in the party and/or Israeli intelligence to undermine Corbyn's leadership. No surprises here, since identical allegations proliferate on numerous websites associated with the Corbynista and Palestinian causes. Then there is the claim that *opposition* to anti-Semitism was being 'weaponised' to undertime Corbyn's leadership, an inversion of the traditional left-wing thesis that *anti-Semitism itself,* not opposition to it, was whipped up by the far right to divert the masses from the struggle against capitalism. But the one that merits the most interest because of its provenance are the repeated allusions to the existence of a world Jewish conspiracy, almost invariably personified by the Rothschilds family. Here we have, in its purest and most explicit form, the thesis of *The Protocols of the Learned Elders of Zion,* one that found full favour both with the Nazis and has more recently in the Muslim world and on the left, that Jews, largely by stealth, control the entire world's banking system and, by doing so, virtually everything else on our planet. It was Hitler's ruling obsession, one he returned to it again and again in his *Mien Kampf,* and one which led directly to the gas chambers of the Holocaust. *It is also an obsession shared by members of the Labour Party.*

In the cited cases of anti-Semitism listed above, no fewer than 23 contain direct references by Labour Party members to the Rothschilds. A search online quickly brought up a dozen or more websites that could have been the source of these references, all overtly anti-Semitic and in some case, also Nazi. One, titled *Real Jew News,* listed no fewer than 13 articles on the alleged conspiratorial activities of the Rothschilds, with titles such as 'Greek Riots and the Rothschild Bankers', 'The Rothschilds' Secret Operations', 'George Soros: An Evil Rothschild Agent', 'England's Jews Control Europe', 'The Rothschild-Israeli Occult Connection' and 'How the Rothschild Dynasty Operates'. So much information…and yet strange, because all this and much more is supposed to be a closely-guarded secret. Another revealed 'how the Rothschilds own Israel and direct its genocidal policy', like all the others I surveyed, more grist to the mill of gullible Jew-baiting Corbynites, as at the London anti-Trump rally addressed by Corbyn on June 9. 2019, where one of the audience displayed a large poster with the legend: 'They All [underlined] Work for Rothschild'.

In the normal run of things, these are the kinds of opinions that one would expect to find being voiced by members of a fully-fledged Nazi movement. But today, those that advertise them are quite at home in the Corbynista wing of the Labour Party, with many of them being protected from disciplinary action by their Dear Leader's personal staff. This is only to be expected when, as we have already seen, Corbyn himself is no stranger to Jewish conspiracy theory. Another example, devastating in the extreme, came to light in April 2019 when the *Sunday Times* carried a story concerning a 3,500-word Foreword Corbyn had written in 2010 for a new edition by Spokesman Books of John Hobson's *Imperialism,* first published in 1902. One passage of the work (which Lenin used as source material for his own book on same subject some 14 years later) advances the same claim that features prominently on Corbynista websites and postings by his Labour Party supporters, namely, that the Jews, usually personified by the Rothschilds, control the world economy through their monopoly of the banking system…precisely Bebel's 'socialism of fools'. Hobson confined himself to Europe, but the thesis is essentially the same, even down to the Rothchilds as the main villains of the piece:

> United by the strongest bonds of organisation, always in closest and quickest touch with one another, situated in the very heart of the business capital of every state,

controlled, so far as Europe is concerned, by men of a single and peculiar race, who have behind them many centuries of financial experience, they are in a unique position to control the policy of nations.

He continues in the same vein:

'Does anyone seriously believe that any great war can be undertaken by any European state if the House of Rothschild [sic] and their connections set their face against it?' Then Hobson goes even further down the path of Jewish conspiracy theory, in doing so anticipating the claim made by Hitler in *Mein Kampf*, which he in turn derived from the *Protocols*, that the Jews not only control the world of finance but its ostensible, enemy, the revolutionary Left: First' Hitler: '[Germany's economy had] fallen victim to the united attack of [Jewish] finance capital, which carried on its fight with the special help of its faithful comrade, the [likewise Jewish] Marxist movement.' Now Hobson: 'There is not a war, a revolution, an anarchist assassination or any other public shock' from which these 'harpies' (sic) cannot 'suck their gains'. And the *Protocols*: 'We [that is, the "Learned Elders of Zion"] shall create by all secret subterranean methods open to us with the gold that is in all our hands, a universal economic crisis whereby we shall throw upon the streets whole mobs of workers simultaneously in all the countries of Europe.' Not least in view of its provenance, how come Corbyn managed to pass over without comment Hobson's thesis? But so he had the identical allegation of his Hamas 'friends' in their Manifesto that all left wing movements since the French Revolution have been the work of the Jews...including, it must follow, his very own Momentum.

The core of Hobson's economic argument, one that was endorsed by Lenin, minus the anti-Semitism, was that in order to boost its profits, capitalism is compelled to find new markets, sources of raw materials and fresh outlets for investment. by means of colonial conquest and exploitation, which in turn leads to rivalry and eventually war between the competing imperial powers. And, masterminding the entire process, is an international conspiracy of Jewish bankers. Even though one of the central messages of Hobson's book is therefore that rich Jews conspire to conquer and suck dry the riches of the world, as depicted in the anti-Semitic Tower Hamlets mural which he initially praised, Corbyn found his study exemplary in its exposure of the evils of capitalism: 'brilliant', 'correct and prescient [sic], a 'great tome' no less. As for its diatribes against the Jews...not a word. Instead, he titles his Forward 'Internationalist at Work'! If it is the case, as a Labour Party statement claimed, that 'Jeremy completely rejects the anti-Semitic elements of his [i.e., Hobson's] analysis', given that Hobson the 'internationalist' is known to have harboured and advertised in other writings his prejudices against the Jews, and that they formed a central component of his 'analysis' in *Imperialism*, why didn't Corbyn, the dedicated anti-racist, immediately spot them, and then take the opportunity to condemn them in his Foreword, and when he spoke at the launching of the book on January 12, 2011? Far from condemning Hobson's 'analysis', this is how Corbyn responded to it:

For someone who was revered by Marxists, and quoted by Lenin, for his analysis of the pressures to extend empire, his analysis of the then current empire and its future, was not very revolutionary. What is brilliant, and very controversial at the time, is his analysis of the pressures that were hard at work in pushing for a vast national effort in grabbing new outposts of empire on distant lands and shores.

But who was doing the 'pushing' and 'grabbing'? Hobson says, Jewish finance, which 'control[s] the policy of nations'. Corbyn must had read those passages where this central element of Hobson's 'brilliant' analysis is developed. But he passes them over without comment. Instead, he declares Hobson's anti-Semitic book to be a work that 'deserves enormous credit and recognition'. How did Corbyn reply to the well-founded accusation that once again, he had uncritically praised a work with an undisguised anti-Semitic theme?

> This accusation is the latest in a series of equally ill-founded accusations of anti-Jewish racism that Labour's political opponents have made against me. [In fact, as Corbyn was only too well aware, most of them have come from within his own party.] I note that the Foreword story was written by a Conservative Party peer [as if that *ipso facto* renders it untrue] in a newspaper whose editorial policy and owner [Rupert Murdoch - more *ad hominem*] have long been hostile to Labour. At a time when Jewish communities in the UK and indeed, across Europe feel [sic] under attack, it is a matter of great regret that the issue of anti-Semitism is often politicised in this way.

Corbyn cannot even bring himself to acknowledge that Jews actually *are* 'under attack', including by his supporters in the Labour Party, only that they 'feel' they are. It's all in the mind. And yet, as he must have known, in France Jews were leaving in their thousands because of anti-Semitic violence, including murder, and that Jewish MPs of his own party were being subjected to death and even rape threats. On the same day that the Campaign Against Anti-Semitism website carried Corbyn's defence of his uncritical treatment of Hobson's book, Corbyn's Hamas 'friends' fired more than 600 rockets supplied by his former Iranian employers into Israeli territory, killing four civilians and wounding more than 100. Again, on that day, the same source reported two expressions of viciously anti-Jewish attitudes in the UK. Omar Choudhury, 'Black and [?] Minority Ethnic Officer' of Bristol University Students Union, told a Jewish student that he should be like Israel and 'cease to exit'. So much for 'minorities'. Despite a petition calling for his removal being signed by more than a thousand students, and his employers agreeing that his comment was anti-Semitic, Choudhury was not even given a formal warning, but merely required to apologise to the student he had insulted. The second case concerned Kamran Ishtiaq, President of the British Pakistani Youth Council since 2009. In 2014, he posted a picture of Hitler on his Facebook page. When another Facebook user objected that 'Hitler was a racist bro', Ishtiaq, obviously unaware that Hitler had allied himself with Muslim leaders in the Second World War, replied, 'I know that and to be honest he would have killed Muslims too if he got the chance'. But then he continued, 'But do you know what, I would salute him still if he killed 90 Muslims and 92 Jews.' Hitler was his hero 'cuz he just killed Jews, didn't get a chance to kill Muslims.' All in the mind? When these comments came to light five years later, he told the *Birmingham Post* that he stood by them, adding that the number of Jews killed in the Holocaust had been 'exaggerated' in order to justify what he called Jewish 'revenge'.

Should Jews be concerned about such cases of flagrant anti-Semitism exhibited by individuals who hold offices of influence within British society including, as we have seen, in one of the UK's two largest political parties? Or is it the case, as Corbyn implies, that Jewish concerns are unfounded, that the issue has been stirred up by his party's enemies, that opposition to anti-Semitism is being 'weaponised', in his case by the Tory peer in question, the Jewish Lord Finkelstein, and a Tory press magnate? Not that Corbyn has any objection *per se* to Tory peers, only those who expose his indulgence of anti-Semitism. He accompanied a Muslim one, Lord Sheikh, on two freebees to the lands of Arabia, the first as guest of President Assad of Syria (who later played host (twice) to the Neo-Nazi Nick Griffin), the second to attend a Hamas council of war against Israel in Tunisia, where he laid a wreath at the graveside of Fatah operatives involved in the planning of the hostage-taking operation that led to the massacre of the Israeli team at the 1972 Munch Olympics.

Ad hominem arguments avail Corbyn nothing. The plain fact, one that Corbyn takes care to avoid, is that the book he had unreservedly and fulsomely praised (I have read his *Foreword*) was flagrantly and deeply flawed by its anti-Semitism, and that fact is true irrespective of who reports it, even when the reporter is a Jewish Tory. Is it any wonder then that with a track record such as his on the 'Jewish question', a poll conducted in April 2019, revealed that 55% of voters agreed with the statement that 'Jeremy Corbyn's failure to tackle anti-Semitism within his own party shows he is unfit to be Prime Minister'?

How the Labour Leadership responded, or as many have claimed, failed to respond, to this extraordinary surge of Jew-hatred, became a subject of adverse comment both by anti-Corbyn Labour MPs and sections of the media, being partly informed by leaks of documents officially privy only to Corbyn's central staff. In March, 2019, the *Sunday Times* acquired access to confidential information held at Labour Party HQ which revealed that of 863 Labour Party members reported to have made anti-Semitic comments, 249 had not been investigated, and another 454 remained unresolved. Of the 409 cases resolved, 191 required no further action, 145 received a formal warning, and 15 were expelled. One party member, on Corbyn's staff, said Israel was excused being an 'apartheid state' 'because of the Holocaust'. No action was taken...hardly a surprise, since this is a routine Corbynista accusation against Israel. Also restored to full membership were Labour Councillor Ben Lloyd-Shogbesan, who had compared Israel to Nazi Germany, and Council candidate Alan Myers, who had posted a comment about 'Zionist leaders and their billionaire masters'. (Who might they be, one wonders?) A Lancashire Councillor who was expelled for posting claims that the media were controlled by the Jews, was re-admitted after explaining she used 'Jewish' as 'a blanket term of description without any racist connotations'. A blanket term for whom? She gave a clue when she also attacked the Rothschilds in the same posting. Make of this arcane excuse what you like, the fact is that prominent party members were being licensed to say virtually anything derogatory about the Jews. For example, in another case, a member who described Labour's Jewish MPs as 'Zionist infiltrators' was let off because he was a council candidate. Incredibly, even a member who posted on-line 'Heil Hitler, fuck the Jews' escaped expulsion, while Thomas Gardiner, a close ally of Corbyn, blocked the fast-track expulsion of a party member who described two Jewish Labour MPs, obviously both women, as 'shit-stirring cunt buckets'. What a nice bunch these Corbynistas are.

The same report revealed that in violation of the required procedure, cases involving members whom Corbyn's Chief of Staff, Karie Murphy defined as 'elected politicians or candidates', were being referred to Corbyn's office, resulting in the blocking or delaying of 101 complaints, refuting the assurance Corbyn gave to Margaret Hodge that 'I do not involve myself in a complaint at all.' (In October 2020, Labour confirmed that the now-ousted Murphy was under investigation for having conducted a vendetta against a number of anti-Corbyn MPs. When seven of them, including the Jewish Luciana Berger, who had endured years of Jew-baiting by Corbynistas in her constituency party, resigned, she messaged on WhatsApp, 'Fucking idiots. All the work I did to trigger them and they leave before I had the pleasure.' A kinder politics.) Understandably, in view of this assurance, MPs were outraged when they learned that both veteran Stalinist Andrew Murray and his daughter Laura, described as 'Stakeholder Manager' on Corbyn's staff, (tying things up nicely, Corbyn's son Seb, also 'appointed on merit', is on McDonnell's) had for at least a year been blocking and reversing disciplinary actions against members charged with anti-Semitism, usurping the role ascribed to Labour's disputes committee. Murray junior's role as Corbyn's overseer was regularised when she was appointed Head of Complaints in April 2019. Responding to accusations of political favouritism and nepotism, a party source said she was 'the best person for the job'...just like Corbyn junior.

One case binned by Murray senior was a claim by a party member that ISIS was a creation of Mossad, while Murray junior cleared a member who, like Corbyn, had approved of the Tower Hamlets anti-Semitic mural. In March of 2018, she had also reversed, *but only after consulting Corbyn*, the suspension of Patricia Sheerin: 'LTO [Leader of the Opposition] recommendations are that you investigate but without suspension as although her tweets are drawing upon conspiracy theories, they are about Israel and no mention [sic] of Jews or Jewishness etc'. Conspiracy theories about the Jewish state of Israel are OK, as long as there is no actual mention of the Jews. Just a nod and wink will do, as with Corbyn when on Press TV in August 2012, he referred to the 'hand of Israel' but not the Jews. A year later, Sheerin was one of three party members arrested by police on charges of inciting racial hatred against Jews. Another member who had recycled a cartoon on a Nazi website (sic!) was cleared by Corbyn himself, on the grounds that it was not anti-Jew but anti-Israel.

Days later, the *Sunday Times* revealed that Murray senior and yet another Corbyn insider, his 'Director of Strategy and Communications', fellow Stalin apologist Seumas Milne, had intervened to lift the suspension of Glyn Secker, a member of the viciously anti-Zionist and frequently no less anti-Semitic secret website Palestine Live that Corbyn, its highest profile member, visited at least 30 times, until withdrawing after being elected Labour leader in September 2015. After Secker had been suspended for postings on its website, including one which said 'Jew=Zionist=Israel=Jew', Murray and Milne sprang to his defence, emailing the party's Disputes Committee that 'none of the posts can be identified as anti-Semitic in the terms we have adopted as a party,' adding, as a clincher, that Corbyn 'was interested in this one'. The suspension was promptly lifted, as it was for Momentum activist Marlene Ellis, suspended in 2016 for declaring in an Open Letter to Corbyn that by suspending Livingstone for claiming that Zionists collaborated with the Nazis (a claim she endorsed) the party had 'played right into the hands of the Zionist criminals' by 'seeking to curry favour with the pro-

Zionist lobby in and beyond the media.' Commenting on these revelations, Labour MP Wes Streeting said he did not understand 'how anyone on the left can even try and defend Labour's handling of anti-Semitism - or continued to deny the problem.' He had 'absolutely no confidence in the Labour Party's approach to tackling anti-Semitism and will discuss next steps with colleagues.' In a secretly taped interview with Margaret Hodge, Corbyn can be heard admitting that evidence of anti-Semitism was 'either being mislaid, ignored or not used'.

Interviewed by Andrew Marr on BBC TV on February 23, 2019, Deputy Leader Tom Watson revealed that he had a file of 50 cases still waiting to be processed, while MP Margaret Hodge said she had personally submitted another 200. Watson's included: an accusation that Jews were guilty of 'double-dealing, back stabbing, cheating'; that Jews were 'pervert[ing] democracy in the UK'; that 'Jews murder people and children'; the claim that Hitler was an 'illegitimate Rothschild'(sic!), that the numbers of Jews said to be have been killed in the Holocaust 'don't add up'; and that Jewish MPs Ruth Smeeth and Louise Ellman 'don't know what runs through their veins, not human blood'. Yes, these are the expressed views of *Labour Party members*, the same 'socialism of fools' derided by Bebel and Engels, views which, before the election of Corbyn as Leader, no-one would have dared to voice so brazenly. Now, Labour's anti-Semites wanted to tell the world what they think of the Jews, and those who defend them. In the on-line *Daily Mirror* story covering the Watson interview, there were the following comments: 'You [Watson] need to join the right-wing Blairites. Good riddance.' 'With deputy leaders like Watson who needs a Tory party.' 'Always follow the money. Who's paying them…Israel.'

Labour's anti-Semitism crisis deepened still further when on July 10, 2019, it was the subject of a Panorama investigation on BBC1. Corbyn had been invited to appear on the programme to answer the charges made against him by former members of his staff, but he declined the offer. Instead, Panorama screened a series of statements issued by the party in answer to the charges made against it. Anticipating that the programme will remain accessible on line, I simply draw attention to one damning fact of many that emerged from it, namely that out of the thousands of cases processed, thanks largely to the efforts of Milne and the Murrays, as of July 2019, only 15 had resulted in expulsions. After turning down the invitation to state his case, following the programme's screening, Corbyn claimed it had 'many, many inaccuracies,' though he did not say what they were, merely that it had a 'pre-determined position'…again unspecified. A predictable response, not least in that on Iran's Press TV, Corbyn had accused the BBC of a pro-Israel bias emanating from the country's London embassy. His dismissal of the programme's findings proved too much for one-time loyalist Emily Thornberry, who said it was mistake to 'attack the messengers' when it was so obvious that the party had an 'ongoing problem with anti-Semitism'. This was confirmed when, only a matter of days later, fully a third of Labour Peers - 67 - signed an Open Letter to their party leader titled, 'This is your Legacy, Mr Corbyn', protesting at his continued failure (at best) to weed out the party's anti-Semites. It concluded: 'You have failed to defend our party's anti-racist values. You have therefore failed the test of leadership.' (Acting with an alacrity and severity rarely if ever in evidence even in cases of proven anti-Semitism, within the week, the Sunderland Labour Party expelled Hilary Armstrong for signing the Open Letter to Corbyn.)

The peers' devasting letter followed the resignation from the party of three other Labour peers, not by accident two Jews and one of Armenian origin. Then, days later, came a revolt of the plebs, as all the staff at Labour's Newcastle-based Membership Department walked out when, on first her first day as Corbyn's new appointment as the Department's Head, it was discovered that Jules Rutherford had previously tweeted that allegations of anti-Semitism were 'smears against the Party Leader'. Not for the first time, a Labour spokesman refused to comment and, following the example of her Leader, that the tweet was quickly consigned to the memory hole.

Three conclusions arising from facts presented in this work are undeniable. One, that despite repeated claims to the contrary, Labour's anti-Semitism has been on the rise only since the election of Corbyn as leader; Two, those who promote it get more often than not an easy ride from the top party leadership. Three, with the election of a party leader widely celebrated in the 'Muslim community' as a champion of Islam and the enemy of Israel, it was now considered safe for some Labour Party Muslims to voice openly views about the Jews which hitherto had been, as one Muslim commentator has described it, their 'dirty little secret'. Symptomatic of the tolerant attitude towards Labour Party Jew-baiting is the scandal that led in March 2018 to the resignation of Corbyn loyalist Christine Shawcross from both the Labour Party National Executive Committee and as head the Labour Party's Disputes Panel. Her duties in the latter office included investigating accusations of anti-Semitism made against party members. One such charge was made against Allan Bull, who was due to stand as a Labour candidate in that hot-bed of anti-Zionism and dubious voting practices, Peterborough, in the local elections due in May 2018. Bull had been suspended from his local party after posting on Facebook an article saying the Holocaust was a 'hoax'. Shawcross, also a Director of the Corbynista Momentum, lifted his suspension and then, after an outcry, resigned. Reversing the old adage by appointing a thief to protect many others, Corbyn proposed as her replacement another loyalist, Claudia Webbe, a councillor in Corbyn's Islington North constituency and former Mayoral adviser to and election agent of the disgraced Livingstone. Webbe defended him when in 2005, as Mayor of London, he was suspended for a month for likening a Jewish journalist to a Nazi concentration camp guard.

Aside from the Islington connection, it is easy to see why Webbe was Corbyn's choice. She did not even believe Labour had an anti-Semitism problem, having previously tweeted that it was a plot engineered by the 'combined machinery of state, political and mainstream elite' to undermine Corbyn's leadership. Not only this. Webbe had also shared platforms with three Labour Party members who had been suspended on charges of anti-Semitism. Webbe was assisted by yet another Corbyn loyalist, party General Secretary Jennie Formby, who then, in her turn, found herself usurped by the super loyalists Milne and the Murray dynasty. Labour Peer Lord Falconer, appointed to bring some sort of order to a disciplinary process that had escaped control, when questioned about the interventions of Milne and the Murrays on Radio 4, asked 'what on earth is going on?... how can we ask people to vote for a party that is anti-Semitic?' How indeed. Days later, there came a truly surrealist moment when a MP who likens herself to Jesus entered the chamber of the Commons wearing an electronic leg tag after her early release from prison. (At the time of writing, Webbe, MP for Leicester East since 2019, narrowly avoided jail, having been found guilty on

October 12, 2021, of harassment, which included threats of an acid attack on and showing naked pictures of a female friend of her partner, despite the efforts of Corbyn, John McDonnell and Dianne Abbott, who testified as character witnesses on her behalf.)

Of the cases of alleged or proven anti-Semitism I have culled from various sources, no fewer than six involved members of Corbyn's Shadow cabinet, seven were back-bench MPs, five were Parliamentary candidates, one a candidate for the EU Parliament, 38 were councillors, 17 were council candidates, and 16 had Muslim names. Nevertheless, her master's (often very confused) voice Diane Abbott, who is herself an anti-white racist, is quoted as saying on May 1, 2016, that 'it is a smear to say that Labour has a problem with anti-Semitism', a position that in the wake of the 'Corbyn mural' scandal, finally became indefensible. Comments that occasioned accusations of anti-Semitism ran the usual gamut from Jews are no better than Nazis to praise for Hitler as 'the greatest man in history' who 'killed six million Zionists', and from denying the Holocaust to applauding it. And yet again we have the Rothschilds, Jews kidnapping Palestinian children (whether for their body organs or their blood was left unsaid), a Jewish Holocaust of the Palestinians, a Jewish world conspiracy, ISIS created by Mossad, 'ZioNazi vermin', a Mossad conspiracy against Corbyn, a David Duke video, praise for David Icke, 'Jews have big noses and slaughter the oppressed', 'Israel has Tory and Labour parties under [its] control', Hamas justified in killing Israeli civilians, 'Zionist Jews' a 'disgrace to humanity', '150,000 Jewish SS personally involved in the Holocaust', BBC and press controlled by Zionists, 'apartheid' Israel, Jews the chief financiers of the slave trade, the 'Zionist conspiracy', the 'the filthy history of paedophilia, murder and bigotry', and inevitably, much praise for Jew-baiter number one, Ken Livingstone.

These are beliefs quite openly promoted and recycled by members, not of Hamas or of a Nazi movement but *of the Labour Party*, many of them having been elected or chosen to represent the party in the UK's democratic institutions up to the very highest level. They have served in Corbyn's Shadow Cabinet and in Livingstone's case, as his adviser on defence policy. The *Sunday Times* of April 1, 2018, revealed that twelve of Corbyn's and McDonnell's staff, and McDonnell himself, were members of 20 social media groups which featured more than 2,000 violently abusive and anti-Semitic postings, among them, the Corbyn cultist 'We Support Jeremy Corbyn', 'Jeremy Corbyn leads us to victory' and 'Let's help make Jeremy Prime Minister'. Another, 'Supporting Jeremy Corbyn and John McDonnell', carried a posting which read; 'Adolph, [sic] you should have finished the job.' The same day, Corbyn announced that he had consigned his own personal Facebook account to the same Orwellian memory hole that swallowed up his adulatory postings on Venezuela.

On April 12, 2018, the *Jewish News* reported that at a screening of his film *I, Daniel Blake* at the Kingswood Constituency Labour Party, Corbynista film director, one-time Healyite and Patron of the Palestine Solidarity Campaign Ken Loach called for 30 Labour MPs who attended a demonstration outside Parliament against Labour anti-Semitism to be de-selected. At the same event, he recommended to the audience a series of programmes on Al-jazeera TV titled *The Lobby*: 'It explains the role of the Israeli government in infiltrating and undermining the Labour left.' He followed this up by posting online the prediction that 'it will get worse because if the Labour Party gets into power and if they stick with their manifesto and go even further you will have the full range of international capital [sic] against us.' In other words, the Israeli government is undermining Labour by supporting the campaign against anti-Semitism on behalf of 'international capital', or what the Nazis called 'international Jewish finance'. This excursion into classic Jewish conspiracy theory evidently proved an embarrassment to a Corbyn leadership already deeply mired in the party's anti-Semitic scandal, because Loach's services as producer of Labour's TV local election broadcasts were promptly dispensed with. So why not offer them to Al-jazeera or better still, Hamas TV?

A survey of Labour Party anti-Semitism would not be complete without recognition of the pioneering contributions of that doyen of leftist Jew-baiters, Ken Livingstone, who after more than two years of suspension for making remarks concerning Hitler and Zionism that were considered to be anti-Semitic, resigned in May 2018. (The reader will recall that Livingstone does not regard anti-Semitism as racism.) The first was that Hitler 'supported Zionism' an assertion on a par in its mendacity with professional Holocaust denier David Irving's claim that Hitler was 'probably the biggest friend the Jews had in the Third Reich'. Another no less Holocaust revisionist, was that the SS 'set up training camps so that German Jews that were going to go [to Palestine] could be trained to cope with a very different sort of country when then got there.' As any *bona fide* historian of the Holocaust will tell Livingstone, the 'different sort of country' the SS dispatched the Jews to was not Palestine, then under the British Mandate, and therefore rendering such an operation impossible, but the six death camps in Poland: Treblinka, Sobibor, Belzec, Maidenek, Auschwitz and Chelmno. (Could it be that Livingstone is confusing his imaginary Jewish SS division with the all-too-real Muslim Handschar Division trained by the Waffen SS to hunt down and murder Jews and communist partisans in Yugoslavia?)

This was not the first time Livingstone has been suspended for anti-Semitism. When Leader of the Greater London Council, he was suspended from office for four weeks for likening a Jewish journalist to a Nazi concentration camp guard. The friendship and political collaboration of Livingstone and Corbyn goes back a long way, at least as far as 1982, when they jointly founded the forerunner of that proven stamping-ground for anti-Semites, the Palestinian Solidarity Campaign. Corbyn was first elected as a Labour MP the next year, while Livingstone had been Leader of the Greater London Council since 1981, with Corbyn's current Shadow Chancellor John McDonnell as his Deputy. While Corbyn moved in the orbit of what was to become the Stalinist British Communist Party, contributing frequently, as we have seen, to its daily paper, the *Morning Star*, Livingstone was co-editing the *Labour Herald*, a weekly journal that began publication in September 1981, printed by Astmoor Litho, the same printers that printed both the publications of the *soi-disant* Trotskyist Workers Revolutionary Party led by Gerry Healy and the English language version of the Gaddafi regime's weekly bulletin, *The Green March*. (Corbyn however shared Livingstone's admiration for the *Herald's* paymaster. Addressing a meeting called to protest at western involvement in the dictator's overthrow, his gushing praise for Gaddafi's 'achievements' was met by groans from what was an overwhelmingly far left audience.)

Those conversant with the history of communism might indeed find it odd that Corbyn, a fellow-traveller of the ultra-Stalinists, and Livingstone, not only an editor of a journal closely aligned with an avowedly Trotskyist party, but a prominently featured guest speaker at its public meetings and an interviewee in its daily paper, *News Line*, could collaborate so harmoniously for more than two decades. Even with their limited knowledge of history, they both must have been aware that Stalin not only had Trotsky assassinated in Mexico in August 1940 but ordered the murder of thousands of his followers in the Soviet Union in the terror purges of the 1930s. The key to solving this riddle is to be found in the issue that first brought them together...anti-Zionism. When the common enemy is the Jewish state, other issues that may divide must be put to one side. Here Livingstone, at least initially, led the way, by virtue of his intimate relationship with the WRP, beginning in 1981.

An internal WRP document acquired from a former member by the *Sunday Times* revealed that the party began to receive funding from Libya following a secret agreement between the WRP and Gaddafi, concluded in April 1976 in Tripoli by Corrine Redgrave and a representative of the Libyan regime. In addition to promoting Gaddafi's politics in its press, the WRP undertook to supply information to Libya's anti-Semitic dictator on the 'activities, names and positions held in finance, politics, business, the communications, media and elsewhere' of 'Zionists', the standard code word for Jews. The same document itemised WRP funding between the years 1977 and 1983 by no fewer than five Arab states and the PLO. The five states were Libya (£542,267) with smaller sums from Iraq, Kuwait, (invaded by Iraq in 1990) Qatar, and Abu Dhabi, in toto, around £813,000. These sums might not have been the whole picture. An Arab journalist was told by an employee of the Libyan news agency in London that the agency was in receipt annually of £1.5 million, part of which was then used to pay far above cost for printing work done by Astmoor Litho, the WRP's printers, thus providing in effect a hidden subsidy.

These publications included the Libyan embassy's *Green March*, an English language propaganda journal, and no fewer than 250,000 copies of an English edition of Gaddafi's *Green Book,* launched in 1980 in London by Vanessa Redgrave. The WRP 1981 manifesto's enthusiasm for the Libyan dictator's at best semi-coherent ramblings knew no bounds: 'The WRP salutes the courageous struggle of Colonel Gaddafi, whose Green Book has guided the struggle to introduce workers' control of factories, government offices and the diplomatic service, and in opposing the reactionary maneuverers of [Egypt's] Sadat, [Israel's] Begin and Washington.' Gadhafi's excursion into high theory found equal favour with another anti-Zionist organisation: 'This vital book cannot be obtained from any other book suppliers in Britain. Read the ideas which the Zionists and capitalists want to suppress. Only £3.00 p&p.' This puff appeared in the journal of the Neo-Nazi National Front, *NF News*, and it raised a number of intriguing questions. If the NF's claim to have a monopoly on sales of the *Green Book* in the UK was true, where did they get their supplies of the book from? Did there operate a novel division labour, with Healy's Gaddafi-subsidised printing press printing the book, and the National Front selling it?

The WRP's financial dependency on Gaddafi was immediately reflected in the party's almost daily reporting in its press of the Libyan dictator's sayings and deeds, and vituperative attacks not only on Israel but exposures of what were claimed to be the sinister Zionist manipulation of British political organisations. For example, an editorial in the *News Line* of December 8, 1980, claimed to have detected a 'deep Zionist influence' in the Anti-Nazi League, the proof being that its Secretary, Paul Holborow, had said that 'the main fight is now against anti-Semitism'. 'The sudden switch to anti-Semitic issues', claimed *News Line,* was to 'facilitate the participation of another pro-Zionist Mr Anthony Wedgwood Benn, whose attempts to groom himself for the Labour leadership have become positively offensive'. This is now what is known in the same trade as 'weaponising anti-Semitism'. Having unearthed yet another Zionist conspiracy, this being a hijacking of the Labour Party, the Editorial then offered its own version of a now-fashionable left-wing Holocaust revisionism, the purpose of which was to deny its uniquely anti-Jewish nature and genocidal objective, and to down play the need to combat anti-Semitism: 'No one will forget that the gas chambers of the Third Reich did not discriminate. They were used to exterminate Jews, Christians, gypsies, Russians, Poles, Czechs, socialists and communists.' No-one can forget it, for the simple reason, as I have said before in relation to three other identical leftist subterfuges, it did not happen. This statement is blatantly false and whoever wrote it, unless they were as ignorant of the history of the Holocaust as Livingstone, must have known it. The gas chambers *did* discriminate, on the grounds of race. Of this list, only Jews and Gypsies were gassed, though unlike the Jews, the Nazis had no plans to exterminate all the Gypsies. Those deemed to be of 'pure gypsy blood', whom the Nazis believed were 'Aryan' in origin, were exempted. Of Europe's roughly one million gypsies, some 220,000 are believed to have died at the hands of the Nazis during the war compared with six million of Europe's ten million Jews.

Corbyn has deployed exactly this particular version of Holocaust revisionism as part of his campaign to de-Judaize Holocaust Memorial Day, to this end, sponsoring a motion in the House of Commons proposed by fellow anti-Zionist zealot John McDonnell on January 27, 2011, to change its name to 'Genocide Memorial Day' on the same specious grounds that 'Nazis targeted not only Jewish people.' but the 'disabled', 'working class activists and trade unionists', 'Roma, Jehovahs Witnesses, lesbian, gay and bisexual people and others they considered undesirable.' How historically and semantically illiterate can you get? To repeat, save for Roma, none of these categories is a race, and therefore, could not have been a victim of 'genocide', which means the killing, or the attempt to kill, an entire race. Neither were they, unlike the Jews, targeted for total extermination, and that includes the 'disabled', because the aborted Nazi euthanasia programme put to death not all the 'disabled', for example victims of accidents and war injuries, but only those specifically deemed genetically unfit to procreate or live a useful life. But what do such piffling details matter when the objective of the exercise is to deJudaify the Holocaust?

Public Health expert Professor John Ashton of the University of Bristol, who featured in TV reports on the Coronavirus epidemic, in addition to tweeting the standard repertoire of Corbynista anti-Zionist slanders...that it was 'sickening to see Zionists behaving like Nazis' and 'is Israel now satisfied about how many children it has murdered'...has also engaged in the now-obligatory leftist version of Holocaust revisionism, tweeting on 2017 Holocaust Remembrance Day that 'it would be helpful [sic...to whom exactly?] if everybody remembered that the Holocaust was about Gays, Gypsies and the disabled as well as the Jews.' In another tweet, in addition to gays and the disabled, Ashton introduced a new category of imaginary victims of the Holocaust... 'those with learning difficulties'...clear evidence that when it comes to history and not epidemics, Professor Ashton also suffers from a similar deficiency.

By the time Livingstone had been attracted into the magnetic field of the WRP, and this would have been no later than 1981, the party was operating as little more than a propaganda vehicle for not only Gaddafi, but Saddam Hussein and the PLO, while pumping out daily doses of venom against Israel and its supporters in the British labour movement. With Livingstone as one of its three editors, this role was now also taken on by the *Labour Herald*, like the WRP's *News Line*, printed by Astmoor Litho and sold at well below cost price. Livingstone was obviously in his element, the viciousness of the journal's tone exceeding even that of what was in effect its parent publication, the WRP's *News Line*, with one issue of June 25, 1982 featuring a cartoon of a huge and hook-nosed Israel Prime Menachem Begin in a Nazi uniform, standing on a heap of corpses oozing with blood and giving a Nazi salute, with the caption, *The Final Solution*; and another, a favourable review of a book which claimed Zionists collaborated with the Nazis in the Holocaust.

In letters to *Tribune*, the socialist weekly, of October 22, 1982 both Livingstone for the *Labour Herald* and Alex Mitchell of *News Line* naturally and lyingly denied the allegation made in a letter the previous week that their respective publications were in any way connected with, or dependent on the Libyan regime. 'We completely reject these insinuations' said Livingstone. True to form, Mitchell sniffed out the nature of the conspiracy at work:

> The Zionists were comprehensively thrashed at the TUC in Brighton and the Labour Party conference in Blackpool. It ended their *35-year grip* on the Middle East policies of the Labour and trade union movement. For the first time, the leadership of the Palestinian Liberation Organisation and the national rights of the Palestinian people were unequivocally recognised. Is it any wonder that a policy of retaliation should be put in motion and that the Workers Revolutionary Party and its daily newspaper, the *News Line*, are prime targets?... The Zionists work on the "big lie" theory that if you tell the 'Libyan gold' story often enough, then some people are bound to believe it. (emphasis added)

As the WRP internal documents proved, it was Mitchell and Livingstone who were doing the lying, big time. A year on, the *Daily Express* of December 21 carried an amusing and revealing item by 'William Hickey'. Livingstone had been spotted in the exclusive five-star West End restaurant *L'Ecu De France* dining with two officials from the Libyan embassy. In reply to enquiries at County Hall, Hickey was told the two Libyans 'wanted to talk to Ken about a programme they want to do for Libya. It's supposed to be [sic] about left-wing politics in Britain. They wanted him to advise on the planning of it as well as taking part.' There are reasonable grounds for suspecting that this too was another 'big lie' or as his one time-mentor Healy used to say, a 'class truth'.

While Leader of the GLC, Livingstone made a number of public comments about the Jews which attracted considerable criticism, the gist of some being that British Jews were going fascist. Following the 1981 election victory in Israel of Menachem Begin's rightist Likud, British Jews 'suddenly became reactionary, turned right, nearly to fascists.' In London and elsewhere, 'extremist Jews' were organising 'para-military groups, which resemble fascist organisations' - though presumably not, as in Nazi Germany, under SS supervision. As for the Holocaust, while careful not to deny it happened, Livingstone insisted there were far worse crimes than those committed by the Nazis, another claim that has recently gained currency on the left, in many cases motivated by a concern not to provide ammunition to justify the creation of the state of Israel. 'Every year [sic] the international finance system kills more people than World War Two. But at least Hitler was mad.' Yet again, Livingstone was talking nonsense, and even he must have known it. Something in the region of 70 million people were killed in World War Two, more than 80% by the Nazis and their allies. As for Livingstone's claim that Hitler was mad (which he repeated in the remarks that led to his suspension) the implication is that his unbalanced state of mind exonerated him from any legal or moral responsibility for the Holocaust. Hitler was not 'mad'. He was an anti-Semite...like Livingstone, who is also not mad and who, again like Hitler, subscribes to the belief that Jews conspire to gain political power. Back in 1982, in his *Labour Herald*, Livingstone made a scarcely veiled allusion to the existence of an undue Jewish influence in the Labour Party: 'There is a distortion [sic!] running right the way through British politics...a majority of Jews in this country supported the Labour Party and elected a number of Labour MPs.' We can be sure that if Jews had been equally prominent in the Tory party, that too would have been seized on as even stronger proof of the same conspiracy.

Faced with the prospect of unemployment when the Thatcher government announced its intention to close down the GLC, Livingstone made a bid to become selected as a candidate in the safe but not vacant Labour seat of Brent East, whose current occupant was the Jewish Reginald Freeson. Freeson was also a prominent supporter of Israel, and Chairman of Poale Zion, a Jewish socialist group affiliated to the Labour Party, now called the Jewish Labour Movement, which, at this very time, Livingstone, together with Corbyn, was campaigning to have expelled from the Labour Party. Freeson was on the Labour left, having opposed the US military involvement in Vietnam, marched with CND against British possession of nuclear weapons, and supported a united Ireland. Impeccable socialist credentials, one might have thought. However, things were not so simple, because Freeson was also a Jew and a Zionist. Only Livingstone knows for certain what his motives were in choosing this particular seat to launch his Parliamentary career. But one is entitled to guess.

The constituency had a large first and second-generation Irish population, many of whom were possibly influenced in their attitude towards the Jews by their church's historical antipathy towards those its good book and up to 1959, its Good Friday liturgy ('the perfidious Jews') say betrayed the (no less Jewish) son of God. How much this favoured Livingstone's bid for the seat it is impossible to say, but certainly, a remark made by Livingstone on Irish radio on August 6, 1983 would have done him no harm in what was to become his battleground with Freeson for the Brent East seat in 1985. In the interview, Livingstone presented his own version of Holocaust revisionism, like the WRP's in that it minimised the uniqueness and scale of the Nazi genocide of the Jews, and similar to Corbyn's insistence that any refence to the Holocaust must always be accompanied by one 'in the same breath' to slavery: 'What Britain has done for [sic] the Irish nation is, although it is spread over 800 years, worse than what Hitler did to the Jews.' And remember, unlike the British, at least Hitler had the excuse that he was mad.

Comments like these were bound to, and maybe designed to produce a response from prominent Jews. Replying to the claim that British Jews were going fascist, in a letter to the *Jewish Chronicle,* Freeson said Livingstone should stop being 'his master's voice' to the WRP. After Livingstone ousted him from the Brent East seat in 1985, Freeson said his support, albeit at times critical, for Israel, had resulted in him being branded as 'that bloody Jew'. In his capacity as Chairman of Poale Zion, Freeson wrote to the Labour's Party's National Executive Committee to warn of the likely consequences of Livingstone's unrelenting attacks on Jews:

> This letter is by way of a friendly warning about a situation that I fear could deteriorate soon if the Party does not dissociate itself from the crude populism which Mr Livingston's anti-zionism and anti-Jewish remarks represent. It could permanently alienate the Jewish community collectively from the very Party to which so many members of our community have looked for support and their own political involvement.

Proof that the Brent East Constituency Labour Party had been de-Zionised' was forthcoming when in October 1985 the Chief Rabbi, Emmanuel Jakobovits, declined an invitation to attend a lunch at which Livingstone would be present. He was attacked in a letter to the *North West London Press* as 'rude, bigoted and narrow minded' by Livingstone acolyte Emma Tait, Chairperson of Brent East Labour Party. She in turn received a stinging response from Dr Jacob Gewirtz of the Board of Deputies of British Jews:

> As a close colleague of Mr Ken Livingstone, she is well aware of the reasons why no self-respecting Jewish personality would wish to appear on a public platform with the GLC leader. Mr Livingstone has hardly missed an opportunity to take a swipe at the Jewish community, referring to its leading members as 'near-fascists' and to Israel as 'a racist state not entitled to secure borders'… Instead of vilification by Ms Tait, the Chief Rabbi is deserving of the highest praise for his principled refusal to lunch with Mr Livingstone.

Elected MP for Brent East in the 1987 General Election Labour, Livingstone returned to big-time London politics in 2000 when, after narrowly losing the Labour Party nomination for mayor, he ran and won as an independent, resulting in his expulsion from the party. From his new vantage point, following 9/11, he became deeply involved in a number of anti-Zionist campaigns with Corbyn, along the way taking time out, as we have already seen, to raise the profile in the UK of the Hitler-admiring Muslim cleric Yusuf al-Qaradawi. Here are just two typical examples of the preacher's message so admired by Livingstone:

> Throughout history, Allah has imposed upon the Jews people who would punish them for their corruption…The last punishment was carried out by Hitler…He put them in their place. [sic] This was divine punishment for them. Allah willing, the next time [sic] will be at the hands of the believers. [i.e., Muslims]. (Al Jazeera TV, January 28, 2009)

and:

> Oh Allah, take the treacherous Jews. Oh Allah, take this profligate, cunning arrogant band of people. Oh Allah, they have spread much corruption and tyranny in the land. Pour your wrath upon them Oh our God. Lie in wait from them… Oh

Allah, take this oppressive Jewish, Zionist band of people. Oh Allah, do not spare a single one of them. Oh Allah, count their numbers, and kill them, down to the very last one. (Sermon on Al-Jazeera TV, January 9, 2009)

In the *Muslim News* of September 2010, that is, *after* his *protégé* had made these statements extolling Hitler and advocating the extermination of the Jews, Livingstone praised their author as 'one of the leading progressive voices in the Islamic world'. Following his election as Leader of the Labour Party in September 2015, Corbyn appointed his comrade of more than thirty years standing as his adviser on defence, or rather disarmament policy.

As a consequence of the upsurge of anti-Semitism in the Labour Party after the election of Jeremy Corbyn as its Leader in September 2015, on April 10, 2018, Avi Gabbay, Chairperson of the Israel Labour party, sent the following letter.

Dear Mr Corbyn: The Labour Party of Israel and the Labour Party of the UK have a long history of friendship We remember fondly the warm relations that Prime Ministers Wilson, Blair and Brown had with Israel's Labour Party and the State of Israel and the Jewish community in the UK, along with the ongoing visits and friendship with many Labour Party UK MPs and Labour Israel MPs. And yet, it is my responsibility to acknowledge the hostility you have shown to the Jewish community and the anti-Semitic statements and actions you have allowed as Leader of the Labour Party UK. This is in addition to your very public hatred of the polices of the government of the State of Israel, many of which regard the security of our citizens and the actions of our soldiers - policies where the coalition and the opposition in Israel are aligned. As Israel approaches Holocaust and Heroism Remembrance Day this week, we are reminded of the horrors of anti-Semitism in Europe and our commitment to combatting anti-Semitism in all forms and in all places. As such, I write to you to inform you of the temporary suspension of all formal relations between the Israel Labour Party and the Leader of the Labour Party UK. While there are many areas where our respective parties can and will cooperate, we cannot maintain relations with you, Leader of the Labour Party UK, while you fail to address adequately the anti-Semitism within Labour Party UK. I have informed all Labour Israel staff, Members of Knesset, and elected Leaders of the Labour Party Israel of the suspension of ties with your office. I have asked the International Secretary of the Labour Party Israel to update me quarterly on this situation, and should this suspension change, you will be updated accordingly.

On the same day, Jennifer Gerber, Director of (UK) Labour Friends of Israel, said:

We fully understand why the Israeli Labour Party has decided to suspend relations with Jeremy Corbyn. He has failed to respond to their repeated offers of dialogue, including offers to host him at Yad Vashem, Israel's National Holocaust Museum. LFI's relations with the Israeli Labour Party remains unaffected and we will continue our close cooperation.

Also on the same day, Joan Ryan MP, Chair of the Labour Friends of Israel sent Corbyn the following letter:

As you will be aware, the leader of the Israeli Labour Party, Avi Gabby, announced today that he is suspending relations with you due to your failure to deal with anti-Semitism in the Labour Party and your hostility to the state of Israel. I fully understand why Mr Gabby has taken this course of action and I am ashamed that one of sister parties has no option but to take this unprecedented step. [This is correct. Founded in 1889, never before in the entire history of the Socialist International, of which the UK and the Israeli Labour Party are fraternal members, has one of its parties felt obliged to break off all relations with the leader of another. Neither, prior to the election of Corbyn in 2015, had any of its party leaders in the International's entire history been accused by its own members of anti-Semitism.

Comparable in shame and context is the letter sent by the outlawed Social Democratic Party of Germany from its exile headquarters in Prague in April 1937 to a former Labour Leader who, like a future one, had been singing the praises of an anti-Semite as a man of peace, in this case, not one of Corbyn's Hezbollah and Hamas 'friends', but Adolf Hitler. Within weeks of coming to power on January 30, 1933, Hitler's regime had declared war on the German workers' movement, arresting and some cases murdering its leaders and activists, and banning its trade unions and political parties, the largest of which was the Social Democrats. Like Corbyn, Lansbury placed the cause of peace above all others, even at the price of seeking friendship with a regime that had murdered his socialist comrades. (Corbyn's services as a highly-paid broadcaster for a regime that has also murdered socialists and trade unionists also seems to have caused him no qualms of conscience.) The letter in question, like that of the Israeli Labour Party to Corbyn, pulled no punches, accusing Lansbury (again like Corbyn) of violating the traditions and obligations of international working-class solidarity, his actions being 'inconsistent with the decisions of the Socialist Labour International regarding the attitude of the socialists to Hitler Germany, and furthermore wound'[ing] the feelings of the German Socialist Democrats who are out to exterminate Hitler.' Like his useful idiot counterpart Corbyn in Iran, Tunisia, the West Bank and Syria, Lansbury had allowed himself to be beguiled as to host's benign intentions, after a Corbyn-style Potemkin visit of two days declaring on his return that 'German youth are being educated in the spirit of peace'…just as they are in Gaza by Hamas, if we were to believe Corbyn. The letter concluded by declaring that 'the leaders of the Social Democratic Party of Germany make a resolute protest against this private action of Lansbury's which is hostile to the German battle for freedom.' Considering Corbyn's no less demeaning fool's errands, who says history does not repeat itself? John Ryan's letter continues:]

As you know, in 2016, the leader of the [Israeli Knesset] Opposition, Isaac Herzog, invited you to visit Israel and offered to take you to Yad Vashem. I remain perplexed as to why you were happy to sit down with Hamas and Hezbollah but could not find the time to meet with those who are working to advance the cause of peace, reconciliation and a two-state solution. I would now urge you to consider why it is that Israeli Labour feels it cannot have a relationship with you. Leadership is about taking responsibility and it is yours to urgently heal this breach and take action to reassure our comrades in Israel.

And yet again on the same day, April 10, 2018, Holocaust-denying Nick Griffin (he once referred to it as the 'Holohoax') and former *Fuehrer* of the British National Party, announced that he would vote Labour if Corbyn opposed British military action against the regime of Syria's President Assad:

If he sticks to his guns then for the 1st time in my life I will vote Labour - right now nothing is more important to me than resisting the psychotic rush to #WW3 of Boris [Johnson] and the #neocons. Corbyn refuses to blame Assad for chemical attack in #Syria…

True to form, just as he did when he opposed the removal of a Saddam Hussein guilty of the same war crime, Chemical Corbyn did indeed 'stick to his guns'. Quite a day for Jeremy...Israeli Labour out, Nick Griffin in. Some would say, more than a fair swap. This was not the first occasion on which Griffin had aligned himself with the far left. He had previously claimed the western military interventions in Afghanistan and Iraq were 'illegal' and accused the British military of committing war crimes by participating in them. In June 2013, Griffin visited Syria at the invitation of President Assad's Ba'ath Party. He was there again in November 2014 as a guest of the Syrian Justice (sic) Ministry, following in the footsteps of Corbyn, who made the same pilgrimage in 2011, accompanied by Tory Peer Lord Sheikh and Baroness 'body parts' Tonge.

In October 2016, Corbyn wrote an account in the Communist Party's *Morning Star* of his Syria trip, funded to the tune of £1,300 by the Hamas-affiliated UK-based Palestine Return Centre. (By accepting President Assad's hospitality, Corbyn was evidently prepared to overlook the fact that unlike Israel, his Ba'athist host did not recognise the existence of a distinct Palestinian nation.) During that visit, from October 31 to November 2, 2011, Corbyn recalled, Assad had provided him with evidence that 'the Israeli tail wags the US dog', a notion revisited by the *New York Times* when on April 25, 2019, it published a cartoon worthy of the Nazi *Der Sturmer*, with Trump wearing opaque dark classes and Jewish skull cap being pulled along on a leash by a hooked-nosed dog with a star of David collar and the face of Netanyahu. (This is the world-famous journal which, despite its being protected by the First Amendment, along with the entire US media, lacked the courage shown by many of its European counterparts to reproduce as an act of solidarity the Danish cartoons that triggered riots across the Muslim world. What was the mind set of those who sanctioned the publishing of this filth, safe in the knowledge that unlike those of the Muslim rioters, the inevitable Jewish protests would be peaceful and dignified?)

As for Griffin, he must have felt very much at home in Damascus as the guest of a regime that elevates to its summits Jew-baiters such as Defence Minister Mustafa Tlass, author of *The Matzah of Zion*, a work which dredges up from the sewers the Islamo-Christian legend of the Jewish blood libel and gives them contemporary political twist with the assertion that 'the Jew can kill you and take your blood to make his Zionist [sic] bread.' So yes, Griffin we can understand...but what was Corbyn doing in the same company?

With relations suspended between Corbyn and the Israeli Labour Party, Shadow Foreign Secretary Emily Thornberry was a matter of days later dispatched to the West Bank, where she was among an audience that was addressed for three hours by Palestinian Authority President Mahmood Abbas. Abbas is the proud possessor of a Doctorate from Moscow University in Holocaust revisionism, titled, 'The Other Side: The Secret Relationship between Nazism and Zionism', a subject that would have all too familiar to Thornberry, as it was saying Hitler supported Zionism that had led to the suspension of Corbyn intimate Ken Livingstone. In the course of his address, Abbas gave the assembled delegates the benefit of his grasp of this highly demanding subject. The misfortunes of the Jews, he explained, were their own fault, brought on by their 'social behaviour, usury, charging interest and financial matters'. An old refrain sung by anti-Semites down the ages, as for example by the UK's most notorious Nazi, Sir Oswald Mosley: 'The Jew himself has created anti-Semitism - created as he has always done, by letting people see him and his methods. Even Hitler was not an anti-Semite before he saw a Jew.'

Thornberry's Facebook comment on the speech, far from condemning these outrageous slanders on the Jews, said that it had been a 'privilege' to represent her party at the Palestinian National Council. Only when challenged by journalists did she issue a subsequent statement deploring the PA President's 'anti-Semitic remarks'. One has to ask…what was an official delegate of the Labour Party doing at a gathering where the featured speaker hurled insults at the Jews that would not have been out of place at a Nuremberg Rally…or for that matter, on websites frequented by her Leader?

One could also ask the same question of Dianne Abbott, who similarly let her in this instance Maoist sympathies get the better of her when, in November 2020, she spoke at an event hosted by the pro-Chinese No Cold War group. Her address was preceded by that of Jing Jing Li, an employee of the state-controlled broadcaster CGTN, who accused foreign media of 'trying to create a racial conflict in China' by reporting human rights violations of Muslims in Xinjiang (formerly Sin-Kiang). Such reports, she said, were 'fabrications'. Abbott, who followed Jing Jing Li, began her talk by saying she was 'pleased' to be 'speaking at this important meeting'…just like Thornberry was to be present at Fatah's. And also like Thornberry, only when Abbott's involvement at an event whose prime purpose was to white-wash Peking's brutalisation of the Uyghur Muslims became public knowledge did she issue an apology. It is easy to see why Abbott raised no objections to the proceedings at the time. Her boss has always been highly selective when it comes to speaking up for Muslims. He will sign a declaration that lyingly accuses Israel of the genocide of the Palestinians, but remain silent when Palestinians are killed in their thousands by his Syrian hosts, and deny in Parliament that the Serbs committed similar atrocities against the Muslims of Bosnia and Kosovo. Nor has he, so far as I have been able to ascertain, issued any public denunciation of China's persecution of the Muslims of Xinjiang. Hence her master's voice silence when the opportunity and obligation arose to do so.

Perhaps the ultimate humiliation for Corbyn came in the House of Commons on April 17, 2018. Only once before had anti-Semitism been a matter formally brought before the House. This was on December 17, 1942, when MPs stood for one minute in silence in remembrance of the millions of Jews being murdered in Hitler's Holocaust. Now anti-Semitism was back, only with Corbyn in the firing line, not Hitler, in a formal three-hour debate on Labour Party Jew-baiting. Two years previously, Corbyn had been summoned to appear before the House of Commons Home Affairs Select Committee to answer charges that he had failed to combat anti-Semitism in his party following his election as its Leader in September 2015. Now the issue was back again at Westminster…with a vengeance. Even though he was its prime target, Corbyn chose to absent himself for most of the debate, and while present in the chamber, remained silent. The debate was opened by Sajid Javid, Secretary of State for Communities and Local Government:

> We cannot and must not ignore the particular [anti-Semitic] elements within the Labour Party, and nor can we ignore the fact that this particular concern is currently corelating with the Leader of the Opposition and the waves of activists that have come with him…Is there a culture that attracts them and is allowed to fester? Unfortunately, when it comes to the Leader of the Opposition, there are simply too

many of his apparently accidental [sic] associations to list. As the Board of Deputies of British Jews put it in a letter to the Leader of the Opposition, 'Rightly or wrongly, those who push this offensive material regard Jeremy Corbyn as their figurehead'. [At this point, an outraged Corbynista loyalist intervened, asking, 'is that allowed in the Chamber - such shameless personal abuse?'. The Deputy Speaker explained that the Secretary of State was quoting from a letter.]

When Andrew Gwynne, Javid's Shadow, replying on behalf of the opposition, made the ringing declaration that 'there is no place for anti-Semitism in the Labour Party', Tory MP Simon Hoare retorted that 'actions speak louder than words', and pointed out that 'Mr Livingstone remains a member of the hon. Gentleman's party'. Gwynne lamely replied that 'due process was going on' - one that had taken over two years, with Jew-baiter Livingstone still not expelled, and threatening legal action if he was. This laid-back attitude was too much for Labour's Ian Austin:

> Let me be clear about this. Ken Livingstone claimed that Hitler was a Zionist. That is anti-Semitism pure and simple. It happened more than two years ago, and there has been ample time to deal with it. It is a disgrace that it has not been dealt with. Kick him out immediately... My hon. Friend should stand at the dispatch box and tell the leader of the Labour Party that Livingstone must be booted out. Boot him out!

A Jewish Tory MP, Robert Halfon, went for the Corbynista jugular:

> I genuinely believe that the current Labour leadership is, at best, turning a blind eye to the problem and, at worst condoning anti-Semitism...I see the membership of dubious Facebook groups, the defence of anti-Semitic murals and the phoney reports produced by the now Baroness Chakrabarti and they indicate three unwise monkeys: see no anti-Semitism, hear no anti-Semitism, and do not speak out against anti-Semitism.

He then went off-piste by demanding his own government 'must go further in stamping out all extremist terror groups, including proscribing Hezbollah's political arm. People should not be allowed to march down Trafalgar Square and Whitehall waving Hezbollah flags.' He could have added, neither should the Leader of the Opposition be a featured speaker at such rallies, where banners and posters are displayed demanding the destruction of the state of Israel and likening it to Nazi Germany. Labour's Luciana Berger, who is also Jewish, spoke of anti-Semitic insults directed at herself from the Corbynista wing of her own party:

> It pains me to say this as the proud parliamentary chair of the Jewish Labour Movement that in 2018, anti-Semitism is now more commonplace, more conspicuous and more corrosive within the Labour Party. That is why I have no words for the people purporting to be both members and supporters of our party and using the hashtag JCforPM who have attacked me in recent weeks for my comments, for speaking at the rally against anti-Semitism, and for questioning the remarks of those endorsing the anti-Semitic mural...There are people who have accused me of having two masters. They have said that I am Tel Aviv's servant, and called me a paid-up Israeli operative...They have called me Judas, a Zionazi and an absolute parasite, and they have told me to get out of this country and go back to Israel...My party urgently needs to address this issue publicly and consistently, and

we need to expel from our ranks those people who hold these views, including Ken Livingstone.

Berger was followed by another Jewish MP, Tory Andrew Percy. He related how in a recent visit to the Jewish community in Brussels, he saw 'people living in genuine fear not just behind security guards in their schools, but behind 10-foot or 15-foot gates with military personnel and tanks [!!!] outside.' Blunt-speaking Percy evidently has no time for the Corbyn/Clinton/Cameron/Blair/Papal 'nothing to do with Islam': 'A recent study undertaken by the Institute for Jewish Policy Research found that certain communities in this country, particularly the Muslim communities, are twice as likely to hold deeply anti-Semitic views'. As for Labour Party anti-Semitism, the topic under debate, he noted that Corbynista Andrew Gwynne's contribution had focused on anti-Semitism that came from the far right. 'What I did not hear him talk about quite so much, however, are the Labour members who have been defended by some of the people sitting beside him [on Labour's front Bench]. One Labour member, who said that the Jews were responsible for the slave trade [Momentum activist Jackie Walker, then suspended, for the second time, on charges of anti-Semitism] was defended by a [Corbynista] Member who sits behind him'. Percy was now getting into his stride, homing in on the main target:

> What I saw throughout this debate was the Leader of the Opposition chuntering repeatedly when anyone stood up and tried to hold him to account for some of the things that people have said and done in his name., This a leader of the Labour Party who found himself not in one, but in four or five racist anti-Semitic Facebook groups by accident. He did not look at the material. He did not read the material. He did not know the material was there. He did not understand the material. He looked at the mural and made a comment on the mural, but he did not know about it. How are we supposed to believe any of this?

At this point, another Tory MP, Alec Shelbrooke, recalled that while campaigning at the 2016 General Election, after shaking Percy's hand, a Labour Party member had said, 'I now have to go and wash my hands'. Percy then continued]:

> I am sorry the Leader of the Opposition has left his place., because he needs to be held to account. The question I would like to ask him is why he has still not taken the opportunity to respond to the invite from the Labour Party in Israel to visit Israel and to visit Yad Vashem [the Holocaust Museum] ... Labour member after Labour member has made all sorts of disgusting comments about Jews...Laura Stuart felt the need to post a picture on Facebook of a photograph from the Holocaust Educational Trust that had been changed to include the words 'Zionist fairy tales' and 'Fat Zionist conference'. A Labour Party member did this. There are countless other examples. I have to say to the leadership of the Labour Party: this is in your name by people who are being motivated by the actions of the Labour Leader. [Here the Deputy Speaker asked Percy to moderate his tone, to which he replied]: How can one possibly be moderate in one's language when we are dealing with a leader of a political party in this country who has stood up and described people who want to wipe Jews off the planet as his friends?...I have spent several years campaigning in politics. The last general election was the first time anybody stood up and told me I was Israeli scum and did so having named the Leader of the Opposition as a

motivation for saying it.

Next up was Labour's John Mann, for thirteen years the outspoken Chair of the all-party group against anti-Semitism, who for this very reason, had been singled out by Corbynistas for special treatment:

> When I took this voluntary cross-party role, I did not expect today, when Labour members [of Parliament] stand in solidarity with our Jewish colleagues and with the Jewish community, to be targeted by an organisation called Momentum, which has happened to all of us which stood in solidarity. But worse than that, explicitly targeting Jewish members of the Parliamentary Labour Party because they are Jewish. That is what is going on at the moment. I did not expect, when I took on this cross-party role, my wife to be sent, by a Labour Marxist anti-Semite, a dead bird through the post. I did not expect my son, after an Islamist death threat, to open the door to the bomb squad. I did not expect my wife, in the last few weeks, from a leftist anti-Semite in response to the demonstration, to be threatened with rape...We identified 13 years ago the three forms of anti-Semitism: Islamist anti-Semitism, traditional right anti-Semitism, and the anti-Semitism of the new left...Those who say it is a smear in raising this issue need to publicly apologise...Where this stuff ends is what happened in Copenhagen, is what happened in Brussels, it's what happened in France repeatedly...people murdered because they are Jewish, that's where this ends...it's constant, explicit anti-Semitism. And then the bigger group, the excusers of anti-Semitism, who say it is something to do with challenging the Leader of the Labour Party. No, it isn't. What Jewish people say to me now is different to what they said thirteen years ago. I'm stopped in the street by Jewish people who say to me very discreetly, 'I am scared'...People - young Jewish members - are scared to go to Labour Party meetings with me, because they are fearful they will be intimidated and threatened and that their identity will be challenged...Any Jewish person, as the vast majority do, has the right to say, 'I am a Zionist', and I have no right to deny him that right, and those that do are racists. And just that change in language, by making the word Zionist as a pejorative insult by the Labour Party, just that change, would alter the dialogue in this country in a very big way.

The other highlight of the session, one which exposed the vile, concerted Jew-baiting by Corbynistas, was Labour's Ruth Smeeth reading out milder examples of emails sent to her that she described as 'the poison of anti-Semitism that is engulfing parts of my own party and wider political discourse']:

> Hang yourself you vile treacherous Zionist Tory filth. You are a cancer of humanity. Smeeth is a Zionist; she has no shame and trades on the murder of Jews by Hitler whom the Zionists betrayed.
> Ruth Smeeth must surely be travelling 1st class to Tel Aviv with all that slush. After all, she's complicit in trying to bring Corbyn down.
> First job for Jeremy Corbyn tomorrow: expel the Zionist BICOM smear hag bitch Ruth Smeeth from the Party.
> This Ruth Smeeth bitch is Britainophobic, we need to cleanse our nation of these types.
> #JC4PM Deselect Ruth Smeeth ASAP. Poke the pig – get all Zionist child killer scum out of Labour.
> You are a spy! You are evil, satanic! Leave! #Labour #Corbyn.
> Ruth you are a Zionist plant. I am ashamed you in Labour. Better suited to the murderous Knesset! #I Support Ken.

Your fellow traitor Tony Blair abolished hanging for treason. Your kind need to leave before we bring it back. #Smeeth Is Filth.
The gallows would be fine and fitting place for this dyke piece of Yid shit to swing from.

Two that she did not read out were: 'Yid cunt' and 'Fucking traitor.' As the mantra has it, a kinder politics...As if on cue, Labour's Stephen Doughty then rose to inform the House that he had 'just seen a tweet from someone claiming to be a member of Momentum suggesting that those of us who have spoken out about anti-Semitism have taken a bounty of £1 million from Israel to undermine the leader of the Labour Party.' Tory MP Simon Clarke returned to Corbyn's role in furthering the rise of Labour anti-Semitism:

> The leadership of the Labour Party has been captured by a man who, more than any other, embodies the selective blindness of his political beliefs in regard to anti-Semitism. It is worth noticing that, after defending the despicable mural in Tower Hamlets, the Leader of the Opposition condemned himself in his own excuses. He said, I didn't notice the anti-Semitism. I believe him, for failing to notice blatant anti-Semitism is precisely the problem. Perhaps he has become immune. The problem is that he sets the tone...The former Member for Sunderland South, Chris Mullin, tweeted on 26 March: 'Sorry to see Jewish leaders ganging up on Corbyn...' [Clarke put the question to Corbyn]: Will he now utterly disassociate himself from Hamas and Hezbollah? Is he proud that Salim Mulla, who said that Israel was responsible for the Sandy Hook massacre and ISIS, is still representing his party as a councillor in Blackburn?

But answer came there none, because Corbyn was not in the Chamber to answer it. Ian Austin, Labour, related an embarrassing encounter with a Holocaust survivor he had recently met in Poland:

> The first words he said to me when he learned I was a Labour MP were: 'Are you not ashamed to be in the Labour Party, with all the anti-Semitism?' [Austin admitted that he was indeed 'deeply ashamed'.] We have witnessed appalling anti-Semitic claims. We have seen Labour candidates denying the Holocaust. At last year's conference, one speaker said, 'The Holocaust, yes or no?' What does he mean by 'yes or no'? Was it right? Did it happen? [Austin then broke off to comment with biting irony that he was] pleased that the leader of the Labour Party has returned, because the current crisis was triggered by the shocking discovery that he had defended a grotesque racist caricature. For three days he issued excuses. Only on the fourth day, with that unprecedented protest planned, did he manage to say sorry. Labour Party members, all of us, have to ask ourselves what we would be saying - what he would be saying - if a senior member of the Conservative Party had defended a racist caricature of anybody else. I am afraid - I want to say this very directly to him - that he spent decades defending these people. Hamas's charter is avowedly anti-Semitic, Hezbollah too, yet our leader describes them as 'friends' and invites them to Parliament. Raed Salah, found guilty in court of the blood libel, was described as a 'very honoured citizen' and invited here too. Stephen Sizer, a Church of England vicar, was disciplined by his own church when he spread ideas that were 'clearly anti-Semitic', yet our leader defended him and claimed he was 'under attack' by a pro-Israeli smear campaign.

In answer to these charges, Corbyn said not a word. He did not need to, because he knew that while most Labour MPs were revolted by his pandering to anti-Semitism, those whose opinions counted in the Labour Party, and a sufficient number of its rank and file activists, believed that their Dear Leader had been the victim of a Zionist plot.

Rounding off this easily the most sordid episode in the entire history of the Labour Party came the adoption on July 17, 2018 by the Labour Party National Executive Committee, of its new definition of anti-Semitism, one that was supposedly intended to create a 'more thorough and detailed code for members which can actually be put into practice' to combat anti-Semitism. To their credit, and at last showing some moral backbone, the previous day, Labour MPs, with only four votes against, supported a resolution rejecting the Corbyn code. By deleting four classic examples of anti-Semitism that did the rounds in the Corbynista wing of the party from the almost universally recognised definition of anti-Semitism advanced by the Intentional Holocaust Remembrance Alliance, the NEC had given official approval to some of the very views that triggered the Labour Party anti-Semitic scandal in the first place. Under the proposed new, Corbynista, code it would *not* be anti-Semitic to:
Accuse British Jews of being more loyal to Israel than the UK;
Describe the policies of Israel as racist and comparable to those of Nazi Germany;
Argue that Israel should not exist;
Hold Israel to standards of conduct not demanded of any other country.

Let me anticipate what I hope will be the incredulous reactions of the reader: Accusing Jews of treason or Israel of being a Nazi state are *not* examples of anti-Semitism, but of opinions that are perfectly compatible with membership of a thoroughly Corbynised and de-Zionised Labour Party. Corbyn loyalists objected to the four examples on the grounds that including them would stifle 'legitimate criticism of Israel'. It is as if for them the prime task of the Labour Party is combatting Zionism, even at the risk of splitting the party, thereby possibly facilitating its exclusion from government for the next decade or more, as the Social Democratic split did in the Thatcher years. (I wrote this some months before a split did occur on February 18, 2019) Furthermore, in order to prove that a statement vilifying Israel is anti-Semitic, it would be necessary to have 'evidence of anti-Semitic intent.'. Unless the person making the statement, admitted that it was deliberately intended to be anti-Semitic (and none had done), how did one prove such intent? It is as if the party's definition of anti-Semitism had been tailored to accommodate the fanatical anti-Zionism of the Corbynistas and the anti-Semitism of many of Labour's increasing number of Muslim members. This included Corbyn himself with regard to all four excluded examples.
Not only this. With his reference on Press TV to the 'hand of Israel', Corbyn has dabbled in Jewish conspiracy theory, which contravened even his own faction's proposed code He has also implied that the same 'hand' is at work on the domestic UK scene. In 2013, during a speech made to the Palestine Return Centre, he demanded, without giving any proof that they were not, that schools 'should start teaching a lot of people [sic] the history of the Middle East in a more accurate and balanced way'. Corbyn then outlined his 'accurate' and 'balanced'

version of the history of the Middle East, in which the policies of Israel were likened to those of Nazis Germany: 'The West Bank is under occupation of the very sort [sic] that is recognisable by many people in Europe who suffered occupation during the Second World War'. Interviewed by Iran's Press TV in 2012 on the subject of what he believed was BBC bias towards Israel, an accusation repeated *ad nauseum* by anti-Semites on pro-Palestinian and Corbynista websites, Corbyn said:

> There seems to be [so again, he has no proof] a great deal of pressure on the BBC from the Israeli government and the Israeli embassy and they are very assertive toward all [sic] journalists and the BBC itself. They challenge every single thing [sic] on the reporting all the time [sic]. I think there is a bias towards saying that Israel is a democracy in the Middle East, *that Israel has a right to exist, that Israel has its security concerns.* [Emphasis added]

The previous year, Corbyn had claimed in the *Morning Star* that Israel exerted 'unbelievably [sic] high levels of influence' over 'upper echelons of parts of the media'... more conspiracy theory, in contravention of his own party's already watered-down definition of anti-Semitism. Here we have the key to understanding why throughout his political career, Corbyn has aligned himself with movements that were or still are opposed to the existence of a Jewish state in the Middle East. Shortly before being first elected as Labour MP for Islington North in 1983, Corbyn became one of the founders, and a sponsor, of the Labour Movement Campaign for Palestine, the predecessor to the current movement also founded and patronised by Corbyn, the Palestine Solidarity Campaign. The central demand of the LMCP was the replacement of Israel by a secular state of Palestine with equal rights for all its Jewish and Arab citizens, one that by including the West Bank and the Gaza Strip, would have a Palestinian majority, with consequences for its Jewish minority that need no elucidation here. This was also the stated policy of the PLO until its acceptance of the Oslo Accords of 1993, which embraced the goal of the so-called 'two-state solution' rejected by Corbyn and his fellow anti-Zionists. In its 'mission statement,', the LMCP pledged itself to 'eradicate Zionism' within the Labour party and the broader labour movement; that is to say, 'eradicate' support, no matter how critical of its polices and actions, for the existence of Israel.

Shortly joined by Livingstone, Corbyn became a high profile and active member of the LCMP through the 1980s, speaking at and chairing its meetings. Even at this early stage in his career as an MP, it was evident that opposing Zionism was not only for him one his most pressing concerns. He believed it should also be for every Labour Party member: 'The Labour Movement Campaign is the only campaign rooted in the Labour Movement whose platform really tackles the important issues in relation to this question. Its activities ought to be supported by every [sic] Labour Party member'- including, presumably, its Jewish ones, nearly all of whom would have counted themselves as supporters of the state of Israel. In this already obsessional fight against Zionism, Corbyn's initial allegiance was to the PLO, with its goal of a secular Palestine 'from the river to the sea'. With the PLO's and Fatah's acceptance of a 'two state solution' in 1993, followed by the rise of a Jihadi, theocratic terrorist Islam that repudiated it, Corbyn turned his back on the PLO and found new allies in Hamas and

Hezbollah, with their goal of a Palestine founded on the ruins of Israel and the corpses of its Jewish population. First Fatah and the PLO, then Hamas and Hezbollah.... Why the switch of allegiance by Corbyn? Because in each case, the shared objective was unchanging...the elimination of the 'Zionist entity', which the PLO, at least on paper, had repudiated in 1993. The only substantial distinction to be made between Corbyn and the anti-Zionist movements he has associated with over the years are not their objectives, but their division of labour. For Corbyn it has been a matter of meetings, conferences and speeches, while his Jihadi partners get on with the other end of the business...killing Jews.

If the elimination of Israel is not his goal, why then does Corbyn imply the BBC should be constantly emphasising, when covering Middle Eastern events, that Israel is *not* a democratic country, has *no* right to exist, and has *no* security concerns? As in the case of the teaching of Middle Eastern history in British schools, because the BBC does not do what Corbyn wants, this for him is conclusive proof, as it is for many Jewish conspiracy theorists who frequent Corbynista websites, of the BBC's pro-Zionist bias, a claim that is impossible to sustain in the light of the occasions, some of them cited in this work, were the BBC has revealed itself as being hostile not only to Zionism, but to Jews as such. Corbyn perhaps forgets that the BBC has a different remit from the channel on which he made his accusation, one which obliges it to be neutral and objective in its news reporting. There can be only one possible construction to put on these remarks. Israel *is* conspiring in various ways to subvert British institutions, is *not* a democracy (though it is indisputably in the Middle East), has *no* right to exist, and despite its being the target of attacks by Corbyn's terrorist 'friends' that have killed more than a thousand Jewish civilians and three attempts by Arab armies to 'wipe it off the map', Israel has *no* legitimate security concerns, and is to boot carrying out Nazi policies. Remarks such as these reveal Corbyn as someone who believes that when things are not as he would like, it is because a 'hand' is at work, whether it is directed against the Palestinians, staging 'false flag' terrorist attacks in the Middle East, controlling the BBC and schools, or undermining his leadership of the Labour Party. I invite the reader to surmise whose hand that might be.

Just how deeply runs anti-Semitism in the Corbynista wing of the Labour Party was confirmed by two on-line outbursts in August 2018. When Party Chairman Tom Watson, hitherto mute on the issue, demanded that Corbyn support the adoption of the international definition of anti-Semitism, George McManus, Chairman of the Labour Party's National Policy Forum, tweeted that 'Watson received £50,000+ from Jewish donors. At least Judas only got 30 pieces of silver.' Days previously, after making yet another *pro-forma* commitment to combat anti-Semitism in his party, there appeared on Corbyn's website the following postings, none of which was deleted:

'This is such a distraction issue. Where exactly is the anti-Semitism in the UK? This is all about the Friends of Israel being the biggest lobby group in Parliament.'

'Notice how and when this started. When the polls started putting Labour ahead of the Conservatives. I support you JC.'

'Perhaps the issue should be the murderous brutality and active Apartheid of the Israeli Zionists. Worse than the Nazis.'

'But Jeremy Corbyn these Jewish people are very violent people. They are the 21st century terrorists.'

'Why is it that Jews are so established in this country of ours. They control the media and have a powerful influence on the political stage now that should be looked into ASAP.'

'Giving way to a cabal [again!] of Zionists, Tories and right-wing Labour MPs and letting them set the agenda is a serious mistake.'

Still the skeletons continued to float to the surface of the latrine. On August 23, 2018 the *Daily Mail* released a video of Corbyn addressing in 2013 a London conference sponsored by the Qassem Brigades, the military wing of Hamas, the clerical Nazi movement dedicated to the destruction of the state of Israel and the extermination of the world's Jews. Another speaker was the Reverend Stephen Sizer, whom Corbyn had defended when suspended by his bishop for claiming that 9/11 was the work of the Jews. In the course of making a number of derogatory remarks about a particular group of Zionists, Corbyn said the following: 'One is, they don't want to study history, and secondly, they don't understand English irony either, having lived in this country for a very long time, probably all their lives, they don't understand English irony either [sic]. I think they need two lessons we [sic!!!] can help them with.' Had these remarks been made about British Muslims, Corbyn would have been the first to condemn them as racial stereotyping. But since they were made about British Jews at a gathering promoted by a movement that seeks their extermination, it is reasonable to assume that no-one objected.

Less than two weeks later, it became clear that Hamas was not alone in its genocidal designs on the Jews. On September 4, the day that the Labour Party National Executive Committee met to either adopt or amend the party's proposed definition of anti-Semitism, the media reported that the Metropolitan Police had received from the London radio station LBC a leaked dossier of more than 80 pages on 45 cases of anti-Semitic conduct by Labour Party members currently being investigated by the party's disciplinary disputes panel. Of these, at least 17 were considered serious enough to be investigated as race-hate crimes. One party member called the Jews 'devils', adding, 'We shall be rid of the Jews who are a cancer on us all', and suggesting that the Red Sea would be an 'ideal destination' for them. 'No need for gas chambers anyway as gas is so expensive and we need it in England.' Another posting by a Labour MP no less called for a woman Jewish Labour MP to 'get a good kicking'. A third member posted, 'One cannot understand the state of the world without understanding Jewish power, and one cannot understand the nature of Jewish power until one understands the nature of Jewish thinking'.

These are the thoughts and words of Nazis, and judging by their tone, they would, if given the opportunity, act upon them. Yet they are those of paid-up members of the *Labour Party*, one of them an MP. The body supposedly investigating these cases, the party's Disputes Panel, was headed by Corbyn's appointee, Claudia Webbe, despite (or could it because of?) her previous public defence of Ken Livingstone against well-founded charges of anti-Semitism. Incredibly, she retained this strategic position even after tweeting on August 13, 2018, that the 'combined machinery of state, political and mainstream elite' had 'join[ed] together' to 'make false allegations and pretended [sic] claims' of anti-Semitism. A mole with a conscience ensured that the file, which included

274

evidence of death threats against Jewish Labour MPs, evidence which had been withheld by Claudia Webbe, ended up in the hands of the one branch of the 'combined machinery of state' empowered by law to act on what it contained. On November 2, the Metropolitan Police announced that (contrary to Webbe's claim) the file contained evidence that criminal offences had been committed, and that it had begun legal proceedings against those Labour Party members deemed responsible. A kinder politics.

On September 13, 2018, for the third time in two years, Parliament addressed itself to the virus of anti-Semitism in the Labour party. The occasion was a 90-minute debate in the House of Lords. Following the example of her Leader, absent from the proceedings was Baroness Chakrabarti, Corbyn's appointment to the chamber as her reward for whitewashing Labour Party anti-Semitism. (Chakrabarti then leapfrogged over far more experienced and less malleable party colleagues into the post of shadow Attorney General, despite - or more likely because of - her previous endorsement of more than 2,000 false war crimes accusations cases corruptly pursued for financial gain against British servicemen in Iraq by solicitor Phil Shiner. After an investigation by the Solicitors Disciplinary Tribunal, in 2017, Shiner was struck off.) Extracts from some of the speeches follow.

Lord Popot (Con): Jews have long felt safe in this country. Regardless of what was happening elsewhere in the world, here in the UK - like us - they felt at home...So when my Jewish friends say they fear for their children's safety in schools, in synagogues and universities; when they are afraid of openly identifying as Jewish, and when they start to question their future in this country, the rest of us have a duty first to listen and then to ask: How has it come to this? Why has it come to this? Unlike the anti-Semitism of the past, which was rooted in religious and racial hatred of the Jews, modern anti-Semitism is expressed through the anti-Israel and anti-Zionist movements. How many times have we heard that the problem today is not with the Jews but with Zionists? Yet the connection between anti-Zionism and anti-Semitism is not always understood. Zionism is the proposition that the Jews have a right to their own state in their ancient homeland. Anti-Zionism advocates the opposite.

Present-day anti-Zionists also believe that the Jewish state is not only illegitimate but should be dismantled. They argue that they are simply standing up to colonial oppression and for human rights and that it has nothing to do with anti-Semitism. But would they also, on anti-colonial and humanitarian grounds, question the legitimacy of the USA, Pakistan, Bangladesh, Australia and most modern states in the Middle East-countries created through colonial intervention? Would they question the legality of practically the whole of Europe, the borders of which were shaped, destroyed and redrawn through centuries of war? There are many Hindu, Christian and Muslim countries across the world, but just one Jewish state. Why is Israel–this tiny strip of land the size of Wales–singled out for criticism with so much intensity and loathing?... Look up Israel on social media and you will be shocked to see the level of hate directed against Jews There are phrases such as 'Zionists controlling the media, financial institutions and foreign policy'. It is not long before you find yourself in Holocaust denial or blood-libel territory...These age-old anti-Semitic tropes have found a new audience in both the far right and the far left of the political spectrum. Whether it comes from the left or the right, make no mistake: today the word 'Zionist' is code for Jews. Jews have long suspected it. Anti-Zionists have always known it. Recent events have exposed it.

Lord Mendelsohn (Lab): How did things get so far that recent polls have shown that nearly 40% of Jews in Britain feel so uncomfortable that they are thinking of leaving the country? Close to 90% are convinced that the leader of a main political party is an anti-Semite, as does a staggering 39% of the general public How is it that a part of the UK no longer feels that a party which has always stood up for justice, liberty and progress is the one to which they can entrust their lives and those of their children? They feel this so intensely that many are considering emigration?... In 1984, an anti-Zionist Jew, Steve Cohen, wrote a book calling out the far left for its anti-Semitism, called *That's Funny, You Don't Look Anti-Semitic*. I commend it to everyone It is as relevant today as it was then. Far too few of the non-Labour Party left were prepared to accept it then. But it illustrates a direct line the politics of which have entered the Labour Party en masse and are now causing this current crisis. That crisis has never been gripped since the start of Jeremy Corbyn's leadership and it has, over the summer, placed his position - his record, his views and his conduct - at the heart of it. It astounds me that it is a revelation no longer worthy of questioning that I too believe that the leader of my party, Jeremy Corbyn, has been a perpetrator of anti-Semitism.

Lord Sugar (Ex Labour, now Cross Bencher): The real question should be put to the leader of the Opposition. The Labour leader allowed the issue of alleged anti-Semitism in the Labour Party to ramble on for months. What kind of leader is he not to take his party by the scruff of the neck, making it see sense and kill the matter off once and for all? He should terminate the obsession of the hard left with Israel and Palestine [and focus instead] on far more pressing matters, such as Brexit and jobs [The trouble was, it was Corbyn's own obsession too] Labour eventually adopted the IHRA but, from what I hear, Mr Corbyn tried to add an 11th-hour rider [permitting members to call Israel a racist state] which resulted in hours of debate among his own people; people such as Peter Willsman who once accused Jewish 'Trump fanatics' of fabricating allegations of anti-Semitism. What a complete and utter clown; everyone knows that no Jew in the UK| in their right mind would be a Trump fanatic. Mr Corbyn allowed matters to rumble on because, frankly, he does not give two hoots about what Jews in the UK think. He simply does not care. Of some 250,000 Jews in the UK, let us say 220,000 may be eligible to vote. If it comes to an election, 220,000 votes are a drop in the ocean. We mean nothing to him.

Lord Pannick (Cross-Bencher): There have always been anti-Semites and I am afraid there always will be. But what is so alarming is that in this great country - a country that gave refuge to my great-grandparents when they were fleeing pogroms at the end of the 19th century - the leadership of one of our major political parties is incubating anti-Semitism. When the leader of the Labour Party calls representatives of Hamas his friends, despite the fact that their policy is to kill as many Jews - I emphasise Jews - as possible, when he applauds graffiti that shows the working man oppressed by Jewish bankers, when he expresses support for a vicar who suggests that Mossad was responsible for the 9/11 outrage, and when he contends that British citizens who are Zionists do not really understand this country, it is not surprising that his shameful conduct encourages the release into the political atmosphere of a poison that is polluting our civil society. No politician who tolerates, far less encourages, such a virus is fit for public office. [This was not a view shared by Robin Rowles, a Church of England lay preacher. On the website of the Friends of Jeremy Corbyn Facebook group, he claimed that the Jews would 'vote Corbyn out as leader so that they would lose the next elections (sic), which is what the Jews want']

On June 20, 2019, the Lords returned to the subject of anti-Semitism. For the third time, Corbyn was in the dock, under attack yet again not only from the Tories, but from his own party. And for the second time, nothing was heard from his specialist on the topic, Baroness Chakrabarti. Lord Harris (Labour), after acknowledging the rise of Jew-hatred across continental Europe, and barely concealing, because he made little or no attempt to do so, his contempt for Corbyn, then continued:

> However, I want to focus nearer to home, on this country; with a deep sense of shame, I want to talk about the party I have been a member of for almost 50 years. Labour has a proud history of combatting racism and discrimination, and of opposing fascism and anti-Semitism. It is therefore profoundly shocking for those of us brought up on that tradition to find our party now the subject of a formal investigation by the Equality and Human Rights Commission. This is nothing short of humiliating for those of us on these benches. It is causing dismay among party members outside this House, and is deeply alienating for those we might hope would vote for us, whether they are from the Jewish community or not. It undermines the Labour Party's whole ethos, the values of equality, decency and solidarity that brought so many of us here on these benches into the Labour Party in the first place. Over three months ago, I wrote as chair of the Labour Peers' group to Jeremy Corbyn, the leader of the party. That letter expressed our dismay - no, worse than that, our alarm - at the continuing failure to remove anti-Semites from our party. I have not had the courtesy of a reply. Last week, I met two women who had been verbally and physically harassed at a meeting of their local Labour Party because they were Jewish.
>
> I wish I could say this was an isolated instance but, alas it was not. [How times had changed from before Corbyn, when just one such 'isolated instance' would have been unthinkable.] The process of dealing with complaints of anti-Semitic behaviours within the party has been slow, tortuous and frequently inconclusive. Too often individuals are suspended [and as often as not, then quietly re-instated by Corbyn's vetting team] only when their cases receive external publicity. Action was taken against one member of the party's National Executive Committee only after a second anti-Semitic rant was recorded and publicised; he had been let off with a warning after the first one. Too often those who have complained about anti-Semitism have been dismissed as apologist for, or even in the pay of, the Israeli government or Mossad, or we are told that the cases are few and far between. Any anti-Semite in the Labour Party is one too many. The party's abject failure to deal effectively with anti-Semitism over the last three years cannot be ascribed to inadequate resourcing of the complaints and compliance function in the Labour Party head office, or blamed on an inadequate or outdated process. The failure is a political one; it is a failure of leadership. Those of your Lordships who have been responsible for major organisations know that that the tone, style and ethos of such organisations are set at the top. That is what leadership means. Leadership is not about hiding behind procedure by blaming more junior officials or allowing you acolytes to dismiss legitimate complaints to spite those who disagree with your political approach. We on these benches must take the task of cleansing our party of anti-Semitism and those who condone and foster it.

Lord Pickles (Conservative) witnessed leftist anti-semites in action at his party's annual conference in Manchester in 2017:

> A young man wearing a kippah was abused by a very well-dressed middle-class left-wing crowd the Y[id] word, the c[unt] word and the f[uck] word was used.

There were references to the smoking chimneys of Auschwitz. He was spat upon and to their eternal shame, the police stood by and did nothing,

Corbyn had two defenders, but their apologias were of such a nature that he could have best done without them. The debate, officially listed on Hansard as one about anti-Semitism, was for them simply one more opportunity to put the boot into Israel. First Lord Campbell-Savours, who sought to attribute the rise of anti-Semitism to the policies of the Israeli government. He began by denying that his party was 'institutionally racist' and that while Labour did have what he called 'a problem' so did all the other parties. Having put his party's critics in their place, this zealous Corbynista homed in on the real villain of the piece - Israel:

> What is happening is that many in my party are deeply concerned and confused by Netanyahu's attitude to the settlements and calls for annexations. There is a particular problem in Labour-supporting ethnic minority communities [only one, actually, the Muslim] who join with Palestinians in feeling targeted as fellow Muslims, and a small minority of whom are clearly anti-Semitic. The treatment of the Palestinians is being used by racists across Europe to foster prejudice against Jews. It is all very frightening, *and Israel needs to reflect.* (Emphasis added)

What does he mean, '*and Israel needs to reflect*'? That the Jews of Israel have brought this hatred upon their fellow Jews in Europe? And who precisely are those supposedly 'targeting' UK Muslims? Certainly not his own party, unless we are talking about their votes, legally or otherwise, nor the various public agencies. including Labour Councils, that it is now acknowledged, either connived at or at best, ignored what one official report described as 'industrial scale' Muslim sexual 'targeting', grooming, trafficking and gang rape of non-Muslim under-age girls, nor the media, which while aware of the rape gangs scandal, decided to say nothing about it. Neither, finally, can he mean successive governments, Labour and Tory alike who, in the name of multi-culturalism and promoting 'diversity', have gone far beyond what is either reasonable or necessary in accommodating aspects of their religion and culture which are incompatible with the norms and even in some cases, as with FGM and Sharia courts, laws of British society. Since he associates this 'targeting' of Muslims with that supposedly inflicted on their co-religionists in Palestine, the only inference one can draw is that those 'targeting' British Muslims are British Jews. And so what was supposed to be a speech against anti-Semitism morphed seamlessly into an attack on Zionism and the Jews, and an apologia for the anti-Semitism of Muslims. As for his Dear Leader]:

> I do not believe that Corbyn is prejudiced. [What are we then to make of his allegations that Israel controls the BBC and US foreign policy, and influences the curricula of UK schools?] Caught in the headlamps of public outrage, he is agonising [poor Jeremy] over how to respond...People simply do not understand what Corbyn is all about. He is obsessed with human rights and sometimes he gets the nuances [!!!!] wrong.

We are asked to believe that the Leader of the Labour Party and of her Majesty's Opposition, the life-long campaigner against racism, with his two E grade A levels and an uncompleted course in 'trade union studies', cannot explain himself coherently in such a straightforward matter as anti-Semitism? It is akin to a feminist finding herself being repeatedly accused of defending rape or wife-beating. One would assume, surely, that as in all other intellectual endeavours, here too an obsession would be an aid to focus and clarity, not its complete opposite. That aside, there are no 'nuances' to human rights. You are either for them, for everybody, everywhere, or you are not. Corbyn is most definitely not. As we have seen in his highly selective attitude towards human rights, such as his support for repressive regimes in Iran, Syria, Russia, Cuba, Nicaragua and Venezuela, and movements that murder Jewish civilians, 'nuance' is in effect a euphemism for his rejection of that principle.

The other defence, for want of a better word, came from a fellow anti-Semite, Baroness Tonge. As someone who has re-cycled the accusation that an Israeli relief team harvested body organs from dead victims of the 2010 Haiti earthquake; resigned from the Liberal Democrats as a result of her involvement in an anti-Semitic scandal; as one its Patrons, also resigned from the Palestine Solidarity Campaign after associating the massacre on October 27, 2018, by a Neo-Nazi, of eleven Jews at their Pittsburgh synagogue with the polices of the Israeli government and, in 2011, accompanied Corbyn on a junket to Syria funded by Hamas-related Palestine Return, as the guest of an anti-Semitic President who, like Corbyn, has a highly nuanced approach to human rights; after all this and more, not surprisingly, most of her speech was devoted to an unrestrained attack on Israel. Her defence of Corbyn replicated that of Campbell-Savours: 'He is not an anti-Semite; he is a man who feels passionately about human rights and, like me does not always express it in the right sort of way.' No wonder he is misunderstood when these 'ways' include associating with avowed Holocaust deniers and Jewish conspiracy theorists, and describing as his 'friends' and even 'brothers' terrorists who murder Jewish civilians. As one Tory Lord put succinctly: 'I understand what Jeremy Corbyn is about and I do not approve of it. It is as near to anti-Semitic as one can get'.

Sharing with most religions their Manichean view of the world as one of a struggle to the death between the forces of absolute good and absolute evil, every totalitarian movement and ideology needs an 'other', a mortal enemy which fulfils two functions; one that personifies the absolute evil and, no less essential, by conspiring to bring about the defeat of the absolute good embodied in the movement and, above all, in its beloved Leader, is the sole cause of all the set-backs and betrayals that befall the sacred cause. Such was role ascribed by Islam, the Catholic Church and the Nazis to the Jews, and by the anti-Semitic Stalin to the Jewish Trotsky. Not by co-incidence, the Corbynista 'other' is also, like those of Mohammed, the Vatican, Hitler and Stalin, Jewish, in this case principally personified by the state of Israel and its various agencies and supporters, the 'hand' behind terrorist acts blamed on Muslims and which controls ISIS, the BBC, the UK's school history syllabus, the media, the Conservative Party and US foreign policy, which suborns Jewish Labour MPs and is responsible for the 'weaponising' of a spurious anti-Semitism against the Dear Leader, that rules the state which is the seat of the world dominance of the Rothschilds and responsible for the apartheid and genocide of the Palestinians, whose operatives harvest body organs and variously exploits, invents and facilitates the Holocaust to further the aims of Zionism etc etc…Small wonder then that after enduring more than three years under a Leader who throughout his political career has bootlicked and hobnobbed with dictators, associated intimately with Stalinists, terrorists, anti-Semites, Jew-killers and Holocaust deniers, and whose cultic supporters accuse his Jewish critics of working for Israeli intelligence and threaten them with death and their female ones with rape; that on the morning of Monday, February 18, 2019, seven Labour MPs announced their resignation from the Labour Party and their formation of the centrist and pro-European Union Independent Group. One of their number, Mike Gates, MP for Ilford South, 52 years a Labour Party member, gave some of their reasons for doing so:

> I am sickened that the Labour Party is now a racist, anti-Semitic party. I am furious that the Labour leadership is complicit in facilitating Brexit which will cause great economic political and social damage to our country. Jeremy Corbyn and those around him are on the wrong side in so many international issues from Russia to Syria to Venezuela. A Corbyn government would threaten our national security and international alliances.

The same day, a YouGov poll revealed that 34% of voters thought Corbyn was an anti-Semite, while nearly 40% of potential Labour voters said that anti-Semitism made them less likely to vote Labour. This was in vivid contrast to a majority of party members, 77% of whom when polled by YouGov in March 2108, said they believed claims of anti-Semitism had been deliberately exaggerated to undermine Corbyn's leadership.

The next day, Corbynista loyalist MP Ruth George demonstrated yet again why the break had occurred, claiming on Facebook that 'support [for the new Group] from the state of Israel' was 'possible', because one of the seven, the Jewish MP Luciana Berger, whom zealous Corbynista activists had called 'a dirty little Zionist rat', was a former Chair of the PLP Labour friends of Israel. Also the same day, it was reported that at a meeting of the Wimbledon Labour Party, Sir Duncan Michael, knighted in 2001 for services to engineering, claimed the anti-Semitism controversy had been contrived, that it was 'a storm that had started after we elected Jeremy', and had been directed at him by a 'very undemocratic elite from within our party', because Corbyn was 'kindly [sic] to Palestine and others [sic]'. 'Attacking Corbyn', he continued, had failed. He passed three democratic tests, so the Jewish community [sic] plans to attack our party'. This clear accusation that there is a collective conspiracy by the 'Jewish community' to unseat Corbyn was ruled by party officials not to be anti-Semitic.

The eighth MP to resign, the non-Jewish Joan Ryan, Chair of Labour Friends of Israel, went for Corbyn's jugular: 'Until Corbyn became its leader in September 2015, Labour did not have a problem with anti-Jewish racism…Having spent so long in the company of Holocaust deniers, anti-Semites and terrorists who murder Jews, he is simply blind to the problem.' Corbyn, she said, had surrounded himself with a 'Stalinist clique.' In reply, the party's *Corybynjugend*, Young Labour, tweeted, 'Joan Ryan gone - Palestine lives', yet more evidence Corbyn is a rallying point for all those who see Labour chiefly as vehicle for promoting their hatred of Israel and the Jews. Meanwhile, two unsavoury blasts from the past who fit this description to perfection, the Saddamista George Galloway, who claimed that accusations of Labour anti-Semitism were 'pure Goebbelsian propaganda', and Derek Liverpool redundancy notices by taxi Hatton, sought readmission to the party. Galloway was turned down, but Hatton was admitted on the Monday, only for him two days later to be suspended (surely a record) after a tweet dating from 2012 came to light saying 'Jewish people with any sense of humanity need to start speaking out publicly against the ruthless murdering being carried out by Israel.' A bemused Hatton claimed his tweet was 'innocuous', which by normal Corbynista standards, it was. But then these were not normal times. With the suspension of Williamson, no fewer than 16 Labour MPs elected in 2017 were for various reasons no longer taking the party whip, a state of affairs unprecedented in the history of Parliament. Also unprecedented in the history of major UK political parties was the announcement on March 7, 2019, by the Equality and Human Rights Commission, established the Blair administration in 2008, that it was to investigate whether the Labour Party under Corbyn's leadership had 'unlawfully discriminated against people because of their ethnicity and religious beliefs'. The only other party to have been investigated on the basis of the same charge is the neo-Nazi British National Party. Let us hope Corbyn and his Stalinist clique receive the 'Jew process' they so richly deserve. (They did.)

Addendum

Labour's nomination of candidates for the UK General Election of December 12, 2019 called forth a new batch of anti-Semites in addition to those listed above. Pride of place must surely go to Maria Carroll, Corbynista candidate for Carmarthen East. Carroll was the organiser of a secret Facebook group which advised Labour Party members on how to beat charges of anti-Semitism. Amongst those so advised was Peterborough Labour Councillor Alan Bull who, in June 2015, posted a link on Facebook claiming 'the murder of six million Jews is a hoax', shared posts asserting that Labour under Tony Blair had been a 'Mossad front' and that the same Israeli intelligence agency had murdered Princess Diana. When investigated by Labour's Compliance Unit, Bull was advised by Carroll's secret group, which goes by the very official-sounding name of 'Labour Party Compliance: Suspensions, Expulsions, Rejections Co-Op [sic]'. In addition to being given legal advice, which in previous cases had led to investigators 'backing off', Bull was told the postings were 'anti-Zionist but not anti-Semitic'. The 'Co-Op' also advised former Weymouth Labour Councillor Mollie Collins who, in January 2016, posted a link on Facebook to a web site which claimed to know 'how the Holocaust was faked', and another in 2015 that the Rothschilds 'took down' the missing Malaysian MH370 airliner, and that the BBC was a 'mouthpiece for Israel'. Another 'client' of the group, Exeter party activist Sue Grant, shared a Facebook post accusing the Israeli Jews of being as bad as the Nazis and, a tad inconsistently, a link to a film which claimed the Nazi extermination camps were 'not DEATH CAMPS!

Running Carroll close is Dan Greef, Labour's candidate for South Cambridgeshire. Greef posted on Facebook in 2013 that he 'had great day out at a concentration camp' and that he had voted for the BNP. I will repeat that, that he had voted for the BNP. In another posting, he declared, 'Bloody Israel, I sometimes want to rip it all up.' He can be seen in a photo op with a smiling

Corbyn.

Next, we have Alana Bates, Labour's candidate for St Ives. She plays bass in a group called The Tribunes, which describes itself as a 'radical-political alternative rock four-piece band'. One of its 'radical' songs is titled 'From the River to the Sea', which also happens to be the anthem of the anti-Israel Boycott, Disinvestment and Sanctions campaign endorsed by her party Leader, the river being the Jordan and the sea, the Mediterranean, and in between, a Palestinian state and no Israel. A quatrain in the song, which she can be seen and heard singing on YouTube, goes like this:

'Justice should not have to wait
Israel's an apartheid state
Justice should not have to wait
Israel is a racist state.'

And a promo couplet goes:

'Ethnic cleansing and the rest [sic]
Support BDS.'

Bates claimed the song did not call for the destruction of Israel.

Gideon Bull, Labour's candidate for Clacton, stood down after it was revealed that he had called a Jewish fellow Labour councillor in Haringey a 'Shylock'. Laura McAlpine, Labour's candidate for Harlow, stood by her chief campaigner Brett Hawksbee after a 2018 blog came to light in which he claimed that some Israelis would be happy to see a 'pogrom in Gaza and the West Bank, a Jewish final solution to the Palestine problem'. Kate Ramsden, Labour's candidate for Gordon in Scotland, stood down after it emerged she had compared Israel's policies to the actions of a child abuser. (She can be seen on a demo proudly displaying the front page of the Stalinist *Morning Star*) Zara Sultana, Labour's Corbynista candidate for Coventry South, refused to stand down when it was revealed that she had declared in a posting that she would 'celebrate' the deaths of two Prime Ministers; her own party's Tony Blair, and Israel's Benjamin Netanyahu. Jane Aitchison, Labour's candidate for Pudsey, came to her defence, saying that 'some people celebrated the death of Hitler'. Ali Malini, Labour's Momentum-backed candidate for Uxbridge, promoted 9/11 conspiracy theories on line, and used the tag '#jew' and the word 'Zionist' as forms of insult in messages. Corbynista Kate Linnegar, Labour's candidate for North Swindon, posted messages about 'Holocaust mongers' and liked a post titled 'How Israel lobby manufactured UK Labour party's anti-Semitism crisis'. She also likened Israel to Nazi Germany, described Livingstone as a 'decent' man', and liked another post calling Israel a 'so-called country'. Salma Yaqoob, Labour's Mayoral candidate for the West Midlands, was formerly Leader and Vice-Chair of George Galloway's Muslim-based Respect, and is a Patron of the Corbynista Stop the War Coalition. She appeared on a YouTube video speaking at an anti-Israel rally where in the course of an anti-Zionist diatribe, she described Jews as pigs (*a la Koran*).

In the General Election of July 5, 1945, which under the leadership of Clement Attlee, Labour won with 47.7% of the total vote and a majority over all other parties of 145 seats, 18 Jews were newly-elected to Parliament. Of these 18, 17 were Labour and one, a communist. As I write these lines, Labour goes into the General Election of December12, 2019, as a party in which 13 MPs and three peers, five of them Jews, have resigned in disgust at their party's failure to rid itself of its Jew-baiters, a party the overwhelming majority of British Jews not only believe is led by an anti-Semite, but one that the prospect of it winning that election has led to nearly half of Britain's Jews seriously considering leaving the UK. The findings of a survey conducted by YouGov and devised and analysed by Dr Daniel Allington of Kings College London were published by the Campaign Against Anti-Semitism on December 1, 2019. They confirm what I have argued in this work, that non-Islamic anti-Semitism has migrated from the far right to the far left, to the extent that Corbyn and his party is seen by anti-Semites and Jews alike as far and away the most hostile to the Jews, and that judged by their responses to a wide range of questions relating to the Jews, two thirds of self-identifying Corbynistas are anti-Semitic.

Consistent with these findings is the following: Among the many examples of anti-Semitism submitted by the Jewish Labour Movement to the Equalities and Human Rights Commission investigation into Labour Party anti-Semitism were:

One Jewish party member at his local branch was called a 'Tory Jew', a 'child killer, 'Zio scum' and told 'Hitler was right'.

MP Margaret Hodge received Facebook messages calling her a' Zionist Bitch' and 'Zionist remedial cancer'. Two others accused her of 'damaging Labour in the interests of Israel' and being 'under the orders of her paymaster in Israel'.

A Jewish 2017 General Election candidate was told on social media, 'You and your Zionist cult are not welcome. This is London, not Tel Aviv.'

A party member was defended by other members for saying at a branch meeting that it was 'the over-representation of Jews in the capitalist ruling class that gives the Isaeli-Zonist lobby its power'…Bebel's 'socialism of fools'.

Likewise consistent is the Labour Party General Election video promoting its concern for the UK's religious and ethnic minorities. Two are missing from the 20 or so listed…the Jews, and Judaism.

On December 8, 2019, the *Sunday Times* published a selection of comments made by Labour Party members about the Jews. Four with explicit genocidal intent read:

'The Jew is worse than the Black Death, worse than Ebola virus. The Jew represents pure evil'. (Bear in mind that this, like the three comments that follow, is not a posting by a member of the BNP or some similar Nazi outfit, but of the *Labour Party.*)

'You have to think with a scientific method...with clarity of thought. No emotion. We need to eliminate this infection. We kill viruses every day.'

'Can we hope for the complete extinction of all Jews by 2017?'

'I call for the complete annihilation and [sic!] extermination of every Jew on the planet.'

In the General Election that followed four days later, it was the author's party that was annihilated, recording its worst performance since the General Election of 1935.

In the contest for a new Labour Leader that followed Corbyn's electoral humiliation (after a campaign in which, according to a report by the Campaign Against Anti-Semitism, Labour candidates were responsible for 82% of all recorded anti-Semitic comments and incidents) the centrist candidate Sir Keith Starmer also 'annihilated' his Corbynista rival Rebecca Long-Bailey, who received less than half of Starmer's first preference votes - 27.6% to his 56.2%.

For one of the two High Priestesses of the Corbyn cult, (the other being old flame Dianne Abbot), despite Labour's crushing defeat, Long-Bailey's faith in and love for her fallen leader remained undiminished: 'Jeremy was [sic] one of the most honest, kind, principled politicians that I ever met. [What kind of political bubble had she been living in?] I'd give him ten out of ten.' And if she had won the leadership contest, she would have offered him a place in her shadow Cabinet because, she said, 'I love him so', affirmations of loyalty and devotion matching if not excelling Dianne Abbott's 'I would never say that Jeremy was wrong'...the inverse form of the Italian fascist mantra, 'Mussolini is always right'. Students of cults should take note that whereas since 1870, Popes have only claimed infallibility in matters of faith and morals, Saint Jeremy, at least in Abbott's estimation, is infallible *tout court*. Let us recall that in his sensational 'Secret Speech' to the 20th Soviet Communist Congress on February 24 1956 exposing the crimes of Stalin, Khrushchev related that the Soviet dictator (who, as we have had cause to record, enjoyed a high standing among Corbyn's immediate entourage) likewise 'considered that he never erred, that he was always right'. An identical claim for another mass murderer, one who enjoys a like status among some of Corbyn's admirers, was made by Nazi Labour Front boss Robert Ley in a speech on November 3, 1936, assuring his audience that 'the *Fuehrer* is always right.' If we allow Mao his miracles and overlook Jeremy's aborted attempt to walk on water, here then we have a faultless five. Yet whatever their devotees might say, each is also numbered among history's greatest failures. But let us banish from our minds the thought that the devotion of Long-Bailey and Abbott, avowed feminists both, has the remotest resemblance to that of impressionable women turned on by close proximity to a boss who hangs out with men whose profession is murder. Even so, let me offer some advice. I strongly recommend that they give serious consideration to what Marx had to say on the subject of cults, that when he and Engels first joined the communist movement, they did so 'on condition that everything making for superstitious worship of authority would be deleted from its statute.'

Within hours of the news of Starmer's victory, Corbynista loyalists struck back. A posting on the Corbynista website, 'Jeremy Corbyn Group Supports Richard Burgon [who came third] for Deputy Leader' claimed that Labour's new Leader (notwithstanding Starmer's membership of Labour Friends of Palestine, non-membership of Labour Friends of Israel and unqualified support of Corbyn's foreign policy) was 'just another Israeli lickspittle', while another posting, evidently mindful of the fact that Dominic Raab, then deputising for the Coronavirus-incapacitated Boris Johnson, was Jewish, deplored that the UK was now a 'one party state run by the Jews'. In an article on the general election in the blog *Middle East Eye*, Medical doctor Dr Ghada Karmi, a Research Fellow at the University of Essex, insisted that 'while much has been made of the capitalist establishment's role in Corbyn's downfall due to his socialist economics, it was the pro-Israel lobby [again, the same Corbynista code for the Jewish conspiracy] that dealt the final blow', one, she claimed, 'likely coordinated by the Israeli embassy.' (As we have seen, Corbyn has made identical allegations, using the same terminology, about US foreign policy, and about the Israeli embassy regarding media coverage of the Israel-Palestine conflict and UK schools' teaching of Middle East history.) Dr Karmi was greatly concerned by Starmer's describing himself as 'a supporter of Zionism' and his seeming inability to understand, unlike Corbyn, that 'terminating Zionism [sic] is the only way to a permanent peace [sic]'. We get the picture. Just as the Nazis once used to say, all the 'Israeli lobby' has to do is tug a hidden string - hidden that is not from the likes of Dr Karmi, but the ever-gullible voter - and a leader dedicated to the 'termination of Zionism' falls, and is replaced by one no less opposed to it.

Despite his previous reticence on the subject, I applaud Starmer's stated determination to 'tear out this poison [of anti-Semitism] by its roots'. By electing a leader prepared to give such a pledge, and moreover, as a bonus, one with a three-digit I.Q., the majority of Labour members had put an end to the Corbyn ascendency and their party's simultaneous descent into the sewer of institutional Jew-baiting. However, Starmer's appointment of Afzal Khan as his shadow Deputy Leader of the House was not consistent with his stated aim. Like other Labour Muslims, Khan had posted on social media his belief in a Jewish conspiracy, namely an 'Israel-British-Swiss crime syndicate' and 'mass murdering Rothschilds Israeli mafia criminal liars' - not views, I suggest, that are consistent with Starmer's vision of a post-Corbyn Labour Party cleansed of anti-Semitic poison. The same goes for his appointment of John McDonnell *protégé* Naz Shah to his shadow cabinet. Suspended from party membership for anti-Semitism after her on-line proposal to deport the entire Jewish population of Israel to the USA, not long after her re-instatement, she re-tweeted in good faith a spoof tweet which said that 'those abused girls in Rotherham and elsewhere just need to shut their mouths. For the good of diversity', and launched a petition, signed by more than a hundred Labour MPs, decrying as a Nazi (sic) the editor of the *Sun*, Kevin Mackenzie, for running an article by fellow Labour MP for Rotherham, Sarah Champion, which exposed the identity of her town's rape gangs. Of all the posts not to give Shah, for reasons best known to himself, Starmer awarded her with that of Shadow Minister of Community Cohesion.

He also would have been well-advised to appoint one of his two main rivals for the leadership, Lisa Nandy, to a post other than shadow Foreign Secretary, given her ambiguous attitude towards the state of Israel. At the time of her appointment, she had served for seven years, first as vice chair, then chair, of the PLP's Labour Friends of Palestine, as well as being a member of the viciously anti-Zionist and frequently anti-Semitic Palestine Solidarity Campaign, two of its Patrons being Corbyn and Loach. On the one hand, Nandy has been unequivocal in her denunciation of leftist anti-Semitism, and that 'Jewish people have a right to national self-determination', a standpoint that 'makes me a Zionist'. Yet on the other hand, she has no less unequivocally declared that 'we cannot allow the selling of arms to Israel'. How can one support the right of Israel to exist, while at the same time deny to it the right to defend itself against those who seek to 'wipe it off the map', to quote the former employer of Starmer's predecessor? As of October 2021, there are no indications as to in what ways if any Labour's policy towards Israel will differ from that of Corbyn's. Labour's response to the renewed fighting between Hamas and Israel in May 2021 suggested that the anti-Zionism of the Corbyn era died hard. Perhaps it had something to do with the composition of Starmer's shadow cabinet. As of October 2021, of its 30 House of Commons members, 16 were members of Labour Friends of Palestine, including Starmer, and only six, members of Labour Friends of Israel, three of whom were also members of the Friends of Palestine. Down below, in the constituencies, hatred of Israel continued to seethe, a loathing reflected in the carrying, by majority of two to one, of a totally one-sided resolution on Israel at the September 2021 Labour Party conference. Moving the resolution, a delegate from Momentum-dominated Young Labour compared Israel to Franco Spain, and described it as a colonial-settler state, without specifying to which colonial empire Israel belonged. At least it made a change from likening Israel to Nazi Germany.

However, in comparing Israel to fascist Spain, the mover of the resolution must surely have been unaware that Franco had always been on the best terms with a leftist hero, Fidel Castro, who ordered three days of official mourning after Franco's death in 1975. Always hostile to Israel, the Cuban regime broke off diplomatic relations with the Jewish state after the Yom Kippur war of October 1973 and has never resumed them. For his part, Franco never recognized the state of Israel, like Hitler during the Second World War, and like anti-Zionists today, adopting an alliance with the Jews' Arab enemies.

As for the resolution, drafted by Omar Mofeed, the son of a former Hamas health official (when it comes to anti-Zionism, there's nothing quite like the touch of a professional), it accused Israel of a long list of crimes that as always, included apartheid, while saying not a word, as one would expect, given its authorship, about Hamas's rocket attacks on Israel, its rejection of a two-state solution and its goal of exterminating the Jews. And for all the talk of a Jew-friendly Labour, with respect to these omissions, the movers of the resolution were simply following the example set by the party's post-Corbyn leadership.

While they both deplored the loss of Palestinian lives, neither Starmer nor Nandy in their initial comments on the Israel-Hamas conflict of May 2021 condemned or even mentioned the Hamas rocket attacks which triggered the conflict and killed six Jews, or that the avowed aim of Hamas was not a two-state solution but the elimination of the state of Israel and murder of all its Jews. On June 15, 2021, in a debate in the House of Commons on two anti-Israel petitions, Labour's shadow Middle East minister, Wayne David, tried to have it both ways, saying that Labour 'strongly condemns the firing of rockets by Hamas' (which to, be fair is more than what Starmer and Nandy did) but then added 'we also strongly condemn the air attacks that led to such a large loss of life', ignoring two indisputable facts: firstly that if Hamas had not initiated the conflict with its rocket attack, there would have been no loss of life, and secondly, that Israel has the right under international law to take military action in response to such attacks.

David also tied himself in knots in his attempt to define his party's attitude towards anti-Semitism...another bone of furious contention in the Corbyn era. Again, it was a case of on the one hand and on the other: 'There can be no justification for anti-Semitism in any shape of form, whatever people's views are on the Israel-Palestine conflict.' But some of those 'views', as we have seen, are themselves anti-Semitic, including denying the right of Israel to exist, equating Zionism with Nazism, denying the Holocaust, accusing Israel of exploiting the Holocaust, of apartheid and the genocide of the Palestinians... all views which Labour officially condemns as anti-Semitic and as such, hypothetically at least, incompatible with membership of the party. The simple truth is, and even Israel's worst enemies must know it, that if Hamas left Israel alone, Israel would leave Hamas alone. It has better things to do with its time and resources. But Hamas won't, because it hasn't.

As Starmer went about the business of choosing his team, his enemies continued in their attempt to undermine his leadership by depicting him as a stooge of Israel. Very much in the same vein as the previously cited three postings, Darius Cooper, an officer of the Hackney South Labour Party, claimed that by accepting a donation of £50,000 for his election campaign from the Jewish Sir Trevor Chinn, Starmer had been 'bought' and was now, yes, yet again, 'in the pocket of the Israeli lobby.' However, Corbyn's accepting donations amounting to £10,000 for his election campaign of 2015 from avowed supporters of Hamas and advocates of terrorism against Jewish civilians we are assured does not lead to the same dependency. A scrutiny of the Electoral Commission's records by the Campaign against anti-Semitism revealed that one of the donors was London-based GP Dr Ibrahim Hamami, who is a columnist for the official Hamas journal *The Filastin*. On his Facebook page, Hamami had praised attacks on Jewish civilians in the West Bank as acts of 'dignity, freedom and honour.' Killing Jews an 'honour'? Another doner, Professor Ted Honderich, who gave £5,000, in 2011 wrote in the *Guardian* (once again one asks, where else?) that 'Palestinians have a moral right to terrorism [sic!] within historic Palestine.' A 'moral right' to kill Jews? So all Jews, whether they live in the West Bank or the state of Israel, are fair game, because , according to the Hamas Charter, this 'historic Palestine' includes the current state of Israel, home to 6.6 million Jews as well as 1.9 million Arabs. Article 6 says that Hamas 'strives to raise the banner of Allah over every inch of Palestine.' What would happen to these 6.6 million Jews if the strivings of Corbyn's benefactors became a reality is not a prospect for idle conjecture. The West, if it again acted, or rather failed to act, as it did in the first Holocaust of the Jews, would be witnesses to a second. As the BDS chant has, it, 'From the river [Jordan] to the [Mediterranean] Sea, Palestine shall be free'. When these and other similar donations came to light, a spokesman for Corbyn insisted that 'nothing dodgy is going on'. Soliciting and accepting donations from advocates of Jew-killing not dodgy?

Addendum

'What immortal hand or eye could frame thy fearful symmetry?'
The Tyger, by William Blake

287

Repeatedly in this work, I have drawn attention to the overlap and, in some cases, identity, of far left and right hostility towards Israel and the Jews. As one would expect, this convergence, and the degree of virulence with which this loathing is conveyed, is most in evidence when the subject matter, at least ostensibly, is the Middle East. What follows are comments made on websites about the Jews culled and published by the website Canary Mission, which monitors on-line anti-Semitism. It reproduced in two vertical columns and paired according to subject matter, on the left comments made by pro-Palestinians, members of the leftist Students for Justice in Palestine, and on the right, by white supremacists, Neo-Nazis and like ilk. I have reversed some the pairings, and invite readers to spot which they are.

Hitler should have took you all	Hitler missed a few
The Holocaust: 20th century's biggest lie	Lies told in school about the Holocaust
A Jew in the oven is worth two in the FEMA [?] camp	Let's stuff the Jews in the oven
Sorry if your Pizza tastes a little bit like kike.	What's the difference between a Jew and a Pizza?
All our ovens are dual purpose.	The Pizza leaves the oven.
How many Jews can you fit in a VW Beetle?	How to fit 6 million Jews in a VW Beetle.
54. 2 in the front, 2 in the back, 50 in the ash tray.	Put 'em in the ash tray.
Set fire to the Jews	Gas the kikes. Race war now.
Hitler was a boss	Hitler. Cuz he's a boss
I would relish the chance to see a Zionist Holocaust	We need to put Zionists in a concentration Camp.

As we have seen, Corbyn has won plaudits from some of the leading figures of the contemporary extreme right for his stance on the 'Jewish question'...notably David Duke, Nick Griffin and David Irving. Yet like Corbyn, and many others on the left who share his anti-Zionist animus, they each deny they are anti-Semitic. Below are statements to this effect which, as with those cited above, have been made by political figures located on the left and right, together with other public utterances by the same individuals on the same subject which suggest they are lying. Again, I challenge the reader to identify who is of the left and who of the right.

We stand against anti-Semitism.	The Zionist figures who hold an American passport and American citizenship suffer from a syndrome called double loyalty.

I am the least anti-Semitic person you've ever met.	I don't need your Jewish money…fuck you!
How can you call us anti-Semites?	The Zionist Jew is the party of Satan.
I am a friend of the Jews.	Auschwitz is total fucking bullshit.
I'm not anti-Semitic!	I hate to say it, but the Nazis were right!
Racism in any form is wrong and deplorable.	It's not Muslims that are going to kill us. It's Jews.
I am not what you call a racist.	There can be no compromise with the Jewish supremacist agenda. Either we win or they destroy us.

Like Students for Justice in Palestine, BDS, Boycott, Disinvestment and Sanctions, is another anti-Zionist campaign active in the Anglo-Saxon world that attracts leftist support, especially on university campuses. But as we have seen, the left, or to be more precise, the far left, does not have a monopoly in this field. Former KKK Grand Wizard, Hitler admirer and white supremacist David Duke is a case in point. (It was Duke, remember, who enthused over Corbyn's election as Labour leader, describing it as a ray of sunshine, and who shared with him both the hospitality of the mass murdering President Assad of Syrian and employment by Iran's Press TV channel.) I list below six comments by Duke and BDS supporters on a number of themes that feature prominently in the anti-Zionist movement. Once again, I challenge the reader to identify who said what.

When you study the statements of Jewish Leaders' billion-dollar Jewish organisations you realise they suffer from a syndrome called 'double loyalty'.	Zionist figures who hold an American passport [have shown] that Jewish disloyalty is far worse than 'dual loyalty'.
The US is an Israeli occupied territory.	Occupied Congress doing the (Chosen) people's Business.
How can you be against white supremacy in the USA but support a state like Israel that is built on the idea that Jews are supreme to everyone else?	I coined the term 'Jewish supremacism' in 2003? Now it is recognized as a valid term by anti- Zionists.
Israel has hypnotised the world, may God awaken the people and help them see the evil doings of Israel	Israel has hypnotised the world, may Allah awaken the people and help them see the evil doings of Israel
From the river to the see, Palestine will be free.	From the river to the see, Palestine will be free.
I'm shocked at the racist, genocidal state	Definitely, most definitely we oppose a

known as Israel still exists. Kudos to whoever brings it down.

state in any part of Palestine.

Below we have again examples of far left and right comments on the same subject, this being Jewish/Zionist control of the USA. And also again, the challenge is to guess which is which.

Holocaust guilt and manufactured anti-Semitism are contributing factors to the subservient relationship the USA enjoys with the state of Israel.

Israel has a hold on Congress. They know how to bully, how to intimidate. Congress is bought and paid for by the Israel lobby.

The Zionist movement's cultural influence includes the media as well as Hollywood.

I've come to realist this is a demonic stranglehold that's destroying America... Zionism. This thing is choking the life out of America.

New York Police Department equals Ku Klux Klan equals Israeli Defence Force.

I will not serve in a foreign government. The Republicans are nothing but Zionist stooges.

Take a look at the type of names on the buildings Around campus – Haas, Zellerbach – and decide who controls the university.

The real threat to America is not the Chinese. It's the Zionists who control our country.

For those who see politics purely in terms of the conventional left-right spectrum, not only the convergence of their views on certain topics, as above, but the actual collaboration of white supremacists and even avowed Nazis with self-appointed leaders of the USA's black population defies any rational explanation. Yet it remains a fact. Back in the early 1960s, the rise of the civil rights movement produced a white segregationist backlash, mainly in the south, that breathed new life into Lincoln Rockwell's moribund American Nazi Party. This was paralleled by a similar resurgence of the Nation of Islam under the joint leadership of Elijah Poole (AKA Elijah Mohammed) and Malcom Little (AKA Malcom X). Founded in 1930, it advocated, like the US Nazi Party (along with the KKK) total separation of blacks and whites. Contact was established between the two movements, resulting in a delegation of the US Nazi Party, led by Rockwell in full brown-shirted uniform, complete with swastika arm-band, attending a Washington Black Muslim convention as guests of honour. The scene was captured for posterity by photographer Eve Arnold. Aware that Arnold was Jewish, Rockwell rounded on her, threatening to turn her into a 'bar of soap'.

Rockwell was even a featured speaker at another Black Muslim event, at the Chicago International Amphitheatre, where he proposed to his all-black audience of 12,000 that their best option was an alliance, albeit of convenience, with his Nazis, since both stood for segregation: 'You know we call you niggers, but wouldn't you rather be confronted by honest white men who tell you to your face what the others say behind your back.?' Malcom X's solution to anti-Black racism was for blacks to be 'permanently separated from our former slavemaster and placed on some land that we can call our own.' (This policy continues in a watered-down form with Black Lives Matter demands for campus black 'safe spaces' and racially segregated dormitories.)

Rockwell made no secret of his admiration for Hitler, calling him 'a gift from providence'. And neither did Elijah Mohammed's successor, Louis Farrakhan, describing him as a 'very great man'. And, also like Rockwell, he was not exactly enamoured of the Jews. 'I don't care what they put on me...the powerful Jews are my enemy.' 'Did you know that the *Koran* says the Jews are the most violent of people? I didn't write it, but I'm living to see it.' An avowed opponent of racial integration, ('I'm not into integration...you can't integrate with wickedness if you want righteousness') he was one of the first prominent black personalities to come out for Black Lives Matter ...'these are young leaders for the future'...but true to form, he criticised whites who had joined the movement with the intention of broadening its appeal....'they wanted to change the narrative'. Possibly. But very few on the 'white' left have taken issue with Farrakhan's 'systemic' anti-Semitism and his veneration for Hitler, or the manifestations of violent anti-Semitism that have accompanied a number of BLM riots, with attacks on Jewish-owned stores, Jewish schools and synagogues, and its leaders' hostility towards Israel, an issue that has no bearing whatsoever on the race question in the USA.

Perhaps the most extraordinary recent left-right convergence in the USA was the 2021 videoed zoom meeting of minds on the 'Jewish question' between former black Democratic Congresswomen for Georgia from 1993 to 2005, Cynthia McKinney, and four white supremacists, among them Angelo John Gage of the KKK. McKinney has never made a secret of her opinions about the Jews. On June 28, 2021 she tweeted a jigsaw puzzle of a burning World Trade Centre captioned 'The final piece of the puzzle'. The last piece is about to be slotted into place, with the word 'Zionists' written on it, completing the sentence, 'Zionists did it.' She has also denied on Twitter that six million Jews died in the Holocaust, and been active in the anti-Zionist cause, being aboard two boats that attempted to break the Israeli naval blockade of Gaza in 2008 and 2009, and in Black Lives Matter, taking to task Democratic politicians for whom 'all of a sudden, Black Lives Matter just before the [2020] election'. She also 'liked' a posting which claimed to have detected the 'liberal hand of Zionism in Antifa'. Excerpts of their conversation follow:

It's what we ought to do, even though it's what we are told we can't do. Black people are supposed to be afraid of 'white nationalists'...we are supposed to be afraid. So if you are afraid, you don't reach out, you don't talk to, you don't work with...the stove-piping of the US electorate means you and I never talk to each other... we only talk to people like us, so that we are never able to really come together effectively to work against the one per cent, which is now the half percent [i.e., the Jews].

[One of the group, 'C T', talks about a black professor, Tony Martin, who] got into a lot of trouble in his Black Studies class at Wellesley College. He introduced the truth of the secret relationship between Blacks and Jews, talking about the secret involvement of the Jews in the slave trade [a favourite subject of Corbynista and Momentum activist Jackie Walker] ... he wrote this book [he holds it up] called *The Jewish Onslaught*...this fits with what you were saying about white nationalists and black nationalists. White nationalists are typical white working-class people [her head nods], who are seeing demographic change, who are poor and struggling, but they see an anti-white narrative, so they think, we have to collectively organise too, because no one is speaking up for us. So they have the same mentality as black people [she nods again]. So why shouldn't there be dialogue…But when you look at black organisations like the NAACP, they are started by Jewish people. [she nods again] Slowly but surely, they put black people in power once they have been trained properly. Tony Martin says this: 'Black people will continue to be the pawn in other people's games until the elusive quest for power is realised. And maybe the Jewish establishment has concluded that a prostrate African-American population oppressed or paternalized [she nods vigorously] will continue to be its insurance against a Euro-American reversion to European anti-Jewish activity. [sic!] They [the Jews] will use races against each other, so as long as we are at each other's throats, we will never look up at the ivory tower.'

[McKinney]: That's right. I don't call them ['the Jews'] an elite. That gives them a kind of nobility. They are not noble at all. These are very evil people. The Jews in Atlanta wanted to join the Pilgrim driving and social clubs, economic clubs…so they [also] joined the civil rights movement and road on the backs of black people…they were interested in their own advancement, so they used the civil rights movement as a tool for their advancement…the Jews use the civil rights movement for their purposes. And that wouldn't have been the first time. {This was also the view of Malcom X. There is an awkward moment when C.T. responds by saying that Jews have been involved in Black Lives Matter. But it quickly passes. McKinney continues]: These people [the Jews] are heartless. A song is called, 'Who is your God', right? It's sung by an Israeli woman. And they're killing the Palestinians…Israel is preparing for a strike against Iran…they've been striking on Syria…you can't wait these people out, because this is an inter-generational crime syndicate…and they don't have a god, because no god would justify what they do…all the killing… [She then expounds a convoluted argument intended to prove that the Covid pandemic was started by Ashkenazi Jews whom, she claimed, were immune to it. This goes down a treat with all four white supremacists. One says, 'if we need any more reasons, they keep giving it to us.']

Back in the 1970s, when in the UK, the neo-Nazi National Front was on the rise, there was a chant used on anti-racist marches: 'Black and white, unite and fight!' Then, the 'fight' was against Nazis. Today, for McKinney, it's the same slogan, but the 'fight' is alongside the Nazis against the Jews.

One of Corbyn's several associations with the far right was revealed after the eruption in late July 2020 of the anti-Semitic scandal involving the rapper Richard Cowie M.B.E, aka Wiley. He had posted on Twitter a series of vicious attacks on the Jews, one calling for their extermination, and another, a recycling of a Neo-Nazi justification (not denial) of the Holocaust, and a vintage Protocols exposition of Jewish conspiracy theory, accompanied by a picture gallery of the guilty parties, all German Jewish revolutionaries of the early 20th century. Another posting, repeating the allegation first put into circulation by the Corbynista Momentum activist Jackie Walker, alleged that 'at the height of American slavery, 78% of slave owners were ethnic Jews'. Some of his outraged fans' reactions were commendably unprintable. Condemnations by public figures and politicians, while more measured, were no less severe. Wiley responded with more anti-Semitic invective – 'Black people don't call the police but Jewish cowards do when Wiley speaks his mind. FUCK YOU' and 'Israel is not yours…can you hear me…' This last riposte might explain why Corbyn was not among those politicians who denounced Wiley's racism. Both are not only vocal supporters of the supposedly anti-racist Black Lives Matter but, also like BLM, hostile in the extreme to Israel. According to the *Shropshire Star* of November25, 2019, 'Brit-Awards winning grime artist Stormzy [aka Wiley] was 'among the rappers and musicians to back Labour at the 2019 general election. Accompanying the report is a large photo of Wiley and Corbyn posing together. Wiley had tweeted Corbyn, 'Big up @jeremycorbyn' to which Corbyn replied 'Thank you Wiley'. As soon as the story broke of Wiley's racist outburst, Corbyn, as he invariably does when he is caught with his anti-Semitic trousers down, deleted the tweets.

What might be called the Wiley affair had a sequel that highlights how not only Wiley but a number of prominent blacks both in the UK and the USA who regard themselves as committed anti-racists seem to have a problem when it comes to anti-Semitism, something they share with Livingstone, for whom anti-Semitism is 'not the same thing as racism.' Whoopi Goldberg seems to agree, judging by her comments on the subject, as reported in the *Daily Mail* of February 1, 2022, which she made in an interview on the US TV show, The View. She claimed that the Holocaust 'wasn't about race' because it was a conflict between 'two groups of white people', the Jews and the Nazis. 'This is white people doing it to white people so y'all go fight amongst yourselves.' Replying to the backlash on her own The Late Show, she explained that 'being black, when we talk about race it's a very different thing to me, so I said the Holocaust wasn't about race.' The reason, she said, 'you can't call this [anti-Semitism] racism' was because 'this [the Holocaust] wasn't based on skin. You couldn't tell who was Jewish.' How come then that apart from gypsies, who were also 'white', only Jews ended up in the gas chambers and that down the centuries, Christian mobs have never had any difficulty in spotting who was a Jew when it was time for another pogrom? She then gave an example: 'If the Klan is coming down the street and I'm standing with a Jewish friend, I'm going to run. But if my friend decides not to run, they'll get passed by most times.' So, according to Goldberg, the Nazis were not racist, and the Klan didn't have designs on the Jews because they couldn't tell who they were. Two utter, disgraceful falsehoods The KKK did lynch Jews, and Hitler was a racist. Listen to former KKK Grand Wizard, anti-Zionist and Corbyn enthusiast David Duke on the Jews: 'They [the Jews] are trying to exterminate our race...they probably deserve to go into the ashbin of history.' Now Hitler, who did his best to put them there, on race: 'For as long as a people remain racially pure and are conscious of the treasure of their blood, they can never be overcome by the Jew... Nations that make mongrels of their people, or allow their people to be turned into mongrels, sin against the will of eternal Providence...If a people refuses to guard and uphold the qualities with which it has been endowed by nature and which have their roots in the racial blood, then such a people has no right to complain over the loss of its earthly existence.'

Now to the Wiley sequel.

The *Jewish Chronicle* of January 25, 2022 carried a story, together with a photo, concerning the black Manchester United footballer Marcus Rashford, who won nationwide public support for his successful campaign to persuade the government to provide free meals in holiday time for needy school children during the pandemic. So far, so good, indeed, very good. Now we come to the photo, which is not so good. It was clearly posed, because Rashford and his two companions were looking straight at the camera. They are at a Wiley gig in a Dubai hotel venue. Rashford has his left arm around Wiley, with to his right, his also black club mate Jesse Lingard. Rashford was questioned as to why he was, so to speak 'hanging out' with an anti-Semite (one who happened to be on tweeting terms with Corbyn) so notorious that he couldn't get a gig in the UK (Islamic Dubai seems not to have had the same objections), had been disowned by his fans, dumped by his manager, banned from twitter and investigated by the police for hate crime. In reply, a pro *forma* explanation, not an apology, was issued in Rashford's name, one clearly crafted by someone versed in such matters, because it was almost identical in its legalistic wording to the one issued on behalf of Lingard. It said that given its 'context', the photo could be 'misconstrued', thought it did not say what the correct construction was, neither did it condemn or even refer to Wiley's anti-Semitism. However, as to the 'context' of the photo, it could not be clearer, and it does not sit easily with the two statements' assurances that both Rashford and Lingard were opposed to anti-Semitism. In Rashford's defence, it could be said that this encounter was perhaps a one-off, which is more than can be said for another self-proclaimed anti-racist, who has made it a habit to hang out not for one evening, but for the best part of two decades, with anti-Semites who not only spouted Jew-hate, but were at the business end of translating it into action.

U The Corbynistas Strike Back

In the main body of this work, I posed the question, if, after being elected Labour Leader, he was faced with the choice of remaining true to his anti-Zionist convictions and commitments, or yielding to those who favoured a slightly more nuanced attitude towards Israel and the Jews, would Corbyn re-enact the role of a Prince Hal now crowned king, and say to his boon Jew-baiting and killing companions of yesteryear, 'Anti-Semites and Holocaust deniers, I know you not'? The answer came in the extraordinary events surrounding the meeting of the Labour Party National Executive Committee on September 4, 20018, convened to make a final decision on whether to adopt *in toto* the International Holocaust Remembrance Alliance definition of anti-Semitism, or retain the existing version known to be favoured by Corbyn, which excluded four of the IHRA's eleven examples of what constitutes anti-Semitism. As within Labour Party HQ, the NEC deliberated, outside, unprecedented scenes unfolded. Demonstrating Momentum storm troopers demanded a firm stand against any revision of their favoured draft, which permitted members to say that Jews are disloyal to Britain, and that Israel is a racist state that should not exist, while Jews and their supporters called for the full IRHA version. Could this really be London in the year 2018, and not Berlin in 1933? After three hours of heated debate and despite a personal intervention by Corbyn with a 500-word amendment in support of a minority who wanted to stand firm on the original draft, the overwhelmingly Corbynista NEC announced its decision. It had adopted the full IRHA definition, but with a caveat that rendered it ineffective: 'The NEC has today adopted all of the IHRA examples of anti-Semitism in addition to the IRHA which Labour adopted in 2016, alongside a statement which ensures that this will not *in any way* undermine freedom of expression on Israel or the rights of the Palestinians.' (emphasis added)

In other words, anti-Semitic party members could exercise their unlimited freedom of expression (one which their Leader would deny to critics of Islam) by continuing to liken Israel to Nazi Germany or deny its right to exist. But would it have been legitimate to oppose the right of Palestinians to their own state, or for that matter, as Corbyn's Syrian hosts have done, to deny that there is even such an entity as a Palestinian people? To ask is to answer. The reference to 'freedom of expression' is therefore selective, hypocritical and a red herring. Hypocritical because beginning with their leader, the politically correct Corbynistas do not believe in free speech, the proof being that in addition to Corbyn's outspoken views on the subject at a pro-censorship rally in Trafalgar Square in 2006, nowhere in Labour's policies can there be found proposals to repeal any of the accumulation of laws dating back to the Thatcher and Blairite scum eras that criminalise making statements that could have (not necessarily have) given offence; and a red herring because, while anyone should be free to say what they like about Israel or any other subject as members of society, once they freely choose to join a party that finds some of what they advocate incompatible with its principles and rules, different rules necessarily apply. Would the current Labour Party NEC for example uphold in the name of free expression the right of members to claim that all Muslims are terrorist and rapists? It would not, and rightly so. Why, then, make an exception for insulting lies about Israel and its Jewish inhabitants and diaspora supporters? There are, however a number of organisations that will gladly accept those who wish to vent such feelings about Israel, and provide them with every opportunity to do so. In the event, the NEC's patent subversion of the intent of the IRHA code was for Corbyn insufficient. With the full support of his Shadow Chancellor John McDonnell, who is on record as being opposed to the very existence of the state of Israel, he had submitted to the NEC at its meeting a clause which said openly what the NEC wanted to permit by a nod and a wink, namely that it should not be regarded as racist to 'describe Israel, its policies or the circumstances around its foundation as racist because of their discriminatory impact.'

These 'circumstances' that Corbyn alluded to but failed to elucidate were firstly a resolution passed by the United Nations on November 29, 1947 establishing two states west of the River Jordan in the former British Palestinian Mandate, one Jewish, the other Palestinian; thereby in fact if not in name, establishing what is now called the 'two state solution' agreed between Israel and the PLO at Oslo in 1993. The Zionists unconditionally accepted the resolution, while all the Arab states voted against and unconditionally rejected it, and then proceeded to invade Israel on the first day of its independence on May 14, 1948. Defeated by tiny Israel, Jordan and Egypt cut their losses by annexing respectively the West Bank and the Gaza Strip, *the two territories designated by the UN for the proposed Palestinian state.* So much for Arab and Muslim brotherhood. If they had instead of making war on Israel, accepted the UN resolution, there would be no 'refugee' issue today or 'occupied territories', but a predominantly Jewish and a Palestinian state living, one hopes, peacefully as neighbours, as was the UN's intention and that of the Zionist leadership. Those Palestinians, far from all, who fled Israel in 1948 did so as a result of the Arab invasion, not, as Corbyn appears to be implying, as result of any policy or actions by the Israeli authorities, who pleaded with them to stay.

So much for Corbyn's accusation that British schools do not teach the true, anti-Zionist version of Middle Eastern history. And history was also made when for the first time, the Dear Leader was rebuffed by his devotees, who in rejecting his clause, made it clear that they had gone as far as they dare in accommodating his fanatical anti-Zionism. Their leader publicly defeated, and indeed humiliated by the lukewarm, the hard-core Corbynistas of London Palestine Action struck back the next day, when posters illegally displayed on bus stops informed Londoners that 'Israel is a racist endeavour'. Corbyn's fixation on Israel had already divided the Labour Party. Now it was threating to tear apart his own faction. The same day, the *Jewish Chronicle* reported that a survey of British Jews indicated that around 40% would consider leaving the UK if Corbyn became Prime Minister. The day after that, September 6, *The Times of Israel* carried a report of a UK school teacher who had been cleared of charges of anti-Semitic conduct. He had posted on Facebook the following comments:

> Every sane human is anti-Semitic. Because you bastards have made Zionism synonymous with the mistreatment of Palestinians. Billions are anti-Semitic and proud of it...Of course we hate Jews. Israel is the evillest regime on the planet. Supported by Jews from within, and around the world...Israel should be wiped off the planet. [Could this last be a crib from Corbyn's former employer, Iran's

296

The same day, the Corbynista counter-attack shifted up a gear with Joan Ryan, Labour MP for Enfield North and more to the point, Chair of the Labour Friends of Israel, losing a vote of confidence in her local party by 94 to 92 after being accused by what she described as an alliance of 'Trots, Stalinists and communists and asserted hard lefts' of 'smearing' Corbyn and 'fuelling and indeed inflaming' his 'trial by media'. One posting on the 'Corbyn True Socialism' website said she should be 'shoved right back in the gas ovens'. The proceedings were illegally filmed by Corbyn's former employers, Press TN, banned from the UK since 2011 for screening a forced confession by an Iranian journalist. Dismiss the thought that targeting in this way the one Labour MP who more than any other is most closely identified with the Israeli cause was a co-incidence. A party founded by the trade unions to represent the working class was being transformed into one whose prime purpose, no matter with whose support, or at what cost, was to wage war on Zionism. The next day, two more anti-Corbyn MPs lost votes of confidence. All this in less than a week.

At the Labour Party Conference in Liverpool the next month, proceedings began with the now ritual Nuremberg chanting of the Dear Leader's name and his signing a life-size cardboard cut-out of himself. As for his own responsibility for the explosion of anti-Semitism in the Labour Party after his election as its Leader, his only regret, he told reporters, was 'the stuff I've had thrown at me and the ill-informed nature of it.'

Ignoring all the human rights abuses rampant in the world, from Venezuela, Nicaragua, Turkey, Syria, Russia, Iran and the entire Islamic world to China and Myanmar, where Muslims were being interned, persecuted and murdered in their thousands, and doubtless buoyed by the knowledge that in the name of a free speech neither they nor their leader believes in, they could continue to say exactly what they liked about Israel, delegates waving Palestinian flags passed just one foreign policy resolution, condemning Israel for its response to the attempted illegal incursions into its territory by Hamas. Can this really be the UK in 2018 and not Germany in 1933? No wonder British Jews are seriously considering packing their bags.

V Nightmare in Tunisia (with apologies to Dizzy Gillespie)

On August 11, 2018, the *Daily Mail* published a story refuting Corbyn's claim that the wreath-laying ceremony he attended in Tunisia in 2014 had only been for the victims of an air attack in 1986 by Israel on a PLO camp in the same country. Photos published by the *Mail* clearly showed Corbyn praying (Islamic fashion) and standing, massive wreath in hand, in front of the graves of leading members of the PLO involved in the planning and execution of the failed Black September hostage operation at the 1972 Munich Olympics, all of whom, it is generally believed, had been hunted down and killed by Mossad. Pressed to explain what he was doing there, Corbyn told the *Independent,* using the passive, that 'a wreath was laid by some of those who attended the conference [sic] for those who were killed in Paris in 1992. I was present when it was laid. I don't think [sic] I was actually involved in it.' This proved to be a lie, contradicted by his later admission that he did lay a wreath. In a photo published by the *Mail*, he is seen actually holding the wreath as he stands, prominently, among a group in front of the graves. On August 13 during a visit to Walsall, Corbyn now confirmed that the wreath in question had been 'laid to those who were killed in Paris in 1992', that is, the Black September Munich operatives, not the victims of the Israeli air attack in 1986. On the same day, he told Channel Four News, 'I laid one wreath along with many other people'. However, in the several photos of the ceremony, only one person is carrying a wreath, Comrade Corbyn. But then on the 14th, back in London, there came a denial from Labour HQ, with a statement claiming that the PLO operativities in question were not even buried in the Tunisia cemetery, and therefore there was no ceremony for them, with or without Corbyn. If so, for whom was Corbyn praying and holding a wreath in the photos? Yet the Facebook page of Fatah, the organisation behind the Munich massacre, carries a tribute to Atel Belson, who it says 'joined in the planning of the Munich operation' and who after being killed in the Meridian Hotel in Paris in 1992, was buried in the Tunisian cemetery.

> As I was going up the stair
> I met a man who wasn't there!
> He wasn't there again today
> Oh how I wish he'd go away!

The 'conference' which Corbyn refers to in the *Independent* (which he addressed and is pictured by the *Mail* seated at the speaker's table) he described as one for 'peace'. But then everything Jeremy does is for peace, even though what he was participating in was in fact a council of war against Israel. One of Corbyn's 'friends', top Hamas commander Oussama Hamdan, outlined, quote, a 'four-point vision to fight against Israel', in the course of which he praised his movement's, quote, 'great success on the military and national levels.' 'Violence' he said, was, quote, 'magnificent' albeit to be sure in the interests of what Corbyn

298

invariably describes as 'peace and dialogue'. Hamdan is not only, as he says, a successful military commander. He is also something of an authority on the so-called 'Jewish blood libel' in which Jews are supposed to drink the blood of Christian children. Interviewed on Lebanon TV, he assured viewers (many of whom would not have needed reassuring) that 'it is not a figment of imagination or taken from a film. It is a fact.' The reader will recall the no less virulently anti-Semitic Hamas preacher, Sheikh Raed Salah, who recycled the same myth, and of whom Corbyn subsequently said, 'I look forward to giving you tea on the [House of Commons] terrace because you deserve it', and praised as an 'honoured citizen' with a 'voice that must be heard'. What nice people Corbyn chooses to associate with and call his friends. Also in attendance at the 'peace conference', though not at the wreath-laying, was a Tory Peer, Lord Sheikh. Questioned as to his presence at such a gathering, he said, 'there may have been [sic] Hamas. I did not meet any Hamas people. I am very careful, obviously'. Unlike Corbyn, who just can't keep way from the action.

But this also proved not to be the whole story. The Tory Peer had protested too much, because the *Daily Mail* then carried a feature which showed the 'ever careful' Lord Sheikh, again in the company of Corbyn (never one to miss out on a freebee, no matter how vile his host) shaking hands with the blood-drenched President of Syria, Bashar al-Assad, having arrived with Corbyn and Baroness 'body parts' Tonge in November 2009 on the same road to Damascus as later travelled twice by the Neo-Nazi Nick Griffin and, in April 2018, by former KKK Grand Wizard, white supremacist, Holocaust denier, conspiracy theorist, anti-Zionist and, like Griffin, anti-Semite and Corbyn admirer David Duke. On his website, Duke related how he 'spoke for peace [sic] to 50,000 Syrians' in 'the largest square in Damascus'. What a crew! It was the same rainbow coalition that in the same joint enterprise took turns in the TV studios of the Ayatollahs, with the Left on both occasions represented, not co-coincidentally, by Corbyn and the Liberal Democrats by the anti-Semitic Baroness Tonge and, in Damascus, for the Tories, by a Lord, and for the extreme right, by a notorious British Neo-Nazi and an American white supremacist.

Their high-profile presence in Syria raises some intriguing questions. One can understand the appeal of being so honoured in a country whose rulers, together with their Arab brothers in the Middle East, three times waged wars to 'wipe Israel off the map'. But did any of these anti-Zionists zealots know, or if they did, did they care that while sharing in full measure their loathing of Israel, Assad does not even recognise the existence of a Palestinian people, and that what Corbyn, Baroness Tonge, Lord Sheikh, Griffin and Duke understand as Palestine their host has territorial claims on and regards as 'South Syria'? And what of the Syrian regime's promotion of anti-Semitism? True, this will not be an issue with several of its guests...but what of Comrade Corbyn, the life-long opponent of racism? I choose two of many examples, the Jewish 'blood libel'...'The Talmud's instructions [to commit ritual murder], soaked in hatred and hostility towards humanity, are stamped in the Jewish soul' says Jbara Al-Barghuthi, writing in the Damascus literary magazine *Al-Usbu' Al-Adabi;* and Holocaust denial... 'all the stories about this matter were exaggerated and fabricated' claimed Damascus Radio, the proof being that 'many Jewish officers served in the Nazi command, among whom several were close to Hitler'. That's a new one on me. Then we have the declaration on the website of Corbyn's former employer, Press TV, on

January 27, 2008, International Holocaust Remembrance Day, that 'we all need to mull over the faking of history and the Greatest lie every told.' The same year, the same website published an article by the British Holocaust denier Nicholas Kollerstrom titled *The Walls of Auschwitz: A Review of the Chemical Studies*. The article claimed that the gas chambers at Auschwitz were used for 'benign' purposes only. When the *Jerusalem Post* and the anti-fascist magazine *Searchlight* exposed the Press TV article, the author, described by the website as a 'distinguished academic', was removed as an honorary fellow by University College London.

Whether or not these lies passed Corbyn by, a year on, we find Corbyn beginning his stint with the TV Channel that promoted them. On more than one occasion he has made clear that his support for what he construes as the Palestinian cause necessarily finds him acting in concert with those whose views on other matters he does not necessarily share...like, for example, Holocaust denial, Jewish conspiracies, the extermination of the Jews, the *Protocols*, 9/11, 7/7, the blood libel, Jews as Nazis...etc. etc. This 'convergence of convenience' as I call it demonstrates yet again how politicians from widely-separated segments of the political spectrum can put aside their petty party squabbles when the common enemy is the J... sorry, I meant Zionism. I call Assad's regime 'blood-drenched' with good reason. In February 2017, Amnesty International released a report giving details of 13,000 executions by hanging carried out by Corbyn's hosts between September 2011 and December 2015 at Saydnaya prison north of Damascus, sometimes as many as fifty a day. 'Trials' (before a military court) of those condemned to death lasted between one and three minutes. As we have noted, Jeremy is of course opposed to capital punishment just as we can be sure he is to the torture and beating of prisoners. Both were routine in Saydnaya prison. In April 2020, in Berlin, two former 'intelligence officers' of the Assad regime went on trial, accused of 'crimes against humanity', specifically, torture. What with Cuba, Venezuela, Nicaragua, Iran, Syria and Hamas, one cannot help but wonder how it is that for all his advocacy of a 'kinder politics', Jeremy somehow keeps finding himself in the company and as a guest of movements and regimes that murder and commit the most appalling acts of cruelty against their own people.

And still the Jeremy stories kept coming, as is the way when the press senses it has struck a particularly rich vein. The *Daily Telegraph* carried a photo of Corbyn, taken at 'his' notorious Finsbury Park Mosque in February 2016, a year and half after he became Labour Leader, giving the four-finger salute of the Muslim Brotherhood, sponsor of Corbyn's 'friends' Hamas and, during the Second World War, deeply involved in collaboration with the Nazis in north Africa. Then the *Times* published a photo of Corbyn at the wreath-laying ceremony standing next to Maher el-Taher, whose Popular Front for the Liberation of Palestine one month later murdered four rabbis in a Jerusalem synagogue, hacking them to death with an axe while they prayed. All no doubt in the interests of peace and dialogue.

The 'Black September wreath' story broke after the *Mail* had dispatched a photographer to Tunisia to check out and photograph the relative positions of the two groups of graves. They are 15 yards apart, and the photos of Corbyn beyond any doubt show him standing close to and facing those of the Black September operatives. The Corbyn spin machine went into over-drive. As ever-more damning evidence of his involvement in the ceremony accumulated almost by the hour, so Corbyn's story was recalibrated accordingly. Beginning with an official

Labour Party no comment, by the end of the day, Corbyn had been compelled to confess all. He had no choice. The evidence was visual, unambiguous and overwhelming. But no matter. He had his reasons. His now active role in a ceremony commemorating a Jew-killing terrorist was in the interests of... yes, 'peace': 'You cannot pursue peace by a cycle of violence. The only way you can pursue peace is by dialogue.' And, it seems, by honouring those who, far from conducting a 'dialogue' in the 'pursuit of peace', were leading members of a terrorist organisation, Fatah, dedicated to the destruction of Israel, and themselves, personally responsible for the slaughter of the entire Israeli team in Munich in 1972.

Corbyn's lies caught up with him yet again when the Howie's Corner website reproduced an article by Corbyn for the British Communist Party's *Morning Star* dated October 5, 2014, with the headline, *Palestine United*, and subtitled: 'Unity was in evidence during a major meeting [sic] in Tunisia, writes Jeremy Corbyn'. The fifth paragraph of Corbyn's article related that after 'wreaths were laid on the graves of those who died on that day [that of the Israel air attack] and *on the graves of others [sic] killed by Mossad agents in Paris in 1991*, we [n.b.] moved on to the poignant statue in the main avenue of the coastal town of Ben Arous.' (emphasis added) Three years later, in an interview on Sky TV, Corbyn contradicted this account, which proved to be the true one, claiming he had only attended the ceremony commemorating those killed in the Israeli air attack. How easily lies trip off his tongue.

Rounding off what had been a lively week for Corbyn came a report in the Jewish online *Forward* that in his last appearance on Press TV in August 2012, Corbyn had described Hamas terrorists released in a prisoner swap with Israel, who had been convicted of killing seven Jews in Jerusalem in 2003, as his 'brothers', a step up from just being his 'friends'. For Corbynista loyalists, as on all previous occasions when their Dear Leader's anti-Semitism had been exposed, there could be only one possible explanation for these latest revelations. Union chief Len McCluskey could be relied upon to provide it. Disingenuously claiming he was 'at a loss to understand the motives of the leadership of the Jewish community', he then proceeded to specify what they in fact were. He accused those Labour MPs who had spoken out against anti-Semitism of being involved in a conspiracy 'embracing capitalism, the free market and the alliance with Trump's America'. It reads just like the *Protocols*, as did another union chief's explanation of why the Labour Party was being wracked by accusation of anti-Semitism. Speaking at a Palestine Solidarity Campaign event at the 2018 Trades Union Congress, far leftist Mark Serwolka, General Secretary of the Public and Commercial Service Union claimed that accusations of Labour Party anti-Semitism had been invented to divert attention from the killing of 'dozens of Palestinians...unarmed innocent civilians' by Israeli troops. Having assured his audience that he was 'not a conspiracy theorist', though had he told them that he was, that would not have worried them in the least, he then went on to prove the exact opposite:

> ...but I'll tell you what - one of the best forms of trying to hide from [sic] the atrocities that you are committing [the Hamas-instigated clashes on the Israel border were screened on TV and fully reported in all the media.... How else did Serwolka know about them?] is to go one the offensive and to create a story that does not

301

actually exist [sic] for people on this platform, the trade union movement or, I have to say, for the Leader of the Labour Party.

How does Serwolka know the minds of Britain's 6.23 million trade unionists, some of whom will be Jews, and others will be like Unite's Assistant General Secretary, Steve Turner, who rejects the Left's double standards on human rights. Addressing an anti-racist event at the same TUC, Turner acknowdged that because of the left's refusal to speak the truth about Islamic terrorism, traditional working-class Labour supporters were looking elsewhere for those that did. They were saying,

You're protesting austerity. I see you advertising the protest against Trump. I see you protesting against the Israeli government, against this and that. But where were you protesting when someone used a car as a weapon to mow people down on Waterloo Bridge? Where was the left? Where were we? Where were we when the Manchester bomb went off? [like Shamima Begum, the would-be returnee Jihadi bride from the Islamic State, Corbyn was blaming it on British foreign policy.] Where were we on Westminster Bridge? Where was the left? Where's the left criticisms of the state of Iran for instance, who whipped trade unionists for taking strike action, who denies women human rights, who runs an obscene regime. [Surely a thrust at Corbyn] Saudi Arabia, where we welcome the head of state of Saudi Arabia to the UK. Did we protest? No, we didn't. Why not? What's so sensitive in the left about having discussions about these issues that leaves a vacuum that the right, for no reasons, are only too willing to fill.... They are filling a vacuum that in part is being left by us. We need to talk to those people who are attracted by it and stop talking to ourselves. And we don't do it. And it's uncomfortable.

That says it all. To return to Corbyn's escapade in Tunisia, which epitomises what Turner was objecting to. What on earth was a Labour MP, soon to be elected Leader of the Labour Party, doing in Tunisia on an undeclared freebee, hobnobbing with terrorists and praying and laying a wreath at the graves of Jew-killers, and when caught out, resorting to torturous evasions of the truth more fitting for a career criminal caught in the act on CCTV than the Leader of Her Majesty's Opposition?

W Stalin's Final Solution of the Zionist Question

'The Jews are a spying nation.' J. V Stalin, December 1, 1952

'I knew all too well my father's obsession with "Zionist" plots around every corner.' Stalin's daughter, Svetlana Allilueva.

The accusation that the first loyalty of the Jews is to Israel, which we have seen has featured prominently in the Corbynista abuse heaped on Jewish Labour MPs, (one being referred to by Corbyn as 'the Honourable member for Tel Aviv') and excluded, one suspects for that very reason, from the Labour Party's first definition, later amended, of anti-Semitism, has an intriguing pedigree, antedating by decades the actual creation of the Jewish state in 1948. For all his alleged (by Ken Livingstone) pro-Zionism, Hitler asserts this claim in his *Mein Kampf*, in the same passage cited with approval by Corbyn *confidante* Elleanne Green on her secret *Palestine Live* website ninety years later. Following the Second World War, it re-surfaced, this time on the left, with Stalin's state-sponsored pogrom of Soviet Jewry who, after the creation of the state of Israel, were accused, under the rubric of being 'cosmopolitans without kith and kin', of 'subservience towards things foreign', in effect, to be guilty of treason to the Soviet State.

Even during the war, anti-Semitism in the USSR was never far below the surface. There was no official acknowledgment, either then or up to end of the Soviet Union in 1991, of the extermination by Nazi death squads of more than two million Jews in territories occupied by the German invaders, or that 142,000 Jews died fighting in the Soviet armed forces against the *Wehrmacht*. As Jewish Red Army men battled the Nazis in the outskirts of Moscow, Stalin told a Polish delegation in the Kremlin on December 3, 1941, that 'Jews are bad soldiers'. A diary found on a dead German soldier which chronicled his role in the Holocaust, when published in *Pravda*, was doctored to erase all references to his killing of Jews. In 1944, the Tsarist *'numerus clausus'* was revived to limit Jewish students to 10% of the total in higher education …a Stalinist version of 'affirmative action', on behalf of Russian dunces. As Lenin used to say, 'if you meet a clever Russian, the chances are he's a Jew, an opinion evidently not shared by Stalin, who claimed in 1945 that it was Russians who were especially endowed with 'a clear mind'. These were straws in the wind of the hurricane to come. Stalin's anti-Zionist campaign only really began in earnest in 1948, the year of the birth of the Jewish state. As one of Stalin's top intelligence operatives, Pavel Sudoplatov, later related in his memoirs, *Special Tasks*, 'Israel's victory in its war of independence greatly strengthened awareness among Soviet Jews of their cultural identity. Israel presented a new magnet for emigration. The anti-cosmopolitan campaign quickly turned anti-Semitic. Now the battle was against "rootless cosmopolitanism", meaning Jews who had Western ties or ideas and might not hold the Soviet Union first in their hearts.'

To generate the pogrom atmosphere conducive to the planned onslaught on

Soviet Jewry, Stalin's secret police put into circulation rumours that in any civilised country would have been dismissed as the ravings of lunatics. One that went the rounds was that of a tunnel being dug by actors from the soon to be closed Jewish Theatre to the Kremlin a full two kilometres away, with the intention of blowing it up, together with all its occupants. Jews were purged from leading positions in the armed forces and party apparatus. Previously overrepresented by a sizable margin, by 1951, there was only one Jew out of more than 1,000 party secretaries. There then followed the arrest, torture and on August 12, 1952, execution as US and Israeli spies of all the members of the Soviet Jewish Anti-Fascist Committee. Miron Vorsi, a cousin of the moving spirit of the Committee, the world-famous actor Solomon Mikheols, whom the secret police had murdered on Stalin's orders in 1948, was made to confess that he was the leader of a 'terrorist group' consisting of Jewish doctors and 'a number of Jewish nationalists', which, 'by means of criminal methods of treatment', would attempt to 'destroy the health of leading [government] workers'. According to Vorsi's scripted confession, his cousin was the mastermind of a classic *Protocols* international Jewish conspiracy:

> Mikheols said that for us Jews, it was necessary at all times to maintain key positions in science, art, literature and in pedagogical institutions, and only then would we be able to unite the uncoordinated strengths and preserve the unity of the Jewish population…In this way, it was already clear to me that the name Jewish Ant-fascist Committee was only a smokescreen under which Jewish nationalists realised their anti-Soviet, nationalist goals; and the fact that the Committee directed to the USA various kinds of information about the Soviet Union, directly shows that he essentially served the interests of Zionists circles in the USA.

This and other similarly scripted confessions, followed by the purging of all leading Soviet institutions of Jews, climaxed in late 1952 in the fabrication and then 'unmasking' of the so-called 'Doctors Plot', in which the cream of the Soviet medical profession, many of them Jews, were accused of planning to poison the entire Soviet party and state leadership on behalf of their US and Zionist paymasters. It was not only Jewish doctors who were targeted. There was an *in-camera* trial of Jewish poets and their associates, 13 of whom were convicted of treason and also shot on August 12, 1952. Jewish managers of the Stalin (sic) car plant were charged with Zionism after sending a telegram to the world-famous (but soon to be murdered on Stalin's instructions) Jewish actor Solomon Mikheols celebrating the founding of Israel. Learning of this case, Stalin response was to say to Khrushchev, 'the good workers at the factory should be given clubs so they can beat the hell out of those Jews at the end of the working day.' More executions of Jews followed. Sensing that not all his immediate entourage shared his conviction that all Jews were born traitors, he lectured a meeting of the Party's ruling Presidium of December 1, 1952, on the threat they posed to the security of the Soviet Union: 'Every Jew-nationalist is an agent of American intelligence'. Amongst Stalin's inner circle, it was an open secret that he enjoyed 'anti-Semitic anecdotes', on one occasion being convulsed with mirth when his bodyguard viciously parodied the last moments of the executed Jewish Bolshevik leader Zinoviev, on his knees crying out: 'Hear Israel, our God is the only God'.

Stalin's war on the Jews was accompanied by the erasing, *a la* Third Reich, of all visible manifestations of Jewish contributions to world and Soviet culture. Even the portrait of Mendelssohn at the Moscow Conservatoire was removed, just as for the same reason his statue in Leipzig had been demolished by the Nazis a decade previously. But the portrait of the anti-Semite Wagner, Hitler's favourite composer, remained on display. As was the intention, public manifestations of anti-Semitism boiled over as Jews were assaulted in the street, while men accused of being Jewish had to prove their gentile credentials by exposing their genitals. Male party members divorced their Jewish wives, who were then either imprisoned or executed, to be quickly replaced by new gentile partners provided by the party. Molotov, Stalin's most devoted stalwart, duly obeyed an order by his master to divorce his Jewish wife, Polina, who was charged with 'links with Zionism' and 'betrayal of the motherland' and despatched to a labour camp in Kazakhstan.

On Stalin's specific instructions - 'beat, beat and beat again' - Jews accused of treason were tortured remorselessly until they signed pre-fabricated confessions, one of which declared: 'enveloped by nationalist poison, we agreed to the blind conviction that Jews, by virtue of their alleged special qualities of intelligence, were called by history itself to rule the world'... a fair precis of the version of the myth of the world Jewish conspiracy first expounded in 1905 by a Russian priest, Sergei Nilus, in the *Protocols of the Learned Elders of Zion*, a text that has found favour right across political and religious spectra from Nazis to Corbynistas and from Muslims to Christians.

Some of the 'confessions' extracted under torture were absurd even by Soviet standards, at least in one case deliberately so, as related by Sudoplatov. Colonel Naum Schwartzman, before his turn came, had himself been employed to edit the confessions of previous victims. When interrogated for his role in a Jewish plot to overthrow the Soviet regime, in order to prove himself insane, he elaborated on the main charge by confessing to have had 'homosexual relations with [the now arrested previous police chief] Abakumov, his son, and the British Ambassador'. Piling on the lunacy, 'he invented unbelievable stories, like being inspired in his terrorist activities by drinking Zionist soup [sic] by his Jewish aunt, or sleeping with his step daughter, or having homosexual relations with his son.' Just when he seemed to have succeeded in convincing his interrogators that he was indeed mad, Stalin intervened. 'That scoundrel is playing for time. No need for any [medical] expert. Arrest the whole group immediately.' Then 'Stalin ordered the arrest of all Jewish colonels and generals in the Ministry of Security. A total of some fifty senor officers and generals were arrested'. Stalin instructed his investigators to 'put them in handcuffs and beat them until they confess'. One surviving victim of Stalin's pogrom recalled many years later the atmosphere of menace of that time:

Events were mounting to a climax. Horrible news was passed by word of mouth. The MGB [successor to the NKVD, and predecessor of the KGB] had disclosed a Jewish conspiracy at the Moscow automobile plant. Mass arrests had been made, wreaking havoc on the leading engineering and technical personnel...More Jewish plots were unearthed - in the Moscow metro and elsewhere...the medical world was not simply deflated, it was crushed...everyone who was still at large expected arrest that night...Every physician was regarded as a potential murderer. I shall never forget the face of my laboratory assistant, distorted with fury and hatred, as she hissed through clenched teeth 'Damn intellectuals [code for too clever by half Jews R.B.], they all deserve to be cudgelled.' Meetings were held at all factories and

305

offices, some organised, some spontaneous, and almost all openly anti-Semitic. Speakers would vehemently demand that all criminals should be put to a terrible death. Many went so far as to offer their services in carrying out the actual executions.

On December 1, 1952, Stalin addressed the Soviets Union's ruling body, the Presidium of the Party Central Committee: His subject was the political meaning of the Doctors' Plot:

> Every Jew-nationalist [i.e., Zionist] is an agent of America intelligence. The Jew-nationalists think the USA has saved their nation, where they hope may become rich men, bourgeois. They consider themselves obligated to the Americans. Among the doctors are many Jewish nationalists.

On January 13, 1953, *Pravda* [Russian for 'truth'] carried an article drafted by Stalin:

> The unmasking of the band of doctor poisoners dealt a shattering blow to the American-English instigators of war...the whole world can now see once again the true face of the slave-master cannibals from the USA and England ...The bosses of the USA and their English "junior partners" know that success in ruling another country cannot be achieved by peaceful means. Feverishly preparing for a new world war, they urgently sent their spies into the rear of the USSR and into the countries of the People's Democracies [a reference to the series of show trials of alleged agents of Tito] they attempted to implement what had been destroyed among the Hitlerites - to create in the USSR their own subversive 'fifth column.'

Given the context, the message was unambiguous. The capitalist West's Jewish 'fifth column' was resuming Hitler's lost war against the Soviet Union. 58 prominent Jewish intellectuals, writers and artists, fearful with good reason that their turn could be next, sent a letter to *Pravda* denouncing Israel with a venom and themes that are common coin today among leftist anti-Semites. Zionists were' the helpers of the Jewish rich' and Israel 'a kingdom [sic] of exploiters...a kingdom of profit for a small bunch of rich people...a vanguard outpost of war provocateurs...a bridgehead for USA aggression...a war is necessary to Jewish millionaires and billionaires' because 'it is for them a source of great profit.' 'Jewish industrialists and bank magnates' were conspiring to 'unleash a new world war', while Israel itself was ruled by 'a small bunch of rich people' who served the interests of 'Jewish and American capitalism'. What the Zionists claimed to be the homeland of the Jews was in reality the 'homeland of America', a weapon for the development of a new war...a bridgehead for US aggression against the Soviet Union and all peace-loving peoples'. The Soviet people were expected to believe, and assuredly many did, that Israel, one of the smallest countries in the world, with less than one hundredth of the Soviet Union's population and a miniscule and poorly equipped army comprised then as now largely of reservists, was threatening with annihilation a country covering one sixth of the land surface of the globe, possessed of nuclear weapons and the largest army in the world. Even so, it was 'impossible to be an authentic fighter for the affairs of peace and freedom of nations without conducting a struggle against Jewish billionaires and millionaires and their Zionist agents'.

Self-abasement could sink no lower. Yet the letter was not published. Instead *Pravda* carried a story on the 'plot' with the headline, 'Murderers in White Gowns'. Clearly more was required than just attacks on Israel. Denunciations of fellow Jews were now the order of the day.

Once armed with the 'evidence', extracted by torture, that all Jews were either potential or actual traitors, in the last weeks before his death, Stalin set in motion his Bolshevik version of the final solution of the Jewish question. With all existing slave camps already bursting at the seams, he ordered the construction of four new camps in the East to house the first *tranche* of arrested Jews. Convoys of cattle trucks to transport them, Nazi style, to their early deaths were being assembled in the railway marshalling yards of Moscow and other major Soviet cities, while the Soviet press whipped the public into a frenzy of hatred against 'rootless cosmopolitans without kith and kin'...not a difficult task given Russia's appalling history of pogroms and Jew-baiting. As the campaign escalated, so 'spontaneous' mass meetings, no more so than the pogrom set in motion by the Nazis on the 'Night of the Crystals' of November 9-10, 1938, voted unanimously for the planned deportation of Soviet Jewry to the Far East. After interrogating one of the suspects in the 'Doctor's Plot', security chief Mikhail Ryumin included in his report the following comment: 'In Moscow there live more than a million and a half Jews. They have seized the medical posts, the legal profession, the union of composers and the union of writers. I'm not even speaking of the trade networks. Meanwhile, of these Jews, only a handful are useful to us. All the rest are potential enemies of the state'. In his biography of the Soviet composer Dimitri Shostakovich, who despite being himself at this time out of favour for failing to conform to the dictates of 'socialist realism', courageously set Jewish texts to music, Ian MacDonald set the scene for this return to medieval barbarism:

In January 1953, two ominous themes appeared in the Soviet press: a campaign for 'greater vigilance', accompanied by slogans contending that there was no nobler act than denouncing your best friend; and what amounted to a call for a national pogrom of the Jews. The key element was the so called Doctors' Plot', announced by an article in *Pravda* by Stalin himself. According to this, the Jews were literally poisoning Soviet society: Jewish doctors by injecting their patients with carcinogens or syphilis, Jewish pharmacists by serving their customers with pills made of dried fleas.

In their *The Unknown Stalin*, the historians Zhores and Roy Medvedev tell the same story:

These entirely absurd accusations provided the basis for an unrestrained and increasingly hysterical crusade in the press, particularly in *Pravda*. Every day the major papers published some item or other exposing subversive activity in the USSR by American, British, Israeli and various other secret services. The evident signs of an incipient pogrom aroused anxiety throughout the world.

Sergo Beria, the son of Stalin's last but two police chiefs, provides an insider's view of the then prevailing mood:

The entire intelligentsia took part in that shameless campaign against the Jews, whatever they may say nowadays...I say nothing of the masses, who had no need for encouragement. We came close to pogroms. The hounds were unleashed. I saw apparently normal people transformed into mad dogs. The most fantastic stories were spread. The Jews were said to have deliberately inoculated children with diphtheria, to have poisoned vaccines, to have killed new-born babies in the maternity hospitals so as to annihilate the Russian people and so on ['Baby killers']. The human vileness and baseness described so complacently by Dostoyevsky burst forth in every journal. This was the first time that I experienced evil in a purely unreasoned form. It was unbearable, worse than the Nazis' murders. An entire people was being conditioned to kill.'

Stalin died on March 5, 1953, so the last act of his 'final solution', the Kremlin's version of Hitler's Crystal Night pogrom of November 1938, was never staged, but if it had been, this is what it would have entailed. True to the tradition of the autocracy's Black Hundreds, with their war cry of 'Beat the Yids and Save Russia', not the state, but the outraged popular masses were to have delivered the *coup de grace*. Gallows to hang those prominent Jews convicted of treason, 'beasts in human form' as *Pravda* Koranically described them, were to be erected in Red Square, but before the sentences could be carried out, gangs would exact lynch law justice, while other mobs, pure-blooded sons of holy mother Russia, would hunt down and kill Jews at addresses provided by the security police. Supposedly to rescue them from the same fate, the remainder would be deported in cattle trucks to the Soviet far east, there to be left to waste away. These facts have been established by a number of writers on Stalin's last years, most notably the Russian investigative journalist Arkady Vaksberg in his *Stalin Against the Jews*, who had access to previously unseen documents relevant to the case and security officials involved in the operation.

If Stalin had lived to see through his removal of several million Jews to the far east of Siberia, it would have been the last of a long series of similar 'cleansings' and, as such, would therefore have presented no insuperable technical or logistic difficulties. First came 'class cleansing' - the so-called 'liquidation of the kulaks', supposedly better-off peasants, but in reality any peasant who resisted Stalin's forcible collectivization onslaught of the early 1930s. At least three million peasants were deported from the fertile western provinces of the USSR to slave camps in the east and the arctic north. Of those peasants who were left behind, in the famine and cannibalism that ensued, at least ten million died of starvation and disease. In the terror of 1937-38, which saw the physical annihilation of the Bolshevik old guard and the purging of 80% of the military high command, Stalin's xenophobic paranoia ran riot, triggering the murder and deportation of tens of thousands of communist refugees from fascist and authoritarian regimes: Poles, Letts, Finns, Yugoslavs, Estonians, Germans, Austrians, Greeks, Iranians, Chinese, Romanians, Bulgarians, and Macedonians, together with the extermination of the political and cultural elites of the USSR's numerous national minorities. These 'resettlements', to use the Nazi euphemism for the extermination of the Jews, were only the beginning, a trial run, you might say, for what was soon to follow on an even grander scale.

Beginning in 1940, from states and territories allotted to Stalin by his pact with Hitler in August 1939 - Latvia, Lithuania and Estonia, each annexed after rigged referenda in June 1940, Finland, after its defeat in the in the 'Winter War' of 1939-40, and from eastern Poland and the Moldavian province of Romania -

there were deported in cattle trucks to the same destinations in total no less than three million men, women and children. As was the case with the Nazi deportations of the Jews, thousands died of hunger and cold *en route*. In the first months of the Nazi invasion of the USSR in 1941, in the Ukraine and the Baltic States, not surprisingly, Hitler's armies were initially greeted as liberators. The same occurred in the Caucasus and the Crimea a year later, only this time the welcoming party was composed mainly of Muslims from a myriad of nationalities. Even before the war was over, Stalin, the 'Father of the Peoples', took his revenge, deporting not just the guilty, *but their entire nations*: Germans, Chechens, Crimean Tartars, Ingushi, Karachi, Balkars, Kalmucks, Greeks, Armenians, Kemchins, Turks, Kurds – all told, another 3 million...again, thousands of miles to the East, the old dumping ground of the tsars. In 1948, there were more mass deportations from the Baltic states, and, in 1950, 100,000 more from Moldavia. Then it was intended to be the turn of the Jews.

This story has a sequel. In October 1956, the British Communist Party, rocked by revelations of Stalin's crimes in Khrushchev's 'secret speech' earlier that year, sent a delegation to the USSR to investigate the fate of Soviet Jewry under the idol of Corbyn's election strategist and, taking turns with Corbyn, Chairman of the Sharia left Stop the War Coalition. What they learned horrified even these case-hardened loyalists:

> Jewish writers, artists and intellectuals had been tortured and physically destroyed [why not say it, *murdered?*], particularly during the period 1948-52, and this included the whole of the Jewish Anti-fascist Committee...deliberate efforts had been made to repress all expressions of Jewish culture...the Moscow Jewish State Theatre had been shut down, Jewish papers had ceased publication and the Yiddish Publishing House had been closed...The *Soviet Encyclopaedia*, which in its 1932 edition devoted about 160 columns to the Jews, reduced this in the 1952 edition to four columns. The biographies of many eminent Jews have been removed. Marx was no longer referred to as a Jew...the years 1948-52 were known [among Soviet Jews] as 'The Black Years', the period during which many Jews were dismissed and charged with treason and executed...Those arrested and charged in secret were prominent political or cultural workers. Shortly after his arrest, the immediate relatives of the arrested man would be deported to some distant place and there set to work, and often at low wages. Finally, the husband would be shot, perhaps after torture to try to force him to confess or to incriminate others.

In the wake of Israel's victory over Egypt, Syria and Jordan in the 'Six Day War' of June 1967, Soviet anti-Semitism moved up several gears. Hundreds of books and articles were churned out on various aspects of the 'anti-Zionist question', some of them dwelling in imaginary detail on the alleged collaboration of Zionist Jews with the Nazis before and during the Second World War, a theme that was to become popular in later years with the western far left. One such offering, issued under the auspices of the 'Anti-Zionist Committee of the Soviet Public', staffed entirely by Jewish stooges of the KGB, was titled, *Criminal Alliance of Zionism and Nazism*. As one would expect, no reference was made in this or any other publication on the same theme to the actual collaboration of Arab/Islamic leaders with the Nazis in the Holocaust, Stalin's pact with Hitler, or the asylum granted by the Kremlin's Arab allies to Nazis wanted for their part in the extermination of European Jewry. Some titles published were also in English, including *Zionism: Instrument of Imperialist Reaction; Anti-Sovietism, the Profession of Zionists* and *Zionism Counts on Terror.*

One decade on, little had changed. A symphony by Shostakovich was banned because it commemorated the massacre in September 1941 of 40,000 Jews by the Nazis at the Babi Yar ravine outside Kiev. Two decades on, when, on the hundredth anniversary of Lenin's birth in 1870, western scholars referred to the Bolshevik leader's maternal Jewish ancestry, the Kremlin responded with outraged denials, as if Lenin had been falsely accused of some unspeakable crime. Five years later, taken to task by the Israeli delegation for having engineered the United Nations resolution defining Zionism as a racist ideology, Soviet diplomat Yakov Malik retorted, 'do not poke you long [sic] noses into our Soviet Garden. Anyone who pokes his long [sic] nose into our garden will find himself without a nose. You had better carve this on your long [sic] noses, Zionists.'

Five decades and more on, anti-Semitism was and is still the norm amongst Russia's post-Bolshevik political class. More than 150 anti-Semitic newspapers pump out the same bile as *Pravda* did in Stalin's day. Very much in the spirit and letter of Hamas, the manifesto of the anti-Semitic *Pamyat* (memory) movement demands a 'German-Russian alliance [sic...again!] that will finally put an end to Zionism', for which read, the Jews. In December 1998, Chairman of the Russia Duma Security Committee Viktor Ilyukhin accused President Yeltsin's 'Jewish entourage' of committing 'genocide' against the Russian people. (at least it made a change from the Palestinians), while Duma member General Albert Makashov blamed 'the Yids' for Russia's problems and threatened to 'send them to the other world': 'We will remain anti-Semites, and we must triumph.'

Seven decades on, Jewish migration from Europe to Israel has reached record levels, 55,000 from France alone since 2000, fuelled not only by the traditional anti-Semitism of the far right, but the vicious anti-Zionism of the left, and most of all, by the illegal mass immigration of anti-Semitic Muslims orchestrated by German Chancellor Angel Merkel. For the first time since the expulsion of the Jews from England by Edward the First in 1290, British Jews have joined this modern exodus, fearful of the consequences of a government headed by a politician who has counted genocidal Islamic terrorists among his friends, and has presided over a party many of whose members have quite openly and with impunity paraded their hatred of the Jews.

On the very day I wrote these lines, *The Times of Israel* of November 27, 2018, carried a report of a CNN survey of attitudes towards the Jews in seven European countries; the UK, Germany, Poland, Hungary, Austria, France and Sweden, which revealed the following: 20% of Europeans think the Jews have 'too much influence world-wide'; 28% too much influence in business and finance, 25% in wars and conflicts and 32% that they exploit the Holocaust 'to advance their position or achieve certain goals', (predictably, in Poland this was 50%). 34% said they either knew nothing or 'very little' about the Holocaust while 31% said that commemorating the Holocaust distracts attention from other atrocities around the world... all allegations featured prominently on Corbynista websites. On December 11, the same journal reported that the European Union Agency for Fundamental Rights had conducted a survey of Jewish experiences of anti-Semitic attitudes and incidents in 12 EU member states, again including the UK. A third of the 16,395 Jews interviewed said they were considering emigrating as result of a recent sudden increase of hostility towards, them, which included physical attacks as well as verbal abuse, mainly, so it would seem, by Muslim migrants. A final thought. With something like a quarter of Europeans subscribing to a belief in a Jewish world conspiracy, is it any wonder that European Jews feel *persona non grata*?

Addendum: Stalin's Pogrom in Prague

Given Stalin's obsession with the 'Jewish Question', it was only to expected that when Yugoslavia's break from the Kremlin in the spring of 1948 precipitated a series of show trails of suspected Titoites in Eastern Europe, the role of Zionism should be placed at the centre of this imagined conspiracy. Nowhere was this more so than in the trial of prominent Czech state and party leaders conducted in Prague in November 1952. On his way to total power, Stalin had made short work of his leading Jewish opponents in the Soviet communist party...Trotsky, Zinoviev, Kamenev and Radek. Now it was the turn of the Czechoslovaks. Of the 14 defendants, no fewer than 11 were listed in the indictment as Jews, and of these 11, eight were sentenced to death and executed after confessing to and being convicted of treason (all these verdicts were posthumously quashed in 1963). According to the indictment prepared by a team of Soviet advisers known affectionately by their Czech subordinates as 'The Teachers', the accused had organised a 'Trotskyist, Titoist, Zionist, bourgeois nationalist' anti-state conspiracy on behalf of US imperialism. Just as in the 'Doctors Plot', a special role in this mythical operation had been allotted by the prosecutors to Jews, hence their blatant preponderance in the dock. The remaining three non-Jews were obviously included to counter the inevitable accusations from anti-Stalinists that the trial was in reality a judicial pogrom.

The pre-scripted testimonies of the accused Jews made it all too clear that the central theme of the trial was indeed anti-Semitism, disguised not always, and when it, was, thinly, as anti-Zionism. One defendant typically confessed that 'in trade negotiations with capitalist states I concluded commercial agreements that were favourable to capitalist, above all Jewish merchants, but disadvantageous to the Republic'. The highest profile defendant, former Vice Premier and party General Secretary Rudolf Slansky, confessed to 'placing Zionists [that is, Jews] in important posts' because, as Slansky explained:

> Zionists [again, obviously, Jews] were conducting activity aimed at the liquidation of the popular [sic] democratic [sic] regime in Czechoslovakia. These Zionists [Jews] in turn placed other Zionists [Jews] in various posts in the administration and economic offices and through them I was linked with the Zionist [Jewish] organisations. The significance of this lay in the fact that Zionist [Jewish] organisations in Czechoslovakia were in turn connected with similar Zionist [Jewish] organisations in the capitalist countries. The whole world-wide [sic] Zionist [Jewish] movement was in in fact led by the imperialists, in particular the US imperialists, by means of US Zionists. [i.e., the 'Israel lobby' Corbyn and his cohorts assert still control US foreign policy 60 years and more later.]

There we have it.... the world Zionist, i.e., Jewish conspiracy. Once again, it could be the *Protocols*...or for that matter, just as easily, a Corbynista website. As Slansky was the star defendant at the trial, establishing his intrinsic 'Jewishness' - treachery - was integral to the prosecution's case against not only him but his Jewish co-conspirators:

> The witness Oskar Langer, an international Zionist agent, also confirmed that

Slansky was the patron all Jewish bourgeois nationalists, and that he had expressly said that it was necessary to fill important positions in economic, political and public life with Zionists and Jewish bourgeois nationalists....His closest associates from the days of his youth were Germnder, Frejka and Sling [Jewish co-defendants] – all Zionist agents.' [Then came the punch line, line, dictated by the trial's architect in the Kremlin]: '*Slansky cannot deny his Jewish bourgeois character.* (emphasis added)

The message was clear: Ignore the *pro forma* 'bourgeois'. Conspirator-in-chief Slansky was a Jew and Jews have a certain 'character', which impels them to treason. Just as Stalin said, they were a 'spying nation'.

Another aspect of the trial that also features prominently in today's anti-Semitism was the prosecution's associating defendants with both the Nazis and Israel. Two defendants had been inmates of Nazi concentration camps, so this provided the prosecution with the opportunity to accuse them of collaboration with their captors. One admitted that he had 'cooperated with the Nazis and been promoted to foreman. As a Nazi henchman, he had helped the Nazis maintain order by torturing his fellow prisoners and by stealing their food'. Although not a Jew, he nevertheless confessed to his involvement in Zionist plottings. Asked why, he replied:

Slansky, who led the conspiratorial Centre, is himself a Jewish bourgeois nationalist, and a whole number of other members of our centre are also Jewish bourgeois nationalists or even directly Zionists [why the distinction?] The main reason for our [the non-Jewish conspirators'] support, however, was that the Zionists were the most reliable imperialist agency, which gave Slansky the best opportunity for maintaining his link with the imperialist West.

Another former Nazi camp inmate, this time Jewish, was described by the prosecution as 'a bourgeois [i.e., Jewish] nationalist, son of a rich merchant and collaborator of the Nazis', and as if this was not enough to ensure his conviction, he also admitted taking part in 'actions which were organised by the Anglo-US imperialists and their agents in Israel aimed at enriching the Jewish bourgeoisie.' The purpose becomes clear when one notices the linkage between Nazis, the 'Jewish bourgeoisie' and the state of Israel. Asked why he had betrayed his country, the same defendant replied that it was because 'I am a Jewish bourgeois nationalist'...in other words, a Zionist, whose only loyalty is to Israel. Where have we heard that before?

Several other themes will be familiar to those who follow the fortunes of Corbynism. As already noted, the prosecution made great play with the role played by 'Jewish billionaires' in the mythical conspiracies concocted by Stalin's 'teachers. Among those listed were the banking scions of Morgenthau, Baruch, Mandel and...yes. that favourite Corbynista whipping-boy, the Rothschilds. Then there was Slansky's confession that in order to protect his Jewish co-conspirators from exposure, to use the current Corbynista term, he had 'weaponised' anti-Semitism:

I deliberately shielded them by abusing the campaign against so-called [sic!!!] anti-Semitism. By proposing that a big campaign be waged against anti-Semitism, by magnifying the danger of anti-Semitism and by proposing various measures against anti-Semitism – such as the writing of articles, the publication of pamphlets, the holding of

313

lectures - I criminally [sic] prevented the waging of a campaign against Zionism…I deliberately shielded Zionists by publicly speaking out against the people who pointed to the hostile activities of Zionists and by describing these peoples as anti-Semites…

No, this is not Corbyn's Labour Party, *circa* 2019, but Stalinist Prague, 1952. The absurdity and inconsistencies of the charges and the scripted confessions echoed those of Stalin's pre-war frame up trials and purges, as result of which, millions were either executed or dispatched to an early death in remote slave camps, accused, in every case falsely, of having conspired with the Soviet Union's enemies to subvert Bolshevik, or to be more precise, Stalin's rule. For example, in the first of the three Moscow trials, defendants confessed to having begun their collaboration with the Gestapo no later than the Autumn of 1932, several months before Hitler's appointment as German Chancellor on January 30, 1933 and a full half a year before the Gestapo was founded by Herman Goering on April 26, 1933.

The relentless anti-Semitism pervading the Prague trial can be measured by the frequency of the use of certain key words and terms as reported by the far from complete public record of its proceedings. Among these were: Israel: 43; Cosmopolitan: 7; Zionist or Zionism: 124; Jew: 60. Nothing daunted, the British Communist Party loyally rebutted accusations that the Prague trial was in any way anti-Semitic. The party's *Daily Worker* (predecessor to Corbyn's favourite newspaper the *Morning Star*), in insisting that 'Gentiles and Jews stood in the dock together accused of hostile acts against the people's democracy of Czechoslovakia', understandably neglected to add that while Jews, due to the ravages of the Holocaust, comprised only a minuscule fraction of the country's population, they outnumbered the 'gentiles' in the dock by a ratio of 11 to 3. (A precedent for this device had been set in the first of the three Moscow trials of Bolshevik leaders of 1936, 37 and 38. In the dock were no fewer than ten Jews out of out of a total of 16 defendants, all accused of and convicted and executed for collaborating with Nazi Germany…as Jewish communists do. And in August 1939, Stalin did just that, signing his pact with Hitler to partition Poland between them.)

Defiantly, the *Worker* continued: 'The [unspecified] number of Jews involved was decided by the number who participated in the anti-State conspiracy and not by the authorities at all.'. But the truth was, and there surely must have been even loyal Stalinists who secretly entertained the thought, as some certainly did over Moscow show trials (even Stalin admitted to his cronies, strictly off the record, that all their accused were innocent) there was no 'anti-State conspiracy' and therefore those Jews selected for trial had been chosen by the 'authorities', not on the basis of an equally non-existent guilt, but for no other reason than they were Jews.

X Money for Old Rope

Of Livingstone's famous *bon mot*, which later served as title of his autobiography, 'if voting changed anything, they'd ban it', if anyone can be said to have devoted their adult life to chasing after votes, it is Livingstone, from Lambeth Council and Leader of the GLC to MP for Brent East and finally, his crowning glory, in the footsteps of Dick Wittington, to be elected, if only twice, Mayor of London. Simultaneously with this electoral ascent, Livingstone very publicly associated himself with regimes and movements that have indeed banned, rigged or opposed free elections precisely because they could bring about political change...Cuba, Syria, Nicaragua, Venezuela, Iran, the PLO, Hamas, Hezbollah...Then there is Livingstone the anti-racist, a profile he is no doubt able to reconcile with his praise for Yusuf al-Qaradawi as 'one of the leading progressive voices in the Islamic world', a cleric who on Al-Jazeera TV, praised Hitler for visiting Allah's just punishment on six million Jews, and his own insistence that 'anti-Semitism is not the same thing as racism', and in the same vein, that 'it's not anti-Semitic to hate the Jews of Israel,' presumably, all six million of them. Finally, we have gay rights. Throughout his political career, and especially when Leader of the GLC and then Mayor of London, Livingstone acquired a deserved reputation as a promotor of the rights of sexual minorities...at least in the UK. But here too, he was able to reconcile this stance with taking up paid employment as a host for Iran's Press TV, owned by a regime that puts gays, including children, to death by throwing them from tall buildings and publicly hanging them from cranes.

I have previously referred to the unmatched capacity of Livingstone to adjust his stated opinions to what he regards as the needs and milieu of the moment. His old Sharia comrade Jeremy Corbyn is a no less seasoned exponent of the same tactic. They make a fine duo. This is nowhere better demonstrated in their duplicitous attitude towards the death penalty. First, Livingstone: 'I have been opposed to the death penalty throughout my life.' Sangat Television, March 25, 2012, reporting a speech by Livingstone to a Sikh protest in London against the death sentence imposed by an Indian court on Balwant Singh Rajoana, convicted of the murder of former chief Minister Beant Singh. But then: 'One of the things [Venezuelan President] Chavez did when he came to power, he didn't kill all the oligarchs...he allowed them to live, to carry on.' (Livingstone on Talk Radio, as reported by *HuffPost*, August 3, 2017.) One cannot but notice a certain discrepancy between these two statements.

Now Corbyn, with reference to the US killing of Osama Bin Laden, the architect of 9/11: 'I profoundly disagree with the death penalty for anybody.' (Iranian Press TV, August 2011) Next, a letter from Corbyn to Prime Minister David Cameron concerning the impending execution by the Saudis of Ali al Nimr on charges of anti-government activities, as reported on the BBC News website, September 26, 2015: 'As you may be aware, Ali has exhausted all his appeals, and could be executed any day - in a particularly horrific manner, which involves beheading and the public display or "crucifixion" of the body.' Now consider this. In that same year, 2015, Iran carried out 997 'recorded' executions without any public protest that I have been able to trace from its former Press TV employee, Jeremy Corbyn, or for that matter fellow employee Ken Livingstone. According to Amnesty International, Iran, with a population of 80 million, is responsible for half of all executions carried out *in the entire world*, with its population of 7.5 billion. The evidence is indisputable that Corbyn and others with double standards identical to his own have been prepared to take up highly-paid employment with a regime drenched in the blood of tens of thousands of victims of its theocratic tyranny.

There was a repeat performance of Corbyn's selective opposition to the death penalty when in October 2018, the Saudi *Washington Post* journalist Kamal Jashoggi was reported missing, presumed murdered (which proved to be the case) after visiting the Saudi Consulate in Istanbul. Corbyn's Shadow Foreign Secretary Emily Thornberry criticised the Conservative government's response as being 'too little, too late'. In Iran that same week, despite a campaign by Amnesty International to save her from the gallows, Zeinab Sekaanvand Lokran, accused of killing her brute of a husband, for which if true, she deserved a medal, in the name of Allah the Merciful and the Compassionate was hanged in Iran three days after giving birth to her baby, which died. But there were no protests, either too little or too late, from Ms. Thornberry. Why the difference? Could it be because Corbyn regards the Sunni Saudis as fair game, being allegedly allies of the west in the 'war on terror'; that is, though nobody who is supposed to be waging it dares say so, on Jihadi Islam, while he has proved himself a true friend of both Jihadi Islam and the hangmen of Shi'a Iran?

Let me repeat: The evidence is incontestable that together with Saddam useful idiot George Galloway from the far left, and from the far right James Thring, Kevin Barrett, and Manuel Ochsenrieter, editor of the Neo-Nazi monthly *Zuerst!*, Corbyn and Livingstone have taken paid employment from the Iranian Press TV Chanel, in Livingstone's case as a regular presenter. Launched in January 2007, Press TV is funded by the Iranian state, and is a division of Islamic Republic of Iran Broadcasting, the sole legal broadcaster in Iran. Its head is appointed by the Iranian theocracy's Supreme Leader, currently Ayatollah Ali Khamenei. Normal payment per appearance on a programme is around £500. However, as recorded in the House of Commons Register of MPs interests, Corbyn received ten times that amount for four hours work. Concerning Livingstone, the following excerpted item appeared in the London *Evening Standard* on January 11, 2009:

> Ken Livingstone was today accused of 'showing a lack of judgment' after it emerged, he had been paid thousands of pounds to front a programme on Iranian state television. He has presented seven shows on the English-language Press TV channel, three of which have been broadcast since he became Labour's London mayoral candidate in September. The government-funded international news network was launched by Iranian President Mahmoud Ahmadinejad in 2007 and is run by the Islamic Republic of Iran Broadcasting. The broadcaster was investigated last year by Ofcom after interviewing a jailed *Newsweek* journalist who was allegedly under extreme duress at the time in an interrogation room.
>
> Mr Livingstone's appearances, reviewing books on the channel, put him at odds with senior Labour figures including party leader Ed Miliband, who called last month for the release of an Iranian woman sentenced to death by stoning after her alleged confession to her part in her husband's murder was shown on Press TV. [Remember, Livingstone has been 'opposed to the death penalty' throughout his

life.]

Human rights campaigners condemned the channel after its report on Sakineh Mohammadi Ashtiani. In a report on its website, Press TV said she had accompanied a film crew to her house 'to recount details of the killing of her husband at the crime scene.' Activists, however, claim her apparent confession was coerced. The criticism of Mr Livingstone follows calls for his expulsion from Labour in October, after he campaigned openly alongside Tower Hamlets mayor Lutfur Rahman, who had been deselected by the party over alleged links to [Islamic] extremism. [Rahman was subsequently found by a judge to have been corruptly elected and was removed from office.]

Mr Livingstone first appeared on Press TV in March 2009, standing in for former Respect MP George Galloway. Previous presenters on the channel have been paid about £500 per show. [Now we get an insight into Livingstone's literary tastes] Books reviewed on his Epilogue programme include *Zionist Israel and Apartheid South Africa*, *The Invention of the Jewish People* [sic], and *Israel and The Clash* of *Civilisations: Iraq, Iran, And The Plan To Remake The Middle East.*

As we have seen, like Livingstone's, Corbyn's opposition to the death penalty is highly selective. Let us first note that its repeated prescribing in both the *Koran* and Sharia law are overwhelmingly for acts and totally for thoughts that in the civilised world are nowhere treated as crimes, and that the Saudi, Ali al Nimr, had been condemned and was to be punished in accordance with the very same laws that are used to the same effect in Iran. Yet as we have seen, despite voicing his opposition to the death penalty on of all TV channels, one controlled by the state with the highest per capita execution rate in the world, Corbyn wants, in fact, demands, that everybody should show their respect for the faith that has gifted to the world the system of justice which had led to the sentence passed on Ali al Nimr. And why did Corbyn feel free to protest about this particular execution, while he has remained silent in his acquiescence of thousands of others carried out in Iran, including the more than two thousand that took place while he was in the employ of the executioners?

Here we have a case of 'the enemy of my friend is also my enemy'. As I have already said, it is because those who were about to carry it out in Saudi Arabia were, officially at least, allies of the West, principally the USA, in the so-called war on terror, which Corbyn vehemently opposes, and because Saudi Arabia, in its role as the leader of the Sunni branch of Islam, is the sworn enemy of Corbyn's former employers, the Ayatollahs of Iran, rulers of the Islamic world's premier Shi'a power, fighting proxy wars against the Saudis in Yemen and on behalf of President Assad of Syria, and dedicated to 'wiping Israel off the map'. Finally, Iran is the patron and quartermaster of Corbyn's 'friends' Hezbollah.

Though he lied on BBC TV about the dates of his appearances, Corbyn has himself acknowledged receiving the sum the sum of £20,000 in payment for his services to Press TV, earned between 2009 and 2012. The normal payment is £500 a session, but since Corbyn made only four appearances, he was, for some unspecified reason, being paid £5,000 a time, *ten times the normal rate.* Why? Meanwhile, back in Iran, his theocratic pimps were conducting executions at a rate of sometimes more than three a day, including, in that term of service, three of alleged homosexuals. A kinder politics.

Now some facts about the use of the death penalty by the former employers of Livingstone and Corbyn. The offences for which it can be imposed by Iran's legal code, which just like Saudi Arabia's, is based exclusively on Sharia and Koranic law, number more than 300, and include: 'Waging war on God' (a catch-all rubric covering umpteen crimes, including those of violence, political opposition, trade unionism, and corruption); Adultery, Rape, Sodomy, Apostasy from Islam, Blasphemy and Consumption of Alcohol. *These offences are almost identical to those that carry the death penalty in Saudi Arabia.* Since the Ayatollahs came to power in 1979, all executions have by law to be in public, and take place at 4.00 AM, just before the call to morning prayer. Virgin females sentenced to death are raped by guards just before being hanged, because the law says that virgins cannot be executed. Most of those executed are hanged, frequently simultaneously in batches, either from cranes or gallows, the rest, are either stoned or shot by firing squad, except for homosexuals, who are thrown from cliff tops or tall buildings, as prescribed by Sharia law.

As to the frequency of executions, with its highest rate per capita, Iran has not only led Saudi Arabia but the entire world in this abominable competition, without so much as a murmur of protest from either Livingstone or Corbyn as I have been able to locate. As we have seen, just in one year, 1988, more than 30,000 political prisoners were executed on the basis of a *fatwah* issued by Ayatollah Khomeini. According to an Amnesty International report, in 2015, the former employers of Livingstone, Galloway and Corbyn carried out 694 executions in the six months between January 1 and July 15; that is, at a rate of more than three per *day*. In just one day, September 25, 2017, the Ayatollahs hanged 42 alleged 'terrorists', a blanket term that covers a multitude of alleged sins, and on December 24, another 38. But as Livingstone says, he has been opposed to capital punishment throughout his life. Or, to be more precise, just like Corbyn, only when it suits him.

The same double standards were in evidence again when, following the adoption of the Sharia law punishment of death by stoning by the Sultan of Brunei, in March 2019, Corbyn's Shadow Foreign Secretary Emily Thornberry, joined protesters outside the Brunei-owned Dorchester hotel in London. This is the same Thornberry who when called upon to condemn the killing of demonstrators by the Iranian police, refused to do so because it was not clear who was wearing 'the white hats'.

Corbyn excelled even his own exemplary standards of selective outrage when on April 7, 2018, he called on western leaders to condemn the killing of demonstrating Gaza civilians by the Israel Defence Force. (As we have seen, he has failed to do so when the killed civilians have been Israeli Jews, Venezuelans, Syrians, Nicaraguans or Iranians.) As with the conflict of 2014, which began when Hamas kidnaped and killed three Jewish youths, and tunnelled and fired rockets into Israeli territory, the IDF response was also claimed on this occasion to be 'disproportionate', since neither the security of Israel nor its civilian lives were endangered by the Hamas demonstrations while they remained within the border of the Gaza Strip. However, urged on by armed Hamas fighters, who as revealed by a Hamas official, accounted for the bulk of those killed by the IDF, some demonstrators, who included numerous children, a mother with her baby and an invalid in a wheelchair serving as 'human shield' cannon fodder for the Hamas gunmen to their rear, did succeed in breaking into Israeli territory.

As in the Hamas acts of aggression which began the conflict of 2014, this so-called 'March of Return' was also an act of aggression, as defined by the United

Nations General Assembly at its session of 1974, specifically, in Article 1, 'the use of armed force against the sovereignty, territorial integrity or political independence of another state'. To qualify as such, acts of aggression need not be carried by regular armies. Article 3, clause G is quite specific on this point, which covers exactly the incursions into Israel launched by Hamas in April and May 2018: 'The sending by or on behalf of a state armed bands, groups, irregulars, which carry out acts of armed force against another state of such gravity as amount to those listed above, or its substantial involvement therein.'

Hamas claimed that these acts of aggression were in fact simply the asserting the right of the Palestinians of the Gaza Strip to return to their homeland in Israel. Even if this lie were true, and their claimed right to abandon Gaza and settle in Israel justified, these acts are nevertheless described by the UN resolution to be ones of aggression: Article 5, clause 1: 'No consideration of whatever nature, whether political, economic, military or otherwise, may serve as justification for aggression.' As in 2014, Israel exercised the right to defend itself from such acts of aggression, as defined by the UN Charter, Article 51: 'Nothing in the present Charter shall impair the right of individual or collective self-defence if an armed attack occurs against a member of the United Nations, until the Security Council has taken measures necessary to maintain international peace and security.'

Yet once again, Israel, not Hamas, found itself pilloried for exercising its legal right to self-defence, while the cannon fodder manipulated by Hamas were glorified as the heroic victims of Zionist brutality, even though it was obviously the intention of Hamas, virtually friendless in the Arab world (but not in the leadership of the Labour Party), to provide their movement with martyrs and by so doing, win the sympathy of the ever-gullible west. Hamas's tactic of exploiting what, in the Middle East of today, is an entirely bogus refugee problem, has a long tradition in the Arab world.

The real purpose is not 'return', but invasion and conquest, which as far back as 1949, in the aftermath of Israel's defeat of five invading Arab armies, the Egyptian Foreign Minister made very clear when he declared that 'in demanding the return of the refugees to Palestine [by which was meant, the new state of Israel] the Arabs mean their return as masters of their country and not as slaves'. One of the stated aims of BDS is 'promoting the rights of Palestinian refugees to return to their homes and properties.' Only those Palestinians who left Israel as result the Arab invasion of 1948 can be classed as genuine 'refugees', and of those, the vast majority are no longer alive. Their descendants are not refugees, and therefore their 'home'' is not Israel, any more than Russia was the 'home' of the American descendants of the Jews who fled the pogroms of the tsars. The fact that they are treated in most cases as outcasts in the Arab countries where they live is not the responsibility of Israel but of the regimes that refuse, for political reasons, to accord them rights of full citizens in the land of their birth. 'Open Borders? For Muslims arriving in Europe? Of course. But not for Palestinians in the Middle East...unless that is the borders are Israel's.

As in the Hamas-Israel of conflict of 2014, the question that should have been asked, but never was by those whose job it was to do so was: what would any government have done, faced with repeated illegal, violent incursions into its territory by tens of thousands of people, some of them armed, and all reared from early childhood to hate and want to kill its citizens, who were attempting to enforce by an invasion a spurious right to settle in a land they were not born in?

All those who genuinely support the goal of a two-state solution to the Palestinian issue have a both a right and duty to protest at any killings by Israeli forces if they can be proved to have been caused by the deliberate targeting of unarmed civilians. I will be one of them. But neither Hamas, which stands for the destruction of Israel and the extermination of all its Jews and, by staging a series of violent provocations at the Israeli border, seeks to bring about the killing of Palestinian civilians that could then, with the always compliant assistance of the world's media, be blamed on the Israelis, nor Corbyn, who has never condemned the cynical tactics and genocidal goal of Hamas, have any moral right to do so. In Corbyn's case, his hypocrisy over the Gaza killings was compounded by his refusal, when challenged, to condemn the killing of over a hundred Venezuelan demonstrators protesting against the corrupt, bankrupt and election-rigging regime of President Maduro in the summer of 2017, the thousands of civilians killed by the regime of President Assad in Syria with the massive military assistance of President Putin of Russia, including chemical weapons, and the tens of thousands murdered by his former paymasters, the Ayatollahs of Iran. The day after Corbyn issued his statement condemning the deaths at the Gaza border, at least 90 civilians were killed in a chemical attack on the town of Douma near Damascus. A report in the *Guardian* said 'videos showed bodies of dead children and other family members, some foaming at the mouth.' On this occasion, from Corbyn's duplicitous mouth, not a word, proving that sometimes silence can indeed speak louder than words.

Then there are for Corbyn the not inconsequential matters of the atrocious persecution of the Rohingya Muslims of Myanmar (formerly Burma) by the country's Buddhist military, and the incarceration in concentration camps in Sin-Kiang province of more than a million of their co-religionists by China, neither of which has been the occasion for protests outside the London embassies of the regimes responsible for these outrages, because although the victims in both cases are followers of what the Sharia left describes as the religion of the oppressed, their oppressors were not Jews or the USA, but governments hostile to the West. One must always see the 'bigger picture'. Applying the same tactical device, 'the enemy of my enemy is my friend' (with respect to Hamas and Hezbollah, literally so) led Corbyn to support the Kremlin-backed Eastern Orthodox Serbs in their 'ethnic cleansing' campaigns *against* the (belatedly) western-backed Muslims of Bosnia and Kosovo in the early 1990s. Finally, and perhaps most despicable of all, is this self-proclaimed champion of the Palestinians' silence concerning the crimes against their compatriots by the Ba'athist Assad regime which, unlike Israel, neither recognises the existence of a Palestinian people nor its right to nationhood. The website of the Action Group for Palestinians of Syria meticulously documents the persecution of Palestinians by the regime that played host to both Corbyn and the neo-Nazi Nick Griffin. As of May 2019, the number just of those killed stood at 3,946. A kinder politics.

Addendum: Doctor Livingstone, I presume

As legend has it, so said the journalist Henry Stanley on tracking down in 1871 the intrepid physician turned explorer and anti-slavery campaigner on the shore of

320

Lake Tanganyika. Our Livingstone's fame – or notoriety – derives in part at least from another exploration, not of a continent, but for what he believes is the untold story of Hitler's support for Zionism and its goal of a Jewish state in what was then the British Mandate. Driven by his unquenchable hatred for all things Israeli, it was a quest that he first undertook some 110 years after his namesake's for the source of the Nile, while co-editor of the Gaddafi-funded Labour Herald. The fruits of this, for what of a better word, 'research', were not only treated with the derision they deserved by those infinitely more qualified in the subject. When he regurgitated them shortly after being appointed Corbyn's 'defence' adviser, they to led to accusations of anti-Semitism and then his suspension and finally resignation from the Labour Party.

This was not the only time when Livingstone's pontifications on a subject about which he knew nothing resulted in ignominy. Readers might recall a similar occasion when, not content with that of historian, he no less fraudulently assumed the profession of his namesake, with consequences that put human lives at risk.

Following the introduction of the so-called 'triple jab' MMR inoculation of children against measles, mumps and rubella, in 1998, Melanie Phillips led a campaign in the *Daily Mail*, endorsed by its editor, (quite possibly, as in the paper's similarly ill-founded opposition to genetically-modified crops, because the government introducing and promoting MMR was Labour) to have the treatment banned on what were claimed to be sound medical grounds. To support her claim that MMR had unacceptable side effects, she cited what she took to be bona fide evidence of such effects published in *The Lancet* on February 28, 1998 by a medical researcher at the Royal Free Hospital School of Medicine, Andrew Wakefield. In rejecting MMR as unsafe, he recommended the use of an alternative anti-measles vaccine which he had already patented, though this was not known at the time he advertised his objections to MMR. Wakefield also appeared on BBC TV to repeat his warnings against the 'triple jab'.

This, combined with the *Daily Mail* campaign, led, as was intended, to a huge decline in the number of children being inoculated with MMR, inevitably and predictably followed some years later by a return of the three conditions, especially measles, it was designed to eradicate. In this what I suspect was a politically motivated endeavour on the part of the *Mail*, and a pecuniary one by Wakefield, they had the unsolicited support of our intrepid would-be polymath, now in the guise, not of charlatan historian, but quack biologist. (In both capacities, he followed in the footsteps of British academics whose political loyalties required that they defended in print the Stalinist purges and the anti-Darwinian hocus pocus of Trofim Lysenko.) Ever the populist, Doctor Livingstone mark two, elected Mayor of London in 2000, two years later seized on the opportunity to exploit the unwarranted fears of parents stoked up by the (Tory) *Daily Mail*. He would be the champion of those without a voice, speaking 'truth to power', as the saying goes, in this case to the heartless know-alls of the British Medical Association. 'I remember having these three jabs separately. Often you had quite a severe reaction. Why whack [sic] them into a child at the same time? In no way [sic] would I inflict on a child that [unspecified] risk...My advice to all Londoners [sic] is that if you can, get it done separately.'

This 'advice', from someone no more qualified to give it than the children he was claiming to protect, seemed clear enough. If possible, do not let your children have the triple jab. But when members of the medical profession objected to

Livingstone's 'advice', a spokesman for Doctor Livingstone mark two issued a totally different 'spin' on what he had said: 'He was not recommending the single jab over the triple vaccine [He was - lie number one] but was stressing his personal opinion that parents should get their children vaccinated in some way. [lie number two...he said 'get it done separately'].'

Normally, Livingstone got away with double talk like this...being for the death penalty in Venezuela, ignoring it Iran, but against it India, or for gay liberation in London, yet silent about the persecution and execution of gays in the realm of Allah...but not on this occasion, because he had run afoul of the BMA. He was challenging men and women of science, and the stakes were too high. Children's health and even lives were at risk. Addressing the BMA's annual conference, Chairman Ian Bogle bluntly accused Livingstone of making 'an outrageous statement for someone in his position. He will have done irreparable damage, damage that takes a long time to put right. It beggars belief that somebody would do this. I don't tell him how to run London and he should certainly not advise and confuse parents in this way. When London children are disabled or die, Mr Livingstone, as they will unless we change current trends, then you will share the blame.'

Tragically, this prediction was correct. Before the promotion of Wakefield's claims about MMR by the *Daily Mail* and their endorsement by Livingstone, the inoculation rate was 92%. After them, it fell to 80%. As a direct result, the number of measles cases rose from 58 in 1998 to 1,348 in 2008, with two deaths.

And what of Dr Wakefield, the *Mail's* lone warrior against the 'medical establishment'? In 2004, it was discovered that before Wakefield had declared MMR to be unsafe, he had already patented an alternative vaccine to replace it. Then, in 2006, it came to light that he had been paid the undisclosed sum of £400,000 to assist in a failed law suit against the manufacturers of MMR! Finally, in 2010, his 'research' into MMR was found by the General Medical Council of the BMA to be 'dishonest'. The Lancet retracted his paper on MMR and, ultimate humiliation, he was struck off the medical register. What of Dr Livingstone mark two? Despite his never having retracted or apologized for his endorsement of Wakefield's fraudulent claims against MMR, and having the deaths of two children to (let us be charitable) possibly trouble his conscience, Livingstone suffered no such disgrace amongst his political co-thinkers, any more than he has for serving, together with Corbyn, as a highly-paid TV presenter for a regime that has the highest rate of executions in the world while also, again like Corbyn, having been 'opposed to the death penalty throughout my life'.

Y Who Dunnit?

According to *Al-Hayat Al-Jadida,* the official daily of the Palestine Authority, the *Charlie Hebdo* massacre of January 7, 2015, was not the work of the Islamic State. It was 'a carefully executed and fully controlled plan', with the aim of creating in France a climate of terror 'to encourage Jews to emigrate to Israel.' 'The entire operation had been 'planned by Mossad'. The 'crime committed against *Charlie Hebdo* and the Jewish store in Paris were not co-incidences. We believe that there is a conspiracy at work, for the US and Israeli intelligence services are the greatest experts at exploiting the organisations that emerge in areas of conflict.'

This is a none too subtle variation on the theme which proliferates on Corbynista websites that the Islamic State has been created and controlled by Mossad. The same journal, dated March 24, 2016, offers an identical explanation for the Brussels massacres two days previously, in the form of a question:

> …why did the crimes and terrorist massacres of ISIS in France and Brussels coincide with the European Union's first attempt to free itself from the Israeli extortion and of the Jewish persecution complex in Europe, and coincide with European members of parliament's support of the Palestinian right to statehood?

PA Security Forces Spokesman Adnan Al-Damiri repeated and expanded on the question, only to then seemingly struggle for an answer:

> How come Europe has turned into the scene of terror attacks and murder of innocent civilians after the expansion of European boycotts of products made in Israeli settlements? Is it possible that the timing of the targeting of Europe by ISIS and its offshoots is innocent [?] and a coincidence? And why specifically Europe now that the European popular and official support for Palestine is growing? Help me understand and answer.

The answer they were seeking, but not expecting, came in the form of a sermon at Jerusalem's Al-Aqsa mosque on July, 2016, by Sheikh Al-Abu Ahmad:

> Any action carried out, and explosion, and any operation in which a Muslim is killed in Muslim countries, American stands behind it. together with the infidel West that hates Islam and Muslims. It doesn't matter who takes responsibility for the crime and who announces it. We will never believe it. We will never believe it because America is the one that blows up Muslims and is the one that kills Muslims.

Z Orwell on the Corbynistas *(mutatis mutandis)*

There is a minority of intellectual pacifists whose real though unadmitted motive appears to be hatred of western democracy and admiration for totalitarianism. Pacifist propaganda usually boils down to saying that one side is as bad as the other, but if one looks closely at the writings of young intellectual pacifists, one finds that they do not by any means express impartial disapproval, but are directed almost entirely against Britain and the United States [today also, and mainly, Israel]. Moreover, they do not as a rule condemn violence as such, but only violence used in the defence of the Western countries. The Russians, unlike the British, are not blamed for defending themselves [today, for attacking others] by warlike means. (*Notes on Nationalism*, October 1945)

Left-wing intellectuals do not think of themselves as nationalist, because as a rule they transfer their loyalty to some foreign country, such as the USSR, [today, Cuba, Venezuela, Iran, Syria, Nicaragua, Russia, North Korea, ISIS, Hamas and Hezbollah] or indulge it in a merely negative form, in hatred of their own country and its rulers…[O]ne expects governments and newspapers to tell lies. What is worse, to me, is the contempt even of intellectuals for objective truth so long as their own brand of nationalism is being boosted. The most intelligent people seem capable of holding schizophrenic beliefs [However one rates his IQ, this fits the two-faced Livingstone to a T.], or disregarding plain facts, of evading serious questions with debating-society repartees, or swallowing baseless rumours [Zionist plots against the Dear Leader] and of looking on indifferently while history is falsified. [viz., re the Holocaust] (*Partisan Review*, Winter 1944)

You are wrong also in thinking that I dislike wholehearted pacifism, though I do think it is mistaken. What I object to is the circumspect kind of pacifism which denounces one kind of violence while endorsing or avoiding mention of another. [viz., of Jihadis, Assad and Putin] (Letter to the pacifist John Middleton Murry, July 21, 1944)

…a message to English left-wing journalists and intellectuals generally: 'Do remember that dishonesty and cowardice have to be paid for. Don't imagine that for years on end you can make yourself the boot-licking propagandists of the Soviet regime, or any other regime, [viz., Cuba, Venezuela, Iran etc] and then suddenly return to mental decency. Once a whore, always a whore.' (*Tribune*, September 1, 1944)

At present we are all but openly applying the double standard of morality. With one side of our mouth we cry out that mass deportations, concentration camps, forced labour and suppression of freedom of speech are appalling crimes, while with the other we proclaim that those things are perfectly all right if done by the USSR or its satellite states [today, Cuba, Venezuela, Iran etc], and where necessary we make this plausible by doctoring the news and cutting out unpleasant facts. (Unpublished letter to *Tribune* June 1945)

I Churchill on Islam

How dreadful are the curses which Mohammedanism lays on its votaries! Besides the fanatical frenzy, which is dangerous in a man as hydrophobia in a dog, there is this fearful fatalistic apathy. The effects are apparent in many countries. Improvident habits, slovenly systems of agriculture, sluggish methods of commerce, and insecurity of property exist wherever the followers of the Prophet rule or live. A degraded sensualism deprives this life of its grace and refinement; the next of dignity and sanctity. The fact that in Mohammedan law every woman must belong to some man as his absolute property, either as a child, wife, or concubine, must delay the final extinction of slavery until the faith of Islam has ceased to be a great power among men. Individual Moslems may show splendid qualities – but the influence of the religion paralyses the social development of those who follow it. No stronger retrograde force exists in the world. Far from being moribund, Mohammedanism is a militant and proselytizing faith. It has already spread throughout Central Africa, raising fearless warriors at every step; and were it not that Christianity is sheltered in the strong arms of science, the science against which it has vainly struggled, the civilisation of modern Europe might fall, as fell the civilization of ancient Rome.

Winston Churchill: *The River War* (1898)

Arrest that racist!

Churchill was no less pungent in his decrying the hypocrisy of what today is the Islamic interpretation of the right to free speech:

'Some people's idea of free speech is that they are free to say what they like, but if anyone says anything back, there is outrage.'

II What to do about Islam?

Its ideals born out of the Enlightenment triumph over religious superstition and made flesh by the victory of the American and French revolutions, western civilisation, two centuries on, proved strong enough to defeat two mortal challenges to its liberal democratic values and institutions, those of Nazi Germany and Bolshevik Russia. Now we face a third no less totalitarian threat from Islam. Like its forerunners, the avowed goal is world conquest, and the enslavement or elimination of all those who refuse to submit to in this case, the rule of a fictitious god, Allah. In the main body of this work, I have cited numerous texts both from the *Koran* itself, and from all the main schools of Islamic jurisprudence, that unambiguously declare this to be the ultimate goal of Islam. So they need no repetition here. Since the reality of the challenge is not in dispute, at least by those who make their judgements on the basis of incontestable evidence and not ill-informed apologetics, the question is, how should the west respond to it? One solution, the Quisling, favoured by multi-culturalists, the Sharia left, the Swedish *dhimmi* establishment and German Chancellor Merkel, is self-Islamisation, by which Europe, instead of acting as a bulwark against Islamic expansion, surrenders to it peacefully by unlimited Muslim migration and the progressive acceptance of Islamic culture, practises and laws. As we have already seen in the public outrage in Germany after the Cologne sexual assaults and in the UK, the trials of Muslim rape gangs, the problem with this policy is that sooner or later, it will provoke angry and entirely legitimate opposition from those who are called upon to do the submitting.

Those who now accept that multiculturalism has been a total failure, and who instead advocate genuine integration of Muslims into their host society are one step closer to reality. At least they recognise that there is what reform Muslims, some of whom I have cited, have called a 'Muslim problem', not one of western guilt or intolerance, and that its solution, at least at the level of domestic policy, is to persuade, induce and if necessary compel Muslims to integrate into the culture and obey the laws of the host society. I too favour this policy so long as it does not intrude on Muslim rights to believe what they want and say what they believe publicly, and to practice their religion unhindered, provided that doing so conforms to the existing laws of the land. Neither fear nor favour. But such a policy of integration does not, and cannot, solve the much bigger issue of how to meet and defeat the global challenge of Islamic imperialism, one which avowedly seeks the conquest of the entire world for Allah.

We are told by pacifists, Corbynistas and their like that there can be 'no military solutions' to world problems. Sometimes this proves to be the case, at least, up to a point, though the collapse of the Kremlin empire was in large part due to the ability and readiness of the west to match and exceed the military capacity of its cold war opponent and, equally crucially, unlike the rulers of the Soviet bloc, to do so without reducing its own peoples to near-poverty. Even that arch-advocate of 'political solutions', Neville Chamberlain, in the end realised that the only answer to Nazi expansionism was a 'military solution', even though, because he had failed to foresee and prepare for its necessity, it was initially an inadequate one.

Most of those who on principle oppose 'military solutions' would, if pressed, have to admit that the source of Islamic terrorism is the Middle East, the birthplace of the faith that not only justifies and nourishes Jihad, but today funds its fighters and has given birth to a new caliphate, the Islamic State. We in the west shamefully delegated the task of its elimination (an improvement on Obama's 'containment') to Shi'a Iraqis, Hezbollah acting as Iranian proxies, the Kurds and a myriad of largely ineffective feuding Syrian factions, topped up with sporadic token bombing raids and commando operations by the USA. After more than three years of this substitute for a strategy, with each faction pursing its own geopolitical ethnic or theological agenda, what remains of Islamic State, despite military setbacks, is still very much in the business of doing Allah's work, as the massacres in Paris, Brussels, Nice and elsewhere have demonstrated. To add to which, the chaos and misery, death and destruction unleashed by the religious wars in the Middle East have either driven or provided the pretext for millions of Muslims to head for the prosperous heartlands and welfare states of Europe, some from as far afield as Nigeria and Bangladesh. Let us be charitable, and assume that ideally, the vast majority would gladly return to their homelands if circumstances were favourable. If this assumption is wrong, then it would suggest that what they are seeking is not temporary asylum, but permanent residence, that they are not refugees, but economic and welfare migrants. Assuming that as politicians assure us, the former is the case, one would have thought that it was in the best interests of all concerned, refugees as well as their increasingly reluctant hosts, to see to it that the prime cause of this mass migration, the utter inability of the Arab Middle East to regulate its own affairs in a peaceful and civilised manner, was eradicated once and for all, by any and all means necessary. Just to take the case of the Islamic State, not the only, but certainly since its emergence in 2014 the prime cause of the current chaos in the region: How does it come about that the combined might of the western world could not extirpate in three years a band of religious fanatics numbering only a few thousand, and yet the Allies in the Second World War utterly routed the combined forces of Nazi Germany, Imperial Japan and fascist Italy in less than four? What kind of a signal does this send to all those aspiring Jihadis eager to take on the infidel?

Rousseau's insistence that if necessary, a people must be forced to be free, is a nonsense. His disciple Robespierre disagreed with him in this respect, arguing wisely that 'no-one loves missionaries with bayonets'. However, using force to give a people the *opportunity and means* to be free, as the Western Allies did in Germany and Japan at the end of the Second World War, is a different matter entirely. Some council patience, saying that once the Arab oil runs out, or the west develops the technologies that supplant it, Arab-funded Jihadism will go the way of the Spanish empire when the Inca gold ran dry. Even if true, which I doubt, since there was Islam before we found oil, and there will be Islam when it is all gone, how long must we wait? And meantime...

The solution I propose may well fail, but not because the peoples of the Middle East are mentally and physically in any way different from the rest of the human race. It is the deeply entrenched primitive conservative beliefs of their majority which are the problem, not their genes. Therefore, whatever multiculturalist racists might argue to the contrary, they are just as capable, given

328

the necessary time and assistance, of responding to the challenge of creating free and peace-loving societies as the post-war Germans and Japanese, who like the Arabs lacked a deeply rooted tradition of democracy and individual freedom, yet who unlike the Jihadis and theocrats, have been taught and learned that dreams of world conquest and the suppression of freedom and democracy do not pay. Just as was the case in 1945, it is in our interests as much as the peoples of the Middle East to do what we can to help them learn this lesson and take the first steps along the path towards finding their place in the civilized world. Therefore, in abandoning the present failed policy of the appeasement of Islamic Jihadism and theocracy, which not only endangers the security, freedoms and prosperity of the west, but does nothing to end the appalling miseries of those held in their sway, yet in the full knowledge that no such solution would be entertained by those whose responsibility it would be to authorise and implement it, I propose the following:

Preferably with, or, as is far more likely, without the approval of the United Nations, the combined military forces of the west, acting under the leadership of NATO, must occupy and place under its administration the whole of the Middle East with the exception of Israel, Jordan, Egypt and the territories of the Palestinian Authority, with the consent of its ruling powers if possible, but if necessary without it. If deemed militarily necessary, this operation can be carried out in stages. To achieve its aim, which is to eliminate all sources of Islamic terrorism by the de-militarisation, stabilisation, secularisation and democratisation of the entire region, the following states which nourish it will need to be occupied: Saudi Arabia, Iraq, Syria, Lebanon, Yemen and all the Gulf States. All existing governmental agencies will either be dissolved or placed under the direct control of the occupying powers, following the example of the Allies in the occupied Axis states at the end of the Second World War.

Using the same precedent, the occupation and temporary administration of these territories will be assigned to states participating in the operation. They will codify and announce in advance of the operation, and enforce for its duration, criminal and civil laws that will be wholly secular and based on the principles of the United Nations Universal Declaration of Human Rights, which these states, as members of the United Nations, are in theory required to uphold. As their rulers seem to find this task beyond their powers, why not give them some practical assistance? When conditions permit, a schedule will be set for free elections to a constituent assembly in all these states under conditions of complete freedom of association, of belief secular and religious, and of all media and speech. These elections will be held under the direct supervision of the occupying forces, again following the example of the Allies in post-war Germany and Japan. As a barrier to those Muslims who will, as they did in the wake of the so-called 'Arab Spring', seek to vote the Arab world back to the seventh century, each constitution adopted, to receive approval by and consequent withdrawal of the occupying powers, must include 'entrenched', that is to say irremovable articles, protecting, for ever, certain fundamental rights of all the peoples of the region, the majority of which are enshrined in the UN Universal Declaration of Human Rights and which, technically at least, all the states in the region already subscribe to. (There are precedents for this procedure. With the same aim in mind, a number of democratic countries have included similar entrenched provisions in their constitutions, including not only Germany, as one would expect, but also France, the USA, the

Czech Republic, Bosnia and Brazil.) Until such constitutions are adopted by the countries concerned, and then approved by the occupying powers, the countries in question will be suspended from membership of the United Nations and its various subsidiary bodies.

The entrenched constitutional articles will include:

Complete freedom of religious and non-religious belief, including the right to criticise, change, adopt and give up a religion;

Total separation of state and religion, no state religion;

Compulsory free secular education;

Secret, equal and universal adult suffrage, and fixed term elections;

Protection of the rights of homosexuals and other sexual minorities;

Protection of the equal rights of women, and protection of children from sexual exploitation and child marriage;

The right to complete freedom of expression in all its forms;

Freedom of association and non-association;

The right of labour to organise;

A secular legal code.

Call it cultural it imperialism if you like but, unlike racist cultural relativists, I believe the peoples of the countries in question are no less entitled to these rights than we are in the west. And equally to the point, their adoption, while bringing benefits to the vast majority, will harm no-one, any more than they have done in the West. I can list well over a hundred countries whose people today suffer and, in the past, have suffered from a lack of individual freedom. But I know of none whose people have suffered because of it. If, following the withdrawal of the occupying forces, there is made any attempt to defy, remove or subvert any of these entrenched articles, this will be met with immediate economic sanctions and, if these fail, renewed military occupation and the prosecution of those responsible. At the earliest opportunity, all those suspected of committing war crimes will be arrested by the occupying powers, tried at the International Court of Justice in The Hague, and if found guilty, be punished accordingly. The occupied region will be completely and permanently de-militarised, enabling its governments to devote the resources thereby released to the welfare of their peoples instead of their enslavement, the promotion of Islamic terrorism and the waging of religious wars. The protection of the region from external attack will be the responsibility of the occupying powers both during the occupation of the region and after their withdrawal. The states will maintain a police force purely for the purposes of maintaining domestic law and order. Any attempt to reconstitute any armed force for any other purpose will be met with a renewed military occupation and the elimination of the offending forces.

Addendum

I said that even assuming that my proposals for curbing Islam were viable, (reforming Islam is a task that only Muslims can accomplish) it would be unlikely in the extreme that the United Nations would lend them its support. What follows goes a long way to explaining why. It consists of (edited) extracts from an address to a meeting in the House of Lords by Hillel Neuer, Executive Director of UN

Watch, on July 4, 2016. Its subject was the corruption, political bias and anti-Israeli prejudices of the UN Human Rights Council.

The occasion on which we meet is the tenth anniversary of the Human Rights Council, which was established in June 2006.... We also meet on another anniversary, the 70th of the predecessor body, the Commission on Human Rights established by the humanitarian Eleanor Roosevelt in 1946, of which she was the founding chair...The body that replaced it in 2006, the Human Rights Council has 47 [rotating] members.... How has this new Council performed in its first decade? What shall the United Kingdom and its allies in the democratic world do to advance the Council's founding goals? We can best measure the Council's performance by the yardstick of the UN's own standards...These were set out in 2005 by the then Secretary General Kofi Anan...He identified core failings in the previous body.

They were, 1) Countries had sought membership, quote, 'not to strengthen human rights but to protect themselves against criticism or to criticise others.' 2) 'The Commission had been undermined by the politicisation of its sessions and the selectivity of its work.' 3) The Commission suffered from 'declining professionalism and a credibility deficit which casts a shadow on the reputation of the UN as a whole.' This was because over time, the Commission had become a vehicle for governments and, absurdly, governments whose only expertise on human rights lay in systematically violating them. Among regular members were Sudan and China and most famously, the Libyan regime of Colonel Moammar Gaddafi, who was elected Chair of the Commission in 2003. These failings and abuses led to Anan's proposal for a new council. In its resolution 60/-5-1 creating the new Council, the UN General Assembly promised that it would elect to it members committed, quote to 'uphold the highest standards in the promotion and protection of human rights.' [So far as any of the world's 56 Islamic countries were concerned, this would be impossible, because their joint Cairo Declaration of 1990, in explicitly basing itself exclusively on Islamic law, necessarily repudiated all man-made laws, principles and morals.] Those member states of the new Council who committed gross and systematic violations could have their membership suspended by a two-thirds majority vote. The Council would, quote 'address situations of violations of human rights.' The work of the Council would be guided by 'universality, impartiality, objectivity and non-selectivity.' Have these objectives been realised?

Ten years later, the Council membership, in relation to the protection of human rights, has never been worse. 62% of its members failed to meet minimum standards of a free democracy as measured by Freedom House, states like China, Cuba, Russia, Saudi Arabia, Venezuela, Algeria, Burundi, Congo, Qatar, United Arab Emirates and Vietnam. In 2001, speaking of the old Commission, Kenneth Roth of Human Rights Watch said, 'Imagine a jury that includes murderers and rapists, or a police force run in large part by suspected murderers and rapists who are determined to stymie investigation of their crimes.' These words apply even more today. With rare exceptions, the majority on the Human Rights Council has turned a blind eye to the world's worst human rights violations...a Tibetan Buddhist monk who was tortured in China for the crime of creating a video documenting crimes against his people...No resolution on Cuba, where peaceful civic activists are beaten or languish in prison...there has never been an emergency session on Iran, which can be convened by only 16 members, when its regime was slaughtering its own people in June 2009 when they protested against fraudulent elections. [It was in 2009 that Corbyn began working as a presenter for Iran's Press TV channel.] No emergency session for Saudi Arabia after carpet-bombing Yemen, killing hundreds of children, beheading more people than ever before and subjugating its women, tramples on religious freedom; all in the name of a fundamentalist theology which over decades and with billions of petro-dollars, the Saudis have propagated all around the globe. Not only is Saudi Arabia a member of the Council, it was last year made head of a committee that selects human rights experts and one on women's rights, and sits on a committee on the independence of the judiciary, having sentenced a blogger to a thousand lashes and ten years in prison. When Saudi Arabia was listed by the UN as one of the countries responsible for the deaths of children in armed conflicts, the Saudis told Secretary-General Ban Ki-moon if Saudi Arabia was not deleted from the report, we will cut our hundred million contribution to the Palestinians, and convene a meeting of clerics that would issue a fatwa against the United Nations, declaring it to be unislamic. To his shame, he removed Saudi Arabia from the list.

In its ten years of existence, the Human Rights council has only ruled against 14 of the UN's 193 members. Over the same period, between 1991 to 2001, its much-criticised predecessor condemned 24 countries for human rights abuses. What has also to be condemned is that the western democracies on the council - France, Germany, the UK and the USA - have not introduced any resolutions on human rights abuses. [Saudi Arabia, one of the most guilty, is also regarded for economic and geopolitical reasons as a western ally.] One of the reforms introduced by the new Council is Universal Periodic Review (UPR) in which all member states of the UN must be reviewed at least once every four to five years in sessions usually lasting only three hours, in which questions on human rights can be put by other member states and accredited interested parties. [The speaker then described how this procedure is abused by the reciprocal collusion of states with something to hide or deny.] During one session, in 2009, Libya used UPR to praise Cuba for promoting freedom of thought and expression, while China praised Saudi Arabia for its record on women's rights. [sic]. In 2013, China again praised Saudi Arabia, this time for its religious tolerance. [Saudi Arabia bans all religions other than Islam, and all versions of Islam other its own, while China persecutes its Muslims.] The next day, Chinese and Saudi delegates swapped roles, with the Saudis [with the persecuted Tibetans and the Uyghur Muslims obviously in mind] praising the Chinese for, quote, their 'progress in ethnic minority regions at the political, cultural and educational levels.' [This surreal mutual back-scratching act saw the world's most orthodox Islamic state praising one ruled by atheists for what amounted to the cultural genocide of its Muslims.]

No issue at the UN Human Rights Council has been more distorted than racism. [as everywhere else] The example comes to mind of the 3,000 Yazidi women from Iraq and Syria, who were kidnapped and then used as sex slaves by the Islamic State. It is almost impossible to believe that in 2016, thousands of women are being sold in the market as sex slaves…ISIS didn't just kidnap and rape. They have developed a whole theology in which before the rapist rapes her he tells her that what he is about to do is commanded by the Sharia [i.e., Islamic law] …It's a theology of hate because they [the Yazidis] are not believers. [Here the Islamic State rapists were, as the *Koran* instructs them to do, following the example of Mohammed, who raped a Jewish woman whose husband he had killed at the battle with the B. Qurayza…see Appendix L. The *Koran* says: 'Ye have indeed in the Messenger of Allah a beautiful {sic} pattern of conduct for anyone whose hope is in Allah and the Final Day, and who engages much in the Praise of Allah.' Chapter 33, Verse 21] …yet all the experts at the Human Rights Council never mentioned these rape victims or this rape theology. They missed it. Instead, much of the discussion on racism and xenophobia is focused on the West. Yes, these exist in the West, and it is right to discuss it. But the only UN narrative is that white people in the west [here we go again] are abusing people of colour and Muslims. But when [black…R.B.] girls in Africa are kidnapped by Boko Haram because they are Christians, or there is slavery in Mauritania, that does not fit the narrative, [including that of Black Lives Matter] so it is not talked about. [Again, *deja vue*] There are many Cuban resolutions adopted which blame human rights abuses on banks. [sic] Yet the model regime is that of Hugo Chavez [as it is Corbyn's] where people are starving [and five million of its citizens have fled abroad].

Now a word or two about Israel. I have mentioned some of the countries where human rights abuses are ignored. In the Commission, Israel was routinely targeted in a special agenda item devoted exclusively to that country. This practice of 'selectivity' was supposed to be excluded from the work of the Council. But its majority's obsession with demonising not Israel but Israelis, [that is to say, Jews] and denying their human rights has never been worse. Since its creation [in 2006] the Council has adopted 67 resolutions condemning one country, Israel, and only 61 on the rest of the world's 192 [The UN HRC has a regular item on its agenda, number seven, devoted exclusively and uniquely to the alleged war and human rights crimes of one country…Israel. As an accredited NGO (Non-governmental Observer) Hillel Neuer is entitled to take part in sessions of the HRC concerning Israel, which of course does not have a seat on the HRC. As can be seen on YouTube, on nearly every occasion when he does, his allotted three minutes of speaking time is repeatedly interrupted by a succession of obviously pre-arranged spurious points of order, invariably raised by representatives of states such as North Korea, Sudan, Russia, Saudi Arabia, Iran, Venezuela, China and Cuba, who when their turn comes, despite their appalling human rights records, are invariably given a smooth passage.]

Resolutions on Israel are uniquely suffused with political hyperbole, selective reporting and the suppression of any countervailing facts that might provide balance. [By contrast] A commission of inquiry into Hamas which exonerated the [Jew-killing…R.B.] movement initiated a new era whereby a terrorist group has come to rely on the Human Rights Council as an international tool in its war against Israel. In March this year, the UN issued a list of companies doing business across the 1949 armistice line, the purpose of which was to implement the anti-Israel Boycott Disinvestment and Sanctions campaign.

Finally, let us consider the experts on the Council. There are some 70 experts under 50 mandates known as Special Rapporteurs or independent experts or working groups. Some do good work. But far too many are wolves in sheep's clothing appointed by the dictatorships to pursue radical agendas in the name of human rights. In 2008, they appointed Richard Falk, a leading promotor of the 9/11 conspiracy theory [that it was the work of the Jews], a supporter of Hamas and President Ahmadinejad of Iran. In 1979, he wrote an op-ed in the *New York Times* [the US equivalent of the *Guardian*] called 'Trusting [Ayatollah] Khomeini' in which he welcomed his regime as new model of democracy for the world. He was a UN expert for six years, and was so pro-Hamas the Palestinian Authority tried to get rid of him, but failed. In 2014, when Falk's term came to an end, his wife replaced him. [sic!] John Zeigler, the hunger expert, held office for 16 years. He was appointed by Castro of Cuba and Chavez of Venezuela. He has a radical leftist agenda. In 1989 he created the annual Gaddafi Human Rights Prize, worth $250,000. million [This is not a misprint] He rewarded his sponsors by awarding the prize to Castro and Chavez. In other years the prize went to [the Hitler-admiring leader of the Nation of Islam and Black Lives Matter enthusiast] Louis Farrakhan, head of the largest anti-Semitic group in the USA. In 2002, the prize was awarded by Zeigler to [the one-time French Stalinist and then convert to Islam] convicted Holocaust denier Roger Garaudy and, in the same year, to himself. I couldn't make this up if I wanted to. Zeigler is a UN expert who sits on the Advisory Committee of the UN Human Rights Council…If Eleanor Roosevelt were alive today, would she not agree that in the words of Reporters Without Borders, many of these decisions are indeed grotesque.

Four years on, and nothing had changed. In December 2020, the UN General Assembly adopted 21 resolutions, one each on North Korea, Syria and Iran, and 17 on Israel. So, Israel's record on human rights and related issues is 17 times worse than three of the world's most repressive dictatorships. (The far-left dominated actors' union, Equity, once the preserve of Vanessa Redgrave's Gaddafi-funded Workers Revolutionary Party, went one better. As of June 2021, it had adopted 18 resolutions condemning Israel, and none that criticised the government of any other country.) On May 27, 2021, Human Rights Council delegates queued up to accuse Israel, and only Israel, of war crimes committed in its conflict with Hamas. Leading the pack, UN Human Rights President Michelle Bachelet spoke of 'appalling events in Gaza and the occupied Palestinian territories', and 'Israeli attacks' that 'may constitute war crimes.' But she said not a word about the Hamas firing of rockets from civilian locations in Gaza at civilian targets in Israeli territory - a double war crime - that began the conflict, and which most definitely violated resolutions adopted unanimously by the UN General Assembly in December 1974. Its definitions of acts of aggression include, in Article 3, part B, 'bombardment by the armed forces of a State against the territory of another State or the use of weapons against the territory of another State.' All succeeding speakers, we can be sure, as is always the way, by prior agreement, followed her lead by ignoring Hamas' acts of aggression against Israel, as defined by the body under whose auspices they were meeting, and instead read from the same script as the President. Hillel Neuer replied to their lies on behalf of United Nations Watch:

The United Nations was founded to prevent war. Yet today's one-sided session, and the pre-determined investigation it proposes, will achieve the opposite, because they were the very purpose of this war. The purpose of Hamas, backed by the Islamic Republic of Iran, was to attack Israeli cities from within populated areas in Gaza, to incur civilian casualties, and exploit the suffering of their own people, in order to de-legitimise Israel here at the UN, in international courts, and the media. [Elsewhere I cite extracts from a Hamas military manual which says exactly this.] A council for human rights ought to condemn what Hamas is doing. Why then does today's resolution fail to mention that Hamas started this war, firing over 4,000 rockets that deliberately targeted civilians across Israel, and that the rockets were launched from civilian areas, such that each attack constitutes a double war crime? Why is there no mention that hundreds of millions of dollars of international aid money donated to help Gaza's poor population, were diverted by Hamas to build 250 [some say 600] miles of terror tunnels? Why is there no mention that Hamas is recognized world-wide as a terrorist organisation [a designation opposed by Corbyn], and that its founding charter openly calls for the genocide of the Jews? [in Article Seven] Why is there no mention that on May 7 in Gaza, a Hamas leader told Palestinians, quote, 'We want you to cut off the heads of the Jews with knives? [This instruction is in accordance with Chapter 8, Verse 19 of the *Koran*] Why is there no mention that in the past two weeks, Jewish people world-wide from London to LA were threatened, chased and violently assaulted by pro-Palestinian protestors? Madam President, isn't the UN supposed to defend victims of terrorism and racism?

So, the reader will now understand why, even if my proposals for the curbing of Islam and the elimination of the jihadism it spawns were in any sense plausible, they would not only receive no support from the UN, but be met by a huge majority with its active opposition.

III The Rebirth of a Myth: Naz Shah's Adolphe Légalité

'Never forget that everything that Hitler did in Germany was legal'. Naz Shah, Corbynista Labour MP for Bradford West.

Following the fiasco of his 'Munich putsch' of November 1923, Hitler re-thought his strategy, and came to the conclusion that the road to power lay through an adroit exploitation of what proved to be fatal flaws in the Weimar Constitution, most notably the ill-famed Article 48, which entrusted powers to the President that made possible the by-passing of the democratically elected Reichstag and the suspension of civil liberties codified in other articles of the same constitution. This spectacular about-turn earned for Hitler the ironic sobriquet 'Adolphe Légalité' after 'Philippe Légalité', Duke of Orleans, who after the overthrow of his cousin, Louis XVI in 1792, unsuccessfully schemed to replace him as a constitutional monarch. In Hitler's case, the new strategy worked. With the connivance of the upper-class *camarilla* around the senile monarchist President Field Marshall Paul von Hindenburg and supported by intense lobbying from business, agrarian and military interests who wanted to settle accounts with a still powerful left and restore Germany once more to major power status, Hitler was appointed Chancellor on January 30, 1933. Lacking a majority in the Reichstag, and out-voted in the chamber by the two left wing parties, the Social Democrats and the Communists, Hitler was therefore compelled to form a coalition with the Nationalists, but one that still lacked an overall majority. All this was legal, but much of what followed was not, either being spuriously rendered legal by retrospective legislation, or simply outside the law altogether.

Once granted emergency powers after the Reichstag Fire of February 27, Hitler unleashed a reign of terror on the German left. Armed squads of his private army of brown shirted storm troopers went on the rampage, arresting and then beating up, torturing and in many cases murdering thousands of left-wing militants in scores of improvised jails that operated entirely outside the control of Germany's prison system. Feeble attempts by local and government officials to curb the illegal violence were invariably overruled with Hitler's approval by the Nazi Minister of the Interior Wilhelm Frick. Even then, at the Reichstag elections of March 5, held under conditions of a raging murderous terror against the Left, the Nazis failed to secure a majority of the votes cast and deputies elected. Contrary to the claim made by the ignoramus Livingstone that Hitler won an election in 1932, he not only lost all four elections his party contested in that year, but only started winning elections when, like Corbyn's and Livingstone's Ayatollah comrades in Iran, he eliminated all opposition and converted Germany into a one-party state.

Illegality was not reserved exclusively for opponents of the Nazis. When Hitler settled accounts with his unruly Storm Troopers in the 'Night of the Long Knives' of June 30, 1934, the murder of Ernst Rhoem and his associates was entirely outside the law, carried out by the SS and Gestapo purely on Hitler's

335

command, and then sanctioned *post facto* by an all-Nazi Reichstag some days later. *Pace* Naz(i) Shah, Hitler never attempted to claim his action was legal. On the contrary, he asserted his right to act outside and against the laws of his own regime: 'In this hour, I was responsible for the fate of the German people, and thereby I became the supreme judge of the German people.' And not only judge, but jury and executioner: 'I gave the order to shoot the ringleaders in this treason, and further I gave the order to cauterize down to the raw flesh the ulcers of this poisoning of the wells in our domestic life'.

It was also on an order from Hitler that in 1937, offspring of unions between German women and black solders of the French army stationed in the Rhineland after the First World War were illegally compulsorily sterilized. The same applies to the Nazi's secret euthanasia programme that operated between January 1940 and July 1942, which resulted in the murder in gas chambers of at least 70,00 Germans deemed by doctors to be 'unworthy of life' on account of either their real or alleged infirmities. Authorised only by an order from Hitler, the action was never approved by any official German legal or medical body, and of necessity required the violation of the Hippocratic oath by those doctors who took part in the programme, as did the 'experiments' they carried out on Jews in Nazi death camps. Were these doctors also innocent when they were convicted of murder and executed by the Allies after the war? Because all they had done was to obey a policy emanating from their *Fuehrer* whom, we are assured by the MP for Bradford West, never did anything that was illegal.

When we come to the Nazi persecution and then extermination of the Jews, it is the same story. Laws were indeed passed that step by step drove the Jews from public life and deprived them of those few and dwindling rights left to gentile Germans. But the pogrom unleashed by Goebbels on the night of November 9-10, 1938, known as Crystal Night, had no foundation in law, Nazi or otherwise. All it required was for Hitler to give the verbal order. None of the thugs who perpetrated the acts of looting, vandalism and murder was ever prosecuted. Again illegally, the Jews were then made to hand over to the Nazi government an equal sum to compensation paid by insurance companies to cover claims for Jewish property damaged during the riots.

Professional Holocaust deniers, as distinct from the Muslim variety, who lack all academic sophistication, have made great play of the fact that no document has been found where Hitler had authorised or given legal sanction to the extermination of the Jews. (Though Hitler did give several public warnings that this would be their fate in the event of their launching a second world war.) So far as pseudo-academic Holocaust deniers are concerned, the fact that at end of that war, six million European Jews had gone missing counts for nothing, whereas a missing, or rather non-existent document, counts for everything. There is a simple answer to this apparent contradiction. Every attempt was made to keep the fate of the Jews a secret, not only from the Jews destined to die, but also from the Germans themselves, though for obvious reasons, this proved impossible. Verbal commands and coded terms were used to conceal and disguise the real purpose of the operation, such as 'special treatment', 'final solution' and 'resettlement' (rather like Shah's proposed 're-relocation' of Israel's Jews to the USA) and never 'extermination'. Ample testimonies exist that the order to exterminate the Jews was instead passed on verbally, from Hitler to his second-in-command and designated successor Goering, and then to those charged with carrying it out, SS

336

Chief Himmler and his immediate subordinates Heydrich and Eichmann. So again, contrary to what Naz(i) Shah implies, even within the framework of the laws of the Third Reich, the Holocaust had no legal foundations whatsoever.

Sha's insistence that Hitler always acted legally presumably also applies to matters pertaining to Nazi Germany's foreign relations. Even if we exclude from consideration the many treaty obligations the Third Reich inherited from its Weimar predecessor and then violated, such as the Treaty of Versailles, with its limitations on Germany's military capacity, the de-militarisation of the Rhineland and various border changes involving the surrender of German territory, followed by the Locarno Treaty of 1925 and the Kellogg-Briand Pact of 1928, Hitler also unilaterally repudiated or violated agreements his own regime entered into, for example the non-aggression pacts with Poland in 1934 and the USSR in 1939.

Last but far from least, there are the war crimes committed by the German armed forces, principally on the Eastern Front. Here too, Germany's own laws and military regulations, and international rules governing the conduct of warfare, conventions to which Germany was a signatory, were violated on a colossal scale, with the killing, starving and working to death of millions of prisoners of war, and the murder of millions of civilians simply because they were Jews and members of other so-called inferior races, or belonged to banned political organisations. There was also the infamous *Kommissarbefehl* or Commissar Order issued by Hitler on the eve of the Nazi invasion of the Soviet Union in June 1941, which authorised the execution of political officers serving in the Red Army, in flagrant violation of The Hague Conventions of 1899 and 1907, and the Geneva Convention of 1929, each of which Germany was a signatory to. It was for these war crimes and crimes against humanity that Nazi leaders were convicted and sentenced to death at the Nuremberg Trials. Is Shah implying that since their orders came from Hitler, they too, like Hitler, were innocent?

In conclusion, we have to consider the possibility, however remote, that Shah is fully conversant with the history of the Third Reich, and that she is therefore aware that many of the crimes perpetrated by the Nazis were retrospectively legalised either by Hitler personally, as in the case of the murders committed in the 'Night of the Long Knives', or by the courts, as in the cases of the destruction and plunder of property belonging to Jews, trade unions and left-wing parties. If Shah's claim that 'everything that Hitler did in Germany was legal' rests upon what she believes is the legality of retrospective legislation, then this raises no less serious issues concerning her fitness to serve as a law-making member of Parliament, whether for Labour or any other party. All western legal authorities concur that retrospective legislation undermines one of the most central principles of any justice system worthy of the name, namely that all those subject to it have the right to know whether any action they may carry out at that moment in time is either legal or illegal, and if the latter, what the prescribed punishments are for doing so. The principle is, No crime without a law, no punishment without a crime. Retrospective legislation abolishes that principle, leaving those subjects to the law liable to arbitrary punishments for actions that at the time they were committed, were legal, just as it enables others, usually those in power, to commit actions that at the time were illegal, such as the murders authorised *post facto* by Hitler in the 'Night of the Long Knives', which are then retrospectively made legal. Instead of the rule of law, one of the bedrocks of a free, democratic society, we have a principle that suits to perfection the arbitrary rule of a despot. Is that how Naz Shah, an elected legislator, thinks English Law should operate?

With the views that she holds on the Jews and Hitler, how did Shah, who like her defender Livingstone, so far as the history of Nazi Germany is concerned, is either a liar or a total ignoramus, manage to be adopted as a prospective Labour MP? That fact that she did tells us all we need to know about those in the Bradford West Constituency Labour Party who adopted her as a Parliamentary candidate, and those in the party leadership who restored her to full party membership.

IV Leaving Islam...at your Peril

'The Prophet said: "If someone discards his religion, kill him."' Sahih al-Bukhari 4:52:260.

On the evening of October 13, 2016, ITV screened a programme titled 'Islam's Non-Believers', which examined the hostile treatment undergone by Muslim apostates in the UK at the hands of their former co-religionists, in the first place their own families. Even the most zealous Islamophile would think twice before invoking 'but what about' to warrant a programme where the religion in question is any other than Islam. For those readers who did not view the programme, I reproduce below extracts which bear most closely on the subject matter of this work. The programme opens with a masked (sic) ex-Muslim woman describing how her family reacted when they learned of her apostasy:

'They locked me in the house. They hit me. I don't think it would be that hard for them to kill me.'

Another woman, whose scientist and atheist husband was murdered at a book fair in Bangladesh by Muslim zealots, then indicates the machete head wounds that she suffered in the attack. Another young woman, not disguised: 'You are going to get shunned. You are going to get mistreated.'

Presenter: 'I found an underground resistance movement who defy fundamentalists [no, they are orthodox Muslins enforcing the Sharia] here and across the Islamic world.'

A masked man with disguised voice: 'Internet and social media is our battleground. Our numbers are growing each and every day.'

A Muslim cleric addresses a mass meeting in Bangladesh: 'We vow to hang the atheist apostates on the gallows. God willing!'

The audience chants: 'Burn down the houses of atheists!'

Another cleric (in English): 'The Hellfire is awaiting anyone who is reducting [sic]Allah and his Messenger. Moreover, their families should not continue having any kind of relationship with them.' Then follows a brief exposition by the Iranian-born Maryam Namazie of the Council of Ex-Muslims of Britain outlining how and why it helps those doubting or leaving Islam to make good their escape to an Islam-free secular life. Next, a series of accounts by UK and overseas-born young Muslims, some disguised, some not, (mostly women, be it noted) of how they came to leave Islam and the reactions of their families. Sadia, a girl brought up as Muslim in Oxford told her mother when she was 15 that she no longer believed in God. She recalls her mother's reaction:

'You can't tell anybody else because they will kill you.' Sadia then explains, 'because we [i.e., Muslims'] are obliged to kill ex-Muslims'. [correct] She then relates how her brother, an atheist at fourteen, and later chemistry student at Hull University, came to commit suicide after leaving Islam. 'Everybody knew he was an atheist, much more open than I was about it...Your intelligence gets attacked. They make you feel like you are stupid...like you are dirty. You become unimportant within the [Muslim] community. He started hating himself so much because he never experienced real love and compassion...It is the burden of the guilt that you are disappointing family and loved ones. That is what kills you'.

Another masked young woman with disguised voice, speaking in English:

Anger, disgust, sadness. I just felt very empty. I felt very guilty to just be me. I felt like I couldn't think the way that I did or feel the way that I did. You question your sanity, that is how badly it affected me. This whole stigma around ex-Muslims. Everyone judges us negatively. No one wants to listen to our stories...We can't speak up because we live in fear of being harassed, of being discriminated against, of our families leaving us.

She then relates how her self-hate led to cutting herself.

Another masked woman with disguised voice in English, after ten years as a secret atheist, finally told her mother she was 'coming out' as an apostate:

I'll never forget how my mum cried for ages. My dad couldn't talk much. My mum was wailing, begging me not to do this. I told her I have to and I'm sorry. I have to tell you who I am...All of a sudden, here I was perceived as a someone that had no morals...My mum and dad were so heartbroken and it hurts me that I had to tell them and break their hearts. [It is explained that her disguise is also to protect her parents.] I think the community will come to my parents and tell them that their daughter has dishonoured them, that my parents did not do a good job at all to bring up a daughter like me, they should probably have killed me when I was young.

The Presenter then relates how the programme makers wrote to a range of Muslim leaders in the UK asking for their comments on the issue of apostasy. Only one agreed to appear in the programme, Dr. Omer El Hamdoon, Deputy Secretary General of the Muslim Council of Britain, a body that collaborates closely with the Sharia left, and officially welcomed the election of Jeremy Corbyn as leader of the Labour Party in September 2015. The Council has received substantial public funding, despite its having had a policy of boycotting Holocaust Memorial Day ceremonies as a protest against what it called 'the ongoing genocide and human rights violations in the occupied Palestinian territories.' An ideal partner for Corbyn and his Sharia left comrades.

The Presenter prefaces El Hamdoon's comments by telling viewers that 'he says that no one is compelled to be a Muslim'. This is strictly true. However, there are certain complications as Dr El Hamdoon is well aware. If, in a Muslim state, monotheists, namely Christians and Jews, those the *Koran* the calls the 'people of the book', refuse to convert to Islam, they have the choice of accepting *dhimmi* status and paying the infidel's tax, or be killed. If they are not 'people of the

340

book', the choice is reduced to one of convert or be killed. True, no one has to become a Muslim. But the alternatives are such as ensure that most of those who live or come under its rule will do so. It is a pity that the opportunity was missed to ask El Hamdoon to comment on the law of his own faith in this respect, and likewise, on the penalty for the subject of the programme, apostasy, which is invariably death and is, as the programme says, together with blasphemy, the law of the land today in no fewer than twelve Islamic countries, including two Muslim enemies, Corbyn's much-admired Shia' Iran and Sunni Saudi Arabia.

Though he does not say this at any time in his interview, El Hamdoon's position is summarised by the Presenter as being, 'people can leave of their own free will and should not be punished'. The first part of this statement is true, but the second is not. Anyone can stop believing in Islam, just as they can in any other system of ideas they no longer find convincing. But the second part of the statement is totally false because, unlike any other system of ideas, according to the *Koran,* Sharia law and various *hadith* claiming to record faithfully rulings of the prophet himself on this matter, renouncing Islam is punishable only and always by death. This was one of two weakness in the programme, and a serious one at that, in that it failed to inform viewers at the very outset, by citations from Islamic sources, what constitutes the crime of apostasy, and the penalty that inevitably follows it. The second flaw, which I believe stems from the same source as the first, was to depict the response of the 'Muslim community' to apostasy as the result of the influence of 'fundamentalism', (not a term accepted or used by Muslims) whereas all the relevant Islamic sources prove beyond any doubt that the Muslim attitudes depicted in this programme conform precisely to the version of Islam embraced by Dr El Hamdoon's British Council of Muslims:

The Muslim community is a community based on religion. So if a person chooses to stop being a Muslim, they can't really expect that the Muslim community is going to say to them, "you are [still] part of our community", because you have left Islam, you have left the religion...If family holds their religion very deep to their hearts, when they see one of their members has left that religion, they feel a sense of betrayal. And obviously, a lot of people will say, "look, I just can't deal with this, so I just shun [sic] that member out because he has betrayed me". Islam does put a big emphasis on faith, and sometimes someone will have to [sic] reject a certain person because their attitude rewards faith. That can happen.

Bear in mind that this justification of shunning apostates comes from one of the leading figures in 'mainstream' Islam. Given the opportunity to interview him, I would simply have asked him to comment on this *hadith*: 'The Prophet said: "If someone discard his religion, kill him."' (Bukhari: 4:52: 260),

and from Chapter 4, Verse 89 of the *Koran*: '...if they turn renegades, seize them and slay them wherever ye find them.'

The programme then returns to Rayhana, one of the disguised women apostates:

I was planning to run away from home and go to university because my parents didn't want me to move out of home. I think I said I'm not a Muslim any more. I thought that would mean they would let me go. But they locked me in the house, they hit me, they burnt my arms, I still have the scars. My dad said he wished he had already killed me, that he had strangled me when I was born.

With the help of the Council of Ex-Muslims of Britain, she escaped from home, and now has to live under police protection...*in England*. Another young woman brought up in Bangladesh, and now an active member of the Council of Ex-Muslims in London, describes her mother's reaction to 'coming out' as an apostate:

'I was told that it was Allah's command for parents to tame [sic] their children. My mom said, "wherever I beat on your body, that part goes to the heaven"'. We are told that Rayhana's father 'is cursing her on the internet...All they want to do is think a different way and they are not allowed to'. Dr. El Hamdoon now returns to explain why, as the Presenter puts it, 'it is not realistic to expect atheists to be treated the same way by a religious [more precisely, Muslim] community.'

That's the normal perspective. In the eyes of the religion, you have done something wrong, because religion expects you to stay religious, and you don't want to be religious, so they are going to say, "you are no longer favourable in our eyes". It doesn't mean we discriminate against you. It doesn't mean that we treat you badly or incite hatred or whatever...We don't discriminate, but our love cannot be the same. (sic!) It's just human behaviour.

No it is not. It is *Muslim* behaviour. The majority of the rest of mankind does not react in this way when a loved one decides to think for themselves rather than uncritically accept the beliefs of their parents. That is how human progress happens. Being himself a devout and unquestioning Muslim, El Hamdoon cannot see that the suppression of independent thinking has led to hundreds of millions of Muslims remaining trapped in the century Islam was born and is more than any other single factor (least of all the influence of the west) responsible for the endemic violence, and abysmally low cultural and intellectual level so evident today in Islamic society in its homelands and diaspora. Commenting on his remarks, the Presenter describes Dr Hamdoon as a 'mainstream Muslim'. But a 'mainstream Muslim' is still a Muslim. And a Muslim, to be such, must accept, without engaging in any of the 'cherry picking' favoured by liberal Christians, all that the *Koran* proclaims and the Sharia demands. And what both insist on, without any equivocation, is that the crime of apostasy must be punished by death and death alone. So unless Dr. Hamdoon wishes to run the risk of himself being accused of apostasy, he is obliged to accept that this is the law of Islam, and if called upon to do so, uphold it. That is why it is a pity that he was not taxed on this crucial point, and as result of this omission, be allowed to present himself, unchallenged, as the acceptable face of British Islam.

We are now given what the Presenter calls a 'fundamentalist interpretation of Islam'. In fact, as the sources already cited prove, it is entirely, for want of a better term, 'orthodox', as the excerpts illustrate. First, briefly, three clerics:

'If the court had sentenced him to death for apostasy, everybody would have known that Islam was the official religion of this country.'

'The Prophet therefore by confronting apostasy Islam was preserved.'

'I mean that an apostate has to be killed'.

Then Dr Zakir Naik, online from India, 'one of the most popular TV preachers in the world':

'But if the person who reverts, who was a Muslim, and then converts, and becomes a non-Muslim, and propagates his faith, and speaks against Islam, and refutes Islamic rule, the person should be put to death'.

If that is 'fundamentalist', then so are the *Koran's* already-cited Chapter 4, Verse 89, and the *hadith* on the same subject. Next up is the Saudi cleric Sheikh Assim al-Hakeem, who broadcasts in English and visits the UK to preach. Again, what he says concerning apostasy is impeccably orthodox Islam, no less 'mainstream' that that of Dr. Hamdoon

'In Islam, the punishment for apostasy is death penalty'

And so it is.

Haitham al Haddad, a British-based preacher, invokes the image that recurs time and again in the K*oran*:

'The hell-fire is waiting for anyone who rejects Allah and his messenger.'

The programme continues with a survey of the history of the atheist and free-thinking movement in Bangladesh, and of the murderous onslaught against its bloggers by machete-wielding Muslim zealots. We then move to the UK where a similar campaign of hate is being whipped up against apostates among the Muslim diaspora in London and around the UK. Viewers see a meeting celebrating the murder in Bangladesh of the atheist blogger Rajib Haider:

'The black sheep has died, Rajib, the atheist…even taking the names in our mouths is dirty…it's a dirty name. May he get the punishment [presumably in hell] he deserves. This is what we demand. He called the Prophet Mohammed a fool.' The crowd cry 'Allah' and a man calls out, 'burn the atheists' houses down'. The crowd then chants, 'Enemy of Islam, beware, be careful!'

Another speaker then continues: 'He is the martyr of Hell. He is the chief person of Hell!'

We are then told that these 'are not fringe extremist speakers talking in this way about a murdered writer. They are important community leaders.' [ah…the vibrant Muslim community yet again, this time not gang raping but by way of a change, out for the blood of anyone within it who has the temerity to think for themselves.]

One of the speakers is Mufti Shah Sadruddin: We are told

he is one of the most senor religious figures in the Bangladeshi British community. He is the rector of a full-time secondary school and a leading figure in this organisation [we see its committee] Jamiat-E-Ulama UK, the council of Muslim scholars in the UK based in London. He even ran for election as a Conservative councillor, portraying himself liberal, tolerant and opposed to hatred: 'I believe in equality. I believe in fairness. I believe in loving the human race, and I hate to hate anybody.'''

But hate he does. Viewers then see him speaking the previous year, demanding the death sentence for a Bangladeshi atheist blogger: 'Child of a hypocrite, he swore at my Prophet'.

He then calls for the death penalty on people who insult Islam: 'O Bangla's scholars! O Bangla's Muslims! Wake up! No son of a bastard will remain alive after swearing at my Prophet!'

His local Conservative Party declined to respond to questions put by the programme's makers regarding Tory support for Sadruddin's candidacy.

Viewers are told 'a number of these rallies were held around the UK, and they were all organised by senior and respected community leaders.' One in Rochdale is addressed by a speaker who declaims: 'As long as the atheists in Bangla are not hanged, until then, our protests will continue.' [Crowd: "Burn down the houses of the atheists!"]

A London-based Bangladeshi atheist blogger had to go into hiding after he was targeted in leaflets distributed outside Mosques with the obvious intention of inciting zealous Muslims to murder him. A similar leaflet was posted online, naming three bloggers and accusing them of blasphemy. It was posted by Syed Naem Ahmad, Organising Secretary of Jamiat-E-Ulama UK, who is also a charity trustee, and a broadcaster on Islamic TV. The leaflet called for atheist bloggers to be hanged. Viewers then see the first stages of an operation carried out by the Ex-Muslim Council to affect the escape of two apostate young women from their devout Muslim parents, whose family is on holiday in London. This is followed by a number of atheists relating their experiences of persecution and worse in various Islamic countries…Tunisia, Bangladesh, Yemen and Pakistan, where nearly 40 free thinkers are on death row awaiting execution or serving life sentences for blasphemy. For obvious reasons no one can be sure how many atheists there are living - and being murdered - under Islamic thought crime laws, but one estimate, difficult to credit, it must be said, puts the number of atheists in Saudi Arabia alone at one and half million and four million in Pakistan. Whatever the actual number, within four hours of the Ex-Muslim Council launching its new website, it reached number one on Twitter and in two days 72 countries, receiving 118,000 tweets.

This then is the 'tightly knit' Muslim community celebrated by Islamophiles who don't have to live in it, as tightly knit and well-guarded as any Nazi concentration camp, just as efficient and ruthless in its suppression of dissent, and as relentless in its pursuit of those who escape its confines as any Gestapo officer or SS detachment. We should not be surprised, though we should feel nauseated, by the total lack of support afforded by the Corbynista left for the work of the Council for Ex-Muslims, and its total indifference at best to the persecution of atheists, free thinkers, apostates and human rights campaigners in countries governed by Sharia law.

By now, only the most obtuse of readers will not understand why this is the case. The Sharia left in general, and its useful idiot Corbyn in particular, have for more than a decade now forged the most intimate collaborative relationships with several large and well-endowed Muslim pressure groups in the UK, and no less close ones with a wide range of equally well-heeled representatives of Jihadi movements abroad. As Corbyn and his Momentum cohorts must be well aware, all of them, if called upon to do so, would be obliged as Muslims to endorse the repressive measures being unleashed against apostates from their faith. Having in the past always sided with Islam against its critics, as in the cases of *The Satanic Verses*, the Danish cartoons and the *Charlie Hebdo* massacre, there is therefore not the least prospect that either Corbyn or his Sharia left allies will risk antagonising their Muslim comrades by any public protest or action on behalf of persecuted apostates. Then there is of course the Muslim vote. Imagine the backlash against Labour in the 'Muslim Community' once the word gets around that Corbyn has come out in support of apostates from Islam! So...as always in such matters, one must see the bigger picture.

V The Law is a Pig

Tucked away on page 8 of my local paper, the December 31, 2016 Swansea edition of the *South Wales Evening Post*, in a column titled *Around The UK*, was the following item:

'A man jailed after leaving bacon sandwiches outside a mosque has been found dead in his cell. Kevin Crehan, 35, was halfway through a one-year prison sentence he received in July after admitting the racially- [sic] motivated attack [sic] on the Jamia Mosque in Bristol earlier this year.'

Let us now pick our way through what to what many of the *Post's* readers would perhaps have seemed a story of little consequence.

1. Placing bacon sandwiches outside a Mosque is ignorant, bigoted and loutish. However, the following questions involve points of law:

a) The report speaks of an 'attack' on a building, which implies the offence of criminal damage to property, but refers only to the 'leaving' of sandwiches outside it. Was the structure of the building in any way damaged by the placing of bacon sandwiches outside it? If not, in what sense was the mosque 'attacked' other than 'racially'? If 'racially', are we to assume that the mosque itself possessed a racial identity, like the chicken in a Manchester Sainsbury's? If so, which?

b) Were the occupants of the Mosque, if any, at the time of the 'attack', also aware of being or were deemed to have been 'attacked'? If so, in what way?

c) In view of the 'attack' being treated as 'racially motivated', in what sense can placing bacon sandwiches outside a building with a purely religious function be said to have been an attack on racial grounds? If so, which race, or races, were being attacked?

2. Whether this action should constitute a criminal offence and at that, one carrying a prison sentence, in this case of one year, is another matter entirely.

3. The act of placing the bacon sandwiches outside the mosque is described as 'racially motivated'. This begs the question...which race, or races, were the intended target of this action? A Mosque is open to Muslims of all races (though in many cases, they exclude Muslim women).

4. However race is defined, there is no racial group on this planet that can be said collectively to share an aversion to bacon, or any other pig-derived food or non-consumable product. Some might say, with the Old Testament's ban on pork in mind, that Jews fall into this category, but however true this may have been the case in more pious times, this is patently not the case today. Only observant Jews, and especially those strictly orthodox, would feel themselves under an obligation to obey this rule, whereas a Jewish atheist clearly would not. Some, using an analogous argument, might claim that Arabs would feel none too happy if they found themselves in close proximity to a bacon sandwich, but once again, this falls at a similar hurdle as the Jews, since not all Arabs are Muslims, any more than are Pakistanis, Bangladeshis, Indonesians etc etc.

5. In the light of point 4, which is incontestable, we arrive at the inescapable conclusion that specifically and explicitly forbidding the consumption of pig-derived foods, and the aversion that this ban has created, is exclusively the creation of two religions, Judaism and Islam, the second having cribbed it from the first: 'And the swine, though he divide the hoof, and be cloven footed, yet he cheweth not the cud, he is unclean to you'. (Leviticus, Chapter 11, Verse 7)

'Forbidden to you is the flesh of an animal which dies of itself, and the blood and flesh of swine'. (*Koran*, Chapter 5, Verse 4)

6. It follows that the placing of a pig-derived product outside a mosque can only give offence to those defined by and strictly adhering to the teachings of their Islamic faith, their race therefore being immaterial. It is entirely probable that amongst the congregation at this particular mosque, just like many others, there can be found Muslims from a variety of ethnic backgrounds, including possibly converts of Anglo-Saxon or, like the offender, Kevin Crehan, even Celtic stock. It is a belief that has been targeted, not a set of genes.

7. As an exercise in the madness that today invades our otherwise eminently rational legal system once it makes concessions to the dictates of Sharia law, imagine the following scenario. To establish the required proximity of a bacon sandwich to a mosque that would invite the charge of a 'racially motivated attack', a person bearing the said object stands on the pavement let us say, 100 metres from the mosque, and awaits the arrival of a patrolling policeman. In due course, one does arrive, whereupon our would-be racially motivated attacker conspicuously places his bacon sandwich on the pavement, in full view of the policeman, who duly tells him to pick it up or be charged with committing an offence under the Litter Act. Our attacker does what he is told. The next day, our attacker stands one metre nearer the mosque, resulting in the same sequence of events. And so the same operation is repeated each day, one metre at time closer to the mosque. My question, which I address primarily to those responsible for enforcing the law that brought about the arrest, conviction, jailing and, as a tragic if unintended consequence, the supposed suicide of Kevin Crehan, is this: At what precise distance, if any, from the mosque would placing the bacon sandwich on the ground and leaving it there not only be an offence under the Litter Act, punishable by a small fine, but also become a 'racially motivated attack' carrying a prison sentence of one year?

7. If in its wisdom the English justice system deems that the placing of a bacon sandwich outside a mosque causes a degree of harm that merits a prison term of one year, it is surely reasonable to ask why it does not see fit to enforce the law against the female genital mutilation of Muslim girls carrying a maximum jail term of fourteen years, all of whose victims, I would submit, in their hundreds of thousands have experienced an infinitely greater and longer lasting trauma as a result of undergoing this barbaric Islamic misogynist ritual, than any that might be caused by the sight or smell of a bacon sandwich outside their local mosque. They say that the law can sometimes be an ass. It can also be a pig.

VI A Pope Goes a Cherry-Picking

Although this work is chiefly devoted to the doings of Islam and its leftist acolytes, I have found it necessary at times to turn my attentions to one of its main western apologists, namely the Roman Catholic Church. The Vatican is ideally suited to this role, because from its very earliest days, it has been more concerned with the *real politick* of the acquisition of power and wealth than any spiritual mission guided by the teachings of the Bible. In pursuit of these entirely worldly goals the Papacy has never had any qualms about falsifying the principles and laws upon which its mission is supposed to based, namely those which are to be found in the Bible, and in the Bible alone. Let me cite one example. One of the most often-quoted sayings attributed to Jesus is his 'render therefore unto Caesar the things that are Caesar's and unto God the things that are God's.' (Mathew, 22:21) Ever since it became the official religion of the Roman Empire in AD 380, the Papacy has never willingly rendered anything to anyone, so when confronted with the emergence of nation states in late medieval Europe, it concocted its own rather one-sided version of church state-state relations in the Papal Bull *Uman Sanctum* promulgated by Pope Boniface VIII in 1302, a document which in its attempt to provide a theological underpinning for Caesaro-Papism, must rank among the most blatant misinterpretations of a Biblical text ever undertaken in the entire history of Christianity:

> We are told by the word of the gospel that in this His fold there are two swords, a spiritual, namely, and a temporal. For when the apostles said 'Behold here are two swords', when namely, the apostles were speaking in the Church [sic], the Lord did not reply this was too much, but enough. Surely, he who denies that the temporal sword is in the power of Peter wrongly interprets the words of the Lord when he says 'put up thy sword in its scabbard'. Both swords, the spiritual and the temporal, are in the power of the Church.

Let us see who is in fact 'wrongly interpreting the words of the Lord'. The scene with the two swords does not take place 'in the Church', or a synagogue for that matter, which would at least render this piece of fiction more plausible. Luke, if he is to believed, tells us what really happened. It is the Feast of the Passover, the setting for the Last Supper. The twelve apostles are gathered together with Jesus, not in a 'Church', but a private home's 'guest chamber', a 'large upper room furnished'. (22: 11-12), where they partake of the bread and the wine. (22: 19-20) There is no talk of swords. This occurs later, in the garden of Gethsemane, and here, swords are real, not figures of speech:

> And he [Jesus] said unto them, When I sent you without purse, and scrip, and shoes, lacked ye anything? And they said, Nothing. Then he said unto them, but now, he that hath a purse, let him take it and likewise his scrip; and he that hath no sword let him sell his garment, and buy one. For I say unto you, that this is written must yet be accomplished in me. And he was reckoned among the transgressors: for things concerning me have an end. And they said, Lord, behold, *here are two swords*. And

he said unto them, It is enough. (22: 35-38, my emphasis)

See what then follows, again not in a 'church' but the garden of Gethsemane: When Jesus is about to be arrested, an unnamed but obviously armed apostle asks him, 'Lord, shall we smite with the sword?' Instead of telling Peter (if indeed it is he) to 'put up his sword', *Jesus says nothing*, whereupon 'one them smote the servant of the high priest and cut off his right ear'. Only now does Jesus intervene, but not to reprimand the sword-wielding apostle, but to condone his action: 'Suffer ye thus far'. (Luke: 22:49-51)

The cited passage has no bearing whatsoever on Church-State relations in the sense claimed by the Papal Bull. As a Jew, Jesus, so the Gospels say, preached not in a 'church', but in synagogues (Mathew 13:54) and the Jerusalem temple. The passage in question describes the arrest of Jesus in the Garden of Gethsemane by the Roman state, by a 'great multitude with swords and staves' (Mark 14:43), a Roman 'cohort', which consisted of between 360 and 800 armed soldiers. In all four Gospels, Jesus (in Luke after an authorised act of defiance) 'goes quietly', submitting to the authority of pagan Rome, thereby 'rendering unto Caesar'. The manner in which this passage has been misused and mistold to sanctity and augment the secular power of the Roman church tells all we need to know about the cynicism and mendacity of the Papacy.

In addition to manipulating Biblical passages and faking documents, such as the notorious Donation of Constantine, and fleecing and conning the faithful with bogus holy relics by the wagon-load, over the centuries the Papacy has taken from the Bible (having already subjected its texts to numerous redactions) what suits its purposes, while ignoring or even denying that which obstructs them, as for example the already-cited ruling of Pope John XXII that the first Christians did not hold all property in common, even though Acts 5:32 says they did. The sheer scale and audacity of the lying is quite breath-taking and still continues today. Here we have a prime example: The current *Catechism* asserts that Mary was 'ever-virgin'. Mathew however, in Chapter 1, verse 25, says of her husband Joseph that he 'knew her [i.e., had sexual intercourse with her] not till she had brought forth her first-born son'. First-born? Yes, because, if we are to believe what the Catholic Church calls the 'true word of God' (which, when it is inconvenient, as in this instance, it chooses not to) the 'ever-virgin' Mary, in addition to Jesus, *gave birth to at least six more children*; four sons and an unspecified number of daughters:

And when he [Jesus] was come into his own country, he taught them in their synagogue, insomuch that they were astonished, and said, whence hath this man this wisdom and these mighty works? 'Is not this the carpenter's son? Is not his mother called Mary? And his brethren, James and Jo-ses, and Simon and Judas? And his sisters, are they not all with us? (Mathew: 13: 54-56)

Once again, God gets it wrong. The *Catechism* assures its readers that 'Jesus is Mary's only son' and that 'James and Joseph, "brothers of Jesus", are the sons of another [sic] Mary'! Why, if they were not the sons and daughters of the mother of Jesus, does Mathew say they were? On this point, the *Catechism* is silent, and wisely so. Was Mathew 13 reporting, perhaps unwittingly, a case of mistaken

349

identity? Not Jesus preaching, but a look-alike Jesus tribute act touring the synagogues of the Holy Land, the itinerant son of a mother calling herself Mary and of a father claiming to be a carpenter who had four other sons and several daughters? No source for this both laughable and lamentable attempt to refute Mathew is supplied, because none exists. Just another barefaced lie, concocted to sustain in the gullible flock the lucrative cult of the Virgin Mary, and exalt the superior state of celibacy shared (officially at any rate) by the clergy. No wonder Pope Francis II was able to find so much sweetness and light in the *Koran* when his own holy book can be subjected to such cavalier interpretations.

The official negative stance of the Roman Church towards divorce is well known, though exceptions to it have been made on numerous occasions when expediency, usually political, has dictated a more flexible approach. (That is why Henry VIII assumed his divorce from Catherine would be rubber-stamped by Clement VII. The problem was, she was the aunt of Holy Roman Emperor Charles V, who had the Pope in his pocket.) Nevertheless, the current (1994) edition of the *Catechism of the Catholic Church* is very clear: Divorce 'objectively contravenes God's law'. Even the Catholic Church, which over the centuries has created a whole body of Papally-derived doctrine that has little or no foundation in any Biblical text, such as the 'mystery' of the Trinity, a concept nowhere to be found in the Bible and only imposed on the Church by Emperor Constantine three centuries after the death of Jesus, the ban on the use of contraceptives, and the invention of five additional sacraments to the two derived from the New Testament, would be hard put to deny that 'God's law' can only be found in the Bible. Clearly, a quotation from the good book is therefore called for to prove the point, so we are presented with one to suit the Vatican's purpose, Mark, Chapter 10, Verses 11 and 12:

'Whoever divorces his wife and marries another, commits adultery against her, and if she divorces her husband, and marries another, she commits adultery'. [Even here, divorce *per se* is not condemned, but the act of re-marriage following it.]

For Catholics who do not know their Bible (the vast majority, I suspect, which is exactly how the Vatican likes it) that would seem to settle the matter. Not so. While Luke (17: 18) says almost word for word the same as Mark (hence 'synoptic gospels'), Mathew, although also regarded as one of the three synoptic gospels, does not:

'Whosoever putteth away his wife, *except it be for fornication*, and shall marry another, committeth adultery; and whoso marrieth her which is put away doth committee adultery.' (my emphasis) In modern parlance, Mathew has Jesus say that adultery is sufficient grounds for divorce. As the Roman Catholic Church thinks to the contrary, it naturally prefers to cite Mark. It also has the same problem with Deuteronomy, which goes one better than Mathew by also sanctioning bigamy:

If a man have two wives [sic], one beloved, and another hated, and they have born him children, both the beloved and the hated; and if the first born son be hers that was hated: Then it shall be, that when he maketh his sons to inherit that which he

350

hath, that he may not make the son of the beloved first born before the son of the hated, which is indeed the first born. (21: 15-16)

As to divorce:

When a man hath taken a wife, and married her, and it come to pass that she finds no favour in his eyes because he hath found some uncleanness [sic] in her: then let him write her a bill of divorcement and give it in her hand and send her out of his house. And when she is departed out of his house, she may go and be another man's wife. (24: 1-2)

Here we have a ruling that not only re-enforces that of Mathew but goes further by granting grounds for divorce that do not involve adultery. Leviticus, which together with Deuteronomy comprises the core of 'The Law' of the Old Testament, takes divorce for granted. Laying down the rules for the conduct of the priesthood, 'the sons of Aaron' (21: 1), one such given to Moses by Jehovah was that 'they shall not take a wife that is a whore, or profane, neither shall they take a woman put away from her husband'. (21:7) Obviously then, divorce was not forbidden, for how else 21: 14: 'A widow, or a divorced woman, or profane, or a harlot, these shall he not take; but he shall take a virgin of his own people to wife'. Divorced women, along with those others specified, were regarded as 'unclean', and therefore not fit to be the wives of the priesthood. But they could only have existed if divorce was legal. (Also forbidden to priests was necrophilia: 'Neither shall he go into any dead body' [21: 11] ...but that is another story.)

Given the irreconcilability of Mark and Luke on the one hand, and Mathew, Leviticus and Deuteronomy on the other, there is reasonable cause to suspect that like other passages in the Gospels that are now or initially were at variance with the Old Testament, Mark and Luke could have been subjected to some judicious editing. Unless Jehovah is in the habit of contradicting himself, which all theologians would argue is incompatible with his infinite wisdom, of one fact we can be certain: With respect to divorce, Mark and Mathew cannot both be 'God's law'. And Leviticus and Deuteronomy, contrary to what many Catholics assume, are accorded by their Church no less authority than the gospels. Again, we turn to the *Catechism* for confirmation that this is so:

The Old Testament is an indispensable part of Sacred Scripture. Its books are divinely inspired [including therefore Leviticus and Deuteronomy, with their bigamy and divorce] *and retain a permanent value, for the Old Covenant has never been revoked...Christians venerate the Old Testament as the True Word of God.* The Church has always vigorously opposed the idea of rejecting the Old Testament and the pretext that the New has rendered it void. (my emphasis)

And does not Mathew have Jesus say, 'Think not that I come to destroy the law, or the prophets: I am not come to destroy but to fulfil.' (5: 17) Fulfil what exactly? 'For verily I say unto you, till heaven and earth pass, one jot or one tittle shall in wise pass from the law, till all be fulfilled.' What law? That fabricated by Popes perhaps? For Jesus the Jew, there could be no other law than that dictated by his father to Moses, the law of Leviticus and Deuteronomy.

Catholics, confronted and perplexed by these contradictory teachings on the

351

matter of divorce in a book that they are told is wholly inspired by god, perhaps might take comfort from the fact that a supreme head of their Church has resolved matters not only to his own satisfaction, but in so doing, also for all those 1.2 billion Catholics who owed him their spiritual obedience. In his introduction to the *Catechism*, Pope John-Paul II says of the text that it is 'a statement of the Churches' faith and of Catholic doctrine, attested to or illuminated by [sic] Sacred Scripture, the Apostolic Tradition and the Church's Magisterium'…Vaticanese for Papal cherry   picking.

VII Hate Speech?

'I want to spend the next four years making sure that every non-Muslim in London knows and understands Mohammed's words and message. That will help to cement our city as a beacon that demonstrates the meaning of the words of the prophet'.

(Ken Livingstone, mayoral election campaign speech to the North London Central Mosque, March 16, 2012.)

It does not require much imagination to envisage the legal consequences that might well ensue in not only the UK but a growing number of Western countries if the following comments were to be made about Muslims in public, whether by word of mouth, in print or on-line:

'In their hearts is a disease'

'Deaf, dumb and blind, they are void of all wisdom'.

'The worst of beasts.

'Unclean'.

'apes and swine'

The message of the book containing these and other statements of a similarly vituperative nature too numerous to cite here has been commended by the heir apparent to throne of the Great Britain and Northern Ireland, as well as by politicians ranging from the extreme right, starting with Adolf Hitler and Heinrich Himmler, through the centre to the far left, ending with Ken Livingston and Jeremy Corbyn, and clerics of a wide variety of denominations, including the current Pope. It is readily accessible to the general public on line, in bookshops and public libraries, and to students in university libraries, and is on the shelves of hundreds of thousands of homes across the UK. It is also used as an instructional text in thousands of schools, many of them publicly funded, and for sermons in religious services.

As their content and context make clear beyond any doubt, these hateful statements are directed at specific groups of people, namely those who do not subscribe to the beliefs of the author who made them. And yet their wide dissemination has not resulted in any prosecutions under the UK's hate speech laws. Could it be because they are the 'words of the prophet' that Livingstone wanted 'every non-Muslim in London to know and understand'? Since the choice epithets cited above were aimed explicitly at those London voters Livingstone sought to introduce to the teachings of the prophet, had he succeeded in this undertaking, his margin of defeat at the hands of Boris Johnson would in all probability have exceeded the record for a previous incumbent of such a high office.

Koran citations, respectively:
2:11, 2:172, 8:56, 9:29. 5: 61

VIII Stalin's Man of Peace

'I know how much the German nation loves its Fuehrer. I should therefore like to drink his health.' J. V. Stalin, the Kremlin, August 24 1939, toasting the signing of his pact with Hitler.

'We are all Stalinists'. Andrew Murray, Jeremy Corbyn's General Election strategist, in the Communist Party *Morning Star* on the 120th anniversary of Stalin's birth.

'...the dirtiest, the most criminal and most repulsive figure in history.' Leon Trotsky on Stalin, March 4, 1939.

'I Think history will regard Hitler as one of the great men of our time...with no love for pomp and show, Christianity in its purest form might stand a chance with him.' George Lansbury, Labour Party Leader from 1932 to 1935, after his meeting with Hitler, April 1937.

Ever since his agreement at Munich on September 29, 1938 to hand over the Czech Sudetenland to Hitler, Tory Prime Minister Neville Chamberlain's name has become a by-word for the appeasement of dictators bent on conquest. And rightly so. But it is a measure of the double standards of much to today's left that no such opprobrium attaches itself to the name of Stalin for his pact with Hitler of August 23, 1939, which lit the fuse of the Second World War by unleashing the Nazi invasion and enslavement of Poland, and sanctioned the country's partitioning between the Third Reich and the USSR. And yet Stalin's collaboration with Hitler in the destruction of Poland was of a different order to that of Chamberlain's role in the dismemberment of Czechoslovakia, shameful as it nevertheless was. While Chamberlain, together with French Prime Minister Daladier and Mussolini, sanctioned the annexation of the Sudentland by Hitler, unlike Stalin, he did not take part in its seizure, or acquire a share of the spoils. Neither did Britain, from May 10, 1940, under Churchill's leadership, deny sanctuary and continued diplomatic recognition to exiled governments driven from their homelands by the Nazi war machine. But in what proved to be a futile attempt to appease Hitter, that is exactly what Stalin did, expelling the ambassadors of countries under Nazi occupation from Moscow, while at the same granting full diplomatic recognition to the quisling regime of Petain in Vichy France. So it is strange indeed that whatever crimes Stalin has been accused of (and we have noted that within the Corbynista inner circle, they count for little when weighed against his alleged achievements) insofar as the broader public takes an interest in this period of history, unlike Chamberlain's, their knowledge of Stalin's role in the Second World War is unlikely to include his appeasement of and collaboration with Adolf Hitler. Stalin, born Jughashvili, chose for himself a name that means man of steel. And yet although merciless in crushing his domestic enemies, all being defenceless and almost all imaginary, in Hitler's hands, he proved to be putty.

In the light of these facts concerning the truly monumental crimes of Stalin, it should be surely a cause for concern that at the very highest levels of the Labour Party's leadership, Corbyn has seen fit to employ adviser for defence, Ken Livingstone, Seumas Milne as Director of Communications and Andrew Murray, General Election strategist and political adviser, each of whom have credited Hitler's partner in crime with what they obviously regard as his great contributions to the cause of socialism. Livingstone, who as I write, is serving the second year of his suspension for remarks deemed anti-Semitic, in his inimitable double-think fashion, writing in the British Communist Party *Morning Star* of September 25, 1991, was able to reconcile his years of collaboration with a number of self-styled Trotskyist, and therefore ostensibly at least anti-Stalinist groups, with his attributing the sweeping reforms of the post-war Attlee government 'largely' [yes, 'largely'] to 'the presence of post-war developments [sic] in eastern Europe', 'developments' which largely consisted of the region's enslavement, terrorising, military occupation, exploitation and near economic ruin by Stalin. By this reading of post-war history, on a par with Livingstone's excursions into that of Nazi Germany and the Holocaust, Stalin is the true author of the British welfare state! One wonders what Aneurin Bevan, the real architect of the UK's National Health Service and who, unlike Livingstone, Milne, Murray and for all one knows, Corbyn, despised Stalin and all his works, would have thought of Livingstone's absurd claim. In the same manner, again according to Livingstone, the process of post-war decolonisation in the 'third world' was the result of the Soviet Union acting in its support as an 'anti-capitalist force'. Be that as it may, while the west de-colonised, closer to home, the Kremlin stubbornly clung on to its own east European empire, putting down national uprisings in East Germany in 1953, Hungary in 1956 and Czechoslovakia in 1968, each with massive military force. Within the USSR's own borders, only with its collapse in 1991 did it become possible for some of its national minorities to achieve their independence. Livingstone's version of Soviet history is no less fanciful than his of Nazi Germany.

Just as *dhimmi* feminists today simulate envy of the Muslim woman's lot without for one moment entertaining the least intention of sharing it, so their Stalinophile counterparts in the Soviet era likewise looked nostalgically to the East for their political inspiration while continuing to enjoy all the benefits of the democratic liberal order they so despised. (Judged by their public comments, Corbyn's Shadow Chancellor John McDonnell and Shadow Home Secretary Diane Abbott are more enamoured of a purely oriental version of Bolshevism, with Mao's 50 million plus victims, more than double those of Stalin's. All good Corbynistas are however united in their admiration of Castro's one-party dictatorship, and in their support for attempts by the besieged Chavista President Maduro to establish a similar regime in Venezuela.)

Just what it is that attracts Corbynistas to dictators? In the darkest days of the Second World war, George Orwell took comfort from his conviction that the British, for all their faults, and he was never slow to criticise them, were by tradition resistant to the appeals of the totalitarianism and leader cultism that had extinguished democracy on the European continent. 'No party rallies, no Youth Movements, no coloured shirts, no Jew-baiting, or spontaneous demonstrations.'

That was then. The Corbynista hero-worship of dictators is all of a piece with the preposterous but also sinister cult of Corbyn himself, an exotic *melange* of disparate and discordant elements, united and unified primarily by a shared hostility to liberal democracy. Incredibly, under the aegis of the Corbyn *Fuehrerprinzip,* there has been an inherently unstable melding of Stalinism, *faux* Trotskyism, Maoism, utopian socialism, anti-Semitism, advocates of Sharia law, anti-Americanism, anti-Westernism, millenniumism, political correctness, misogyny, cultural relativism, Nazism, messianism, conspiracy theorism, jihadism, thuggery, Islamophilia, anti-Zionism and X Factor celebrity culture, this last with its Jeremy pop song, oil painting, T-shirts and Nuremberg-style chanting of his name at rallies and rock concerts.

Such was the extent of the Corbyn craze among the politically illiterate that the 2017 edition of the Collins dictionary even included the word 'Corbynmania', defined as 'fervent enthusiasm for Jeremy Corbyn, the leader of the UK Labour Party.' And as cults are want to do, Corbyn's spawned a vast memorabilia industry of kitsch: colouring-in books, miniaturised and life-size card-board cut-outs, garden gnomes, playing cards, broaches, knitwear, under-pants, Corbyn Lenin-style cloth caps, fake tattoos, shopping bags, pillow-cases, mugs (sic), teddy bears and Lego figurines. (In view of his long association with the Muscovites of the *Morning Star,* why no Jeremy the Tank Engine?) To dramatise Corbyn's quasi-saintly status, there was even a plan to have him walk on water at the 2017 Brighton Labour Party conference, only to be thwarted, unlike Jesus, by the elements. All the features that Orwell describes as integral to a totalitarian movement are present, down to the shirts, the Jew-baiting, the Momentum 'youth movement', comprised mainly of students, and the carefully-staged 'spontaneous' chanting at pop concerts. This ludicrous and demeaning cult is without precedent in a mainstream British political party. Until now, such fawning adulation of leaders, be they of the left or right, has always been confined to the fringes of the political spectrum. No longer. It has moved centre stage.

History never repeats itself exactly, since every event is unique. But sometimes it comes pretty close to doing so. Today, nearly the entire left, along with the rest of the political establishment, vehemently insists that whatever the evidence to the contrary might suggest (such as the repeated summons to Jihad in the *Koran* and terroristic acts in the name of Islam by those describing themselves as Muslims) Islam is a (or even the) religion of peace. Similar claims were made for Hitler by pacifists, the Stalinist left and its fellow travellers in the wake of the Nazi-Soviet Pact of August 23, 1939, again despite evidence to the contrary, such as the repeated summons in *Mein Kampf* to wage war in the East for *Lebensraum,* the rearmament of Germany after the Nazi conquest of power in 1933, the logistic and military support provided for Franco in the Spanish Civil War, the annexation of Austria in 1938 and the destruction of Czechoslovakia in 1939.

In his *Mein Kampf,* the one foreign policy option Hitler beyond all doubt excluded, both on ideological and geopolitical grounds, was an alliance with the Soviet Union: 'The fight against Jewish world Bolshevism requires a clear attitude towards Soviet Russia. You cannot drive out the Devil with Beelzebub.' And, prophetically as it turned out, he warned that 'the very fact of the conclusion of an alliance with Russia embodies a plan for the next war. Its outcome would be the end of Germany'. Instead, it was to be a war of conquest against the USSR, for 'soil' and 'living space':

We take up where we broke off six hundred years ago. We stop the endless German movement to the south and west and turn our gaze toward the land in the east. At long last we break off the colonial and commercial policy of the pre-war period, [so much for Lansbury's plan] and shift to the soil policy of the future. If we speak of soil in Europe today, we can primarily have in mind only Russia and her vassal border states.

Those western Stalinists familiar with these and similar statements where Hitler outlined his foreign policy can therefore perhaps be forgiven for assuming that when also considering the official (but soon to be proved bogus) hostility of the Soviet leadership towards fascism, there could not be the remotest possibility of a deal between the Third Reich and the (anti-Semitic) leader of 'Jewish world Bolshevism'. They would therefore have rejected as an outrageous slander on the Kremlin's anti-fascist integrity when at the height of the Czech crisis, on September 22, 1938, Trotsky predicted, as he had done repeatedly since the Nazis came to power in 1933, that 'Stalin will seek [an] accord with Hitler'. They would have found the proof for their disbelief in the Soviet press, which mocked Chamberlain for his now infamous claim that handing over the Sudentland to Hitler had secured 'peace in our time', and the assertion in *Izvestia* of October 4, 1938, 'it is the first time we know of that the seizure of someone else's territory, the shift of borders guaranteed by international treaties, is nothing less than a "triumph" or "victory" for peace'. Never for one moment did Stalinists the world over anticipate that within the year they would be using identical terms to applaud the treaty that not only sanctioned Stalin and Hitler doing precisely to Poland what Chamberlain and Hitler had just done to Czechoslovakia., but gave the green light for Stalin to extend his allotted 'sphere of influence' by annexing all three Baltic states, Finland and Romania's province of Bessarabia.. When confronted with the sensational news of Stalin's conclusion of his pact with Berlin after having spent the best part of the previous six years denouncing Hitler as the butcher of the left, the prime threat to the USSR in particular and the security of the world in general, in the Autumn of 1939, Stalinists were everywhere saddled, not for the first or last time, with the task of totally reversing their previous strategy and policies. Hitherto, shifts in the party line had evolved incrementally at least over a period of months. Now, the reversal was accomplished in a matter of hours and in a manner and on a scale that revealed Stalin's cynical indifference to the humiliations it would inevitably inflict on his loyal minions in the Comintern.

Football historians have recorded that infamous day in May 1938 when, to further Chamberlain's policy of appeasing Hitler, the British ambassador to Germany, Sir Neville Henderson, acting on instructions from the Foreign Office, ordered the English football team to give the Nazi salute before their match against Germany in the Berlin Olympic stadium. As Stanley Mathews recalled in his autobiography, *Feet First*, 'all the England players were livid and totally opposed to this, myself included'. Within little more than a year, Britain was at war with the country whose dictator they were honouring. For all Stalin's similar exercises in placatory multi-culturalism, they also ended in the same result, just as the west's have done since 9/11 in its appeasement of Islam. When Ribbentrop stepped from his plane at Moscow Airport, he was greeted not only by Deputy

Foreign Minister Potyomkin, but by the familiar strains of a Soviet band playing the Nazi anthem, the Horst Wessel Song, allegedly composed by a storm trooper killed in a street battle with communists, and the sight of Swastika flags, one flying from the bonnet of Stalin's personal bullet-proof limousine taking him to the German embassy, flags that had been hastily purloined from a nearby film studio that was still busy making an anti-Nazi movie.

Dutifully following the lead of the Kremlin, in the manner of the Jesuits, black became white, and white, black, but only after several weeks of confusion and indecision, in which for want of a clear lead from Moscow, the various sections of the Communist International improvised a policy which attempted to combine opposition to the Nazi invasion of Poland with support for the pact that had sanctioned it. Blissfully unaware that the secret protocol attached to the pact made provision for the conquest, partition and annexation of Poland by its signatories, on the day the pact was signed, the British Communist Party's *Daily Worker* carried an Orwellian headline which saluted Stalin's deal with Hitler as a 'dramatic peace move to halt aggression'. *Tribune*, the socialist weekly founded in 1937 to campaign for a popular front against fascism, faithfully echoed this delusion. A pact between Hitler and Stalin would be 'a great re-enforcement for peace in Eastern Europe'. And it was 'a lie to suggest that it leaves Germany a free hand against Poland or anyone else'. On the very day, September 1, that Hitler attacked Poland, the editorial in *Tribune* again insisted that the pact had 'strongly re-enforced the power for peace in Europe', while an article by Stalinist fellow-traveller Konni Zilliacus, titled *Stalin - Architect of Peace,* complained of 'malicious or ignorant commentators' who 'pretend[ed] that the Soviet-German pact is an arrangement to give Germany a free hand in Europe'. The very idea! Another article demanded that readers 'dismiss the tales of a secret Nazi-Soviet alliance for the partition of Poland', the existence of which, though long known in the west, was only finally acknowledged by the Soviet leadership, like the Katyn massacre of 22,000 Polish officers by the NKVD in 1940, in the brief era of *Glasnost* that preceded the collapse of the USSR in 1991. Following their governments' declarations of war on Germany on September 3, so far as the Communist Parties of Britain and France were concerned, support for Poland and their own countries' war efforts were still in operation when on September 7, Stalin explained to two of his political intimates the real purpose of the pact. The aim was to unleash a war between Germany and the Anglo-French allies.

'We [sic...here Stalin, as he was often wont to do, is using the Bolshevik equivalent of the royal plural] see nothing wrong in their having a good fight and weakening each other. It would be fine if at the hands of Germany, the position of the richest capitalist countries, especially England, were shaken. Hitler, without understanding it or desiring it, is shaking and undermining. the capitalist system. [Just as today many on the left no less naively believe and hope Islam is doing.]'

Only after a delay of nearly a month from the signing of the pact did the Comintern bother to convey to its sections that Hitler was no longer the enemy, and that the warmongers were located in Warsaw, London and Paris. And when it became clear, after the Red Army marched into its allotted eastern zone of Poland on September 17, that the USSR had joined the ranks of those hitherto denounced as 'aggressors', even the most obtuse Stalinist could see that the old line had to go. But in France, like Britain at war with Germany since September 3, party leaders understandably found the switch from anti-fascist patriotism to pro-Nazi defeatism hard to swallow, let alone sell to their bewildered rank and file. (Even within the Soviet Union, where two decades of terror and brain-washing had produced a seeming total unanimity of opinion, Molotov found it necessary to denounce 'short-sighted people in our country' who had been 'carried away by simplistic [sic] anti-fascist propaganda' [all of it emanating from the Kremlin] and were therefore unable to grasp the necessity and virtues of their wise leader's deal with Hitler.)

In France, L'Humanité, the party's daily, had experienced similar difficulties, having initially greeted the news of a pact that a bare week later, with Stalin's connivance and assistance, would unleash a war to enslave Poland, with a front-page photo of Stalin and the caption, 'Stalin, the Champion of Peace and the Independence of Peoples'. When not peace but war came, and as yet unaware that Stalin had agreed with Hitler to erase Poland from the map of Europe, on September 2, the party had unanimously voted its support for war credits in the National Assembly. Then, on September 19, still trying to square the same circle even two days after the Red Army had invaded eastern Poland, the party announced its 'unshakable resolve' to defend France from Nazi aggression. This was not at all what Stalin had in mind when he signed his pact with Hitler. So on September 28, the Comintern informed the French party that 'in this war a position of national defence is not a correct one for the French communists.' Instead, it was to be treason. (One of the many ironies of Stalin's alliance with Hitler was that over the three previous years, he had staged a series of purges and show trials in which Lenin's former comrades and leaders of the Red Army were convicted and executed on fictitious charges of serving, on Trotsky's instructions naturally, as accomplices of Hitler. Another was that in helping Hitler eliminate Poland from the map of Europe, Stalin had removed the only barrier that stood between the USSR and an invasion by Nazi Germany. As a direct result of the pact, when the time came for Barbarossa, the Wehrmacht launched its invasion of the Soviet Union from a border 250 miles closer to Moscow. And yet three years previously, in one of his rare interviews with a western journalist, Stalin had observed, correctly, that 'when a state wishes to attack a state with which it does not have a border, it begins to create new borders until it neighbours the state it wishes to attack'.)

With the unambiguous Comintern directive of September 28 that unlike Nazi Germany, the war was being waged by France and Britain purely to further their imperial interests, Stalin's pro-Nazi pfennig had finally dropped. On October 1, the now-outlawed party called on the French government to accept Hitler's peace proposals, and with them, necessarily, the destruction and partioning of Poland. Three days later, party leader Maurice Thorez, who at the outbreak of war, had volunteered for military service, deserted his unit by slipping over the Belgian border and making his way to Moscow, from where he promoted the new line that Hitler was a man of peace, and that it was the French and the British who were the war-mongers. Pursuant to this policy, after the fall of Paris to the Wehrmacht on June 14, 1940, two top officials of the French Communist Party, Maurice Treand and Jean Catelas, approached the city's Nazi occupiers to request permission to resume legal publication of L'Humanité, which had been banned by the French government for its support of the Stalin-Hitler Pact. Despite their undertaking that the paper would 'denounce the activities of the agents of British imperialism' and promote 'a policy of European pacification', that is, submission to Nazi rule, the Stalinist duo failed in their attempt to outbid the sundry French fascists as France's quislings. But this setback had no impact on the party line, which was neatly summed up in its favourite slogan: 'Neither De Gaulle nor Petain'. The result was that only after Germany invaded the USSR on June 22, 1941, after a full year of Nazi occupation, did the French communists take part in the resistance to the enslavement of their country. The British party also had its knuckles rapped. It too had been slow to embrace the new pro-Hitler line. For those acquainted with the Chomsky principle and the anti-Western stance of the Corbynista Stop the War Coalition, the Comintern instruction has a familiar ring:

> Each party must fight against reaction in its own country, not against fascist reaction in a foreign country. It is not fascist Germany, which [has] concluded an agreement with the USSR, but reactionary anti-Soviet England, with its enormous colonial empire, which is the bulwark of capitalism. Therefore, the tactic of anti-fascist struggle is also not applicable here.

One can only imagine how the party's Jewish membership, greatly augmented during the popular front period when anti-fascism was the order of the day, truly felt about having to promote the raging anti-Semite Hitler as a man of peace. And yet there had been ample warning that such a policy switch could be in the offing. From the very the first days of the Hitler regime, as it set about rounding up, torturing and murdering members of the German Communist Party, Stalin's diplomats assured their Nazis counterparts that so far as the Kremlin was concerned, it was to be business as usual. In the words of *Izvestia* on May 6, 1933, less than a week after the destruction of the German trade union movement, 'the Soviet Union does not wish to alter anything in its attitude to Germany.' Then, in February 1934, none other than Stalin gave a broad hint at the 17th Soviet Party Congress that a deal with Hitler could not be ruled out: 'Fascism in Italy, for example, has not kept the USSR from establishing the best of relations with that country'. Yes indeed. If Mussolini, then why not Hitler? And so it proved. The fact that both Germany and the USSR had concluded ten-year non-aggression pacts with Poland in 1934 never entered into either Hitler's or Stalin's calculations when they agreed to partition Poland any more than did the latter's concern for the difficulties they would inevitably cause in the sections of the Comintern affected in one way or another by the consequences s of the pact.

Only one deviation from the new policy of defeatism was sanctioned...*in Nazi Germany*. There, the mercilessly-hounded remnants of a once-powerful party (at least 20,000 murdered) were informed by its leader, Walter Ulbricht, beyond the reach of the Gestapo in Moscow, that not the Third Reich, but Britain, was 'the most reactionary power in the world'. The public bench mark for this new policy was set with statements made by Stalin and his Foreign and Prime Minister Molotov. In a speech to the Supreme Council of the USSR on October 31, 1939, a little more than a month after Poland had been subjugated by and divided between the forces of Hitler and Stalin, Molotov depicted Poland and its French and British allies as the 'aggressors', and Nazi Germany, their innocent victim. (After the Sharia left's reaction to 9/11 and subsequent Jihadi atrocities too numerous to list here, does this not sound familiar?)

In reading the relevant excerpts of Molotov's address, one that gloats over the crushing of Poland's heroic though doomed resistance to Nazi aggression, and exudes sympathy towards poor Germany for its treatment at the hands of British and French imperialism, bear in mind that already, in the Nazi zone of occupation, specially trained SS murder squads were well on the way to achieving Himmler's goal of exterminating the Polish intelligentsia, and had already begun the rounding up and slaughter of Jews that constituted the first stage in what was to culminate in the Holocaust. (Thousands of Jews who fled the Nazi pogrom by crossing into the Soviet zone were driven back by the Red Army, to almost certain death in the gas chambers of the Final Solution.)

> The ruling circles of Poland boasted quite a lot about the "stability" of their State, and the "might" of their army. However, one swift blow to by Poland, first by the German army and then by the Red Army, and nothing was left of this ugly offspring of the Versailles treaty which had existed by oppressing non-Polish nationalities.

In view of Stalin's repressions of the Soviet Union's national minorities, this was rich indeed. Molotov neglected to add that this 'one swift blow' was delivered in the east by seven Soviet armies comprised of one million troops, who faced a disorganised remnant of an already defeated Polish army numbering at most 25,000 effectives, while in the west, Stalin's Nazi partners did the 'heavy lifting', mobilising 11 tanks divisions to Poland's one, and forty infantry divisions to Poland's thirty. In the air, Germany's 850 bombers and 400 fighters vastly outnumbered and outperformed Poland's antiquated fleet. Despite the Red Army's minimal contribution to Poland's defeat (996 killed compared to Germany's 10,570) Stalin replied to Hitler's 'true and sincere greetings' on his 60th birthday that his alliance with the Third Reich had been 'sealed in blood', one that was celebrated with a filmed joint victory parade in Brest Litovsk by the two conquering armies. No protest was forthcoming from Polish communists against the dismemberment of their country because the previous year Stalin had taken the precaution of dissolving their party on the grounds that virtually the entire membership was 'following the instructions of the Polish counter-revolutionary intelligence'. All twelve members of the party's central committee living in Soviet exile were executed, along with almost every other member Stalin could lay his hands on. Ironically, in 1936, at the high tide of the Stalinist popular front against fascism, a time when Poland was being courted as a potential ally against Nazi Germany, the Polish Communist Party was taken to task by the Comintern for its 'national nihilism'. Molotov continued:

> Today, as far as the European great Powers are concerned, *Germany's position is that of a State which is striving for the earliest termination of war* [which it began], while Britain and France, which but yesterday were declaiming against aggression, are in favour of continuing the war, and are opposed to the conclusion of peace. [emphasis added] The roles as you see are changing. Everybody realises that there can be no question of restoring old Poland. It is, therefore, absurd to continue the present war under the flag of restoration of the former Polish State. [In other words, we and the Nazis have Poland, and no one is going to take it away from us, least of all the Poles.]...The ruling circles of Britain and France have lately been attempting to depict themselves as champions of the democratic rights of nations against Hitlerism, and the British government has announced that its aim in the war with

Germany is nothing more nor less than the 'destruction of Hitlerism'. It amounts to this. One may accept or reject the ideology of Hitlerism as well as any other ideological system, that is a matter of political opinion. [sic!] But everybody should understand that an ideology cannot be destroyed by force, that it cannot be eliminated by war. It is therefore not only senseless *but criminal* to wage such as war as a war for the 'destruction of Hitlerism' camouflaged as a fight for 'democracy'. (emphasis added)

The USSR's foreign policy, Molotov made clear, was not one of a plague on all imperialist houses, but one 'built on the basis of friendly relations, on readiness to support Germany's [i.e., Hitler's] aspirations for peace'. To ensure there were no misunderstandings in Berlin on this point, on November 30, *Pravda* carried the following statement by Stalin:

It was not Germany that attacked France and England, but France and England that attacked Germany and bore the responsibility for the current war. [That the war began with Germany's invasion of Poland and was the reason why Britain and France honoured their treaty obligations to Poland by declaring war on Germany was passed over by Stalin as it had to be, because he had joined in the attack on Poland.] After the onset of hostilities [sic] Germany made peace proposals to England and France, and the Soviet Union openly supported Germany's peace proposals [those of September 28] since it continues to consider that a speedy end to the war would radically ease the situation of all countries and peoples. The ruling circles in England and France crudely [sic!] rejected Germany's peace proposals as well as the attempts of the Soviet Union to end the war as soon as possible.

In the twinkling of an eye, Chamberlain had been transformed by Stalin from an appeaser of Nazi Germany into a war monger, and Hitler from a warmonger into an apostle of peace and a bulwark against western 'plutocratic' imperialism. And not only of peace. In a conversation with Comintern chief George Dimitrov, Stalin even speculated on the possibility that now Hitler had aligned himself with the Soviet Union, the Nazis might take their socialist claims more seriously than hitherto: 'In Germany, the petty-bourgeois nationalists are capable of a sharp turn – they are flexible – not tied to capitalist traditions unlike bourgeois leaders like Chamberlain and his ilk'. In the same tradition, in the words of Seumas Milne, today it is Russia that plays the role of a 'check to unbridled US power', just as we have seen, emanating from the same far left quarter, similar expectations for Islam, depicting it not only as an anti-imperialist force (while nevertheless remaining a religion of peace) but also a faith with a progressive, even left-wing social agenda. And just as Corbyn's anti-NATO and pro-Jihadi foreign policy has won him praise from the west's enemies, so Stalin's pro-Hitler line found favour in Berlin. In April 1940, after the Nazis had invaded and subdued Denmark and Norway, Molotov issued a statement emphasising that 'the Soviet government understands that Germany was forced to such measures…We wish Germany a total victory [sic] in its defensive [sic] measures'. Going to extraordinary lengths to justify the Nazi onslaught on Scandinavia, *Izvestia* of April 11 insisted 'there can be no doubt that Germany [for which read Hitler] has been forced [sic] to act [sic] in Norway and Denmark because of prior moves by Britain and France.' Just so. (Corbyn likewise claimed that Putin's assault on the Ukraine was a defensive response to an imaginary 'US drive eastwards' and the Sharia left that Hamas and

Hezbollah, both bent on destroying Israel, are 'resistance movements'.) When in yet another 'defensive measure' Nazi troops entered Paris on June 14, Molotov offered its conquerors his government's 'warmest congratulations.'

Following these Soviet endorsements of the peace-loving Hitler's new conquests, a Gestapo report of June 20, 1940, acknowledged that the government of the USSR had

> on numerous occasions shown that it considers the measures taken by Germany in the war – the taking [sic] of Norway, Denmark and the entrance [sic] into Holland and Belgium – as necessary and proper…In its press, the Comintern is adapting to the present foreign policy of the Soviet Union *and recognises that Germany is waging a just war.* (emphasis added)

The previous November, at a conference of Naval officers, Hitler had expressed his confidence that 'as long as Stalin is in power, it is certain that she [Russia] will adhere strictly to the pact made.' As Lenin would say, Stalin was now Hitler's 'useful idiot'. The pact also bought about no less dramatic reversals in Soviet domestic policy. The word 'fascist' disappeared, literally overnight, from the Soviet media and all political discourse. Anti-Nazi books vanished from libraries, while the anti-Nazi film *Alexander Nevsky*, ostensibly about the 13th century Russian Prince's defeat of the Teutonic Knights in the battle of Lake Peipus, made way for hitherto banned operas by Hitler's favourite (and anti-Semitic) composer. In pursuance of the new pro-Hitler line emanating from the Kremlin, as Stalin put it to Dimitrov, that 'we will not come out against governments that favour peace', the British Communist Party launched its prototypical stop the war coalition, which like its Corbynista successor, directed all its fire at the 'enemy at home' and none against the regime of peace in Berlin. Even as the *Luftwaffe*, fuelled by Soviet oil, blitzed its way across Britain, and on the continent, Himmler's rounding up, deportation and murder of Jews gathered its genocidal momentum, Stalin's stooges climaxed their quisling campaign with the launching of a 'People's Convention' at a rally in London on January 12, 1941. Fronted by D.N. Pritt K.C., notorious as the chief apologist in the UK for Stalin's purges and show trial frame-ups of the 1930s, the Convention adopted a six-point manifesto which said not a word about, let alone against Hitler's subjugation of Europe and his continued war against Britain, but instead, in point number four, advocated 'friendship with the Soviet Union', which was then still allied with Nazi Germany, and in number six a Corbynesque 'People's Peace that gets rid of the causes of war'.

For as long as the pact endured, Stalin and his Comintern minions performed two invaluable services for Hitler. One, political, was the promotion of defeatism in countries either overrun by the Nazis or, as in the case of Britain, still successfully defying them. The other, economic and logistic, involved the USSR conveying to or supplying the Third Reich with raw materials, especially oil, essential to Hitler's war machine that the British naval blockade prevented Germany from importing by sea, in Trotsky's apt phrase, thereby becoming 'Hitler's quartermaster'. And as an unsolicited bonus for Hitler, Stalin handed over to the tender mercies of the Gestapo 570 German Communists, some of whom were Jews who, after fleeing the Nazi terror, like so many other Comintern refugees, had fallen out of favour with their Soviet hosts. Then came June 22,

1941, the Soviet Union's 9/11. Here too Trotsky had proved infinitely more far-sighted than those in the Kremlin who, prior to Stalin's taking on the role himself, had accused Trotsky of being Hitler's accomplice. (According to one Stalinist publication, following Stalin's pact with Hitler, Trotsky had switched masters by transforming himself into an agent of the FBI and yes, 'international Jewry'.) Trotsky had predicted, again correctly, that within no more than two years after the signing of his pact with Stalin, Hitler would turn east to execute the mission of conquering 'living space' in the vastness of the USSR. Despite numerous warnings from his own intelligence sources in Germany that the Nazis were preparing to attack, Stalin refused to believe that Hitler, a man of peace, was capable of such treachery. A report by Soviet intelligence, dated June 17, 1941, warning of an imminent Nazi invasion, was rejected by Stalin with the appended comment: 'You can send your "source" from German aviation HQ to his fucking mother. This is not a "source" but disinformation.' On June 21, 1941, the very eve of the Nazi invasion of the USSR, *Challenge*, the British Communist Party's youth paper, faithfully echoed Stalin's trust in Hitler's peaceful intentions towards the Soviet Union by airily dismissing what it called 'the hullabaloo in the press about Germany and Russia'. It was still on sale as the *Wehrmacht's* panzers roared towards Moscow, Leningrad and Kiev. As for Stalin, even when numerous reports reached him that the Germany army had penetrated scores of miles into Soviet territory, he tried to persuade front line commanders bearing the brunt of the Blitzkrieg that the invasion then underway was the unauthorised actions of reactionary Germany officers seeking to provoke a war between the Third Reich and the Soviet Union. Stalin gave the order not to return their fire: 'This is provocation by the German military. Do not open fire to avoid unleashing wider action.' Still convinced that Hitler was a man of peace, at least so far as the Soviet Union was concerned, Stalin insisted that 'Hitler surely doesn't know about this'. Once the horrific reality of Barbarossa sunk in, again overnight, literally, Stalinists world-wide performed another spectacular somersault, in Germany from defencism to defeatism, and everywhere else, from defeatism to patriotism *a l'outrance,* though one that was *sui generis,* since it was in defence of a county other their own.

Though always prominent in so-called 'peace movements', Stalinists are not pacifists (think only of the Red Army, for decades the largest in the world, and Stalin's terror which claimed at least 20 million lives), when it suits their purposes, they can, like Richard, Duke of Gloucester, 'play the chameleon' by resembling them. Over the years, Stalinists have been remarkably effective in both penetrating and manipulating initially independent peace movements as well running their own, like the 'British Peace Committee', these latter being always fronted by compliant useful idiots. The strategic aim in either case was and still is to ensure that their general thrust is directed chiefly against the actual or potential enemies of what was once the Soviet Union and is now Putin's Russia. The best examples of the success of this strategy are the initially independent Campaign for [UK unilateral] Disarmament, founded in 1957, which the pro-Moscow Corbyn first joined in 1966 at the height of the Cold War and in which he later held the office of Vice-President, and the pro-Putin Stop the War Coalition, co-founded and successively chaired by Corbyn and the ultra-Stalinist Andrew Murray, and one of whose Patrons is Kamil Majid, founder of the British Stalin Society. Unlike 'peace campaigner' Corbyn, who for the major part of his political career has kept some very non-pacific company, first as a long-time fellow-traveller of the pro-Kremlin 'tankie' faction within the British communist movement, and more recently as an advocate and apologist for various Irish and Islamic terrorist movements, one of his predecessors, George Lansbury, Labour Leader from 1932 to 1935, was a fully paid-up pacifist. For him, there never had been and never could be a 'just war'. War was the greatest evil known to mankind, and everything else that humanity valued, not only its material and cultural well-being, but even its most elementary freedoms, had if necessary to be sacrificed to avoid it. This stance him put out of step with the mainstream of the British labour movement, and after being savaged by trade union boss Ernest Bevin at the 1935 Labour Party conference for his utter lack of realism at a time when Hitler and Mussolini were so obviously preparing for war, was replaced as party leader by Clement Attlee. Now a free agent, Lansbury spent the rest of the pre-war years trying to convince the British public that for all the appearances to the contrary, the leaders of Nazi Germany and Fascist Italy could be persuaded to take the path of peace. His efforts in this direction coincided with the launching in 1936 of the pacifist Peace Pledge Union by the Reverend Dick Sheppard, with its members' undertaking that 'I renounce war and never again, directly or indirectly, will I support another.' Meantime, in Berlin, Tokyo and Rome, where not pacifism, but re-armament and conquest were the orders of the day, preparations were well in hand to subject the effectiveness of Sheppard's pledge to the test of reality.

Undeterred by what seemed to many to be the war-like intentions of the Axis powers, Lansbury advanced a now-familiar argument deployed by the Corbynistas and the broader Sharia left to either excuse or justify Islamic terrorism and Russian expansionism; namely that the danger of a new world war was the fault of the major western democratic nations. What Germany, Italy and Japan lacked was what Britain and France especially possessed in abundance and what was more to the point, to excess: colonies, and all the economic advantages that went with them. To right matters, Lansbury proposed that all the world's colonies should come under international control, and all their resources allocated fairly amongst the world's major powers, this arrangement serving, so far as the major beneficiaries of this redistribution were concerned, namely Germany, Italy and Japan, as a kind of 'Axis geld', akin to today's 'Jihadi geld'. Granting these colonies their independence was not, and could not have been part of the plan, since the overriding priority was the preservation of peace, and not justice for the peoples of the colonial empires. True to his word, in 1937, Lansbury embarked on what he described an 'embassy of reconciliation', visiting Berlin in April and Rome in July. (Similar fool's errands have taken Corbyn to Damascus, Cairo, Tunisia, Tehran, the West Bank and Gaza with identical results.) It needed only a two-hour audience with Hitler to convince him that it was 'sheer nonsensical folly' to believe that his host wanted war. His useful idiocy even extended beyond praising Hitler as a man of peace: 'I think history will regard Hitler as one of the great men of our time. He appeared to me to be free of personal ambition.... With no love of pomp and show...Christianity in its purest form might stands a chance with him'. And at this point a digression is called for. If we replace Christianity with Islam, one cannot but help being reminded of a YouTube video where Corbyn can be seen and heard uttering no less delusional platitudes about his similarly anti-Semitic terrorist 'friends' Hamas and Hezbollah:

It will be my pleasure and my honour to host an event in Parliament where our friends [sic] from Hezbollah will be speaking. I have also invited friends [sic] from Hamas to come and speak as well...so we can promote that peace, that understanding and that dialogue. [As Corbyn knew full well, both of his guests rejected as matter of principle any 'peace', 'understanding' or 'dialogue' with Israel.] The idea that an organisation that is dedicated towards the good of the Palestinian people [and he could have added, like Lansbury's Berlin host, the extermination of the Jews] and bringing back long-term peace [the Hamas Charter said nothing about 'long term peace'. Article 13 declared: 'There is no solution to the Palestinian problem except by Jihad'] and social justice and political justice [likewise absent from the Charter] in the whole region should be labelled as terrorist organisations by the British government is really a big, big, historical mistake. [Corbyn's hapless syntax has the 'idea' making the mistake, not the government.]

Like Lansbury in his estimation of Hitler, it is Corbyn who is making the 'big mistake'. The way Corbyn describes Hamas and Hezbollah, they could easily be mistaken for the Middle Eastern equivalents of a European social democratic party rather than terrorist movements dedicated to the elimination of a member state of the United Nations. In fact, both Hamas and Hezbollah are theocratically-driven war machines pure and simple, awash with the most advanced weaponry that money can buy, and they make no secret of it. The Shia militia, Hezbollah, does not attempt to disguise that it is little more than an Irian proxy, and its sponsors have seen to it that it is better equipped for war than the armed forces of its Lebanese hosts. Both movements' intentions towards the Jews and Israel, defined with total clarity in their respective charters and numerous public statements by their leaders, those whom Corbyn described as his 'friends', are no different in intention and no less transparent than were those of Hitler towards the Jews and the Soviet Union. Given his close relationship over the years with both the Iranian theocracy and his Hezbollah and Hamas 'friends', Corbyn must have been fully aware of this. Just one example of many of Hezbollah's dedication to peace is the tenfold increase in its stock of missiles, a purely offensive weapon, in the period between 2006 and 2015, giving it the capacity to launch 1,000 missiles *per day* into Israeli territory for a period of two months. Yet although equipped for and pledged to a war of aggression and elimination against the 'Zionist entity', in true Orwellian fashion, Hezbollah invariably refers to itself in its *Manifesto* as a 'resistance' movement.

And how does Corbyn reconcile his description of Hamas as a movement dedicated to 'bringing back long-term peace' with its suicide attacks on restaurants, cafes, markets and buses, its tunnelling into Israel's territory, the kidnapping and murder of its civilians and the bombarding of civilian targets with thousands of rockets, and the round-the-clock pumping out of genocidal hatred towards the Jews on its TV channels? Just between January 2000 and August 2005, during the so-called 'Second Intifada', Hamas was responsible for more than 40% of all suicide attacks carried out in that period, nearly all of them on civilian targets, such as the Tel Aviv Dolphinarium discothèque of June 1, 2001, with 21 victims, the Haifa bus bombing of December 2 of the same year, with 15 victims, and on March 31, 2002, the Mazta Restaurant bombing, also in Haifa, with another 15 killed. The list goes on. According to Wikipedia, in the twelve years between 1993, the year of the adoption of the Oslo Accords, and 2005, the end of the second 'Intifada', there were 171 suicide attacks, nearly all aimed at civilian targets. Of these attacks, 87 were carried out by Hamas, including one against a school and another against a school bus. Hamas subsequently claimed responsibility for nearly all of these attacks. In the same period, as a result of these 'martyrdom operations', 805 Israelis were killed, 503 by those of Hamas. Of the 964 wounded, 388 were caused by Hamas suicide bombers. And this is not terrorism? Corbyn speaks of 'dialogue', knowing full well that both Hezbollah and Hamas have always on principle rejected any negotiations with Israel on the grounds that the Jewish state has no right to exist. Section Three of Chapter Three of *The New Hezbollah Manifesto* (2009) reads as follows:

> Our stance on the negotiations and compromises made by the Madrid conference, the 'Araba Valley retrospect', the 'Oslo Accords' [between Israel and the PLO], is a total refusal to any kind of compromise with the Zionist entity, which is based on admitting its legitimate presence and giving in [sic] what it occupied from the Palestinian and Islamic land. This stance is predetermined and permanent [n.b.] and isn't set for any compromise, even if the whole world admits to 'Israel'.

Hezbollah leader Sheikh Hassan Nasrallah goes much further; it is not just Israel, but the Jews, *all the Jews*, who must disappear: 'If Jews all gather in Israel it will save us the trouble of going after them worldwide.' Is this what Corbyn means by dialogue? The 2017 Hamas *Declaration of Principles*, like the 1988 Charter (still in force) is likewise unambiguous on its attitude to Israel. Article 21 renounces the Oslo Accords of 1993, with their agreement between the PLO and Israel on the goal of a 'two state solution', because they involve 'commitments that violate the inalienable rights of the Palestinian people'; while Article 18 declares that 'the establishment of "Israel" [sic] is entirely illegal', though it neither cites from nor refers to any legal code or any international body which says that it is. Article 19 likewise resolves that 'there shall be no recognition of the legitimacy of the Zionist entity.' In article two of the *Preamble*, the projected state of Palestine is defined as extending 'from the River Jordan in the East [thereby denying Palestinian nationhood to more than one million non 'refugee' indigenous hereditary Jordanian Palestinians] to the Mediterranean in the West and from Ras al-Naqurah in the North to Umm al-Rashrash in the South', thereby obliterating Israel from the map. So I ask again: What dialogue? Between whom? And about what? Any literate person can see that both Hamas and Hezbollah propose not a two-state solution, but a one-state no-Jew Islamic final solution to the Palestinian question. That is why it must be obvious even to a simpleton such as Corbyn that having learned the lesson of the Holocaust, the Jews of Israel have proved on three occasions, 1948, 1967 and 1973, that they are 'never again' going to submit quietly to their allotted fate.

Now to return to the main narrative.

Other pacifists, most notably John Middleton Murry, went beyond Lansbury's appreciation of Hitler's saintly personal qualities, singing the praises of the regime he had created. Beginning with his axiom that 'pacifism is the belief that any condition of society, any condition of the individual is better than modern war', Murray initiated the progression, one followed by peace campaigners up to the present day, from a plague on all houses to discovering more virtues in the opposed totalitarian camp than there were in their democratic own. To take one example: The atrocities committed by Nazi thugs in the Crystal Night pogrom of November 1938 (91 Jews murdered, 30,000 arrested, 267 synagogues and 7,500 Jewish business premises destroyed or damaged) were reported in *Peace News*, the official weekly journal of the Peace Pledge Union, as minor criminal scuffles of little consequence, and certainly nothing to do with the Nazi regime. Some windows were smashed, resulting in 'an odd case or two' where thieves had 'angle[d] one or two objects through holes in the shop windows'. Reports of widespread violence against Jews and their property were put down to anti-German propaganda. And anyway, Britain was guilty of far worse crimes in its colonies, so any criticism of Hitler in the matter was 'unctuous'.

Here again we see at work the Chomsky principle, that one is only entitled to criticise the misdeeds of one's own government, and also, *a la* Corbyn, how readily 'peace campaigners' deny, overlook, minimise or even excuse acts of violence so long as they are not committed by their own or their country's allies, and all the more so if they are directed against them. In the same spirit, and with the same purpose as its non-reporting of the Crystal Night, in June 1939, *Peace News* featured a pacifist tourist's impression of a Third Reich that was in the last stages of preparing itself for war against Poland: '...no scowls, but many smiles in the villages, much waving, few swastika flags, no postcards of Hitler so far as I could see, no militarism, no airplanes, no searchlights and in fact no trace of the war-mindedness there is here [i.e., in Britain], either outwardly or in conversation.' With its track record of appeasing totalitarian gangsters, it was only to be expected *Peace News* recognised a kindred spirit in Corbyn, with its issue of October-November 2015 hailing his election as Labour Leader as a 'huge opportunity for the peace movement', and listing his many endeavours in the same cause:

> He has been a passionate supporter of non-violent protest and non-violent solutions to conflict As Vice-Chairman of CND, he opposes Trident nuclear weapons and NATO, Currently Chair of the Stop the War Coalition, he has opposed all Britain's recent major wars – the Falklands in 1982, the 1991 Gulf War, Kosovo in 1999 [to protect Muslims from ethnic cleansing by the Serbs], the invasion of Afghanistan in 2001, Iraq in 2003 and Libya and Syria in 2013. A Patron of the Palestine Solidarity Campaign, Corbyn is a long-time critic of Israel's occupation of Palestine.

And, the pacifist *Peace News* could have added, in the light of its history of overlooking or excusing anti-western totalitarian militarism, a friend of the terrorist movements that are pledged to bring about the destruction of Israel and the murder of all its Jews. *Peace News* also published in June 1939 a collection of writings in an identically delusional vein, entitled *Germany's Will for Peace*...if we are to believe Corbyn, just like that of Hamas and Hezbollah. Unfortunately for *Peace News*, not to speak of the people of Poland, Germany's will for peace did not extend to its relations with its eastern neighbour, any more than does that of Hamas and Hezbollah to their Jewish neighbours. Within less than three months, Europe would be at war. The question then became, how to stop it. It was at this point that the pacifist anti-war campaigning merged with that of sundry British, mainly upper-class pro-Nazis and the Communist Party, committed as the latter now was, following the lead of its puppet master in the Kremlin, to endorsing Hitler's peace proposals issued after his conquest, with the assistance of

Stalin, of Poland. Anticipating by some six decades the Sharia left/Stalinist operation of the same name, the Peace Pledge Union, re-enforced after May 1940 by recruits from the banned Mosleyite pro-Hitler British Union of Fascists, launched a 'Stop the War' campaign, one which necessarily involved acceding to most of Hitler's territorial demands. With the Nazis poised to invade Britain after the fall of France, Middleton Murry concluded that Hitler's regime had demonstrated the superiority of totalitarian methods over those of liberal democracy, not least on the battlefield, though some might say this was an odd criterion for an avowed pacifist to employ. It followed that Britain, and more generally, all democratic countries, had to accept and adjust themselves to this new reality: 'Totalitarianism has come to stay. The question at issue between the British genius and its mortal instruments [i.e., its means of defending itself] is not, as we tend to imagine, how to resist totalitarianism, but how to accept from it only what is necessary and good while rejecting all that is retrograde and evil.'

This theme was taken up by another pacifist, Wilfred Wellock. The two still-aligned totalitarian giants, Nazi Germany and the USSR, had provided a model of society greatly superior that of the liberal capitalist west, sacrificing individual freedom in exchange for more social cohesion and greater economic efficiency. Even the Nazi military conquest and enslavement of Poland, France, Holland, Luxemburg, Belgium, Denmark and Norway was painted in approving colours. *Peace News* (sic) saw the seemingly irresistible onslaught of the Nazi war machine as the 'destined instrument' of European unification. 'National Socialism, relative to any [sic!!!] other form of society, is a good thing'…even for Jews, presumably. What Hitler had achieved for his people, especially the workers (now relieved of their encumbering trade unions and two political parties) was 'beyond the wildest dreams of socialists', that is, of the more conventional kind. At times, the same journal, like the Stalinist press of the same period, was reduced to re-cycling Nazi war propaganda. For example, the German invasions of Denmark and Norway in April 1940 were, like Corbyn would have us believe of Putin's seizure of the Crimea and eastern Ukraine, a purely defensive response to the threat of British operations in the Scandinavian region. Pacifists, beguiled and overawed by what seemed to be the unstoppable might of the Nazi Juggernaut, were assuming the role of self-appointed *Wehrmacht* cheerleaders.

Following the Nazi invasion of the Soviet in Union on June 22, 1941, unlike the Stalinists, totalitarian pacifists were now confronted with having to make a choice between the two warring parties. This caused a split in the PPU, between supporters of Murry, who sided with Nazi Germany, and a pro-Soviet faction. By this time, for many self-styled pacifists, opposition to all forms of violence had been displaced by a preference for one of two systems of totalitarian militarism and a concomitant rejection of western liberal democracy. While his opponents rooted for a Stalin (but not western) victory, the pro-Hitler Murry favoured an armistice between the USSR and Germany that would leave the Nazis with most of European Russia, which, as Murry must have known, was precisely Hitler's well-advertised war aim of securing 'living space' in the east. Only towards the war's end, when, after initially rejecting reports of the Holocaust as anti-German propaganda (like *dhimmi* feminist dismissals of what one called 'horror stories' of Muslim misogyny and Milne's of Stalin's terror), he finally accepted them as true, did Murry endorse the moral necessity of defeating the Nazis. Unmoved by the enormity of the Holocaust, other pro-Nazi pacifists held out to the end, after

370

which they effortlessly switched from being useful idiots for Hitler to serving Stalin and his successors in the same capacity, just as Corbyn does the Jihadis. Did it ever occur to Hitler's useful pacifists that by opposing the employment of military force to defeat Nazi Germany, they were in effect saying, better that every Jew in Europe be murdered in a gas chamber rather than one German soldier be killed on a battlefield; that it is better to reject a lesser evil even when doing so leads inevitably to an infinitely greater one? We hear similar arguments today when proposals are made to take military action against Islamic Jihadis. And pacifists and 'peace campaigners' would claim the 'moral high ground'?

Addendum: Don't be Beastly to the Nazis (With apologies to Noel Coward)

In 2001, in anticipation of the USA invasion of Afghanistan to remove a Taliban regime believed to be harbouring Osama Bin Laden, the architect of 9/11, a motley collection of far leftists launched their 'Stop the War Coalition'. As we have seen, the prime movers in this enterprise were the ex-Trotskyist Socialist Workers Party, two unreconstructed Stalinists, Andrew Murray and Kamal Majid, and, inevitably, all-purpose useful idiot Jeremy Corbyn. And as we have also seen in the main body of this work, the Coalition from the very beginning has been highly selective concerning its choice of wars it wanted to stop. All military operations by western powers have been opposed on principle, irrespective of their motive or political nature of their target, while those directed against the west are endorsed, again no matter what the nature and motives of the regime or movement conducting them. All such self-styled peace movements and campaigns that operate in democratic countries have exhibited the same tendencies, even if in a less flagrant and cynical manner than the Corbynite Coalition; that is, they represent the motives, policies and behaviour of their domestic governments in the darkest possible colours, while doing the opposite for those regimes or movements with which they either are at war or in some other way opposed to. (See Appendix Z for Orwell's acute observations on this phenomenon) Classic examples of this tendency (for some it is a principle) are the pro-Nazi Peace Pledge Union, the pro-Soviet British Peace Committee, the later years of the Campaign for Nuclear Disarmament, and the campaigns against the Falklands war and the three US-led military operations against Saddam in Iraq (twice) and the Taliban in Afghanistan. More recently, we have seen how Corbyn has performed the same service on behalf of his 'friends' Hamas and Hezbollah and his former employer Iran, while attributing Jihadi atrocities to the foreign policies of the countries so targeted... the UK, USA, France, Israel and Germany. But how then explain and justify similar atrocities elsewhere? Must we also attribute them to the crimes of Egyptian, Kenyan, Nigerian, Syrian, Iraqi, Afghan, Australian, Belgian, Danish, Finish, Austrian and Swiss imperialism? Yet the one country whose rulers do have imperial ambitions and have waged brutal wars in pursuit of them against

371

Muslims in Syria, Afghanistan and Chechnya, is provided with all manner of tortuous excuses for its expansionist policies and crimes.

The sudden reversal of Stalin's foreign policy following the conclusion of his pact with Hitler of August 23, 1939 set in motion a similarly selective stop the war campaign by the parties of the Communist International, even to the extent of denying the expansionist goals of Hitler's foreign policy as Corbyn's Coalition has done on behalf of Islam and Russia, and the repressive nature of his domestic regime, as Corbyn does for Iran's. What follows are extracts from the verbatim record of meetings of the Central Committee of the Communist Party of Great Britain that were held between September 24 and October 2, 1939. The full record was reproduced in 1990 in the book *About Turn* edited by Francis King and former *Daily Worker* Editor George Mathews. These extracts reveal a party leadership struggling to absorb the implications of transforming a peace campaign that had for the previous four years been directed towards forming an anti-fascist alliance of Britain, France and the USSR against a re-arming and belligerent Nazi Germany into one supporting the joint peace proposals of Nazi Germany and the USSR issued on September 28 after their military defeat of Poland. Now that Stalin and Hitler were allies, this new peace campaign was directed against what was described as the imperialist aggression of Britain and France for declaring war on Nazi German following its invasion of Poland two days previously on September 1. For example, Neville Chamberlain, who had been remorselessly pilloried by the Communist Party for his betrayal of the Czechs at Munich, was now, according to Stalin's new orientation, to be denounced for going to war over Poland, while Hitler, like Mohammed (whom as we have seen, Hitler, together others in his immediate circle, admired for his martial qualities) was transformed from a predatory imperialist into a man of peace. Some, as we shall see, unlike Corbyn and his Coalition comrades, found this selective peace campaigning too much to swallow.

The new line was finalised in Moscow on September 7 at a meeting between Stalin and Comintern chief Georgi Dimitrov. It reached London on September 10, but Party General Secretary Harry Pollitt, with his pamphlet *How to Win the War* [sic] due out on the 14th, and still committed, as was his party, despite Stalin's pact with Hitler, to supporting the war of France and Britain against Nazi Germany, suppressed it. Consequently confirmation of the new line only came to the rest of the party leadership on the 25th, following the arrival from Moscow of David Springhall, who had been briefed by Dimitrov. He quickly disabused his comrades of their naïve delusion that they could support a war against Stalin's new ally and partner in crime: 'Whereas formerly the working class and the Communist Parties fought to preserve peace, now that imperialist [sic] conflicts had led to open war, the working class in the various countries [here was meant, as we shall see, Britain and France, but not Germany] must fight against the war…' It had to be understood 'that the Communist Party in the Soviet Union had to carry out complicated manoeuvres. In this respect, Comrade Dimitrov spoke about the photos of Stalin and Ribbentrop shaking hands [and, he could have added, Stalin's toast to Hitler].' In other words, from being the worst of enemies, Stalin and Hitler were now the best of pals, so cut out the anti-Nazi stuff. One stupefied comrade asked if the new line on Hitler meant that British communists now had 'to work not only against our own bourgeoisie but for their [i.e., Britain's] military defeat.' Back came Springhall's answer, hot from the Kremlin :

372

'Yes, that is correct'. This was a perverted version of the 'revolutionary defeatism' promoted by Lenin during the First World War, in which workers in all its participant countries were to regard their own ruling class as their main enemy. In the Second, until the Nazi invasion of the USSR, while it applied to those countries at war with the Axis powers, it did not to Nazi Germany, now the ally of the USSR. When on June 22, 1941, Hitler tore up his pact with Stalin, the asymmetric tactic remained the same, but in reverse, with Allied defeatism replaced by defencism, while what remained of the exiled leadership of the German Communist Party called for an all-out war against Germany.

The most vigorous defence of the new line came, in addition to Springhall, from one of the party's two representatives on the Comintern's Executive Committee, William Rust, and Rajani Palme Dutt, the party's leading theoretician. It was in this capacity that the latter opened the discussion at the Party' second session on October 2, only a matter of days after Nazi Germany and the USSR jointly issued on September 28 their terms for a 'peace' settlement to the war that began on September 1. This followed a second visit to Moscow by Ribbentrop, which 'finally settled by the treaty signed today the questions arising from the dissolution [sic] of the Polish State, and having thereby [that is, by the elimination of Poland] created a firm foundation for a lasting [sic] peace[sic] in eastern Europe'. Now that the state for which Britain and France went to war against Germany no longer existed, why pursue a hopelessly lost cause? It necessarily followed that 'the liquidation of the present war between Germany on the one hand and England and France on the other would be in the interest of all nations'…presumably, Poland included.

Now came the 'peace offer' which committed the British Communist Party, together with all other sections of the Comintern, to the new, pro-Nazi, line: '…both governments [i.e., those of Nazi Germany and the Soviet Union] will direct their common [sic] efforts, if necessary in accord with other friendly powers [for example, fascist Italy], to attain this aim [the 'liquidation' of the war] as soon as possible.' And finally, the punch line, one that required the adaption of defeatism by the communist parties of France and Britain: 'If, however, these efforts of both governments remain unsuccessful it will be established thereby that England and France bear responsibility for the continuation of the war, and in the event of the continuation of the war *the governments of Germany and the USSR will consult each other on the necessary measures.*' (emphasis added)

It was Britain's adherence to this conquerors' 'peace' that the communist party, subordinated as it was to the iron discipline of the Communist International (which meant Stalin), was now obliged to pursue, a 'peace' that required…and this became explicit…underwriting not only the territorial acquisitions Hitler had gifted to Stalin in eastern Poland and subsequently in Finland, all three Baltic states and a part of Rumania, but Hitler's in Austria, Czechoslovakia and Poland. Integral to the new line was the party's adopting and pursuing at home the strategy of 'revolutionary defeatism' - effectively, treason - in the name of a 'people's peace'. The nature and implications of this policy will become evident in the discussion that follows. This, then, was the Communist Party's 'stop the war' campaign, mark one.

Depositing into Stalin's memory hole the fact that only a few days previously, the party had been demanding a more vigorous prosecution of a war being waged on behalf of Poland, Dutt now averred that 'the international working class may under no conditions defend Fascist [sic] Poland'. Then, reverting to the strategy of the 'Third Period,' one that prevailed between 1928 and 1934, according to which the non-communist left and all bourgeois states were fascist, Dutt explained why: 'The division of states into fascist and democratic states has now lost its former sense'. *Ipso facto*, not only 'fascist' Poland was fascist. So were Hitler's remaining enemies, Britain and France. Meanwhile, Hitler's Germany, hitherto fascism incarnate, was mending its evil ways because, thanks to Stalin, 'German fascism', previously 'the spearhead of international reaction', had been 'compelled to amend itself [sic!!!] in such a way that it [had] abandoned its offensive against the Soviet Union'. Poland, unlike Nazi Germany, was irredeemably 'fascist', worthy only of partition and obliteration, guilty, so Dutt claimed in defiance of both all the facts and his own party's previous policies, of 'having brought on the war' by 'enter[ing] into an imperialist coalition with Chamberlain' and by so doing 'defeating and sabotaging the peace [sic] front'. He would have no truck with objections that Poland was just as much a victim of Nazi aggression as Czechoslovakia and Austria, even though the latter was far more removed from democracy than 'fascist' Poland. Communists had opposed the Nazi conquest of the first two. Why then, not Poland? Because Stalinist alchemy worthy of *1984* had transformed Hitler's invasion of Poland into a provocation against the 'peace' *by Poland*, while Chamberlain's honouring of his government's guarantee on March 31, 1939 to uphold Poland's national integrity, which the Communist Party, Dutt included, had previously supported, was now a ruse on Poland's part to further its rulers' 'imperialist [an empire without colonies] and class interests'.

By rejecting Hitler's demands on its territory and then defending it, Poland, with the support of Chamberlain, had 'wrecked the peace front, and by doing that they brought international disaster [sic...a combined Nazi-Soviet invasion] on their people...they [the Poles] did bring forth the war.' If we recall how the SWP derided the Kurds as 'western pawns' for accepting (far too little) western aid in their fight against the Islamic State, we can see a direct parallel with the role ascribed to Poland by Dutt and his puppet-masters in the Kremlin. The Poles were likewise, 'pawns of British imperialism', for accepting what proved to be token (like the West's for the Kurds) support from Chamberlain in their resistance to Germany. Indeed Rust used this very term when he, like Dutt, accused Poland of having allowed itself to become 'a pawn in the game' being played by 'British imperialism'.

In this 'new situation' Dutt continued, 'we have to adjust our perspective.' This adjustment not only required re-appraising the nature of German fascism and its role in world politics, but of 'the significance of the distinction between fascist and democratic states', which now 'no longer applied'. The 'historical role of British imperialism as the leader of world counter-revolution' required the abandonment of the party's existing policy of a 'war on two fronts' - against Chamberlain and against Hitler – and the adoption of a single war, 'the struggle on one front against our own imperialism'. Dutt made no attempt to disguise the reason for his overnight re-discovery of the manifest sins of his own imperialism and the downgrading of Hitler's: '...we have had a certain [sic] change in the situation by this week, because the peace proposals [of Hitler and Stalin] have forced [sic] a new situation.' Consequently, there had to an end to talk of the 'restoration of Poland' and 'the overthrow of Hitlerism'. There was also a danger that Britain and France would endeavour to 'tear [Germany] away from the Soviet Union and turn it against the Soviet Union.' The party would counter such moves by 'our demand for peace negotiations and a peace conference including the Soviet Union.' And if that failed, as it was sure to, there must follow the 'war on one front'.

Ranged against the party's intelligentsia and Muscovite apparatchiks were three former proletarians who understood better than anyone the impossibility of selling to the working class what amounted to treason to their country and surrender to Hitler. (Unlike to many among the British upper class.) They were *Daily Worker* editor and former Clydeside worker Johnny Campbell, former boiler-maker and party General Secretary Pollitt and Willie Gallacher, former engineering worker from the Clyde and the party's only MP. They were soon to capitulate to the new line, albeit with a bad conscience, but considering their rank, standing and length of membership in the party, their resistance, a combination of pride, horse sense and a residual spark of human decency, was unprecedented.

Gallacher was the first of the three to take the field against Dutt. 'He [Dutt] accepts the [Comintern] thesis. He is for the fight on one front. He has every conceivable phrase in the course of his speech that makes him absolutely correct and a devoted servant to the Communist International, and surely the Communist International will all be happy to know that.' While Gallacher waxed sarcastic to a degree that barely disguised his contempt, Campbell was bluntness itself. 'Calling off the war [of Britain and France against Germany] would be a descent from Marxism to Mosleyism', the point being that the stance of Mosley's British Union of Fascists and National Socialists on the war was no different to that of Stalin, Dimitrov and Molotov and their Comintern puppets. 'At the outset of the war, we started by saying that we had an interest in defeating the Nazis, we now recognize that our prime interest is the defeat of France and Great Britain...We started out by proclaiming the defence of the British people from fascism, we are now told that the defence of the British people from fascism is imperialism.' (Today, advocating doing the same for the UK and the West generally against Jihadi Islam is for many on the left Islamophobia and racism.)

Ramming home his point, Campbell quoted from the Soviet press articles claiming that the war was all Poland's fault, and her misfortunes of her own making. First, *Pravda* ('Truth'): 'Poland's ill-starred rulers, instigated by the incendiaries of world war [these 'incendiaries' being the former Hitler-appeasers Chamberlain and Daladier] attempted to disrupt the peace [again] established in Eastern Europe'...a 'peace' to be imposed by Stalin and Hitler on a crushed, partioned and obliterated Poland. And *Izvestia* ('News'): 'First Poland, then France and Britain with her numerous vassals and dominions have entered the war against Germany' ...Poland by cunningly having itself invaded by the Nazis. (During the 'old line' of the 'Popular Front against Fascism and War', in which Britain had been allotted a central role, the question of the UK's 'vassals and dominions'...i.e., empire, had taken a back seat in order to facilitate an alliance with anti-appeasement empire Tories like Churchill and Eden.) The danger, said Campbell, now also waxing sarcastic, 'is no longer one of a fascist domination of Europe,' but one of 'British and French imperialism miraculously breaking through the Siegfried Line, over-running Germany, installing a [democratic] government in Germany which will fight the Soviet Union and then going on to a war against the Soviet Union.' All this, said Campbell, 'is the stuff of which dreams are made'.

Campbell did not exaggerate. Welsh Party Secretary Idris Cox, a true loyalist, was entirely 'on message'. Given that 'Hitler is not now [sic] the chief menace to the Soviet Union but British imperialism', 'we [that is, British communists] have to work for the defeat of British imperialism'. By whom, exactly, was this defeat to be inflicted? The only possible conclusion was, by the only country with which it was at war and had the means to do so, Nazi Germany. And a good job too. You could say, as the USA did after 9/11, Britain 'had it coming'. But surely this was to jump from the British imperialist pan into the Nazi fire? Not so. Life under Hitler was not as bad as only a few days previously, Cox and his comrades had made it out to be. It was all very well, said Cox, for Pollitt to say he wanted to 'crush the fascist bastards'. But, countered Cox, 'it is not a question of how many have been put [sic] into concentration camps in Nazi Germany' (among whom were thousands of communists, soon to be added to in their millions by Jews in death camps) because 'there are even worse [sic] cases of oppression and ill-treatment in our own colonies under British imperialism'...a classic case of 'but what about?'. So, when it came to having to choose...and that choice had to be made...Nazi Germany was by a long way the lesser of two evils.

As for Britain being the main, indeed, only threat to the USSR now that Hitler and Stalin were on such good terms, had Cox consulted an atlas, he would have seen that because of their elimination of Poland, Nazi Germany and the USSR now shared a common border, one that was 250 miles nearer Moscow than Germany's had been hitherto. However, for Britain to attack the USSR, it would have to mount sea-born invasions via the German-controlled Baltic, via the Black Sea (in a re-run of the Crimean War) and, to land in the Soviet arctic, via the North and White Sea. A land invasion could only be mounted from India via independent Afghanistan into Soviet central Asia. But who needs bourgeois geography when we have the genius of the great Stalin as our guide? So, 'the danger to the Soviet Union arises now from a military strengthening of British imperialism'. (a clear invitation to desertion and sabotage) 'British imperialism', Cox continued, 'and not Nazi Germany in this new situation is the chief menace to the Soviet Union.' And then came Barbarossa, 25 million Soviet war dead and British Arctic convoys carrying at enormous risk desperately-needed military hardware to Murmansk.

Understandably, as the events of the spring and summer of 1940 were to prove, the likelihood of Britain sharing the fate of France and Poland was not a matter of idle speculation. Perhaps for this reason, 'revolutionary defeatism' for some was a tad too indigestible. Scottish organizer Peter Kerrigan (I knew his daughter Jean, who like me, broke from the Communist Party to join Healy's Socialist Labour League) shared them. 'I still cannot agree that we were wrong to put forward the proposition of the fight on two fronts.' (that is, against both Hitler and Chamberlain.) In the same vein, he was none too happy with his conclusion that 'when we argued for the defeat of our own government', it meant 'the defeat of the country militarily and this always means to me a victory for German fascism.' Correct. So why did he at the end of the discussion vote for the resolution which endorsed this very policy, leaving only Pollitt, Campbell and Gallagher in opposition?

More than these four had their doubts. But not Yorkshire organiser Marian Jessop. After airily dismissing concerns shown by some speakers for the plight of the Poles – 'The only thing I am concerned about is that there has been an extension of the Soviet territory' - this of course was not imperialism - she waxed lyrical about the fact that Stalin's pact with Hitler would mean he would now 'prefer, if he has to fight, to fight a war in the direction of the West'...precisely Hitler's purpose in signing the pact, to avoid the dreaded 'war on two fronts' that led to Germany's defeat in the First World War. That Hitler could, as a result of his pact with Stalin, feel free to unleash the Wehrmacht on France and then, possibly, Britain, was for Jessop a prospect 'we have to rejoice about and feel proud of'... 'perspectives' 'about which we can feel very happy'. Nine months later, on June 14, 1940, proud and happy Nazi troops were marching up the Champs Elysees, a matter of days after the routed British army barely escaped capture at Dunkirk. So much for the two greatest threats to the Soviet Union. That same month, Hitler instructed Staff General Erich Marcks to beginning planning the invasion of the Soviet Union, named by Hitler Operation Barbarossa on December 18, 1940. So much for Stalin's 'perspectives'.

Others, as I have said, were not so sanguine as Cox and Jessop. One delegate wanted to sugar the defeatist pill by suggesting 'it has not got to put that way'... the 'way' being 'the victory of Nazi domination'. Instead, he proposed a re-enactment of Christmas 1914, asking, as if it was simply a matter of finalizing the details, 'how are we going to approach the question of fraternization at the front?'... perhaps with the crews of Nazi panzers as they swarmed at top speed on Soviet fuel across France and southern England. Not so party philosopher Maurice Cornforth. Belying his allotted task to promote Marxist materialism, Cornforth's approach to the subject under discussion smacked more of a devout Roman Catholic than an atheist communist. Confessing (appropriately) that the literally overnight 180 degree policy reversal on the war 'had been something of a surprise and something of a shock', he then explained that his initial disorientation had been overcome by his 'faith in the Soviet Union', a faith that if lost or questioned, would mean 'one is done for as a Communist and Socialist...the fact of the matter is that a socialist state in that position can do no wrong [like, in matters of faith and morals the Pope] and that is what we have to stick to...' Of course what he really meant, and everyone must have known it, was an unquestioning faith in Stalin. Cornforth then tied himself in dialectical knots in trying to explain what his faith consisted of. Once again, the target was the plain-speaking, non-dialectical Campbell. He had argued that, contrary to the predictions of the supporters of the new line, 'war exhaustion' would not lead to demands for 'peace' but, as Cornforth put it, if 'exploited' by supporters of the war against Germany, to 'a rise of feeling against German fascism.' Cornford saw such a development as dangerous in the extreme, because this would be 'exploited into a rise of feeling against the Soviet Union' as 'the friend of German fascism'...which indeed it was. Cornford concluded that 'we have to be very careful [sic] about arguments of this sort.' So we have, *a la* Hegel, thesis; a 'rising feeling against German fascism'; antithesis; this spilling over into a 'rising feeling' against the Soviet Union, 'the friend of German fascism'; and synthesis; that hostility towards fascism must be opposed, because it will spill over into hostility towards the Soviet Union. Q.E.D.

Perhaps the most extraordinary contribution in the discussion came from North East organiser Hymie Lee; even more so if we quite reasonably consider the possibility that he was Jewish. If this was indeed the case, it would, on the face of it, have led one to assume that he would have been amongst those most uneasy, to say the least, about his party's new orientation towards the peace initiative of Stalin's Nazi partners. But then Stalin's blatantly post-war anti-Semitic policies and purges did not significantly dent the allegiance of the party's considerable Jewish membership, unlike the reaction of the vast majority of the Labour Party's Jewish members and supporters to similar prejudices harboured by Comrade Corbyn and proclaimed in the crudest form by many of his cultic following.

Jewish or not, Lee opened his remarks by referring in the most grandiloquent terms to the 'great historical significance of the Soviet-German Pact' and the 'tremendous importance of the day of signing of the Pact in general [sic] history'. It was as if the pact with the Nazis had been a long-sought and prized goal of the world communist movement (and in fact, so far as Stalin was concerned, it was, and had been almost from the first days of Hitler's regime) and now, at last, it had been realized. Lee put the issue bluntly, and quite accurately. Complaining that members had 'not appreciated the diminishing, the almost disappearance [sic] of the difference between the fascist regime [of Hitler] and the so-called [sic] democratic regime [of Britain and France]', he continued, 'we cannot hold this position [of the opposition of fascism and democracy] at all.' Now we come to it: 'We have to choose therefore between a fascism [sic] which is suppressing the Communist Party in France [for being opposed to the war against Nazi Germany it should be added] and a fascism [that of Nazi Germany] that is prepared to make a pact with the Soviet Union...The change is that we have Germany in contact'. And how! This 'contact', as Lee coyly put it, included not only combined military operations against Poland, a joint victory parade of the Red Army and the Wehrmacht in Lvov after Poland's defeat, an agreement to divide eastern Europe into Nazi and Soviet 'spheres of influence' and the supply of raw materials and fuel essential for the Nazi war machine, but a clause in the pact's supplementary secret protocol of September 28 that provided for the security agencies of its two parties to suppress 'any sort of Polish agitation affecting the territory of the other country'.

Once established, this 'contact' between Stalin's NKVD and its Nazi counterparts led to the former rounding up and handing over to the tender cares of the latter at least 500 refugee German communists, several of them Jews, who had been arrested and convicted of spying for the Nazis during the Stalin purges of the later 1930s. Two who lived to tell their story were Margarete Buber, who after two years in a Soviet slave camp, survived four more years in a Nazi one, the Ravensbruck women's camp. She was liberated by the arrival of the western imperialists, who fortunately for her, got to the area before the Red Army. Her *Under Two Dictators* records her extraordinary story. Her husband, Heinz Neumann, an exiled former leader of the German Communist Party, was not so lucky. He was executed on Stalin's orders in 1937. Another victim then survivor of Lee's 'contact' between Hitler and Stalin was the Austrian Jewish physicist Alexander Weisberg, who after being arrested for spying on behalf of Nazi Germany and then saved from almost certain death at the hand of Stalin's secret police by the intervention of Albert Einstein, was also handed over to the Gestapo. Interned in the Cracow Jewish ghetto, he escaped, was caught, escaped again and took part in the Warsaw Ghetto uprising of April-May 1943 and the Warsaw uprising of August-October 1944. At the war's end, like Buber, he managed to avoid 'liberation' by the Red Army, ending up in Malmo. His extraordinary story is told in his *Conspiracy of Silence*.

In Lee's estimation (and not his alone) the mere fact that Stalin and Hitler were now 'in contact' had by osmosis transformed Nazi Germany into a progressive force in world politics, while 'Britain and France' were not only 'against having a pact with the Soviet Union' but (one could easily infer, unlike the Nazis) 'suppressing the Communist party and working-class movement.' So, there was fascism and fascism. Under the Nazi version, as another comrade explained, 'the German people are coping [sic!!!] with [but not opposing, as that would threaten the pact] German imperialism', and, according to Springhall, were even engaged, under, we must suppose, the benevolent eye of the Gestapo, in 'revolutionary discussions' in 'German factories'. (Readers will recall Corbyn's similarly fanciful tale of 'lively', 'robust' - but also 'dangerous' - 'debates' in clerical fascist Iran.) How different from 'fascist France', where such talk could get workers locked up.

Very much in the same spirit, Rust took issue with Campbell's objection to the claim that the once crucial distinction between fascism and democracy had now been obliterated. 'In his anxiety [sic!] to develop the arguments for his case at the dread prospect of letting in Hitler fascism, we get a distorted picture of the actual situation, because the plain fact is not the power of Germany, but the weakness of Germany.' Two years on to the day, 'weak' Germany's tanks stood at the outskirts of Moscow. The proof of Hitler's 'weakness' was that he, and not the war-mongering Chamberlain and Daladier, was 'suing for peace', the inference being that only those who are weak and in danger of losing 'sue' for peace. The problem was, Hitler had not lost, but just won a war, together Stalin, and was now, also together with Stalin, and, for it was worth, the likes of Dutt, Springhall and Rust, seeking to impose on Europe a 'peace' of conquerors.

Pollitt was having none of this make-believe. The new line meant that 'the fight against fascism has disappeared' and worse still, as a consequence, 'fascism has now because of its non-aggression pact with the Soviet Union, taken on [he obviously means been ascribed] a progressive role.' Referring to the effect on party policy of what he described derisively as the 'Soviet-fascist' peace proposals, he pointed out that the party slogans no longer made any mention of the fight against fascism. In fact 'it is becoming unfashionable to mention the word'. (In the Soviet Union, it had disappeared entirely.) Things had come to such a pass that one comrade in the discussion reported that at a meeting in London, a member had said that 'there was no difference between living in Britain today and living in Nazi Germany'. If the reader will recall, have we not been warned by a Guardianista feminist not to believe the 'horror stories' about the lot of women in the realm of Allah, and by Corbyn's former Press Officer, Seumas Milne, to give no more credence to those about Stalin's Russia? *Plus la change…*

Footnote

Picture the scene…one politically not far removed from reality. It is late 1940, at the height of the *Luftwaffe* blitz on London. Two Stalinists are somewhere on the Kent coast. A bomber approaches from the sea, making for the London docks. Believing it to be a British plane, heading home after a raid on Stalin's Nazi ally, our two intrepid Stalinists, brandishing their fists, bellow 'imperialist warmonger' as it flies overhead. Then one of them spots the German cross on the Heinkel's wings. He cries out, exultantly, 'it's one of ours!' Now the fist-brandishing mutates into a Bolshevik clenched-fist salute, to the cry of, 'let Churchill have it, Adolf'.

IX A Corbynista King in Waiting?

Since Oliver Cromwell's exercise in regicide, British monarchs have been well advised to keep their noses out of religion and politics. Two that failed to heed the salutary example of Charles the First, who dabbled disastrously in both, have come to a sticky end, living out their days in exile and ignominy; the first, James II, for seeking to restore the rule of Rome, and the second, Edward VIII, not only for his dalliance with an American whore, double-divorcee and possible Nazi agent, but his ambition to play the part of a people's king. At the height of the abdication crisis, fascists and Stalinists, each seeing Edward as the enemy of the British establishment, rallied to his cause, with demonstrations by Mosley's Black Shirts and the Communist Party outside Buckingham Palace. There was even talk of a 'King's Party' headed by another outsider, Winston Churchill. Once in exile however, Edward, fobbed off with the title of Duke of Windsor, revealed another dimension to his political agenda with his enthusiasm for the Nazi regime in Germany.

Now we have an heir to throne that seems not to have heeded the lesson of his great uncle's and his namesake's fates. Unlike his mother, who throughout her reign has been an exemplar of discretion and official impartiality, Charles has for many years publicly aired his often-cranky views on a range of subjects that traditionally have been off-limits to the crown. To facilitate this interventionism, and to prepare him for the day when he takes up office as head of state, Charles has surrounded himself with a team of advisers, some say tame yes men and woman, who by a process of natural selection either share or have learned to defer to his idiosyncratic and often extremely reactionary opinions, with the most valued and trusted *confidante* of this circle having been the Jungian disciple Laurens van der Post. Now we get to heart of the matter.

In November 2017, a letter from Charles to van der Post was discovered in a public archive. Dated November 24, 1986, it provides an insight into to the heir to the throne's thinking on a subject which is if anything of greater import today than when Charles broached it to his *guru*. It was written after the Prince had paid a visit to his fellow royals in the feudal despotisms of Saudi Arabia, Bahrain and Qatar. The experience had helped him, he writes, 'to understand better [the Arabs'] point of view about Israel. Never realised they see it as a US colony'. But that is not how Charles saw the relationship, rather the reverse: 'Surely some US president has to have the courage to stand up and take on the Jewish lobby in US'. Corbyn also holds this view of US-Israeli relations, revealing in the Stalinist *Morning Star* his agreement with his host President Assad of Syria's comment that 'the Israeli tail wags the US dog'. The US and international far right has a term for what Charles and Corbyn are describing: ZOG…Zionist Occupation Government, a concept also shared with Qais Qadri, a Palestinian journalist: 'There is no difference between the Republicans and the Democrats with regard to their hostility towards the Palestinian cause. We are weaker than the Jewish lobby [sic] to cause any changes in American policy.'

As Charles sees it, not only do the Jews pull the strings in the White House; they are the prime cause of terrorism in the Middle East: '...it is the influx of foreign, European Jews (especially from Poland they [his Arab friends] say) which has helped to cause great problems...how can there ever be an end to terrorism unless the causes are eliminated?' The cause being, since he mentions only one, the presence of European Jews in what not only the Jihadis, but his royal friends regard as exclusively Arab and Islamic territory. References to a 'Jewish lobby' that determines US Middle Eastern policy, and to a solution to the Palestinian issue that by implication involves the 'elimination' of Israel's European Jews (who comprise the vast majority of Israel's total Jewish population) produced a furious response from the editor of the *Jewish Chronicle*, Stephen Pollard:

> To me this the most astonishing element of the prince's letter. The "Jewish lobby" is one of the anti-Semitic themes that have endured for centuries. It is the myth there are these very powerful Jews who control foreign policy or the media or banks or whatever...That [this] comes from the heir to throne is unsettling, to put it mildly.

There are those, however, and we know exactly who they are, who will have reason to find in these comments not for cause for condemnation, but for hope. Just imagine... a head of state committed to the anti-Zionist cause. And, as a bonus, as we shall see, to promoting the virtues of the religion of peace. Charles's thinking, for want of a better word, on the Arab-Israeli conflict has not changed over time. In 2003, it was revealed that because of his critical attitude towards American support for Israel, the Foreign Office had vetoed any visits by the Prince to the USA over the previous six years. In May 2017, the Foreign Office intervened with the Prince's itinerary again, cancelling what would been the first visit by British royal to Israel, the concern being that his presence there would harm relations with Arab leaders, where he has always been a welcome guest. When he did go finally to Israel in January 2020, to attend the commemoration of the 75th anniversary of liberation of Auschwitz, he made amends by nipping over the border to commiserate with the Palestinians on their alleged sufferings under Israeli occupation.

Is it no secret that Charles is, to put it as politely as one can, no Einstein or Aristotle. Considerable time, resources and effort, at public expense, were invested in the attempt to enhance his modest mental capacity, only to produce results that are no less meagre than those we find, after the failure of a similar exercise, in what was until December 2019, his potential Prime Ministerial partner in the Palestinian and Islamic causes. Charles's gullibility is of such a magnitude that he believes in magic, namely, the efficacy of quack, so-called 'alternative' medicine, and what is worse, has had no compunction in exploiting his royal status to demand public funding to promote it. It is worth recalling that in this fraudulent enterprise he had the support of the no less credulous Corbyn, who backed a House of Commons motion moved by Tory MP David Tredinnick deploring a Health Select Committee report's dismissal of claims made for the effectiveness of homeopathy. Anyone who believes that water has a (selective) memory is capable of believing in anything. As if to prove it, we have Charles, who like Corbyn believes that Islam is a (or better still, the) religion of peace, and with Charlotte Church, attributes the mass influx of Muslims into Europe to global warming and not the depredations of Islam, and Corbyn, who believes that 9/11 was 'manipulated', and that Hamas and Hezbollah are dedicated to 'long-term peace'. As for his Tory colleague, he only believes in astrology, and that blood does not clot under a full moon. (Another of Charles's cretinous obsessions is that trendy fad of the overly well-heeled, 'organic farming', and opposition to GM crops, which, unlike his own methods, have proved to be the only answer to the challenge of feeding those hungry billions at the other end of the social scale.)

But to really capture the intellectual horizons of he who will one day be king, it is necessary to follow him in his quest for 'spirituality'. Charles has let it be known that when he comes to the throne, he will change one item of the many in his job description. It is inscribed on all coins of the realm; 'Fid Def', *Fidei Defensor*, Defender of the Faith, that faith being, ironically, since it was awarded by a Pope to Henry VIII for attacking Luther, not that of the *soi-disant* Protestant Church of England, but the Vatican's. Charles sees this title as being out of step with modern multicultural (or in this case, multifaith) Britain, and instead prefers that of Defender of Faiths, the one in particular he has in mind being of course Islam. But not only on the grounds of 'inclusiveness'. Islam, as we shall see from what follows, has much to teach we benighted western infidels. Like lost Biblical sheep, we have allowed ourselves to be seduced down the path of the false claims of science and to succumb to the corrupting temptations of materialism. (Be it noted that when it comes to things material, Charles wants for nothing, being one of the richest subjects in his mother's kingdom. He also has a predilection for high-powered top of the market cars.) It is Islam, he believes, that will lead us back to the proper appreciation and achievement of a truly spiritual life. Now follow excerpts from a speech, with my interpolations, given by Prince Charles on December 13, 1993 at Wilton Park, Sussex, a facility maintained by the Foreign and Commonwealth Office as a forum for debate on global issues.

****

I start from the belief that Islamic civilisation at its best has an important message for the West in the way it has retained an integrated and integral view of the sanctity of the world around us. I feel [sic] that we in the West could be helped to rediscover the roots of our own understanding by an appreciation of the Islamic tradition's deep respect for the timeless traditions of the natural order.

[An order about which it knew next to nothing, for example something as elementary as the dimensions and shape of the earth and its motion around the sun, which 'we in the west', namely the pagan Greek, Aristarchus of Samos, had discovered a full eight centuries before the birth of Islam, and who, had he lived under Sharia law, as a polytheist would have been faced with the choice of either converting to Islam or be put to death. Yet to this day, there are clerics in Charles's favourite Muslim realm who continue to insist that as in all other things, so in matters of astronomy, Galileo, Copernicus and the Ancient Greeks were wrong, and the *Koran*, correct. After all, since Allah created the universe, he must know its every detail.]

'I believe that process could help in the task of bringing our two [why only two?] faiths closer together.'

383

[This assertion begs many questions. Suffice it to mention but one, that the *Koran* forbids what Charles is proposing, not once, but *six* times, for example: 'O you who believe, do not take the Jews and the Christians as friends.' (Chapter 5, Verse 31) Charles has a copy of the *Koran*, since he quotes from it in this address. Since they are germane to his case, how come then he passed these passages over?]

'It [the "bringing closer together of our two faiths"] could also help us in the West to rethink, and for the better, our practical stewardship of man and his environment in fields such as health care, the natural environment and agriculture, as well as in architecture and urban planning.'

[What mental world does Charles inhabit? There are Muslim critics of the Islamic world who would dismiss every one of these claims as sheer fantasy. I would suggest they are probably the consequence of his only encounters with Islamic culture being that of the Mosques and air-conditioned palaces of his Arab potentate hosts. Our philosopher-prince continues]

'Modern materialism is unbalanced and increasingly damaging in its long-term consequences.'

[Speaking of a craving for things material, we have seen that Islam's holy book contains detailed rules governing the seizure and allocation of what it calls 'booty' and 'the spoils of war', these being both human as well as material. Neither are the rulers of the modern Muslim world noted for spurning the material pleasures of life, as Charles well knows from first-hand experience, as do those immensely rich Muslims who frequent the fashionable shopping centres of most western capitals.]

'Yet nearly all the great religions of the world have held an integral view of the sanctity of the world. [But not, when it comes to deviations from the true faith, the sanctity of human life.] The Christian message with, for example, its deeply mystical and symbolic doctrine of the Incarnation...'

[The Incarnation, together with the crucifixion and resurrection of Jesus, one of the defining tenets of the Christian faith, is denied by Islam. The Muslims he so reveres for their spirituality are obliged to believe that the church of which one day he will be the head is founded on a series of lies: viz.: 'It is not befitting to the majesty of God that He should beget a son'. (*Koran*, 19:35) and: 'They {the Jews} say in boast, "We killed Christ Jesus the son of Mary, the Messenger of Allah" {sic} but they killed him not, not crucified him.' (ibid, 4:157)]

'...has been traditionally a message of the unity of the worlds of spirit and matter, and of God's manifestation in this world and in mankind. But during the past three centuries...'

[which, be it noted, beginning with the Enlightenment and the birth of modern science, are also those of Locke, Hume, Voltaire, Diderot, Kant, Hegel, Newton,

Paine, Darwin, Galileo, Gaus, Brunel, Pasteur and Stephenson, and standing on their shoulders, made broad by the power of reason, in the centuries that followed, Faraday, Turing, Higgs, Hawking, Einstein, Pasteur, Curie and Heisenberg]

'…in the Western world at least…'

[the East having had the good sense not to have been led astray by such thinkers as these]

'…a dangerous division has occurred in the way we perceive the world around us. Science has tried to assume a monopoly, even a tyranny [sic!!!] over our understanding.'

[Here Charles is right. The one 'tyranny' Islam cannot be accused of imposing is that of science. Sweden, with its population of 9.9 million, generates in one year as many papers in scientific journals as the entire Arab world, with its population of 422 million.]

'Science has tried to take over [no, explain] the natural world from God; it has fragmented [again, no, it has begun to explain] the cosmos and relegated the sacred to a separate and secondary compartment of our understanding, divorced from practical, day to day existence.'

[Which is exactly where it belongs, and despite what Charles says, most western Christians today would agree. What he is describing, with his bewailing of the triumphs of modern science, is a second fall of man, like the first, brought about by an irresistible thirst for knowledge, for the truth of reality, mythologised in the original sin of curiosity of Pandora and Eve. However much Charles may regret the passing of a world of blind faith, this thirst can never be slaked, nor its results undone. It is of the essence of the human condition.]

X 'Enormous Contributions'

Following his election as Labour Leader in September 2015, come Eid and Ramadan, Corbyn never missed an opportunity to lavish praise on a faith that if it he was to find himself living under its laws, would confront him with the choice of either converting to Islam or be put to death:

> On behalf of the Labour Party I want to send my best wishes to all Muslims in the United Kingdom celebrating Eid al-Adha. This is a special time for Muslims, and an opportunity to celebrate the values of Islam. These are the values of family ['honour killing', marrying off children to aging relatives, polygamy, grooming and gang-raping children, wife beating, FGM, marital rape], community [self-ghettoisation] and of charity [funding terrorism and ripping off the welfare state]. At a time when so many people are facing hardship [most of them living under and because of Islam], these values seem more important than ever. I also want to take this chance to recognise the enormous contribution Muslims across Britain make to our country, our communities and to our way life. (*The Muslim News*, September, 24, 2015)

As in the example cited above, we are rarely if ever told what precisely these 'enormous contributions' consist of, how they enhance of the lives of non-Muslims, and in what ways they differ from those made by the rest of the UK population. If they are unique to Islam, why is it that millions of Muslims are risking their lives to escape from lands where these highly esteemed 'contributions' abound and flourish in all their unalloyed glory? I challenge Corbyn and indeed all those infidels who extol the virtues of Islam, to name but one single country where it constitutes the dominant faith that operates a functioning pluralist democracy and upholds those human rights codified in the United Nations Universal Declaration of 1948. Yet there are ample examples to hand Corbyn could have cited to prove his point. The contributions of Islam are indeed manifold and varied. But they are also in nearly every instance, not only hitherto virtually unknown in western society, but, as several surveys have shown, are regarded by the majority of its peoples to be totally alien to its ethos and laws. Not only in the UK, but everywhere they have settled in large numbers in the non-Islamic world, Muslims are statistically over-represented in prisons, the committing of horrendously vile sex crimes, honour killings, female genital mutilation, bogus asylum claims, polygamy, forced marriages, terrorism, political corruption, subversion of the educational system…and so the list can go on. True, those on the receiving end of these 'contributions'…one can hardly call them beneficiaries…would I suspect evaluate them in a less positive light than does Comrade Corbyn, thereby inviting the accusation of 'Islamophobia' from the usual chorus of *dhimmis*, as would for certain what follows:

> The terror attack that unfortunately took place in London was a vehicular attack. This time it was near a mosque, if you follow the news. How can anyone decide to carry out a terror attack near a place of worship, near a mosque, a church or any temple where God is worshipped? In all the previous vehicular attacks, at least in 2016 and 2017, the "heroes", unfortunately, were Muslims. And then people wonder

why they hate us? Why do they hate us? If they didn't, there would be something mentally wrong with them. [sic!!!] We use weapons all the time, slaughter people all the time flay people all the time, burn people alive all the time run people over all the time, and plant explosive devices and car bombs all the time. Why do you still expect them to love you? Tell me what the Muslims have contributed to the world throughout the twentieth century? Nothing. What have the Turkish Muslims of the Ottoman state contributed to the West? Slaughter, massacres, the impaling of Europeans on spears...It's true. That's what the Turks did in Europe in the 16th and 17th centuries. What did the Muslim Turks do to their Arab neighbours, most of whom are Muslims? They enslaved them, tortured them, imposed inflated taxes upon them. They made their lives unbearable.

What did the Muslims contribute to the West in the 19th and 20th centuries, except for the theories of [advocates of terrorism such as] Maududi, Sayyid Qutb, Abu Bakr Naji and Osama Bin Laden? What did the Muslims contribute to the West? Don't say to me: 'The literature of Naguib Mahfouz and the science of Ahmed Zewail'. The achievements of these people cannot be attributed to their being Muslims. What have the Muslims shown the West other than the bombing of their capital cities? What have the Muslims shown them other than their vehicular attacks? What have the Muslims shown them other than shooting at them? What have the Muslims shown them other than burning them alive in cages? They burn alive other Muslims as well. They all claim to have a monopoly over Islam. What have the Muslims shown the Westerners to make them love them and welcome them in their countries? After all this, you still ask me why they hate us?

And then people invent new terms, like 'a global conspiracy against Islam'. Man, a global conspiracy against Islam would mean that Muslims are being massacred around the world. The opposite is true. It is the non-Muslims who are being massacred. Am I right or what? Then you say to me: have you considered the Muslim minorities in India or Mali? To tell you the truth, what I see is Muslims perpetrating massacres against Christians and other majorities across the globe. The Muslims are constantly whining, lamenting and wailing: The West is constantly conspiring against us. Fine, let's assume that the West is conspiring against you and only sees your negative image. Where is your positive image? The Muslims of the Abbasid state [of Baghdad] presented a positive image. [750 to 1258] They exported scientific research through so-called [sic] "Muslim" scholars, most of whom by the way, were not from the Arabian Peninsula. None of them were from the Arabia peninsula. They were all from North Africa, and from what are now called the former Soviet Islamic republics of central Asia. What have the Arab countries contributed to the world? Nothing. Two, three, four or ten scientists in the course of 1,435 years? C'mon, man! Let's forget about 435 years and keep just one millennium. Ten important scientists in 1,000 years?! Who invented the airplane? The missile? The space shuttle? Centrifuges? Quantum mechanics? The theory of relativity? Who? Where did the most important philosophers come from? Not from here. And you still expect them to love us? And then you say: 'Terror-sponsoring countries like Britain deserve...' [No, he is not addressing Corbyn, but he could be] Nonsense! People do not deserve to be killed, slaughtered or run over by a car.

Youssef Al-Husseini, Egypt TV, June 19, 2017

Though they would outrage devotees of the Corbyn cult, and unlike analogous comments about the Jews, provide more than sufficient grounds for a fast-tracked expulsion from the Labour Party, these views are shared by a significant and growing portion of Egypt's semi-secular establishment. What is far more significant is that they are even beginning to be publicly aired in the heartlands of

Islamic conservatism. Here we have an interview with an Arab Islamic cleric, screened via the internet on July 23, 2012:

We Arabs are a consumer society, though there has been some change. But to what extent? Are we about to leave our backwardness? Oh no, we haven't even begun because we have yet to acknowledge that we are backward. Perhaps 10%-20% of the people are aware of this backwardness but the majority do not even realise it [amongst whom we must number Corbyn and Prince Charles]. So the problem is that we are backward and we don't know it. On the contrary, we treat the people who created this great and lofty [Western] civilisation as if they were carpenters and blacksmiths. We view them as mere labourers while we consider ourselves to be men of thought, science and culture who embody everything you aspire to in life. This is the exact opposite of how things should be…That's the reality. If we were to send back to the prosperous West everything we got from it, what would be left? Even the *Aqqal* head band you are wearing [points to interviewer's head] was made in Britain. [So maybe Corbyn and Cameron are right after all. Islam creates jobs in the UK and boosts its exports] We are incapable of producing anything. We can't do without the West. If you have a headache, you need to swallow the aspirin that they make. If you want to travel, you must take a plane or a car. If you want to get some sleep, you turn on the air conditioning, and the same is true of all the implements of civilisation. Civilisations complement one another. Complement?! What have we given them? ['Oil, the religion of Islam', interrupts the interviewer.]

The oil came from Allah, and on top of that, we need the West to extract it. If not for their industry, our oil would be worthless. It had been in this land for centuries, but we did not benefit from it in any way. Oil became valuable only when others came up with inventions, and later came here to extract it from our land. Civilisations are measured by their ability to change, we are exactly the other way around. We believe that the measure of success is unchangeability and this is a great problem. [a virtue, according to Prince Charles] If societies remained static, civilisation would not develop. Their development is dependent on their willingness to change. The reason that the West developed is that it stemmed from Greek culture, which was founded on the objective use of reason. When this great beacon of light was extinguished in the Middle Ages, the great mathematics of the Arabs had a role in the development of the West, but I still believe that Anglo-Saxon culture is superior. [So much for the PC shibboleth that all cultures are equal, with Islam's being more equal than all the others. Now comes perhaps the greatest heresy of them all.] The problem for the Arabs in societies that were occupied, like Egypt or Iraq, was that the colonists left too early, before they had established democracy. As a result of the British occupation or colonisation, Egypt was preparing to become a democratic country. There was cultural and political pluralism. Egypt was on its way to becoming a democratic country, if not for the 1952 [military] coup which was dubbed a 'revolution' [and evolved rapidly into the one-party dictatorship of President Nasser and his obsession with destroying Israel].

Are we enslaved by our identity or should it serve for our development? History, identity and culture should belong to society, and not vice versa. Otherwise, it is as if you are locking yourself in a cage. People are not unchanging, like rocks or trees. A person needs to change. [and some, especially Muslims, more than others] One should choose one's identity, rather than have it imposed upon him [could this be a coded plea for the right to leave Islam? There are believed to be possibly as many as three million secret apostates in Saudi Arabia, where the penalty for leaving Islam is death.] …When I talk about the development of the West, some people say to me, "What about Japan and China?". [I reply] If these countries had not emulated the West, they would not have progressed. Their progress was determined by the extent to which they borrowed from the West.

388

The interviewer concludes the proceedings by asking the cleric, 'so our opening up to the West will determine our development?', to which he replies, 'Absolutely'.

Postscript

'The history of all hitherto existing human society is the history of class struggle.' (K. Marx and F. Engels: *The Manifesto of the Communist Party*.).

'A hallmark of effective teaching is racial awareness.' (Yale Centre For Teaching and Learning)

'We must do all in our power to foster this racial awareness until it attains the same standard as obtained in Rome in the days of her glory.' (Adolf Hitler, July 5, 1942, as recorded in *Hitler's Table Talk*)

'A practical approach to developing racial awareness in schools.' (Course prospectus at Goldsmiths College, London)

'The entire work of education and training must be to burn the racial sense and racial feeling into the instinct and the intellect, the heart and the brain of the young entrusted to it.' (Adolf Hitler: *Mein Kampf*)

The unlawful killing of an arrested black man, George Floyd, by four policemen in Minneapolis on May 25, 2020 was followed by massive street demonstration, some of them violent, not only in the USA, but cities across the Western world, and the rise to prominence of Black Lives Matter, a movement dedicated to opposing the dominance of what it calls the white patriarchy. As we have seen, the killing of George Floyd also provided an impetus and the pretext for the promotion of critical race theory, not only at the highest levels of US, and to a lesser extent, UK, academe, but in schools, public institutions and work places. There was also not only an academic but physical assault on the two countries' past, with attacks on statutes and monuments deemed in some way racist. I am far from being alone in saying that in so many ways, both BLM and CRT, far from offering viable solutions to the racial problems they claim to address, compound them, because both are based on shared false premises. Before explaining why, let me say this. I am not opposed to the removal from public places (to museums) of statues of and monuments to personages from the past whose actions, by the standards of today, were palpably motivated or justified by racism, such as the slave trade. But these gestures, because that is all they are, have had and will have no impact whatsoever on the quality of life of the UK's or the USA's ethnic minorities.

What I do take issue with...and in this I am far from being alone on the left...was the targeting and even vandalising with graffiti of statues of those who, for all their faults (and who, apart from the virtue-signallers demanding their removal, is without them?) and even what today would be judged as their war crimes, served better than others of their day the cause of freedom and democracy: Oliver Cromwell, to whom we owe the supremacy of Parliament by his defeat of the royalists in the English Civil War of the mid 17th century, and Winston

Churchill, who far from being a slave trader, more than any other single individual, saved Britain from enslavement by the Nazis. It was for this reason that in 2002, in a field of 100 candidates, he was voted the Greatest Briton by BBC viewers, with just under half of the slightly more than a million votes cast. (Cromwell came tenth) It is to Churchill's opposition to the appeasement of Hitler when other Tories were prepared to put their class before country, and then his inspired and inspiring leadership in the dark and desperate days after Dunkirk, when all seemed, and indeed could have been lost, that we owe that today do not live under the heel of a racist Gestapo, and that Britain can therefore be a home to not only a quarter of a million Jews, but for all the claims of BLM that Britain is a racist country, also for umpteen ethnic, religious and racial minorities. Yes, Churchill and Cromwell were white and heterosexual. But for those who value above all else democracy and liberty, even above political correctness, our debt to them is beyond measure. But Black Lives Matter, who evidently had other priorities, wanted to have their statues removed. (At the time of writing, a boarded-up Churchill has survived the BLM iconoclastic onslaught, unlike Ulysses Grant, the General who led the Unionist armies to victory over the slave states of the Confederacy, whose statue was pulled down, as police stood by, in San Francisco's Golden Gate Park on June 19, 2020 and in Portland on October 10, 2020, that of Abraham Lincoln, who issued the Emancipation Decree on January 1, 1863, and who paid for it with his life when he was assassinated on April 15, 1865.)

Then there is the ever-present issue of double standards when and where today's left is involved. In April 2021, at the very time when not only US, but western public interest was focused on the trial of Dereck Chauvin, who was charged with (unintentional homicide for the illegal killing of George Floyd by using improper methods of restraint on him, Mario Gonzalez died in police custody in almost identical circumstances to those of Floyd. One would have thought then that this case would have attracted not only media interest, but public protests. But there was neither because, as the apt saying goes, it did not 'fit the narrative', the reason being, Gonzalez's skin was not black. Some lives matter more than others, even when they are taken by the police.

The kind and level of global international solidarity mounted for George Floyd was also in short supply in the wake of another killing, this time not unintentionally, of a criminal suspect illegally resisting arrest by the police, but a targeted assassination of a French school teacher for doing his job. On October 16, 2020, Samuel Paty was murdered and decapitated as per the *Koran*, chapter 8, verse 12, by a Muslim for showing a cartoon of Mohammed to a class on freedom of expression. At a ceremony conducted by President Macron, Paty was posthumously awarded his country's highest tribute, the *Légion d'Honneur*. Millions took to the streets of France to protest his ritualistic murder and to defend their country's secular traditions and constitution. The USA also has a secular constitution, and its First Amendment protects the same freedom of expression that Paty was murdered for teaching. But no one in the US stirred, any more than did anyone else outside of France. No politicians condemned Paty's murder It was as if it had never happened, because here we not only had another 'wrong narrative, but fear that that an official public show of outrage at a murder so obviously inspired by the religion of peace could easily give offense to those who shared it. Had Paty been a small-time black career criminal wrongfully killed by a police officer after resisting arrest, the world's righteous would have erupted onto the streets. But he wasn't, so…silence.

Then we have the double standards, coupled with gross political ignorance and posturing, on the part of BLM's sole leader. BLM founder Patrisse Cullors says she is a 'trained Marxist', even though the movement she has spawned is devoted almost exclusively to racial issues rather than those of class. Hardly surprising, given those she cites as responsible for her 'training', among them the white middle class urban terrorist Weathermen, the Black Panthers ('The revolution has come, it's time to pick up the gun. Off the pigs.!') the native American movement, the 'Young Lords', a Chicago 'turf war' group, the 'Brown Berets', another Latino outfit from the same city, and 'the great revolutionary rainbow experiments [sic] of the 1970s'. As one would expect, with such a parochial, nationalist and ethnic rather than class background, when it comes to the history and traditions of the international workers' movement, she is something of an ignoramus. Otherwise, she would have either never allowed her followers to pull down the statue of Lincoln, or instructed her comrades in the UK to mete out the same treatment to a certain famous (or notorious) monument in London's Highgate cemetery. Because if she is what she claims to be, Cullors would have known that Marx and Lincoln were on the friendliest of terms. It was Marx who, in his capacity as Secretary of the International Workingmens' Association, wrote to Lincoln to congratulate him on his re-election as President in 1864, and it was Lincoln who, through his London ambassador Charles Adams, sent his thanks to Marx and his 'sincere and anxious desire that he may be able to prove himself not unworthy of the confidence which has recently been extended to him by his fellow citizens and by so many friends of humanity and progress throughout the world.'

So, Lincoln regarded Marx as a 'friend'. And indeed he should have done, because it was thanks to Marx that the voices of the recognized leaders of the (entirely white) European working class were raised in solidarity and brotherhood with the victims of American slavery. In Marx's own words, 'from the commencement of the titanic American strife, the workingmen of Europe felt instinctively that the star-spangled banner carried the destinies of their class.' These were no idle platitudes. At great personal sacrifice, to a man and woman, the (white, let us remind exponents of critical race theory) textile workers of Lancashire for the entire duration of the civil war refused to touch raw cotton imported from the slave states of the south.

I would not be in the least surprised to learn that neither BLM founder Cullors nor any of her collaborators has any knowledge either of this exemplary act of international solidarity and brotherhood with the victims of American slavery, or of the movement founded by Marx, and, even less likely, that he was the author of its founding principle, that 'the emancipation of the working classes must be conquered by the working classes themselves'. I say this, because for want of a better term, her leadership style has a distinctly elitist flavour. Until her resignation early in 2021, she was sole leader of BLM, answerable to no-once since its two other co-founders departed in 2020, leaving her in sole control of its assets, valued at $90 million in 2021, but believed to be much larger. No-one knows for sure, because BLM does not issue financial statements, just as it doesn't elect its leaders(s) or hold annual conferences to decide policy. Everything, especially the cash, was in the sole hands of Cullors, a state of affairs that led to protests by ten of BLM's US chapters, who in a joint statement

392

claimed that none of them had received a dime from Cullors since their founding in 2016. Cullors' life style is also distinctly at odds with three of BLM's main objectives, which are to abolish the police, capitalism and the nuclear family. Cullors lives with her partner, Janaya Khan, and their two children, and owns four up-market properties in fashionable, nearly all-white locations, three in Los Angeles and the other in Atlanta, Georgia. One has a swimming pool and runway and hanger for a private plane. As of April 2021, she was reported to be checking out a fifth property in the Bahamas which, if she purchased it, would make her a neighbor of Justin Timberlake and Tiger Woods. When she received death threats after the news broke of her bourgeoning property portfolio, she asked and was given round the clock police protection. Don't do as I do…

Shortly after the story of her property acquisitions broke, Cullors announced her resignation from BLM to focus, she said, on her projected second book, *An Abolitionists Handbook*, and on her new media career with Warner Brothers. Her departure left several questions unanswered as to the size and whereabouts of BLM's assets, not least because of the lack of any proper auditing, and the complex multi-tiered structure of BLM. According to William Cunningham, writing in the black-oriented business journal *Black Enterprise*, dated June 20, 2020, US corporations had pledged $1.678 billion to BLM and its various causes. It is impossible, for the reasons stated, to discover to what extent these pledges were made good. What we do know is that precious little found its way down to the grass roots of the movement, a scandal that led to the resignation of several high-profile activists and denunciations of Cullors by long-standing black critics of the movement. More outrage exploded when in April 2022, it was revealed that in October 2020, with cash pouring in to BLM coffers on the back of the killing of George Floyd, Cullors, together with the other two founders of BLM, Alicia Garza and Melina Abdullah, had secretly purchased with BLM funds, via a third party, a $6 million, 6,500 square foot, seven bedroom, seven bathroom plus swimming pool South California mansion for their own exclusive private use. Let me engage in a little speculation…an appropriate word for its subject matter. While it has served the purpose of its rightist critics to leave unexplored the authenticity of BLM's claim to be a leftist, even Marxist movement, let us for a moment be charitable, and grant the possibility, however remote, that she has at least waded her way through the first few chapters of Volume One of Marx's *magnum opus*, *Das Kapital*, in which he examines the process of capitalist production and accumulation. He expresses this in a simple formula: The first cycle begins, Money (M) invested in Capital (C), realising more Money (M1); then the next, M 1, C 1, M 2 and so on. Cullors' property portfolio, purchased with M, represents stage 2 of the first cycle, Capital. If it increases in market value, highly likely given its exclusive, predominately white, locations, it can then be sold for more than she paid for it, stage three, M1, and so on. As the saying goes, you speculate to accumulate. Goodbye George…thanks for the ride.

On February 18, 2020, reports appeared in the media that Amazon had suspended from its charity platform Black Lives Matter Global Network Foundation, the holding company that Cullors used to collect and control all BLM funds, which were believed to amount to at least $60 million but could be substantially more. The decision followed California's Department of Justice decision to hold the leaders of BLM personally responsible for the Foundation's missing financial records (assuming that they existed in the first place). Riding on the back of the killing of George Floyd, by the end of 2020, BLM was awash with donations from big corporations, registering itself as a charity in December of that year. Since then, it has failed to provide tax returns. (Its 2019 filing was from a non-existent address.) BLM's three founders are no longer officially connected with the movement, while the *Washington Examiner* stated that no-one connected with BLM knew who was currently running the movement or who was managing BLM's assets. Just as Trever Phillips said, BLM is 'a scam'.

As for Amazon, no one can accuse the company of not doing its very best to promote the woke agenda. While it was allowing BLM to violate charity regulations, Amazon had responded to accusations that the camera (that is, not just its own cameras, but the camera *per se*) was racist (I will also repeat that, 'that the camera was racist') by, and I quote 'working to re-work the algorithms and tweak the training data that power the Pixel camera in order to more accurately and brilliantly capture people of colour.' Fittingly, Amazon has termed the project 'Image Equity'...pure wokespeak. And not a moment too soon. Already a series of articles had been published, exposing camera racism, starting with the *New York Times* (where else) in April 2019 ('The Racial Bias Built into Photography'), then *The Atlantic* in January 2020 ('Digital Cameras Still [sic] Racist'), the *Calgary Journal* in February 2020 ('Time for a new lens: The hidden racism behind photography') and *Illumination* in July 2021 ('Is Your Camera Racist?'). The anti-racist zeal unleashed by the illegal killing of George Floyd has led to the unmasking of camera racism in more than just conventional commercial models: The on-line *Streetsblog* found that 'speed cameras are racist', (one has to assume by being able to detect the skin colour, even at night, of whoever was at the wheel) while an article in *Time* asked 'Are Face-detection Cameras Racist?', the answer being a resounding yes. So well done, Amazon. By at least making your cameras as you say 'less racist', you have gone some way towards atoning for what some would judge as you institutionally racist treatment of BLM by requiring that the movement should conform to laws devised by white men purely for the benefit of white men.

Cullors' and her movement's world is not that of the working class, of the trade unions and parties it has created over the best part of two centuries to advance its own interests, but one of race war against a 'white patriarchy', the vast majority of whom do not enjoy the privileges and share the political power of the world's propertied classes but, like a similar majority of the world's other races, earn their living by working for them. It would be an interesting exercise to see just how many (or rather, as I suspect, how few) BLM activists in the UK belong to a trade union. As for political parties, they have had since 2020 the choice of two claiming to represent Black Lives Matter. Both intend to stand candidates on platforms corresponding to the policies of BLM UK. Insofar as they succeed in attracting support from the UK's ethnic minorities, it will be to the detriment of the Labour Party and the advantage of the Conservatives.

Ironically, when it comes to Marx's *forté,* BLM are no better informed of the economics of the 21st century than they are of the politics of the nineteenth. As the saying goes, money talks, and a huge and ever-increasing share of it is speaking Asian, especially Chinese, Japanese and Arabic, not English or, for that matter, any Indo-European tongue. So much so, that just as Marx predicted and welcomed in his *Communist Manifesto* of 1848, the process of globalization (opposed, like much else, by far right and left alike, with their reactionary anti-

European Union dystopias of either capitalism or socialism in one country - *vide* my comments on the Trump-Corbyn convergence) has created a single *world* market and economic system. As such, it is one in which today, white workers increasingly are employed and, as Cullors, the 'trained Marxist', would surely agree, exploited, by non-white employers and investors, just as is the case with the reverse. A few miles from where I live is an example of the former, the UK's largest steel plant, at Port Talbot, South Wales. Due to the ethnic composition of the region, its work force is overwhelmingly 'white', while its owners, the Indian multi-billionaire Tata family, are not. This is an inevitable and increasingly prevalent consequence of the spread of capitalism from west to east and from north to south, a process which embraces all sectors of the world economy from mining, energy, basic industry and agriculture to manufacture, transport, high-tech communications and finance.

Another result of this process of globalization is the increasing irrelevance of the parochial view of politics and society shared by critical race theory and its wokista practitioners, in the first place, Black Lives Matter. To take but one example of scores, if not hundreds. The Bombay-based Tata group, two thirds of whose operations are located overseas in more than a *hundred* countries, employs world-wide a multi-racial work force of *750,000*, a typical multinational conglomerate, with a revenue in 2020 of $106 billion. According to 'critical race theory', by virtue of their genes, the work force, not only at Port Talbot but other Tata steel plants on the European continent, where it numbers 20,000, is enjoying all the privileges and therefore sharing all the prejudices of the white patriarchy, unlike their racially disadvantaged billionaire employers. Closer to my home, in fact just outside my front door, at the crack of dawn, come rain, shine and Covid19, a team comprised entirely of members of the white patriarchy collect my bagged up-garbage. I must ask them two questions: do they agree with critical race theory and, if they do, how does it feel to be ruling the world.

But victimhood can have its compensations. While the average wage rate at Tata UK for the year 2020 was £31,870, and for refuse collectors, £17,172, (both before tax), in the same year, the fortune of Ratan Tata, the owner of Tata UK, was valued at $1 billion. To put this in perspective, he was not even remotely sufficiently wealthy to be listed in Forbes' top ten richest Indians, with at number one, Mukesh Ambani (petro-chemicals, oil and gas), $36.8 billion. Ratan Tata came in at *number 61*. Heading 'Communist' China's richest capitalists is Mua Huateng, with $59.95 billion, the ninth richest man in the world. Saudi Arabia's Prince Alwaleed bin Talal is worth $18.7 billion, United Arab Emirates' Majid Al Futtaim $10.94, Indonesia's two Hartono brothers, a combined $26.2 million, South Korea's Lee Kun-hee, $17.3 billion, Malaysia's Robert Kuok, $11.5 billion, Charoen Sirivadhanabhakdi, Thailand, $20 billion, Singapore's Lee Ziting $17.8 billion, Japan's Tadashi Yani $22.3 billion, and Jeremy's 'friends', Hamas chiefs Khaled Mashal, $2.6 billion, and Masu Abu Marzook, between $2 and $3 billion. A case of for the very few, and not the many.

Of the 45 richest people in the world, *nine are Chinese*. The UK, the world's first capitalist country and industrial power, is represented by one, the *Indian*-born and *Bombay*-based N.J. Hinduja. We are assured by critical race theory that only whites are and can be racist, because racism is about power, and whites have all the power. Tell that to those I have listed above. They will reply that power is not about race, but about wealth, which has no colour and which today, knows no borders. I find it both instructive and amusing, that capitalists can give a lesson in Marxism to so-called 'cultural Marxists'.

To return to the point where we began…Lincoln's statue. Let us leave the last word on this instructive episode to Martin Luther King, who had a foot, so to speak, in the camps of the two friends. Of Marx, King said though he rejected his central theory, he saw as morally wrong the 'gulf between superfluous wealth and abject poverty' that existed in capitalist societies. As for Lincoln, King would have been horrified that his statue would have been pulled down simply because his views on racial matters, though more enlightened than most, were of his time and place. Of the relations between the two contemporary champions of exploited labour, King said that Lincoln not only 'welcomed the support of Karl Marx during the civil war', but also 'corresponded with him freely.' But then who is King, the advocate of that most insidious of all forms of racism, 'colour blindness', with his humanist nostrums about judging a person by their character and not their skin? So down came Lincoln, emancipator of the slaves, and the General who defeated their masters. The indiscriminate nature of the iconoclastic orgy was such that when the Rochester, New York, statue of Frederick Douglass, the pioneer black abolitionist, was pulled down on April 3, 2022, the 156th anniversary of one of his most famous speeches, commentators were left puzzling as to the motive of those who had done it, because it could just as easily have been the work of anti-white racists of the BLM left as anti-black racists of the far right. Was Douglass a coon for collaborating, albeit critically, with the paternalist Lincoln, or an uppity nigger threatening the rule of the white man?

It was for lunacies such as this that Black Lives Matter was seen by some commentators as Trump's not so secret weapon in his bid to retain the Presidency. (The BLM vandalising of war memorials to those who died fighting Hitler's racist Reich led to the UK government, with post-Corbyn Labour support, proposing a ten-year prison sentence for this crime.) Not being white is no insurance against such acts, as the citizens of Leicester, many of them of Indian origin, discovered, when their city's statue of the non-violent anti-imperialist campaigner Gandhi was defaced, absurdly, with the legend, 'fascist'.

No less absurd in its own ecclesiastical way was the announcement by Justin Welby, the Archcoward of Canterbury, that the depiction of Jesus as a white man was under review, a classic case of when a juggernaut starts rolling towards you, the best tactic is to get behind it and start pushing. (Amongst those joining Welby in this obscene stampede to avid accusations of racism were the managements of the British Museum, the British Library, the BBC, Amnesty International, departing, as it has in the Middle East, from its original brief of defending Prisoners of Conscience, the Football Association, Argos and Sainsbury, with their racially segregated 'safe spaces' for black employees, and the cadet branch of the House of Windsor. In the USA, after the killing of George Floyd, BLM gained enormous traction, adding to its $100 million grant from the Ford Foundation a portfolio of endorsements from dozens of Wall-Street quoted companies and a promotional contract with Warner Brothers. Amongst 'progressives', expressing dissent from the BLM and CRT agendas was something best confined to family and closest of friends.)

And so, like many of his calling, not being cut of the same cloth as the early Christian martyrs, Welby, along with an entire army of equally spineless politicians, celebrities and media people, started pushing. Going round the world, he said, 'you go into churches and you don't see a white Jesus. You see a black Jesus, a Chinese Jesus, a Middle Eastern [sic!] Jesus - which is of course the most accurate - you see a Fijian Jesus.' Albeit without intending to, Welby was acknowledging what has been known from the days of the ancient Greeks and Romans, that man makes god or gods in his own image, and not the reverse. That however is not my point. First, if the Chinese, black Africans or Fijians can make Jesus in their (wrong) image - and good luck to them - why should not white Christians in theirs? How is that racist? My main problem, however, is this: Why did he not, instead of 'a Middle Eastern Jesus', say 'you see a *Jewish* Jesus, which is *totally* accurate.'? 'Middle Eastern' could just as easily be Arab, Kurd, or any number of other Middle Eastern ethnic groups. Could it be that the Primate entertained the expectation that a de-whitened, 'Middle Eastern' Jesus would resonate better with Black Lives Matter's well-advertised anti-Zionism, as in its posting of June 28, 2020. It claimed, with more than hint of Jewish conspiracy theory, that 'mainstream British politics is gagged [by whom?] of the right to criticise Zionism' (even though in his four years of leadership of the Labour Party, as in his previous thirty as a backbencher, there were times when Corbyn had done little else), and that the movement (like its US counterpart) stood 'loudly and clearly with our Palestinian comrades [sic]', in stark contrast it must be said to its calculated, cowardly and cynical failure to condemn 'loudly and clearly' the black slave markets of Libya. But then again, did not Islam convert Jonathen Brown assure his University of Georgetown audience that as long as the owner was a Muslim (as is the case in Libya) 'it is not immoral for one human to own another'?

If BLM were, like, for all its doctrinal anti-Semitism, Islam, to claim Jesus as one of its own, I suggest they first consult Welby's own holy book, written almost entirely by and about Jews, and the only source we have about Jesus. It tells us that Jesus was born a Jew, a descendent of King David, Israel's national hero (Mathew 1:1), was called and addressed as rabbi, correctly translated in the King James version as 'master' (Mark 12:14,19, Luke 17:13, 18:18, 20:21,39), preached only to Jews (Mathew 10: 5-6), preached in synagogues (Mathew 13:54, Mark 1:21-22,39) and the Jerusalem temple (Mathew 21: 12-15), was hailed, mocked or described as king of the Jews (Mathew 27:11,37, Mark 11:9-10, 15:9, John 19:19) and was arrested, 'scourged' and executed by Pontius Pilate for plotting a Jewish rebellion to liberate Israel from Roman rule (Luke 22:35-38, 23:2-3,5,12, John 19:12) and, finally, in Luke 1:68-74, that John the Baptist was described by his father in terms that today, would qualify him as a militant Zionist: 'Blessed be the Lord God of Israel; for he hath visited and redeemed his people' and 'raised up a horn of salvation for us in the servant of the House of David' (again), that 'we should be saved from our enemies, and from all that hate us', 'that we be delivered out of the hand of our enemies.' (Then, the legions of Caesar, today, of Allah) These are not the kinds of C.V. to endear their owner to the anti-Zionists of Black Lives Matter. So, let's just say instead of being a Jew, Jesus was 'Middle Eastern' or, even better, after the name the Romans gave to Israel when they conquered it, a Palestinian, thereby rendering him eligible for posthumous membership of one of today's Jihadi movements dedicated to the conquest of the land of his birth and the extermination of all its Jewish inhabitants. I joke not. Did not the Jew-killing PLO Chairman Arafat once famously say that 'Jesus was the first Palestinian *fedayeen* militant who carried

397

his sword along the path on which the Palestinians today carry their cross [sic].'?

Britain, we have been told over and again by Black Lives Matter, and by others who, because of their public office or profile, dare not say otherwise, is a racist society. We should be careful about making such an allegation without making clear what is meant by it. No-one would deny that there are British people who harbour, exhibit and act upon prejudices they hold against members of other races. But does this indisputable fact alone render Britain a racist society? By way of an analogy, there are, no less indisputably, paedophiles who prey on and sexually abuse children. But does this fact alone render Britain a paedophiliac society? In both cases it is surely, at least in part, a question of the extent of their prevalence, and whether, for want of a better term, the balance of 'public opinion' approves of or condemns, and the law tolerates or punishes the behaviour in question.

Let us grant for the moment at least that Britain's is, as BLM claims, a racist society. This would still leave circumstances like the following to be accounted for. The Jay and Casey reports into Rotherham's Muslim rape gangs both attributed the failure to report and prevent their activities to *fear of accusations of racism*, together with all the attendant negative professional and social consequences for the public officials involved. The same explanation has also been found to account for identical behaviour in other locations where rape gangs have operated with impunity. If racism is as prevalent in society as some would have us believe, that it is, so to speak, 'institutional', 'systemic' or the 'default position', then firstly, why in that case would a charge of racism instil such fear, and secondly, and this is my main point, a fear so all-pervading and profound, that over a period of at least three decades, it led tens of thousands of otherwise mostly decent and conscientious public officials, not just in Rotherham, but in dozens of town and cities across England, to permit and even facilitate rather than report and prevent the organised rape of white working class children, a trade conducted quite openly on what the Jay report describes as an 'industrial scale'?

Surely, given that the UK is as racist as some claim and, as was indeed the case, that nearly all the victims of this 'industry' were white, and nearly all the paedophile rapists were, to use the official euphemism, of 'Pakistani heritage', here was an opportunity for racists with the power to do so to quite legally give the hated 'Pakis' the treatment they deserved. But, as we now know, the exact opposite happened, because, far from being racist, the default position, certainly in all sectors of public life, was then and remains, as Casey puts it, a 'right on' anti-racism carried, as in what follows, to a ludicrous and indeed possibly criminal degree. The Jay Report relates that when two fathers tracked their daughters to 'safe houses' where they were being gang raped, after calling the police, they, and not the rapists, were arrested, as was a girl being gang raped, for being 'drunk and disorderly'. Girls who reported their abuse to the police, one with fresh blood stains on the crotch of her jeans, were told not to make trouble and turned away, as were their parents. A police officer who requested permission to continue investigating gang rape was told by his superior officer that if he persisted in his inquiries he would be relegated to traffic duties. Were these police officers, and hundreds like them, presented as they repeatedly were in such cases with the pretext and opportunity to vent to their supposedly racist prejudices, doing so, or were they rather concerned above else to demonstrate to their superiors that they harboured none?

They acted as did thousands of other public officials, covering up and even abetting the gang rape of children...as we have seen, social workers were especially guilty in this respect...because in addition to fearing accusations of a racially-motivated 'over-policing' of Muslims by amongst others, Muslim-vote seeking local Labour politicians, they thought that to act otherwise, that is to enforce the law on rape and under-age sex, could undermine so-called 'community cohesion', whose preservation required turning a blind eye to crime within the 'Muslim community', and finally and perhaps most crucially, because they were under strict instructions to do so, one of the proofs being the already-cited letter sent by Labour Home Secretary Jacqui Smith in 2008 to all police authorities in England and Wales ordering them not to take action against Muslim rape gangs because the children they were raping 'had made an informed choice about their sexual behaviour'. The Casey report provides statistical evidence strongly suggesting that similar directives were in operation long before Smith issued hers. (No doubt Ms. Smith regards herself no less a feminist than an anti-racist. She is of course entitled to her self-delusions. One thing is for sure. Were they to learn of her giving a green light to gang rape, those who were reduced to sexual slavery as its consequence would use less complimentary epithets to describe her.)

For all this, let me say it again. Of course the UK has its racists, though until proved otherwise, whatever their number might be, I do not believe it is increasing. In fact there are grounds for believing that apart from an increasing anti-Semitism, about and against which, given its official anti-Zionist stance and antecedents in Farrakhan's anti-Jewish Nation of Islam, Black Lives Matter has nothing to say, (and in the USA, did nothing to prevent Nazi-style attacks on synagogues and looting of Jewish-owned stores by black demonstrators) the trend is in the opposite direction, whatever the anti-racist industry might assert to the contrary. Understandably so, since nobody likes to be out of a job.

In addition to BLM's accommodation, to use no stronger word, with anti-Semitism, no less to be deplored is that despite their exposure by a CNN documentary in 2017, the slave markets of Libya, have thus far escaped condemnation by a movement seemingly more concerned with the obliteration of all traces of those responsible for the white (but not Arab) slave trade of centuries past than the enslavement of black Africans today. (According to the Global Slavery Index, as of 2020, there were 9.2 million slaves in Africa, all of them black). Could this be because those conducting and profiting from the slave markets of Libya are not long-dead wealthy white Christians, but very much alive and wealthy Arab Muslims, an indifference to certain black lives analogous to the refusal of BLM both in the USA and the UK to deplore the fact that young black men are being killed by young black men on the streets of London and Chicago on a scale that dwarfs that of black victims of unlawful white police violence? Both are met with the same shameful silence as the Sharia left's concerning the fact that the vast majority of Muslims who have met a violent end over the last four decades have been killed, not by 'western imperialism' or the 'Zionist entity', but by an eastern, Slav imperialism, as in Bosnia, Afghanistan and Chechnya, and in the Arab world, by fellow Muslims.

Having included in its 2016 policy statement the lying allegation that Israel is guilty of simultaneously committing 'genocide' against and imposing 'apartheid' on the Palestinians, it was only to be expected that BLM would exploit the killing

399

of George Floyd to ramp up its anti-Israel rhetoric. Addressing a BLM demonstration of 1,000 at Oriel College Oxford on June 12, 2020 demanding the removal of a statue of Cecil Rhodes, Oxford University, the speaker said to cheers, 'like many others, invests in Israeli apartheid', while 'the American police are trained by the Israeli oppressor army.' This was pure Corbynism, which perhaps explains why it was first put into circulation by the *Morning Stalin*, with its front page headline of June 1, 'Minnesota cops "trained by Israeli forces in restraint techniques"', and then recycled by defeated Corbynista Labour leadership candidate Rebecca Long-Bailey. On June 27, 2020, perhaps momentarily forgetting that beloved Comrade Ten out of Ten was no longer her boss, she tweeted that actress Maxine Peake was an 'absolute diamond' for her interview in the *Independent* in which she had made the same false claim (subsequently demolished by Channel 4 News and withdrawn by Peake, Long-Bailey and the *Independent,* but not the *Morning Star* or BLM) that kneeling on the neck 'was learned [by US police] from seminars with Israeli secret services.' How come so many anti-Semites have privileged access to Israel's 'secrets'?

That same day, to a synchronised chorus of protests by Momentum and Corbynista councillors and MPs, Labour Leader Kier Starmer sacked Long-Bailey from her post as shadow Education Secretary for refusing to take down a tweet sharing an article which 'contained an anti-Semitic conspiracy theory'. Her defiance and then retraction called to mind Jonathan Swift's epigram, 'falsehood flies and truth comes limping after it'. There was no retraction however after another posting making the same allegation, this time, in a re-run of the Stalin-Hitler pact, by a Michigan-based Neo-Nazi on her website by the *Protocols*-promoting Nannette White ('everything evil and destructive happening is their [i.e., the Jews'] handiwork'), specifically, that 'Minn cops [are] trained by Israeli police, who often use knee-on-neck restraint'. The next day, the anti-Israeli action moved to Paris, where BLM demonstrators waved PLO flags and carried anti-Israeli posters, one of which read: 'Enough of Israel's Massacres' and another, 'Israel, the laboratory for police violence'. 'Anti-racists' supposedly protesting against the killing of George Floyd chanted 'dirty Jews' and 'Jewish whores'. Back in the UK the previous day, two young black men were shot dead at a illegal rave in Moss Side, Manchester, followed, on June 18, by the drive-by shooting to death of another black man, a father of two, in Cheam, London. At the time of writing, the ethnic identity of their killers is not known. But one thing is certain. They were not killed by white policemen. So, as is the case in the USA, none of these killings elicited any comment, let alone condemnation, from Black Lives Matter.

Neither did two massacres of black Africans by Islamic State affiliates. In the first, in Mozambique on November 6, 2020, the victims, totalling more than 50, were decapitated on a football pitch to cries of 'Allah is the Greatest', followed by the abduction of a number of women. The second massacre occurred in northern Nigeria on the 28th of the same month, the victims, farm workers, numbering at least 110. Like the slave auctions in Libya, these atrocities passed BLM UK by, perhaps because it had a more important issue on its anti-racist plate...the proposal by Labour councillors in Newham to re-name the Maryland train station in east London because of its supposed links to the slavery once practiced in the US state of the same name. Supposed, because in an essay on the subject of place names, retired professor Ged Martin had traced the station's name back to the Old English word for boundary, 'maere'.

In another similar fool's errand, staff at the British Library were set to work, at tax-payers expense, tracing the antecedents of 300 famous Britons to see if they were connected in any way with slavery and colonialism. Three literary names they came up with were Lord Byron, Oscar Wilde and George Orwell…all men of the Left, avowed enemies of the British establishment, and not connected in any way, unlike their relatives, with either slavery or colonialism. Byron spoke up in parliament for Catholic emancipation and the Luddites, supported Napoleon at the battle of Waterloo and died while helping the Greeks in their war of liberation against the Turks. Socialist and gay Oscar Wilde was an Irish subject of the British empire, while Orwell's political radicalism was born of his disgust at the treatment of the Burmese while serving in the colony's police force. So what is the point of this exercise?…unless one subscribes to the Biblical 'lapsarian' doctrine of inherited sin which, ironically, many of the left now do, the sin in question being born white, male and heterosexual. It was initially claimed that an antecedent of a fourth sinner, the poet Ted Hughes, a certain Nicholas Ferrar, born in 1592, was involved in the colonization of Virginia. This allegation (for what it was worth) not only proved to be false, because Ferrar died childless, but a slander, Farrar being the author of a pamphlet attacking slavery.

It requires only the most basic of maths and a modicum of historical knowledge to demonstrate how ill-informed and mendacious is this exercise in BLM-inspired hereditary McCarthyism. Let us assume that the current generational gap is 25 years. I will hold this constant as we go back in time, even though it will in reality contract as increasingly, parents have children at a younger age. If I take the British Library staff engaged on this enterprise or, better still, those of the library management who devised and authorised it, each of them will have two parents, four grandparents and so on, doubling at each generation every 25 years. So we have, working back from 2020 in 25 year intervals to the time when the non-ancestor of Ted Hughes was engaged (allegedly) in colonialism, the following accumulation of directly related ancestors of one young adult living today: 2, 4, 8, 16, 32, 64, 128, 56, 512, 1024, (this takes us back to the year 1805) 2048, 4095, 8192, 16,334, (now to 1705) 32,384, 65,536, 65,536, 131,072 and finally, 262,144 in the year 1605, when the population of England was around a tenth of the 65 million it is now. Who would exclude, not just the possibility, but the probability, that among that number of ancestors, there were none connected with the slave trade?

Working forward in time from 1605, and assuming one slave trader has two children, as do all their descendants (again, a conservative projection because, until recently, the birth rate was above this number) we get the same progression; that is, just one slave trader will have by the year 2020 passed on his genetic iniquities to 262,144 young adults. It has been estimated that at its peak in the 18th century, around 2% of the British population (say of around ten million) were engaged in the slave business. So even if only a small number of that 2% passed on an unbroken line of descendants, doubling with each generation, hypothetically, their number alive today would exceed that of the UK's current population. In reality, this is of course impossible. They will have been interbreeding over time both with an increasing number of other descendants of slavers and a diminishing number of those who were not.

It will objected that except for a minority who are the product of inter-racial marriages and liaisons, (which currently number around one million, and, the more they increase, the better, not least, because it will put out of business the race warriors of right and left) all of today's descendants of slave traders in the UK will be white. Not so. Given that every human society has practiced slavery going back, not just to 400 years ago, as in North America by European colonists, but at least to the dawn of recorded history, it is a statistical certainty that, irrespective of their ethnic identity, not just the staff of the British Library but the current population of the UK and indeed the entire world will have ancestors who were both slave owners and slaves, a fact that renders the notion and practical implementation of 'restitution' a nonsense…unless, that is, as seems to be the intention, it only applies to white owners of black slaves and, not, as in two of many examples, to Muslim traders in white Christian slaves (the so-called 'Barbary' trade), or black African owners of fellow black Africans, as was the case long before the Europeans arrived on the scene, and long after they departed it.

I wonder how many students of 'Black History' are taught that after Britain's white patriarchal Parliament abolished the slave trade in 1807 (more than two centuries on, and it is still flourishing in Africa) the Royal Navy established a squadron of warships, eventually comprising one sixth of its entire fleet, to suppress the slave trade along the coast of west Africa? All told, 1,600 slave ships were intercepted, and 150,000 slaves liberated. Someone should tell the BBC wokistas who, to appease Black Lives Matter, unsuccessfully tried to ban a certain composition traditionally performed at the last night of the Proms, that England was only able to free the slaves because Britannia ruled the waves. Such facts however count for nothing. Whites are born and stay in sin. The best they can do is to confess it and as with all religions, hope for forgiveness.

With this in mind, white Parliamentary staff were exhorted by 'diversity'-promoting 'Parli-REACH' to write poems acknowledging their 'internal racism' on a digital wall. They were also encouraged to attend BLM demonstrations protesting the death of George Floyd, some of which involved breaking laws passed by their employer. But would they have been prepared to do so on behalf of another victim of US police violence, Tony Timpa, who, on August 10, 2016, died in circumstances almost identical to those of George Floyd? He had called the police from a parking lot in Dallas. He was in some distress, being a schizophrenic off his medicine. By the time the police arrived, he had been handcuffed by security guards. Camcorder footage shows him then being manhandled by police and repeatedly shouting 'you're going to kill me.' Timpa was pinned to the ground, face down, for thirteen minutes, while his captors, waiting for an ambulance, laughed and joked about his mental state. Even after he lost consciousness, the joking continued, one officer exclaiming 'Back to school! Come on, wake up!' By this time, their captive was probably already dead, a victim of US police violence no less lethal than that meted out to George Floyd four years later. But unlike Floyd, he was white. That is why no-one in the UK has heard of, let alone marched for Tony Timpa, partly at least because, so the legend goes, in the USA, white cops only kill unarmed blacks. In fact, readily available FBI statistics prove that US police are 20% more likely to kill an unarmed white person such as Tony Timpa than a black one such as George Floyd. But dare to say it, and you may well be accused of racism. This possibility has proved sufficient to induce compliance on the part of public figures and institutions with ideas and policies that those acquiescing in them must surely know to be both deeply flawed and based on false premises and, above all, injurious to social harmony and individual freedom, a shamefaced, spineless conformism that contrasts with times when men and women were prepared to undergo torture and be burned at the stake rather than assent to beliefs they held to be false. I would dearly like to ask them...do they really want the abolition of the police and the nuclear family? And if indeed it is the case that what we have here is not conformity but conviction, then one can only marvel that such credulity can flourish amongst the highly educated in the 21st century.

What is for sure flourishing, if that is the right word, is a poisoned, intimidatory incipiently totalitarian atmosphere, not only in public but private life, one of fear of being seen to be less than fully on board with BLM groupthink and racial blackmail as it intrudes, virtually unopposed, into almost every aspect of British society, from universities, politics, sport and supermarkets to all branches of culture, the media, pressure groups such as Amnesty International and hitherto non-political institutions such as the National Trust, the BBC, the British Museum and the British Library. It has invaded the work-place and yes, even gardening, a once innocent pastime now deemed by BBC botanist James Wong to be saturated with racism. Apparently, 'UK gardening culture has racism baked into its DNA' because of its use of terms such as 'native' and 'heritage'. And so the list of trigger words continues to grow exponentially and our vocabulary of permissible terms (and expressible thoughts) shrink proportionately, as it did in the Newspeak of 1984. Dissenting from the prevailing, almost semi-official 'narrative', be it on race, gender or Islam, can be a risky business, as a number of prominent public figures have found out, notably the actor Laurence Fox, children's writer J. K. Rowling and psychologist Jordan Peterson.

Another pervasive myth one is expected to defer to in respectable company is that the entirety of American society, not just the US police force, is 'institutionally racist' to the very core. Some go as far as to compare Nazi Germany's treatment of the Jews with the USA's of its blacks (a variant of Israel's with the Palestinians). So I ask: Would Hitler have appointed a Jew as his Foreign Minister, as George Bush junior did two blacks, one a women, who served him in that capacity as Secretaries of State, Colin Powell from 2001 to 2005, and Condoleezza Rice from 2005 to 2009? Would Hitler have appointed a Jew as Chief of Staff of his armed forces, as Bush senior did Powell, a four-star general, as his Chairman of the Joint Chiefs of Staff from 1989 to 1993? Would Hitler have chosen a Jew as head of his country's security agencies, as Bush junior did Rice, who served as National Security Adviser between 2005 and 2009? Nazi Germany murdered every Jew it could lay its hands on. The USA twice elected a black man, Barack Obama as its President. Nazi Germany enacted laws that reduced its Jews to the status of pariahs and outcasts. Beginning in 1961, the USA enacted laws that not only rendered illegal all such treatment of its black population, but conferred on them certain advantages in the spheres of education and employment. So wherein then resides the comparison?

True, much to their shame, states in the deep south once had laws banning racially mixed marriages and sexual relations akin to those that outlawed sexual relations and marriages between so-called Aryans and Jews in Nazi Germany. Following on from the Civil Rights Acts of 1964 and 1965, these laws were overturned by a Supreme Court ruling in 1967, since when, racially mixed marriages in the USA have been steadily on the rise, as has public approval of them, now at 97%. In 1980, whites married to blacks numbered 167,000. In the year 2009, it was 550,000 and is still rising. Since attitudes towards sexual relations has always been at the very core of the race question, in the light of the above statistics, in what sense can the USA today be said to be a racist country?

The belief that the USA is racist is for many on the left an article of faith and, as such, impervious to evidence, for example, that Nigerians, currently numbering a little over a quarter of a million, are far and away the most successful of all recent immigrants to the USA. In the sphere where in a meritocracy it matters most, education, as of 2016, 61% of Nigerians over the age of 25 held degrees, double the rate for native-born Americans. They also out-perform native Americans in the elite professions, especially medicine and academe.

It is the same story in the no less racist UK, with Nigerians scoring 21% higher in O and A level exams than the national average. At degree level, all black university students (not just Nigerians), along with all other ethnic minorities, are over-represented in relation to their share of the total UK population, with under-performing whites again anchored firmly at the bottom. As for Asians, Indian students outperform white students at every level of the UK's educational system, with 31% going on to pursue employment in the top professions, especially medicine, engineering and the law. Indian graduates earn on average £28,500 per year compared to their white counterparts' £26,100. The employment rate of Indians between the ages of 16 and 64 is 76% ...exactly the same as whites. Average household income of Indians and whites is also exactly the same. 76% of Indian households own their own home, compared to 68% of white. Indians are far less likely to be arrested by the UK's institutionally racist police than whites, with 6.7 for every 1,000 Indians compared to 12.2 for every 1,000 whites. As of 2020, Hindus comprised 2% of the UK's population but only 0.4%, of its prisoners...under represented by a factor of five. Contrast this with Muslims, the vast majority of whom hail, like Hindus, from the sub-continent. They comprise 4% of the UK's population, but account for 16% of its prisoners...over represented by a factor of 4. Thus, a Muslim is 20 times more likely than a Hindu to end up in jail...a discrepancy that has nothing to with race or for that matter, 'institutionalised racism', but a great deal to do with culture and religion.

Finally, the UK's law makers. December 12 2019 saw the election of the most diverse Parliament and government in British history, with 14.4% of MPs from ethnic minorities...1.4% above their share of the UK population. The four highest posts in the government elected were held by Prime Minister Boris Johnson, part Turkish, Chancellor of the Exchequer Rishi Sunak, Punjabi, Home Secretary Priti Patel, Ugandan-Indian (preceded by Sajid Javid, Pakistani), and Foreign Secretary Dominic Raab, Jewish. Is all this evidence...and I could furnish if I chose so much more...proof of the UK's 'institutional' or 'systemic' racism?

How right then was Trevor Phillips, the black former Chairman of the Equalities and Human Rights Commission, to deride Black Lives Matter as 'a scam' that 'uses race as a battering ram to change society'. And so far as the UK's ethnic minorities are concerned, that change has been for the worse, stoking up racial tensions where little or none existed, just as feminazis, another branch of the same retrogressive movement, have done to relations between the sexes, with their hashtag 'kill all men'. This of course is not 'hate speech, any more than is its anti-racist (sic) analogue, 'kill all whites'. Is it any surprise that a 2018 poll suggested that only 20% of UK women now identify as 'feminist', while four times as many believe in gender equality (which man-hating feminazis have made very clear they do not)? Likewise, in an October 2020 poll, a paltry 17% disagreed with the proposition that BLM had harmed, not helped, race relations in the UK. Even more damning, the percentage for ethnic minorities, on whose behalf, supposedly, BLM's battle against racism is being waged, was only nine points higher at 25%.

Because far too few are prepared to challenge its bogus claim to represent the interests of black people, Black Lives Matter in its various manifestation is being allowed to pollute all political, intellectual and cultural life and in doing so, impede progress towards a world where race counts for nothing. Some will for sure consider this judgment more than little a little harsh, possibly even motivated by racism. So I say, let the reader draw their own conclusions as to the sincerity of those who determine the movement's policies and actions.

Metropolitan Police statistics reveal that half of all victims of London knife crime, and 44% of all its murder victims, are black, even though, according to the 2011 census, blacks make up only 13% of the city's total population. Their increase in recent years has been partly attributed to swingeing cuts in the police under successive Tory governments since 2010. Coincidentally, it so happens that one of the demands of Black Lives Matter UK is 'abolition of police' and, in in all fairness, it cannot be denied that for all their law and order rhetoric, the Conservatives have gone some considerable way towards achieving this goal, reducing front-line police in England and Wales from 140,000 in 2010 to 120,00 in 2020, office staff also by 20,000 over the same period, and community police officers from 17,000 to 10,000. In London, where black lives are most at risk, the reduction has been by a staggering 47%, most under mayor Boris Johnson. I ask the reader in all seriousness...since none of the 27,000 knife attacks on and the several hundred murders of blacks in the same period had been carried out by the police, how would BLM's policy of abolishing the police contribute in any way towards making London's black lives any more secure?

In 2020, BLM UK conducted its campaigns on the back of the death in custody of George Floyd as if police relations with blacks in the UK replicated in every detail those in the USA, even to the extent of its young (white) female demonstrators screaming 'don't shoot' at unarmed law officers. Charades such as this, one of which occurred during the attempted storming of Downing Street in response to a police killing 3,000 miles away, happened because BLM UK saw itself as a clone of its more glamourous US parent and mentor, as if the history, politics and racial anatomy of the two countries were identical, seemingly unaware that unlike the USA, slavery (as distinct from the slave trade) has never had any legal foundation in Britain, any more, again unlike the USA, than has discrimination against any race. Sasha Johnson of Oxford BLM even took this imitation to the point of wearing a Black Panther uniform, complete with beret, affecting a rather unconvincing American gangster drawl, calling for a 'black militia' such as she must have seen images of parading in the USA armed with sub-machine guns, describing a black man who disagreed with her a 'coon' and promising to personally give him a beating. Perhaps with her macho posturings she saw herself as the UK incarnation of the black American gun-running ultra-Stalinist and BDS campaigner Angela Davis. The fantasy became all too real when she was seriously wounded after being shot in what some believed to have been a Chicago South Side-style gangland shootout, at a garden party in south

London on May 23, 2021. (A man was also wounded in the foot by a gun-shot.) Initial claims that the shooting was politically motivated were not endorsed by a friend of Johnson's, who told the BBC, 'The incident is more related to rival gangs as opposed to her activism.' Confirmation of this came when police (whom BLM want to abolish) were reported to be looking for 'four black men' in connection with the incident. A month later, four men were charged with conspiracy to murder a person or persons not named. Let me say this very clearly: For all my many political differences with Johnson, and criticisms of the manner with which she promotes her cause, unlike some depraved white racists, I am glad that she survived the shooting. The UK, and the west generally, needs to have a free and open debate on the race question, and BLM, in its various manifestations, is part of that debate no less than those like myself who see its policies and tactics as largely counter-productive and based on false claims. As I have said repeatedly in this work, I defend the right of anyone to express their political or religious beliefs publicly, just I do the right of others to criticise those beliefs in any manner or medium they choose. Also unlike some I could name (starting with Patrisse Cullors) I do not doubt the sincerity of Johnson's anti-racism, though I profoundly disagree with her methods of furthering it.

That being said, she is still young, and like anyone of her age, has a lot to learn, not least perhaps being more selective about some of the company she keeps. As for her politics, let us hope that the experience of being the (unintended) victim of an attempted black on black murder will persuade her that this is an issue that can no longer be ignored or denied by those who say that black lives matter. The fact that shortly before the shooting incident, she conducted a civilized exchange of views with the supposedly 'far-right racist' Tommy Robinson (it can be seen on YouTube) and distanced herself from of some the policies of BLM that Robinson and a black friend criticized, such as the abolition of the police and the nuclear family, suggests that she might well do so. To that end, I would like her and her movement to consider the following: For the two years between March 2018 and March 2020, Home Office statistics for homicide in England and Wales record that of 886 persons convicted for murder in that period, 180 were classified as black, 21% of the total. Yet blacks make up only 3.4% of the population of England and Wales, therefore being over-represented as murderers by a factor of six. Of the 124 black murder victims, *99 were murdered by other blacks*, 80% of the total, while the number of blacks killed by the 'institutionally' and 'systemically' racist police in the same period was…zero.

In the 11 years between 2008 and 2018, according to Metropolitan Police statistics, there were 133,918 victims of knife attacks in the capital, 31,317 of them black, 23% of the total. Those charged with (but not necessarily convicted of) knife crime numbered 3,486, of whom *nearly half*, 1,452, were black. But only 13% of London's population is black. So again, blacks are hugely over-represented in this category of crime, by a factor of a little under 4. Here we have, in part at least, the answer to why blacks are also over-represented in the UK's prison system by a factor of 3. Black Lives Matter attributes these racial discrepancies solely to 'institutional racism', as does its counterpart in the USA. It also shares its belief that the solution is the abolition or 'defunding' of the police and the closing of the prisons and law courts, with the inevitable but it would seem, unforeseen consequence that these measures would leave un-punished, or release onto the streets, perpetrators of murders, including of blacks, and racist and sexual crimes. Less radical solutions that could be adopted either singly or in combination are 1) When passing custodial sentences for the same crime, judges could reduce the jail time for blacks, or recommend that they receive earlier remission than the statutory norm. 2) Crimes that normally carry a prison sentence could, again at the judge's discretion, for blacks be replaced by a non-custodial penalty. 3) Each police authority could be set a racial quota of arrests that corresponds with the ethnic composition of the population in its jurisdiction. If the quota for black arrests is reached before the end of a given period, say a year, no further arrests of blacks will be made in the remainder of that year. (Since her election in 2016, black Cook County District Attorney Kim Foxx has pursued a policy known as 'prison reform', wokespeak for going soft on black crime. In the first three years of office, she dropped all charges against 30% of felony defendants, 8.1% of which were homicide case, compared with 19% dropped under her predecessor, of which 5.3% were homicides. By November 2019, Foxx had dismissed 25,000 felony cases, the most famous being that of black TV actor Jussie Smollett, who after staging a racist attacked on himself in Chicago by two masked black associates wearing MAGA caps, was charged with filing a false police report. Foxx then had all charges dropped, and the public court file containing the evidence against Smollett sealed. This transparent attempt to protect Smollett failed, when three years later, he was found guilty in a Chicago court on five of six felony counts of falsely reporting a hate crime.)

Human nature being what it is, I suspect that each of the above proposals would result in blacks committing more crime, just as they would for any other racial group so favored. While they would certainly have the effect of reducing the UK's black prison population, in doing so, they would also violate a long held and cherished legal principle that all should be equal before and under the law. That is why I propose a remedy consistent with that principle, which is for blacks to commit less crime.

Why is there a taboo against discussing these admittedly difficult issues? Instead, we had a tweeted comment on the Johnson shooting by Corbynista Labour MP Dianne Abbott, which strongly implied that the gunman who shot Johnson had a racist motive, and was therefore almost certainly white, despite witnesses to the shooting saying the gunman was black: 'Black activist Sasha Johnson in hospital in critical condition after sustaining a gunshot wound to the head. No-one should have to potentially pay with their life because they stood up or racial justice'. And no-one, least of all an MP, should make such a public and potentially inflammatory comment without first being fully informed of the facts, especially after a police spokesman called on the public to 'avoid speculating as to the motives [behind the shooting]'. In the interest of racial harmony, she would have been well-advised to wait for an official police statement on the incident, which said 'Around 3.00 am a group of four black males dressed in dark clothing entered the garden of the property and discharged a firearm. They left the scene before officers arrived.' Social activist Lin Mei did wait, and only then tweeted: 'Sasha Johnson was shot by people in our own community. Will we be out on the streets like we were when police do the same? An activist who stands up for black people, to the point of putting down white people, but it was her own people that shot her. Community: Silence.' This included the silence of Abbott, who quickly lost interest in the case once it became clear that Johnson had not been the victim of a race crime, proving yet again that black lives matter only when they 'fit the narrative'.

Two weeks later, police investigating the shooting revealed that none of the forty or so friends and comrades present at the party had come forward as a witness to the incident. Was this out of fear...or a 'closing of black ranks'? Possibly both, but certainly the second. Blacks comprise by far the largest ethnic minority in London. Yet despite it being headline news for days, none of their 1.1 million raised so much as a whisper of protest at the shooting of a young mother of two children who has devoted herself to campaigning on their behalf. Evidently her life stopped mattering when the finger on the trigger proved not to be white.

Among the policies of the party Johnson launched in 2020 [the 'Taking the Initiative Party' – TTIP] was a register recording the names of all those deemed to be guilty of racism as defined by the ubiquitous critical race theory, which includes the use of 'trigger words' that unintentionally induce trauma, and involuntary 'micro-aggressions' only visible or audible to the theory's exponents. Johnson's calling a black man a 'coon' does not qualify as racist because, again according to critical race theory, since racism is about power relationships, and the white patriarchy has all the power (but surely not in 'black' Africa and all of Asia) only white men can be and are racist. Q.E.D. Those (white only) persons so listed on her proposed register would lose a number of their legal rights, which would include being barred from living with or near non-whites, and from occupations that could bring them into contact with members of ethnic minorities - a reverse apartheid. I await the first election her party contests with interest.

Black Lives Matter UK feeds not only on its young white activists' obsession with 'virtue signalling', but on their political naivety, in the first place, the illusion that Britain is in matters racial and policing identical to the USA. Yet while they behave as if they believe, wrongly, that in the USA, most blacks who meet a violent death (yearly around 10,000) are, like George Floyd, killed by the police, even the most ill-informed about US affairs must surely be aware that in the UK, the yearly total not of blacks but of all those killed by the police is always in single figures, and usually low ones at that. The happy co-existence of such flagrantly contradictory beliefs, and the fervour of those that believe in them, are proof that as Sam Harris has said, what passes for anti-racism today is essentially a religious movement, impervious, like all others, to evidence and logical argument. How many of those screaming at the gates of Downing Street for the blood of British politicians, in revenge for a still to be legally proved crime committed in another continent, were aware that in a number of ways that bear upon the race question, the USA and the UK are not remotely comparable? The fantasy world inhabited by their US counterparts was revealed by a survey conducted after the death of George Floyd. 17% of those who defined themselves as on the left believed that the number of un-armed, repeat, un-armed blacks killed by police in 2019 was 10,000 or more, and 29% that it was about 1,000. *The actual number was 17.* The number of blacks killed by police in the same year was 259, all but 17 of whom would have been armed. In the same year, 2019, the number of blacks killed by other than police, and of whom the identity was known (roughly one third of all black homicides) was 2,906, of whom 2,754, 80%, were killed by other blacks, and whose lives therefore did not matter.

If we take the total number of black homicide victims in the year 2020, 9,913, approximately 90% of which, as in each year, were murdered by other blacks, and compare that number to the number of blacks killed by police, lawfully or otherwise, 192, we have a ratio of 52 to 1. This ratio changed drastically in 2021, approaching 100 to 1, when with officers backing off and police authorities in Democratic cities subject to defunding, police killings of blacks fell to 131, while the number of black homicides, not surprisingly, increased to well over 10,000. To get a clearer picture of the growing scale of black-on-black murder in the USA since the killing of George Floyd, it can be seen in microcosm in one small area with an overwhelmingly black population, the 15th Ward of New Orleans, Algeria. It has a population of 26,000, 90% of whom are black. In 2019, there were 118 homicides, one per *220* of the population, far and away above the national rate of 5 per *100,000*. In the year of Floyd, this number soared to 190, and in 2021, reached 217, an increase of 84% in two years. On a much larger scale, we see the same trend in St Louis, population 302,000, 43% of whom are black, compared to a national percentage of 12. In the year of Floyd, the murder rate reached its highest level ever, with 263 homicides, compared to 73 in 2003, when the city's population was 50,000 greater. The black-on-black carnage reached such a scale that St Louis was not only rated the most dangerous city in the USA, at 66 homicides per 100,000, compared to the national rate of 5, *but 13th in the world.* New Hampshire, with a black population of 2.5%, has a murder rate of less than one per 100,000.

Taking a broader view, in 2021, with three weeks to go before the end of the year, 12 Democrat-run cities, with some operating the BLM policy of defunding the police and 'reforming' the justice system, broke their records for homicides, with Philadelphia leading the way with 521 murders, surpassing that in the much more populous cities of New York (443) and Los Angeles (352). This can partly be explained by Philadelphia's demographic, 44.1% black and only 35.8 white. It is of course not politic to say this, but it is still nevertheless the case that not only in Philadelphia but in nearly every urban area, there is a strong co-relation between the murder rate and the percentage of its population who are black. And what is more, the impact of BLM's campaigns against the police have accentuated this trend, with police cut backs and courts granting bail to black murder suspects emboldening criminal black gangs to step up their fratricidal turf wars.

According to on-line FBI data, in 2019, of the 11,495 perpetrators of homicide whose racial identity was known, those who were identified as black totalled 6,425, 64%. But this is only part of the picture. Females accounted for only 9% of all perpetrators, meaning that around 90% of murderers were males. So we are looking primarily not at the 12% of the US population who are black, but the 6 % who are black males. Then we have age. Those murderers who were black were considerably younger than those who were white; of those aged from 13 to 16, 165 were white, 260 black, from 17 to 19, 492 and 891, 20 to 24, 790 and 1441. From then on, the age-related murder rate begins to even out. Insofar as we are allowed to talk about a 'black crime' issue, (and there are black commentators who are far more ready to do so than white ones) it is primarily one of young black males killing mainly those of an identical demographic. Wokistas will say this is 'stereotyping' or 'profiling'. If so, so is saying that murder in general is primarily an adult male issue, a proposition which all feminists would endorse without any risk of being accused of either sexism or ageism.

The statistics I have cited, and others that tell the same story, are crying out for serious, objective debate, though out of fear of being accused of racism, few public figures are preprepared to engage in one, with those on the left preferring instead the easy options of virtue-signaling and parroting the white-blaming hocus pocus of critical race theory. No doubt many do so with honorable intentions, but with consequences that are the direct opposite of those they seek. By propagating the lie that the US constitution and justice system exist only to hold down and exploit blacks, and decrying the subjects and teaching methods of the US educational system as so many means of indoctrinating blacks in 'white' 'ways of knowing', leftist academics have legitimised, even glorified the anti-social and criminal behavior of what in the vernacular is known as the 'bad-assed mother fucker', and in white speak, a black 'noble savage'. The result is increasing black failure and violence in the schools, and more black corpses on the streets. (According to Wikipedia, Chicago has at least 60 street gangs and more than 100,000 active gang members, who between them are responsible for 60% of all the city's homicides.) 'And 'black lives matter'?

The data I have cited is readily available, so it is inexcusable that Democratic politicians, many of whom represent cities where violent black crime is out of control, should make public statements that ignore the tragic consequences of black-on-black murder, while grossly misrepresenting the relationship between police and the USA's black population. Take for example Joe Biden's ludicrous comment in June 2020 that black children must be taught to tolerate police abuse so that they can 'make it back home', and Obama's, with his in 2016 that black parents were right to fear that their children would be killed by police every time they go outside. According to the pro-Democrat *Washington Post* of April 16, 2021, a total of 22 children (not just black children) under the age of 16 had been fatally shot by police since 2015, three accidentally. Of the remaining 19, eight of those killed were armed, another four were armed with knives and three were holding toy guns...an average of four a year. So, not exactly the massacre conjured up by Biden and Obama, and not remotely comparable to the 3,410 children killed and 18,227 wounded by non-police gun violence in just one year, 2017, with 41% of the fatalities being black children, most caught in crossfire by rival black gangs.)

Let me pose a number questions to UK BLM activists: How many know the following:

That those defined as 'black' comprise only 3% of the UK population, compared to 12% in the USA?

That the number of *legally* owned firearms in the USA is 393 million, some of them semi-automatics 60 million in excess of the US population, while the number in the UK is approximately 600,000 shotguns and 10,0000 firearms, roughly 1% of the UK population?

That the USA murder rate is 5.30 per 100,000 persons, compared to the UK's 1.20? (in Jeremy's socialist dystopia, Venezuela, it is the world's third highest, at 56.30 per 100,000)

That at 330 million, the USA population is five times greater than the UK's?

That while there are no laws in the USA which discriminate adversely against blacks, and have not been since they were made illegal in 1965, there are laws which favour them?

That US blacks are seven times as likely to commit murder as whites because blacks, who make up 12% of the US population, in a typical year, 2018, committed 155 more murders, 3,177, 48.4% of the total, 6570, than whites and Latinos, 3011, who constitute 85% of the population? (Again, this relates to homicides whose perpetrators are known)

That a number of studies by both black and white academics show that in the USA, unarmed blacks, again like George Floyd, are significantly less likely to be killed by police than unarmed whites?

That when it comes to so-called 'hate crimes' ('hate speech' is protected by the First Amendment; to be such, a 'hate crime' must be accompanied by the committing of an already existing crime such as assault) according to FBI data for 2018, a black person was less likely to a victim of this offence, 5.5 per 100,000, than a Muslim, 6.6, and a Jew, 14.8 per 100,000?

Given that racism is encountered among all sectors of the US population, albeit in various proportions and degrees of virulence, only an idiot would deny there are racists among its police. With a total force of 700,000, two thirds of them white, how could there not be? But the claim on a poster held aloft by a (white) BLM activist that there are 'no good cops in a racist system' is absurd, no less so than the BLM criminal-friendly demand to 'abolish the police'. What needs to be done is not abolish the police, but improve their training and pay, and root out the bad ones. Of course, due to a failure of leadership, individual forces can be infected by racism, leading to excessive or unwarranted force such as that used on some occasions against (mainly white be it said) BLM demonstrators. Commentators contrasted such behaviour with that of police officers charged with guarding the Washington Capitol on January 6, 2021, when some patently offered no effective resistance to an invasion by white Trumpists bent on preventing the confirmation of Biden as winner of the 2020 presidential election. Once again, left and right converged. The next day in New York, BLM marchers, instead of calling for the disciplining of these officers and the beefing up of security against Trumpist law-breakers, held aloft a banner demanding 'Disarm, Defund, Abolish [the police]'. Had that demand been in operation at the Capitol on January 6, Trump's attempted coup would at the very least have ensured there would have been no certification of Biden's victory, and possibly even unleashed a massacre of politicians who had been vocal in their support of BLM following the killing of George Floyd in May 2020.

Ironically, in the summer of 2020, some of the police BLM want to abolish colluded with law-breakers on a far greater scale than on January 6, 2021 in cities across the USA, 'taking the knee' and standing by as BLM activists pulled down statues, looted shops, burned cars and buildings, assaulted and killed by-standers, vandalized property, attacked synagogues and besieged state and federal institutions in what Sam Harris has called a 'sickening eruption of criminality'. (In justifying BLM thuggery, CNN's Chris Cuomo also demonstrated his ignorance of his country's constitution, when he asked, rhetorically, 'show me where it says protestors are supposed to be polite and peaceful.') Yet for all the talk of racist, trigger-happy police, none of the 25 deaths that occurred during these demonstrations were caused by police action, though several were by BLM activists. But an insurrectionist white female Trumpist was shot dead by a white policeman on January 6, and a white police officer was killed by white Trumpists. 'Abolish the police'? At the very moment when US democracy was under siege from white supremacists mobilised by Trump, just whose side were BLM on?

Those who argue that the over-representation of blacks killed by police is proof of a nation-wide police *systemic* racism (like many others in large cities across the USA, the current Superintendent of the Chicago police is black, as is the city's Mayor), that it is a result of a deliberate policy, need to explain why this is not reflected in recruitment, since the percentage of black police is slightly more than their share of the population, 12%, just as it is slightly less so for whites, 66%. One could, using the same argument, claim that a much larger over-representation of men as compared with women killed by police - twenty to one - is proof of 'systemic misandry', or the existence of a matriarchal conspiracy. Research has proved - as one would have expected - those police killings almost always occur in the course of a confrontation between an officer or officers and a suspect or suspects either known or with good reason suspected to be armed. And given that the number of just *legally* owned firearm in the USA is a good three times more than the adult male population, this would be a reasonable assumption. Since men and blacks are over-represented in violent crime statistics, one would therefore also expect that disproportion to be reflected, albeit not exactly, in statistics related to police killings...and so it is. In 2020, 192 blacks were killed by police out of total of 1038 – some 20% of all police killings. Since blacks are 12% of the US population, so the argument goes, this is proof positive of a significant police racial bias...by a factor of 1.6. And so it would be, but for the fact that the black share of violent crimes ranges, depending on the crime, from 2 to 4 times their share of the population. In 2017, *53%* of all murders and non-negligent manslaughters, 28.7 of rapes, 33% of aggravated assaults, and all violent crimes, 37.5%, were committed by blacks. This last percentage is almost exactly equal to the percentage of blacks in US prisons in the same year... 37.3, hardly evidence of 'institutional racism' in the US justice system. The remedy for the excess of black prisoners is not to abolish the police and prisons, as proposed by BLM, or to jail fewer black criminals and let the rest go free to commit more crime, but for blacks to commit less crime. And like Obama, Denzel Washington says just this, that black crime 'starts in the home. If the father's not in the home, the boy will find his father in the streets.'

But blacks are not alone in this. The same FBI statistics show that men are far more likely to kill than are women, with the same consequences as for blacks compared to whites...police are more likely to kill men than women. There were 5713 homicides committed by men in 2018, but only 705 by women, eight times more, while in the same year, police killed 940 men, and only 45 women, 20 times more. Yet no-one talks about a gender bias in police killings, or one of age, even though most police killings are of those ranging in age from the late teens to mid-thirties, because it is this age group that is responsible for most violent crimes, including homicide. Only when it comes to race, where the same applies, with blacks committing on average 50% of all homicides, are there claims of bias in police killings. Focusing exclusively on racism leads to the ignoring of what is the most effective means of reducing the number of blacks killed by police and in prison, *which is to reduce the black crime rate*, a solution that requires radical changes in black culture of the kind indicated by Obama and Coleman Hughes (see below).

412

White supremacists will also see the 'black question' as a race question, one of genes, that blacks are racially inferior, a claim impossible to reconcile with their achievements at the very highest level and in every field of American society, from Jessie Owens and Joe Louis, both of whom in their own ways refuted Nazi race theory, Owens by winning four gold medals at the 1936 Berlin Olympics as Hitler and his party elite looked on aghast, and Louis by knocking out in the first round and hospitalising for ten days German World Heavyweight contender Max Schmeling (who was not a racist and had a Jewish manager, Joe Jacobs), to two of the most gifted, accomplished, innovative and influential musicians of the 20th century, Louis Armstrong and Charlie Parker, both of whom were born into and grew up in poverty and segregation. They and the mainly black musicians they inspired not only re-discovered the lost art of improvisation that once flourished in the baroque and early classical eras. They raised it to unprecedented levels of creativity and technical prowess, setting in train a revolution in music no less radical and enriching in its consequences than that of Beethoven and Wagner, and no less universal.

To master his instrument and the elements of what the new 'official science' describes as 'white' musical theory, Parker practised 15 hours a day for three years. Armstrong was abandoned by his father, and with his teen-age mother unable to cope, for a while lived with his grandmother. When seven, he did odd jobs for a Jewish family. He quicky became aware that they too suffered from racial prejudice: 'I was only seven years old, but I could easily see the ungodly treatment that the white folks were handing the poor Jewish family I worked for.' They taught him, he recalled, 'how to live – real life and determination.' They also bought him his first instrument, a cornet. As a mark of respect and gratitude, he wore a star of David pendent for the rest of his life…again, like Jesus's Zionism, hardly likely to endear his memory to the anti-Zionists of BLM. Instead of feeding young American blacks with alibis for failure, glorifying victimhood and sanctifying George Floyd, I would tell them the inspiring life stories of Owens, Louis, Parker and Armstrong, each one a child of Jim Crow, but each life story one of triumph over adversities that today's young blacks can have little conception of, and those like myself, none at all.

Ironically, Wokistas, like white supremacists, also see the black issue as a race question, only a white one, attributing it entirely to the legacy of slavery, Jim Crow and the continued domination of the white patriarchy. If this is true, how then account for the well-documented spectacular success of recent black immigrants to the USA from Nigeria and the West Indies, whose ancestors also experienced the humiliations and deprivations of white colonial rule and in the case of West Indians, also slavery? And surely they too will have been exposed to the same prejudices as native black Americans. I, along with a growing number of black academics, and a much smaller number of white commentators such as Sam Harris, while not denying the historical dimensions to the USA's black question, (which, with the passing of time, must become less important) place most emphasis not on race as such but on culture, which has nothing to with genes, but is about those elements in our lives that are the product of the interaction of the entire inheritance of the past with the present… material factors such climate, topography, technology, and those that are intellectual/ideological…literacy, numeracy, the arts, politics, religion etc. Our particular interest is in those elements of the black sub-culture that breed crime, self-segregation and under-achievement, and in what ways they can be surmounted. One obvious factor is the decline of the black nuclear family (the stated goal of Black Lives Matter, not only in the USA but in the UK, is its *abolition*), from 75 % to 35% over the last 50 or so years. In 1990, the number of fatherless black families was 3.4 million. By 2019, it had risen to 4.1 million. One of the results is that a boy from a black fatherless family will be 20 times more likely to end up in jail than a black boy from a family with a father…that is, if he is not killed first in a drugs gang turf war. I find it both extraordinary and deplorable that the two of BLM's objectives which will drag down young blacks even further into a life…and death… of crime – fatherless families and abolition of the police – have escaped criticism by all but a handful of public figures.

Another consequence of absentee fathers is that with black mothers having their hands full raising a (BLM-approved) non-nuclear family single-handed, their children will spend more time than any other ethnic group unsupervised, taking to the street, or watching television, and therefore less on homework and other activities that will raise their cultural level. In a speech delivered on Father's Day, 2008, none other than Barak Obama spoke of the damage done by the absence of black fathers. 'They have abandoned their responsibilities, acting like boys instead of men. And the foundations of our families are weaker because of it.' He continued, not for one moment, I am sure, expecting that such home truths could have him condemned as a stooge of the white patriarchy: 'We know that more than half of all black children live in single-parent households – a number that has doubled - doubled since we were children. We know the statistics – [now, 'white maths'] that children who grow up without a father are five times more likely to live in poverty and commit crime; nine times more likely to drop out of schools and 20 times more likely to end up in prison…We need fathers to realise that responsibility does not end at conception. We need them to realise that what makes a man is not the ability to have a child – it's the courage to raise one.' And it took some courage to say it. Because it seems that rather than telling black fathers what they badly needed to hear, according to *Washington Post* black columnist Mychal Smith, Obama was playing the coon or Uncle Tom by 'focusing on the supposed [sic…at the beginning of his article, he cites Obama's statistics proving that it was all too real] absence of black fathers', while ignoring 'institutionalised [that is, white] oppression'. So, the message should be, if not stated in so many words, stop blaming ourselves, and focus instead on problems that can only be attributed to the white man.

But let us look more closely at the issue raised by Obama…absentee fathers…that Smith wanted his readers to ignore, since it is a life-style choice freely made by black men, and not a result of white racism. As stated, in 2020, 65% of black families in the USA were fatherless. First, compare this figure with the percentage of fatherless Asian families in the USA…15%. Now compare some other percentages which, Obama argued, were closely related to the first. Blacks, who constitute 12% of the US population, account for around 50% of all US homicides, while Asians, who comprise 6% of the US population, account for only 1.4%. Blacks are therefore over-represented by a factor of four, Asians under-represented by a factor of five. So, a black person is 20 times more likely to commit homicide than an Asian, just as he or she is for that reason to be far more likely to be killed by the police. In fact the percentage of Asians killed by police is so small it does not even show up on FBI annual statistics.

414

And then we have the observation made by Coleman Hughes, that in the USA, Asian children watch the least TV, black children, the most, this being one of the several reasons why blacks are at the bottom of the educational ladder, while Chinese are at the top. So much so in fact that as they once did to the children of impoverished Jewish immigrants, Ivy League universities have colluded in adopting an unofficial *numerus clausus* to keep their numbers down (16% of admissions whereas on merit it should be 40%), only this time not to make room for the not so industrious offspring of prosperous Wasps, but less qualified 'affirmative action' black students...the so-called 'bamboo ceiling'. (It is a sign of our times that when a Chinese student challenged Harvard's racially discriminative policy in a court of law, he received no backing from the warriors for social justice. He lost the case, suggesting that some minorities are considered more ethnic than others)

In the academic year 2011-12, only 57% of black school pupils had the maths and science qualifications required for college entrance, compared with 71% for white pupils, and 81% for Asian. Is this all down to 'systemic racism' as Smith would have his readers believe, or at the very least, also due to watching too much TV and having no dad to make sure his son does his homework, and to check up on his progress at school parents evenings? The 'racialisation' (specifically 'Africanisation') of subject curricula and teaching methods, and a more general dumbing down of the educational ethos such as has been proposed and, in some cases, implemented in black neighbourhoods by Democratic Party-controlled school boards and teachers unions, will not equip black children for a successful and rewarding life in a high tech 21st century superpower. Such schools certainly need more funding, but not academic racial engineering.

With these facts in mind, anyone should be able to see that white-blaming has done and will do nothing to solve the problems that are preventing millions of young American blacks from fulfilling their potential. It has made some of them more difficult – providing not practical solutions, but instead implanting in young blacks contempt for 'white' learning, feeding racist, often violent rage, and even justifying organized looting as 'reparations' for a slavery that ended a nearly century and half before they were born, while middle class guilt-ridden whites perform rituals such as Catholic-style confessions of 'white privilege', knee-taking, collective grovelling before standing blacks (I have seen this on YouTube), mutual and self-flagellation and breast-beating. Worst of all, BLM has generated among blacks the cult of an ennobling but also fatalistic victimhood.

Yet despite this Manichean orgy - all whites bad, all blacks good - unleashed by Black Lives Matter, the fact remains that there are no laws in the USA which, as they once did, discriminate against blacks. On the contrary there are laws passed by mainly white legislators and upheld by no less white courts which offer them preferential treatment in education and employment, a policy which by lowering expectations for black students, some black academics argue has done more harm than good for those they were intended to benefit.

I say Manichean with justification. In December 2020, the (Democratic) Mayor of Boston ordered the pulling down of his city's statute of Lincoln, holding his Emancipation decree in one hand, and of a liberated slave he is reaching across to with the other. (The statue and its message closely resembles the one outside the Trades Union Congress headquarter in London.) Despite the statue having stood since *1876* without anyone noticing anything amiss, Mayor Marty Walsh said it had to be removed 'because of its reductive [sic] representation of the black man's [sic - only 'black *men*'? - this is surely 'reductive' of black women] role in the abolitionist movement.' One commentator even described it as 'a monument to white supremacy'. As was said in the realm of Big Brother, 'freedom is slavery'. US press reports described the former slave as 'kneeling' before Lincoln as if he was submitting to him like a slave, (videoed mass white knee-taking to standing blacks is a different matter entirely) whereas, with only one knee on the ground he is depicted rising. He is not looking down in submission but upwards in hope, as he rises. Otherwise, why the statue?

What all the reports on this outrage failed to mention was that the Boston statue is an exact copy of the original by Thomas Ball, which stands in the Lincoln Park, Washington D.C. The Wikipedia entry, obviously not up to speed on critical race theory, shares my take on its message: 'The ex-slave is depicted on one knee, *about to stand up*, with one fist clenched, shirtless, and broken shackles at the President's feet.' (emphasis added) And whatever critical race historians might say, it was Lincoln more than anyone else, black or white, who by defeating the slavers of the south, had actually made it possible for him, like the rest of America's emancipated slaves, to stand erect on his feet. But BLM history prevailed over truth, so down came the Boston statue, despite the certainty that without Lincoln's waging war on the Confederacy, emancipation would have been delayed for decades and the former slave of the statue, freed by Lincoln's decree, would still be on both his knees to his master.

Who would have believed that all it would take to posthumously enrol Abraham Lincoln in the ranks of the KKK would be the police killing of a black man in Minneapolis in May 2020? The lesson of this truly revolting episode is that no matter what white men like Lincoln did and however well intentioned, it will never be enough, and in what they did do and whatever their motives for doing it, fatal flaws in their character and unforgivable faults in their deeds will always be found and used to discredit or cancel out their contributions to human progress. So after Boston, next stop, Lincoln Park, then Mount Rushmore…but it will need dynamite…and finally, to crown this campaign to cast into the BLM memory hole one of the greatest political achievements in the history not only of the United States, but all humanity, must come the erasing of the words inscribed on a Washington Capitol desecrated and vandalised by Trumpist insurgents: 'In this temple as in the hearts of the people for whom he saved the union the memory of Abraham Lincoln is enshrined for ever.' But that's if Confederate-flag waving white supremacist Trumpists don't beat them to it.

With George Floyd, another historic fiction has been concocted, again by Black Lives Matter. It is a totally different though no less instructive story. Just as there are no good whites so there are no bad blacks…excepting of course race-traitor 'coons' and 'Uncle Toms' who disagree with this proposition, like Obama for example, and Coleman Hughes. Drug addict Floyd left behind him a trail of five children he was never a proper father to, and for much of his adult life, spent it as what more than one black commentator has described as a small-time career criminal, with a string of convictions and jail terms numbering eight in all. His last offence, for which, after a plea bargain, he received five years, was for his involvement in an armed house robbery in which he held a loaded gun against a pregnant woman's stomach…hardly Oprah Winfrey's 'gentle giant'. He was not killed, like Lincoln, in or for his pursuit of a noble cause, but by four policemen, illegally though not deliberately, after being apprehended for reportedly passing a forged banknote at a shop. Yet it is Floyd who has acquired the status of semi-sainthood as an anti-racist martyr, and Lincoln, assassinated on April 14, 1865, by John Wilkes Booth in revenge for the north's victory over the slave states, one of a white supremacist.

Like all worthwhile historic progress, as Marx said of the proletariat's, those of America's blacks can only and therefore must come ultimately from within, by their own efforts, and not via the begging bowl. And as it has in the past, it will continue to come, not overnight, but in stages. According to Marx's schema, Labours' great advance had to await the victory of the bourgeoisie over feudalism, a struggle in which it could only play, like the slaves in the north's against the Confederacy, a supplementary, subordinate role. As Lincoln's great achievement was to abolish slavery (comparable to the European bourgeoisie's overthrow of feudalism), so King's a century later, by mobilizing impoverished, segregated and disenfranchised blacks, was to secure the legal and constitutional foundation necessary for their further advancement, with the enactment by Congress of the civil rights acts of 1964-5. What Obama was advocating in his Fathers' Day speech was for blacks to build on that foundation by self-reform of their own culture, not, as BLM does, by idealizing and justifying its most retrogressive features. To argue otherwise is to condemn millions of blacks to decades more self-ghettoisation, criminality, turf wars, drug addiction, and educational under-achievement, demeaning them as incapable of self-help by fostering instead a culture of dependency that places their fates in the hands of a mythical and incurably racist white patriarchy. Because this is what, for all the white virtue signalling, iconoclasm, looting, vandalism, armed militia parading, pitched battles with the police and street violence, BLM policies and tactics amount to.

To further compound the problem, many Democratic politicians, white as well as black, seeing blacks as voting fodder, would rather maintain their state of dependency than address such issues as those raised by Obama and black academics like Coleman Hughes, an outspoken critic of Black Lives Matter, and a registered Independent who votes Democrat. He, like Obama, has listed some of the 'life style' choices that he believes contribute to under-performance of many of the USA's native blacks. One he has highlighted is that on average, black women spend more on cars, clothes and jewellery than do white women, and therefore have less to allocate to savings and cultural and educational items that will benefit their children. As these choices cannot plausibly be blamed on the white patriarchy or the police, but can only be altered by those who make them, critical race theorists like Mychel Smith either deny their significance, ignore them, or accuse those who do not of racism. Again, the same Manicheanism: blacks as eternally innocent victims of wicked whites. Two black academics see the now *de rigueur* white (self) blaming as a perverse form of white paternalism, analysed by Jason Riley, in his book, *Please Stop Helping Us,* and Shelby Steel in his *White Guilt.* If we ignore the vacuous, non-evidenced flim flam, what critical race theory boils down to is not a solution to, but an alibi for black failure.

And what of the UK police's 'systemic racism', supposedly as endemic as that of the USA's? How many BLM activists know that in the UK between 2010 and 2020, blacks were 25% less likely to die in custody than whites? That all fatalities caused by police shootings in the USA in 2019 numbered 1,004, in the UK, three, none of which were of blacks, and one, of a Muslim terrorist who had stabbed five people? That the number of US police officers killed 'in the line of duty' in 2020 was 296, while in the UK, it was one, again, by a Muslim terrorist? That the UK, except for Northern Ireland, is one of 17 of the world's 193 nations whose police, unlike in the USA, do not routinely carry firearms? Yet play-acting young white women, perhaps needing a buzz from a simulated sensation of danger as well as from signalling their virtue, were hysterically screeching 'don't shoot'. (Indulging in the same fantasy, some young 'street' blacks in the UK refer to the police as 'the feds'.) I could cite many more statistics than those above, all pointing to the same two conclusions, that US society is violent in ways that the UK, at least until Allah burst upon the scene, is not; and that the race issue in the USA has from its very beginnings, shaped its political life in ways that in the UK, at least until Black Lives Matter imposed its racially divisive agenda, was played by class.

In the USA, more often than not, race and violence have worked in tandem so to speak, first against America's indigenous peoples, then its imported slaves. In the eras of slavery and then Jim Crow, it was exclusively a matter of white violence, inflicted both by the state and civilians (as with the KKK) on blacks. Today, the statistics are telling a different story. Although police and (criminal) white on black violence - and we are talking here about lethal violence - continues, by far the greater proportion of blacks are killed by other blacks, annually around 90%.. Bearing in mind again that only one third of black homicides are recorded by the FBI, because the other two-thirds that do not come to court, mainly for lack of witnesses (mainly out fear or a perverted sense of 'black solidarity'), in 2019 there were 2,925 black victims of civilian homicide, 2,600 of whom were killed by other blacks and 234 by whites. (more than twice as many whites - 524 - were killed by blacks) Blacks killed by police in the same year numbered 209. So, adding together police (some of whom would not have been white) and white killings of blacks, we have a total of 443. These numbers vary only marginally over the years, meaning that a black person in the USA today is at the very least *six times* more likely to be killed by another black civilian than a police officer or a white civilian. Yet the only killings of blacks BLM demonstrates against are those committed by the police - one 15th of the total of all black fatalities, 3134. As for the rest, 2,925, their lives seem not to matter, any more than does the freedom of black slaves in Africa, estimated in 2017 by the International Labour Organisation (yet another white patriarchal institution) as 7.1 million.

I have been advised by Paul Bridges of Amnesty International that statistics can be made to 'prove almost anything' (see Addendum). In that case, I would like to see it demonstrated, without invoking 'critical race theory' objections to 'white maths', how the FBI statistics I have cited can be made to prove that the black population of the USA is today the victim of 'systemic' white racist violence, as indeed it once was under slavery and Jim Crow.

Although one might assume it from the slogans and activities of Black Lives Matter, Social Justice Warriors and Antifa, and those disheartened Corbynistas searching for and finding pastures new in their company, racism is not exclusively a preserve of whites. Not only 'western', but all societies have their racists, although to be sure, in widely varying proportions of their total populations, as do all races, though many self-proclaimed anti-racists deny this...itself a racist assumption, as if the brains of certain peoples are incapable of having racist thoughts. If so, how then explain the Turkish genocide of the Armenians, the Hutu 'tribalcide' of Tutsis in Rwanda, the Arab genocide of the black Darfuris in Sudan, and the eviscerating hatred of millions of Arabs for Jews, and of some Israeli Jews for Arabs? Yet for all that, we can read articles explicitly inspired by 'critical race theory', like Luke Visconti's, headed by a huge Black Lives Matter banner, proclaiming that 'black people can't be racist', and by 'Marley K', insisting that 'all whites are racist'. Maybe one day far in the future, historians will be puzzling over how it came about that in the land of Yale, Harvard and Princeton, this racist nonsense became the new orthodoxy on countless US campuses. And that in the same land of the First Amendment, woe betided anyone, student or staff, who openly dissented from it.

How is a 'racist society' to be defined? By a certain percentage of its population who are racists? If so, what should that percentage be? And how is to be measured, and by what criteria? What some regard as racism others might dismiss as nothing more than overly exuberant patriotism at international sporting contests, or simply a critical attitude towards certain aspects of a culture or cultures other their own. So here too, care must be taken to ensure we are talking about the same thing. I define racism as the belief that one racial group is biologically superior or inferior to another, mentally if not necessarily physically, and that this difference in abilities is genetically inherited, and not determined by cultural or any other external factors. As for a racist society, such as the UK and the USA supposedly are, it could be and indeed has been defined, rightly in my opinion, on the basis of its racially discriminatory laws, as in Nazi Germany and Tsarist Russia against Jews, apartheid South Africa against all non-whites, and Jim Crow USA against Blacks. I stand to be corrected, but I believe that the UK has never had such laws as regards race, any more than on its soil it has legally allowed slavery, though until they were repealed in the 19th century, there were laws that discriminated against (non-Anglican) religious minorities and unbelievers.

The issues so far as the UK is concerned are, firstly, what is racism and what causes it, next, having defined it, in what ways and to what extent does it manifest itself in public life (for example, in the justice system and policing, legislation, public services, health, education, employment etc) and finally, what proportion of the UK's overall population, irrespective of their race, are afflicted with it. In the main body of this work, I have cited examples of surveys of attitudes towards the Jews, both in the UK and in continental Europe, that in each case provided results that with small variations, revealed that anti-Semitism was deeply embedded in each country investigated, to the order of around 30% of their populations. This is the kind of information that is needed if prejudicial attitudes towards and treatment of black and other racial minorities in the UK are to be tackled effectively. Otherwise, we will be fighting in the dark. (I note in passing that whereas in the UK, following the killing of George Floyd, BLM was able, in a matter of a few days, to mobilise thousands of demonstrators at locations right across the country, the vast majority of whom were not black, two rallies outside Parliament called by the Campaign Against Anti-Semitism to protest against Labour Party anti-Semitism attracted at most two thousand supporters, most of whom were Jews. I leave to the reader to draw their own conclusions from these disparities.)

I think that once equipped with these indispensable, though not in every case, easily ascertained facts, it should be possible to target and then reduce, if not eliminate, most overt manifestations of racism by a variety of means both legal and educational, though not by waging a racial and sexually divisive all-out war against a 'cis white patriarchy' as advocated by BLM's wokista soul mates, the Social Justice Warriors. The two entirely unsustainable assumptions those using this term make are that white women are not, or cannot be racist, and that all heterosexual white males are. With respect to the latter claim, I would like those that believe this to be so to explain precisely how homosexual anal intercourse inoculates its practitioners against white patriarchal racism.

What today goes by the name of anti-racism can assume the most perverse guises, as in the extraordinary response of Cambridge University to Churchill (sic!) College Professor Priyamvada Gopal's tweets that 'white lives don't matter' and 'abolish whiteness'. Defending her right to express her 'lawful opinions' on the race question (though what her 'white' students might have thought about them is another matter), her employers went further, seemingly endorsing her comments by promoting her. In the McCarthyite groupthink climate that had been generated by Black Lives Matter, any academic who dissented from her racist 'lawful opinions' and having the courage, some might say foolhardiness, to publicly say so, would have run the very real risk of themselves being accused of racism, to say nothing of all its attendant consequences, none of which would have involved promotion.

No such concerns however seemed to have troubled black Oxford BLM activist Sasha Johnson, who in 2020, posted a video of herself repeatedly calling a black man a 'coon' for challenging her account of the death of George Floyd, tweeted that she favoured the enslavement of whites, and announced that she would be founding a new political party that will exclude whites from its leadership. In 2016, Toronto BLM leader Yusra Khogali went even further down the same Orwellian Road of racist anti-racism with her claim on Facebook that 'white people are a genetic defect of blackness', white skin being 'subhuman', while blacks are 'the strongest of all humans.' Also more intelligent, because 'black skin captures light and holds it in its memory bank mode, which reveals blackness converts light into knowledge.' (Here we have an example of one of the fruits of anti-racist 'official science'…black optics.) Imagine this being said about whites in ultra woke Canada. The cuffs would on them in no time.

We are given an altogether different 'take' on the cerebral dimension of the race question by the US National Museum of African American History. It lists features of 'white culture' which, regrettably, have been 'internalised' by 'people of colour'. Among them are, I quote: Self-reliance, independence and autonomy, in control of their own environment, Protestant work ethic, the nuclear family, father and mother, objective, rational linear thinking, hard work the key to success, plan for the future, follow rigid time schedules, (BLM speak for punctuality), decision making, must always 'do something about a situation'. We are encouraged to infer that the current problems of the USA's black population partly at least derive from their imbibing, to one extent or another, these features of 'white culture', and that therefore it would be well advised to reject them. Ironically, if they did so, they would confirm the stereotype white racists have always attributed to blacks: lazy, stupid, lacking initiative, fatalistic, unreliable, feckless, superstitious, profligate.

It is no less ironic that race, once the monopoly of the far right, has displaced class as the prism through which, together with gender, the left sees and analyses

420

the prime divisions in society. And yet as it has always done, Hitler's 'racial awareness', in a new, pseudo-radical guise, serves those who have a vested in obscuring the class cleavages that constitute the economic and social foundations of all capitalist societies. No wonder then that billionaire celebrities took BLM to their hearts, as did Wall Street, with massive funding, compulsory 'anti-racist' training sessions for all its staff, and fast track race and gender promotions to the board room. And yet on both left and right, this is what passes for 'Marxism', a 'Marxism' that as the statistics prove, leaves intact the greatest gulf between haves and have nots in the western world, with currently, 716 multi-racial and gender US billionaires, second only to 'communist' China's 1,113, and growing poverty among black and white men and women alike. But speak not about class, only race and gender. I often wonder what the authors of the first citation at the head of this Postscript would make of all this. Perhaps if I were to press an ear tightly against the wall of a certain tomb in a Highgate cemetery, I would a rattling sound as the skeleton revolved of a cis-patriarchal Jew.

Addendum: The Black Deaths That Don't Matter

Shortly after compiling the above statistics on crime in the USA, there appeared on December 7, 2021, an online posting by Zac Kriegman, a statistician who had just been fired by his employer, Thomson Reuters, for an (internal) posting critical of Black Lives Matter. I reproduce excerpts below. The full text is now available online. My comments are in square brackets.

I believe the Black Lives Matter movement arose out of a passionate desire to protect black people from racism and to move our whole society towards healing from a legacy of centuries of brutal oppression. Unfortunately, over the past few years I have grown more and more concerned about the damage that movement is doing to many low-income black communities. I have avidly followed the research on the movement and its impacts, which has led me, inexorably, to the conclusion that the claim at the heart of the movement, that the police more readily shoot black people, is false and likely responsible for thousands of black people being murdered in the most disadvantaged communities in the country…

At BLM protests, and from BLM proponents, we have since heard that it's 'open season' for the police to kill black people, and those police are 'hunting' black people. According to the BLM website itself, 'Black lives are systematically and intentionally targeted for demise' by 'state sanctioned violence against Black people.'

The only problem: it's completely untrue. According to the *Washington Post's* database of police shootings, over the last five years there have typically been between 30% and 100% more unarmed whites killed by police than unarmed blacks. (It's worth noting that in the vast majority of police shootings of both blacks and whites, police gunfire was justified in response to an armed and threatening suspect.)

[Kriegman then addresses the claim that proportionate to their share of the population (12/13%) blacks are more likely to be shot by the police than whites.] Police are not supposed to distribute lethal force randomly [i.e., evenly] throughout the population in order to ensure equal application to each racial group. [This would necessitate police not engaging in confrontations with blacks who are acting illegally, shooting whites who are not, or a combination of both.] Instead, police are supposed to use lethal force only in response to threats of serious violence during encounters with criminal suspects...[Therefore] the correct benchmark for measuring bias in police use of lethal force is the number of high-risk encounters for each group, and not the population of each group.

This is a critical distinction because there are definite reasons to believe that police have very different rates of high risk encounters per member of different racial groups [as they do with males and females and certain age groups] *for reasons related to entirely legitimate policing objectives.* [all emphases in original] For instance, as the evidence in the following section demonstrates, on *average*, violent crime rates are dramatically higher in predominately black communities than they are in predominately white communities. This violence takes a severe toll on those communities, can traumatize residents, makes it virtually impossible for children to focus on school and academic success, and worse. Because, on *average*, there is so much greater violence in predominantly black neighbourhoods, in order to protect and defend the (mostly) black residents in those communities, police are disproportionately required to confront criminal suspects in those communities. [In an average year, around 90 % of black victims of homicide are killed by other blacks, and around 2%, nearly all of whom will have been armed, by police.] Therefore, we should expect there to be more encounters in those communities for the purpose of achieving entirely legitimate and laudable policing objectives...Therefore, if we want to investigate whether there is [racial] bias in the application of lethal force, we need to look at the rate of police shootings per potentially violent encounter with criminal suspects and not per member of a group's overall population (most of whom are law-abiding, peaceful citizens). When you do so, the supposed anti-black bias disappears completely, and possibly, even reverses...

Here the evidence is very clear. For instance, the *Wall Street Journal* reports that 'African-Americans make up 53% of known homicide offenders in the US and commit about 60% of robberies, though they are [only] 13% of the population. [other sources say 12%] ...But, as referred to above, over the past five years, police have killed 39% more unarmed whites than blacks. There are many more whites killed by police, even though whites account for a similar absolute number of violent offenders. [Thus, the bias is against whites, not blacks.]

[Kriegman then refers to the work of Roland G. Fryer, a 'star economist at Harvard University'.] Without doubt, he is one of the top researchers in the field of economics. He is also black, grew up poor, personally witnessed episodes of his peers being roughed up by the police and, initially at least, supported the BLM movement. He set out to lay the empirical foundations of the BLM movement by conducting a study exactly like that described above. In what he describes as 'the most surprising result of my career', his study 'didn't find evidence for anti-black or anti–Hispanic disparity in police use of force across all shootings, and, if anything, found anti-white disparities when controlling for race-specific crime.' [see above] ...Thus far, Fryer's research finding that there was no [race] bias in shootings stands as the gold standard for investigating the question of police bias in use of force...[For this very reason, even though the author is black and has impeccable academic credentials, it is ignored by the Left, because it underpins the 'wrong narrative'.]

In order to investigate whether one group of suspects is more likely to be shot than another in similar circumstances, you must know the number of such circumstances where nobody is shot, and this is what sets Roland Fryer's study apart from all others. He had access not just to death reports, but to incident reports in general, including those where lethal force was not used. And he was able to code the specifics of the circumstances according to 290 variables. [sic!] This allowed him to calculate the rates that a given set of circumstances would lead to the use of lethal force for different groups. And the result clearly showed that there was no detectable bias towards shooting black suspects...

[Kriegman then discussed the relationship between reported crimes and arrests for different racial groups, in relation to whether there was a racial bias in arrests.] The Justice Department's Bureau of Justice Statistics released a report looking into this question on a national scale. It found that 'for non-fatal violent crimes that victims said were reported to police, whites accounted for 48% of all offenders and 46% of arrestees, Blacks accounted for 35% of offenders and 33% of arrestees. Asians accounted for 2% of offenders and 1% of arrestees.'...In plain English, the number of arrests for violent crime is proportional to the number of violent crimes actually committed by each group.

[Finally, the 'Ferguson Effect', the impact on policing and crime caused by public and media reactions to what is generally believed to be an illegal killing of a citizen by police, so called after the killing by police of the black Michael Brown.in Fergusson, Missouri, in 2014. Police reportedly became reluctant to challenge black suspects, while thousands left the force. Nationwide, murder rates, mainly of blacks, soared, from 4.5 per 100,000 in 2014 to 5.4 per 100,000 in 2016. An even greater surge occurred after the killing of George Floyd in May 2020, with again, most victims as well as perpetrators being black. Initially sceptical, Fryer studied the impact of the 'Ferguson Effect' on black lives. Kriegman continues:]

After an exhaustive statistical analysis, he [Fryer] concluded that not only was something like the Ferguson Effect real, but in just the five cities that he examined, it caused a staggering 900 excess murders and 34,000 felonies that would not have otherwise occurred, and it was expected to cause hundreds more murders in those cities in the following years. Extrapolated to other cities and time periods, these results suggested thousands of additional murders victims nationwide.

In 2020, the theory was tested again when protests and riots swept across the country following George Floyd's death while in police custody...as anti-police rhetoric and propaganda increased after Floyd's death, once again, police reduced pro-active policing and murders spiked. This time, even more than in 2016. One top expert in the field estimates that the result of de-policing [as distinct from 'de-funding'] during June and July of 2020 alone resulted in an additional 1,520 murders. Crime rates are increasing only for a few specific categories – namely homicides and shootings. These categories are particularly responsive to reductions in pro-active policing. [Thus, we have 'defund the police' = more blacks killing blacks] The data also pinpoint the timing of the spikes to late May 2020, which corresponds with the death of George Floyd [on May 25] while in police custody in Minneapolis and subsequent anti-police protests, protests that likely led to declines in law enforcement, such as street stops and other forms of policing designed to prevent firearms crimes.

[There then follows a graph which shows weekly homicides per 100,000 city population from January 2017 to October 2020. In April 2020, pre-Floyd, it was a little over 2 per 100,000. By July, post Floyd, *it was just under 8 per 100*,000. Various studies of the Floyd or Minneapolis Effect have shown extra homicides ranging from 2,500 to 10,000. But even the pro-BLM CNN agrees that whatever the number, the effect is real. It can be charted graphically in the tragic case of Philadelphia, the city of brotherly love founded by the Quaker William Penn (thus Pennsylvania) but now, thanks to BLM, one of black fratricide waged amidst 44% of the city's population. In 2014, homicides were at their lowest level since 1970, 248. Then the Fergusson Effect kicked in, plateauing in 2018 at 353 and in 2019 at 356. Even though it only kicked in at the end of May 2020, by the end of that year, the Floyd Effect had raised the number of homicides even higher, to 499. In 2021, it reached 557, the highest ever, as did the number of female victims, 70. In that year, Philadelphia's homicide rate was six times the national rate. Over the same period, as a result of BLM activism and political decisions by its supporters, police pulled out of predominately black, high crime neighbourhoods, with the inevitable and totally predictable consequence that as the number of police arrests declined, from 40,000 in 2019 to 24,000 in 2021, so at an almost identical rate, the number of murders rose. In the first three weeks of 2022, the lethal Floyd Effect was still working, with 38 homicides, an increase of 3% over the previous year in the same period. 77% of the victims were black, and 14% younger than 18. All told, there were 125 victims of gun violence, an average of six per day.

Baltimore, with a population only one third of Philadelphia's 1.5 million, still registered 31 homicides in the first 25 days of 2022. All of those whose race was reported were black. Out of the total of 31, two were triple homicides and four double homicides...six multiple shootings in less than a month, in just one city little larger than Cardiff, whose Crown Court in an entire year, 2021. convicted just one man for murder. Like Fergusson, Baltimore had its own 'effect', beginning 2015, when six police officers were charged by state attorney Marilyn Mosby after the death in custody of Freddy Gray, a black suspect, on April 19 of that year. A local crime reporter described the reaction this produced amongst police officers: 'What Mosby basically did was to send a message to the Baltimore Police department:" I'm going to put you into jail for making a bad arrest." So, officers figured it out. "I can go to jail for making the wrong arrest, so I am not going to get out of my car to clear a corner", and that's exactly what happened post-Freddie Gray.' Arrests fell from 40,000 in 2014 to 18,000 in 2017, while homicides soared from 214 in 2014 to 344 in 2015 and then plateaued. So again, there is a clear (inverse) relation between arrest and homicide rates, just as there is an equally evident (positive) one between race and homicide rates. Baltimore is 62% black, and its homicide rate, at 57.1 per 1000,000 in 2020, was *seven times* that of the USA as whole, at 7.8 per 100,000. Cleveland Ohio is 49% black. In 2014, just prior to the death of Michael Brown, the murder rate was 16 per 100,000, already three times the national rate. By 2016, it had more than doubled, to 35 per 100,000. in 2021, it was 43 per 100.000 compared to the national rate of 7 per 100,000. And so we could go on, with in each case, a similar pattern recurring again and again.

Across the USA over the years, the percentage of blacks murdered by other blacks has not varied by more than one or two percentage points. The same is true of whites murdered by whites, a phenomenon that is by no means unique to the USA. Most killing is within ethnic groups, not across them, except when it comes to violence inspired by race hatred. The third column indicates the share of the total number of homicides that each year are perpetrated in the USA by blacks. This percentage also varies only slightly. Extrapolating from FBI homicide data for the ten years from 2010 to 2019, we get the following. Note that black on black homicide is significantly more common than it is for white on white. This means that proportionally, twice as many whites are murdered by blacks than blacks are by whites. Take a typical year...2019. In that year, of the 3299 white victims of homicide, 566 were murdered by blacks, 17%, while in the same year, of the 2906 black victims of homicide, only 246 were killed by whites, 8.5%.... again, not the right 'narrative'.

Year	White on white (%)	Black on Black (%)	Homicide (%)
2010	82	89	49
2011	83	92	50
2012	84	91	49

2013	83	90	52
2014	79	90	51
2015	82	89	51
2016	82	90	53
2017	80	88	53
2018	81	89	53
2019	79	89	51

With blacks making up 12% of the US population, while accounting for let us say 52% of all homicides, and the rest of the US population, 88%, for the other 48 %, this leads to the following. With blacks over-represented by a factor of 4.3, and the rest of the US population under-represented by a factor of 1.8, this means that a black person, who nine times out ten will be a male, is about eight times more likely to commit murder than a non-black person, with the likelihood being nine out of ten that their victim or victims will also be black. Anyone who doubts the validity of these conclusions should check for themselves the on-line FBI data on which they are based.

Let us pause for a moment and consider the following. According to records kept by the Tuskegee Institute, the number of black lynchings perpetrated by the Ku Klux Klan between 1882 and 1968 was 3446, an average of 40 per year. (The last Klan lynching was in 1981.) Very few of those who acknowledge the crimes of America's racist past are prepared to publicly state the terrible truth that blacks are now killing *each other* at a rate not of 40 a year, but of no less than 20 *a day*. And even if we take the lowest estimation of excess black murders due to the Fergusson and Minneapolis Effects, far more blacks have died as a result of BLM activism in the space of seven years than at the hands of the Klan over an entire century. Such are the 'strange fruits' of BLM anti-racism. Now Kriegman continues:]

It's worth taking a moment to put these numbers [of 'excess' homicides] in perspective:
18 unarmed blacks [are] shot by the police annually;
26 unarmed whites [are] shot by the police annually;
2,500 at least, but possibly well over 10,000 additional murders – mostly black – as a result of the de-policing prompted by BLM falsehoods;
8,000 blacks murdered by criminals annually. [In 2021, it reached 10,000]

It would take roughly 140 years for police to shoot as many unarmed black people as have been murdered as a result of BLM falsehoods in just the past few years. But, the thousands of additional black murders are just the tip of the iceberg of devastation that BLM falsehoods have inflicted on black communities. For each victim murdered by criminals there are dozens of lives derailed; hundreds of chidden traumatized. Perhaps even greater than the deaths and trauma that result directly from BLM's falsehoods is the damage done by drawing attention away from the real solutions to the approximately 8,000 black people murdered annually. The tragedy of the BLM movement is not just the *additional* murders and devastations to low-income black communities that its falsehoods have caused directly [looting, arson etc] but also how those falsehoods retard progress on tackling the violence that was already plaguing those communities before BLM came along. How could we possibly have gone so wrong?...

The best explanation I can come up with for why a person (white, black or any other race) would support the BLM movement is ignorance of even the most rudimentary facts. [CRT advocates and BLM activists do not like facts, especially statistical ones like the above.] For example, support for BLM correlates very highly with being more liberal [in the USA, this means 'left wing', often very far from liberal in the traditional sense]. More than 50% believe law enforcement killed 1,000 or more unarmed [sic] black men in 2019. Nearly 8% believed they killed more than 10,000! [That is, 27 *per day*. Compare this estimate of *unarmed* blacks killed every day by police with the actual number of *armed* blacks killed by police every day, *less than one*. Whoever drew up this survey should have included the following question: 'What is the source of your data on police killings?'] According to the *Washington Post*, the real number of unarmed black men shot and killed by the police in 2019 was 11. That's a difference of three orders of magnitude [a thousand times too high. Bear in mind that nearly all these estimates would have been made by highly educated people in positions of influence and even power, including politicians, academics, school teachers and journalists.] It is impossible to reason intelligently when your beliefs about the relevant facts are so completely divorced from reality. [as it is with flat earthers, geocentrists, creationists, Holocaust deniers and Covid conspiracists].

I have cited only excerpts of this paper that relate directly to the subject under review – the dire, indeed lethal, consequences of critical race theory when translated into mass action on the streets and the decisions of politicians. Not for the first time in history, race-obsessed professors have the blood of thousands on their hands, only this time it is that of blacks, not Jews.

Addendum

A data base on US police shootings published by the *Washington Post* on February 9, 2022 shows that the per capita rate for police shootings of blacks in 2021 was a little over twice that for whites. It also shows that police shoot 20 times more men than women. This latter statistic, which, like the shootings of blacks, varies only slightly each year, has never been attributed to police bias against men, the reason being that FBI crime statistics show that males are far more likely than females to engage in the kinds of crime that lead to fatal encounters with police. Annually, females commit around 25% of all violent crime, and 10% of homicides, while being around 30% of all homicide victims. The same applies to age, also shown in the *Post* data base, with more than half of those shot by police being between 20 and 40. Below and above this age group, data show police shootings tapering off to zero, as do FBI rates of homicide. Toddlers and geriatrics tend not to engage in violent crime, least of all murder.

But when it comes to race, the data-based approach that is applied to age and gender, one that discounts deliberate or 'institutional' bias, and focuses on the incidence of *criminal behaviour*, is abandoned by those on the left who concern themselves with this subject. The fact - and it is a fact - that police are more than twice as likely to fatally shoot a black person than a white one is nearly always attributed solely to race bias, that as BLM puts it, police, including black officers, who make up 12% of the US police force yet account for *more than* 12% of fatal police shootings of 'fellow' blacks, are 'hunting down' innocent black men.

However, employing the same criteria as in the cases of gender and age, namely *the propensity of the group in question to commit violent crime*, we have the following: Over the years, with very little variation either way, annual FBI data show blacks committing 50% of all homicides, and 37% of all violent crime. Therefore, just was the case with males and those between the ages of 20 and 40, so also in this case blacks are far more likely to be engaged in potentially lethal encounters with police than those of other races.

Prior to 2021, the number of blacks killed by police annually averaged around 230, with all but a dozen or so being armed. Following the killing of George Floyd in May 2020 came another nationwide backlash against the police, who once again pulled back from urban black areas, handing over the streets to black criminal gangs, with the same results as before. Arrests fell, as did fatal police shootings of blacks, down to 195, while the number of *all* recorded black homicide victims in 2020 soared to 9,913, compared to the 2,906 black homicide victims as recorded by the FBI for 2019. However, neither number gives us the whole picture. Firstly, we have to bear in mind that while 9,913 is the number of *all* reported homicides of blacks as recorded by Statistica, unlike FBI homicide data, we are not given any information as to the racial identity of their killers. Secondly, at the time of writing, FBI homicide data for the year 2020 had not been released, so we have to make extrapolations from the last year for which FBI data was available, 2019. Only then are we in a position to make a reasonable assumption about the racial identity of the perpetrators for the year 2020. Over the previous ten years, and we can safely assume for a good many before that, an average of around 90% of blacks whose murder is recorded by the FBI data were killed by other blacks. As for the rest of the victims, the police were unable to identify their killers because of a lack of witnesses or sufficient forensic evidence, the former because of the well-known 'no snitching' code that prevails in the black 'community'. It is therefore more than likely that the percentage of these 'extra' victims killed by blacks in 2020, as in previous years, will be higher than the usual 90% for which the police, and therefore the FBI, will have sufficient evidence to identify their killers as black. If so, this raises the share of blacks killed other blacks in 2020 to something in the region of 95%.

By the same token, this also affects the share of all homicides committed by blacks, which the FBI annually records as around 50%. For 2019, FBI data give the number of white perpetrators as 3,448, and of black, as 3,218, pretty much equal, as are the number of victims, white, 3,299, and black, 2,906. But as to the latter, there is a dramatic change in the year of Floyd, 2020. Citing now not FBI data, but again Statistica, the *total* number of homicides (not just those recorded by the FBI) jumped by 30% from 16,324 in 2019 to 21,570 in 2020, of which 7,029 victims were white, and 9,913 black. Thus the total number of black victims is three times that recorded by the FBI for the previous year, and white, twice. Even when allowing for a possible comparable rise of 30% in the number of black homicide victims for 2020 recorded by the FBI, say to around 4,000, this still leaves us with around 6,000 black homicide victims - 60% - having no identified killer, the vast majority of whom, for the reason already stated, will be black. With white homicide victims it is a similar, but far from identical story. Assuming again that the number of FBI-recorded white victims of homicide rose in 2020 by 30%, to around 4,000, this leaves us with a potential 3,000 - 40 % - who will for the same reason be victims of mainly whites, only less so, because twice as many

427

whites are annually killed by blacks than blacks by whites. This, together with the far greater increase in black than white homicide victims, means that the percentage of homicides committed by blacks will be significantly greater than the annual average of around 50% recorded by the FBI. Here we have the tragic consequences of the 'no snitching' code, observed partly out fear, but also a misplaced feeling of 'black solidarity'. As a result, something like two thirds of all black murderers of blacks are never arrested, tried and convicted. Most will in all likelihood kill again...and then more some. Politicians and officials in Democrat-run cities no less than BLM activists are fully aware of the scale and causes of the carnage they have facilitated, in particular with their 'Bail Reform', which enables suspects charged even with murder to be out on the streets within 24 hours of their arrest. But to acknowledge, discuss and confront it is taboo.

At the very heart of this crisis among America's young black males (even back in 2008 when they made up 18% of all US male youths, they were responsible for nearly 60% of all youth homicides) is a cult of nihilistic, sadistic, predatory violence, which has reached a new degree of depravity with the rise of the so-called Super Gremlins; amoral, merciless gang killers celebrated by rappers in lyrics such as the following:

'Say you my nigga, I'm be your killer
Nobody gon' play with you when I'm with you.'

and

'Damn, my nigga, you trippen'
We could've been superstars
Remember when we was jackin' cars
Now, it's not safe for you
You switched like a pussy, lil' bitch.'

(Rapping itself is a dangerous business. Every year, scores are murdered by rival gangs.)

Then there is' Demon Time', defined in the *Urban Dictionary* as 'any time of the night past 11 pm. A time of pure fuckery. When the fuck boys come out to play. People's feelings are not taken into account.' Or their lives, as here:

'Ha haha, demon time, nigga
Yeah gang, uh, gang, gang,
Give 'em hell, brr bah
I got bells, bah bah bah
I got shells...
Shoot a nigga up
'Cause I ain't worried 'bout shit.'

But it is the police, so we are told, who are waging war on America's blacks.

In recent years, to increase their body count, Super Gremlins have taken to murdering Chinese, seen as 'soft' targets. 2021 saw a 450% rise in the number of

Chinese murdered in New York, un-protested as one would expect by BLM and un-reported by the left media, partly because of who is killing them, but also because Chinese have been far too successful to 'fit the narrative' of an oppressed ethnic minority. Double standards also allow gangster rappers to refer to blacks as 'niggas' without being accused of legitimising white racism, because it is public knowledge that no-one on the black 'street' uses terms devised for them by paternalist white academics, such as 'Afro-American' and more recently, the ridiculous 'people of colour', as if everybody else is colourless. (Throughout this work I have described black Americans as blacks, as do many American black academics and commentators, just as everybody describes white Americans as whites, and not 'Euro-Americans' or 'people of no colour'). Even so, I would much rather live in a world where skin colour has no more significance than a person's inside leg measurement or shoe size, a world where, if I can misquote Dr. King, a person is identified and treated as a unique individual, not as a member of a racial 'community', as is the case today with politicians and pundits of both left and right. I truly believe that in the civilised world at least, the former is how the majority wishes it to be, and does so as best it can, despite all the pressures to behave otherwise, to be, as the CRT mantra has it, 'racially aware'...like Nazis or the KKK for example. And contrary to what their respective anti-racist industries claim, having studied the relevant data, I simply do not believe that the USA and the UK are, when judged by any objective criteria, racist societies. The problem is that far too many have political, career and financial motives for sustaining the lie that they are - hence the invention of terms like 'micro-aggression', 'triggers', 'systemic' and 'institutional' racism and 'unconscious racial bias', and the manufacturing of fake hate crimes - racist graffiti, attacks and hoaxes *a la* Jussie Smollett, all designed to keep the wheels of the anti-racist industry turning as supply increasing fails to match demand.)

The havoc and carnage wreaked within and on the black 'community', much of it by young black American males, many still in their mid-teens, is graphically measured in the statistics I have cited. They are just as readily accessible as those on police shootings, but are rarely if ever quoted in articles on the subject, even though they are no less essential for a proper understanding of the rate of police shootings of blacks as they are for the rates of police shootings of men and those aged between 20 and 40. The problem is, they do not 'fit the narrative', because blacks, at 12% of the US population, are over-represented as perpetrators of homicides by a factor of at least four, and of all violent crime, by one of three, while being, as the target of lethal police shootings, over-represented by a factor of only just over two. This points towards only one conclusion, however unpalatable for the politically correct. If there is a race bias in police shootings, it is not blacks who are its victims. A number of studies have established that for reasons which in the post-Floyd political climate should be self-evident, white police officers, who make up nearly 90% of the total force, are more likely to use deadly force against an armed white suspect than a black one.

Similar claims have been made for a racial bias in the US prison population to those regarding the fatal shooting of blacks by police officers. They are also refuted by the same evidence. As already stated, at the very least, blacks are responsible for 50% of all US homicides, and for reasons I have argued above, probably substantially more. But let us stay with 50%. Blacks account on average for 37% of all violent crime, and if my surmise is correct about unsolved homicides, this percentage will also be somewhat higher. But again, let us stay with the FBI's 37%. Even if we work on the false assumption that only violent crimes attract custodial sentences (40% of black prisoners are in fact drug offenders) and that there is no racial bias against blacks in sentencing, we would expect the incarceration rate for blacks to approximate this percentage, and if there is a racial bias against blacks in sentencing, to significantly exceed it. But as with police shootings of blacks in relation to the black homicide rate, it does neither. According to Pewresearch, as of 2017, the black incarceration rate was not 37%, but *33%*. If we do include incarcerated black drug and other non-violent offenders, say 50%, of all black prisoners, this reduces from 33% to around 15% of the US prison population those blacks incarcerated for violent crime, *despite their having committed* 37% *of all US violent crime*. That is the why the black violent crime rate of 37% rarely if ever finds its way on to the pages of leftist publications. Instead they invariably ignore all data on the black violent crime rate, and always point to the over-representation of blacks in prison as proof of a racial bias in the justice system, as does for example Ashley Nellis in an article published in *The Sentencing Project* in October 2021, titled 'The Colour of Justice: Racial and Ethnic Disparities in State Prison'. Nowhere in this lengthy article, replete with statistics on racial disparities in incarceration rates, is there an allusion to, let along comparable data on, racial disparities in *crime rates*, which renders his contribution to the subject at best worthless, and at worst, dishonest.

His claim that blacks are discriminated against in the justice system rest upon a confusion, if indeed that is what it is, between the *size* of an ethnic/racial group and the *level*, *nature* and *distribution* of criminal behaviour *within* that group. He consequently finds evidence of racial bias in the incarceration rate of blacks in the disparity between the 33% share of black criminals in US prisons and the share of blacks in the US population, 12%, leaving entirely out of consideration the fact that blacks commit not 12% of all US crime annually, but around 27%, and most crucially, 37% of all *violent* crime. The logic of his argument would, if implemented as a policy, lead to the creation of a woke prison utopia, based on the CRT principle of 'equity', where insofar as crime occurs at all, each ethnic/racial group in the USA will be 'represented' so to speak by exactly the same share of prisoners as its share of the total population of the USA, a kind of criminal proportional representation. Thus the percentage of blacks in US prisons would be reduced from 33% to 12%, while those of other racial/ethnic groups with a crime rate below their share of the US population would increase, necessarily in both cases irrespective of their actual rates of crime. What sort of justice system would this be, in which punishment bears no relationship to crime? One wonders what world such academics live in. Do they not realise, as most 'ordinary' people do, that that due to a host of factors - historical, geographical, cultural, economic etc - the nature and rates of crime among the USA's myriad racial/ethnic groups, does now, and will for the foreseeable future, vary enormously, and therefore by the same token, their comparative rates of incarceration. Whites are 76% of the US population, and in 2019 committed 69% of its crimes, and blacks, 12%, and 27% of all crimes. Like their crime rate, the highest incarceration rate is that of blacks, at 465 per 100,000 of the black population, more than 20 times the rate for Asians, who also have by far the lowest crime rate, ten times less than that of blacks.. Coincidence? Race bias? If so, why not also for Asians? What more proof do we need of the causal relationship between crime in its various aspects and incarceration rates?

Wikipedia, which unlike Nellis has no ideological axe to grind, states the following in its entry on 'Race and crime in the United States': 'According to the FBI, African-Americans accounted for 55% of all homicide offenders in 2019, with whites 41.1% and "Other" 3.0% in cases where the race was known...The per capita offending rate for African-Americans was roughly *eight times* [my emphasis] higher than that of whites and their victim rate was similar.' How is it possible to argue that this enormous disparity in offending rates does (and it would seem, should) not have any bearing on the two groups' rates of incarceration? As well as an ethnic/racial group's overall crime rate, the distribution of criminal behaviour within the group will also affect its share of the total prison population. If crime is concentrated in a very small number of family-related, mature, experienced, full-time professional criminals, other things being equal, their ethnic/racial group's share of the total prison population - even supposing they all get caught - will be significantly less than that of an ethnic/racial group with same size population and level of crime, but with its criminals far more numerous, not concentrated in a few families but widely distributed among its population, mainly young and lacking in sophistication and therefore more likely to be apprehended. Mafia-era Chicago is a perfect example of the former (superbly portrayed in the Godfather movies), where highly organised, family-based, economically-motivated professional crime was concentrated in very few, mainly Sicilian hands, run as a 'business', with rivalries and violence kept to a minimum; and its diametric opposite in every way, black crime - unorganised, street gang-based, murder-oriented, unsophisticated, predatory, peer group, not family related, diffuse, life-style obsessed, opportunist - a textbook example of the latter. Whereas a small number of Mafia families for decades effectively controlled the crime of entire cities with relatively few convictions, it today takes 60-odd black gangs with a combined *active* membership of 100,000 to exert the same level of control just over the crime of Chicago's South Side.

In 2019, the total number of blacks in US jails was 452,000, 1.3 % of the total black population and around 3.5 % of its adult male population, by far the largest criminal percentage of any ethnic/racial group in the USA. Even though a large proportion, some 40%, would have been serving sentences for drug offences and others again for other non-violent crimes, this still left a very large number of young, mainly part-time criminals, the majority of whom lacked even the most basic skills of their trade. But because they were so numerous, they were still able between them to account for 37% of all US violent crime. The fact that blacks accounted for only 30% of property crime again points to a low level of black criminal 'productivity', contrasting with white crime, where the difference was the reverse. The diffuse, 'labour intensive', 'low tech', or, less politely, primitive, lumpen, nature of black crime, focused primarily on killing and drug dealing, goes a long way, unlike race bias, to explaining why blacks comprise 33% of the US prison population compared to their 12% of the US population. If black crime were to be conducted with anything like the proficiency of the Mafia's, there is no doubt that the black share of the US prison population would be reduced to single figures. As it is, but for the 'no snitching' code, which enables two thirds of black murderers to avoid detection, conviction and imprisonment, it would be higher than its current 33%. (The 'no snitching code' is also in force among the UK's black population. It led to the collapse of the trial of four black men accused of involvement in the near fatal shooting of BLM activist Sasha Johnson in May 2021. None of the more than 30 black guests at the party where she was shot would testify as a witness to the crime. Yet another case of the 'wrong narrative'.)

With so many black criminals meeting early deaths, some still in their teens (of the approximately 11,000 murders committed by blacks in 2020, the majority of the victims were members of rival black gangs) is it any wonder that few survive long enough to acquire the skills and experience essential for a more respectable performance?

FBI crime data for 2019 reveal this prevalence amongst black criminals to engage in low skill, violent crime, which is more likely to attract a prison sentence. Their highest shares of all US crime were 53% for robbery, 51% for homicide and 42% for weapon possession, compared with financial and property offences varying between 30 and 36%, whereas for Asians, it was the reverse, 1% of homicides compared with fraud, 1.5%, and embezzlement, 1.8%. These variations have nothing to do with differences of race per se. They are the product of different cultures.

I find it quite extraordinary that an academic such as Nellis can produce a paper so flawed in its methodology that he excludes entirely from any consideration the main determinant - the nature and incidence of black crime - of the subject he is discussing, preferring instead to talk only about anti-black race bias, which undeniably still does exist, but as the relevant data show, does not have remotely the same impact on the black incarceration rate as does that of black crime. I suspect that this lacuna is due not so much to a lapse in scholarship as a lack of courage, because he must surely be no less aware of this data than I am. If so, it is an omission that does no service to those who in their vast majority are the victims of blacks who commit crime...other blacks.

How times change. Who remembers now Barrack Obama reading the riot act to black men who fail to measure up to their parental responsibilities, with the result that black boys with no father are 20 times more likely to end up in jail than boys who have one? Or Denzel Washington's warning that a black boy with no father at home will always find one on the street? Today, with 70% of black families fatherless and black teenage mothers on welfare spawning from a series of brief sexual liaisons children they can neither properly parent nor educate, Black Lives Matter, instead of waging war on the scourge of violent black crime, facilitates lawlessness by demanding the abolition of the police, the release without bail conditions of violent crime suspects and the closing of prisons; legitimises it by attributing all the problems of black communities to white racism and a supposed racial bias in the US's laws, and incites and even participates in crime with looting, arson, vandalism, assaults on police officers and attacks on public buildings and synagogues; and in instead of condemning the failings of black fathers, exonerates them by calling for an end to the nuclear family. With allies like this, who needs enemies?

Afterword

I began the postscript by contrasting the global outrage at the killing of George Floyd, a crime that while it had world-wide political repercussions, had no political motive, with the total lack of similar reactions to the virtually identical killing of Mario Gonzalez, and to another that most certainly did have a motive, albeit one of a religious nature, namely that of Samuel Paty. To which I must add, the near-total silence both within and outside the 'black community' that greeted the shooting on May 23, 2021, of UK BLM activist Sasha Johnson by an alleged black suspect, simply because, like the killing of Gonzalez and Paty, it did not 'fit the narrative'. White cop killing white man, black killing white, or black killing black (like Muslim killing Muslim), is the wrong 'narrative'. Only white killing black, especially if the white man, no matter what the circumstances, is wearing a police uniform, is the correct 'narrative'. This may well explain why the shooting dead by US police of fifty white men in the first three months of 2021, at a time when the media were focused as never before on the failings of US policing revealed in the trial of Derrick Chauvin, also passed without media comment, as did the manslaughter of Jack Barnes in February 2021 by Manchester transport police, even though the circumstances of his death were identical to those of George Floyd...knee on neck, as he gasped 'I can't breathe'. Here was a golden opportunity, one might have supposed, with the impending Chauvin trial constantly in the news, for BLM UK to make its case for defunding or abolishing the police. But again, silence, because, like Tony Timpa and Mario Gonzalez, Barnes had the wrong colour skin.

Silence was again the order of the day on the part of the UK political establishment when, following two days of Muslim protests at the school's entrance, on March 26, 2021, a teacher at Batley (Yorkshire) Grammar School was suspended after showing a cartoon of Mohammed in a scheduled religious studies lesson on blasphemy. Again, it was question of the wrong narrative, with continued Muslim demonstrations outside the school leading to the teacher's suspension and the school's closing early for the Easter holidays. Despite the tragic case of fellow school teacher Samuel Paty being still fresh in many minds, there was no public outrage or statements of sympathy by politicians when, after his suspension and fearing for his life, the Batley teacher, together with his wife and four children, had to leave his home for a secret accommodation under police protection after his name and address were publicised by a Muslim activist. It just so happened that he had previously received a donation of £3,000 towards his 'Purpose of Life [sic] Charity' (who says Muslims don't have a sense of humour?) from the Kirklees branch of the far leftist-dominated National Education Union, the very same union *to which the teacher belonged*. As if to rub salt into his wounds, his union was also one of the sponsors of the third of the succession of rallies held in London two months later in support of Hamas in its war against Israel. None of this could you make up. A year later, the teacher (together with his family) was still in hiding under police protection from death threats by devotees the religion of peace, possibly facing the prospect of re-living the fate that befell Salman Rushdie.

It was a devasting comment on the cowardice of the UK's political leaders that it was a Muslim, Deputy Leader of Slough Council, Sabia Akram, who at great risk to herself, alone publicly extended the hand of solidarity to the besieged teacher, bravely tweeting 'Come to Slough. We welcome you and your family.' (she also received the usual Religion of Peace death threats) Why could not the Labour, Tory and Liberal Democrat candidates in the Batley and Spen by-election of June 1, together with their party leaders, display the same solidarity as a Muslim politician, who must have known that making such a courageous offer placed herself in danger? Their silence…and one suspects that it is was by mutual agreement…tells us that they placed a higher value on the pursuit of Muslim votes than the defence of a teacher facing the prospect of sharing same fate that befell Samuel Paty and the staff of *Charlie Hebdo*.

The suspension, not to speak of the threat of assassination, of a trade unionist simply for doing his job, was of no concern to the ultra-Islamophile Socialist Workers (aka Sharia Wahabi) Party. Instead, it took the side of his employers. Having previously found that Paty's showing a cartoon to his class was 'rightly seen as an insult' and that France's defence of its secularism was somehow proof that the country was 'drenched in Islamophobia', the party naturally endorsed the Batley teacher's suspension and the Muslim protests. Its weekly, *Socialist Worker,* conflating, as Islamophiles always do, religion and race, claimed that 'insulting the prophet is not freedom speech, it is racist abuse'. Sadly for the SWP, as was made clear in the House of Commons in a ruling by Justice Minister Jonathen Djanogly in 2012, English law does not treat abuse, libel or slander of the dead as a crime, not even when their target, as it also was on that occasion, is Mohammed, just as Islam does not treat 'insulting the prophet' as racism, but as *blasphemy.*

Following the teacher's suspension, one of the pupils in the class revealed that he had also shown cartoons of Donald Trump, Boris Johnson and the Pope. Had only these three been on display, we can be sure of two things. One, that he would not have been suspended and two, even if, hypothetically, he had been, the SWP would have been the most vociferous in his defence, arguing that unlike Mohammed, the Pope (not to speak of Trump and Johnson), as a white infidel, was fair game. (Proof of the former came when the Head announced that only cartoons of Mohammed would be no longer be used in future classes. Need I add that there were no Catholic or Tory demonstrations at the school gates?)

What the SWP was in effect implying with its accusation of racism was that to protect the sensitivities of Muslims (and with gang rapists and wife-beaters especially in mind, we know how sensitive some Muslim men can be), infidel UK citizens should be subject to the same blasphemy laws that up till now, have only been applicable to Muslims and at that, only enforceable, at least officially, in countries ruled by Islamic law. Here, not for the first time, in its pursuit of the chimerical Muslim masses, the SWP found itself in company that in its now long past 'orthodox' Marxist years, with religion, including Islam, being 'the opium of the people', would have been unthinkable; a Primate of the Church of England, Rowan Williams, who proposed that Islamic law be incorporated into English law, and the Third World-dominated United Nations Human Rights [sic] Council, which on several occasions has approved resolutions demanding that blasphemy should be made a crime in all the UN's 193 member states.

434

Like so many public figures today, be they clerics, politicians or pundits of various persuasions, the Socialist Workers Party is ever-ready to say what freedom of speech is not, but never, what it is. The general consensus on the left is that the kind of speech protected by the US First Amendment is somehow 'right wing', because it permits saying all sorts of things which can supposedly give offence to what are defined as 'protected' identities, with each needing to be treated like threatened species on the verge of extinction, rather than as *homo sapiens* with a skin as thick and backbone as strong as everybody else's, and with all their mental faculties in working order.

There was a time, now long past, when speech and press freedom were an integral part of the left/liberal agenda, beginning with the Enlightenment (Voltaire) and the French and American revolutions which it inspired, and then continuing with the English radical battles against clerical and Tory censorship (the Blasphemy and Stamp Acts) waged by the likes of Paine and Shelly, followed by the Chartist, socialist and workers movements, advanced liberals of later years like J.S. Mill and Bradlaugh and yes, the founders of modern communism, Marx and Engels and their successors August Bebel, Karl Kautsky and Rosa Luxemburg (but not, after 1917, Lenin and Trotsky).

Those days are long gone. UK Governments of both the left and right have for decades, beginning with Thatcher's Public Order Act of 1986, been engaged in progressively restricting what can be publicly said about an ever-expanding number of important issues. And what is truly ironic is that none of these laws are today opposed by the far left, laws approved by the UK's capitalist parliament and enforced by its capitalist police and law courts. In fact, the SWP's (belated) hostile reaction to Salman Rushdie's *Satanic Verses*, and to the Danish, French and Batley cartoon affairs, suggests that where Islam is concerned, these laws do not go far enough. (Predictably, one law the SWP have demanded should be repealed is legalisation passed in 1985 and amended in 2003 making female genital mutilation a criminal offence carrying a penalty of up to 14 years' imprisonment. But the SWP's fear that the law would lead to the conviction of Muslim parents for this abominable crime have, with but one exception, thus far proved groundless.)

Let me issue a challenge, not just to the SWP, but to all to those who favour, how ill and variously-defined, what goes by the name of 'responsible' free speech. Can they name one country, now or in the past, that has suffered in any way from what they regard as an excess of free speech? I can, however, name a good many that have suffered as a result of its suppression, among them countries whose authoritarian regimes have the support of the SWP and its Corbynista and Stalinist comrades of the 'Stop the War Coalition'. The record of history speaks for itself, even if the left is not listening: everywhere and always, censorship has served as the weapon of the rich and the powerful, be they Muslim or of any other faith or ideology, not of those whose voices of protest and rebellion in Islamic countries it silences.

In addition to finding the Batley teacher guilty of racism, the *Socialist Worker* also brought another charge against him no less flawed, what is known in the trade as 'punching down'. Applying the Chomsky principle that, unless it is Israel, the enemy is always 'at home' and 'above', it argued that 'there is a big difference between ridiculing the establishment-backed Church of England and mocking the beliefs of the poor and the oppressed'. The 'poor and oppressed' Wahabi Saudi royal family perhaps? Or the Sunni Gulf petro-sheikhs? Or the two Muslim billionaires who from the safety and sensuous pleasures of their Qatar exile, manage the affairs of the SWP's favorite Jew-killing terrorist movement, Hamas? Or that intransigent foe of the 'Zionist entity', Iran's Shi'a 'Supreme Leader' Ayatollah Khamenei? This spiritual man of God also disposes of the material assets of SETED, the 'Headquarters for Executing the Order of the Imam', valued in 2013 by Reuters at $95 billon, and consisting of holdings in land, industry, oil, farming and tele-communications. A clear case of for the one, and precious little for nearly everyone else. This last item of the cleric's portfolio paid the salaries of Comrades Corbyn (at £5,000 a time), Galloway and Livingstone, who took turns as presenters with a no less zealously anti-Zionist team of holocaust deniers and Jewish conspiracy theorists when they worked for Iran's Press TV.

As the SWP well knows, those Muslims who do fit the description of those it calls the 'poor and oppressed' do not live in the UK or any other western country, but in Asia, the Middle East and Africa. There, they are indeed mostly poor and oppressed, because they live in failing Islamic societies, governed by an immensely rich, brutal, (they are responsible for nearly all the world's recorded executions) corrupt - *and also Muslim* - ruling class, one which cares nothing for their subjects' welfare, let alone their freedoms. That is why millions of Muslims have risked their lives in the bid to flee the miseries and lethal dangers of the realm of Allah and settle in the free, peaceful and prosperous lands of the despised *kuffar,* where they know they will not be oppressed, or killed in a fratricidal theological war, and where, if they are entitled to stay, they will enjoy exactly the same rights, women as well as men, as their infidel fellow citizens; the right to vote in free elections, stand for public office, attend universities, join free trade unions and have the opportunity not to stay poor. In fact, far from being in any way oppressed, save by their religion, UK Muslims, at least male ones, have been the beneficiaries of privileges not available to any other members of society. Legally, they are allowed to operate Sharia courts which, as a matter of principle, discriminate against women, and consequently make rulings that are contrary to UK law. Muslim men have also, with the connivance of those charged with enforcing the law, been allowed to break it, going unpunished for the genital mutilation of their daughters and becoming rich on the proceeds of the trafficking, pimping and raping of under-age girls.

As for the Church of England being exclusively the church of the privileged, was it the three million-strong, mainly black Anglican church of Bishop Desmond Tutu that supported the white 'establishment' in the Apartheid era, or the all-white, segregationist Afrikaner Dutch Reformed Church? And contrary to what the SWP implies, only 33% of Anglicans live in the UK. 55%, 43 million, live in sub-Saharan Africa, most, the SWP will surely agree, being poor if not in every case oppressed. Few in the West realise, because much of the media and all but a few Christian clergy have chosen for obvious reasons to say nothing about it, in Africa and the Middle East, black and Arab Christians, among them Anglicans, have been and are still being murdered, kidnapped, raped and enslaved in their thousands by Muslim militias, each, as we have seen, endorsed, critically, of course, by the SWP.

In May 2019, the normally Islam-friendly *Guardian* featured a report commissioned by the then Home Secretary Jeremy Hunt which had revealed that the proportion of Christians in the populations of the Middle East and north Africa had fallen over the last hundred or so years from 20% to 5%. As one would expect (this was the *Guardian* remember) nothing was said about the religious identity of those responsible for this catastrophic decline, which it most certainly would not have been the case if their relationship had been the reverse. (For all its talk of 'Islamophobia', the *Guardian*, like the left generally, knows full well that in the west, Islam is not persecuted in any way, which, together with a higher Muslim birth rate and migration, helps to explain why it is the only religion experiencing growth in an increasingly secular western world.) Those Christians that remained in the two regions, said Hunt, were 'some of the poorest people on the planet.' So, not quite the picture conjured up by *Socialist Worker* to bolster its case for banning free speech about Islam. As for those Muslims protesting at the gates of Batley Grammar School, many of them being men who, it was said, were not parents but imported muscle, none of them looked remotely either poor or oppressed. On the contrary, they were doing the oppressing, getting a teacher suspended and exercising an Islamic veto over what can be taught to his school's pupils. One might have thought that unlike the fanatically Islamophile far left, which has a particularly large theological axe to grind, all the UK's party leaders would have shown at least a modicum of solidarity with this victim of Islamic intolerance, if not of the exemplary kind President Macron accorded Samuel Paty. But instead, there was silence. After all, there is the Muslim vote. One must always see the bigger picture.

A final thought on the subject of censorship. If the post-Corbyn Labour Party is to regain, as I hope it will, the lost support of its working-class voters, without which it cannot hope to win a general election, it will have to demonstrably cease to function as a vehicle for the self-serving identity politics and life-style fads and fancies of the censorious metropolitan middle classes who dominated the party in the Corbyn era. Like religion, and especially in a political party, they should remain a private matter. Together with other policies that have broad public support (one being a commitment to apply for re-admission to the EU, and two others, the secularisation of the UK's education system on the lines adopted in France and the USA, and the abolition of fee-paying private schools) it needs to re-cast itself as the party of individual freedom and above all, of free expression in all its forms. This is by no means a secondary issue. A survey conducted in February 2021 suggested that something like half the UK population were 'afraid to speak their mind' in the presence of a police officer. And this was in Boris Johnson's post-Brexit 'Mother of the Free' in 2021, not Hitler's Germany and Stalin's Soviet Union in the late 1930s, or Kim Jong un's North Korea and the Ayatollahs' Iran today.

As a first step in such a transformation, Labour should pledge that one of its first measures on coming to power will be the repeal of all existing legislation (much, if not most, Tory) that is currently stifling free speech, to be replaced by an entrenched, that is to say, irremovable act, protecting it. This could also serve as a precedent for a badly needed fully-written constitution. Such an act should take as its model the free speech clause of the First Amendment to the US constitution, together with the exemptions, each of them on balance justifiable in my opinion, that have been added as a consequence of a number of Supreme Court rulings. (However, one ruling rejected the claim that so-called 'hate speech', illegal in the UK, should be added to this list.) Among the most important of these exemptions are speech integral to illegal conduct, 'fighting words', that is, speech that incites lawless action, and 'true threats' (in English law, comparable to 'common assault'). Also excluded is the so-called 'hecklers' veto', which has been invoked in recent years by leftists who in the name of free speech, shout down speakers they disapprove of.

Like many others who are deeply troubled by the progressive erosion of free expression in the UK, not to speak of the western world generally, I am convinced that such an act as the one I propose will have overwhelming public approval. As well as harming no-one (being 'offended' is not being harmed) and benefitting everyone (assuming that everyone wishes to speak freely…if some don't, no one will make them) unlike most government legislation, free speech costs the tax payer nothing. In fact, it will free up much-needed resources in the policing and justice systems currently being used to suppress it, resources which can then be deployed to combat crimes that do cause genuine (bodily) harm, and that until recently, as a matter of policy, have been totally ignored, such as Muslim gang rape and FGM. (Let us not forget that it was fear of being accused of racism and 'Islamophobia that greatly contributed to the failure to take action against both these barbaric crimes.) Such is the level of public concern over this issue that I do not rule out the possibility that free speech could help to sweep Labour to power if the party has the courage to make it the law of the land

However, at the time of writing (July 2021,) all the signs are that under the party's current leadership, no such courage will be forthcoming. On July 11, Labour announced that it would be voting against a government bill to prevent universities suppressing freedom of speech on their campuses. The party's shadow education secretary called the measure a 'hate speech bill', one that would give 'Holocaust deniers, anti-vaxxers and people harmful to public interest the opportunity to sue their way to a platform at universities'. That was not the bill's purpose, as the shadow minister knew full well. It contained no such provision. It did not, as was implied, give the right of any non-student to speak at a university and on a subject of their choosing…an absurdity. As well as protecting the free speech of students and teaching staff, it protected an *already invited* outside speaker from being 'cancelled'. Opposition to the bill was also forthcoming, as one would expect, from the far-left dominated National Union of Students.

As for 'the public interest' and topics that constitute 'hate speech', who will decide what they might be? It seems Labour intends that the decision will made by speech police before university students have had the opportunity to decide this for themselves. Labour's policy of 'not in front of the students' found itself at odds with two men of the left, John Milton and Karl Marx. His *Areopagitica* was Milton's reply to an act by parliament under Charles I to license the press: 'Nor is it to common people less than a reproach; for if we be so jealous over them, as we dare not trust them with an English pamphlet, what do we but censure them for a giddy, vicious and ungrounded people; in such a sick and weak estate of faith as to be able to take nothing down but through the pipe of a licenser.' Two centuries later, Marx also waged a similar battle for a free press against another King who could not trust his people…William IV of Prussia. For those who advocated censorship, 'true education consists in keeping a person swaddled in a cradle all his life, for as soon as he learns to walk, he also learns to fall, and it is only through falling that he learns to walk. But if we all remain children in swaddling clothes, who is to swaddle us? If we lie in a cradle, who is to cradle us? If we are all in jail, who will be the jail warden.' Or as Aristotle famously asked, 'who will guard the guardians?' Keir Starmer? Certainly, as a former Director of Public Prosecutions, he has a sharp eye when it comes to speech crime. When Labour MP Rosie Duffield, acting on security advice after receiving threats for saying only women have a cervix, decided not to attend her party's 2021 annual conference, instead of defending her right to say something that has been known to medical science for centuries, Starmer's response was to say 'it is something that should not be said'. Starmer delivered no such rebuke to the editors of the prestigious medical journal, *The Lancet*, when a matter of days later, in its issue of September 25, 2021, in deference to the trans lobby, the journal used the term 'bodies with vaginas' instead of women. Starmer dug himself even deeper into the woke hole in an LBC phone-in on March 28, 2022, when during a discussion about trans 'women' competing in women's sporting events, he not only refused to take a position on the issue, but declined to say whether a women could have a penis, both extraordinary responses for a former lawyer, barrister, Q.C., Director of Public Prosecutions and Head of the Crown Prosecutions Service. But then the habit seems to be catching, because Biden's nominee for the US Supreme Court, Ketanji Brown Jackson, when asked to provide a definition of a woman, was unable to do so. (In January 2022, there were press reports that staff at Bristol University were demanding the banning of the use of the word 'maternity', and that a feminist activist had been accused of 'transphobia' and investigated for saying that only women could give birth. Meanwhile, men claiming to be women had been given permission to use the women's facilities at the university's swimming pool. What price Thomas Paine's *Age of Reason*?)

Instead of paternalist mollycoddling, why not treat students as the adults they are, and let them debate and then make up their minds on the important questions of the day, however 'hateful' some might find them? And anyway, nobody will be compelled to attend the kind of events Labour wants to ban, and if they are properly conducted, those who do will have the opportunity to contest ideas they disagree with. That is how free speech in a democracy works. Does Labour really think that history students are incapable of refuting lies about the Holocaust, or biology students conspiracy theories about Covid19? If such subjects, and others no less controversial (the age of the universe, 'critical race theory', capital punishment, the Arab-Israeli conflict, assisted dying and transgenders in women's sport are just a few of many) cannot be debated at university, where does Labour think they should be, if indeed at all? In view of the party's reaction to the government bill, are we to assume that when (or if) Labour is returned to power, it will outlaw debates at universities on subjects it deems to be promoting 'hate speech'? Sadly, Labour has made a serious error of political judgment as well as of moral principle in supporting a policy best expressed in a slogan chanted by leftist mobs on US campuses to shout down speakers they do not approve of...'Free speech is hate speech.'.

Footnote

As noted above, the Socialist Workers Party has joined the chorus of voices from across political and clerical spectra demanding what goes by the name of 'responsible free speech'. Each has its own special reasons for doing so...for example, trans-gender activists want to silence and criminalise feminists who insist there are only two sexes. (Notable among them is Labour Shadow Foreign Secretary Lisa Nandy.) As I write (June 2021), a Scottish woman, Marion Millar, is about to stand trial under the Communications Act for tweeting a photograph of a bow of ribbons in the green, white and purple colours of the Suffragettes, tied to a tree outside a Glasgow BBC TV studio. A member of the public had complained that the bow looked like a noose. This was enough to set in motion the wheels of Scotland's criminal justice system. While I am reasonably confident that the super-woke SWP approves of the prosecution, its main concern since 9/11, which it approved, has been the protection of Islam from criticism, especially from those who, like *Charlie Hebdo,* see it as legitimate subject for humorous comment, just like any other religion. Thus, after initially defending Salman Rushdie, sentenced to death by Ayatollah Khomeini in 1989 for his novel, the *Satanic Verses,* under the new post 9/11 dispensation, the SWP performed a Stalinist-vintage 180-degree summersault, adding its voice, albeit belatedly, to those of the 'establishment', from Tory Prime Minister Margaret Thatcher and historian Hugh Trevor-Roper to Labour Deputy Leader Roy Hattersley, who had accused Rushdie of 'Islamophobia' and even racism. In doing so, the SWP demonstrably repudiated the libertarian tradition that had always been integral to authentic Marxism which, in its formative years as the International Socialists, the party had defended against its Leninist and Stalinist perversions. It was in defence of that tradition that its first major literary undertaking was the publication of a biography of Lenin's most incisive, perceptive and prophetic critic, Rosa Luxemburg, by their leading theoretician Tony Cliffe. (Its second edition underwent textual revisions that reflected the evolution of the IS into a classic Leninist 'vanguard' party.)

To put the record straight so speak, below are citations from the writings of Marx and Luxemburg that should dispel any doubts as to their stance on the most important right of all, without which all others are in constant jeopardy, the right to free expression of speech and press, and their opposition to censorship of any kind. First, Marx:

[Censorship] 'exercises tutelage over the highest interests of the citizens, their minds.' 'To fight [i.e., to oppose] freedom of the press, one must maintain the thesis of the permanent immaturity of the human race [hence the need for "responsible free speech"].'

'A free press is the ever-vigilant eye of the people's spirit, the embodiment of the people's trust in itself…It is a spiritual mirror, in which a people discover itself.' Yes. Warts and all.

Now Rosa Luxemburg;

'Freedom only for the supporters of the government, only for the members of one party [and, inevitably, in the end, only for its one leader] - however numerous they may be - is no freedom at all. Freedom is always and exclusively freedom for the one who thinks differently. Not because of any fanatical concept of "justice" but because all that is instructive, wholesome and purifying in political freedom depends on this essential characteristic [exactly!], and its effectiveness vanishes when "freedom" become a special privilege.'
     'Without general elections, without *unrestricted* freedom of the press, without a free struggle of opinion, life dies out in every public institution, becomes a mere

semblance of life, in which only the bureaucracy remains an active element.'
(emphasis added)

Luxemburg is alluding here to two events; the dispersal, on January 19, 1918, by armed force, of the Russian Constituent Assembly, in which the Bolsheviks had only one quarter of its delegates; and when two days after their coup in Petrograd on November 7, 1917, the Bolsheviks approved a decree banning (temporarily of course) freedom of the press established after the overthrow of Tsar Nicholas II on March 8 of the same year. It was never repealed.

Finally, we have Trotsky, whose attitude to press freedom, unlike that of Marx and Luxemburg, was ambiguous, to say the least, in part contingent on the circumstances of the moment. From the Bolshevik-Menshevik split of 1903, provoked to large degree by Lenin's obsessive centralism, until the very eve of the revolution of March 1917, Trotsky could be seen as a representative of the more libertarian wing of Russian Marxism. But after throwing his lot in with the Bolsheviks on his return from exile in the USA, as Commissar for War, he either approved or initiated all the repressive measures of the early Bolshevik years of power, only then to find himself their prime target with the rise of Stalin. Confronted in his final years in exile, from 1929 to 1940, with rise and then brutal consolidation of Stalin's tyranny, Trotsky reverted to the quasi-libertarianism of his pre-Bolshevik years, upholding the complete freedom of the press in a capitalist society, while still, unlike Luxemburg, defending the right of a revolutionary regime to impose restrictions on press freedom if the situation warranted it, as in this article, written in Mexico and dating from 1938. However, he added this proviso, that 'the interdiction or censorship [by a revolutionary regime] of bourgeois papers is not at all a matter of "programme" or "principle", not an ideal situation.' When it came to the question of press freedom in a capitalist society, Trotsky position was unequivocal, unlike his latter-day epigones. His defence of press freedom is particularly relevant in our censorious times, because Trotsky is not defending the freedom of a left-wing publication under attack from the right, but the reverse:

A campaign [by the Stalinists] against the reactionary press is developing in Mexico...The object is to 'curb' the reactionary press, either by submitting it to censorship, or by banning it completely... [as the Bolsheviks did in Russia] It is not difficult to see that, even if this campaign were to triumph and bring concrete results to the liking of Lombardo Toledano [a Stalinist trade union leader], the ultimate consequences would fall on the working class. Theory, as well as historic experience, testify that any [n.b.] restriction to democracy in bourgeois society is eventually directed against the proletariat...any workers 'leader' who arms the bourgeois state with special means to control public opinion in general [laws against 'hate speech'] and the press in particular, is a traitor.'

Well said, Comrade Trotsky! Corbyn, who has called for laws ('we demand') that require 'respect' for religion, and the SWP, who demand special protection for Islam, are precisely traitors, not just to the working class, but to democracy and to the right of everyone to express their opinions publicly, no matter how offensive some may find them.

441

So free speech is a right-wing cause? Each of these defenses of press freedom come from the revolutionary left. This how the right, or rather, the far right, dealt with it. In Germany on February 27, 1933, a fire broke out in the Reichstag debating chamber. To this day, disputes as to how the blaze started continue. What is not in dispute is that the Nazis, who with Hitler as Chancellor, had formed a coalition government with the Nationalists on January 30, used the fire to secure the passing of an emergency decree the next day. It read in part: 'Articles 114, 115, 117, 118, 123, and 153 of the Constitution of the German Reich are suspended until further notice. It is therefore permissible to restrict the rights of personal freedom [*habeas corpus*] freedom of expression, *including freedom of the press*, the freedom to organise and assemble, the privacy of postal, telegraphic and telephonic communications.' (emphasis added) Article 118 affirmed the right to free expression of opinion, article 123 to freedom of assembly without prior permission. So freedom of expression is *right wing*? I rest my case.

Addendum: Lies, Damned Lies and BLM Statistics

Back in 2010, along with head of Gender Affairs unit Gita Saghal and several of its high profile supporters, I resigned my membership of Amnesty International because of its decision to employ the services of a known sympathizer of the Taliban, Moazzam Beg. I still, however, receive their bulletins, one of which, promoting the World Day Against the Death Penalty of October 10, 2020, gave rise to the following amicable exchanges between myself and Paul Bridges, Chair of the Amnesty Anti-Death Penalty Project. I had taken issue with its endorsement of the Black Lives Matter claim that, as Bridges put it, in the USA, 'the death penalty is an issue of racial justice'. He referred to 'several studies conducted across the USA' that established 'clear links regarding a racialized death penalty'. He cited 'a particular statistic' that showed that "43%" of those who have been executed in the US have been people of colour"'.

I wrote to him as follows:

As a life-long opponent of racism, slavery and the death penalty, I do not want BLM propaganda. This organization promotes anti-white racism. The founder of BLM Toronto has posted on line the claim that whites are 'sub-human', and the leader of BLM Oxford that whites should be enslaved by blacks. BLM also refuses to acknowledge, let alone condemn, the death penalty and slavery practiced in non-western countries. It is not proof of racism that 43% of those executed in the USA are black, given that 52% of all murders in the USA are committed by blacks.

This is his reply:

Thank you for coming back on this. I just wanted to say that we of course, utterly condemn the types of racist statements you have highlighted. All racism whether white on black, black one white [whose existence is denied by so-called 'critical race theory] is wrong. Sadly, most movements contain extreme and unsavoury elements but I do not believe that this is a widespread view within the BLM movement. As regards the death penalty statistics that you mentioned we do not offer it [sic] as proof of racism [he did just that!] but we do believe that is evidence of a skewed social justice system in the USA. [But Bridge says that 'the death penalty is an issue of *racial*, not social justice.] Finally, I'd like to thank you for you continued support in opposing the death penalty.

I replied as follows:

Thank you for your prompt reply. Re the death penalty. The statistic I cited suggested if anything its use is skewed against non-blacks, contrary to the claims of BLM. Re BLM racism. Perhaps you do, but I know of no other movement whose prominent activists make such outrageous statements and, what is worse, without their being repudiated by others in the movement. The same Oxford BLM leader, I might add, called a black student 'a coon', promising to have him beaten up simply for disagreeing with her 'take' on the race issue. Black looting of Chicago shops was justified by a BLM activist as 'reparations' [for slavery, abolished in 1863], again, without being repudiated. And so I could go on. As for slavery, I ask you, do you not find it troubling, to say the least, that a movement that makes it its business to pull down statues of white slave-traders of times long gone [and also of those who fought to abolish it], had nothing to say about the auctioning of black Africans in Libya by Arab slave traders, as revealed by CNN as recently as 2017? And of course, there is BLM's attitude towards Israel, which did indeed stir a few consciences but shamefully left the majority unmoved.

I know it is all the rage right now, with everybody who is anybody scrambling to jump on the BLM bandwagon without first checking what it stands for and does, but in the light of the evidence I have presented (but a small sample of the mountain that exists) I think you are making a serious error of judgment in joining the pack.

Finally, Bridges' reply to the above:

As you are aware statistics, reports and events can be selected, interpreted and presented so as to 'prove' almost anything. [Which is what he tried but failed to do with his '43%'] So we could trade claim and counter-claim forever but I don't intend to do so. [Advisedly, as his case is hopeless flawed] More importantly I believe we can agree that both racism and the death penalty are wrong and we both agree that racist statements, whatever the source, are wrong and that we should both continue to campaign against these twin evils whoever they are perpetrated by.

Agreed.

Finally, I say goodbye to the reader with one last observation for their consideration. As I have argued throughout this work, in the overwhelming majority of instances, today's anti-Zionism serves those who promote, propagate and even kill Jews for it as a secular cloak for an ages-old protean prejudice whose origins are located in the scriptures of two monotheistic religions. How else explain that anti-Semitism first took root and then flourished not in pagan societies, only in regions and then countries that are historically Christian, and in others that are still by law Islamic. Yet none of these countries today has a territorial dispute with Israel (Islam is not the state religion of Syria, which is the only that has), while some, the prime example being Pakistan, do have one with a neighbouring state. First it was killing Christ and rejecting Allah, then, compounding these crimes against god, there followed those against society...greed and conspiracy, poisoning wells, spreading plagues (in 1349, the Black Death, and in 2020, Covid19), the 'blood libel', treason. Today for anti-Semites on both left and right alike, it is the 'hidden hand' of Mossad and the Rothschilds, the genocide of the Palestinians. Any stick will do to beat the Yids, because as I have already said, and I will repeat it now, today's anti-Semitism is, as it has always been, not about where the Jews are, but just that they are.

'The anti-Semite rejoices at any opportunity to vent his malice. The times have made it unpopular in the West to proclaim a hatred of the Jews. This being the case, the anti-Semite must constantly seek new forms and forums for his poison. How he must revel in the new masquerade. He does not hate the Jews, he is just an anti-Zionist!'

Martin Luther King, letter to an anti-Zionist friend.

NEMESIS

On October 29, 2020, the Equality and Human Rights Commission announced the result of its investigation of Labour Party anti-Semitism. It found that under the leadership of Jeremy Corbyn, the Labour Party had broken the law, specifically with respect to:

'three breaches of the Equalities Act (2010) relating to:

Political interference in anti-Semitism complaints
Failure to provide adequate training to those handling complaints
Harassment'

Amongst other breaches of the law, it found that 'political interference in anti-Semitism complaints' by Corbyn's own office, LOTO, was 'discriminatory and unlawful, and that the Labour Party was legally responsible for it.' And, I would submit, *ipso facto*, its Leader when this and other breaches of the law were committed. The EHCRC agreed, finding that Corbyn was 'ultimately accountable and responsible for what happened at that time.' The same day, Corbyn was suspended from the Labour Party and had the whip withdrawn for saying the whole business of Labour Party anti-Semitism had been 'dramatically overstated', the proverbial 'storm in a tea cup', or as McCluskey had it, 'mood music', probably generated by the Special Branch. In the light of the evidence, I have presented in this book, I leave it to the reader to decide if they are right.

The Merry Wokes of Windsor

On September 9, 2021, the story broke that Queen and her family were supporters of Black Lives Matter. In an interview with Channel Four TV, Sir Ken Olisa, the (black) Lord Lieutenant for London, revealed that he 'discussed with the royal household this whole issue of race, particularly in the last 12 months since the George Floyd incident.' Asked if the palace supported Black Lives Matter, he replied, 'The answer is easily [sic] yes.' This raises a number of very interesting questions. Constitutionally, the UK now has a Head of State that supports, so we are led to believe, a movement that is campaigning for the abolition of Her Majesty's police service, prisons and justice system, and a legislature dominated by a monarchist, 'law and order' party that has been outspoken in its opposition to the policies of this same movement. Given their divided loyalties, it is difficult to predict how the Conservative government and party will react to this announcement. No less intriguing is the predicament this places the far left in, which has from the beginning been the most vocal in its endorsement and active in the protests of Black Lives Matter. Now these intransigent republicans and enemies of the 'establishment' will find themselves marching in lock step with the House of Windsor. As they have spent the last two decades and more doing exactly the same with racist, anti-socialist enemies of Israel, I foresee see no insurmountable obstacles to their making a similar accommodation, albeit one of convenience, with the royals.

Putin's Useful Idiots

'The EU and Nato have become tools of US foreign policy.' (Jeremy Corbyn, *Nato belligerence endangers us all*, in the Communist Party *Morning Star*, April 16, 2014)

'The United States has overstepped its borders, and in every area.' (Russian President Vladimir Putin, February 10, 2007)

'[Russia's] challenge to western [sic] expansion and intervention in Georgia, Syria and Ukraine [has] provided some check to unbridled US power.' (Corbyn's former Communications Officer Seumas Milne, *The Guardian*, October 29, 2014)

'The main enemy is at home' (*Socialist Worker*, February 28, 2022)

'Ukraine isn't a real country. It's always been part of Russia.' (US President Donald Trump, November 2017

'Russians and Ukrainians are one and the same people.' (Russian President Vladimir Putin, February 2020)

'...by its ceaseless meddling in the affairs of the West, it [Russia] cripples and disturbs our normal development, and this with the object of conquering geographical positions which will assure to Russia the mastery over Europe, and thus crush every chance of progress...' (Frederick Engels: *Foreign Policy of Russian Tsardom*, April 1890.)

'We are astonished that in the current discussion of the Oriental question the English journals have not more boldly demonstrated the vital interests which should render Great Britain the earnest and unyielding opponent of the Russia projects of annexation and aggrandisement.' (Karl Marx, *New York Herald Tribune*, April 12, 1853)

'...in all essential points Russia has steadily, one after another, gained her ends, thanks to the ignorance, dullness and consequent inconsistency and cowardice of Western governments.' (Karl Marx, ibid, April 19,1853)

'In spite of diplomatic tradition, these constant and successful encroachments of Russia have at last roused in the Western cabinets of Europe a very dim distant apprehension of the approaching danger.' (Karl Marx, ibid, April 19, 1853)

Not from the first time, the far left found itself marching in step with the far right and Russia's President Putin when the Ukraine crisis erupted in early 2022. As part of his larger strategy to reclaim the lost territories of the Stalin and Tsarist empires, Putin had stationed 130,000 troops, 1,300 tanks, 1,680 artillery and 3,700 armoured vehicles on Russia's border with Ukraine, plus another 30,000 troops in

Belarus and 1,000 in Moldova, thereby surrounding Ukraine on three sides. The response of the Corbynista 'Stop the War Coalition' was to accuse the UK and the USA of 'ramping up the threat of war' and to demand 'Stop Nato [sic] Expansion'. (Honesty requires that on this occasion, I must give Corbyn credit for a rare moment of political vision. As long ago as April 2014, in an article in the Stalinist *Morning Star* with the Orwellian title 'Nato belligerence endangers us all', he complained that the 'expansion of Nato into Poland and the Czech Republic' had 'particularly increased tensions with Russia'. As for the Ukraine, while he 'would not condone Russian behaviour or expansion' it was 'not unprovoked' because 'there are huge questions around [?] the West's intentions in Ukraine' – but not, so it would seem, Putin's. The problem was, Nato was acting 'outside its own area' [as defined, naturally, by comrades Corbyn and Putin] and that the EU and Nato had formed a 'mutual alliance of interference and domination [sic] reaching ever eastwards'. Again, nothing about Putin's reaching ever westwards to expand his 'own area'.)

Two weeks before Putin's invasion, featured speakers at an anti-Nato online Coalition event scheduled for February 11, 2022, included not only Putin's useful idiot Corbyn but his former political adviser, the life-long Stalinist Andrew Murray and with Corbyn, Coalition founder and Chair, and Dianne Abbott, high priestess of the Corbyn cult and Mao apologist. Its subject was an Orwellian 'No war in the Ukraine: Stop Nato expansion'. The panel of guests would be 'speaking out against Nato's nuclear aggression and interventionist agenda'. (A small detail: The only nuclear threats were those made by Putin. Likewise, his was the only 'intervention'.) The Communist Party's '*Morning Star*, whose pages over the years had been graced by both comrades Murray and Corbyn, likewise directed its fire against the west. 'Russia's concerns are far from absurd. It demands [sic] no further Nato expansion...The anti-war movement should fight the inane war-mongering of the British government and oppose Nato's further expansion.' Putin's were another matter, with troops permanently stationed in north Georgia, Belarus and Moldova, the illegal annexation of Crimea, and the sponsoring of two puppet regimes in eastern Ukraine.

On the very outermost fringes of Leninist lunacy, the last remaining remnant of Healy's Workers Revolutionary Party summoned the masses to the barricades in defence of what in its eyes remained in all but name the former USSR: 'Workers must support Russia: The UK-USA trade unions must stop war drive by bringing down Johnson-Biden governments.' And replacing them, presumably, with regimes answerable to the WRP. (For all its comic aping of Leninist orthodoxy, the WRP's *Newsline* couldn't manage to give the correct date for the Paris Commune, back-dating it by one year to 1870.) On February 16, the *Newsline's* admittedly limited circle of readers were assured that 'Russian troops have completed their training drills [sic] in Belarus' and 'will begin returning to their bases'. A week later, as Russian tanks rolled in to eastern Ukraine and a brigade of Chechen assassins held a Muslim prayer session before hunting down Ukrainian government officials, its headline read: 'Russia defies Imperialism: Time for the World Socialist Revolution'. Putin's ambitions were more modest, being described by a regime spokesman as a 'peace-keeping' mission - just like Poland in 1939, Hungary, 1956, Czechoslovakia 1968, and Afghanistan, 1979.

As with Hitler's invasion of Poland after the betrayal by the UK and France of the Czechs at Munich, Putin may well have seen the West's no less pusillanimous surrender to the Taliban as proof that he could move against the Ukraine without risking any serious international percussions. He certainly had no need to fear the reaction of the far left. Corbyn's 'Peace and Justice Project' also went into Orwellian overdrive, demanding 'No war in Ukraine' and 'Stop NATO Expansion', while Corbyn's Coalition partner, the Socialist Workers Party, who had also been singing the same Quisling song that 'the West's expansion is behind the threat of Ukraine war', was pleased to report that 'more than half of the people in the US [most for sure being Trumpists] say America should "stay out"' of any involvement in the Ukraine crisis.

In yet another Orwellian strophe, Boris Johnson was accused by the SWP of inventing pretexts 'for a Western military intervention' at the very moment Putin was doing exactly that, staging fake border 'incidents', just as Hitler did on the eve of his invasion of Poland, to justify his seizure of the eastern Ukraine. In fact Johnson, whose party had been the beneficiary of Russian funding to the tune of at least £7 million, came under attack from both sides of the House for what was seen as his token response to Putin's aggression, with financial sanctions promised not in a matter of hours or days, but 'weeks' and even 'months'. With the UK serving as a tax, residential and investment haven for Russian oligarchs, and the UK desperately in need of new markets after its exit from the EU, Johnson, for all his anti-Putin rhetoric, was obviously going through the motions, even warning against 'Russophobia'. (Two revelations involving Johnson caused outrage among European politicians. On February 25, as Putin's tanks rolled across the Ukrainian border, Johnson was hosting a fund-raising event in the presence of a Russian oligarch's wife who had donated £2 million to the Tories. Then in a speech at a party conference on March 19, he likened Brussels to Putin, and the UK's Brexit vote to Ukraine's fight for freedom, in the full knowledge that only days previously, Ukraine had applied for EU membership, and that it was the EU which had provided the mechanisms and means for Ukraine to continue fighting, and unlike Brexit Britain, opened its doors to the millions fleeing Putin's terror.) The UK, with the support of a Labour opposition full committed under Starmer to 'making Brexit work', was also the only country not to grant unrestricted asylum to Ukrainian refugees fleeing the Russian onslaught.

With Putin's invasion looming, the SWP had prepared the ground for its anti-western stance by invoking Lenin's policy of 'revolutionary defeatism' which he adopted at the outset of the First World War. Stated briefly, it demanded that revolutionaries on both sides of a war between two imperialist powers or alliances, should, as the *Socialist Worker* correctly explained, 'target their own ruling class'. Although the SWP stance was tactically 'softened' by its hypocritical claim that 'we do not seek to cover up Putin's crimes in Ukraine, Belarus, Kazakhstan, Chechnya and beyond' (but neither had they been the cause of any public protest by the party) it nevertheless made clear that 'our starting point is to say we want an end to the system that produces war - *and therefore our primary enemy is the government at home'* (emphasis added) - music, if he had by chance been listening - to Putin's ears. Here we have once again what I have called the Chomsky principle, that the only government one is called upon to criticise or oppose is one's own - unless of course it happens to be that of the USA or Israel. Peter Tatchell made this very same point about a second London demo, when he was shouted down by stewards armed with loud hailers when he attempted to start a chant in support of arming the Ukrainians and sanctioning Russia. 'The Left has abandoned its anti-imperialism unless it's against the USA or Israel.'

A policy of defeatism is all very well in a country like the UK, where political opposition to its overseas military operations can be conducted with impunity, as it was during the two Iraq wars and the Falklands conflict, when some on the far left quite openly supported armies at war with the UK. But even in peace time, Putin has never tolerated political opposition in domestic matters, let alone to his foreign policy, arresting and even murdering anyone who posed the slightest threat to his rule. So it was only to be expected that when demonstrators took to the streets of Moscow and St Petersburg to protest Putin's invasion of Ukraine they would be beaten and arrested in their thousands, without any protests from not only from the far left, which was only to be expected, but the UK government and the Labour Party. The SWP's anti-western defeatism was therefore knowingly asymmetric, because its anti-Putin counterpart could not be replicated in Russia. By contrast, the SWP could demand, without fear of legal (or extra-legal) repercussions, that 'all Western [sic] forces are withdrawn from the countries that border Russia and that Nato is dissolved, not extended', while anti-Putin Russians, lacking a legal voice, could not make equivalent demands of their own government in relation to its occupation of the Ukraine. The SWP's policy was, despite all the anti-Putin rhetoric, in its effects, therefore pro-Russian, as demonstrated by the conspicuous absence of the customary slogans normally adopted by western leftists when a country is subjected to an unprovoked attack by an imperialist power, such as 'Solidarity with Ukraine' and 'Putin Out'. If challenged to explain their silence, the SWP would argue that according to the rules of 'revolutionary defeatism', demanding that Russian troop leave the Ukraine was the sole responsibility of Ukrainians and anti-Putin Russians, despite all the hazards it necessarily involved, while the SWP's task was to 'target' only 'the enemy at home', knowing full well that under the much maligned 'bourgeois democracy' of the West, there would be no legal repercussions, even if the left's fire was directed solely against the only two organisation that were capable of providing support, inadequate though it initially was, to the people of Ukraine - the EU and Nato. So there would there be no Coalition demonstrations outside the Russian embassy, unlike those routinely staged over the years outside those of Israel and the USA. The far lefts' quarrel was only with Nato and the EU, not Putin, just as the Ukraine's was with Putin and not the West. So as far as the far left was concerned, when it came to it, the Ukrainians were on their own And this was internationalism?

With the prospect looming of a Russian invasion leading to massive civilian casualties, readers of *Socialist Worker* were advised of another Leninist axiom, that 'the key issue is not who fires the shot in the war [i.e., Putin]. It's who is responsible for the conditions that produced the conflict' - that is to say, Nato and the EU, who had not fired any shots and understandably, as both the SWP and Putin well knew, had no intention of doing so.

(Less inhibited in its support of Putin than the SWP, the Muscovite *Morning Star* carried on its front page the lead story with the heading: 'Russian communists call for anti-fascist front against "Nato-led Nazification of Ukraine"', Kremlinspeak for 'invade, occupy, and install a puppet regime', as in Hungary in 1956, Czechoslovakia in 1968 and Afghanistan in 1979.) Veteran Trotskyists will recall that up to its collapse in 1991, unlike its more 'orthodox' Trotskyist rivals, the SWP defined the USSR not as an essentially 'progressive' though 'deformed' workers' state, but as 'state capitalist', thereby deeming it unworthy of any support by the Left, however 'critical'. In a political summersault rivalling Stalin's pact with Hitler, by echoing the Stalinist *Morning Star* in its attack solely against Nato and the EU, the SWP took the side of a capitalist, imperialist, authoritarian, expansionist Russia against a West whose freedoms allow potentially treasonous movements like the SWP to function without let or hindrance.

Undeterred by Putin's almost total economic, financial, political, diplomatic, transport, cultural, sporting and moral isolation, and demonstrators across the world proclaiming their solidarity with Ukraine's embattled but defiant people (over 100,000 at Berlin's Brandenburg Gate) the SWP line on the conflict if anything hardened in a feature article by Nick Clarke in the *Socialist Worker* of February 26. Titled 'Why Nato is an alliance built on war', there is no way that an uninformed reader could glean from its more than 1,200 words that the people of the Ukraine, civilians as well as soldiers, women as well men from the age of 16 to 60, were engaged in a desperate and truly heroic struggle to defend their county's existence as an independent nation. Ukraine is mentioned but once, and even then, simply to lay the blame for what it calls 'the war [sic] in [sic] the Ukraine' (not Putin's invasion of the Ukraine) solely on 'Nato's expansion into eastern Europe'...exactly the pretext used by Putin to justify his invasion. Putin's name does not occur once in the entire article. Instead, the reader is conducted through a catalogue of crimes committed by Nato dating back to its foundation in 1949, the purpose of this exercise being to refute the claim that 'whether it's corrupt Russia, authoritarian China or "backward" Islamism' (note the quotes - as we have seen, the SWP does not think "Islamism - i.e. , Jihadism - is 'backward'), 'the West, for all its shortcomings, mistakes and excesses, has been the spearhead of progress, democracy and freedom in a hostile world.' So, the argument continues, 'when a reactionary, authoritarian regime in Russia invades a country [sic] friendly to the West', (that is near as we get to any reference to Putin's' invasion of Ukraine) 'it can be tempting [sic] to try and decide which is the "lesser evil"'. As he wrote these quite extraordinary lines, millions of Ukrainians were heading for sanctuary in this same 'West'. They were not 'tempted'. The decision was made in an instant, instinctively. Like the countless millions who had made the same journey over the centuries, they *knew* with total certainty that their only hope of freedom and safety lay in the very countries Clarke so obviously despises, their democracy protected by the military alliance he so obviously would dearly love to see fall apart, just as he would the EU. He and those who share his detestation of both, be they of the left or the right, are due for a disappointment. The Ukraine crisis, far from weakening Nato and the EU, made them both stronger by proving their necessity for Europe's defence of its freedoms. However, it must be a source of much needed comfort for the SWP that its campaign for a leave vote in the EU referendum contributed, albeit modestly, to the marginalisation of the UK's role in the resistance to Putin's aggression against the West, and that its government now speaks to the free world with a voice that few listen to, and makes promises of action in its defence that even fewer take seriously. How ironic that as the UK waved goodbye to Europe to regain, so we were told, its lost freedoms, Ukraine should apply to join the EU to preserve them.

I have this to say to Putin useful idiot Clarke and those like Trump and Farage who share his Natophobia and Europhobia : If the choice of Ukraine's refugees was grounded in an illusion as to the freedoms of the West, let Clarke name one occasion in history in which the movement of refugees and migrants has been in the opposite direction, away from the west to the embrace of mother Russia, or south to the realm of Allah. Perhaps influenced, like all leftists today seem to be, by critical race theory, Clarke has not one good word to say for the West. He tells us that the 'version of capitalism adopted by most of the West didn't come from any particular enlightened thinking. Instead it was due to sheer economic interests on behalf of the US and profit for American industry' - without which, amongst many other things, the Allies could well have lost the Second World War. But then, in that war too, the Trotskyist movement, true to Lenin's 'revolutionary defeatism', regarded each side as bad as the other. How Marx would have enjoyed trashing Clarke's vulgar, crude, economic determinism, with all of western civilisation's achievements being reduced to a quest for profit - the Enlightenment, its classical music, art, literature, science, technology, philosophy, political and social reforms...the list goes on.

So much for the manifold sins of the West. However, true to the principles of 'revolutionary defeatism', with its insistence that the main - indeed it would seem in this instance, the only - enemy being 'at home', we learn nothing of the sins of the 'East' - the Soviet-controlled Warsaw Pact's crushing of the Hungarian Revolution of 1956 and Czechoslovakia's 'Prague Spring' of 1968, or of the totalitarian puppet regimes it maintained in power for more than four decades. Even more to the point, nowhere in this disgusting, shameful, cynical article is the case or a call made for solidarity with the Ukrainian people in their resistance to Putin's invasion, or with those brave Russians who have taken to streets to show their support for the Ukrainians. After his gratuitous denigrating, belittling and sneering at the achievements and values of western civilisation, Clarke concludes by accusing not Putin, but Nato, of having brought not 'peace or democracy, but war' and demanding that 'any true socialist should stand up and oppose Nato and the system of imperialist rivalries that it represents.' On the same day that Clarke's article appeared, February 26, two days after Putin launched his unprovoked invasion of Ukraine, CND, Stop the War Coalition, Codepink and No to NATO Network held what was billed as an 'International Emergency Online Rally, under the rubric: 'No War in Ukraine - No to Nato'. Anyone not *au fait* with the real situation would have reasonably assumed that it was Nato who were invading Ukraine, not Putin. At the head of the list of speakers was, inevitably, that very personification of anti-Natoism, the veteran all -purpose useful, in this instance, to Putin, idiot, Jeremy Corbyn.

Across the world, millions were united in their support for Ukraine, and outraged at the megalomaniac seeking to subjugate and colonise its people. Only on the far left and right was there silence, or even worse, awestruck admiration for the heir of Stalin and Ivan the Terrible. Others on the left attempted to finesse their stance, even though in Clarke's case it still necessarily followed that opposition to Nato and all its works required that 'true socialists' - that is, the SWP and its Coalition partners in treason Murray, Corbyn, Abbott et al - should do all in their power to hinder the supply of desperately-needed military hardware to the Ukrainians, while doing nothing to inhibit Putin's bid to enslave them. Readers will recall that the SWP adopted a similar policy towards the Kurds, who they denounced as 'western pawns' for accepting US military aid in their war against the Islamic State, while at the same time supporting Islamic State offshoots in Nigeria and east Africa. And while demanding the disbanding of Nato, neither did the SWP oppose Russian arms supplies to Iran, Syria, and via these two states to their terrorist, anti-Semitic clients Hamas and Hezbollah. Yet again, the same double standards the same selective solidarity. Ukrainians, like the Kurds, must not accept arms from Nato, but regimes and terrorists who will use them to kill Jews can accept them from Russia, since it is a question of supporting what Lenin called the 'revolutionary East' against the 'counter-revolutionary West'. I suggest to comrade Clarke that he puts this thesis on the relative merits of the East and West, one that he clearly endorses, to the test by taking up residence in Russia and then publishing in his name an article as hostile to the Putin regime as he is to the political system which upholds his right to hurl insults at it week after week, and allows him to demand the disbanding of the military alliance which protects his and his comrades' right to do so.

Just as one would expect, the SWP's duplicitous stance on Ukraine was endorsed by hard core Corbynista MPs, eleven of them Labour, and two from whom the Labour whip had been withdrawn, Corbyn himself for his denial of the scale of Labour anti-Semitism under his leadership, and Claudia Webbe after her conviction for harassment, which included threats of an acid attack on a woman. They had signed a Stop the War Coalition statement which opposed the 'eastwards expansion' of Nato (Putin's pretext for his invasion of Ukraine), accused the UK government, not Putin, of 'sabre -rattling' and denied Ukraine's right to apply for membership of Nato, which as a sovereign state, it has every right to exercise. But like Putin, whatever international law might say, his useful idiots do not believe that Ukraine should be allowed to act like a sovereign state. Since Ukraine supposedly lays within the Russian 'sphere of interest', its policies, as also those of Nato's, should be subject to veto by Moscow. (A matter of days after the Russian invasion of Ukraine, Sweden and Finland, also located within this same 'sphere', were warned that a similar fate also awaited them if they applied to join Nato. Until 1917, Finland, like the Ukraine, had been part of the Russian empire, and had then successfully defied Stalin's attempt to reclaim it in the so-called Winter War' of 1939-40.) After reportedly being advised that 'you can be a mouthpiece of the Kremlin or a Labour MP, but not both', to the scorn of the SWP, all eleven Labour MPs beat a tactical retreat and withdrew their names from the Coalition statement. With nothing to lose, those of Kremlin mouthpieces Corbyn and Webbe remained.

Tactical adjustments in the far left's public stance on Ukraine became increasingly necessary as media coverage exposed the wanton brutality of Putin's invasion, and reported both the resistance of the Ukrainians to it and the flood of refugees, some two million by March 10, fleeing from it. What did not change were the unrelenting attacks on Nato, without whose military support, Ukraine's continued defiance of Putin would have been impossible. So we had Dianne Abbott's insistence that 'the claims that Russia is the aggressor should be treated skeptically', that 'the destabilization [sic] in the region comes from a continued eastern expansion of Nato', and her *non-sequitur* that 'the public is opposed to war with Russia.' No-one of course had proposed 'war with Russia', as even Abbott must have known, though Putin had threatened a nuclear one against the West. As for Nato, it was avoiding any actions that could possibly lead to one.

And as always, there was the ever-present 'hand of Israel', to quote Corbyn, with allegations on the wearecorbyn website that Jewish Ukrainian President Volodymyr Zelensky was the front man for a Zionist/neo-Nazi plot against Russia. Then we had the Corbynista 'Labour Left Alliance', with its opposition to 'sending "lethal" aid to Ukraine or imposing sanctions on Russia' and as two of its slogans, the Corbynesque 'abolish Nato' and the SWP's 'the main enemy is at home.' (UK Dock workers obviously did not agree, because in the best tradition of international working-class solidarity, they refused to touch Russian vessels moored at British ports.) Like the comments on wearecorbyn, the LLA had detected evidence of a Jewish conspiracy in Ukraine's resistance to Putin's demands. Zelensky was 'a Zionist who works with fascists'. In Ukraine's most recent general election, in 2019, the far-right ultra-nationalist Svoboda, Ukraine's 'Nazis', secured, 2.15% of the votes and no seats. This was the party, *with I repeat zero seats*, that Putin's invasion was supposedly to liberate Ukraine from. The election was won by the centrist Servant of the People party, with 43.16% of the vote and 256 seats of a total of 450. In the Presidential elections of the same year, Zelensky, of the same party, won 73.22% of the second-round vote.

The *Guardian's* reporting was more nuanced that Abbott's typically clumsy re-hashing of the pre-invasion Corbynite anti-Nato line, but it still a made a fleeting appearance in its coverage of an allegedly 'pacifist' rally in Rome on March 6, a 'procession of peace' that was 'demonstrating against Putin but also Nato'. Yet marchers only chanted 'No base, no soldiers, Italy out of Nato'…but not 'Putin out of Ukraine', a selective pacifism reminiscent of Stalin's Stockholm-based campaign against western nuclear weapons while he was developing and testing his own 'peace bomb' (c.f. Chapter 13) and of the Peace Pledge Union's during the Second World War, in which it dismissed reports of the Holocaust as anti-German propaganda and supported a Nazi victory that would bring to the world (save for the Jews and other *untermenschen*) peace and social justice. (c.f. Appendix VIII) With the invasion into its second week, and as Putin's tanks and artillery laid siege to Ukraine's largest cities, bombing and shelling civilian targets, still we had 'the enemy is at home', the 'enemy' being Nato, the one force that stood between Putin and the crushing of Ukrainian resistance. As one of the Rome demonstrators explained, 'here no one believes we make peace with arms, that we make it by sending arms to one of the parties [i.e., Ukraine].'

The next day, March 7, central London, beginning outside the BBC headquarters and ending in Trafalgar Square, (not the Russian embassy in South Kensington be it noted) was the scene for a classic far leftist hijacking operation staged by march organisers the Corbynista/SWP/Stalinist Stop the War Coalition and the Campaign for Nuclear Disarmament. (Corbyn was a co-founder and Chairperson of the first and was at this time Vice President of the second.) Doubtless most of those marching, many displaying Ukrainian flags and carrying home-made placards attacking only Putin, were motivated purely by their solidarity with Ukraine, and unlike the demo's organisers, would have had no problem with its seeking military and other aid from the West. But most of the placards did, a clear indication of the rally's prime purpose. One held aloft said: 'No to War No to Nato Expansion' - but not to Putin's. (Putin's pretext for his invasion was 'Nato expansion.') Others were more nuanced (after all, it was supposed to be an anti-Putin demo), saying: 'Stop the war Russian Troops Out' and 'No to Nato Expansion', thereby maintaining, albeit in a necessarily attenuated form, the Leninist orthodoxy of 'revolutionary defeatism'. Posters on display at other similar, smaller scale events included 'We say no war with Russia', 'Disband Nato's war machine' (but not Putin's), 'End Nato and US imperialism' (again, but not Putin's), 'Raise wages, not wars' (sic), 'Oppose US/EU/Nato Axis of domination', 'Hands off Donetsk and Lugansk (Ukraine's hands that is, both being Russian puppet states in eastern Ukraine) and a couple from across the pond, 'No war with Russia for Wall Street' and 'US/Nato: No war on Russia and Donbass' {where the two Putin puppet states are located).

(The rank opportunism of the far left on another issue than the Ukraine had an ironic twist. For all their vaunted internationalism, the pro-Brexit stance of Corbyn and the SWP had over the years complemented, albeit in a modest way, Putin's anti-EU intrigues, and both came to fruition when charity vans carrying essential supplies to Ukrainian refugees were turned away at Dover because they had not fully complied with Brexit regulations. Movement was also restricted in the opposite direction, again due to the Brexit campaigned for by the far left. While EU states had already opened their borders to 2 million Ukrainian refugees fleeing the Putin terror, granting them a minimum stay of three years, in two weeks, the Home Office, which over the best part of two decades had put out the welcome mat for bent Russian oligarchs, no questions asked, had managed to issue 50 visas to those fleeing the predations of their benefactor in the Kremlin, and at that, only to refugees with close relatives in the UK. There was no protest at this outrage by a Labour Party newly bent on 'getting Brexit done' better than the Tories. Meanwhile, EU Ireland, population five million compared to Brexit Britain's 67 million, agreed to accept 100,00 refugees. The UK did, however, still have room for upwards of 97 Russian oligarchs who had thus far escaped any sanctions. If, as seemed likely, party-political resistance to accepting the UK's share of Ukrainian refuges was motivated by a cynical desire to appease Brexiteers, it was a serious miscalculation. The normally pro-Tory press and 75% of the public favoured the same 'open door' adopted by EU member states. Sensing the public mood, with polls showing a 60% majority critical of the government's abject failure to match the level of sanctions being applied by the EU, from the leftist *Guardian*, *Independent* and *Mirror* to the Tory *Telegraph*, *Daily Mail* and *Express* and the Murdoch *Times*, the press reveled in uncovering the labyrinthine dependency on 'dirty' Russian money of hallowed UK institutions from football clubs, the Tate gallery, the House of Lords [Boris Johnson overrode MI6 objections to award a peerage to Moscow-born oligarch Evgeny Lebedev] and the Tory Party to academe and symphony orchestras. Intentionally or not, what they were exposing was what had been for years a tacit Tory policy of Brussels out, Moscow in. With Moscow now on the way out, Allah could be confidently expected to take up the slack, augmenting his already powerful grip on the same institutions colonised by Moscow. Like the Kremlin's, Allah's gold buys compliance with and silence about his realm's vile practices, as Newcastle United manager Eddie Howe discovered when he found himself unable to condemn the 81 executions carried out in one day by his Saudi employers.)

At the very moment the London demo marchers were assembling behind the far left's cryptic placards, with their opposition to Nato's eastward expansion mingling with calls for 'peace' (but no attacks on Putin), 2,000 kilometers away, Ukraine's leaders were imploring Nato not to halt its extension to the east, but to continue it, to take more resolute action against their invaders, if not by creating a no-fly zone over their country, then at least by supplying it with fighters that could enable the Ukrainians to do so for themselves, a proposal agreed to by Poland, but vetoed by Biden.

Rarely if ever could there have been a demonstration whose ostensible purpose was so utterly opposed to the real intentions and principles of its organisers, the Coalition, which saw its enemy as being always 'at home', and a no less 'defeatist' CND, which as an advocate of unilateral nuclear disarmament, opposes the UK's possession of nuclear weapons as it does the UK's membership of Nato, but not the nuclear weapons of Russia and its creation of puppet regimes beyond its borders. Ironically, far from Putin's attack on Ukraine having divided and weakened Nato and the EU, as many on the extremes of left and right would have hoped, it has united both as never before, and at the same time and for the same reason, lengthened the queues of nations seeking to join them as the UK followed its chosen course towards global isolation, impotence and irrelevance.

On March 2, with the war now in its second week, and Putin palpably failing to achieve any of his objectives, Corbyn came up with a proposal that if accepted by Ukraine's leaders, would help him to do so. Drawing on all his long and rich experience of total failure to solve any of the world's conflicts, he said: 'Why don't we [sic] cut out the fighting zone, and go straight to the talking zone?' And why not indeed, seeing as 'all wars end with dialogue'. Or at least, so said Corbyn. Admittedly, I was only nine years old at the time. Even so, I still have a very clear recollection of the Second World War ending, not with a Corbynesque 'dialogue' for 'peace' between Hitler and the Allies, but Nazi Germany's military defeat and unconditional surrender, and trial, conviction and execution of most of its leaders at the Nuremberg Trials. But then, like much else requiring factual knowledge, at a minimum, average powers of reasoning and something at least resembling a grip on reality, history is not Corbyn's strongest suit, though playing the role of useful idiot most certainly is.

When, on March 7, Putin got into Corbyn's 'talking zone' (while continuing to rain down terror on Ukraine's civilians), it was not so much to have a 'dialogue' as to confront Ukraine's leaders with an ultimatum, one comprising terms that they had already rejected as non-negotiable because they would require Ukraine surrendering its sovereignty and large tracts of its territory. In return for a cessation of hostilities that were begun by Russia, Ukraine would be required to, quote 'make amendments to [its] constitution according to which Ukraine would reject any aims to enter any bloc', this also being the demand made both by Corbyn and his Coalition that there should be no 'eastward extension of Nato'. Ukraine would also have to 'recognize that Crimea is Russian territory' (seized illegally in 2014) and 'recognize that Donetsk and Lugansk are independent [in reality, Russian puppet] states. So there we had it, Corbyn's 'talking zone.' and 'dialogue'. As Ukraine's leaders did not respond in a like spirit, that is, make the concessions demanded, those who wanted 'peace' above all else knew whom to blame.

Perhaps tiring of repeating the 'No Eastern Expansion of Nato' mantra, on March 8, *Socialist Worker* directed an 'enemy at home' broadside against Nato's partner in crime, the European Union. (Let me remind the reader again that the SWP joined forces with the Euro-sceptic right (and far right) in calling and campaigning for a leave vote in the referendum of 2016.) The article, *European Union leaders use war to extend military influence in region'* claimed to have uncovered a conspiracy by EU leaders to exploit a 'fear of Russian influence '[sic...not tanks] among state leaders in eastern Europe' to enlarge the EU and create 'an EU military force'. Note that while Putin, despite his invasion of Ukraine (nowhere condemned) only has 'influence', the EU plans 'a military force' whose real purpose is not defence but an intrusion into Putin's expanding bailiwick. And *Socialist Worker*, with its sights trained on the 'enemy at home', not Moscow, was none too pleased: 'Georgia, which sits on the Black Sea, to the south of Russia, and Moldova, which is west of Ukraine [wrong; to its south], last week submitted applications to join the bloc. They joined Ukrainian President Volodymyr Zelensky's plea for rapid entry at the European parliament last week.' Why Zelensky would do this, and with such urgency, remained a mystery. Could it have been that his country had just been invaded by Russia? And it gets worse for the SWP: 'For the first time last week the EU announced it would purchase and deliver weapons in its own right', this being totally contrary, like sanctions against Russia and oligarchs, to SWP, Coalition and Corbynista policy. That denying Ukraine access to Nato weapons would undermine its resistance to Putin's invasion was of no concern to the revolutionary defeatists of the SWP, who as always, had their eyes firmly trained on 'the enemy at home', not only Nato, but an enlarged, eastern-oriented EU: 'As Ukraine burns [by spontaneous combustion perhaps?], we are already seeing the new shape of the European Union. Expansionist empire building [not by Putin, *ca vas sans dire*], rising budgets for new military forces and more emboldened "interventionist" [western we can be sure] politicians will help ensure the cycle of conflict has many more years to run.' As for solidarity with Ukraine...not a word.

There was, however, solidarity on display - with Putin - at the United Nations General Assembly when, on March 2, it overrode the previous Russian veto on the Security Council by approving, 141 votes to 5, (Russia, Belarus, Eritrea, North Korean, Syria - Venezuela did not vote) a resolution condemning Russia's invasion of Ukraine. Among the 35 nations abstaining was Iran, which it had been not been engaged in negotiations with western powers to end sanctions against its nuclear programme, would in all likelihood have voted in the same spirit as the speech of its delegate during the debate on the resolution. It could have just as easily been an article in *Socialist Worker* or on a Corbynista website, with its attack on the 'provocative actions and decisions of the US and Nato', and its demand that 'the security concerns of Russia must be respected.' Syria, in all but name a Russian colony, being totally dependent on Russian military intervention for the survival of the Assad regime, denounced in SWPspeak 'the West's policy of hegemony' and in a Corbynesque 'but what about', demanded that delegates who had voted for the UN resolution 'should show their same enthusiasm against Israel's continued occupation of Arab lands', which as we have seen, many had been doing *ad nauseum* for decades, with their permanent anti-Israel majorities in both the General Assembly and the so-called 'Human Rights Council'. As for 'occupation of Arab lands', Syria occupied Lebanon from 1976 to 2005, reducing much of its capital to rubble without any condemnation by the UN, as it crushed Palestinian and leftist movements in pursuit of the Ba'athist regime's goal of a 'Greater Syria'. This includes not only Lebanon and Jordan, but the Palestinian West Bank and Gaza Strip, which are to be transferred from one occupation to another, and even Israel.

Following its withdrawal in 2005, Syria has maintained a pernicious grip on

Lebanese political life via its proxy militia and one of Jeremy's 'friends', Hezbollah, the 'Party of God', which exercises an unofficial veto on the composition of Lebanon's ever-changing coalition governments. Western hegemony bad, Syrian hegemony good. And despite the protests of its victims at their meetings, the UK anti-Zionist left agrees. Understandably, Hezbollah's leader, Hassan Nasrallah, was none too pleased with the Lebanon delegate's vote for the UN resolution. 'You could have abstained. What are you worried about?' 'America and its ally Britain, the rest of [sic] the European Union', had 'pushed Ukraine into the mouth of the dragon'...the same lie being dispensed by the far left in the UK. Moscow also felt let down by Lebanon's vote, not least because 'Russia [had] spared no effort in contributing to the advancement and stability of the Lebanese Republic.' Another of Jeremy's terrorist 'friends', Mousa Abu Marzouq of the Hamas Political Bureau, was more upbeat. 'One lesson of the Russian-Ukrainian war is that the era of US unipolar domination has ended. The US was not in a position to declare war on Russia. Those who cannot declare war will not set the international agenda. From here we can begin to talk about the future [i.e., destruction] of the Zionist entity.'

Here also we have the explicit linkage, which Moscow, with its ruthless grip on its post-war European empire and diplomatic and military involvements in the Middle East, first recognized in the mid-1950s: namely, the interdependence of the two fronts where the civilisation of the West confronts the twin barbarisms of the East: *Dar al-Islam*, the 'Domain of Islam', and the patrimony of Genghis Khan, Tamburlaine, Ivan the Terrible and Stalin. I am only too well aware that it is not done nowadays to call Islam barbaric. But how else to describe those practices it prescribes and its clergy sanction which are outlawed, if not always punished, in every civilised country? Time was when calling something by its right name was not a potential crime but normal practice, as we have seen with Churchill's pungent comments on Islam as he experienced it at first hand in Sudan. (c.f. Appendix I) We also saw that reading out these comments in public a century and more later in an English town led to an arrest that was approved by Mohammed Shaffiq of the Ramadan Foundation. I suspect that had they learned of it, it would have also won the approval of woke leftists, all the more so because despite his dalliance with the Liberals, Churchill was essentially a man of the Right. The same cannot be said of the author of these lines, which describe in decidedly Islamophobic terms the conduct of Muslims of Constantinople at the time of the Crimean War, one that 'in their original nomadic state, consisted in robbing caravans; and now that they are a little more civilised consists in all sorts of arbitrary and oppressive exactions.' The writer continues: 'Were it not for their monopoly of civil and military power they would soon disappear. But that monopoly has become impossible for the future, and their power is turned into impotence except for obstructions in the way of progress. The fact is, they must be got rid of.' There is more in the same vein:

> It maintains with great jealousy the imaginary superiority and real impunity for excesses which the privileges of Islam confer upon it as compared with Christians. It is well known that this mob in every *coup d'état* has to be won over by bribes and flattery. It is this mob alone, with the exception of a few colonised districts, which offers a compact and imposing mass of the Turkish population in Europe. And certainly, there will be, sooner or later, an absolute necessity for freeing one of the

finest parts of this continent from the rule of the mob, compared with which the mob of Imperial Rome was an assemblage of sages and heroes.

So much for the religion of peace, and its 'contributions' to Western civilisation. And the author? Not an up-market Tommy Robinson, but Karl Marx, in one of the series of articles (some possibly ghosted by Engels) he wrote for the *New York Herald Tribune* on the 'Eastern Question' in the mid- 1850s, in which as now, Islam and Russia were the principal players, then as enemies, today as allies. Today, this alignment is well understood not only by Moscow, but in the Middle East by the Shi'a axis of Iran and Syria and their terrorist proxies, and no less by their enemy Israel, where Jews of Russian and Ukrainian heritage demonstrated their opposition to Putin's war, and at the United Nations, where Israel's delegation co-sponsored the General Assembly resolution condemning the Russian invasion, while Syria opposed it and Iran, reluctantly, abstained. Inevitably, given its participants and geographic hinterlands, the confrontation took on a religious dimension. Following on from the deployment of his Chechen Muslim 'hit' squad, on March 11, the Islamic connection was further strengthened and extended when Putin approved the formation of a division of up to 16,000 Arab, mainly Syrian 'volunteers', to bolster his hard-pressed army in eastern Ukraine. They were matched by what must have been a tacitly-approved 'volunteer' force of former elite service men and women from the Israeli Defence Force, yet more evidence that the war was going global along the fault lines of western civilisation and eastern barbarism.

This is not an arbitrary construction. For at least two decades, former KGB operative Putin, for whom, like two long standing comrades of Corbyn, George Galloway and Andrew Murray, the downfall of the USSR was the greatest tragedy of the 20th century, has singlemindedly pursued the goal not only of reclaiming the lost lands of the Romanov and Stalin empires, but the fulfilment of the Pan-Slavist dream of a realm reaching westwards to the heart of Europe, and south to the warm waters of the Mediterranean Sea and the Persian Gulf. He is said to have been inspired to set himself this goal by the historian Aleksandr Dugin, known as 'Putin's philosopher', and in particular, by his book *Foundations of Geopolitics*, in which he advocates the creation of an Orwellian 'Eurasia' 'from Dublin to Vladivostok'. Key to this undertaking for Dugin (and obviously no less so for Putin) is the reintegration of Ukraine into the Russian body politic, without which there would be 'enormous dangers for all of Eurasia', since it forms a vast land bridge connecting East, North, West and South Europe, bordering on Russia, Belarus, Poland, Slovakia, Hungary, Romania and Moldova

Via the internet, Dugin has attracted interest from a wide circle of politicians and intellectuals across the spectrum who to one degree or another, share his goals. Domestically, his writings are required reading for the Russian military leadership. Anti-Semitic in the old Russian Orthodox tradition that produced the *Protocols*, Dugin has also reached out to Islam, being a featured speaker alongside Ayatollah Maqami and a Hezbollah MP at a 'New Horizon Conference' in Tehran. It is all too easy to dismiss Putin's geopolitical ambitions as utopian, which indeed they are, and can therefore be safely ignored. But then so were Hitlers.

(Indeed, there is an uncanny similarity in the expansion of their respective domains. Both were preceded by political collapse, economic decline and loss of empire, followed by first, a seizure of power and the silencing of opposition, then domestic recovery and finally a new phase of expansion facilitated in both cases by Western appeasement - the promotion of irridentists by Hitler in the Sudetenland, Austria and Poland, and by Putin in Georgia, Crimea and the Ukrainian Donbas. Then came territorial occupations either directly or via proxies; Hitler's *Anschluss* with Austria and dismemberment of Czechoslaviai, Putin's in north Georgia and eastern Ukraine, and the seizure of Crimea. Both dictators sought to establish and secure diplomatic recognition for 'spheres of influence', Hitler and Putin in Eastern Europe, and Putin in the Middle East. Both engaged in military interventions in civil wars far from their own borders, Hitler in Spain to support Franco's fascist rebellion, and Putin in Syria to rescue the beleaguered regime of President Assad, in the course of which, Hitler's Condor Legion blitzed Guernica, and Putin's bombers levelled Aleppo. [As I write, Putin is about do the same to Kiev.] Both leaders found favour on the British left and right, Hitler with Labour Leader George Lansbury and Tory Prime Minster Neville Chamberlain, and Putin with Labour Leader Jeremy Corbyn and Tory Foreign Secretary and then Prime Minister Boris Johnson. With the expansionist momentum now unstoppable for the two regimes, and finally intolerable for the western powers, came staged border incidents and then war, with Hitler's invasion of Poland, and Putin's, of Ukraine. The similarities, in fact, near identities, do not stop there. Western Communist Party support for Stalin's pact with Hitler, and the far left's campaign against Nato and the European Union led in both cases to their directing their invective against 'the enemy at home', and not Hitler and Putin.)

The neo-Leninist left, with its fanatical anti-Zionism and frenetic opposition to the 'eastwards extension' of 'western imperialism', has made no secret of where it stands in this centuries-old contest between East and West, the outcome of which, as Marx well understood, will determine the future of mankind. Unlike Marx, who took to task western statesmen for their 'manifest impotency to guard the interests of European civilisation against Russian encroachment', his epigones, in their various manifestations and guises, act on the principle that the enemy is never abroad, but always 'at home' - in the first place, Nato and the European Union, the two ramparts the West has erected to protect its freedoms and ensure its material progress, and which Brexit, with the support of Putin and the far left, has put in jeopardy.

In this great historical reckoning, in which, as they were in the time of Marx, not just territory, but fundamental principles are at stake, there are in Russia and the world of Islam countless millions, mostly among the young, who yearn for the freedoms and quality of life that the West alone can provide, and of which the direction in which the tides of migrants and refugees have travelled in recent times are the irrefutable proof. Likewise, among us, but far fewer, are those who despise these very same freedoms, our Quislings in waiting, who by stealth and deceit have exploited these very same freedoms and the spirit of tolerance that goes with them to gain strategic positions in every walk of society. From political parties, pressure groups and trade unions to the media, public institutions and academe, they exercise an influence on events and attitudes out of all proportion to their numbers, some of whom are, to be sure, well-intentioned but naïve dupes. In one instance of many, following Russia's invasion of Ukraine, the SWP faction in the National Education Union secured the approval of an amendment to the union executive's resolution which had initially condemned it, but without making any reference to Nato. This could not be allowed to pass unchallenged. Invoking the spectre of Abbott's non-existent imminent Nato intervention, the amendment read: 'We believe the deployment of British and Nato forces in Ukraine would be a dangerous escalation in this war' – a tactically necessary soft variant on the theme of 'the enemy is at home'.

Those individuals and organisations who have been devising and directing the anti-Western, defeatist policies and activities of the far left have been the subject of scrutiny in this work, so their names need no repetition here. What does require repeating is that unlike Prime Minister David Cameron's enacting measures without parliamentary sanction to deny Jihadists free speech, and the Labour Party's proposed ban on what topics can be debated at universities, I am an advocate of unlimited free speech except when it incites criminal acts, and consequently, totally opposed to any witch hunt against the far left, such as it has conducted at universities against those who dissent from its woke agenda. Their policies and the ideology that underpins them need to be contested, as I have attempted to do in this work and elsewhere, in open, free polemic and debate, not by bans, prospections and dismissals, as we saw advocated by the SWP in the case of the Batley school teacher suspended and then driven into hiding after conducting a class on freedom of expression.

For those who have not only made a study of the *modus operandi* of the far left, but have like myself also been actively involved in its application, the manner in which it pursued this policy of defeatism in the various phases of the Ukraine crisis was entirely predictable. It proceeded according to Lenin's formula, first advocated in his *Revolutionary Catechism* by that *bête noir* of Karl Marx, the Russian terrorist Sergey Nechayev, that for the cause, all its permitted - lies, deception, simulation (thus being for 'peace' when the real goal is either surrender or conquest), manipulation, duplicity, slander...literally, anything goes.

No less predictably, the only regimes to rally to the support of Putin were ones that Corbyn has been closely identified with over the years: those of the Taliban, Iran, Bolivia, Venezuela, Nicaragua, Syria and Cuba, with dictator Nicolas Maduro being the most outspoken as well as Orwellian: 'Venezuela announces its full support to President Vladimir Putin in the defence [sic] of Russia's peace [!!!]. Venezuela is with Putin, with Russia [in that order], with the brave [!] and just [!] causes of the world and we are going to strengthen our alliance [with Russia] more and more.'...from a distance of 10,000 kilometres. In their own contribution to the Orwellian genre, Russian authorities announced that any media outlet using the words 'war' and 'invasion' would be banned and fined. When on March 1, Russian Foreign Minister Sergei Lavrov addressed by a pre-recorded video the Geneva disarmament conference, nearly all the delegates walked out, leaving behind them two from comrade Corbyn's closest international allies, Syria and Venezuela. In yet another Orwellian moment Lavrov claimed Putin's invasion was in response to the threat of nuclear attack by Ukraine.

As we have noted, the far left began its so-called 'peace' campaign by directing its fire first at Nato, then the European Union, in each case, for their 'eastwards extension' into Russia's legitimate 'sphere of influence', which in turn, so the argument went, provoked Putin's invasion of a Ukraine that by right, lay within it. As the war developed, with Ukraine inflicting devastating casualties and material destruction on the invaders, the far left now retrained its verbal artillery on the Ukrainian leadership. Hitherto, there had been accusations that President

461

Zelensky was a far-right, Zionist agent at the head of a no less far right regime, but now, the emphasis shifted. Just as the Kurds, by accepting American military aid to fight the Islamic State, had become 'Western pawns', so now the Ukrainians were performing the same function as proxies for Nato by requesting and accepting its military assistance. (It should by now go without saying that Russian separatists in the Donbas receiving military support from Putin were never denounced as 'Kremlin pawns'.) Heralding this shift, the *Socialist Worker* of March 27 published an article with the revealing subtitle, 'The war in Ukraine [not Russian invasion of Ukraine] is an ongoing battle between imperialist rivals, driven forward by capitalist competition' - not a struggle by the Ukrainians to preserve their national independence from Russian imperialism. The author, veteran SWP theorist. Alex Callinicos, warned of the dire consequences of a Ukrainian victory over the Russians. He asked, if Ukraine defeated Russia, 'would the US and its allies react by disarming and dissolving Nato? Of course, they wouldn't. They would celebrate this outcome as their victory, and boost Nato further. The US would feel invigorated in its world-historic competition with the real challenger to its hegemony, China.' So once again, the main and here, seemingly, the only enemy, is Nato, with the much to be feared prospect of its being emboldened by a Ukrainian victory over Russia.

Let us pause for moment to consider some very obvious, but for the SWP and its Coalition partners and demonstrating dupes, irrelevant facts. The SWP did not contest those Russian forces had committed atrocities on a vast scale, including the mass murder and deportation to Russia of civilians, rapes, destruction of civilian buildings and facilities and the rest. But if they were honest, they would also have had to concede that for all their alleged 'belligerence' and 'warmongering', neither Nato nor its partner in crime, the European Union, had fired a single bullet or dropped a single bomb in the entire conflict, let alone engaged in any of the atrocities committed by Putin's invading army. Yet the SWP not only treated 'the West' and Putin's 'Russia'. as if they shared responsibility for the rape of Ukraine, but insisted that this guilt was not shared equally, but rested mainly with Nato and the EU in their bid to use the Ukraine as a proxy for an 'eastwards extension' to the borders of Russia. Again, a fantasy. At Russian fuel-dependent Germany's insistence, Ukraine's application for membership of Nato was rejected as long ago as 2008.

To bolster his thesis, Callinicos invoked the authority of Lenin's writings on imperialism, ignoring that in them, Lenin had argued, against those on the left who said otherwise, that even in the midst of a war between two imperialist powers or alliances, as in the First World War, it was correct to support the struggle of oppressed nations for national independence: 'A war against imperialist, i.e., oppressing powers by oppressed people, for example colonial nations, is a genuine national war. It is possible today too.' (This was written in 1916, at the height of the First World War.) Lenin gave two examples of where the struggle of oppressed nations in eastern Europe retained a progressive character in the imperialist era, and therefore deserved the unconditional support of revolutionaries: 'As far as the Ukrainians and Byelorussians, for instance, are concerned, only a Martian dreamer [sic] could deny that the national movement has not yet been consummated there…There the "defence of the fatherland" can *still* [Lenin's emphasis] be a defence of democracy' - just as is it is again in the Ukraine of today.

On the same grounds, Lenin supported the Irish 'Easter Rising' of 1916 against British rule, despite the (abortive) military assistance it also received from a Germany at war with Ireland's master, just as Britain exploited Arab hostility towards the Turks, and Germany Poland's towards Russia, while in the Second World War, Britain gave what assistance it could to resistance movements in countries occupied by the Nazis. In all four cases, genuine, 'progressive' struggles for national independence took place in world wars, despite their being supported for ulterior purposes by one or other of the warring alliances. And let us not forget that it was none other than Lenin who, in April 1917, accepted the offer from the German General Staff of a train to transport himself and his comrades from Switzerland via neutral Sweden to Russia to prepare and then execute the coup that carried his party to power eight months later, and then led, as had been the intention, to Russia's making peace with Germany at Brest Litvosk in March 1918. Did Lenin's deal with the Kaiser, as some have argued, make Lenin a 'German pawn'?

Unlike Lenin and even more so Marx and Engels - see the quotes above - the SWP treats all (western) capitalist countries as equally and totally reactionary, and their support for national movements no less so…again the Kurds are one case in point, and another the (belated) western military inventions on behalf of ethnic and religious minorities subjected to genocide by Serbia following the break-up of Yugoslavia, where Corbyn, together with others on the far left, took the side of the Russian-backed Serbs against the Muslims of Bosnia and Kosovo because the latter were supported by the West.

Thus for the far left, the fact that Ukraine was not an imperialist power, but was invaded by one that was, and that EU membership was restricted to countries, none of whom possessed an empire, that were expected to conform to certain basic democratic criteria, and were extending aid to enable another democratic country to survive an invasion by a power that was imperialist and anything but democratic, was irrelevant. All that counted was that the 'West' is capitalist, and therefore, since all true socialists are opposed to capitalism, it is to be opposed by all available means, including, as we have seen, those forthcoming from regimes and movements totally opposed to the democratic norms of western civilisation; for example, by what the SWP describes as the 'militant Islamism' which inspired 9/11, gave birth to the Islamic State and its African offshoots, and fuels the genocidal anti-Semitism of Corbyn's 'friends' Hamas and Hezbollah and the Ayatollahs of Iran..

Given this 'orientation' - in both senses of the word - it is easy to see why the SWP depicted the support, such as it was, of the West for Ukraine's struggle against Putin as proof that the Ukraine government was serving as the vehicle for Nato's 'eastern expansion', just as the SWP had depicted the Kurd's relationship with the USA as one of 'Western pawns'. From this anti-westernism, all else of the far left's policy on Ukraine flowed. (A spokesman for the four TDs of People Before Profit, which follows the same policy in Ireland as the UK's SWP, explained why they had refused to join in the applause for President Zelensky's address to the Irish parliament: '…we have consistently said we don't agree with President Zelensky's call for a Nato-imposed no-fly zone… [A Russian fly-zone over Ukraine then in operation was a different matter.] In addition, we don't agree with the extension of sanctions which are hurting ordinary Russian people…' As to the first pretext, when his request for a Nato no-fly zone was rejected, President

Zelensky asked for, and was initially offered, Russian-made Polish jet fighters which would be flown by Ukrainian pilots. This too was rejected by Nato when vetoed by President Biden. As to the second objection, it had not been invoked to oppose BDS sanctions on Israel or, for that matter, on Apartheid-era South Africa.)

As fate would have it, the emergence of the new line, in effect, simply a logical development of the existing anti-Nato policy, coincided with revelations of Nazi-style atrocities committed by Russian troops in the liberated, if the SWP will permit the term, town of Bucha, north of Kiev. They require no repetition here, since the whole world learned of them in a matter of hours, in every gruesome detail. Suffice it to say that several world leaders and human rights organisations described them as not only war crimes, but as constituting genocide. What concerns us is that the SWP and, we can safely assume, its collaborators in the Coalition, had shifted their focus on to those organising and leading the fight against the perpetrators of these atrocities, namely the government and, by extension, the people of Ukraine, a 'collective guilt' of a kind similar to that imputed by the SWP to all Zionist Jews

What Callinicos only implied, the *Socialist Worker* of April 3 baldly stated: 'If either Russia *or the West* wins in Ukraine, it will be disastrous for the country's people and lay the basis for future wars.' (emphasis added) Ukraine as an independent force, fighting for its own goals, has here vanished, subsumed into a conflict between two imperialisms in which the people of Ukraine act merely as a proxy for one of the combatants. (Kremlin propagandists said exactly this.) Having outlined the probable consequences of a Russian victory, we are advised that 'a victory for the Ukrainian government of Volodymyr Zelensky based on the weaponry and military backing of the US-Nato forces would be ruinous.' I will repeat that: '*would be ruinous.*' And, as such, worse, so it would seem, than conquest by Russia, because 'Ukraine *would be wholly reliant on the West economically and militarily.* [emphasis in original] It would be a barracks society acting as a Nato outpost on Russia's border', a 'vassal of the West' instead of, as Putin intended, a Russian outpost on Nato's border, an outcome, given that Nato is the 'main enemy', to be preferred to a Western victory in the greater scheme of things, whatever the consequences for the Ukrainians.

Even worse, 'emboldened by success with Western backing, the Ukrainian government might seek to drive Russia out of the [illegally occupied] eastern provinces of Donetsk and Lugansk and even Crimea [illegally annexed by Russia in 2014].' ('Militant Islamists' driving out, or rather, exterminating, the Jews of Israel is an altogether different matter.) As the article warms to its theme, its endorsement of the Kremlin's imperialist concerns become unashamedly explicit, as do the euphemisms: '…a defeat for Russia would warm up a series of "frozen conflicts". A number of statelets – Artsakh [illegally seized from Azerbaijan by Armenia in 1991], South Ossetia [illegally seized by Russia from Georgia in 2008], Abkhazia [illegally seized from Georgia by Russia in 2008] and Transnistria [illegally seized from Moldavia by the USSR in 1990] – survive largely because of Russian military protection. [sic!!!] If Nato defeats Russia, then Georgian forces might enter Abkhazia and South Ossetia, Moldova or Ukraine could seek to eliminate the existence of Transnistria. Azerbaijan, an ally of Nato member Turkey, could grab Artsakh.' Note that while Russia 'protects' illegally annexed territories, their former owners conspire to 'grab' what is under international law legally theirs, a classic example far left double standards. But the hypocrisy does not stop there. The far left has for years described Israel as a 'colonial enterprise' that has no right to exist, and compares its occupation (not annexation) of the West Bank to the predatory conquests of Nazi Germany, while here it refers to Putin's illegal annexations and occupations as 'military protection'.

The SWP's solution to the Ukraine crisis naturally excluded an independent Ukraine resulting from what it called 'a defeat for Russia' by Nato. On the contrary, 'it would have to based on the resistance to the war and Putin in Russia and to Nato in Ukraine and elsewhere.' This required that the Ukrainians 'resist' Nato no   less than the Russians, the very same military alliance that was supplying them with the means to defeat Putin, in effect a 'war on two   fronts'. As for the prospects of a successful domestic resistance to Putin essential for the execution of the SWP's master plan, with opposition to his war confined   largely to the educated   urban young and approval ratings topping 80%, they were remote in the extreme. Let us recall that twice in its history, has had the opportunity to opt for freedom, in 1917, with the overthrow of the last tsar, and in 1991, with the break-up of the USSR. In both cases, it succumbed, with very little resistance, to the knout and the yoke of ancient Rus, first under Stalin and then Putin. In doing so, it leant substance to the validity of the judgment on his countrymen by a 19th century revolutionary   Nicolai Chernyshevsky much admired by Lenin, who cited it with full approval: The Russians were 'a wretched nation, a nation of slaves from top to bottom, all slaves.' But for   its reference to Poland (possibly next on Putin's list), Lenin's endorsement could have written in March or April 2022: 'Nobody is to be blamed for being born a slave, but a slave who not only eschews a struggle for freedom, but justifies and eulogises his slavery by calling the throttling of Poland and the Ukraine the "defence of the fatherland" is a lickspittle and a boor who arouses legitimate feelings of indignation, contempt and loathing.' Harsh words, to be sure. But closer to reality, one suspects, than the SWP scenario of a successful uprising against Putin. His removal from power, if it occurs at all, will most likely be the result of a conspiracy within the Russian elite, possibly akin to that which nearly succeeded in assassinating Hitler in July 1944.

The headline of the *Socialist Worker* of April 4 developed the obscene logic of the 'new line': 'Don't let the foul Russian crimes in Bucha widen Ukraine war.' True, 'Russian imperialism has perpetrated horrific war crimes, [but] Nato escalation [sic] isn't the answer...' By 'escalation' is meant Nato military aid for the Ukrainians., which the far left had opposed from day one of the war, as it had sanctions against Russia, which harmed 'ordinary people', unlike BDS sanctions against the Jews of Israel, who being collectively guilty of genocide and apartheid, do not qualify as 'ordinary people'. We are then given graphic details of these atrocities, which could possibly have been prevented or at least minimized if Nato, contrary to the policy of the SWP, had responded with more urgency and less political inhibitions to the military requests of the Ukrainian government. Having attacked President Zelensky for 'pushing for more arms to be rushed by western allies' - why the 'rush'- what does he need them for? - the reader awaits the solution, the correct 'answer' to this terrible war. It never comes. Instead, we are given the obligatory list of crimes committed by the West (none of those by Russians) as if this *ipso facto* debars (or prevents) any western power from acting in a good cause in the present or future. The article concludes thus: 'Bucha is the future promised to the whole of Ukraine if Russia's invasion goes on *and Nato continues to beat the drums* of *war'*. (my emphasis) One can only deduce from this that if Nato stops 'beating the drums of war', Russia will stop committing atrocities. Yet the SWP knew full well that if Nato did what the SWP demanded, that it stop arming the Ukrainians, Russia would indeed, in double quick time, with more atrocities on the way, overrun 'the whole of Ukraine'. Then the far left would have achieved its goal, which was, to 'Stop the War', thereby bringing 'peace'. And the quicker the better. Such was the theme of a Stop the War Coalition event scheduled for April 9. Not 'Solidarity with Ukraine', let alone 'Victory to Ukraine', because Ukraine was seen as the spearhead of Nato's and the EU's provocative 'extension' to the East, into the realm of Putin, but 'Peace Now'.

One of the features of the far left's campaign to subvert genuine solidarity with Ukraine was how it drew together the very same individuals, some of them clearly anti-Semitic, who have played a leading role in the anti-Zionist movement. Corbyn of course we have already noted. Then we have another disgraced ex-Labour MP, Chris Williamson, who like Corbyn, has been employed by Iran's Press TV channel as a host. On March 14, 2022, his guests included two other disgraced anti-Semites, former Bristol University Professor David Miller, and the rapper and Stop the War Coalition activist Lowkey, who after protests by Jewish students, had his appearance at the 100th anniversary bash of the National Union of Students cancelled. The topic for discussion was Ukraine, but given the political profile of the participants, it immediately acquired a Jewish dimension, with Williamson's opening observation that 'the Jewish identity of President Zelensky has been used by many in the West to cover Nato's clear alliance with neo-Nazi battalions in the war against Russia'...not, Russia's war against Ukraine.

Anti-Semite Lowkey took the bait, responding that 'there is a push [by Nato] to put the Ukrainian state at the need of [sic] these [unnamed] Neo-Nazi groups'... 'Zelensky has overseen the integration into the Ukrainian state of several explicitly neo-Nazi movements.' Then Miller developed this idea in a familiar direction. Zelensky was not only a Neo-Nazi accomplice of Nato's 'war against Russia', but 'strongly oriented toward Israel', further proof of his being 'oriented really towards the far right.' (This claim presumably derived from a speech by Zelensky in which he said that 'we must become like Icelanders in soccer, Israelis in defence of their native land, the Japanese in their technology, and the Swiss in their ability to live in harmony with all their differences.' Just how more Nazi can you get?).

With one more Jewish conspiracy unmasked, Lowkey moved on to another familiar theme - Nato's 'eastwards extension'. There was a 'general Nato policy of pumping Ukraine full of weapons', the purpose being to 'draw the Russian state into a quagmire.' (This was as near as the discussion got to acknowledging Russia's invasion.) Russia was the victim of a Nato-Jewish-Neo-Nazi plot, using sanctions to 'bring down the Russian government and balkanize Russia or even to bring Russia into Nato itself', which would extend Nato as far eastwards as Vladivostok and the Bering Straits. Professor Miller ventured even further into the realms of political science fiction: 'There will be blowback in terms of the Neo-Nazis, so people who have gone to fight there will come back to this country and will commit attacks like has been the case in the past, when Ukrainian terrorists [sic] in this country have committed attacks and killed people.' Could he be getting confused with the Muslim terrorists responsible for 7/7 and the Manchester Arena bombing? (Two days later, Williamson convened a meeting of his 'Resistance Movement', composed largely of Corbynistas expelled or suspended from the Labour Party for anti-Semitism. The topic, surprise surprise, was 'Zionism in Ukraine', and once more Professor Miller was in attendance, unmasking a Jewish conspiracy that bore a striking resemblance to that peddled at the time of the killing of George Floyd, attributed on both the far right and left to Israeli training of Minneapolis police in restraint techniques. According to Miller, 'the Ukrainian military have been trained by IDF people in their [Ukrainian] training schools'.)

In dwelling on the alleged Nazification of the Ukrainian government, all three participants in the March 14 broadcast were simply echoing the Kremlin's claim that its 'special military operation' (it was a crime in Russia to call it a war or an invasion) had as its aim the liberation of the Ukrainians from the Nazi regime of President Zelensky. Such was the resistance of the mass of the Ukrainians to their liberation, however, that a new and even more sinister note was struck in Moscow, one which not by accident, coincided with the committing of a series of atrocities against Ukrainian civilians that observers suspected had a genocidal purpose and character. On April 3, the state news agency Novosti published an item titled, 'What should Russia do with Ukraine?'. It was no longer a question of just removing a Nazi government, because 'a significant part of the popular mass, which are passive Nazis, accomplices of Nazism, is also guilty.' Consequently, 'total purification must be carried out.'...Putin's final solution of the Ukrainian Question.' To further this objective Putin drafted into battle the notorious mercenary neo-Nazi Wagner Group, one of whose officers, Alexei Milchakov, had posted pictures of himself on social media slicing off the ears of dead soldiers as war trophies, and images of the Slavic swastika, the *Kolovrat*. But for the far left, these developments changed nothing. They were not even worthy of comment in its press. It was business as usual. Nato and EU were the main enemy, and President Zelensky their accomplice.

As always when the West found itself obliged to defend its security and freedoms, public figures could be found who were only willing to take the side of those endangering them, as here: Putin's invasion of the Ukraine was 'a consequence of EU and Nato expansion in 2014. It made no sense to poke the Russian bear with a stick. If Vladimir Putin's one demand is that we state clearly Ukraine is not going to join Nato, why don't we do it?' It could be, almost word for word, Corbyn. But it was in fact fellow Brexiteer Nigel Farage, a super patriot advocating that not only the Ukraine but his own country should take orders from a Russian despot. Across the pond, hard-line Trumpists were hewing to the same pro-Putin line. Like Corbyn and his Coalition, the Communist Party and the SWP, Trump had always been opposed to Nato and the European Union, just as he shared their opposition to the US removal of the Taliban in Afghanistan and Saddam Hussein in Iraq. Speaking for pro-Putin Republicans, Donald Trump Jr. denied the Russian leader had any designs on the Ukraine, and described as 'crazy' Biden's sending of troops to Europe. James Vance, possible Republican Senate candidate for Ohio, reprised Chamberlain's dismissal of the Czechs as 'a people of whom we know nothing' with his 'I gotta be honest with you. I don't really care what happens to Ukraine one way or another', while another election hopeful, potential Republican Presidential contestant Mike Pompeo, found Putin to be a 'very talented statesman' with 'lots of gifts'. Perhaps the most spectacular affirmation of American pro-Putin sympathies came at a white supremacist America First convention two days after he unleashed his military on the Ukraine. Just before guest speaker Representative Marjorie Taylor Greene took the stage, convention host Nick Greene, a Holocaust denier, called for a 'round for Russia', to which the all-white delegates responded with a rhythmic chant of 'Putin' as Greene pumped his fist in the air. Trumpist Fox TV host and pundit Tucker Carlson played it more archly, asking on his show, 'Why would we take Ukraine's side and not Russia's side?' Russian state TV repeatedly played clips of his comments in the run-up to the invasion of Ukraine. As to Carlson's clearly rhetorical question, Trump senior gave the answer in an appearance on the Clay Travis & Buck Sexton Show a matter of hours after Putin had launched his invasion of the Ukraine. 'This is genius. Putin declares a big portion of the Ukraine independent [sic] Oh, that's wonderful.' Putin had made a 'smart move' by sending in 'the strongest peace force [sic] I've ever seen.' This was too much for some Republicans, with Liz Cheney tweeting that Trump's statement' 'aids our enemies. Trump's interests don't seems to align with the interests of the USA.' Neither did the votes eight hardcore Trumpists cast on March 17 against the USA's ending its normal trade relations with Russia and Belarus. Another Republican Congressman, Madison Cawthorn, called President Zelensky a 'thug' and his government, 'corrupt' and 'evil'. Like the far left, their enemy was also not Putin, but at home...in the White House. I wonder what Trump would say if his genius friend decided to reclaim another lost Russian territory...Alaska...which Tsar Alexander II sold to the USA in 1867 for the sum of $7.2 million? Who knows? 'Make Russia Big Again'?

I began this work, with Corbyn specifically in mind, by likening the far left's alliance with Islam against the West to Stalin's with Hitler against Poland, little expecting that it would end, as it does now, again with Corbyn in mind, with another alliance of the Quisling far left, this time not with the legions of Allah, but with Stalin's successor against the Ukraine. History cannot repeat itself exactly. But there are times when it has a good try.

Lightning Source UK Ltd.
Milton Keynes UK
UKHW011838180722
406042UK00002B/128